SHIPWRECKS
OF THE
NORTH OF SCOTLAND

SHIPWRECKS
OF THE
NORTH OF SCOTLAND

R.N. Baird

Birlinn

First published in 2003 by
Birlinn Limited
West Newington House
10 Newington Road
Edinburgh EH9 1QS

www.birlinn.co.uk

ISBN 1 84158 233 6

British Library Cataloguing in Publication Data
A catalogue record for this book is available from the British Library

Image origination and scanning by the author
Typesetting and page makeup by Brinnoven, Livingston
Printed and bound by the Bath Press, Glasgow

CONTENTS

INTRODUCTION

Shipwrecks of the North of Scotland is a reference guide to shipping losses off the coast of Scotland from Stonehaven, south of Aberdeen, northwards to Duncansby Head, then westwards to Cape Wrath and the Minch, and includes the waters around Orkney and Shetland.

This book covers the area between the finishing points of the author's two previous books: *Shipwrecks of the Forth* and *Shipwrecks of the West of Scotland*.

I cannot remember a time when I was not interested in ships, wrecks and marine salvage, and since taking up diving as a hobby more than twenty years ago, my interest has been further developed and focused mainly on wrecks in Scottish waters. My research is continuous, but can never be wholly complete. I am aware of many exciting on-going activities, which are likely to bear fruit in the coming months, in terms of new wreck finds, and expansion of our knowledge of the wrecks in our waters. One has to stop at some point, however, to produce a book of this nature. This book contains details of over 450 ships lost off the north-east and north of Scotland. This area saw considerable action during both the First and Second World Wars, and many wartime losses are described for the first time.

Wreck Research

The information in this book has been gleaned over a number of years from many sources, including newspaper files, the Admiralty Hydrographic Department, Lloyds and the Public Records Office. In addition, many books and other publications have provided useful information, as indeed have many individuals.

I have done my best to select what I consider to be perhaps the most accurate of the sometimes vague and conflicting information available. When an exact position is not known, I have endeavoured to provide as close an estimate as the information currently available to me will permit, and this is indicated in the text. By far the most common causes of shipwrecks are running aground and collisions. During both wars, submarine torpedoes, mines, and attack by aircraft were additional hazards, which accounted for a substantial number of the wrecks.

Wartime losses are particularly challenging to research, because the strict censorship that applied during these periods suppressed information from the public domain. As a result, wartime newspapers are not very helpful. The three volumes of *Lloyds War Losses* (one volume covering WW1, and two for WW2) were extremely useful in providing a starting point for further research into the many ships lost during both wars. These provided details of what was known at the time by the Allies during both wars. They have never been updated in the light of subsequent knowledge.

Prof. Dr Jürgen Rohwer's *Axis Submarine Successes 1939–1945*, first published in 1983, and the revised edition, *Axis Submarine Successes of World War Two*, published in 1999, have also been of inestimable value for information from the German side during the Second World War.

Acknowledgements

Quite a number of individuals have provided useful information, but I would especially like to thank the following persons to whom I am particularly indebted:

Kevin Heath for his outstanding knowledge of Northern wrecks, and for his invaluable assistance with hydrographic information and research into Second World War German U-boat documents.

Dr Andrew Jeffrey for his marvellous research into Second World War documents held in the PRO and elsewhere, and for the benefit of his vast range of experience in many other fields.

Brian Malley, particularly for his assistance with regard to First World War research.

Roger Mathison for the benefit of his extensive knowledge of Buchan wrecks.

Ian Whittaker for the benefit of his encyclopaedic knowledge of wrecks everywhere.

I have been stunned by the quantity and quality of the information they have been able to provide.

I should also like to thank them all for their encouragement and humour.

It has been great fun working with them all!

Diving the Wrecks

Most of the wrecks are too far offshore for transits to be useful, and therefore the wrecks must be located by some other means. Apart from seaworthy boats, echo sounders and GPS navigation and position-fixing equipment are absolutely essential for finding a great many of the wrecks. A magnetometer is also very useful. One should never overlook fishing boat skippers. Their knowledge of the seas they operate in is second to none, and they can often provide wreck positions – although these sometimes turn out to be 'wrock' positions!

To compensate for the lack of available transits for the majority of the wrecks, I have endeavoured to give GPS positions.

GPS Positions

At a late stage during the writing of this book, the Admiralty Hydrographic Department announced that they will be revising and reprinting the Admiralty charts from the present OSGB36 datum to a new standard datum – WGS84. The chart itself will remain unchanged, but the lines of latitude will be moved to the south, and the lines of longitude to the east. This means that the latitude and longitude of a fixed position (e.g. a wreck) will change. Latitude will increase in all areas of the UK, while longitude will increase west of the Greenwich meridian, and decrease east of the Greenwich meridian. A complication is that the amount of the change is not constant – it will vary by about 175 metres in the south of the UK to about 110 metres in the north.

A change of this magnitude may not seem very significant in the middle of an ocean. Close to shore, however, or when seeking to avoid hazards such as reefs near the surface, it does require care to be taken in ensuring that your GPS is set to the datum of the chart you are using. When searching for a wreck, the GPS should be set to the datum of the position given for the wreck. All of the positions given in this book are in OSGB36 datum.

I considered whether I should adjust all the positions to the WGS84 datum, but decided against doing so for several reasons. Apart from the enormous amount of work that would entail, almost all of the positions given in my source material are quoted in OSGB36 standard. That is the datum of most of the charts we have all been using up to now, and therefore wreck positions taken from the paper charts are in OSGB36. The charts include a note regarding satellite-derived positions, and the adjustments which should be made to each chart when using WGS84-standard GPS positions. (Note that these adjustments vary from one chart to another.) Different makes of GPS set also use slightly different calculations for converting OSGB36 positions to WGS84 (and vice versa). Avoiding making any adjustments myself eliminates the possibility of me introducing yet another error.

Charts

For maximum comprehension of, and benefit from, the information provided in this book, it is recommended that it should be read in conjunction with the Admiralty charts listed below:

Chart No.	Area
1407	Montrose to Berwick
190	Montrose to Fife Ness
210	Newburgh to Montrose
1446	Aberdeen Harbour and Approaches
1409	Buckie to Arbroath
213	Fraserburgh to Newburgh
222	Buckie to Fraserburgh
223	Dunrobin Point to Buckie
1077	Approaches to Cromarty Firth and Inverness Firth
1889	Cromarty Firth – Cromarty Bank to Invergordon/Invergordon
1078	Inverness Firth
115	Moray Firth
2162	Pentland Firth and Approaches
1954	Cape Wrath to Pentland Firth, including the Orkney Islands
1942	Fair Isle to Wick
219	Western Approaches to the Orkney and Shetland Islands
2249	Orkney Islands – Western Sheet
2250	Orkney Islands – Eastern Sheet
35	Scapa Flow and Approaches
1785	North Minch – Northern Part

Computerised charts such as C-Map World for Windows are a good alternative. (Only in WGS84.)

Boats are required to reach virtually all of the wrecks. Hiring one of the specialist dive boats which operate in the area, or a local trawler, is still probably the best practical solution for divers who wish to explore those wrecks located a long way offshore, and has the additional advantage of the skipper's local knowledge and experience, along with all the technological equipment and comfort provided by a relatively large vessel. Contact the local divers via the Internet. The area covered by this book includes Sea Areas Forth, Cromarty, Fair Isle and Hebrides.

Strong tidal streams run around headlands, and in the narrow sounds separating islands, or between islands and the mainland. The tidal streams in the Pentland Firth are notoriously powerful. Ships have long avoided trying to navigate through the Pentland Firth against the wind or tide. Tankers are prohibited from navigating through here at all! Underwater visibility is generally very good, gin clear in places, particularly towards the north and west, and marine life of all sorts is prolific. Near the coast, from Kinnaird Head southwards, underwater visibility is not nearly so good as in the Moray area and northwards. In early spring (March/April) the increasing sunlight causes a burst of plant activity, producing a plankton bloom which temporarily reduces underwater visibility to as little as 2 to 3 metres. By May, this has largely disappeared, but in September, the autumn storms bring nutrient-rich deeper waters to the surface where there is still sufficient light to allow the plankton to bloom again briefly.

Many of the wrecks in this book are not charted, but most of the charted wrecks in the area have been included. When I first started writing books, I imagined I was writing almost exclusively for the interest of fellow divers, although I was well aware that many of the wrecks were too deep for sport diving, and therefore likely to be only of academic interest to divers. I have since found out that there are many other types of people interested in shipwrecks!

In the introduction to *Shipwrecks of the West of Scotland*, published in 1995, I predicted that the advent of *technical diving* and further developments, which will inevitably follow in the future, would bring some of the deeper wrecks within the reach of divers. This has already happened, and the number of divers able to visit the deeper wrecks is growing.

Further Information

To add to my own knowledge, I should be grateful for any further information which readers may be able to provide. Knowing a date for the sinking of a vessel provides a good starting point for personal research through the files of local newspapers, unless the date is during the First or Second World War, when censorship prevented newspapers from publishing information which would now be useful to wreck detectives.

Some of the named wrecks, whose positions are not accurately known, will no doubt tie up with some of the charted wrecks which have yet to be identified, while others will be the remains of vessels for which, through lack of sufficient information, I am presently unable to suggest a possible name with any degree of confidence. A few of the wrecks are well known to divers, but many more are not. I should welcome information from divers visiting any of the wrecks, to let me know what was found, possibly enabling identification of an *Unknown*, or to correct any errors of fact or omission I may have made. My database contains information on many more wrecks than are included in this book, and I would be willing to have a go at identifying any wreck not included herein.

Side Scan Sonar

Side Scan Sonar was originally developed to assist anti-submarine vessels to identify submarines sitting on the bottom. This is a function for which the equipment is admirably suited, and which it performs well. It has since been used to examine all kinds of bottom features, but the equipment is less suited to finding the least depth over wrecks, or for measuring their dimensions.

More accurate methods are employed to determine the least depth over wrecks – Oropesa or drift sweeps, and echo sounder transducers pointing vertically downwards.

There is no dedicated equipment designed solely for the purpose of accurately measuring the dimensions of wrecks.

On the image provided by side scan sonar sets the horizontal and vertical scales are different. To achieve any degree of accuracy in assessing the length of a wreck, it is therefore imperative, when using this equipment, that the surveying ship's course must be parallel to the orientation of the wreck, and that the wreck echo and shadow should lie vertically on the recording paper. The performance of sideways-looking sonar varies with the depth of the water, the quality of the bottom, and the water conditions.

The interpretation of the sonar trace is also dependent on the experience and judgement of the operator, and this inevitably introduces the possibility of human error.

Although equipment is being continuously developed and improved, many years can elapse between hydrographic surveys of an area.

The apparent dimensions given for a wreck should therefore be regarded in the light of the above.

Loss Analysis

Excluding the *Unknown* wrecks, whose cause of loss can only be speculation, an analysis of the causes of loss of the vessels included in this book reveals the following:

Ran aground	184	43.60%	
Collision	32	7.58%	
Fire	2	0.47%	
Foundered	23	5.45%	
Total Non-War Causes	*241*	*57.11%*	
By submarine	102	24.17%	Incl. torpedo, gunfire and scuttling charges
Mined	38	9.00%	
By aircraft	37	8.77%	Incl. bombs and torpedoes
Depth-charged	4	0.95%	
Total War Causes	*181*	*42.89%*	
Totals	*422*	*100.00%*	

It is interesting to note that 43 per cent of the vessels included in this book were war losses. Why should this figure be so high? The extent of war activities in Scottish waters during both World Wars is not generally appreciated. As an island nation, Britain has always been reliant on overseas trade for exporting its own products and for importing food, oil, raw materials and other goods. Until the Second World War Britain had by far the largest mercantile fleet in the world, and a commensurately large naval fleet to protect it.

Britain was very vulnerable to attack on its shipping – a point ruthlessly exploited by Germany in both World Wars. With her land borders, Germany was much less exposed to this type of attack. Activity in the waters around Scotland during both wars was much greater than in peacetime. Many ships which would normally have been routed through the English Channel, for example, were diverted, for safety, around the north of Scotland instead.

For illustrative purposes, let us consider the situation in the early days of the Second World War, the first six months of which was often referred to as 'the phoney war'.

This ended with the invasion of Norway and Denmark on 9 April 1940, but there was nothing phoney about the war in the waters around Scotland during that time! Ships were being attacked and sunk, and men were dying.

English south coast ports were shut during the Second World War, and a very large part of the import and export trade of the nation was being routed through Scottish ports. I am indebted to the historian Dr Andrew Jeffrey for the following description of the scene.

Prior to the Allied collapse in Norway and France, the main OA (Outbound Atlantic) convoys assembled off Southend and steamed round the south coast of England, collecting ships from Southampton and other ports before heading into the Atlantic via the South-Western Approaches. Outbound convoys from Liverpool and the Clyde, the OB series, rendezvoused with OA convoys in the South Western Approaches. Inbound convoys followed the reverse route but, from July 1940, most ocean traffic began using the North Channel and the North Western Approaches. This route kept the convoys as far away as possible from Axis-held territory and Luftwaffe airfields, but it also caused massive disruption, particularly for traffic to and from British east coast ports.

Pre-war British imports had exceeded 50 million tons p.a., but this figure was dramatically reduced from the beginning of the war. The following table shows imports and net consumption of imported supplies in millions of tons from Ministry of War Transport data:

	Imports	Changes in stock level	Net consumption
First year of war	44.2	+0.9	43.3
Second year of war	31.5	+1.9	29.6
Calendar year 1941	30.5	+1.4	29.1
Calendar year 1942	22.9	-2.45	25.35
Calendar year 1943	26.4	+2.8	23.6
Calendar year 1944	25.1	-1.9	27.0

Merchant Shipping and the Demands of War, HMSO, 1978, p. 201

Despite the dramatic reductions in imports, even at full capacity, the principal west coast ports on the Clyde, the Mersey and at Avonmouth could only handle about two-thirds of trade in 1940, in addition to military traffic. So, under pressure from the Ministry of Shipping, the Admiralty began escorting coastal convoys around the north of Scotland to and from east-coast ports. FS and FN convoys between the Thames and Forth began on 9 July when FN1 sailed Southend for Methil. From there it became EN1 for the passage northabout to the Clyde, eventually to feed Atlantic convoy OA180. Convoys from the Clyde to Methil began immediately, and convoys between Methil and the Tyne began running in December 1940.

Much of the trade between Norway and Scotland was carried in neutral ships, and their losses to U-boat attack were perceived to encourage the sympathy of neutrals towards the Allied cause.

From the outbreak of war until June 1940 transatlantic traffic had been principally routed through the Western Approaches south of Ireland to ports in southern England, but German troops entered Paris on 14 June 1940 and the French government asked for an armistice three days later. With France now enemy territory and ports on the south coast of England untenably close to Luftwaffe airfields, all Atlantic convoys were rerouted through the North Channel. Outbound OA convoys from Southend continued until 24 October 1940, though they were diverted northabout round Scotland, and, from 9 July, OB and OG convoys outbound from west-coast ports were sent through the North Channel.

On the outbreak of war 25 per cent of normal shipping traffic was diverted away from east-coast and channel ports in September and October 1939. This demonstrated that it was never going to be possible for the facilities in the Clyde and the Mersey to handle all Atlantic cargoes, so a system of coastal convoys to link up with ocean convoys had been instituted. FN and FS convoys between Methil and the Thames began on 6 September 1939. And from November 1939 Methil was also the southern terminus of the convoys to and from Norway, though this placed such a strain on the few escorts available that the northern terminus of the FN and FS convoys was moved south to the Tyne. Ships were then forced to sail independently between the Tyne and the Forth, but they proved to be easy targets, so convoys were resumed between the Thames and Methil in February 1940. Further disruption was caused by the Norway campaign in April and May, but FN and FS convoys between the Thames and Methil recommenced on 9 July and EN and WN convoys northabout between Methil and the Clyde began operating in conjunction with ocean convoys.

The minesweeping effort around Scotland was principally directed at keeping the coastal convoy lanes clear. Minesweeper flotillas were based on principal ports and naval bases around Scotland including Ardrossan, Greenock, Scapa Flow, Invergordon, Peterhead, Aberdeen, Dundee and Port Edgar. Declared minefields – real or fictitious – limited the areas to be closely protected by the Royal Navy, and forced shipping to follow narrow swept channels. That tended to concentrate ships in relatively confined routes around the coast, making it easier to defend them, but conversely attracted unwelcome attention from the enemy U-boats.

But the North Sea is also shallow, and A/S measures could be focused on the convoy routes, making patrols by even small Type IIC and IID U-boats in coastal waters during long summer days hazardous. When new bases became available on the coast of France in mid-1940, U-boat patrols off the east coast of Scotland were abandoned, and the seven surviving Type IIC and IID boats undertook short Atlantic patrols, mainly off the North Channel and often within sight of the Scottish coast. In six patrols during July these boats sank 64,600 tons of shipping, and these patrols were useful training for crews. They also spotted outbound convoys and created considerable confusion.

Contraband control involved stopping neutral ships bound for enemy ports and, on the rare occasions when the weather allowed, boarding them to check on their cargo. Otherwise, the ship would be escorted in to the examination base at Kirkwall, where its cargo would be inspected. Ships carrying cargo to neutral countries adjacent to Germany were invited to call at Kirkwall. But diversions to Kirkwall were unpopular with neutrals as they not only involved long detours, but they also took the ships into the U-boat and air attack danger zone close to Scapa Flow, as many ships found to their cost. American ships were forbidden to enter the 'combat zone'. Special arrangements had to be made so that they did not have to call at Kirkwall, and noticeably few American wrecks lie in Scottish waters.

The waters between Scotland and Scandinavia were dangerous, yet trade with Norway and Sweden included important exports of coal and vital imports of timber and, above all, iron ore. It had to continue, and despite the fact that almost all of the ships involved were neutral, convoy was essential. The first Scandinavian convoy had sailed from Norway on 14 October 1939 and arrived off the Forth two days later only to steam into the first air raid on Britain of the war. The second convoy of twelve ships followed on 26 October, ten of them arriving safely at Methil on 31 October, the other two proceeding independently to the Clyde. The first outbound convoy for Norway sailed from Methil on 4 November 1939.

Methil and Bergen were assembly points and the routing and escorting of Scandinavian convoys was the responsibility of the Rosyth escort force. The cycle varied

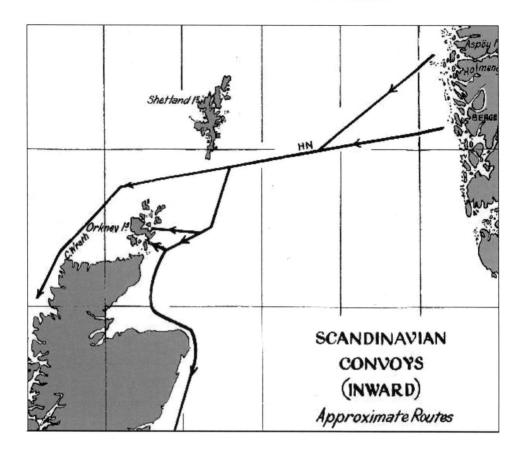

SCANDINAVIAN

CONVOYS

(INWARD)

Approximate Routes

with the weather and the volume of trade but by early February 1940 two convoys, one inbound and the other outbound, sailed every four days. ON convoys sailed from Methil during the afternoon, passed through the Moray Firth west of the normal track to bring the convoy under fighter cover, and were timed to pass the Fair Isle Channel, a focal point for U-boats, in darkness. Arrivals off Norway were timed carefully to avoid twilight, the best time for U-boat attack. The escort would then loiter offshore for four hours to await a Methil-bound HN convoy.

On 28 October 1939 the trawlers *Lynx II* and *St Nidan* were sunk off Shetland by *U-59*, and on 30 October, the *Cairnmona* was torpedoed three miles off Rattray Head by *U-13*. That same evening *U-59* sank the patrol trawler *Northern Rover* off Orkney.

U-18, *U-21* and *U-22* operated off the Moray Firth during November, and *U-22* sank the Kirkwall-bound collier *Parkhill* 17 miles north of Troup Head on the 17th. The trawler *Trinity NB* was attacked by aircraft and sunk 17 miles NE of Rattray Head that same day.

U-18 sank the Grimsby trawler *Wigmore*, part of an Iceland-bound fishing convoy, 25 miles north of Rattray Head on the 18th. On 20 November a torpedo fired by *U-18* at the tanker *Athelking* exploded in the wake of the destroyer *Inglefield* off Rattray Head. Four more U-boats also operated in Scottish waters during November: *U-47* in the Minch, *U-35* in the Pentland Firth and *U-31* and *U-48* off Orkney. The operation was planned in conjunction with the sortie by *Scharnhorst* and *Gneisenau* and the four boats formed a trap for Royal Navy units tempted out after the German ships. A large explosion in the wake of the cruiser *Norfolk* east of Shetland on 28 November, assumed to have been caused by an aircraft bomb, was in fact caused by a torpedo fired by Prien in *U-47*. Prien had intercepted *Norfolk* after receiving a sighting report from *U-35*, but *U-35* was

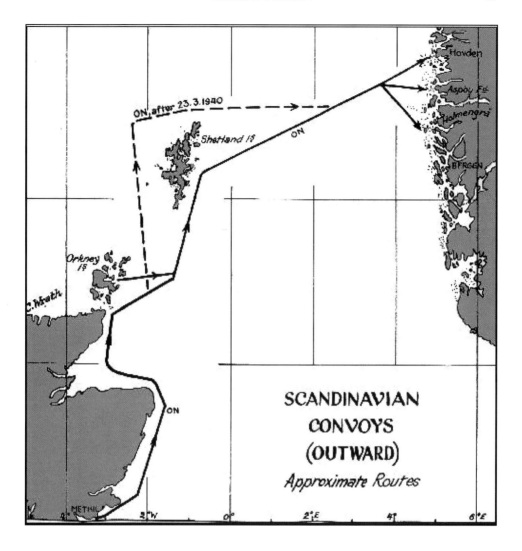

sunk the following day by the destroyers *Kingston*, *Icarus* and *Kashmir* and her crew were taken prisoner. The Swedish tanker *Gustav E Reuter* was torpedoed by *U-48* off Sumburgh Head early on 27 November. The Finnish *Mercator*, Leith for Helsinki, was torpedoed off Buchan Ness on 1 December by *U-21*. Later that day, 85 miles to the east, *U-31* sank the Norwegian *Arcturus*, Burntisland for Trondheim. Also on 1 December *U-56* attacked convoy HN3, inward-bound from Norway, east of Fife Ness, first blowing the stern off the Swedish collier *Rudolf* with a torpedo, killing nine of her crew. Then a short while later, he torpedoed the timber-laden straggler *Eskdene*. Captain Niblett and his crew were landed at Dundee but *Eskdene* was kept afloat by her cargo. She was found on 6 December by the Danish steamer *Grenra* and towed to the Forth.

This book describes shipping disasters which have occurred off the North of Scotland during a little over the past 100 years, but the above précis only gives a flavour of some of the events off Scotland during a few weeks at the beginning of the Second World War. Many vessels had already come to grief in these waters, and this was only a foretaste of further losses to come as the war progressed.

With ships being routed in swept channels close to the land, a number were also lost through the normal marine risk of running ashore. For example *Baron Minto,* Texas City to Hull with scrap metal, and *Simonburn,* Montreal for London with wheat, were both driven ashore near Rattray Head in a storm on 30 October 1940. Many more losses were to follow.

The Wreck Details

Detailed information on each wreck is given immediately under the vessel's name. This is followed by details of the circumstances of loss of the vessel, its present whereabouts and condition (where known) and other more general information where this is known. Any wreck can be found by reference to the two indexes – a name index and a latitude index. These give both the page number and the wreck number (these are assigned sequentially throughout the book).

In general, the wrecks are described in latitude order, which is fine as long as the coast runs north/south. The Moray coast and the north coast, however, run east/west, and therefore the numbering sequence and order of inclusion has been rather arbitrarily adjusted so that the wrecks are grouped together in a slightly more geographically convenient order.

Wrecks around Orkney and Shetland have been described in an anti-clockwise direction.

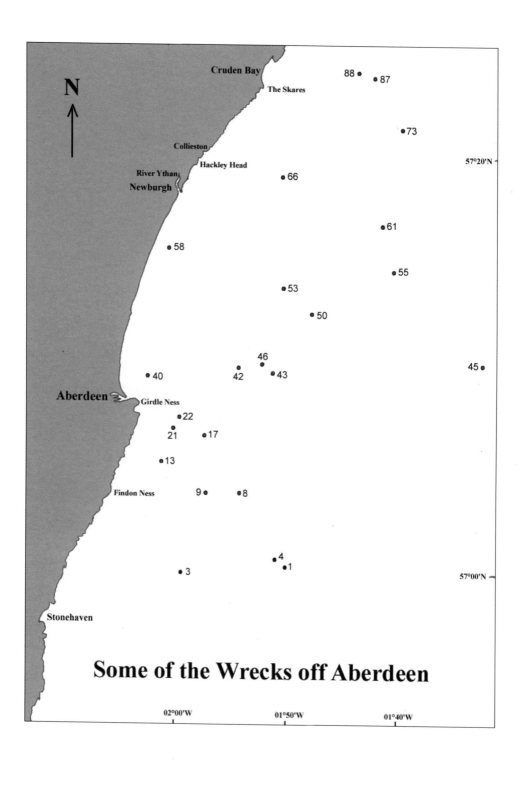

Some of the Wrecks off Aberdeen

1

ABERDEEN

U-40

Wreck No: 1	Date Sunk: 23 06 1915
Latitude: 57 00 00 N PA	Longitude: 01 50 00 W PA
GPS Lat: 5700.000 N	GPS Long: 0150.000 W
Location: 11½ miles SE by S of Girdleness	Area: Aberdeen
Type: Submarine	Tonnage: 685 tons
Length: 212.3 ft Beam: 20.7 ft.	Draught: 11.8 ft
How Sunk: HM S/M *C-24* & *Taranaki*	Depth: metres

During the First World War, a large number of British merchant ships and fishing vessels were captured by U-boats, which would surface nearby and threaten to sink the ship with torpedoes or gunfire if it did not stop and surrender. The merchant ship's crew were then ordered into their lifeboats, and their ship would then be either torpedoed, or sunk by gunfire, or boarded and scuttled with time bombs. One method of discouraging such tactics was to use a decoy trawler to tow a submerged submarine. A telephone cable allowed communication between the trawler and the submarine. The trawler would act as bait to attract a U-boat, and when one was sighted on the surface, the trawler would inform its hidden submarine, and the tow would be slipped at the critical moment.

On 23 June 1915, when *U-40* (KL Gerhardt Furbringer) sighted the trawler *Taranaki* off Girdleness, he believed the trawler would be an easy victim. Submerged behind the trawler, however, was the British submarine *C-24* commanded by Lt Taylor. *Taranaki* advised *C-24* by telephone that a U-boat had surfaced 1,500 yards off the port beam. Things did not go quite to plan, however, as the towing mechanism on the submarine jammed, preventing the tow rope from being released. A phone call was made to *Taranaki*, asking her to let go her end. Weighed down by the heavy wire still attached to her fore end, *C-24* tilted down by the bow as she manoeuvred to attack the U-boat. The hawser fouled *C-24*'s propellers, but despite this, Taylor succeeded in manoeuvring into an attacking position and at 9.55am fired one torpedo, which struck *U-40* just below the conning tower. Twenty-nine of *U-40*'s crew were killed when the U-boat sank, but KL Furbringer and two of his crew were rescued. Furbringer complained, on being brought aboard the *Taranaki*, that he had been sunk by a dirty trick.

The inevitable result, of course, was that U-boats eventually started to torpedo their victims without warning.

U-40 displaced 685 tons surfaced, 878 tons submerged.

The Hydrographic Department gives the position of *U-40* as 570000N, 015000W PA, 11 miles SE of Girdleness, or 12 miles East of Stonehaven.

Two further estimates of her position are 570800N, 015000W PA or 563500N, 010200W PA.

The Hydrographic Department also gives 570000N, 015000W PD (Position Doubtful) for MFV *Our Merit* (LT291).

VINEYARD

Wreck No: 2	Date Sunk: 08 11 1916
Latitude: 57 01 00 N PA	Longitude: 01 51 30 W PA
GPS Lat: 5701.000 N	GPS Long: 0151.500 W
Location: 10 miles S by E ¾E Aberdeen	Area: Aberdeen
Type: Trawler	Tonnage: 126 grt
Length: 95.2 ft	Beam: 19.6 ft Draught: 10.5 ft
How Sunk: Mined	Depth: metres

The steel screw steam trawler *Vineyard* was built in 1896 by Hall Russell of Aberdeen.

Eight of the crew were lost, including the skipper when she was mined on 8 November 1916.

British Vessels Lost at Sea 1914–18 gives the position as 10 miles S by E ¾E from Aberdeen.

This would be in the vicinity of 570100N, 015130W PA.

Lloyds World War One Losses gives 14 miles S by E ½E of Aberdeen.

I.G. Whittaker gives position 565700N, 015130W, 13 miles from Aberdeen.

UNKNOWN – PRE-1960 – NORWOOD?

Wreck No: 3	Date Sunk: Pre 1960
Latitude: 57 01 06 N	Longitude: 01 59 30 W
GPS Lat: 5701.100 N	GPS Long: 0159.500 W
Location: 7.4 miles E of Stonehaven	Area: Aberdeen
Type:	Tonnage: grt
Length: ft	Beam: ft Draught: ft
How Sunk:	Depth: 65 metres

An obstruction which seems to be a wreck standing up 7 metres from the bottom, in a total depth of 60 metres of water, is charted 7.5 miles S of Girdleness. It was discovered in 1960, when a trawler fouled her nets on it. Bearings for this wreck are:

346° to Girdleness Lighthouse.

302° to the radio masts at Sunnyside.

240° to Dunottar Castle.

This would appear to be quite a large wreck, judging by the height it stands up from the bottom, and I had thought that it might possibly be the *Creemuir*.

The wreck was dived in 1999 and again in April 2000. It was found to be the wreck of a single screw steamship in a depth of 65 metres. There is a gun on the stern deck housing. This confirms her as a war loss – almost certainly a British First World War loss. She has a single boiler, two silt-filled holds forward of the bridge, and a raised foc'sle. There is quite a lot of netting near the stern.

The divers estimated the wreck to be about 230 ft long x 30 ft beam, and about 8-900grt.

It is too small to be the *Creemuir*.

It is probably the British steamship *Norwood* (798grt, 220.8 x 30.2 x 15.1 ft, built by Hall Russell, Aberdeen in 1895 – Yard No.286). The *Norwood* was en route from Middlesbrough to Aberdeen with a general cargo. She was last seen by the *St Rognvald* early on 11 February 1917, when she left the company of that ship to avoid mines in Aberdeen Bay. The *Norwood* was torpedoed and sunk off Aberdeen by the *UC-29* at 05.10 hrs on 11 February 1917. Her entire crew of eighteen were lost.

CREEMUIR

Wreck No: 4	Date Sunk: 11 11 1940
Latitude: 57 01 08 N PA	Longitude: 01 50 00 W PA
GPS Lat: 5701.133 N	GPS Long: 0150.000 W
Location: 10 miles SE of Aberdeen	Area: Aberdeen
Type: Steamship	Tonnage: 3997 grt
Length: 360.2 ft Beam: 51.0 ft	Draught: 24.7 ft
How Sunk: Aircraft Torpedo	Depth: 82 metres

The British steamship *Creemuir* (ex-*Langleemere*, ex-*Medomsley*) which was en route from Hull to Sydney, Nova Scotia in ballast, was sunk by a German aircraft on 11 November 1940 between Stonehaven and Aberdeen, and sank in three minutes. Twenty-six of the crew and one gunner were lost. Her Chief Officer and twelve of her forty-five crew were picked up.

British Vessels Lost at Sea describes the position as 10 miles SE of Aberdeen.

This would plot in 570300N, 014700W PA.

She is recorded by the Hydrographic Department at 570108N, 015000W PA.

ALIRMAY

Wreck No: 5:	Date Sunk: 23 09 1949
Latitude: 57 02 48 N	Longitude: 02 07 00 W
GPS Lat: 5702.800 N	GPS Long: 0207.000 W
Location: Downies, S of Portlethen	Area: Aberdeen
Type: Fishing Boat	Tonnage: 46 grt
Length: ft Beam: ft	Draught: ft
How Sunk: Ran aground	Depth: 4 metres

The Aberdeen fishing boat *Alirmay* (A210) ran aground in dense fog, in a rocky bay overlooked by the hamlet of Downies, just south of Portlethen, and sank within 15 minutes.

The crew were able to jump the 6 feet to the shore, and were led up the 100-foot cliffs to safety.

GARRAWALT

Wreck No: 6	Date Sunk: 06 03 1887
Latitude: 57 03 11 N	Longitude: 02 06 30 W
GPS Lat: 5703.183 N	GPS Long: 0206.500 W
Location: Craigmaroinn, Portlethen	Area: Aberdeen
Type: Steamship	Tonnage: 313 grt
Length: 165.2 ft Beam: 23.4 ft	Draught: ft
How Sunk: Ran aground	Depth: metres

While en route from Sunderland to Aberdeen in ballast, the steamship *Garrawalt* struck one of a small group of rocks at the southern entrance to the narrow channel between the mainland and a large rock known as Craig Maron (Craigmaroinn), off Portlethen village.

There have apparently been several other shipping casualties at the same spot over the years – indeed it would be surprising if there had not been – and following the loss of the *Garrawalt*, there were calls for a lighthouse to be built.

CITY OF ABERDEEN

Wreck No: 7	Date Sunk: 27 01 1871
Latitude: 57 03 30 N PA	Longitude: 02 06 30 W PA
GPS Lat: 5703.500 N	GPS Long: 0206.500 W
Location: Portlethen	Area: Aberdeen
Type: Paddle Steamer	Tonnage: 682 grt
Length: 227.7 ft Beam: 29.7 ft	Draught: ft
How Sunk: Ran aground	Depth: metres

The paddle steamer *City of Aberdeen*, owned by the Aberdeen Steam Navigation Co., stranded at Portlethen on 21 January 1871.

SUSANNA

Wreck No: 8	Date Sunk: 22 03 1917
Latitude: 57 04 00 N PA	Longitude: 01 54 00 W PA
GPS Lat: 5704.000 N	GPS Long: 0154.000 W
Location: 5 miles SE of Girdleness	Area: Aberdeen
Type: Steamship	Tonnage: 442 grt
Length: 149.6 ft Beam: 24.6 ft	Draught: 12.0 ft
How Sunk: By *UC-45*	Depth: 58 metres

Charted as Wk PA with at least 50 metres of water over it in a general depth of about 62 metres.

This is the position recorded for the loss of the Norwegian steamship *Susanna*, captured and sunk by the *UC-45* on 22 March 1917, while en route from Haugesund to Hull with a cargo of herrings.

Lloyds World War One Losses describes the position as 6 miles SE by S ½S of Aberdeen.

A.J. Tennent gives the position as 5740N, 0120W.

The *Susanna* (ex-*Jaederen*) was built by Grangemouth Dockyard Co. in 1894.

SILVERBURN

Wreck No: 9	Date Sunk: 13 06 1917
Latitude: 57 04 00 N PA	Longitude: 01 57 00 W PA
GPS Lat: 5704.000 N	GPS Long: 0157.000 W
Location: 4 miles SE of Cove Bay	Area: Aberdeen
Type: Steamship	Tonnage: 284 grt

Length: 121.0 ft   Beam: 22.1 ft   Draught: 9.5 ft
How Sunk: Submarine – Gunfire   Depth: 60 metres

The steel screw steamship *Silverburn* was built in 1914 at Maryport, engine by Gauldie, Gillespie & Co., Glasgow. She had one deck with machinery aft, and a welldeck forward.

The vessel was captured by a submarine and sunk by gunfire on 13 June 1917.

British Vessels Lost at Sea 1914-18 gives the position as 4 miles SE of Cove Bay, where she is charted as Wk PA with at least 50 metres over her in a general depth of about 60 metres.

TEUTONIA

Wreck No: 10   Date Sunk: 29 10 1915
Latitude: 57 04 00 N PA   Longitude: 02 05 30 W PA
GPS Lat: 5704.000 N   GPS Long: 0205.500 W
Location: Findon Ness   Area: Aberdeen
Type: Barque   Tonnage: 647 grt
Length: 151.8 ft   Beam: 33.0 ft   Draught: ft
How Sunk: Ran aground   Depth: metres

The barque *Teutonia* of Langesund was bound for Leith with a cargo of pit props and had reached the Firth of Forth when heavy seas whipped up by a severe south-easterly storm swept some of the deck cargo away. With the vessel shipping water, the remaining deck cargo was jettisoned overboard. Unable to make headway towards her destination against the wind and sea, the ship was blown before the storm as far north as Findon Ness where she was rapidly dashed to pieces on the rocks. The stern section was washed into the inlet at Arnot Boo, where some of the crew were able to reach the shore, but five others were lost.

There is lots of broken wreckage from more than one vessel on Findon Ness, including a winch, and a propeller shaft tunnel. These obviously did not come from the sailing vessels *Teutonia* or *Dunstaffnage*!

DUNSTAFFNAGE

Wreck No: 11   Date Sunk: 17 03 1883
Latitude: 57 04 00 N PA   Longitude: 02 05 30 W PA
GPS Lat: 5704.000 N   GPS Long: 0205.500 W
Location: Findon Ness   Area: Aberdeen
Type: Sailing Ship   Tonnage: 1945 grt
Length: 268.4 ft   Beam: 38.1 ft   Draught: 19.4 ft
How Sunk: Ran aground   Depth: metres

The sailing ship *Dunstaffnage* was built in 1881 by Oswald Mordaunt & Co., Southampton, and registered in Liverpool.

She had discharged a cargo of jute from Calcutta at Dundee, and was being towed, in ballast, by the tug *Recovery* from the Tay to Liverpool. The weather at the time was atrocious, with heavy snow blown by storm force winds from the north east. By midnight on 16 March 1883, the two vessels had reached a point about twelve miles south-east of Girdle Ness, but in the appalling sea conditions, the vessels were hardly able to make any progress.

At about 2.00 a.m., the towing hook on the tug was carried away, along with the hawser. In such stormy conditions, there was no possibility of reconnecting the tow, and the tug turned southwards to run before the storm, noting as she passed the *Dunstaffnage* that her crew were setting sail, obviously intending to do likewise. Indeed, the sailing ship's crew would have no alternative.

The *Dunstaffnage* was never seen again, and it has been supposed that she struck Findon Ness in the storm and broke up, as wreckage including a lifebuoy bearing the ship's name was washed ashore there. The entire crew of twenty-three were lost, including the captain's wife, son and young daughter. Several mutilated bodies were found washed ashore.

ULSTER

Wreck No: 12		Date Sunk: 23 01 1925
Latitude: 57 04 30 N PA		Longitude: 02 05 30 W PA
GPS Lat: 5704.500 N		GPS Long: 0205.500 W
Location: Earnsheugh Bay, Cove/Portlethen		Area: Aberdeen
Type: Trawler		Tonnage: 185 grt
Length: 110.6 ft	Beam: 21.1 ft	Draught: 11.3 ft
How Sunk: Ran aground		Depth: metres

The trawler *Ulster* left Aberdeen shortly before midnight on 22 January 1925, bound for Granton to fuel up with coal before proceeding to the fishing grounds. Less than two hours after setting out, she encountered fog, and ran aground on rocks below the cliffs at Earnsheugh Bay, between Cove and Portlethen, some five miles south of Aberdeen. An attempt to attract attention with the siren was prematurely cut short after only two blasts, when the inrushing water extinguished the boiler fires. Three of the crew scrambled on to the rocks, and two of them succeeded in climbing the 100-foot-high cliffs in their bare feet. Staggering across fields, they came to Blackhills farm, Cairnrobin. A message was sent to the Cove coastguard, who despatched the lifesaving team to the top of the cliffs, where they were met by a fourth survivor. The third man, who had been left at the foot of the cliffs when he was unable to make the climb with the first two, was hauled up by rope. The five crewmen who had remained on board were all lost.

LUFFNESS

Wreck No: 13		Date Sunk: 21 01 1958
Latitude: 57 05 30 N		Longitude: 02 01 00 W
GPS Lat: 5705.500 N		GPS Long: 0201.000 W
Location: 3 miles S of Girdleness		Area: Aberdeen
Type: Trawler		Tonnage: 254 grt
Length: 127.0 ft	Beam: 23.2 ft	Draught: ft
How Sunk: Ran aground		Depth: 28 metres

The trawler *Luffness* originally stranded in Aberdeen harbour, but was removed and sunk 1¾ miles ESE of Cove Bay, where it is charted as a wreck with at least 28 metres over it in a general depth of about 40 metres.

Two or three lumps on the seabed rise 4–5 metres from the bottom in 45 metres of water.

ALWYN

Wreck No: 14		Date Sunk: 12 06 1917
Latitude: 57 05 30 N PA		Longitude: 01 55 30 W PA
GPS Lat: 5705.500 N		GPS Long: 0155.500 W
Location: 5 miles SE of Girdleness		Area: Aberdeen
Type: Sailing Vessel		Tonnage: 73 grt
Length: 73.6 ft	Beam: 19.3 ft	Draught: 9.1 ft
How Sunk: Submarine – bomb		Depth: metres

On 12 June 1917 the sailing vessel *Alwyn* was captured by a German submarine, and sunk by a bomb placed aboard.

British Vessels Lost at Sea 1914–18 gives her position as 5 miles SE of Girdleness.

Allowing for the annual magnetic variation, this would plot in 570530N, 015530W PA.

COUNTESS OF ABERDEEN

Wreck No: 15		Date Sunk: 15 04 1894
Latitude: 57 05 42 N		Longitude: 02 04 30 W
GPS Lat: 5705.700 N		GPS Long: 0204.500 W
Location: Cove Bay, 3 miles S of Aberdeen		Area: Aberdeen
Type: Steamship		Tonnage: 575 grt
Length: 201.2 ft	Beam: 26.8 ft	Draught: 13.8 ft
How Sunk: Ran aground		Depth: 12 metres

Built in 1878, the *Countess of Aberdeen* ran aground in fog on the north side of Cove Bay while en route from Hull to Aberdeen on 15 April 1894. Not long after stranding, she went on fire and burned until the following day when a heavy swell started to break her up, and she disappeared beneath the surface. The wreck is less than 100 metres southwest of the end of the pier and is very broken up. Debris, including many portholes, lies in 6-13 metres.

Her position has also been described as near the entrance to Cove creek, at the extreme SE end of the rocks jutting out at right angles from the entrance to the creek. The bow points north, and the hull is parallel to the shore, listing about 45° to starboard.

The Hydrographic Department gives the position as 570540.1N, 020421W.

TREBARTHA

Wreck No: 16	Date Sunk: 11 11 1940
Latitude: 57 06 08 N	Longitude: 02 04 12 W
GPS Lat: 5706.133 N	GPS Long: 0204.200 W
Location: Cove Bay, 3 miles S of Aberdeen	Area: Aberdeen
Type: Steamship	Tonnage: 4597 grt

Length: 396.0 ft   Beam: 52.8 ft   Draught: 26.4 ft
How Sunk: Bombed and gunned   Depth: 13 metres

The *Trebartha* was built in 1920 by J. Redhead & Sons of South Shields, and was owned by the Hain Steamship Co., part of P&O group.

She was bombed and gunned by German aircraft on 11 November 1940, while en route, in ballast, from London to Philadelphia. Four of her crew were lost. One bomb hit the port side, killing a gunner. Fire also broke out trapping three operators in the W/T shack. The rest of the crew abandoned ship and were strafed while taking to the boats. The survivors were picked up by *SS Oberon* and landed at Aberdeen.

British Vessels Lost at Sea 1939-45 gives the position as 4 miles SE of Aberdeen, and a wreck is charted as PA with at least 50 metres of water over it in a general depth of 60 metres at 570745N, 015700W.

This, however, must refer to the position of attack on the 11th, when the *Trebartha* was abandoned, but she did not sink until the 12th, after drifting ashore 3 miles south of Aberdeen. She is now in two parts lying about 50ft apart in 13 metres of water close to the shore at the north end of Cove Bay, just below the Cove Bay hotel. Lots of wreckage, including brass, is spread over a wide area.

GELSINA

Wreck No: 17	Date Sunk: 25 06 1917
Latitude: 57 06 45 N PA	Longitude: 01 57 00 W PA
GPS Lat: 5706.750 N	GPS Long: 0157.000 W
Location: Mined off Girdleness	Area: Aberdeen
Type: Trawler	Tonnage: 227 grt
Length: 118.8 ft Beam: 23.1 ft	Draught: ft
How Sunk: Mined	Depth: metres

The 227-ton steam trawler *Gelsina* was mined off Girdleness on 25 June 1917 while on Admiralty service. She was armed with one 3-prd. gun.

PRINCE CONSORT

Wreck No: 18	Date Sunk: 11 05 1867
Latitude: 57 06 46 N	Longitude: 02 03 30 W
GPS Lat: 5706.767 N	GPS Long: 0203.500 W
Location: Hasman Rock, N of Altens Haven	Area: Aberdeen
Type: Paddle Steamer	Tonnage: 623 grt
Length: 224.0 ft Beam: 25.3 ft	Draught: 14.2 ft
How Sunk: Ran aground	Depth: metres

The iron paddle steamer *Prince Consort*, en route from Granton to Kirkwall and Lerwick with seventy-three passengers and a general cargo, stranded on Altens Rock, alternatively known as Hasman Rock, off Burnbanks Haven on 11 May 1867. The passengers and crew were taken off by fishermen from Altens.

The ship broke in two and a considerable amount of wreckage and cargo was washed ashore.

The very broken remains of a metal ship have been found amongst the Hasman Rocks at the north of Altens Haven, 2 miles south of Aberdeen.

KENILWORTH

Wreck No: 19	Date Sunk: 30 01 1906
Latitude: 57 06 46 N	Longitude: 02 03 30 W
GPS Lat: 5706.767 N	GPS Long: 0203.500 W
Location: Hasman Rock, N of Altens Haven	Area: Aberdeen
Type: Steamship	Tonnage: 274 grt
Length: 145.2 ft. Beam: 23.1 ft.	Draught: ft.
How Sunk: Ran aground	Depth: metres

While en route to Aberdeen with a cargo of coal on 30 January 1906, the British steamship *Kenilworth* was damaged by hitting rocks at Cove. Although she remained afloat, she was making water. An attempt was made to reach Aberdeen, but the water level was rising so quickly that she had to be run ashore at Burnbanks Haven, south of Altens. Her difficulties had been spotted from the shore, and the Cove lifesaving team set off to follow the steamer northwards. Arriving at Burnbanks, they found the crew had already abandoned ship in their lifeboat, and were attempting to row the rest of the way to Aberdeen. In the heavy seas running, however, they landed at Nigg Bay, south of Girdleness, and set off for Aberdeen on foot. Meanwhile, a tug had left Aberdeen to intercept them at sea, and when it failed to find them as expected, it was assumed their lifeboat had sunk, and a search was mounted. When the men eventually arrived safely in Aberdeen later that day, the search was called off.

The *Kenilworth* finally sank on top of the wreck of the *Prince Consort* at Hasman Rock. The wreck is very broken up and flattened.

Kenilworth *aground at Burnbanks Haven* (Photo: Aberdeen Art Gallery & Museums Collection)

XERXES

Wreck No: 20	Date Sunk: 16 11 1915
Latitude: 57 07 00 N PA	Longitude: 01 50 00 W PA
GPS Lat: 5707.000	GPS Long: 0150.000 W

Location: Off Girdleness		Area: Aberdeen
Type: Trawler		Tonnage: 243 grt
Length: 125.0 ft	Beam: 22.0 ft	Draught: 11.9 ft
How Sunk: Collision		Depth: metres

The steel steam trawler *Xerxes* was built by Cochranes of Selby in 1908. She was sunk in a collision off Girdleness on 16 November 1915.

UNKNOWN – FORT ROYAL?

Wreck No: 21		Date Sunk:
Latitude: 57 07 05 N		Longitude: 01 59 51 W
GPS Lat: 5707.088 N		GPS Long: 0159.849 W
Location: 2½ miles SE ½E of Girdleness		Area: Aberdeen
Type:		Tonnage: grt
Length: ft	Beam: ft	
How Sunk:		Depth: 45 metres

Charted as a wreck with at least 30 metres over it in about 50 metres.

This wreck was found during a survey on 13 August 1976, while the survey vessel was moving from one sonar line to another. Although the wreck lay just outside the survey area, its position was noted as 570707N, 015944W.

The wreck has been dived by Dave Gordon of Aberdeen Water Sports, who described it as a fairly typical steam trawler/minesweeper sitting upright and intact in 50 metres at 5707.088N, 0159.849W.

One unusual feature is that the stern is covered in a mass of twisted aluminium aircraft wreckage.

This might be the *Fort Royal*, and it is possible that the remains of the *Robert Bowen* may lie in the adjacent Spoil Ground. These vessels were both lost in the same aircraft attack while minesweeping off Aberdeen on 9 February 1940.

UNKNOWN

Wreck No: 22		Date Sunk:
Latitude: 57 07 40 N		Longitude: 01 59 11 W
GPS Lat: 5707.667 N		GPS Long: 0159.183 W
Location: 2½ miles SE of Girdleness		Area: Aberdeen
Type:		Tonnage: grt
Length: ft	Beam: ft	Draught: ft
How Sunk:		Depth: 58 metres

Charted as a wreck in 47 metres.

The Hydrographic Department suggested this might be the German torpedo boat *T-6*, which was mined on 7 November 1940, but it is a long way from 575000N, 005000W PA, which was the position given for the *T-6* striking the mine.

The wreck has been reported to be about 80 metres long (264 ft), which closely corresponds to the length of the *T-6*, and lying on a gently sloping seabed. Depth to the top of the bows is 58 metres, and the stern is in 64 metres.

Local divers who have been down to this wreck describe it as an intact steel ship about 150-200ft long and 25-30ft wide. They refer to it as the grass wreck, because according to local fishermen it is reputed to have been carrying a cargo of esparto grass*, although the divers have found no evidence to support this theory.

The wreck is sitting upright, and rises about 10 metres up from the bottom.

There is one mast which sticks up perhaps a further 10 metres, with an old net snagged on it. The net drapes down to the deck of the ship. Portholes seen are made of steel, rather than brass, and there is no sign of any gun. The divers' description in no way matches the *T-6*!

*This is probably a reference to the 1,137 grt steamship *Tasmania*, which drifted northwards with a cargo of esparto grass, and grounded ¾ mile north of the river Don on 10 February 1883. Her twenty-one crew were taken off by breeches buoy. The wreck at 570740N, 015911W is much too far south to be the *Tasmania*, which must be at about 571130N, 020345W, between Findlay Farm and Berryhill, and in any case, the *Tasmania* was a wooden vessel.

BEN TORC

Wreck No: 23		Date Sunk: 06 09 1927	
Latitude: 57 07 42 N		Longitude: 02 02 48 W	
GPS Lat: 5707.700 N		GPS Long: 0202.800 W	
Location: Gregness, ½ mile S of Girdleness		Area: Aberdeen	
Type: Trawler		Tonnage: 199 grt	
Length: 115.8 ft	Beam: 22.1 ft	Draught: 12.0 ft	
How Sunk: Ran aground		Depth: 10 metres	

On 6 September 1927, the steam trawler *Ben Torc* was returning to Aberdeen from a coaling trip to Granton. In fog, fading light and a strong south-easterly wind, she ran on to the rocks at Gregness, about half a mile south of Girdleness. The sound of her whistle attracted the attention of the coastguards to her plight, and two of them swam across a gully to throw a rope to the crew. Despite all that effort on their behalf, the crew refused to leave the vessel by that lifeline, and insisted on waiting for the Aberdeen lifeboat to take them off.

The lifeboat succeeded in approaching the *Ben Torc*, despite the rocks surrounding her, and took off five of the crew. The sixth man, the skipper, had to be rescued from the sea when he fell into the water between the two vessels as he attempted to jump into the lifeboat.

BRANKSEA

Wreck No: 24		Date Sunk: 10 02 1940	
Latitude: 57 08 00 N PA		Longitude: 02 00 00 W PA	
GPS Lat: 5708.000 N		GPS Long: 0200.000 W	
Location: 2 miles ESE of Girdleness		Area: Aberdeen	
Type: Steamship		Tonnage: 214 grt	
Length: 112.3 ft	Beam: 21.1 ft	Draught: 9.1 ft	
How Sunk: Foundered		Depth: metres	

The steamship *Branksea* (ex-*Growler*) was built in 1890 by Edwards & Symes of Millwall, London. Her engine was made by Wilson & Co., London, and the vessel was owned by the Tay Sand Co. Ltd.

She sank suddenly, without warning or explosion, in a smooth sea, 3 miles 90° off Girdleness (cause unknown), while under tow by the tug *Prizeman* to Scapa Flow, where it had been intended to sink her as a blockship to prevent enemy vessels entering the Flow via the sounds between the islands. The blockships sunk for that purpose in both the First and Second World Wars were eventually made redundant by the 'Churchill Barriers' – causeways constructed of concrete blocks made by Italian prisoners of war. These permanent solid links eliminated the security problem by closing the channels completely, and carry the road between the eastern islands.

The *Branksea* was described as a 'Special Service Vessel', which was a description applied to vessels intended to be used as blockships.

The Hydrographic Department has recorded her position as 570000N, 020000W PA.

G KOCH

Wreck No: 25	Date Sunk: 12 01 1913
Latitude: 57 08 18 N	Longitude: 02 02 40 W
GPS Lat: 5708.300 N	GPS Long: 0202.667 W
Location: Below Girdleness Lighthouse	Area: Aberdeen
Type: Steamship	Tonnage: 1609 grt
Length: 260.7 ft Beam: 36.3 ft	Draught: 16.5 ft
How Sunk: Ran aground	Depth: metres

The Danish steel steamship *G Koch* (ex-*Excelsior*) stranded at the foot of Girdleness Lighthouse on 12 January 1913, after being driven before a storm while en route to Burntisland with a cargo of pit props. She was battered to pieces in less than an hour. The cargo and deck fittings from the ship were dashed about by 40-foot waves, whipped up by winds so strong that it was hard for those on the land to stand up. All but seven of the crew of nineteen were rescued by Cove, Torry and Donmouth lifesaving teams with lines fired to the wreck by rockets. Her boiler is visible above water at low tide.

Stern section of G Koch *at Girdleness (Photo: Aberdeen Art Gallery & Museums Collection)*

BEN SCREEL

Wreck No: 26	Date Sunk: 18 01 1933
Latitude: 57 08 20 N PA	Longitude: 02 02 40 W PA
GPS Lat: 5708.333 N	GPS Long: 0202.667 W
Location: Girdleness Lighthouse	Area: Aberdeen
Type: Trawler	Tonnage: 197 grt
Length: 115.5 ft Beam: 23.1 ft	Draught: ft
How Sunk: Ran aground	Depth: metres

On 18 January 1933 the Aberdeen steam trawler *Ben Screel* was returning to Aberdeen in fog, and overshot the harbour entrance, continuing about half a mile too far south. By the time Girdleness foghorn was heard, it was too late to avoid running on to the rocks below the lighthouse. The lighthouse keepers called out the Torry and Aberdeen lifesaving brigades, but by the time they arrived, the crew of the *Ben Screel* had taken to the foremast rigging. The vessel was being pounded by heavy seas, and the men were unable to leave their precarious positions to retrieve the first line fired over the stern of their vessel. The second line was fired within reach of the crew, who were able to secure it to the mast and haul out the breeches buoy. The rope, however, had fouled, preventing the buoy from being used, and while this was being rectified, one of the crew hauled himself along the rope to the rocks. The remaining crewmen were then brought ashore in the breeches buoy, in a cold, wet and exhausted state.

Ben Screel *aground at Girdleness (Photo: Aberdeen Art Gallery & Museums Collection)*

COLLYNIE

Wreck No: 27	Date Sunk: 03 05 1897
Latitude: 57 08 40 N PA	Longitude: 02 02 35 W PA
GPS Lat: 5708.667 N	GPS Long: 0202.583 W
Location: 1 mile WNW of Girdleness	Area: Aberdeen
Type: Steamship	Tonnage: 272 grt
Length: 131.0 ft Beam: 20.7 ft	Draught: 10.3 ft
How Sunk: Collision	Depth: metres

The iron steamship *Collynie* was sunk in a collision with the Wick steamship *Girnigoe* on 3 May 1897, one mile WNW of Girdleness. Eleven lives were lost.

The wreck charted in 9 metres of water at 570846N, 020257W, 1.7 cables 60° from the South Breakwater head may be the *Collynie*, but see also *Empress* below.

EMPRESS

Wreck No: 28	Date Sunk: 23 12 1915
Latitude: 57 08 46 N	Longitude: 02 02 57 W
GPS Lat: 5708.767 N	GPS Long: 0202.950 W
Location: ½ mile N of Girdleness	Area: Aberdeen
Type: Trawler	Tonnage: 104 grt
Length: 93.7 ft Beam: 18.6 ft	Draught: 10.1 ft
How Sunk: Foundered	Depth: 7 metres

The trawler *Empress* foundered off Aberdeen in a severe SE gale on 23 December 1915. All eight members of the crew were lost. Broken wreckage belonging to the *Empress* was washed ashore at Balnagask.

A wreck is charted in 7 metres, ½ mile N of Girdleness, and it may be the *Empress*, but there are at least nine other possibilities for the identity of this one:

Branksea, Robert Bowen, Fort Royal, Gelsina, Xerxes, Nellie Nutten, Era, Yesso, Collynie.

In addition, the steamer *Brilliant* hit ground on the south side of the North Pier, caught fire and sank on 12 December 1839.

YESSO

Wreck No: 29	Date Sunk: 09 02 1917
Latitude: 57 08 57 N	Longitude: 02 03 13 W
GPS Lat: 5708.950 N	GPS Long: 0203.217 W
Location: ½ mile N of Girdleness	Area: Aberdeen
Type: Trawler	Tonnage: 229 grt
Length: 119.9 ft Beam: 22.1 ft	Draught: 11.5 ft
How Sunk: Mined	Depth: 15 metres

The trawler *Yesso* (ex-*Henry Flight*) was in Admiralty service as a minesweeper when she was mined off Aberdeen on 9 February 1917 about 600 yards 45° from the south breakwater at the entrance to Aberdeen harbour. *Yesso* was built by Cochranes of Selby in 1911.

ROBERT BOWEN

Wreck No: 30	Date Sunk: 09 02 1940
Latitude: 57 09 00 N PA	Longitude: 02 00 00 W PA
GPS Lat: 5709.000 N	GPS Long: 0200.000 W
Location: Off Aberdeen	Area: Aberdeen
Type: Trawler	Tonnage: 290 grt

Length: 126.1 ft   Beam: 23.6 ft   Draught: 12.6 ft

How Sunk: By aircraft   Depth: metres

The trawler *Robert Bowen* was built in 1918 by Cook Welton & Gemmel, Beverley. She was requisitioned by the Admiralty for use as a minesweeper in 1939, and broke in two and sank with all hands when bombed while minesweeping off Aberdeen at 11.50 hrs on 9 February 1940.

ONWARD

Wreck No: 31	Date Sunk: 11 07 1916
Latitude: 57 09 00 N PA	Longitude: 02 00 00 W PA
GPS Lat: 5709.000 N	GPS Long: 0200.000 W
Location: 'Off Aberdeen'	Area: Aberdeen
Type: Trawler (H 980)	Tonnage: 266 grt
Length: 143.5 ft Beam: 22.3 ft	Draught: 11.0 ft
How Sunk: Submarine gunfire	Depth: metres

The 266-grt steam trawler *Onward* was built by Cochranes of Selby in 1908. She was requisitioned by the Admiralty in 1915 for use as an armed patrol trawler, and was sunk by a submarine 'off Aberdeen' on 11 July 1916.

The steam trawlers *Onward*, *Nellie Nutten*, and *Era* were together when they were attacked with gunfire by four German U-boats 'off Aberdeen' – hence the approximate position. (This position is rather notional, however. The position has also been described as about 90 miles east of Aberdeen, and given as 5114N, 0111E, which is not even in Scottish waters!)

By 8.35pm on 11 July 1916 *Onward*'s gun was out of action. She was on fire in several places, her engine was damaged and her engine room and stokehold were filling. The vessel was sinking and the crew abandoned ship in their small boat. They tried to reach a nearby Dutch fishing vessel, but were cut off by *U-52*, which took the *Onward*'s crew of fourteen aboard as POWs.

NELLIE NUTTEN

Wreck No: 32	Date Sunk: 11 07 1916
Latitude: 57 09 00 N PA	Longitude: 02 00 00 W PA
GPS Lat: 5709.000 N	GPS Long: 0200.000 W
Location: "Off Aberdeen"	Area: Aberdeen
Type: Trawler (GN 69)	Tonnage: 184 grt
Length: 108.4 ft Beam: 21.6 ft	Draught: 11.5 ft
How Sunk: By *U-52* – gunfire	Depth: metres

The steam trawler *Nellie Nutten* (built by Hall Russell, Aberdeen in 1901) was requisitioned by the Admiralty for use as a minesweeper, and was armed with a single 3-pdr. gun. She was sunk by gunfire from four U-boats: *U-46*, *U-49*, *U-52* and *U-69* 'off Aberdeen' on 11 July 1916.

Nellie Nutten's crew were more fortunate than *Onward*'s crew, in that all but one of them succeeded in boarding the Dutch fishing lugger *SCH 197*, which landed the skipper and ten of *Nellie Nutten*'s crew. The one member of the crew who did not make it on board the lugger was taken prisoner by *U-52*. (Perhaps with fourteen men from *Onward*, and twelve from *Era*, the U-boat was too crowded to accommodate more than one token prisoner from *Nellie Nutten*.)

ERA

Wreck No: 33	Date Sunk: 11 07 1916
Latitude: 57 09 00 N PA	Longitude: 02 00 00 W PA
GPS Lat: 5709.000 N	GPS Long: 0200.000 W
Location: "Off Aberdeen"	Area: Aberdeen
Type: Trawler (H 461)	Tonnage: 168 grt
Length: 104.6 ft Beam: 21.1 ft	Draught: 10.6 ft
How Sunk: *U-52* – gunfire	Depth: metres

The trawler *Era* (built by Mackie & Thomson of Glasgow in 1899) was requisitioned by the Admiralty in 1915 for use as an armed patrol trawler. She was sunk by gunfire from the *U-52* 'off Aberdeen' on 11 July 1916. All twelve of *Era*'s crew were made POWs. Some of the men were injured.

LILLIE

Wreck No: 34	Date Sunk: 19 01 1912
Latitude: 57 09 17 N	Longitude: 02 04 22 W
GPS Lat: 5709.283 N	GPS Long: 0204.367 W
Location: Close ashore, Aberdeen	Area: Aberdeen
Type: Trawler ?	Tonnage: 81 grt
Length: 91.5 ft Beam: 18.3 ft	Draught: 9.3 ft
How Sunk: Ran aground	Depth: 1 metre

This seems to have been a popular place to run aground, as at least seven vessels have come to grief here over the years. Two boilers are charted as an obstruction in one metre of water off the Beach Ballroom. One of them may be all that is left of the *Lillie*, which was lost by stranding in 1912. The Hydrographic Department suggests the other may be the *Cairnie*, a steamship with a cargo of coal, which ran on to the sand opposite the pleasure beach on 13 April 1941.

Notification was given that the wrecks of three vessels were to be blasted in November 1957 – viz. the *Cairnie* (1941), the *James Hall* (1904), and the trawler *Stromness* (1939).

That report does not mention the *Lillie*, nor the *Argosy*, which was wrecked in the same place as the *James Hall* on 17 January 1912.

On 27 November 1852, the crews of the brigs *Venus* and *Armitstead* were swept overboard and the brigs foundered in front of the beach, but obviously the boilers cannot have come from either of these two sailing ships.

The 134-ton *Venus* was apparently lost about one mile north of Aberdeen, when she was run ashore opposite Broad Hill at 5.00am. The tide was fully out at the time, and the vessel grounded 500 yards from the shore, with the sea breaking right over her. Only one of her crew was saved.

The *Armitstead* was run ashore between Footdee and the bathing station, shortly after 11.00am, and broke in two. Five of the crew were washed away and drowned, leaving the captain clinging to a floating plank. He was washed ashore by successive waves, and was the only survivor.

CAIRNIE

Wreck No: 35
Latitude: 57 09 17 N
GPS Lat: 5709.283 N
Location: Close ashore, Aberdeen
Type: Steamship
Length: 120.8 ft
How Sunk: Bombed and ran aground

Date Sunk: 13 04 1941
Longitude: 02 04 22 W
GPS Long: 0204.367 W
Area: Aberdeen
Tonnage: 250 grt
Beam: 20.5 ft   Draught: 10.2 ft
Depth: 1 metre

The 250-grt steamship *Cairnie* was bombed by aircraft 6 to 8 miles S by W of Tod Head, while bound from Methil to Holm, Orkney with 230 tons of coal.

An alternative description of the position of attack is 5 miles E of Johnshaven. She was damaged by a near miss, and subsequently came ashore on 13 April 1941, 320°, 6.5 cables to the North Pier, Aberdeen. Salvage efforts were abandoned, and she was notified for scrap. Only the boiler remains, and this dries at low water.

JAMES HALL

Wreck No: 36
Latitude: 57 09 26 N
GPS Lat: 5709.433 N
Location: Close ashore, Aberdeen
Type: Steamship
Length: 175.0 ft
How Sunk: Collision with *Luddick*

Date Sunk: 23 02 1904
Longitude: 02 04 22 W
GPS Long: 0204.367 W
Area: Aberdeen
Tonnage: 366 grt
Beam: 24.1 ft   Draught: 13.3 ft
Depth: 1 metre

The iron steamship *James Hall* was built by Hall Russell of Aberdeen in 1870. She was unusually long for her gross tonnage. This was because she had a bowsprit and figurehead. While both vessels were making for Aberdeen harbour, the *James Hall* crossed the bows of the *Luddick* and was badly holed on the port quarter. She immediately began to sink and the crew abandoned ship, leaving their vessel heading towards the shore with her engine running. She eventually ran ashore just north of the bathing station.

Although badly damaged about the bow, the *Luddick* picked up the crew of the *James Hall* and limped into Aberdeen. The boiler remains, and dries at low water.

STROMNESS

Wreck No: 37
Latitude: 57 09 30 N PA
GPS Lat: 5709.500 N
Location: Close ashore, Aberdeen
Type: Trawler
Length: 111.0 ft
How Sunk: Ran aground

Date Sunk: 05 10 1939
Longitude: 02 04 15 W PA
GPS Long: 0204.250 W
Area: Aberdeen
Tonnage: 206 grt
Beam: 22.4 ft   Draught: 11.6 ft
Depth: metres

The steam trawler *Stromness* (ex-*Mopsa*) was built by Cook Welton & Gemmel of Beverley in 1907. She drove ashore in a dark night when all the shore lights were blacked out because of the war-time restrictions. Distress rockets were fired, and the crew were rescued by breeches buoy.

The remains of the keel are reported to lie 'abreast of Broad Hill, Aberdeen', near the Beach Ballroom.

STURDEE

Wreck No: 38		Date Sunk: 19 10 1955
Latitude: 57 09 30 N		Longitude: 02 04 15 W
GPS Lat: 5709.500 N		GPS Long: 0204.250 W
Location: Close ashore, Aberdeen		Area: Aberdeen
Type: Trawler		Tonnage: 202 grt
Length: 116.0 ft	Beam: 22.2 ft	Draught: 12.1 ft
How Sunk: Ran aground		Depth: 1 metre

The steam trawler *Sturdee* (ex-*Michael Brian*) was built in 1919 by Hall Russell of Aberdeen. Returning to Aberdeen in fog, she ran aground on the sand just north of the Beach Ballroom. Bridge of Don LSA crew arrived and fired a line to the trawler, which lay in the surf about 150 yards from the shore. Aberdeen lifeboat arrived at the same time and took off all eleven crew in a rescue made difficult by the heavily-breaking seas.

The fish in the trawler's hold was landed the next day, but the *Sturdee* herself was beyond recovery, and was later broken up where she lay, the remains being charted close to the shore in a depth of about one metre.

The wreck is flattened on the seabed, but apparently there are still intact portholes complete with glass to be found in the wreckage.

ERIKSHOLM

Wreck No: 39		Date Sunk: 01 01 1918
Latitude: 57 09 40 N PA		Longitude: 01 51 00 W PA
GPS Lat: 5709.667 N		GPS Long: 0151.000 W
Location: 6 miles ENE of Aberdeen		Area: Aberdeen
Type: Steamship		Tonnage: 2632 grt
Length: 313.0 ft	Beam: 45.0 ft	Draught: 20.0 ft
How Sunk: Mined		Depth: metres

According to one report, the Swedish steamship *Eriksholm* (ex-*Ester*) was mined 6 miles ENE of Aberdeen on 1 January 1918, while en route from Newcastle to Gothenburg with a cargo of coal. The mine was laid by the *UC-58*.

The Hydrographic Department has recorded her at 570940N, 015100W PA.

Lloyds World War One Losses states that she was mined near Stavanger, Norway, and A.J. Tennent gives the position as 5710N, 0151E, and also describes the position as south of Aberdeen.

GLENTANAR

Wreck No: 40	Date Sunk: 03 05 1917
Latitude: 57 09 45 N	Longitude: 02 01 40 W
GPS Lat: 5709.750 N	GPS Long: 0201.667 W
Location: 1 mile NE of Girdleness	Area: Aberdeen
Type: Steamship	Tonnage: 817 grt
Length: 191.4 ft Beam: 29.7 ft	Draught: 10.0 ft
How Sunk: Mined	Depth: 20 metres

The British steamship *Glantanar* was en route from Seaham to Aberdeen with a cargo of coal on 3 May 1917 when she struck a mine laid by the *U-77*, one mile NE of Girdleness.

The wreck lies on a sandy bottom, with a least depth of 20 metres in 27 metres.

She is now upside down and well broken up. The boilers are still there, as is her 4-bladed iron propeller with a diameter of more than six feet.

There may be a restriction on diving her, as the wreck lies within the Aberdeen Harbour Board area.

VIRGILIA

Wreck No: 41	Date Sunk: 03 06 1917
Latitude: 57 09 40 N	Longitude: 01 51 00 W
GPS Lat: 5709.700 N	GPS Long: 0151.000 W
Location: 6 miles E of Girdleness	Area: Aberdeen
Type: Trawler	Tonnage: 209 grt
Length: 116.2 ft Beam: 21.5 ft	Draught: 11.2 ft
How Sunk: Submarine – scuttling charge	Depth: 65 metres

Charted as Wk PA with at least 50 metres over it in a general depth of about 69 metres.

The iron screw steam trawler *Virgilia* was built in 1900 by Schofield, Hagerup & Doughty of Grimsby, engine by C.D. Holmes of Hull.

She was captured by a German submarine and sunk with an explosive charge 5 miles E of Girdleness on 3 June 1917. Her master was taken prisoner.

The Hydrographic Department notes that the *Virgilia* sank in the same position as the *Eriksholm*.

TREVORIAN

Wreck No: 42	Date Sunk: 29 11 1943
Latitude: 57 10 00 N PA	Longitude: 01 54 00 W PA
GPS Lat: 5710.000 N	GPS Long: 0154.000 W
Location: 5 miles E of Girdleness	Area: Aberdeen
Type: Steamship	Tonnage: 4599 grt

Length: 402.6 ft   Beam: 52.8 ft   Draught: ft
How Sunk: Collision with *Ole Garda*   Depth: 62 metres

The steamship *Trevorian* sank in collision with the Icelandic trawler *Ole Garda*, while en route from Hull to the Mediterranean with a cargo of government stores on 29 November 1943.

FORT ROYAL

Wreck No: 43   Date Sunk: 09 02 1940
Latitude: 57 10 00 N PA   Longitude: 01 50 00 W PA
GPS Lat: 5710.000 N   GPS Long: 0150.000 W
Location: Off Aberdeen   Area: Aberdeen
Type: Trawler   Tonnage: 550 grt
Length: 141.0 ft   Beam: 24.1 ft   Draught: 13.2 ft
How Sunk: Aircraft   Depth: metres

The steel trawler *Fort Royal*, built in 1931 by J. Lewis of Aberdeen, was requisitioned in 1939 for use as a minesweeper.

She sank in minutes when attacked by German aircraft while minesweeping off Aberdeen at 11.50 hrs on 9 February 1940. Seven of her crew were killed and twenty-five rescued.

(See Wreck No. 21 at 570705N, 015951W.)

PRINCE OF WALES

Wreck No: 44   Date Sunk: 25 03 1917
Latitude: 57 10 00 N PA   Longitude: 01 32 00 W PA
GPS Lat: 5710.000 N   GPS Long: 0132.000 W
Location: 17 miles E by S of Girdleness Area: Aberdeen
Type: Trawler   Tonnage: 158 grt
Length: 106.6 ft   Beam: 20.5 ft   Draught: 11.0 ft
How Sunk: Mined   Depth: metres

The trawler *Prince of Wales* was built 1891 by Cook Welton & Gemmell of Hull. According to one report she was sunk off Aberdeen on 25 March 1917 by a mine laid by the *UC-77*.

Another report says she was captured by a U-boat and sunk with a scuttling charge after her crew had abandoned ship.

DILSTON CASTLE

Wreck No: 45   Date Sunk: 29 04 1917
Latitude: 57 10 00 N PA   Longitude: 01 32 00 W PA
GPS Lat: 5710.000 N   GPS Long: 0132.000 W
Location: 16 miles E by S of Girdleness Area: Aberdeen
Type: Trawler   Tonnage: 129 grt

Length: 96.7 ft   Beam: 19.4 ft   Draught: 10.4 ft
How Sunk: *UB-22* – scuttling charge   Depth: metres

The steam trawler *Dilston Castle* was built by Clelands Graving Dock, Newcastle in 1900.

She was sunk by the *UB-22* on 29 April 1917, in almost the same position as the *Prince of Wales*.

ST CATHERINE

Wreck No: 46   Date Sunk: 14 11 1940
Latitude: 57 10 10 N PA   Longitude: 01 51 55 W PA
GPS Lat: 5710.167 N   GPS Long: 0151.917 W
Location: 6 miles E of Girdleness   Area: Aberdeen
Type: Steamship   Tonnage: 1216 grt
Length: 243.3 ft   Beam: 34.9 ft   Draught: 15.2 ft
How Sunk: Torpedoed by aircraft   Depth: 66 metres

Built in 1916 by Caledon, Dundee as the *Highlander*, this vessel had succeeded in shooting down two out of three German aircraft attacking her with torpedoes off Tod Head in 5656N, 0204W on 2 August 1940. The first bomber was hit by AA fire and crashed in the sea. The second attack two minutes later saw the enemy aircraft drop bombs, which missed. It then circled and was hit by AA fire, lost height, hit the *Highlander*'s port lifeboat and swung round to crash onto her poop. She made harbour with the wreckage still aboard the following morning. To boost public morale at a time when there was little else in the way of good news to talk about, the incident was widely publicised. An unfortunate repercussion was that from then on, the vessel seemed to attract an excessive amount of unwelcome attention from the Germans, and in an attempt to disguise her identity, she was renamed *St Catherine*.

St Catherine (*as* Highlander) (*Drawing by H.H. Rodmell*)

On 14 November 1940, just after leaving Aberdeen for Kirkwall, she sank in four minutes after being hit by an aircraft torpedo ¼ mile south of the outer buoy in the swept channel. Fourteen of the crew and one passenger were lost, but the steamship *Berriedale*, which was also leaving Aberdeen to join the same convoy, picked up seventeen survivors. Captain Norquoy and the Second Officer were among those lost.

Present-day charts do not show where the swept channel for the approach to Aberdeen was in 1940, but the wreck charted with at least 40 metres over it in about 65 metres at 571010N, 015155W PA looks like a good candidate for closely matching the position description, bearing in mind the leading lights for the approach to Aberdeen require a course of 235° from the East North East.

NURZEC

Wreck No: 47	Date Sunk: 04 01 1974
Latitude: 57 11 00 N PA	Longitude: 02 04 00 W PA
GPS Lat: 5711.000 N	GPS Long: 0204.000 W
Location: Near Balmedie, N of Aberdeen	Area: Aberdeen
Type: Trawler	Tonnage: 686 grt
Length: 179.6 ft Beam: 29.6 ft	Draught: 18.3 ft
How Sunk: Ran aground/salvaged	Depth: metres

Crew members of the Polish trawler *Nurzec* were rescued by helicopter and breeches buoy when she ran aground in a storm at Murcar near Balmedie on the Belhelvie coast on 4 January 1974. The vessel had grounded about 400 yards from the shore. Two of the crew left the trawler in a liferaft which overturned, but they made it ashore through the surf and staggered into Murcar golf clubhouse.

While the rescue services were being alerted, the Russian tug *Gordyy* arrived on the scene and sent a raft with five men over to the stranded trawler, to rescue the twenty-six men still aboard. Eighteen of the crew were successfully taken off before that raft also capsized in the surf, throwing the occupants in the water. Nine survivors made it to Murcar clubhouse.

Although the *Nurzec* had grounded on sand about 400 yards offshore, the coastguards were able to get a line aboard the vessel, but none of the remaining men aboard would leave by that line. Five others were found alive on the beach and were taken to hospital, and four bodies were recovered from the upturned raft.

One of the Russian seamen was found exhausted on the beach about a mile from the stricken trawler, and coastguards gathered up debris from the beach and lit a fire to keep him warm. A helicopter lifted him from the beach and took him to Murcar golf club, where an ambulance was waiting. Police appealed to journalists and other car owners at the scene to ring the 18th green with car headlights to give the helicopter pilot an indication of where to land.

One of the four men still on the *Nurzec* was eventually persuaded to leave by breeches buoy, and the other three, including skipper Bartczak, were taken off by helicopter.

After several unsuccessful attempts, the *Nurzec* was finally refloated on 22 June, and towed to Aberdeen, where she was sold for scrap.

RATTRAY HEAD

Wreck No: 48	Date Sunk: 05 04 1941
Latitude: 57 11 49 N	Longitude: 01 49 36 W

GPS Lat: 5711.817 N	GPS Long: 0149.600 W
Location: 8½ miles ENE of Girdleness	Area: Aberdeen
Type: Steamship	Tonnage: 496 grt
Length: 160.6 ft.	Beam: 25.1 ft. Draught: 9.2 ft.
How Sunk: Bombed	Depth: metres

The 3-masted steamship *Rattray Head* (ex-*Optic*) was built in 1921 by Ardrossan D.D. Co., engine by Hall Russell, Aberdeen.

En route from Leith and Methil Roads for Stromness with 440 tons of bricks and general cargo, she was attacked by aircraft, and sunk. Eight of the crew were saved, but three were lost.

British Vessels Lost at Sea 1939-45 gives the position as 8 miles ENE of Aberdeen.

SHERIFFMUIR

Wreck No: 49	Date Sunk: 01 10 1976
Latitude: 57 12 06 N	Longitude: 02 03 45 W
GPS Lat: 5712.100 N	GPS Long: 0203.750 W
Location: 3 miles N of Aberdeen harbour	Area: Aberdeen
Type: MFV	Tonnage: 180 grt
Length: 100.6 ft	Beam: 22.1 ft Draught: 10.7 ft
How Sunk: Ran aground	Depth: metres

The former Lowestoft trawler *Sheriffmuir* was operating as an oil rig stand-by vessel when she ran aground in dense fog about 3 miles north of Aberdeen harbour entrance on 1 October 1976. She had grounded at 5.00 a.m. 40 yards from the beach just below Murcar golf clubhouse. At about 6.00 a.m. a breeches buoy was secured to the stranded vessel by the coastguards, but the crew had by that time radioed Aberdeen Coastguard HQ to say that they were in no immediate danger, and could wait until low water then walk ashore. As the tide receded, however, a tractor and trailer was driven out to the vessel, and the six crewmen climbed down a ladder into the trailer to be driven ashore. This was a most unusual form of rescue!

The position has also been given as 571145N, 020400W PA.

EMPEROR

Wreck No: 50	Date Sunk: 10 02 1926
Latitude: 57 12 30 N PA	Longitude: 01 47 30 W PA
GPS Lat: 5712.500 N	GPS Long: 0147.500 W
Location: 9½ miles ENE of Aberdeen	Area: Aberdeen
Type: Trawler	Tonnage: 130 grt
Length: 94.0 ft	Beam: 20.5 ft Draught: 11.0 ft
How Sunk: Collision with *Ocean Prince*	Depth: 65 metres

Charted as Wk PA with at least 50 metres over it, in about 70 metres total depth.

The steam trawler *Emperor*, built in 1895, sank in collision with the trawler *Ocean Prince* about 10 miles off Aberdeen on 10 February 1926.

The nine crew took to their small boat and were picked up by the *Ocean Prince*.

IMPERIAL PRINCE

Wreck No: 51		Date Sunk: 19 10 1923	
Latitude: 57 13 00 N PA		Longitude: 02 03 00 W PA	
GPS Lat: 5713.000 N		GPS Long: 0203.000 W	
Location: Belhelvie Sands, at Blackdog		Area: Aberdeen	
Type: Trawler		Tonnage: 128 grt	
Length: 96.6 ft	Beam: 19.2 ft	Draught: 10.6 ft	
How Sunk: Ran aground		Depth: metres	

The steam trawler *Imperial Prince* was built in 1899. She ran aground on Belhelvie sands at Blackdog on 19 October 1923. The lifesaving apparatus did not reach the shore until two and a half hours after her distress flares were spotted, and by then, the nine crew had taken to the rigging. Although she was 400 yards offshore, her masts and funnel still showed above the surface.

After several unsuccessful attempts, a rocket line was finally fired over the trawler, but it was beyond the reach of the men in the rigging.

About five hours after the stranding, the Aberdeen rowing lifeboat arrived on the scene, having been towed there by a tug. While attempting to get alongside the *Imperial Prince*, the lifeboat was broached to by the heavy swell, and four of the lifeboat crew were thrown into the sea, along with all the oars. Although the four men were able to get aboard the lifeboat again, the oars were lost, and with no means of propulsion, the lifeboat was washed ashore one and a half miles north of the wreck. Further rockets were fired from the shore, and although two lines did reach the wreck, the exhausted trawlermen were unable to haul the breeches buoy out, one of the crew falling into the sea and drowning in his effort to do so.

The Newburgh rowing lifeboat, which had been pulled on its cradle for five miles along the beach by horses, next arrived and was launched from a position down-wind of the wreck. Repeated attempts to approach the trawler were thwarted by the heavy seas, until finally, with its crew almost exhausted, a grapnel thrown into the wreck held, and a breeches buoy was attached to one of the rocket lines still hanging from the trawler's mast.

The first trawlerman made the journey across to the lifeboat successfully, but the second fell from the breeches buoy and was lost. A third man just made it before the line was carried away, and the lifeboat made for the shore with the two rescued survivors, leaving five still clinging to the rigging. With a fresh crew from the crowd on the beach, the lifeboat went out again, but was unable to approach the wreck. A further crew of Aberdeen lifeboatmen who had arrived by bus then made an attempt to take the lifeboat out for a third time, but were beaten back by the crashing waves.

As darkness was falling, sailors from two destroyers visiting Aberdeen arrived by taxi and took the lifeboat out. They succeeded in getting alongside the wreck, again by means of a grapnel, and within fifteen minutes rescued the five remaining trawlermen, who by this time had been clinging to the rigging for twelve hours.

COASTAL EMPEROR

Wreck No: 52	Date Sunk: 06 12 1978
Latitude: 57 13 12 N	Longitude: 02 03 06 W

GPS Lat: 5713.200 N

Location: Skelly Rock, 2½ miles N of River Don

Type: Trawler

Length: 114.0 ft   Beam: 25.1 ft

How Sunk: Ran aground

GPS Long: 0203.100 W

Area: Aberdeen

Tonnage: 250 grt

Draught: 12.6 ft

Depth: metres

The former trawler *Coastal Emperor* was employed as an oil rig stand-by vessel. On 6 December 1978 she was driven on to a lee shore in heavy weather on the sandy beach at Skelly Rock off Blackdog Links, 2½ miles north of the mouth of the river Don. Wind conditions at the time were SSE wind force 7-8. The crew were not in any immediate danger, however, as their vessel remained on an even keel on the sand, and the tide was falling. They were all taken off by breeches buoy the following day. It was considered that the vessel would be refloated on a high tide when the weather abated. Several attempts were subsequently made to tow her off the beach, but all were unsuccessful, and on 30 March the next year, she was finally declared a total loss.

The wreck is charted ashore on the beach, but it has long ago been broken up and nothing remains on the site.

Coastal Emperor *driven well up the beach. She was scrapped in situ. Nothing remains.* (Photo: G. Prentise)

UNKNOWN – PRE-1945

Wreck No: 53

Latitude: 57 13 48 N PA

GPS Lat: 5713.800 N

Location: 6½ miles ESE of Balmedie

Type:

Length: ft   Beam: ft

How Sunk:

Date Sunk: Pre 1945

Longitude: 01 50 00 W PA

GPS Long: 0150.000 W

Area: Aberdeen

Tonnage: grt

Draught: ft

Depth: 60 metres

Charted as Wk PA with at least 28 metres over it in about 60 metres. Possibly the *Eriksholm*?

FAIRY

Wreck No: 54		Date Sunk: 25 01 1937	
Latitude: 57 14 00 N PA		Longitude: 02 02 30 W PA	
GPS Lat: 5714.000 N		GPS Long: 0202.500 W	
Location: Off Millden Links, Belhelvie		Area: Aberdeen	
Type: Steamship		Tonnage: 249 grt	
Length: 120.7 ft	Beam: 22.2 ft	Draught: 8.8 ft	
How Sunk: Ran aground		Depth: metres	

The British steamship *Fairy* was en route from Goole to Aberdeen in very heavy weather. On 25 January 1937 she arrived off Aberdeen, only to discover that the port was closed because of the south-east gale force winds and heavy seas. Attempting to ride out the storm off Aberdeen was worse than running before it, and the ship started to take in water, some of it even coming down the funnel. The water level in the boiler room rose to the point that she was unable to maintain steam pressure to operate the pumps or the engine. Her distress signals were seen by the German trawler *Hendrick*, which managed to pass a line to the distressed vessel and take her in tow. The *Hendrick*, however, was not sufficiently powerful to prevent both vessels being blown by the gale towards land, and by nightfall they were off the mouth of the Don.

Distress flares were fired, and both Aberdeen lifeboats set out to assist the two vessels, which continued to be blown north towards the shore. The towline between the two vessels parted, and the *Fairy* was blown ashore on Millden Links, north of Blackdog Rock. Despite being washed partially over the *Fairy* by the huge waves, the Aberdeen lifeboat *Emma Constance* succeeded in taking off the seven crew. The lifeboat was unable to return to Aberdeen against the direction of the wind and waves, and ran before the weather to the relatively sheltered Moray Firth, finally reaching Macduff at 4.30 a.m. on the 26th. The coxswain of the *Emma Constance* was awarded the RNLI silver medal for this exceptionally difficult and dangerous rescue in such appalling conditions.

UNKNOWN

Wreck No: 55		Date Sunk: Pre 1945	
Latitude: 57 14 30 N PA		Longitude: 01 40 00 W PA	
GPS Lat: 5714.500 N		GPS Long: 0140.000 W	
Location: 14 miles S of Buchan Ness		Area: Aberdeen	
Type:		Tonnage: grt	
Length: ft	Beam: ft	Draught: ft	
How Sunk:		Depth: 65 metres	

Charted as Wk PA with at least 31 metres over it in about 65 metres. This wreck was located early in 1945. Possibly the *U-74*?

U-74

Wreck No: 56	Date Sunk: 27 05 1916
Latitude: 57 15 00 N PA	Longitude: 01 15 00 W PA
GPS Lat: 5715.000 N	GPS Long: 0115.000 W

Location: 25 miles SE of Peterhead   Area: Aberdeen
Type: Submarine   Tonnage: 745 tons
Length: 186.4 ft   Beam: 19.4 ft   Draught: ft
How Sunk: Gunfire from trawlers   Depth: metres

UE-Class Ocean Minelaying U-boats were nicknamed 'The Children of Sorrow'.
They displaced 745 tons surfaced, 829 tons submerged.
On 27 May 1916 four armed trawlers (*Sea Ranger*, *Oku*, *Rodino* and *Kimberley*) caught *U-74* (Weisbach) on the surface, using a sail as a disguise, 25 miles SE of Peterhead, and sank her by gunfire and ramming at 12.55 hrs, before she could lay her mines. All thirty-four of her crew were lost.

The description '25 miles SE of Peterhead' would suggest this must have been at about 571500N, 011500W, but the Hydrographic Department gives the position of *U-74* as 5710N, 0120E.

BEN RHYDDING

Wreck No: 57   Date Sunk: 05 03 1881
Latitude: 57 15 00 N PA   Longitude: 02 02 15 W PA
GPS Lat: 5715.000 N   GPS Long: 0202.250 W
Location: Eigie Links, Balmedie   Area: Aberdeen
Type: Sailing Ship   Tonnage: 1267 grt
Length: 238.8 ft   Beam: 36.5 ft   Draught: 21.5 ft
How Sunk: Ran aground   Depth: metres

The British sailing ship *Ben Rhydding*, en route from Calcutta to Dundee, was blown ashore in a storm on the beach at Eigie Links, Balmedie on 5 March 1881. The sandy shore slopes gently for a considerable distance out to sea, and she stranded about 600 yds offshore. As this was beyond the range of the lifesaving brigade's rocket apparatus, the Newburgh lifeboat was taken overland to be launched from the beach nearby. Because of the huge breaking seas, however, it was impossible to approach the *Ben Rhydding*, whose crew had climbed the rigging to escape from the seas. Later that day, the masts were swept away, and the unfortunate crew thrown into the sea and drowned. The captain's body was washed ashore the following day, along with a great mass of flotsam, including her cargo of jute bales.

ARCHANGEL

Wreck No: 58   Date Sunk: 16 05 1941
Latitude: 57 16 00 N PA   Longitude: 02 00 12 W PA
GPS Lat: 5716.000 N   GPS Long: 0200.200 W
Location: 175° 1 mile off CG Belhelvie   Area: Aberdeen
Type: Steamship   Tonnage: 2448 grt
Length: 343.0 ft   Beam: 43.2 ft   Draught: 14.5 ft
How Sunk: Bombed   Depth: 12 metres

The *Archangel* (ex-*St Petersburg*) was built in 1910 by John Brown, Clydebank as a ferry for Great Eastern Railways, which became part of LNER in 1923.

Coal-fired boilers powered steam turbines, which drove her three propellers. Until the outbreak of the First World War she operated on the Harwich–Hook of Holland service, and with her peacetime sleeping accommodation for 450 passengers, was an ideal vessel for the repatriation of POWs after the war.

She was requisitioned by the Admiralty again in the Second World War, for use as a troop ship, and was bombed by three German aircraft (HE111s), while carrying 400 troops and 40 tons of military equipment from Kirkwall to Aberdeen on 16 May 1941.

The position description given in *British Vessels Lost at Sea 1939-45* refers to the original position of attack at 5755N, 0203W, 17 miles north of Kinnaird Head. Despite an intensive AA barrage put up by *Archangel* and her escort, HMS *Blankney*, three direct bomb hits were sustained, as a result of which twelve of the troops aboard and seventeen of the crew were lost. A further seventy were injured. (Another report says fifty-eight were killed and fifty-nine wounded.)

Tugs were sent from Aberdeen and Peterhead and the ship was taken in tow towards Aberdeen, but the tow had to be abandoned, and she was beached 175° one mile from the Coastguard lookout at Belhelvie, seven miles north of Aberdeen. She was later extensively salvaged, and then apparently forgotten.

She was rediscovered in 1952 when the trawler *Kathleen* lost her trawl. Another trawler recovered the trawl, and reported that there was a wreck in 25 feet of water. Divers later visited the wreck and found it to be a large steel ship, but as underwater visibility was only 2-3 feet at the time, they were unable to get any more information on that occasion. It has since been identified as the *Archangel*, and is charted as a wreck at 571600N, 020012W PA, ¾ mile off the shore at Balmedie (1½ miles offshore at high water).

The wreck charted one mile further south at 571500N, 020012W PA, and the wreck charted at 571545N, 020012W ED (Existence Doubtful), are other estimates of the position of the *Archangel*, but there is no wreck in either of these positions. A more accurate estimate of the true position may be 561600N, 020050W.

The wreck is lying at an angle of about 45° to starboard. The forward section is intact, but the after section is broken up. Her three boilers lie almost clear of the hull on the port side, but beware of the hazard of potential entanglement in the lost fishing nets in that area.

With the movement of sand due to sea action, wreckage covers and uncovers.

Archangel (*Photo: Courtesy of World Ship Society*)

ROSS KHARTOUM

Wreck No: 59	Date Sunk: 19 12 1981
Latitude: 57 16 21 N	Longitude: 02 01 00 W
GPS Lat: 5716.350 N	GPS Long: 0201.000 W
Location: 8 miles N of Aberdeen	Area: Aberdeen
Type: Oil Safety Vessel	Tonnage: 197 grt
Length: 163.0 ft Beam: ft	Draught: ft
How Sunk: Ran aground/salvaged	Depth: metres

The *Ross Khartoum* was employed as a standby safety vessel for the offshore oil industry. Her engine failed on 19 December 1981, and she was washed ashore on the beach 8 miles north of Aberdeen. It proved impossible to refloat her, and the wreck was sitting upright, deeply embedded in the sand. She was broken up where she lay, and all of the wreckage was removed.

STAR OF THE WAVE

Wreck No: 60	Date Sunk: 11 01 1926
Latitude: 57 16 24 N	Longitude: 02 01 00 W
GPS Lat: 5716.400 N	GPS Long: 0201.000 W
Location: Ashore near Balmedie	Area: Aberdeen
Type: Trawler	Tonnage: 205 grt
Length: 115.0 ft Beam: 21.9 ft	Draught: 13.0 ft
How Sunk: Ran aground	Depth: metres

The steel trawler *Star of the Wave* was built by Duthies of Aberdeen in 1904. She was blown ashore and wrecked on the Belhelvie coast about 8 miles North of Aberdeen in a south easterly gale during the night of 26 January 1926.

The Belhelvie rocket brigade tried for hours, without success, to get a line to the distressed vessel. The Newburgh lifeboat was transported overland to be launched across the sandy beach from a position south of the *Star of the Wave*. After a struggle to launch it against the waves crashing on the shore, the lifeboat endeavoured to approach the stricken vessel, but was swept past just beyond reach. Eventually, the rocket brigade managed to fire a line aboard and saved ten of the crew. One man was lost. At high tide, the vessel was 150 yards from the shore.

Over the years, many vessels have come to grief on the Belhelvie sands, and one of them – possibly *Star of the Wave* – lies on the sloping sandy beach, covered at high tide, dry at low tide. It is marked as a 'shipwreck' on a notice board with a diagram of the paths through the sand dunes at Belhelvie. A wooden-planked path meandering through the dunes from the south car park leads to the wreck.

UNKNOWN

Wreck No: 61	Date Sunk: Pre April 1945
Latitude: 57 16 42 N	Longitude: 01 41 18 W
GPS Lat: 5716.700 N	GPS Long: 0141.300 W
Location: 11 miles E of Balmedie	Area: Aberdeen

Type:		Tonnage: grt	
Length: 200.0 ft	Beam: ft	Draught: ft	
How Sunk:		Depth: 80 metres	

Charted as a wreck with at least 60 metres over it in about 80 metres.

The wreck dates from pre-April 1945, and is apparently 200 ft long, lying 105/295°. Possibly the *U-74* (27 May 1916)? Or the *Countess* (21 January 1901)?

BELVOIR CASTLE

Wreck No: 62	Date Sunk: 14 02 1917
Latitude: 57 17 00 N PA	Longitude: 01 30 00 W PA
GPS Lat: 5717.000 N	GPS Long: 0130.000 W
Location: 16 miles SE of Buchan Ness	Area: Aberdeen
Type: Trawler	Tonnage: 221 grt
Length: 114.5 ft Beam: 21.7 ft	Draught: 11.5 ft
How Sunk: Mined	Depth: 85 metres

Charted as Wk PA with at least 50 metres over it in about 85 metres.

According to one report the Grimsby steam trawler *Belvoir Castle* was sunk 15 miles SE ½E of Buchan Ness on 14 February 1917 when she struck a mine laid by the *UC-44*.

Lloyds World War One Losses describes the position as 25 miles SE of Buchan Ness.

Another report says she was stopped by a U-boat and sunk by an explosive charge after her crew had abandoned ship, and her skipper was taken prisoner.

ENNISMORE

Wreck No: 63	Date Sunk: 30 12 1917
Latitude: 57 17 00 N PA	Longitude: 01 25 00 W PA
GPS Lat: 5717.000 N	GPS Long: 0125.000 W
Location: 15 miles SE ½E of Buchan Ness	Area: Aberdeen
Type: Steamship	Tonnage: 1499 grt
Length: 260.0 ft Beam: 34.0 ft	Draught: 18.0 ft
How Sunk: By *UC-58*	Depth: metres

The British steamship *Ennismore* was sunk by the German U-boat *UC-58* 15 miles SE ½E of Buchan Ness.

The position has also been described as 20 miles E of Peterhead, and yet a further description of the position has been given as 23 miles E of Girdleness.

ROSLIN

Wreck No: 64	Date Sunk: 04 11 1937
Latitude: 57 18 30 N	Longitude: 01 58 30 W
GPS Lat: 5718.500 N	GPS Long: 0158.500 W
Location: Newburgh Bar, mouth of Ythan	Area: Aberdeen

Type: Trawler	Tonnage: 187 grt
Length: 119.7 ft	Beam: 21.1 ft Draught: 11.3 ft
How Sunk: Ran aground	Depth: metres

A wreck was reported close inshore here in 1938.

The iron-hulled steam trawler *Roslin*, built in 1899 by D. MacGill of Govan, was completed by Cochrane & Cooper of Beverley as the Hull trawler *Windsor Castle*.

She was subsequently sold several times, becoming in turn the *Alcyon*, the *Wostock*, the Russian trawler *T6*, seized by the Navy after the Russian revolution to become the naval trawler *Greataxe*, then the Aberdeen trawler *Roslin*.

On the evening of 4 November 1937 she ran ashore just south of the mouth of the river Ythan, about a mile from Newburgh. Her siren brought out the Newburgh lifeboat, the Collieston and Belhelvie lifesaving brigades and the Aberdeen lifeboat. Two of the crew were eventually saved by the Aberdeen lifeboat, but the other six were swept away and drowned.

KAREMMA

Wreck No: 65	Date Sunk: 20 04 1976
Latitude: 57 18 30 N PA	Longitude: 01 59 00 W PA
GPS Lat: 5718.500 N	GPS Long: 0159.000 W
Location: Beached at Newburgh	Area: Aberdeen
Type: MFV	Tonnage: grt
Length: ft	Beam: ft Draught: ft
How Sunk: Ran aground	Depth: metres

The MFV *Karemma* drifted ashore on the sands at the north end of Aberdeen beach on 12 March 1976 after being abandoned half a mile south of the river Don. The stranded vessel was sold to Seagate Metals Ltd of Peterhead.

The salvage vessel *Minto* failed to pull her off the beach, but a later attempt by the *Minto* and the Aberdeen harbour tug *Sea Griffon* succeeded in refloating her on 20 April. She was then taken in tow towards Fraserburgh, but was taking in so much water that she had to be beached again at Newburgh.

ST CLEMENT

Wreck No: 66	Date Sunk: 05 04 1941
Latitude: 57 19 00 N PA	Longitude: 01 50 00 W PA
GPS Lat: 5719.000 N	GPS Long: 0150.000 W
Location: 20 miles SE of Peterhead	Area: Aberdeen
Type: Steamship	Tonnage: 450 grt
Length: 156.3 ft	Beam: 25.6 ft Draught: 9.8 ft
How Sunk: Bombed	Depth: 40 metres

The steamship *St Clement* was built by Hall Russell, Aberdeen in 1928. Bound from Kirkwall to Aberdeen on 5 April 1941 with 20 tons of general cargo and livestock, she was attacked and sunk by German aircraft. One crewman was lost out of ten crew and one gunner.

The wreck is charted at 571900N, 015000W PA with at least 40 metres over it in 45 metres, 13 miles NE of Aberdeen, or 5 miles E of the mouth of the river Ythan.

St Clement *(Photo: Aberdeen Art Gallery & Museums Collection)*

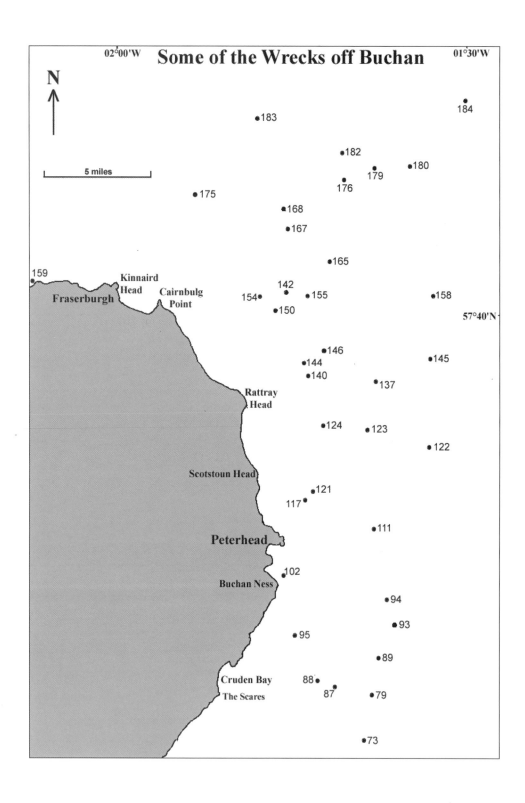

Some of the Wrecks off Buchan

2

BUCHAN

NAIRN

Wreck No: 67	Date Sunk: 02 12 1931
Latitude: 57 20 15 N PA	Longitude: 01 56 45 W PA
GPS Lat: 5720.250 N	GPS Long: 0156.750 W
Location: Broadhaven, S of Collieston	Area: Buchan
Type: Trawler	Tonnage: 197 grt
Length: ft Beam: ft	Draught: ft
How Sunk: Ran aground	Depth: metres

The steam trawler *Nairn* (ex-*Driver*), was blown ashore on the rocks 100 yards off the 150-foot cliffs at Broadhaven, south of Collieston, in a 70mph SSE gale in pitch darkness about 11.00 p.m. on 2 December 1931. Her distress flares were seen, and Aberdeen lifeboat and Collieston lifesaving brigade were called out. Their apparatus had to be dragged a mile across sand dunes and bog to the top of the cliffs overlooking the stranded vessel. From that exposed position, the rockets were unable to reach the trawler in the teeth of the furious gale, and after three abortive attempts, the rocket apparatus was moved to the foot of the cliff.

In extremely difficult conditions, Collieston coastguard and lifesaving brigade eventually succeeded in firing a line aboard at the sixth attempt, and took off the first crewman. After repositioning their line to avoid the risk of the men in the breeches buoy being dashed against intervening rocks by the breaking waves, the other nine crew members were also brought ashore.

Aberdeen lifeboat arrived while all of this shore-based activity was going on, but was unable to approach the *Nairn* in the storm, and stood by offshore until the last of the crew was safely ashore, before returning to Aberdeen.

Collieston Lifesaving Company was awarded the Board of Trade Shield for the best wreck service in 1931, and five of the rescuers were individually awarded Bronze Medals for Gallantry in this rescue.

SANTA CATARINA

Wreck No: 68	Date Sunk: 08 1588
Latitude: 57 20 42 N PA	Longitude: 01 55 36 W PA
GPS Lat: 5720.700 N	GPS Long: 0155.600 W
Location: St Catherine's Dub, Collieston	Area: Buchan
Type: Spanish Galleon	Tonnage: grt
Length: ft Beam: ft	Draught: ft
How Sunk: Ran aground	Depth: metres

This is reputed to be the location of the loss of the Spanish galleon *Santa Catarina* (after which St Catherine's Dub was presumably named). Large quantities of Spanish silver coins, all stuck together with concretion in the shape of the barrels which originally contained them, are reported to have been found.

The position of the *Santa Catarina* has also been given as 572050N, 015543W, 200 yards north of Collieston.

A Danish vessel (name unknown) is also recorded to have been lost here in 1666. The guns of this Danish vessel were salvaged, and used to defend Peterhead.

LESRIX

Wreck No: 69		Date Sunk: 26 01 1942	
Latitude: 57 20 45 N PA		Longitude: 01 57 15 W PA	
GPS Lat: 5720.750 N		GPS Long: 0157.250 W	
Location: Hackley Head, S of Collieston		Area: Buchan	
Type: Steamship		Tonnage: 703 grt	
Length: 175.0 ft	Beam: 30.0 ft	Draught: ft	
How Sunk: Ran aground		Depth: metres	

A storm lashed the east coast for most of January 1942, and shortly after midnight on 25 January, the Hull steamer *Lesrix* ran on to the rocks at Hackley Head, about one mile south of Collieston.

Her distress flares were spotted, but the rescue team at Collieston had already left to attend to the needs of another vessel, the *Empire Pilgrim*, which had gone ashore just north of Old Slains Castle. (She was subsequently refloated in February 1942.)

A merchant navy officer home on leave, along with a local schoolboy, collected what spare equipment was still available, and succeeded in rescuing four of the crew from the bow of the *Lesrix* by breeches buoy. The vessel had broken in two by this time, the stern breaking away and sinking with the loss of ten other crewmembers.

In the meantime, the Newburgh lifeboat had been called out, but was unable to approach the *Lesrix*, which had been driven well up the rocks.

Returning to Newburgh, the lifeboat was capsized off the mouth of the river Ythan by a heavy sea breaking on her beam. All seven of her crew were washed ashore, but two of them died on the beach.

The lifeboat was only very slightly damaged, and continued in service at Newburgh until 1965.

BRIGHTSIDE

Wreck No: 70		Date Sunk: 25 09 1949	
Latitude: 57 20 20 N PA		Longitude: 01 56 30 W PA	
GPS Lat: 5720.333 N		GPS Long: 0156.500 W	
Location: ½ mile S of Collieston		Area: Buchan	
Type: Steamship		Tonnage: 476 grt	
Length: 143.0 ft	Beam: 25.3 ft	Draught: 11.4 ft	
How Sunk: Ran aground		Depth: metres	

The coaster *Brightside* ran on to the rocks ½ mile south of Collieston in fog on 25 September 1949.

She had a cargo of cement. Her crew abandoned ship and were picked up by the drifter *Noontide*, which landed them in Aberdeen.

The steamship Brightside (*Photo: Courtesy of The World Ship Society*)

LADYBIRD

Wreck No: 71
Latitude: 57 20 50 N
GPS Lat: 5720.833 N
Location: Overhill Rock, Collieston
Type: Trawler
Length: 120.7 ft   Beam: 21.5 ft
How Sunk: Ran aground

Date Sunk: 30 09 1906
Longitude: 01 55 48 W
GPS Long: 0155.800 W
Area: Buchan
Tonnage: 218 grt
Draught: 11.4 ft
Depth: metres

The iron steam trawler *Ladybird* was built by Cook Welton & Gemmell in 1901.
She was lost on Overhill Rock, ½ mile north of Collieston, on 30 September 1906.

BELCHER

Wreck No: 72
Latitude: 57 21 00 N PA
GPS Lat: 5721.000 N
Location: ½ miles N of Collieston
Type: Trawler
Length: 101.2 ft   Beam: 20.7 ft
How Sunk: Ran aground

Date Sunk: 04 09 1903
Longitude: 01 55 20 W PA
GPS Long: 0155.333 W
Area: Buchan
Tonnage: 148 grt
Draught: 10.6 ft
Depth: metres

The steel-hulled steam trawler *Belcher* was built by Hall Russell in 1893.
On the morning of 4 September 1903 she ran aground half a mile north of Collieston – presumably on Overhill Rock. The crew were all saved. There may not be much, if any, of this wreck left, as it was sold to a salvage company who were already working on another wreck in Cruden Bay, and presumably they broke it up for scrap.

U-1206

Wreck No: 73		Date Sunk: 14 04 1945	
Latitude: 57 21 18 N		Longitude: 01 39 12 W	
GPS Lat: 5721.300 N		GPS Long: 0139.200 W	
Location: 8½ miles SE of Slains Castle		Area: Buchan	
Type: Submarine		Tonnage: 769 tons	
Length: 220.5 ft	Beam: 20.3 ft	Draught: 15.7 ft	
How Sunk: Foundered		Depth: 70 metres	

Type VIIC/41 U-boat of 769 tons surfaced, 871 tons submerged.

As the Second World War progressed, Allied anti-submarine patrols became more numerous and more effective. The length of time U-boats were forced to remain submerged increased, and they were also forced to go to ever-greater depths. One problem became apparent. The simple two-valve toilet system fitted to U-boats only worked in shallow water. To overcome the problem, a new WC system was designed to work under the greater water pressure of deeper depths, and this new system was fitted to the late VIIC boats. Type VIIC/41 U-boat *U-1206*, built in 1944, was one of them. This new system was so complicated to use that the German navy wrote a handbook on how to operate it, and one man from each new boat was sent to be trained as a 'WC waste disposal unit manager', or as the crew called him, the 'shit-man'. Every member of the crew was ordered to get assistance from this man if he used the system while the boat was deeply submerged.

On 14 April 1945 *U-1206* was off the east coast of Scotland, in depths of around 200 feet.

Her commander, KL Carl-Adolf Schlitt, was a little too proud to ask the 'shit-man' for help – so he read the manual, decided that he understood it, and used the WC system.

But something went wrong, and the first engineer sent the shit-man to the toilet to sort out the problem. There was a little confusion between both men, and the shit-man opened the outside valve while the inside valve was still open. Both of them were suddenly hit by a powerful jet of water, blasting in under a pressure of at least 6 bars. The sea rushed in and quickly flooded the bow compartment. A great amount of water got into the U-boat and found its way to the batteries, which were directly under the WC compartment. Chlorine gas was quickly produced, and everyone in the boat began to be overcome by it.

The first engineer ordered the U-boat to periscope depth. The main ballast tanks were blown and all five torpedo tubes fired to lighten the submarine, which rose to the surface, although still taking in water. The commander ordered the U-boat to surface, and opened the conning tower hatch with his last reserves of strength. As it was obviously impossible for the U-boat to dive again, or to continue its patrol, KL Schlitt ordered the crew to get out.

The crew abandoned the U-boat in four dinghies just before *U-1206* sank by the stern. As far as is known *U-1206* was the only German submarine that was sunk by its own toilet system.

As the dinghies drifted towards the cliff-lined shore, two of them were spotted, and the occupants picked up by HM trawlers *Nodzu* and *Ligny*, and landed at Aberdeen. Another dinghy with ten survivors and one dead rating, was driven ashore two miles south of Buchan Ness lighthouse, where two of the ten who had survived thus far were drowned.

Near Dunbuy Rocks, Captain Schlitt and twelve of his crew were picked up from a fourth dinghy, by the Peterhead lobster fishing boat *Reaper*. The bodies of the three dead crewmembers were buried at Peterhead, but were later exhumed to be buried elsewhere.

According to another version of the story, some members of the crew were found hiding in a cave after drifting ashore in dinghies and landing near Boddam.

A wreck is charted 8½ miles SE of Slains Castle, with at least 40 metres over it in about 70 metres.

This wreck was known to be here in 1944, before the *U-1206* was lost, and it was considered possible that *U-1206* may have sunk on this unknown wreck (which might be the 148-grt Aberdeen iron-hulled steam trawler *Martaban* (A527), captured by a U-boat on 2 May 1915, and sunk by gunfire 22 miles E by N of Aberdeen).

It is said that local fishermen, who claim to know where the wreck of *U-1206* is, say that it is lying on a sandy bottom in a depth of about 40 metres. Efforts to trace these fishermen have been unsuccessful, but their claim was apparently confirmed by commercial divers who reputedly found the wreck while working on a North Sea gas pipeline to St Fergus.

A wreck is charted 3½ miles SE of Old Slains Castle at 571900N, 015000W PA, with at least 40 metres over it, inside the 50 metre contour. The bottom here is sandy, and this might be the *U-1206*, but there is no pipeline in this vicinity.

BEN WYVIS

Wreck No: 74	Date Sunk: 04 12 1908
Latitude: 57 21 30 N PA	Longitude: 01 54 40 W PA
GPS Lat: 5721.500 N	GPS Long: 0154.667 W
Location: 2 miles N of Collieston	Area: Buchan
Type: Trawler	Tonnage: 159 grt
Length: 103.8 ft Beam: 20.6 ft	Draught: 11.3 ft
How Sunk: Ran aground	Depth: metres

The steel steam trawler *Ben Wyvis* ran aground in fog near Old Slains Castle two miles north of Collieston on 4 December 1908. The crew were rescued by the Collieston lifesaving apparatus.

SOLVANG

Wreck No: 75	Date Sunk: 11 11 1905
Latitude: 57 21 45 N PA	Longitude: 01 55 00 W PA
GPS Lat: 5721.750 N	GPS Long: 0155.000 W
Location: At Slains	Area: Buchan
Type: Schooner	Tonnage: 163 grt
Length: 96.5 ft Beam: 23.5 ft	Draught: 12.0 ft
How Sunk: Ran aground	Depth: metres

The Norwegian schooner *Solvang* was driven on the rocks at Slains late on the night of 11 November 1905. The vessel, which was bound for Dysart in ballast, to load a cargo of coal, had been driven before a gale from the Firth of Forth. A very high sea was running, and no-one on the shore saw the vessel strike the rocks, the first news of the wreck being brought to Slains farmhouse about 7.30 the next morning by the two survivors who reached land after a terrible struggle. The Captain, his son and two seamen were drowned.

The comment about reaching land after a terrible struggle might suggest that the *Solvang* ran on to Cruden Scares.

Slains farmhouse is not named on the Ordnance Survey map, and from the above report it is not clear whether the farmhouse referred to is at Mains of Slains just inland from Broadhaven Bay near Collieston, or Slains Lodge, inland from New Slains Castle near Port Erroll. These two possibilities are 5 miles apart.

The position given assumes the former, as the report does not mention the 150-feet cliffs of the latter. These cliffs would virtually rule out any possibility of the crew being able to get ashore.

Confusingly, there are two Slains Castles, 5 miles apart. Old Slains Castle is near Collieston, and the other, New Castle of Slains, near Port Erroll.

CONTENDER

Wreck No: 76		Date Sunk: 12 04 1961
Latitude: 57 22 40 N PA		Longitude: 01 52 45 W PA
GPS Lat: 5722.667 N		GPS Long: 0152.750 W
Location: The Veshels		Area: Buchan
Type: Trawler		Tonnage: 236 grt
Length: 123.1 ft	Beam: 22.7 ft	Draught: 14.5 ft
How Sunk: Ran aground		Depth: metres

The trawler *Contender*, built by Hall Russell of Aberdeen in 1950, ran aground 2 miles south of Cruden Bay in a rocky gully known as 'Big Vessels Reef' (The Veshels). The thirteen crew climbed the cliffs to Ogston farm.

CITY OF OSAKA

Wreck No: 77		Date Sunk: 25 09 1930
Latitude: 57 22 34 N		Longitude: 01 52 52 W
GPS Lat: 5722.576 N		GPS Long: 0152.872 W
Location: Ashore 1 mile S of Cruden Scars		Area: Buchan
Type: Steamship		Tonnage: 6614 grt
Length: 435.5 ft	Beam: 57.7 ft	Draught: 30.3 ft
How Sunk: Ran aground		Depth: 12 metres

The Ellerman steamship *City of Osaka* (ex-*Colorado*) was en route from Newcastle to New York with a cargo of timber. At about 4.00 a.m. on 25 September 1930, she ran aground at Sturdy Point, one mile south of Cruden Scars, below a 150-foot cliff at Ogston, between the shore and an off-lying rock known as The Veshels. There was extremely thick fog at the time, but fortunately the sea was calm. Radio distress messages from the ship were picked up at Wick, and by the destroyer HMS *Walker* in the Cromarty Firth. Wick notified the Peterhead coastguards, and the lifeboat was launched. Meanwhile, Collieston lifesaving brigade set out, with horses dragging their gear across the fields to the top of the cliff overlooking the *City of Osaka*. The breeches buoy apparatus was rigged, and one by one, forty of the crew were hauled safely ashore, and were taken to Aberdeen by bus. Six remaining members of the crew were taken off the stranded vessel later that day by the Peterhead lifeboat, while a boat from HMS *Walker*, which also arrived at the scene in the afternoon, took off the crew's belongings. By 4.30 p.m. the ship, swaying in the seas, and with water breaking over her bows, was abandoned.

Apparently the wreck yielded many trophies to the crews of small boats which left Peterhead as soon as the fog started to lift. Police and Customs searched the boats on their return to harbour, but many items had been well hidden!

The *City of Osaka* lies above an older iron wreck, the *Nymphaea*, which ran aground on 14 July 1914.

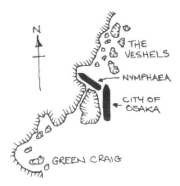

Locations of City of Osaka *and* Nymphaea © RFM 2000

City of Osaka *aground on Sturdy Point.* (*Photo: Aberdeen Art Gallery & Museums Collection*)

NYMPHAEA

Wreck No: 78		Date Sunk: 14 07 1914
Latitude: 57 22 43 N		Longitude: 01 53 00 W
GPS Lat: 5722.717 N		GPS Long: 0153.000 W
Location: 1 mile S of Whinnyfold		Area: Buchan
Type: Steamship		Tonnage: 1969 grt
Length: 286.9 ft	Beam: 37.0 ft	Draught: 21.8 ft
How Sunk: Ran aground		Depth: metres

The British steamship *Nymphaea* was built in 1882 by Tyne Iron S.B. Co. of Newcastle. She was wrecked about one mile South of Whinnyfold, Aberdeenshire while en route in ballast from the Tyne to Cienfuegos on 14 July 1914. The vessel was dashed to pieces by heavy seas.

Nymphaea *aground at Studie Point (Photo: Aberdeen City Art Gallery & Museums) (The point with the flat-topped rock directly below Ogston Farm is variously named Sturdy, Studie or Study – derived from the old scots word for 'anvil'.)*

ORMONDE

Wreck No: 79	Date Sunk: 16 02 1941
Latitude: 57 23 18 N PA	Longitude: 01 38 30 W PA
GPS Lat: 5723.300 N	GPS Long: 0138.500 W
Location: 6½ miles SE of Buchan Ness	Area: Buchan
Type: Trawler	Tonnage: 250 grt
Length: 125.0 ft Beam: 22.0 ft	Draught: 12.4 ft
How Sunk: By aircraft	Depth: 62 metres

The Grimsby trawler *Ormonde* was built in 1906 by Cochranes of Selby. While in Admiralty service, probably as a minesweeper, she was sunk by aircraft 90° off Peterhead, 7 miles from Cruden Scars, on 16 February 1941. There were no survivors.

HMT Chrysolite was also attacked but not hit.

The wreck is charted at 572318N, 013830W PA with at least 55 metres over it in about 62 metres. This was the position recorded in 1945, but a wreck located nearby at 572403N, 013712W in 1975, during a survey of the seabed in connection with the routing of oil pipelines, is thought possibly to be HMS *Ormonde*. (See *Freidrich Bolte*, Wreck No. 89.)

ASTREA

Wreck No: 80	Date Sunk: 14 11 1903
Latitude: 57 23 24 N PA	Longitude: 01 51 00 W PA
GPS Lat: 5723.400 N	GPS Long: 0151.000 W
Location: Cruden Scars, Cruden Bay	Area: Buchan

Type: Brigantine
Length: 126.0 ft.   Beam: 23.8 ft.
How Sunk: Ran aground

Tonnage: 298 grt
Draught: 14.4 ft.
Depth: metres

The Norwegian iron brigantine *Astrea* (ex-*Helga*, ex-*Betsey*), bound for Fraserburgh with a cargo of barrel staves, ran on to the outermost rocks of Cruden Scars directly opposite Whinnyfold. She struck before dawn on 14 November 1903, in a southerly gale and thick fog. The vessel filled rapidly, and her crew took to the rigging.

Port Erroll rocket brigade's lines were unable to reach the stricken vessel as she lay too far from the shore, and it was impossible to launch any of the local boats through the surf.

Peterhead lifeboat was towed to the wreck by a tug and succeeded in rescuing the eight crewmembers from the *Astrea*.

HARTFELL

Wreck No: 81
Latitude: 57 23 24 N PA
GPS Lat: 5723.400 N
Location: Cruden Scars, Cruden Bay
Type: Steamship
Length: 140.0 ft   Beam: 21.6 ft
How Sunk: Ran aground

Date Sunk: 01 03 1902
Longitude: 01 51 00 W PA
GPS Long: 0151.000 W
Area: Buchan
Tonnage: 319 grt
Draught: 10.0 ft
Depth: 18 metres

The Aberdeen steamship *Hartfell* was built by Murdoch & Murray of Port Glasgow in 1883.

On 1 March 1902, while carrying a cargo of coal from Sunderland, she encountered thick fog and ran on to the middle of the outer ledge of Cruden Scars, ¼ mile from the shore.

A mass of copper piping, chain and flattened plates lie in a gully near the SE edge of the Scars, in 11 metres of water at low tide. Portholes have been recovered from this area. The stern of the wreck, with half of a steel or iron propeller, lies about 100 metres SE of the Scars in about 18 metres of water. This wreckage may be the remains of the *Hartfell*, or possibly the *Frederick Snowden*, but several other vessels have also been lost on the Scars.

EASDALE

Wreck No: 82
Latitude: 57 23 24 N PA
GPS Lat: 5723.400 N
Location: Cruden Scars, Cruden Bay
Type: Steamship
Length: 92.5 ft   Beam: 18.5 ft
How Sunk: Ran aground

Date Sunk: 21 09 1906
Longitude: 01 51 00 W PA
GPS Long: 0151.000 W
Area: Buchan
Tonnage: 116 grt
Draught: 8.1 ft
Depth: metres

The iron steam coaster *Easdale* (built 1876) ran aground on the low rocky headland near Whinnyfold at the south of Cruden Bay on 21 September 1906. She was carrying a cargo of coal from South Shields to Portsoy.

The coaster Easdale *aground on Cruden Scars* (*Photo: Author's collection*)

STAR OF THE ISLES

Wreck No: 83

Latitude: 57 23 24 N PA

GPS Lat: 5723.400 N

Location: Cruden Scars, Cruden Bay

Type: Trawler

Length: 112.5 ft　　　　　　Beam: 21.6 ft

How Sunk: Ran aground

Date Sunk: 18 01 1907

Longitude: 01 51 00 W PA

GPS Long: 0151.000 W

Area: Buchan

Tonnage: 197 grt

Draught: 12.4 ft

Depth: metres

The steel-hulled steam trawler *Star of the Isles* was built 1902 by A. Hall & Sons, Aberdeen.

She was wrecked in fog on Cruden Scars off Whinnyfold on 18 January 1907. The crew made it safely ashore at Cruden Bay in their small boat.

Star of the Isles *aground on Cruden Scars* (*Photo: Arbuthnot Museum, Peterhead*)

MILWAUKEE

Wreck No: 84		Date Sunk: 16 09 1898	
Latitude: 57 23 24 N PA		Longitude: 01 50 00 W PA	
GPS Lat: 5723.400 N		GPS Long: 0150.000 W	
Location: Cruden Scars, Cruden Bay		Area: Buchan	
Type: Steamship		Tonnage: 7317 grt	
Length: 472.7 ft	Beam: 56.4 ft	Draught: 31.9 ft	
How Sunk: Ran aground		Depth: metres	

The steamship *Milwaukee*, built in 1897, ran aground in fog on Cruden Scars, 250 yards from the shore. Deck fittings and 1,500 tons of coal were jettisoned to lighten the vessel in an attempt to refloat her, but this was not successful. The stranded vessel was cut in two with explosives, and the stern section towed to the Tyne where a new bow section was built on. The repaired ship was subsequently relaunched in 1899.

The original bow section, 180 ft long, was left on the rocks where she had grounded.

MARIA W

Wreck No: 85		Date Sunk: 22 02 1966	
Latitude: 57 23 31 N		Longitude: 01 51 28 W	
GPS Lat: 5723.516 N		GPS Long: 0151.464 W	
Location: Whinnyfold, near Cruden Bay		Area: Buchan	
Type: Motor Vessel		Tonnage: 241 grt	
Length: 138.8 ft	Beam: 21.5 ft	Draught: 8.0 ft	
How Sunk: Ran aground in fog		Depth: 6 metres	

Location of Maria W © RFM 2000

The Dutch motor vessel *Maria W* (ex-*Twin*), struck Cruden Scars in fog at 3.30 a.m. on 22 February 1966, while en route from Ghent to Scrabster with a cargo of fertiliser.

Her propeller was lost, rendering her helpless, and she was washed stern first into Sandy Haven, just north of the Scars. While the captain sent out distress signals and fired rockets, the other four crewmembers took to the life raft. The Grimsby trawler *Real Madrid* sailed to the area, and using her radar, guided the Peterhead lifeboat alongside the stricken vessel. All five seamen were hauled aboard the lifeboat and taken to Peterhead.

The wreck is very broken up in a gully at the south side of Sandy Haven, about ¼ mile north of Whinnyfold.

FREDRICK SNOWDEN

Wreck No: 86	Date Sunk: 17 01 1912
Latitude: 57 23 24 N PA	Longitude: 01 51 40 W PA
GPS Lat: 5723.400 N	GPS Long: 0151.667 W
Location: Off Whinnyfold, S of Port Erroll	Area: Buchan
Type: Steamship	Tonnage: 725 grt
Length: 201.2 ft Beam: 29.3 ft	Draught: 15.8 ft
How Sunk: Ran aground/foundered	Depth: 40 metres

The Aberdeen steamship *Frederick Snowden*, with a cargo of coal, was wrecked off Whinnyfold, south of Port Erroll, near Cruden Bay in a storm on 17 January 1912.

She was seen listing to port, flying distress signals and heading towards the shore. The lifesaving brigade at Port Errol stood by in readiness, but long before she came within range of the brigade's rockets, the *Frederick Snowden* capsized and sank immediately, close to Cruden Scars, and about 1½ miles from shore. It is thought that the crew may have dropped an anchor in an attempt to avoid running on to the Scars, and this, combined with her heavy list, may have caused the final capsizing.

The vessel was built in Middlesbrough in 1866. There were no survivors from her crew of thirteen.

One board bearing the name *Aberdeen*, and another *Frederick Snowden*, were found.

Thirteen bodies were washed ashore the next day, most of them from the *Wistow Hall*, which was lost on the Tempion Rock only a few hours after the loss of the *Frederick Snowden*.

Frederick Snowden *(Photo: Aberdeen Art Gallery & Museums Collection)*

UNKNOWN – PRETORIA?

Wreck No: 87	Date Sunk:
Latitude: 57 23 43 N	Longitude: 01 41 31 W
GPS Lat: 5723.717 N	GPS Long: 0141.517 W
Location: 5 miles E of Cruden Bay	Area: Buchan
Type:	Tonnage: grt

Length: ft   Beam: ft Draught: ft
How Sunk: Depth: 60 metres

A wreck with at least 28 metres over it in about 60 metres is charted in this position. It was found in 1975 during a seabed survey for oil pipeline routing purposes, and may possibly be the 159-grt trawler *Pretoria,* which was built by Hall Russell in 1900.

While hauling in her gear at 5.00 a.m. on 5 February 1936, six miles SE by S of Buchan Ness, she was struck on the port side by the Aberdeen trawler *Georgette,* and sank in 35 minutes.

The crew were all taken aboard the *Georgette.*

Other possibilities for the identity of this wreck include the *Integrity,* or the *Ormonde.*

INTEGRITY ?

Wreck No: 88   Date Sunk: 02 11 1976
Latitude: 57 24 00 N PA   Longitude: 01 43 00 W PA
GPS Lat: 5724.000 N   GPS Long: 0143.000 W
Location: 4 miles E of Cruden Bay   Area: Buchan
Type: Trawler   Tonnage: grt
Length: ft   Beam: ft Draught: ft
How Sunk: Collision with *Rowanlea* Depth: 60 metres

Charted as Wk PA with at least 31 metres over it in about 60 metres.

This is the approximate position recorded by the Hydrographic Department for the trawler *Integrity,* which sank in a collision with the trawler *Rowanlea* at 9.00 a.m. on 2 November 1976.

According to a report in the *Aberdeen Press & Journal,* however, the collision occurred in perfect visibility about four miles north of Buchan Ness, which would suggest a position of about 573200N, 014600W. The *Integrity*'s port side near the stern was badly damaged, and she sank in minutes. The three crewmembers launched their liferaft, but a rope, which had been used to tie the liferaft to the top of the wheelhouse, snagged, causing the raft to be dragged down by the sinking *Integrity.* With the raft standing on end, just in time, the skipper cut the rope with his knife. The crew were then able to board the raft and were picked up by the Peterhead boat *Harvester.* The *Rowanlea* was undamaged.

FREIDRICH BOLTE

Wreck No: 89   Date Sunk: 22 10 1910
Latitude: 57 24 03 N   Longitude: 01 37 12 W
GPS Lat: 5724.050 N   GPS Long: 0137.200 W
Location: 5½ miles SE of Buchan Ness Area: Buchan
Type: Trawler   Tonnage: 240 grt
Length: 132.0 ft   Beam: 23.1 ft Draught: ft
How Sunk: Foundered   Depth: metres

The German steam trawler *Freidrich Bolte* foundered 5½ miles SE of Buchan Ness on 22 October 1910. The wreck here may be the *Freidrich Bolte,* or possibly the *Ormonde.*

MERCATOR

Wreck No: 90	Date Sunk: 01 12 1939
Latitude: 57 24 28 N	Longitude: 01 34 45 W
GPS Lat: 5724.467 N	GPS Long: 0134.750 W
Location: 8½ miles E of Cruden Bay	Area: Buchan
Type: Steamship	Tonnage: 4,260 grt
Length: 360.0 ft Beam: 48.0 ft	Draught: 20.2 ft
How Sunk: Torpedoed by *U-21*	Depth: 70 metres

The Finnish steamship *Mercator* (ex-*Manchester Mariner*) was built in 1904 by Furness Withy at West Hartlepool. At the end of November 1939 she had arrived safely in Leith from Buenos Aires, and was onward-bound to Helsinki with a cargo of coffee, maize, wheat, linseed, casein and groundnut meal when she was torpedoed off Buchan Ness at 04.53 hrs on 1 December 1939 by *U-21* (KL Fritz Frauenheim).

In the darkness before dawn, Frauenheim had estimated his victim as a ship of about 5,000 grt. He was then in German grid square AN1895, which corresponds to about 572700N, 013600W.

Peterhead lifeboat *Julia Park Barry of Glasgow* was launched, and the *MFV Bread Winner* also put out from Peterhead. Three miles ENE of Peterhead *Bread Winner* found a boat with nineteen aboard and a raft lashed alongside it with another four on that. The sea was washing over the raft, but the men on it were unable to get into the boat as it was full. *Bread Winner* brought all twenty-three into Peterhead. The RNLI also state that a boat with twelve aboard came ashore safely at Boddam. One member of the *Mercator*'s crew was lost.

A wreck charted at 572418N, 013430W PA, 122°, 7½ miles from Buchan Ness Light, was recorded by the Hydrographic Department as the *Mercator*.

The wreck was accurately located, but not identified, at 572428N, 013445W during a pipeline survey in 1975.

PHILORTH

Wreck No: 91	Date Sunk: 06 12 1915
Latitude: 57 24 50 N	Longitude: 01 49 45 W
GPS Lat: 5724.833 N	GPS Long: 0149.750 W
Location: Riddle Skerries, New Slains Castle	Area: Buchan
Type: Drifter	Tonnage: 148 grt
Length: 102.4 ft Beam: 20.7 ft	Draught: 10.7 ft
How Sunk: Ran aground	Depth: metres

The steel-hulled steam drifter *Philorth*, built by Duthies of Aberdeen in 1892, was driven ashore on Riddle Skerries near New Castle of Slains, Cruden Bay during an easterly gale with tremendous seas. Huge waves broke over her, and the trawler was knocked over on her side. Collieston lifesaving brigade arrived with their apparatus after about three hours. The crew were all in the galley, and unable to leave their refuge there to reach the lines fired by rocket from the shore. Eventually, one of the lines was fired within reach, and a breeches buoy was hauled out. Four of the crew made it ashore, but six others were washed away and drowned.

CHICAGO

Wreck No: 92	Date Sunk: 10 10 1894
Latitude: 57 24 57 N	Longitude: 01 49 45 W
GPS Lat: 5724.950 N	GPS Long: 0149.750 W
Location: New Slains Castle, Buchan Ness	Area: Buchan
Type: Steamship	Tonnage: 2381 grt
Length: 293.5 ft Beam: 39.0 ft	Draught: 18.4 ft
How Sunk: Ran aground	Depth: 12 metres

The British steamship *Chicago* (ex-*Lincoln City*), built in 1890 by Short Bros, ran aground at full speed on the Ward of Cruden, immediately below New Slains Castle, north of Cruden Bay, while en route from Rotterdam and Sunderland to Baltimore with a cargo of 50 tons of cement, 50 tons of pickled herrings in small casks, 20 tons of wine, vegetables and mirror glass.

Staff at the castle heard her striking the rocks at 1.00 a.m. on 10 October 1894, and alerted the coastguard. The twenty-seven crew, mainly Dutch, were rescued by the local rocket brigade.

The vessel had struck at low water. The *Chicago*'s forefoot had been carried away and rocks had pierced her starboard side. The ship was lying with a list to port, and although the after section was still reasonably intact, it was being moved about by the action of the waves, and it was feared that she might slip off the rocks into deep water at any moment. Despite this danger, her cargo was salvaged (apart from the cement), but it was impossible to refloat the ship, which lies 50 metres out from the shore in a small bay directly under New Slains Castle.

Wreckage, including a few battered portholes, is scattered all around, while 20 yards to the north east, her double bottom is lodged against rocks. Two boilers lie in 12-13 metres of water, slightly further from the cliff, and beyond them is the stern post and cast iron propeller.

New Castle of Slains is near Port Erroll, and should not be confused with the Old Slains Castle five miles further south, near Collieston.

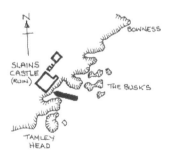

Location of Chicago *at New Slains Castle* © RFM 2000

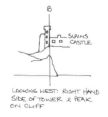

ST GLEN

Wreck No: 93	Date Sunk: 06 09 1940
Latitude: 57 25 51 N	Longitude: 01 35 52 W
GPS Lat: 5725.850 N	GPS Long: 0135.867 W
Location: 6¼ miles SE of Buchan Ness	Area: Buchan
Type: Steamship	Tonnage: 4647 grt
Length: 400.0 ft Beam: 52.1 ft	Draught: 27.0 ft
How Sunk: Bombed	Depth: 60 metres

The 4,647-grt steamship *St Glen* (ex-*City of Swansea*, ex-*Katuna*) was built in 1907 by Armstrong Whitworth of Newcastle. She was bombed and sunk by aircraft on 6 September 1940. The wreck is charted at 572500N, 013800W PA, which was the approximate position given for the attack.

The vessel was en route from Rosario and Buenos Aires to Hull with 4,900 tons of wheat, 1,339 tons of canned beef, 984 tons of salted hides and 221 tons of general cargo. Three of her forty-three crew were lost.

Local fishermen found the wreck at 572551N, 013552W. They know it as 'the Corned-Beefer' due to the large quantity of tins of corned beef trawled up in the vicinity.

SOFIE BAKKE

Wreck No: 94	Date Sunk: 04 08 1940
Latitude: 57 26 05 N	Longitude 01 36 14 W
GPS Lat: 5726.083	GPS Long: 136.233 W
Location: 6 miles SE of Buchan Ness	Area: Buchan
Type: Motorship	Tonnage: 5461 grt
Length: 435.9 ft Beam: 58.5 ft	Draught: 26.0 ft
How Sunk: Collision with *Lima*	Depth: 60 metres

A Peterhead trawler skipper has found a wreck in this position.

This might possibly be the Norwegian motorship *Sofie Bakke,* which sank after a collision with the Swedish vessel *Lima*, off Buchan Ness at 01.00 hrs on 4 August 1940.

She was struck amidships by the *Lima* and sank in 20 to 30 minutes. All her crew were taken off.

The position was recorded as 4 miles 111° from Buchan Ness. This plots in about 5727N, 0140W, but there is no wreck charted in that position.

Sofie Bakke was built in Gothenburg, Sweden in 1938, and was owned by the Knutsen Line of Haugesund, Norway. Her regular route was from the Pacific to the UK, and she was en route from Chile/Peru bound for French ports and Liverpool when France was overrun by the Germans. She was diverted to Gourock, where she joined convoy WN4 to sail for Methil.

The vessel was under the control of Nortraship (i.e. the Norwegian Government) during the war. According to Norwegian records *Sofie Bakke* was carrying materials for ammunition factories. This could be almost anything from chemicals to steel products.

The wreck was recorded at approximately 5725N, 0145W in 50-60 metres, but this is obviously only a rough estimate.

Other wreck positions recorded in this area by Peterhead fishermen include

5727.400N, 0141.000W and 5729.000N, 0137.500W. The *Sofie Bakke* might equally well be one of these.

Peterhead Sea Cadets acquired one of *Sofie Bakke*'s lifeboats.

WINDWARD HO

Wreck No: 95	Date Sunk: 09 05 1917
Latitude: 57 25 37 N	Longitude: 01 45 17 W
GPS Lat: 5726.620 N	GPS Long: 0145.280 W
Location: 2.7 miles 167° from Buchan Ness	Area: Buchan
Type: Trawler	Tonnage: grt
Length: 122.4 ft.	Beam: 21.5 ft. Draught: 11.5 ft.
How Sunk: Mined	Depth: 51 metres

The steam trawler *Windward Ho* was sunk by a mine on 9 May 1917.

Lloyds World War One Losses describes the location as 3 miles south of Peterhead, which would suggest a position of about 572600N, 014500W.

At 11.47 hrs on 16 December 1939, a submarine was bombed 180° 2 miles from Buchan Ness, and HMS *Escort* reported an object on the bottom in 5726N, 0145W. The object is charted as Wk PA with at least 25 metres over it in about 51 metres.

One can imagine euphoric thoughts going through the minds of those aboard HMS *Escort* that they may have located the wreck of the U-boat that had been attacked, but no U-boat is recorded as having been lost that day.

It is almost certain that HMS *Escort* had located the wreck of the *Windward Ho*.

The Hydrographic Department had recorded the position as 572830N, 014430W PA, where it is charted as Wk PA with at least 28 metres over it in about 45 metres, but nothing was found in an echo-sounder search of 0.3 miles radius around that position.

Local fishermen know of a wreck at 5725.620N, 0145.280W, 2.7 miles 167° from Buchan Ness. This equates to 572537N, 014517W, very close to the position reported by HMS *Escort*. As the wreck is already a known 'snag', they dump their damaged nets, ropes and wire on it.

WISTOW HALL

Wreck No: 96	Date Sunk: 18 01 1912
Latitude: 57 26 10 N	Longitude: 01 49 00 W
GPS Lat: 5726.167 N	GPS Long: 0149.000 W
Location: Tempion Rock, North Haven	Area: Buchan
Type: Steamship	Tonnage: 3413 grt
Length: 349.5 ft	Beam: 42.1 ft Draught: 26.7 ft
How Sunk: Ran aground	Depth: metres

The British steamship *Wistow Hall* was built in 1890 by Caird & Co.

On 15 January 1912 she left Jarrow for Glasgow with 500 tons of cargo. En route, she encountered very bad weather. On the 17th her funnel was washed away, two of the crew were killed by falling gear, and the first officer was injured. This was followed by an accident to the captain, who received injuries to his spine, had his right arm broken, and was rendered unconscious.

The boiler room flooded and the fires were extinguished. As the ship was then without power, it was decided to drop anchor off Buchan Ness, but the cable parted and the ship was blown towards the shore, frequently firing distress flares. She was seen by the coastguards at Port Erroll, who followed her drift along the coast. At 8.00 a.m. on the 18th she struck the Tempion Rock, North Haven, close to a stone quarry at the Bullers of Buchan. The quarrymen went to the shore in the hope of helping to rescue those on board, but unfortunately the place where the *Wistow Hall* had come ashore was at the foot of high and inaccessible cliffs, where it was impossible for lifeboats to approach.

As the steamship's boats had been smashed in the gale, the crew were without means of escape and could only cling to the rigging, from which they were swept away by successive seas in full view of the impotent coastguards and quarrymen. Of the fifty-seven crew, only four were saved, one of whom was the captain.

UNKNOWN – ANNEMIEKE ?

Wreck No: 97		Date Sunk:
Latitude: 57 27 24 N		Longitude: 01 22 12 W
GPS Lat: 5727.400 N		GPS Long: 0122.200 W
Location: 13 miles E of Buchan Ness		Area: Buchan
Type:		Tonnage: grt
Length: ft	Beam: ft	Draught: ft
How Sunk:		Depth: 100 metres

A wreck is charted in 100 metres, 13 miles E of Buchan Ness.

This may be the Panamanian vessel *Annemieke*, which foundered on 10 November 1978, 093° true, 13½ miles from Buchan Ness, while en route from Furnace, Argyll to Hamburg with a cargo of granite chips. She sank in a depth of 105 metres.

Near gale force winds were blowing at the time, and the *Annemieke* listed badly after taking in water. A distress message was sent out, and the nine crew abandoned ship in a liferaft. They were picked up twenty minutes later by the Peterhead MFV *Brighter Dawn*, and landed at Peterhead.

CAIRNAVON

Wreck No: 98		Date Sunk: 01 11 1925
Latitude: 57 27 31 N		Longitude: 01 47 11 W
GPS Lat: 5727.520 N		GPS Long: 0147.180 W
Location: 1 mile S of Buchan Ness Light		Area: Buchan
Type: Steamship		Tonnage: 5030 grt
Length: 412.0 ft	Beam: 52.0 ft	Draught: 28.0 ft
How Sunk: Ran aground		Depth: 14 metres

The British steamship *Cairnavon* was built in 1920 by W. Gray & Co. of West Hartlepool.

On 1 November 1925 she ran aground in dense fog while en route from Leith to Montreal with a general cargo, including coal, coke, rags and manganese.

Her SOS was picked up, but because of the fog the coastguards and rocket brigade had difficulty in finding the ship at the bottom of the cliff.

Three of the crew and one passenger climbed down a rope ladder to the rocks immediately below the bow. Carrying torches, they started to climb the cliff in the darkness before the coastguards finally found the stranded vessel and lowered a cliff ladder. In a difficult operation, all forty-nine passengers and crew were brought to safety at the top of the cliffs.

The ship broke in two later that day, and the stern section sank. Wreckage is now spread over a wide area centred on a cleft in the cliffs below South Castle Haven, inshore and south of a large prominent rock named Dundonnie, about half a mile south of Buchan Ness.

Locations of the wrecks of the Cairnavon *and the* Aberdeenshire *(Drawings by Roger Mathison)*

ABERDEENSHIRE

Wreck No: 99	Date Sunk: 21 10 1910
Latitude: 57 27 43 N	Longitude: 01 46 43 W
GPS Lat: 5727.722 N	GPS Long: 0146.718 W
Location: Craig Snow, 1 mile S of Boddam	Area: Buchan
Type: Trawler	Tonnage: 213 grt
Length: 121.2 ft	Beam: 21.5 ft Draught: 12.2 ft
How Sunk: Ran aground	Depth: 13 metres

The steam trawler *Aberdeenshire* was built by Mackie & Thomson of Govan in 1900.

She ran aground on 21 October 1910 at Craig Snow, Dundonnie, one mile south of Boddam. Her nine crew were saved by lifesaving apparatus.

The wreck lies broken up and scattered in a maximum depth of 13 metres in the north end of the channel between Dundonnie and Craig Snow.

The boiler and a steam winch are still recognisable. The builder's plate was recovered in 1995: 'Mackie & Thomson Hull No.26 Shipbuilders Glasgow'.

There is no appreciable current at this site, but the visibility under water here can be dreadful except in extended calm weather.

ZITELLA

Wreck No: 100	Date Sunk: 07 02 1940
Latitude: 57 27 11 N	Longitude: 01 47 52 W
GPS Lat: 5727.189 N	GPS Long: 147.871 W
Location: 1 mile S of Buchan Ness Light	Area: Buchan
Type: Steamship	Tonnage: 4254 grt
Length: 372.9 ft	Beam: 51.6 ft Draught: 25.2 ft
How Sunk: Ran aground	Depth: metres

Built by Burntisland shipyard in 1929, the *Zitella* stranded on Kinnaird Rock, Boddam Bay on 7 February 1940, while en route from Narvik to Middlesbrough with a cargo of iron ore.

She grounded at Longhaven, Buchan Ness in a strong southerly gale, heavy sea and bad visibility. The vessel was holed fore and aft and a total loss. Thirty-three crew landed safely on two rafts. The probable cause of running aground was that she had not been able to take a fix for three days, and fear of the offshore minefields had caused her master to shape a course towards the land, expecting to get into the Moray Firth. He saw no lights nor heard any fog signal before *Zitella* struck.

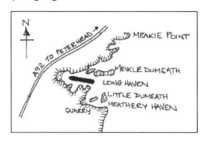

Location of Zitella *(Drawing by Roger Mathison)*

FLOTTA

Wreck No: 101	Date Sunk: 06 11 1941
Latitude: 57 28 30 N PA	Longitude: 01 39 00 W PA
GPS Lat: 5728.500 N	GPS Long: 0139.000 W
Location: Grounded off Buchan Ness	Area: Buchan
Type: Trawler	Tonnage: 545 grt
Length: 164.0 ft Beam: 27.5 ft	Draught: 10.5 ft
How Sunk: Ran aground	Depth: metres

The 545-grt trawler *Flotta* was built as a minesweeper for the Admiralty by Cochranes of Selby in 1941. She was, therefore, almost new when she ran aground on Buchan Ness on 29 October 1941 at 572718N, 014600W PA. She was eventually refloated, but foundered soon after, on 6 November, at about 572830N, 013900W PA.

BEN VENUE

Wreck No: 102	Date Sunk: 06 04 1904
Latitude: 57 28 45 N PA	Longitude: 01 45 50 W PA
GPS Lat: 5728.750 N	GPS Long: 0145.833 W
Location: Skerry Rock, Sandford Bay, Peterhead	Area: Buchan
Type: Trawler	Tonnage: 151 grt
Length: 102.3 ft Beam: 19.8 ft	Draught: 9.9 ft
How Sunk: Ran aground	Depth: 4 metres

The steam trawler *Ben Venue* was built in 1899 by Hall Russell of Aberdeen.

After running on to Skerry Rock in Sandford Bay, Boddam, she got off, but foundered very shortly after, 200 yards south of Skerry Rock, which shows above the surface at low tide.

One report suggests she lies in 54 metres in that position, but the charted depth there is only 4 metres. Her crew of nine got off safely in their small boat and were picked up by the Grimsby trawler *Baltic*.

A fisherman's GPS wreck mark at 5728.833N, 0145.294W, in 40 metres, 0.4 miles, 77° from Skerry Rock, might very well be the *Ben Venue*.

The tide rip around the rocks 200 metres south of Skerry Rock is horrendous!

LOCH WASDALE

Wreck No: 103	Date Sunk: 15 12 1942
Latitude: 57 28 50 N	Longitude: 01 46 09 W
GPS Lat: 5728.838 N	GPS Long: 0146.156 W
Location: Skerry Rock, Sandford Bay, Peterhead	Area: Buchan
Type: Trawler	Tonnage: 210 grt
Length: 116.8 ft Beam: 22.1 ft	Draught: 12.0 ft
How Sunk: Ran aground	Depth: metres

The steel-hulled steam trawler *Loch Wasdale* was built by Duthies of Aberdeen for the White Star Steam Fishing Co. Ltd in 1915, but was transferred to the Royal Navy for minesweeping duties until 1919. In 1939 she was sold to Malcolm Smith Ltd of Aberdeen. During a gale on 12 December 1942 she stranded on Skerry Rock off Boddam, in Sandford Bay.

Peterhead lifeboat was launched at 4.20 a.m. with Harbourmaster James Winter at the helm, due to the illness of the regular cox Johnny McLean. At 4.35 the lifeboat reached Skerry Rock, and despite the horrendous conditions with huge waves whipped up by the gale, succeeded in manoeuvring alongside and managed to take off all twelve of the crew. The lifeboat returned to Peterhead at 5.15 a.m., having been away for only 55 minutes.

Shortly after the crew had been rescued, the *Loch Wasdale* caught fire and sank off the north end of Skerry Rock. She broke up and disappeared within three hours of running aground.

Not much of the *Loch Wasdale* remains – only a few scattered plates, beams and a scotch boiler. The site is subject to strong tidal flows and is best dived at slack. The area is littered with wreckage – some from the *Loch Wasdale*, and some from the more recent *Constant Star*.

CONSTANT STAR

Wreck No: 104	Date Sunk: 27 08 1987
Latitude: 57 28 47 N	Longitude: 01 45 59 W
GPS Lat: 5728.787 N	GPS Long: 0145.976 W
Location: Skerry Rock, Sandford Bay, Peterhead	Area: Buchan
Type: Trawler	Tonnage: 140 grt
Length: 93.0 ft Beam: 20.0 ft	Draught: 11.0 ft
How Sunk: Ran aground	Depth: 8-15 metres

The Peterhead-registered *Constant Star* was making her way back home in a north-easterly gale, force eight when she ran aground on Skerry Rock shortly after midnight on 26 August 1987. Skipper Francis Wood radioed Peterhead Harbour, and the lifeboat was launched. A helicopter was also scrambled from RAF Lossiemouth. When the lifeboat arrived, only the masts of the vessel could be seen due to breaking waves. There were no signs of life aboard, and the life rafts were gone. It was assumed that the crew had abandoned the sinking ship.

The lifeboat, several fishing vessels and the helicopter searched the area, but only an empty liferaft was found. The fishing vessels concentrated on searching the area where this had been found, while the lifeboat returned to Skerry Rock for a last look. The *Constant Star* was almost submerged and the wheelhouse demolished when lifeboat crewmen James Clubb and Sid Chisholm spotted a hand waving above the remains of the wheelhouse. At this moment, a huge sea broke over the lifeboat injuring three of the crew. One member of the lifeboat's crew recalls this as the worst sea condition he has ever been in. At one time the lifeboat was 'pitch-poled'(his description), i.e. caught by a wave, somersaulted fore and aft, and landed back upright! There was no way the lifeboat could approach the *Constant Star*. The helicopter was immediately notified, and successfully winched the eight crew from the wreck.

Note that the wreck is marked on the Admiralty chart in the wrong place – even for her original position aground. Photographs taken at the time clearly show her on the separate northern skerry which dries at LW. The remains now lie in the NW end of the channel between the two skerries at depths ranging from 8 to 15 metres.

The area around Skerry Rock is fiercely tidal but the western side is slightly protected and may be dived at all states of the tide with little difficulty. The remains of the *Constant Star* are well dispersed – the largest remaining sections are hull plates, diesel engine and the hydraulic 'stern-block'. The propeller and other non-ferrous items were commercially salvaged in the late 1980s. As you swim northwards from the site, more wreckage appears – this is from the much older wreck of the *Loch Wasdale*, which sank in 1942.

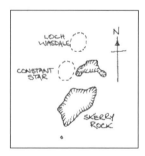

The locations of the Loch Wasdale *and* Constant Star

BEN TARBERT

Wreck No: 105	Date Sunk: 28 11 1975
Latitude: 57 29 46 N	Longitude: 01 46 14 W
GPS Lat: 5729.767 N	GPS Long: 0146.233 W
Location: Entrance to Peterhead Bay	Area: Buchan
Type: Trawler	Tonnage: 280 grt
Length: 121.0 ft Beam: 25.1 ft	Draught: 12.5 ft
How Sunk: Collision with *Aberdeen Venturer*	Depth: 13 metres

The trawler *Ben Tarbert* was lost in a collision with the trawler *Aberdeen Venturer* on 28 November 1975, at the entrance to Peterhead Bay.

Both vessels had developed radar trouble and had gone to Peterhead for repairs. They were instructed to lie off the port until radar engineers could be sent out to them. The

Ben Tarbert was lying at anchor at the entrance to the Bay of Refuge when the *Aberdeen Venturer* manoeuvred to lie alongside her, but in doing so, the *Venturer* struck the *Ben Tarbert* amidships, and she sank in three minutes with the loss of two of her eleven crew. The nine survivors were rescued by Peterhead pilot boat and other vessels.

Her bow was visible above water for a time after she sank, but eventually disappeared beneath the surface. The wreck was demolished with explosives in 1977, but the remains still lie on the bottom, and can be seen on an echo-sounder. This is somewhat academic, however, as the position is within Peterhead Harbour limits, directly under the entrance to the harbour, and Peterhead Harbour Board will not grant permission to dive here.

The trawler Ben Tarbert *(Photo: author's collection)*

RESMILO

Wreck No: 106	Date Sunk: 20 06 1941
Latitude: 57 29 48 N	Longitude: 01 46 12 W
GPS Lat: 5729.800 N	GPS Long: 0146.200 W
Location: Entrance to Peterhead Bay	Area: Buchan
Type: Trawler	Tonnage: 258 grt
Length: 120.5 ft Beam: 22.0 ft	Draught: 12.2 ft
How Sunk: By aircraft	Depth: 13 metres

The trawler *Resmilo* was built in 1917 by Cook Welton & Gemmell, Beverley, engine by C.D. Holmes of Hull. She was requisitioned by the Admiralty in 1940 for use as a minesweeper.

On 20 June 1941 she was sunk by German aircraft at Peterhead. There was no loss of life.

According to Lloyds, she sank in 7 fathoms (13 metres) at the end of the south breakwater, but the wreck is charted in 12.8 metres, between the breakwaters at the entrance to Peterhead Bay, close to the end of the north breakwater. The book *Cook Welton & Gemmell Shipbuilders of Hull and Beverley 1883–1963* by Thompson, Newton, Robinson & Lofthouse, notes that in 1946 she was raised and scrapped.

COLUMBINE

Wreck No: 107	Date Sunk: 24 12 1957
Latitude: 57 30 14 N	Longitude: 01 46 09 W

GPS Lat: 5730.233 N   GPS Long: 0146.150 W
Location: At Northhead, Peterhead   Area: Buchan
Type: Steamship   Tonnage: 347 grt
Length: 149.2 ft   Beam: 23.7 ft   Draught: 11.7 ft
How Sunk: Ran aground   Depth: metres

The coaster *Columbine* (ex-*Thorn*), owned by Hay & Co. of Lerwick, went onto rocks at North Head, Peterhead at 7.34 p.m. on Christmas Eve, 1957. She was en route from Baltasound to Middlesbrough with a cargo of 350 tons of serpentine (for making firebricks). Peterhead lifeboat was called out, and, watched by hundreds of people on the foreshore, manoeuvred alongside the grounded ship. The swell caused the two vessels to surge apart, but the coaster's crew of ten lined the rail and waited for their opportunity to jump into the lifeboat. The *Columbine* was a total loss.

SEA REEFER

Wreck No: 108   Date Sunk: 22 08 1992
Latitude: 57 30 06 N   Longitude: 01 46 12 W
GPS Lat: 5730.100 N   GPS Long: 0146.200 W
Location: South Head, Peterhead.   Area: Buchan
Type: Motor vessel   Tonnage: 1,738 grt
Length: ft   Beam: ft   Draught: ft
How Sunk: Ran aground   Depth: metres

On 22 August 1992 the Antigua-registered refrigerated cargo vessel *Sea Reefer* had arrived off Peterhead to load a cargo of frozen fish. Before she could enter the harbour, however, a storm blew up, and drove her towards the shore. Her anchor was dropped to arrest her drift, but the anchor chain snapped, and the vessel was driven ashore on the rocks at South Head, Keith Inch, north of the harbour entrance. The twenty-two Egyptian crew were all taken off unharmed. When the tide receded, the vessel was left high and dry. The ship's bottom plates were found to be damaged along their whole length, and a pinnacle of rock was sticking up through her tank top. In that condition she could not be refloated, and was declared a total loss.

A 220-metre long road was later built across the rocks to provide access to the wreck, which was completely broken up where she lay. There is nothing left at the site.

Sea Reefer *aground at South Head, Peterhead (Photo: author's collection)*

NORTHMAN

Wreck No: 109

Latitude: 57 30 10 N PA

GPS Lat: 5730.167 N

Location: South Head, Keith Inch, Peterhead.

Type: Trawler

Length: 115.8 ft   Beam: 22.1 ft

How Sunk: Ran aground

Date Sunk: 11 12 1956

Longitude: 01 46 00 W PA

GPS Long: 0146.000 W

Area: Buchan

Tonnage: 199 grt

Draught: 12.1 ft

Depth: metres

On 11 December 1956 the Aberdeen steam trawler *Northman* (built by Hall Russell in 1911) ran aground on South Head, Keith Inch, Peterhead, with such force that the impact was heard over a wide area of the town. In a heavy swell, the Peterhead lifeboat took off the thirteen crew of the *Northman* and landed them in Peterhead.

MARZOCCO

Wreck No: 110

Latitude: 57 30 33 N PA

GPS Lat: 5730.550 N

Location: 2.8 cables, 64° Port Henry pier

Type: Steamship

Length: 285.0 ft.   Beam: 42.1 ft.

How Sunk: Beached

Date Sunk: 14 06 1940

Longitude: 01 45 43 W PA

GPS Long: 0145.717 W

Area: Buchan

Tonnage: 5,106 grt

Draught: 19.1 ft.

Depth: metres

The steel screw steamship *Marzocco* (ex-*Nervier*, ex-*War Tank*) was built in 1918 by Swan Hunter & Wigham Richardson of Sunderland. She was Italian-owned, and registered in Livorno (Leghorn), Italy.

The *Marzocco* had left Sunderland on 9 June 1940, bound for Civitta Veccia with a cargo of coal, and passed St Abbs Head later that day. On the 10th, Italy declared war on Britain, and HM trawler *Stonefly* was sent to intercept her.

The Italian ships *Pamia, Pellice, Barbana G, Moscardin* and *Mugnone*, lying in Methil anchorage and approaches, were taken as prizes and their crews landed for internment.

The breech blocks were also removed from guns on French ships in British ports.

At 04.05 hrs on the 11th *Stonefly* found the *Marzocco* abandoned and low in the water 7 miles 90° from Rattray Head. A party was sent aboard, and the tug *Saucy* sailed from Peterhead to bring her in. At 10.32 hrs on the 11th *Stonefly* reported they were 2½ miles, 027° from Peterhead, speed two knots. They hoped to make the harbour of refuge. At 14.50 hrs *Marzocco* took the ground on North Head Rock in nil visibility. (She was reported to be aground 1½ miles north of Peterhead after being abandoned by her crew, with the tugs *Saucy* and *Iron Axe* standing by.) Her crew were captured but, in accordance with orders sent by W/T, they had scuttled their ship. The salvage vessel *Iron Axe* was sent out but pumps rigged by her crew were unable to contain the flow of water. Divers sent down on 15 June were hastily withdrawn owing to strong tides. *Marzocco* was then abandoned as a total loss with her poop awash at low water.

No trace of the vessel was found by HMS *Scott* in 1958, and Peterhead harbour master said she had broken up some years previously. In August 1967, however, someone made a request to purchase the wreck.

ATLAND

Wreck No: 111	Date Sunk: 25 03 1943
Latitude: 57 29 47 N	Longitude: 01 40 40 W
GPS Lat: 5729.783 N	GPS Long: 0140.667 W
Location: 5 miles ENE of Buchan Ness	Area: Buchan
Type: Steamship	Tonnage: 5,203 grt
Length: 388.9 ft Beam: 52.4 ft	Draught: 26.1 ft
How Sunk: Collision with *Carso*	Depth: metres

The Swedish steamship *Atland* was built in 1910 by W. Doxford & Sons. She was sunk off Peterhead on 25 March 1943, in collision with the SS *Carso*, while en route from Pepel to London with 7,000 tons of iron ore. Nineteen lives were lost.

The wreck is charted at 573050N, 013820W PA, with at least 28 metres over it in about 60 metres, but the true position is as given above. This is known to Peterhead fishermen as the 'Big Wreck'.

The Doxford Turret Ship Atland (*Photo: courtesy of World Ship Society*)

MAGICIAN

Wreck No: 112	Date Sunk: 14 04 1944
Latitude: 57 31 24 N PA	Longitude: 01 47 54 W PA
GPS Lat: 5731.400 N	GPS Long: 0147.900 W
Location: Craigewan Point, N of Peterhead	Area: Buchan
Type: Steamship	Tonnage: 5,105 grt
Length: 394.9 ft. Beam: 52.5 ft.	Draught: 27.9 ft.
How Sunk: Ran aground	Depth: metres

The Harrison Line steamship *Magician*, built in 1925 by New Waterway S.B.Co., was en route from Trinidad via New York (for Atlantic convoy), and Loch Ewe (for coastal convoy), to London with a cargo of 10,000 tons of sugar, several hundred barrels of pitch, and a small quantity of rum.

At some time during 14 April 1944, the convoy ran into dense fog. The ships were proceeding in single file, attempting to navigate by reference to numbered marker buoys indicating the positions of minefields, and to maintain station by following the fog buoy trailed by the vessel ahead, and listening for the sounds of the sirens of the other vessels.

One method used by merchant seafarers to aid station-keeping in convoys was to show a weak blue stern light shining directly downwards on to the water and to listen for propeller sounds. (Very difficult!) In fog conditions things were worse. Sometimes sound signals were used, but during the war a Fog Buoy was adopted. This innovation was a wooden contraption in the form of a cross. It had a metal scoop fixed to the bottom end of the long section. A bridle was fixed to the crosspiece and the device was towed over the stern. When being towed through the water the scoop sent up a spout of water some 5 feet high which was clearly visible. The watch officer of a ship behind constantly judged the distance to this waterspout and adjusted his speed accordingly.

The *Magician* eventually lost contact with the convoy, and turned to starboard after it had been calculated that she should clear Craigewan Point, north of Peterhead, only to run aground there at about 20.30 hrs that evening, on what at first appeared to be a sandy bottom. Some two hours later, the crew heard voices from the shore. These were from the coastguards, who were unable to get a line aboard the *Magician*, which was stranded 200 to 300 yards offshore, directly below Peterhead golf club.

During the night, the ship started to take in water when her bottom was punctured by a pinnacle of rock which pierced No. 4 hold. About 05.30 hrs, the Peterhead lifeboat arrived alongside, and took off all the crew of seventeen British officers and DEMS ratings and about seventy Indians, and landed them at Peterhead some two hours later.

Two salvage vessels, one of which was the *Iron Axe*, were sent from Aberdeen to attempt to pull the *Magician* off the rocks. The rum was salvaged and brought ashore immediately (a natural priority!). The pitch was jettisoned to lighten the ship, and the sugar was ruined by the flooding.

After four weeks of salvage work, and several attempts to pull her off, the *Magician* finally succumbed to severe weather conditions and broke her back, resulting in total loss.

I am indebted to Mr Bill Hodgson, the purser of the *Magician*, for his recollection of the events described above. The episode had a happy ending for him. The first person to help him ashore from the lifeboat was a WAAF radar operator from the local RAF station, who later became his wife.

RENAISSANCE

Wreck No: 113	Date Sunk: 25 03 1928
Latitude: 57 31 30 N PA	Longitude: 01 47 45 W PA
GPS Lat: 5731.500 N	GPS Long: 0147.750 W
Location: Craigewan Point, N of Peterhead	Area: Buchan
Type: Trawler	Tonnage: 199 grt
Length: 115.0 ft Beam: 22.0 ft	Draught: 12.9 ft
How Sunk: Ran aground	Depth: metres

The Aberdeen steam trawler *Rennaissance* (ex-*John H. Irvin*), built in 1913 by Hall Russell, ran onto the rocks in fog at Craigewan Point, about half a mile NE of the mouth of the river Ugie, St Fergus, north of Peterhead.

In an attempt to haul her off, four of the crew rowed out with the trawler's anchor tied to their small boat. Before they could drop it a little way off, their boat was capsized by a wave, and immediately sank, dragged down by the weight of the anchor and chain. The four men in the rowing boat were swept away and disappeared.

Peterhead rocket brigade arrived and had just succeeded in firing a line to the *Rennaissance* when the Peterhead lifeboat also arrived on the scene and took the six remaining crewmen aboard.

En route to the wreck, the lifeboatmen had heard the shouts of one of the four men who had been in the capsized rowing boat, and pulled him from the water after he had drifted more than half a mile from the *Rennaissance*. The three others from the rowing boat were never found.

TRIESTE

Wreck No: 114	Date Sunk: 16 07 1918
Latitude: 57 31 30 N PA	Longitude: 01 47 45 W PA
GPS Lat: 5731.500 N	GPS Long: 0147.750 W
Location: Craigewan Pt, ½ mile N of Peterhead	Area: Buchan
Type: Steamship	Tonnage: 1505 grt
Length: 255.7 ft.	Beam: 34.3 ft Draught: 20.7 ft
How Sunk: Ran aground	Depth: metres

The British steamship *Trieste*, built in 1883 by Whitehaven S.B.Co., was wrecked half a mile north of Peterhead on 16 July 1918, while en route from Swansea to Sarpsborg with a cargo of coal.

CRANSDALE ?

Wreck No: 115	Date Sunk: 21 01 1931
Latitude: 57 31 48 N PA	Longitude: 01 43 00 W PA
GPS Lat: 5731.800 N	GPS Long: 0143.000 W
Location: 2 miles NE of Peterhead	Area: Buchan
Type:	Tonnage: grt
Length: ft	Beam: ft Draught: ft
How Sunk:	Depth: metres

A sonar contact was obtained in this position on 1 April 1945, and it is charted as Wk PA with at least 20 metres over it in about 49 metres.

This might be a slightly inaccurate position for the *Muriel* or the *Bel Lily*.

Alternatively, it may be the Aberdeen steam trawler *Cransdale*, which stranded on Scotstown Head on 21 January 1931. She was refloated that same day and taken under tow towards Peterhead, but sank off Kirkton Head one and a half hours later in 17 fathoms (31 metres). Her crew of nine were saved by Peterhead lifeboat.

Cransdale (ex-*Harry Ross*) (183 grt, 111 x 20 ft) was built in 1901 by Hall Russell, Aberdeen for the Ross Steam Trawling & Fishing Co. Ltd, A453.

BEL LILY

Wreck No: 116	Date Sunk: 14 05 1917
Latitude: 57 32 45 N	Longitude: 01 42 20 W

GPS Lat: 5732.750 N

Location: 0.6 miles 40° from North Head, Peterhead

Type: Trawler

Length: 105.5 ft   Beam: 21.0 ft

How Sunk: Mined

GPS Long: 0142.333 W

Area: Buchan

Tonnage: 168 grt

Draught: ft

Depth: 41 metres

The Grimsby trawler *Bel Lily* was built in 1899 by Irvine S.B. & E. Co. Ltd.

On her way to the fishing grounds on 14 May 1917, she struck a German mine about 1½ miles E by N of Peterhead, and sank with the loss of all her crew of ten.

As all of the crew were lost, it is not clear how this position was ascertained.

The wreck found at 573245N, 014220W was thought to be the *Muriel* – until the *Muriel* was found at 573206N, 014416W in 1999. This wreck must, therefore, be something else.

It was dived in October 1999 and found to be a small steel steam trawler. The wreck is upright and almost intact, and rises about 4 metres up from the seabed. The wheelhouse has gone. There are trawl gallows fore and aft, although the forward portside one is missing, and the hull is damaged in this position – there is a two metre wide hole here, probably mine damage.

(This may be the accurate position for the wreck recorded at 573148N, 014300W PA in 1945.)

MURIEL

Wreck No: 117

Latitude: 57 32 06 N

GPS Lat: 5732.105 N

Location: 2 miles NE of Peterhead

Type: Steamship

Length: 270.0 ft   Beam: 40.6 ft

How Sunk: Torpedoed by *UC-58*

Date Sunk: 17 09 1918

Longitude: 01 44 16 W

GPS Long: 144.262 W

Area: Buchan

Tonnage: 1831 grt

Draught: 18.5 ft

Depth: 53 metres

The steel-hulled collier *Muriel* was built in 1898 by Grangemouth Dockyard Co.

She was torpedoed by the *UC-58* on 17 September 1918, while en route from the Tyne to Scapa Flow with a cargo of coal, and sank in 12 minutes. A naval patrol vessel took off the crew and landed them in Peterhead.

Lloyds World War One Losses described the position of attack as 3½ miles ENE of Peterhead Signal Station, and the wreck was charted 3½ miles NE of Peterhead at 573300N, 014105W PA.

The wreck charted at 573245N, 014220W was also thought possibly to be the *Muriel*.

An unidentified wreck charted at 573206N, 014407W, with a least depth of 36 metres in 48 metres, was recorded in 1958. At that time, the wreck apparently stood up 12 metres from the bottom. This wreck was accurately located at 573206N, 014416W, and dived on 1 September 1999. It was found to be the wreck of an armed steamship with a gun mounted on the stern. (The *Muriel* was defensively armed with a stern gun.) The gun was described by divers as 'short and dumpy' with recoil mechanism above the barrel. Rifles and .303 rounds were found in the bridge area. There is loads of coal about, and two? stern holds are full of coal. She has a well exposed triple-expansion steam engine with two boilers about 20 metres from the stern. In the bridge area, a thin brass ring and 12-inch diameter 'bowl' were found (compass?), along with what looks like a one-meter diameter ship's wheel – wooden with brass reinforcing. Forward of the boiler, the wreck is well flattened. There are two winches on the seabed off the port side. This area has nets, trawl wires and a trawl door entangled – the divers never got further forward than this area.

One 8-inch diameter porthole and two 10-inch diameter prismatic deck-lights were recovered.

The builder's plate recovered from the Muriel. (*Photo: Roger Mathison*)

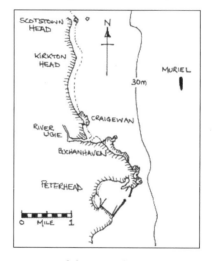

Location of the Muriel © RFM 2000

STRATHBRAN

Wreck No: 118		Date Sunk: 05 10 1924
Latitude: 57 33 00 N PA		Longitude: 01 48 00 W PA
GPS Lat: 5733.000 N		GPS Long: 0148.000 W
Location: ½ mile S of Scotstoun Head		Area: Buchan
Type: Trawler		Tonnage: 212 grt
Length: 115.0 ft	Beam: 22.0 ft	Draught: 13.0 ft
How Sunk: Ran aground		Depth: metres

The steam trawler *Strathbran* was built by Hall Russell, Aberdeen in 1915.

She ran aground half a mile south of Scotstoun Head on 5 October 1924.

DANEARN

Wreck No: 119

Latitude: 57 33 30 N PA

GPS Lat: 5733.500 N

Location: Near Scotstoun Head, N of Peterhead

Type: Trawler

Length: 115.5 ft

How Sunk: Ran aground

Date Sunk: 15 03 1942

Longitude: 01 48 00 W PA

GPS Long: 0148.000 W

Area: Buchan

Tonnage: 231 grt

Beam: 23.1 ft Draught: ft

Depth: metres

The steam trawler *Danearn* (ex-*Pelagos*) was built by Duthies of Aberdeen in 1916, and requisitioned as a minesweeper during the First World War.

She was wrecked by running ashore near Scotstoun Head, north of Peterhead on 15 March 1942.

STRUAN

Wreck No: 120

Latitude: 57 33 30 N PA

GPS Lat: 5733.500 N

Location: Outers Reef, Scotstoun Head

Type: Trawler

Length: 115.5 ft

How Sunk: Ran aground

Date Sunk: 18 01 1933

Longitude: 01 47 45 W PA

GPS Long:0147.750 W

Area: Buchan

Tonnage: 213 grt

Beam: 23.1 ft Draught: ft

Depth: metres

The Admiralty trawler *Struan* (ex-*William Cogswell*), built in 1918, ran aground in fog on the Outers Reef at Scotstoun Head, 4 miles north of Peterhead on 18 January 1933. The sound of her siren attracted attention, and Peterhead lifeboat and the Peterhead lifesaving brigade were called out.

The lifesaving brigade had to transport their gear over more than a mile of sand dunes. Their first rocket fell wide of the trawler, but the second fell across the wreck, and the stranded trawlermen began to haul it in.

At that moment, however, Peterhead lifeboat succeeded at the sixth attempt in closing alongside the wreck, and took off the nine crewmen.

ST MAGNUS

Wreck No: 121

Latitude: 57 32 15.42 N

GPS Lat: 5732.257 N

Location: 3 miles NNE of Peterhead

Type: Steamship

Length: 215.1 ft

How Sunk: Torpedoed by *UC-58*

Date Sunk: 12 02 1918

Longitude: 01 43 35.7 W

GPS Long: 0143.595 W

Area: Buchan

Tonnage: 809 grt

Beam: 31.1 ft Draught: 15.3 ft

Depth: 45 metres

The steamship *St Magnus* was built in 1912 by Ramage & Ferguson, and owned by the North of Scotland and Orkney and Shetland Steam Navigation Co.

On 12 February 1918, while en route from Lerwick to Aberdeen, she was torpedoed by the *UC-58*, three miles NNE of Peterhead. The sea was calm, and all except five of those on board escaped in two of the lifeboats. They were picked up by a minesweeper and taken to Peterhead.

The wreck was first dived in October 1999, and found to be upright with a slight list to starboard, and still reasonably intact. The wheelhouse has gone and the decking has rotted away, leaving the boiler and triple expansion steam engine visible. The starboard side of the wreck is fairly well flattened, but the port side is intact, with a lot of ornate brasswork and a row of portholes.

Depth to the seabed is 51 metres, and the wreck rises 5-6 metres up from the bottom.

St Magnus *at Aberdeen (Photo: Aberdeen Art Gallery & Museums Collection)*

UNKNOWN

Wreck No: 122		Date Sunk:
Latitude: 57 34 35 N		Longitude: 01 33 35 W
GPS Lat: 5734.583 N		GPS Long: 0133.583 W
Location: 8 miles NE of Peterhead		Area: Buchan
Type:		Tonnage: grt
Length: ft	Beam: ft	Draught: ft
How Sunk:		Depth: 86 metres

This wreck was originally charted at 573424N, 013348W PA with at least 50 metres over it in about 86 metres. Possibly the *Skomer*?

UNKNOWN – MALMLAND ?

Wreck No: 123	Date Sunk: 08 08 1915
Latitude: 57 35 22 N PA	Longitude: 01 38 50 W PA
GPS Lat: 5735.367 N	GPS Long: 0138.833 W
Location: 6½ miles NE of Peterhead	Area: Buchan
Type: Steamship	Tonnage: 3779 grt

Length: 336.6 ft   Beam: 50.2 ft   Draught: 22.5 ft
How Sunk: Torpedoed by *U-17*   Depth: 70 metres

The Swedish steamship *Malmland* was built in 1904. She was torpedoed by the *U-17* two miles E by S of Rattray Head on 8 August 1915, while en route from Narvik to Rotterdam with a cargo of iron ore.

The Swedish National Archives give the position as 5 miles N ½E from Peterhead.

A wreck is charted as Wk PA here, with at least 40 metres over it in about 70 metres.

UNKNOWN – ALCORA ?

Wreck No: 124   Date Sunk:
Latitude: 57 35 30 N PA   Longitude: 01 42 40 W PA
GPS Lat: 5735.500 N   GPS Long: 0142.667 W
Location: 4 miles SE of Rattray Head   Area: Buchan
Type: Tonnage: grt
Length: ft   Beam: ft   Draught: ft
How Sunk: Depth: 40 metres

Charted as Wk PA with at least 28 metres over it in about 40 metres.

This is thought by the Hydrographic Department to possibly be the *Alcora*.

The Hydrographic Department notes give the circumstances of loss of the *Alcora* as sunk 2 miles off Rattray Head, but the above PA is 4 miles off Rattray Head.

A further reason to question this position for the *Alcora* is that she has also been reported to have been lost by stranding at Rattray Head, and a position 4 miles offshore in 40 metres of water is not consistent with running aground. (See wreck no. 127.)

ELNA ?

Wreck No: 125   Date Sunk: 27 12 1943
Latitude: 57 35 30 N   Longitude: 01 18 30 W
GPS Lat: 5735.500 N   GPS Long: 0118.500 W
Location: Off Rattray Head   Area: Buchan
Type: Steamship   Tonnage: 1,435 grt
Length: 240.0 ft   Beam: 40.0 ft   Draught: 15.0 ft
How Sunk: Depth: 60 metres

An unknown wreck about 81 metres (267 ft) long, standing up about 10 metres (32 ft) from the bottom, was found at 573530N, 011830W in 1964.

The wreck is lying oriented 340/160°, and the least depth over the wreck is 60 metres in a total depth of about 70 metres.

It may be the US steamship *Elna*, built in 1924 by Hanlon D.D. & S.B. Co. The vessel was taken over by the US Army during the Second World War, and was lost *owing to marine causes* off Rattray Head on 27 December 1943.

UNKNOWN – LORD NELSON ?

Wreck No: 126   Date Sunk: Pre-1973
Latitude: 57 36 36 N   Longitude: 01 43 06 W

GPS Lat: 5736.600 N	GPS Long: 0143.100 W
Location: 3½ miles SE of Rattray Head	Area: Buchan
Type:	Tonnage: grt
Length: ft.	Beam: ft. Draught: ft.
How Sunk:	Depth: 48 metres

The unidentified wreck in this position is oriented 270/90°, with a least depth of 48 metres.

As a result of a diver's report in 1973, it is thought likely to be a trawler, and various suggestions for its identity have been made. These include:

The 151-grt Aberdeen trawler *Skomer* which was sunk off Buchan Ness in collision with the Grimsby trawler *Barbados* on 15 May 1911.

The 295-grt Icelandic trawler *Lord Nelson* which was sunk off Rattray Head on 22 November 1911 when she was involved in a collision with the Aberdeen trawler *Northman*.

TIC No.8 – a dumb dredger which foundered 3½ miles E by S of Rattray Head on 29 October 1911.

The drifter *Victory*, which foundered one mile off Rattray Head on 2 September 1923.

ALCORA

Wreck No: 127	Date Sunk: 30 10 1940
Latitude: 57 34 40 N PA	Longitude: 01 49 00 W PA
GPS Lat: 5734.667 N	GPS Long: 0149.000 W
Location: Stranded 2 miles S of Rattray Head	Area: Buchan
Type: Steamship	Tonnage: 1381 grt
Length: 270.0 ft	Beam: 38.0 ft Draught: 16.0 ft
How Sunk: Ran aground	Depth: metres

The British steamship *Alcora* (ex-*Dundee*), was built by Caledon, Dundee in 1919.

While en route from San Juan to the Tees with a cargo of cement, she was driven ashore in a south-easterly storm, two miles south of Rattray Head at 07.20 hrs on 30 October 1940. The Fraserburgh lifeboat was called out, but the crew of twenty-six were taken off by the local Life Saving Brigade, and *Alcora* was abandoned at 15.00 hrs.

The Hydrographic Department has recorded a wreck at 573530N, 014240W PA (which is 4 miles off Rattray Head in about 40 metres) as possibly the British steamship *Alcora*. This seems unlikely to me, in view of the cause of loss of the *Alcora*, which must have been close enough to the shore for the Life Saving Brigade's lines to be fired to the stranded vessel.

In the south-easterly gale that day, the steamship *Lisbon* was wrecked at Rattray Briggs. All her crew came safely ashore at Fraserburgh. The *Alcora*, *Baron Minto*, *Simonburn* and *Clumberhall* all went ashore at Rattray Head. *Simonburn* was abandoned and sank, and her crew of twenty-four landed at Fraserburgh. The *Baron Minto* was ashore in a good position on a sandspit. Twenty-six of her crew remained aboard and the other thirty-one were put ashore at Fraserburgh. *Clumberhall* was refloated and reached Methil on the 31st, but *Alcora* was abandoned ashore two miles south of Rattray Head. The Fraserburgh lifeboat *John & Charles Kennedy* went to her assistance, but the local LSA team took all the crew of the *Alcora* off by breeches buoy.

LISBON

Wreck No: 128
Latitude: 57 36 36 N PA
GPS Lat: 5736.600
Location: Rattray Head
Type: Steamship
Length: 252.1 ft   Beam: 38.4 ft
How Sunk: Ran aground

Date Sunk: 29 10 1940
Longitude: 01 47 00 W PA
GPS Long: 0147.000
Area: Buchan
Tonnage: 1984 grt
Draught: 17.1 ft
Depth: metres

The Ellerman steamship *Lisbon* was built in 1920 by Hall Russell of Aberdeen.

At 06.50 hrs on 29 October 1940 she was driven ashore in a storm and wrecked one mile east of Rattray Head, while en route from Lisbon to London with a general cargo. Her crew were rescued by Peterhead lifeboat.

EBRO

Wreck No: 129
Latitude: 57 37 30 N PA
GPS Lat: 5737.500 N
Location: 2 miles N of Rattray Head
Type: Steamship
Length: 238.5 ft   Beam: 36.2 ft
How Sunk: Ran aground

Date Sunk: 18 03 1942
Longitude: 01 51 00 W PA
GPS Long: 0151.000 W
Area: Buchan
Tonnage: 1,066 grt
Draught: 20.5 ft
Depth: metres

The Danish steamship *Ebro* ran aground on the sands in Strathbeg Bay 1½ miles from the Coastguard lookout on 18 March 1942 while en route from Reykjavik to Hull with a cargo of fish. Her crew of twelve were saved by Fraserburgh lifeboat. *Ebro* was built by Hall Russell in 1920.

The Danish steamship Ebro *(Photo: author's collection)*

BRAGI

Wreck No: 130
Latitude: 57 37 37 N

Date Sunk: 13 03 1926
Longitude: 01 48 54 W

GPS Lat: 5736.617 N   GPS Long: 0148.900 W
Location: 150 yards N of Rattray Lighthouse   Area: Buchan
Type: Steamship   Tonnage: 850 grt
Length: ft   Beam: ft Draught: ft
How Sunk: Ran aground   Depth: metres

The German steamship *Bragi* ran aground 150 metres north of Rattray lighthouse in wild weather. The vessel was en route from Methil to the Faroes with a cargo of coal, and a deck cargo of coke. The cargo shifted in the high winds and heavy seas causing a list, and in making for the shelter of the land to attempt to rectify the situation, she ran aground. Peterhead lifeboat was unable to approach the *Bragi* because of the ferocity of the breaking waves, and the crew of thirteen were taken off by breeches buoy. She was lying bow on to the shore at a spot where there is a strong eddy tide.

VICTORY

Wreck No: 131   Date Sunk: 02 09 1923
Latitude: 57 36 50 N PA   Longitude: 01 47 00 W PA
GPS Lat: 5736.833 N   GPS Long: 0147.000 W
Location: 1 mile E of Rattray Head   Area: Buchan
Type: Drifter   Tonnage: grt
Length: ft   Beam: ft Draught: ft
How Sunk: Depth: metres

The steel drifter *Victory* was built by Duthies of Aberdeen in 1905.
    She foundered one mile east of Rattray Head on 2 September 1923.

ERNE

Wreck No: 132   Date Sunk: 06 02 1915
Latitude: 57 37 00 N PA   Longitude: 01 49 00 W PA
GPS Lat: 5737.000 N   GPS Long: 0149.000 W
Location: Wrecked off Rattray Head   Area: Buchan
Type: Destroyer   Tonnage: 550 tons
Length: 233.5 ft   Beam: 23.5 ft Draught: 12.0 ft
How Sunk: Ran aground   Depth: metres

The 550-ton destroyer HMS *Erne*, built in 1903, stranded near Rattray Head in a severe easterly gale on 6 February 1915. There was no loss of life and the wreck was later broken up in situ.

UNION

Wreck No: 133   Date Sunk: 29 11 1870
Latitude: 57 37 00 N PA   Longitude: 01 49 00 W PA
GPS Lat: 5737.000 N   GPS Long:0149.000 W
Location: Rattray Briggs   Area: Buchan

Type: Steamship   Tonnage: 2800 grt
Length: ft   Beam: ft   Draught: ft
How Sunk: Ran aground   Depth: metres

The German steamship *Union* was en route to New York with a general cargo, including copper, 1,200 canaries, 310 passengers and 112 crew. Off Buchan Ness the engines were stopped in the hours of darkness to allow a repair to be made to a bearing, and during the two or three hours this was being carried out the ship was steadily drifting northwards. Shortly after getting underway again, about 1.00 a.m. on 29 November 1870, she ran aground on Rattray Briggs. Flares were fired to attract attention to her plight, but they were not seen by anyone on the shore. The weather was calm, and after daybreak, the crew and the passengers landed at Rattray Fishtown, using the ship's own lifeboats. Tugs sent from Aberdeen were unable to pull the *Union* off the rocks, and she eventually broke up in a gale. A large quantity of wreckage was washed ashore.

ST GILES

Wreck No: 134   Date Sunk: 28 09 1902
Latitude: 57 37 00 N PA   Longitude: 01 49 00 W PA
GPS Lat: 5737.000 N   GPS Long: 0149.000 W
Location: The Skellies, Rattray Briggs   Area: Buchan
Type: Steamship   Tonnage: 407 grt
Length: 161.7 ft   Beam: 25.2 ft Draught: 12.0 ft
How Sunk: Ran aground   Depth: metres

The steamship *St Giles* was bound from Lerwick to Aberdeen on 28 September 1902. En route, she encountered dense fog, and ran on to the rocks about ¼ mile north of Rattray Head lighthouse. All of the passengers and crew reached the shore safely in the ship's lifeboats, while cattle on board swam ashore. The vessel broke her back when the tide receded.

BARON MINTO

Wreck No: 135   Date Sunk: 30 10 1940
Latitude: 57 37 06 N   Longitude: 01 47 34 W
GPS Lat: 5737.010 N   GPS Long: 0147.567 W
Location: 50°, 1 mile Rattray CG Station Area: Buchan
Type: Steamship   Tonnage: 4,637 grt
Length: 419.5 ft   Beam: 58.5 ft Draught: 24.2 ft
How Sunk: Ran aground   Depth: metres

The British steamship *Baron Minto*, built in Sunderland in 1937, was owned by Hogarth S.S. Co.

On 30 October 1940, en route from Texas City to Hull with a cargo of scrap metal, she was driven ashore in a storm at Strathbeg Bay, Rattray Head, 50° 1 mile from Rattray Coastguard Station.

The *Baron Minto* was ashore in a good position on a sandspit, and twenty-six of her crew remained aboard, while the other thirty-one were put ashore at Fraserburgh.

While the vessel was stranded in Strathbeg bay she was repeatedly bombed by German aircraft during the following six months, and became a total loss.

Nine thousand tons of her cargo was discharged during the war, but despite this, there must have been sufficient left of the *Baron Minto* and its cargo to make it worthwhile for local divers to carry out further salvage work in the 1970s. These divers apparently made a fair bit of money from the wreck, and with the proceeds they bought a workboat, which they called the *Minto* (they made a 'mint' from the wreck!).

An obstruction charted in the above position in a depth of about 15 metres, one mile NE of Rattray Head light is almost certainly the *Baron Minto*.

KIEV

Wreck No: 136		Date Sunk: 20 10 1916	
Latitude: 57 37 04 N		Longitude: 01 47 21 W	
GPS Lat: 5737.067 N		GPS Long: 0147.350 W	
Location: Rattray Briggs		Area: Buchan	
Type: Steamship		Tonnage: 5,566 grt	
Length: 433.0 ft	Beam: 49.9 ft	Draught: 29.0 ft	
How Sunk: Ran aground		Depth: 15 metres	

The 5566-grt three-decked, twin screw steamship *Kiev* (ex-*Odessa*) was built in 1896 by J. & G. Thomson of Glasgow for Russian owners.

She stranded on Rattray Briggs on 20 October 1916 while en route from Archangel to Leith with a general cargo. Of the sixty-nine crew and twenty-two passengers, eight lives were lost. Peterhead lifeboat saved seventy-four.

An unknown wreck was reported in 1930, 9.5 cables from Rattray Head Light, very close to Rattray Briggs, and may be the *Kiev*, although in this very exposed location, wreckage from a number of vessels is likely to be strewn over a wide area.

The Russian steamship Kiev *(Photo: courtesy of World Ship Society)*

UNKNOWN – PRE-1972

Wreck No: 137	Date Sunk: Pre 1972
Latitude: 57 37 30 N	Longitude: 01 38 00 W
GPS Lat: 5737.500 N	GPS Long: 0138.000 W

Location: 6 miles E of Rattray Head   Area: Buchan
Type: Tonnage: grt
Length: ft   Beam: ft Draught: ft
How Sunk: Depth: 75 metres

This wreck, which is charted with at least 50 metres over it in about 75 metres, was found in 1972.

It might be the trawler *Lochnagar*, lost on 5 January 1909, or the Icelandic trawler *Lord Nelson*, lost in collision with the Aberdeen trawler *Northman* off Rattray Head on 22 November 1911.

BLANKA

Wreck No: 138   Date Sunk: 29 10 1914
Latitude: 57 37 45 N PA   Longitude: 01 52 00 W PA
GPS Lat: 5737.705 N   GPS Long: 0152.000 W
Location: 2 miles N of Rattray Head Lt.   Area: Buchan
Type: Steamship   Tonnage: 1,417 grt
Length: 247.5 ft   Beam: 36.3 ft Draught: 15.3 ft
How Sunk: Ran aground   Depth: metres

The Swedish steamship *Blanka* of Oscarshamn ran ashore about 2 miles north of Rattray Head light at 3.00 a.m. on 29 October 1914, while en route to Hull with a cargo of timber.

During the war the lighthouses were not lit, and in the darkness it had been impossible to establish her position with accuracy. A north-easterly gale was blowing at the time, which perhaps contributed to setting the ship's course further to the west than had been realised. The crew of seventeen were taken off by Peterhead lifeboat.

The *Blanka* (ex-*Mersario*) was built in 1889 by the Tyne Iron Shipbuilding Co. of Newcastle.

TORGRIM

Wreck No: 139   Date Sunk: 31 10 1914
Latitude: 57 37 45 N PA   Longitude: 01 52 00 W PA
GPS Lat: 5737.750 N   GPS Long: 0152.000 W
Location: 2 miles N of Rattray Head Lt.   Area: Buchan
Type: Steamship   Tonnage: 1,617 grt
Length: 260.5 ft   Beam: 37.4 ft Draught: 18.1 ft
How Sunk: Ran aground   Depth: metres

While en route to Grangemouth with a cargo of timber, the Swedish steamship *Torgrim* of Landskrona ran aground close to the *Blanka*, which had gone ashore two days previously. The north-easterly gale was still blowing, and the Peterhead lifeboat had to return to the harbour with engine trouble shortly after setting out. A rowing lifeboat was towed to the stricken ship by a trawler, but was swamped before any of the crew could be rescued, and had to be run ashore. Peterhead and Rattray rocket brigades arrived, but were unable to fire a line to the distressed vessel until a plank with a rope attached was thrown overboard from the grounded ship, and this fouled a rocket line which enabled a breeches buoy to be hauled aboard, and the crew of nineteen were safely brought ashore. The *Torgrim* (ex-*Richard Kelsall*) was built by J. Redhead & Co. of South Shields in 1885.

CAIRNMONA

Wreck No: 140		Date Sunk: 30 10 1939
Latitude: 57 38 40 N		Longitude: 01 43 45 W
GPS Lat: 5738.667 N		GPS Long: 0143.750 W
Location: 3 miles E of Rattray Head		Area: Buchan
Type: Steamship		Tonnage: 4666 grt
Length: 390.7 ft	Draught: 33.7 ft	Draught: 33.7 ft
How Sunk: Torpedoed by *U-13*		Depth: 48 metres

The Newcastle-registered steamship *Cairnmona* was built in 1918 by Sunderland S.B. Co.

Shortly before eleven o'clock on the night of 30 October 1939 she was torpedoed at 5738N, 0145W, 3 miles E of Rattray Head, by the *U-13* (KL Karl Daublebsky von Eichain). The *Cairnmona* had been en route from Montreal and Halifax to Leith and Newcastle with a general cargo, including wheat, zinc and copper ingots. Three of the crew were lost, but forty-two were rescued by the Aberdeen trawler *River Lossie* and the Peterhead lifeboat.

The wreck is charted 3 miles E of Rattray Head at 573748N, 014330W, but the correct position is 573840N, 014345W.

Some of the *Cairnmona*'s cargo of 1,500 tons of copper ingots is recorded as having been recovered on 18 June 1953 by Risdon Beazley's salvage vessel *Foremost 18*. In fact a total of 1,065 tons of the *Cairnmona*'s copper and zinc was recovered by grab from 180-ft depth.

At that time, copper was worth £250 per ton, but has fluctuated in value, with a general upward trend, to almost £1,900 per ton in 1995.

For over forty years, Risdon Beazley was the world's leading marine salvage company. Their main salvage technique was 'smash and grab' from the surface.

At today's prices, the 435 tons of copper not recovered by Risdon Beazley would be worth over £800,000, making this wreck a potentially worthwhile target for modern-style salvage by divers.

The value of the remaining cargo must have been realised by the Northern Shipbreaking Co., however, as they subsequently purchased the wreck and carried out further salvage operations with their vessel *Minto* in 1973/4, recovering the propeller and some of the remaining copper.

In 1974 they reported the wreck to be badly smashed up (probably mainly as a result of Risdon Beazley's and their own salvage activities), lying 320/140°, with a least depth of 48 metres in a total depth of 54 metres.

LOCHNAGAR

Wreck No: 141	Date Sunk: 05 01 1909
Latitude: 57 37 50 N PA	Longitude: 01 41 45 W PA
GPS Lat: 5737.833 N	GPS Long: 0145.750 W

Location: Off Buchan Ness	Area: Buchan
Type: Trawler	Tonnage: 165 grt
Length: 105.4 ft Beam: 21.1 ft	Draught: 11.1ft
How Sunk: Collision with *Margaret*	Depth: metres

The steel-hulled steam trawler *Lochnagar* was built in 1900 by A. Hall & Sons, Aberdeen.

She sank in collision with the Wick steamship *Margaret* off Buchan Ness on 5 January 1909.

The position has also been described as 4 miles E ½ S of Rattray Head.

The *Margaret* picked up the *Lochnagar*'s crew of nine and landed them safely in Aberdeen.

PORT DENISON

Wreck No: 142	Date Sunk: 27 09 1940
Latitude: 57 41 25 N	Longitude: 01 45 36 W
GPS Lat: 5741.666 N	GPS Long: 0145.600 W
Location: 7 miles E of Rattray Head	Area: Buchan
Type: Steamship	Tonnage: 8043 grt
Length: 480.4 ft Beam: 60.3 ft	Draught: 32.3 ft
How Sunk: Bombed	Depth: 82 metres

The twin screw steamship *Port Denison* was built in 1918 by Workman Clark of Belfast.

While in convoy OA220 from London to Liverpool, from where it was intended that she would continue her voyage to Auckland and Lyttleton, New Zealand, she was attacked at 20.05 hrs by German aircraft 107° 9.3 miles from Rattray Head. She was hit first by an aerial torpedo, and then in a second run, flying from stem to stern, with the ship on fire and listing badly, the aircraft sprayed her with machine-gun shells, seriously injuring the signalman and causing many of the crew to jump overboard to escape. Sixteen of them were killed. Forty survivors were landed at Lyness by the escort trawler *Pentland Firth*, and four injured men were taken aboard the *SS Amarapoora*. The tug *Abielle IV* sailed from Aberdeen to the assistance of the *Port Denison*, while the corvette HMS *Bluebell*, commanded by Lt Cdr Robert Sherwood, stood by and picked up eight survivors. Peterhead lifeboat, *Julia Park Barry of Glasgow*, was launched at 20.25 hrs, but according to the lifeboat records, *Port Denison* had sunk by the time she arrived on the scene. Naval vessels were picking up survivors and the lifeboat found a raft with two aboard. At 02.00 hrs on the 27th, HMS *Bluebell* transferred eight survivors to the lifeboat, which landed the master, chief engineer and eight other survivors at Peterhead at 03.00 hrs.

British Vessels Lost at Sea 1939-1945 gives the position of attack on 26 September 1940 as 6 miles NE of Peterhead, but notes that she did not sink until the 27th. During the time she remained afloat she must have either drifted, or perhaps been towed by the *Abeille IV*, for some distance from the position of attack, although it seems unlikely that *Abeille IV* arrived in time to take her in tow, as *Port Denison* had already sunk by the time the lifeboat reached the scene.

Lloyds War Losses gives the position of attack as 6 miles E of Peterhead, and the position of sinking as 7 miles 260° to Rattray Head, in 45 fathoms (82 metres).

The position recorded by the Hydrographic Department in 1940, 7 miles E of

Rattray Head, or 9 miles NE of Peterhead at 573754N, 013548W PA, corresponds to that description.

The wreck found in 1973 at 574125N, 014536W was estimated to be a vessel of about 6,000-8,000 grt. I believe this is the *Port Denison*.

Port Denison (*Photo: National Maritime Museum*)

CRAIG-GOWAN

Wreck No: 143	Date Sunk: 25 04 1977
Latitude: 57 38 00 N PA	Longitude: 01 37 00 W PA
GPS Lat: 5738.000 N	GPS Long: 0137.000 W
Location: 8 miles E of Rattray Head	Area: Buchan
Type: Trawler	Tonnage: 163 grt
Length: 96.0 ft Beam: 22.0 ft	Draught: 11.0 ft
How Sunk: Collision with *Japonica*	Depth: 63 metres

The trawler *Craig-Gowan* (A313) was lost in collision with the trawler *Japonica* about 8 miles E of Rattray Head on 25 April 1977. Eight of the crew were saved, but one man was missing.

This is the position reported in 1977.

SIMONBURN

Wreck No: 144	Date Sunk: 30 10 1940
Latitude: 57 38 12 N	Longitude: 01 43 47 W
GPS Lat: 5738.200 N	GPS Long: 0143.783 W
Location: 3 miles ENE of Rattray Head	Area: Buchan
Type: Steamship	Tonnage: 5,213 grt
Length: 392.3 ft Beam: 53.7 ft	Draught: 28.6 ft
How Sunk: Ran aground	Depth: 38 metres

The wreck originally recorded in 1954 at 573830N, 014430W PA was accurately located and dived in 1973 at 573812N, 014357W, 3 miles ENE of Rattray Head. The divers considered it to be a ship of about 5000 grt, with a least depth of 38 metres in 51 metres.

It is not far from the *Cairnmona* (4,666 grt, at 573840N, 014345W), or the *Port Denison* (8,043 grt, at 574125N, 014536W). It has been suggested that this might be the *Magician* (5,105 grt, recorded at 573124N, 014754W PA), but this suggestion seems most unlikely to me, as the *Magician* stranded only 200 to 300 yards offshore at Craigewan Point, 7 miles further south.

The divers' estimate of the size of this wreck suggests to me that it could be the British steamship *Simonburn* (5,213 grt), which was driven ashore in a storm and stranded 65° one mile from Rattray CG lookout on 30 October 1940. Her crew were rescued by Peterhead lifeboat. The stranded vessel later floated off and sank about four miles east of Rattray Head. (Another reference states about four miles north of Rattray Head.)

The *Simonburn* was built in 1925, and was en route from Montreal to London with a cargo of wheat.

UNKNOWN

Wreck No: 145	Date Sunk:
Latitude: 57 38 30 N PA	Longitude: 01 33 25 W PA
GPS Lat: 5738.500 N	GPS Long: 0133.417 W
Location: 8½ miles E of Rattray Head	Area: Buchan
Type:	Tonnage: grt
Length: ft Beam: ft	Draught: ft
How Sunk:	Depth: 90 metres

Charted as Wk PA with at least 40 metres over it in about 90 metres.

MACEDON ?

Wreck No: 146	Date Sunk: 27 10 1873
Latitude: 57 38 42 N PA	Longitude: 01 42 36 W PA
GPS Lat: 5738.700 N	GPS Long: 0142.600 W
Location: 3½ miles ENE of Rattray Head	Area: Buchan
Type: Steamship	Tonnage: 410 grt
Length: 177.8 ft Beam: 22.7 ft	Draught:
How Sunk: Foundered	Depth: 51 metres

An unknown wreck is charted as Wk PA with at least 28 metres over it in about 51 metres.

This is possibly the iron steamship *Macedon*, built by Armstrong & Co. of Glasgow in 1864.

She sank 10 miles SE of Kinnaird Head on 27 October 1873.

She was carrying a cargo of copper and ore from Spain, and was heading to Glasgow to have a new boiler fitted. En route she called in at Berwick-on-Tweed for inspection, and after leaving there, suffered a series of machinery breakdowns, eventually having to proceed up the east coast of Scotland under sail.

Off Cairnbulg she developed a leak, and as her pumps were useless without the engine to operate them, the crew were forced to bail. Their efforts were not equal to the rate of water ingress, however, and they were finally forced to abandon ship at 4.00 a.m. and reached shore safely. While the crew were still in their lifeboat at 8.00 a.m. they saw the *Macedon* founder.

ANNA

Wreck No: 147	Date Sunk: 07 12 1959
Latitude: 57 39 37 N	Longitude: 01 54 30 W
GPS Lat: 5739.617 N	GPS Long: 0154.500 W
Location: St Combs, SE of Fraserburgh	Area: Buchan
Type: Motorship	Tonnage: 1,045 grt
Length: 240.1 ft Beam: 32.6 ft	Draught: 15.5 ft
How Sunk: Ran aground	Depth: metres

The Finnish vessel *Anna* (ex-*Braemar*, ex-*Havbor*, ex-*Bess*, ex-*Bayard*) began to drift uncontrollably after her engine room flooded and the pumps failed when she was off Rattray Head during a storm, while en route from Riga to Leith with a cargo of timber.

Sea conditions were too severe for a lifeboat to be launched, and the eighteen crew were rescued by breeches buoy by the Rattray and Fraserburgh lifesaving brigades when the vessel grounded at St Combs and became a total loss.

The Anna *aground at St Combs. (Photo: Aberdeen Journals)*

BEN MORE

Wreck No: 148	Date Sunk: 23 12 1911
Latitude: 57 40 00 N PA	Longitude: 01 54 52 W PA
GPS Lat: 5740.000 N	GPS Long: 0154.867 W
Location: Whitelinks Bay, Inverallochy	Area: Buchan
Type: Trawler	Tonnage: 157 grt
Length: 103.0 ft Beam: 20.1ft	Draught: 11.6 ft
How Sunk: Ran aground	Depth: metres

The steam trawler *Ben More* (built 1899 by Hall Russell, Aberdeen) ran aground in Whitelinks Bay, Inverallochy. The crew got away safely in their own boat.

AURIC

Wreck No: 149	Date Sunk: 27 10 1897
Latitude: 57 40 30 N PA	Longitude: 01 55 00 W PA
GPS Lat: 5740.500 N	GPS Long: 0155.000 W
Location: Cairnbulg Rocks	Area: Buchan
Type: Steamship	Tonnage: 454 grt
Length: 174.4 ft Beam: 25.3 ft	Draught: 12.2 ft
How Sunk: Ran aground	Depth: metres

The Belfast steamship *Auric* was carrying a cargo of coal from Seaham to Inverness, when she stranded on the rocks below Inverallochy. It was impossible to salvage the vessel.

CHARLES GOODANEW

Wreck No: 150	Date Sunk: 17 04 1917
Latitude: 57 40 30 N PA	Longitude: 01 46 30 W PA
GPS Lat: 5740.500 N	GPS Long: 0146.500 W
Location: 4 miles NE of Rattray Head	Area: Buchan
Type: Steamship	Tonnage: 791 grt
Length: 195.0 ft Beam: 30.0 ft	Draught: 11.6 ft
How Sunk: Mined	Depth: 47 metres

Charted as a wreck with at least 28 metres over it in 47 metres.

The *Charles Goodanew* was built in 1911, and was described as a store carrier. A total of thirteen lives were lost when she was mined and sunk on 17 April 1917.

In 1919 the position was described as 3½ miles ENE of Rattray Head.

UNKNOWN

Wreck No: 151	Date Sunk:
Latitude: 57 40 30 N	Longitude: 01 45 38 W
GPS Lat: 5740.500 N	GPS Long: 0145.633 W
Location: 5 miles NNE of Rattray Head	Area: Buchan
Type:	Tonnage: grt
Length: ft Beam: ft	Draught: ft
How Sunk:	Depth: 53 metres

Possibly the *Charles Goodanew*?

CHANCELLOR

Wreck No: 152	Date Sunk: 04 09 1913
Latitude: 57 40 40 N	Longitude: 01 34 00 W
GPS Lat: 5740.667 N	GPS Long: 0134.000 W
Location: 9 miles E of Rattray Head	Area: Buchan

Type:		Tonnage: grt
Length: ft	Beam: ft	Draught: ft
How Sunk:		Depth: 80 metres

Charted as a wreck with at least 40 metres over it in about 80 metres.

This may be the *Chancellor*, sunk on 4 September 1913, or possibly the *Bretagne*, sunk on 17 April 1917.

ALDER

Wreck No: 153	Date Sunk: 22 10 1941
Latitude: 57 41 00 N PA	Longitude: 01 56 00 W PA
GPS Lat: 5741.000 N	GPS Long:0156.000 W
Location: Near Cairnbulg Briggs	Area: Buchan
Type: Trawler	Tonnage: 500 grt
Length: 141.0 ft	Beam: 24.1 ft	Draught: 13.3 ft
How Sunk: Ran aground	Depth: metres

The steam trawler *Lord Davidson* (H57) was built by Cochranes of Selby in 1929 for Pickering & Haldane of Hull. Her name was changed to *Alder* when she was bought by the Admiralty in 1939 for use as a minesweeper. She ran aground near Cairnbulg Briggs on 22 October 1941.

ANVERS

Wreck No: 154	Date Sunk: 13 11 1940
Latitude: 57 41 15 N	Longitude: 01 47 30 W
GPS Lat: 5741.250 N	GPS Long: 0147.500 W
Location: 7 miles ESE of Kinnaird Head	Area: Buchan
Type: Steamship	Tonnage: 4398 grt
Length: 383.3 ft	Beam: 52.1 ft	Draught: 25.3 ft
How Sunk: Bombed by aircraft	Depth: 42–53 metres

Charted as a wreck 5 miles E of Cairnbulg Point, or 5 miles N of Rattray Head.

In 1974 divers of the Northern Shipbreaking Co. reported the wreck to be complete, and sitting upright. They estimated it to be a vessel of about 3,500–4,000 grt, with torpedo(?) damage on the port side, and laden with a cargo of mixed steel.

The steamship *Anvers* was built in Belgium in 1908, and was sunk by German aircraft while en route from Philadelphia, via the Clyde, to London, carrying a cargo of 6,000 tons of scrap steel.

The position of attack has been variously described as 4 to 5 miles 45° from Rattray Head, or 6½ miles N of Rattray Head.

One member of crew was killed.

A wreck found in 1974 at 574115N, 014730W, appears to be the *Anvers*.

Depth to the seabed is 53m, and the wreck is lying upright with her deck level. The hull has collapsed outwards so the deck is lying only 2–3 metres off the seabed. The structure is well broken up with some big wheels and ribs rising up above the deck to around 44–46 metres.

There is a huge cargo winch and some bollards, two large boilers and a single propellor.

The cargo appears to be girders and rolls of steel.

UNKNOWN

Wreck No: 155	Date Sunk:
Latitude: 57 41 20 N PA	Longitude: 01 43 50 W PA
GPS Lat: 5741.333 N	GPS Long: 0143.833 W
Location: 7 miles E of Cairnbulg Point	Area: Buchan
Type:	Tonnage: grt
Length: ft	Beam: ft Draught: ft
How Sunk:	Depth: 51 metres

Charted as Wk PA with at least 25 metres over it in about 51 metres.

This is 7 miles E of Cairnbulg Point, or 5½ miles NE of Rattray Head.

Possibly the same wreck as found in 1973 at 574125N, 014536W?

SOVEREIGN

Wreck No: 156	Date Sunk: 10 09 1995
Latitude: 57 40 56 N	Longitude: 01 56 30 W
GPS Lat: 5740.933 N	GPS Long: 0156 500 W
Location: Cairnbulg Point	Area: Buchan
Type: MFV	Tonnage: grt
Length: 60.0 ft	Beam: ft Draught: ft
How Sunk: Ran aground	Depth: metres

The Banff trawler *Sovereign* (BF 367), returning to Fraserburgh after a six-day fishing trip, went aground on the rocks at Cairnbulg Point at high tide, just after 3.00 a.m., on 10 September 1995.

The trawler Sovereign *broken in two at Cairnbulg Point (Photo: Roger Mathison)*

Fraserburgh lifeboat went to her aid. Waves were breaking over the trawler, and it was rolling heavily. In a risky operation, lifeboat coxswain Albert Sutherland managed to get alongside the trawler, despite there being only two feet of water below the lifeboat's keel, and the *Sovereign*'s five crew jumped to safety. The rescue took only 30 seconds. One member of the *Sovereign*'s crew lost a finger and damaged another when his hand became trapped between a taut rope and the trawler's side. An attempt was to be made to refloat the *Sovereign* at the next high tide, but she broke in two, and became a total loss. She was scrapped in situ.

ANTONIO

Wreck No: 157		Date Sunk: 05 06 1979	
Latitude: 57 41 50 N		Longitude: 02 01 31 W	
GPS Lat: 5741.837 N		GPS Long: 0201.518 W	
Location: Just W of Fraserburgh		Area: Buchan	
Type: Motor vessel		Tonnage: 1,333 grt	
Length: 244.0 ft	Beam: 35.0 ft	Draught: ft	
How Sunk: Ran aground		Depth: 10 metres	

The Panamanian-registered motor vessel *Antonio* was on a voyage from Loch Fyne to Hamburg with a cargo of crushed stone when she ran aground in fog just to the west of Fraserburgh on 5 June 1979. Her crew, captain, the captain's wife and an Alsatian dog were taken off by Fraserburgh Lifeboat. The vessel was hard aground with her stern awash. Later reports stated that she had broken her back, and by 18 June she was reported by Moray Coastguard as 'breaking-up'.

The remains (so far un-dived) lie in shallow water about 250 metres off the site of what was the old 'gut-factory' at Fraserburgh – however Fraserburgh's main sewage outfall is directly opposite and the water quality is disgusting, which accounts for the fact that no-one has yet dived the site!

Antonio (ex-*Sylvia*, ex-*Oscar Mathies*) was built by A. Hagelstein in 1957.

MV Antonio *aground off Fraserburgh (Photo: David C. Buchan/Fraserburgh Herald)*

CAPE YORK

Wreck No: 158	Date Sunk: 27 08 1940
Latitude: 57 41 24 N	Longitude: 01 33 20 W
GPS Lat: 5741.400 N	GPS Long: 0133.333 W

Location: 14 miles E of Kinnaird Head		Area: Buchan
Type: Motorship		Tonnage: 5,027 grt
Length: 410.0 ft	Beam: 54.0 ft	Draught: 27.0 ft
How Sunk: Torpedoed by aircraft		Depth: 72 metres

On 26 August 1940, the 5,027-grt motorship *Cape York* was attacked by German aircraft 45°, 10 miles from Kinnaird Head, according to *British Vessels Lost at Sea 1939-1945*. (Lloyds give 45°, 8 miles from Kinnaird Head.)

This twin screw motorship, built in 1926 by Lithgows of Port Glasgow, and belonging to the Lyle Shipping Co., was en route from Vancouver to Hull with a cargo of 3,500 tons of grain, 4,180 tons of timber and 400 tons of lead.

Although very badly damaged by bombs, she was not immediately sunk, and was recorded as being on fire on the 27th at 5745N, 0138W. The tug *Saucy* took the damaged vessel in tow, but this had to be abandoned the day after the attack, when the *Cape York* finally foundered, still in flames, at 574200N, 013305N PA, 55°, 8 miles from Rattray Head. Seventy-four crewmen who had been taken off the burning ship were landed at Peterhead. There were no casualties.

The Hydrographic Department recorded the approximate position for the sinking of the *Cape York* as 574136N, 013306W PA, where it was charted with at least 55 metres over it in about 80 metres total depth, about 10 miles NE of Rattray Head. The wreck is upright and fairly intact.

A salvage contract was taken out in 1971 by Risdon Beazley/Ulrich Harms, who specialised in 'smash and grab' operations to recover non-ferrous metal cargoes, but according to Alan Crothall, who was the managing director of Risdon Beazley/Ulrich Harms Ltd, they never carried out any salvage operation on the *Cape York*.

In 1971 the value of lead was about £100 per ton, making the total value of the lead cargo £40,000. Perhaps this was considered insufficient to justify the costs of a recovery operation at that time, but by 1996 the value of lead had risen to almost £500 per ton. The lead is almost certainly still there, and is now worth some £200,000. In the meantime, of course, the cost of a recovery operation has also risen. Kilburns Salvage identified the wreck in about 1986 at 574124N, 013320W, in a depth of 72 metres, but they did not carry out any salvage work.

The reason that neither Risdon Beazley nor Kilburns Salvage carried out any recovery work on the *Cape York* is that the lead is loaded in the bottom of the ship, and covered with thousands of tons of timber and grain – all of which would have to be removed to get at the lead, which is not considered to be sufficiently valuable to justify the time and cost of removing the overburden.

PRESTONIAN

Wreck No: 159		Date Sunk: 25 05 1915
Latitude: 57 41 00 N		Longitude: 02 09 20 W
GPS Lat: 5741.000 N		GPS Long: 0209.333 W
Location: 50 yards offshore, W of Rosehearty		Area: Buchan
Type: Steamship		Tonnage: 1,152 grt
Length: 223.7 ft	Beam: 33.2 ft	Draught: 14.4 ft
How Sunk: Ran aground		Depth: 13 metres

The British steamship *Prestonian* was built by the Ailsa S.B. Co. in 1901, and was wrecked in Aberdour Bay on 25 May 1915, while carrying a cargo of flax and timber from Archangel to Dundee. The position given by the Hydrographic Department is 574130N, 020830W PA, about ¾ mile west of Quarry Head, but the wreck lies in 12 to 18 metres of water, only about 50 yards offshore, under the cliffs in the bay to the west of Quarry Head. This is within the MOD Firing and Bombing Range, about 1½ miles west of Rosehearty. The top of the boiler is only about 4 metres below the surface. Underwater visibility here is very good.

There are reported to be two double bottoms lying near the *Prestonian*.

On 7 February 1940 the Polish steamship *Bug* went ashore near Rosehearty. Fraserburgh lifeboat took off her crew. The *Bug* might have been refloated, but on the other hand, maybe one of these reported double bottoms is from that ship.

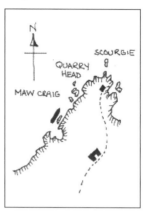

Location of Prestonian © RFM 2000

The Prestonian, *shortly after sinking in Aberdour Bay* (*Photo: Author's collection*)

WILLIAM HOPE

Wreck No: 160	Date Sunk: 28 10 1884
Latitude: 57 40 30 N PA	Longitude: 02 10 30 W PA
GPS Lat: 5740.500 N	GPS Long: 0210.500 W
Location: Aberdour Bay	Area: Buchan
Type: Trawler	Tonnage: 126 grt

Length: 92.5 ft   Beam: 18.5 ft   Draught: 8.1 ft
How Sunk: Ran aground   Depth: metres

The iron steam trawler *William Hope* was built by Hawthorns of Leith in 1882.

While en route from Fraserburgh to Burghead on 28 October 1884, her engine failed off Troup Head. The vessel was blown ashore and wrecked in Aberdour Bay. Jane Whyte, a local farm worker's wife, had gone to check her husband's boat, and found the ship aground. She waded into the sea to catch a rope thrown by one of the crew, and by use of this rope, all the men aboard managed to get safely ashore. Jane Whyte was awarded a Silver Medal by the RNLI for her act, and there is a memorial at the site of her home at Aberdour beach to commemorate the rescue.

NOSS HEAD

Wreck No: 161	Date Sunk: 27 02 1941
Latitude: 57 40 00 N PA	Longitude: 02 20 00 W PA
GPS Lat: 5740.000 N	GPS Long: 0220.000 W
Location: Near Gardenstown	Area: Buchan
Type: Steamship	Tonnage: 438 grt
Length: 150.9 ft Beam: 24.1 ft	Draught: 9.3 ft
How Sunk: Unknown	Depth: metres

Built 1921 by A. Hall, Aberdeen, with machinery aft and a welldeck forward.

With a crew of ten and two gunners, the *Noss Head* left Leith on 25 February 1941, bound for Kirkwall with a cargo of coal and bricks. She sheltered in Gardenstown Bay from 10.00 a.m. on the 26th until 08.30 a.m. on the 27th, when she left to resume her voyage. She was not seen again, but rafts with two bodies were washed ashore at Deerness on 1st March, and Tarracliff Bay on 2nd March. The cause of her loss has never been conclusively established.

The Joint Arbitration Committee, whose responsibility it was to decide the probable cause of loss in circumstances such as hers, where no conclusive evidence was available, considered her loss to be 60 per cent attributable to war risk, and 40 per cent to marine risk. She was finally posted missing at Lloyds on 26 March. This was a formality required to allow insurance to be paid.

G 103

Wreck No: 162	Date Sunk: 25 11 1925
Latitude: 57 41 55 N	Longitude: 02 07 26 W
GPS Lat: 5741.917 N	GPS Long: 0207.433 W
Location: Locheilair Bay, Rosehearty	Area: Buchan
Type: Destroyer	Tonnage: 1,116 tons
Length: 314.4 ft Beam: 30.6 ft	Draught: 12.0 ft
How Sunk: Ran aground	Depth: 5 metres

The German destroyer *G103* was one of the vessels scuttled in Scapa Flow on 21 June 1919. She was raised, and was being towed by the Aberdeen tug *Audax* to Rosyth for scrapping when the tow broke in the Moray Firth, and the destroyer was blown ashore in Locheilair Bay, about one mile west of Rosehearty. On striking the rocks, she broke in two, and the heavy seas quickly pounded her to pieces. The remains lie close to the shore in a depth of 4–10 metres.

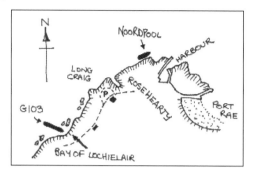

Locations of Noordpool *and* G-103 © RFM 2000

NOORDPOOL

Wreck No: 163	Date Sunk: 01 03 1931
Latitude: 57 42 07 N	Longitude: 02 07 07 W
GPS Lat: 5742.117 N	GPS Long: 0207.117 W
Location: 500 yards W of Rosehearty pier	Area: Buchan
Type: Trawler	Tonnage: grt
Length: ft Beam: ft	Draught: ft
How Sunk: Ran aground	Depth: metres

The Dutch trawler *Noordpool* was washed ashore in a NNE gale about 500 yards west of Rosehearty pier in the early hours of 1 March 1931. The wreck was discovered in the morning, lying on the rocks on its port side, adjacent to the shore. Fourteen crew were lost. The trawler's clock was washed ashore, stopped at one minute to five. Ten bodies were also washed ashore and buried in the local cemetery. The skipper's body was later exhumed and returned to Holland.

The wreck was salvaged from the shore by Camerons of Peterhead. The site is shallow and kelp-covered in the summer. The telegraph and portholes were recovered in 1994/5.

The Dutch trawler Noordpool *ashore near Rosehearty (Photo: Arbuthnot Museum, Peterhead)*

CRAIGFORTH

Wreck No: 164	Date Sunk: 18 10 1884
Latitude: 57 42 02 N	Longitude: 02 03 49 W
GPS Lat: 5742.033 N	GPS Long: 0203.817 W
Location: Pittulie, near Sandhaven	Area: Buchan
Type: Steamship	Tonnage: 1,109 grt
Length: 231.0 ft Beam: 29.7 ft	Draught: ft
How Sunk: Ran aground	Depth: 18 metres

The 1,109-grt Leith-registered steamship *Craigforth* was built in Glasgow in 1869.

En route from Iceland to Leith with sheep and ponies, she went aground at Pittulie just to the west of Sandhaven on 18 October 1894. She had mistaken Rosehearty light for Kinnaird Head light and turned south too soon – stranding to the east of Rosehearty, at Pittulie.

Although this area has been dived quite often, there is no trace of any wreckage apart from an anchor, which lies in about 18m of water just to the west of Sandhaven, off the end of the sewage outfall pipe at the west end of Pittulie.

BRETAGNE

Wreck No: 165	Date Sunk: 17 04 1917
Latitude: 57 42 50 N PA	Longitude: 01 42 00 W PA
GPS Lat: 5742.833 N	GPS Long: 0142.000 W
Location: 8-9 miles NE of Rattray Head	Area: Buchan
Type: Steamship	Tonnage: 1,110 grt
Length: 224.4 ft Beam: 39.6 ft	Draught: 15.8 ft
How Sunk: By *UC-45*	Depth: 70 metres

The Danish steamship *Bretagne* was sunk by the *UC-45* 8 to 9 miles NE of Rattray Head on 17 April 1917, while en route from Newcastle to Copenhagen with a cargo of 1,503 tons of coal.

Charted as Wk PA with at least 40 metres over it in about 70 metres, 7 miles NE of Rattray Head, or 11 miles E of Kinnaird Head.

A wreck has also been charted at 574300N, 014300W PA, with a clearance of at least 40 metres in about 65 metres, 10 miles E of Kinnaird Head. This position was probably a previous approximation for the same wreck, as was 574100N, 014330W PA.

A.J. Tennent gives the position as 9 miles NE (magnetic) of Rattray Head, in 5746N, 0138W.

FRAM

Wreck No: 166		Date Sunk: 01 02 1940
Latitude: 57 42 06 N		Longitude: 02 10 35 W
GPS Lat: 5742.101 N	Bows	GPS Long: 0210.587 W
Latitude: 57 42 45 N		Longitude: 02 13 22 W
GPS Lat: 5742.750 N	Stern	GPS Long: 0213.356 W
Location: Aberdour Bay, W of Rosehearty		Area: Buchan
Type: Steamship		Tonnage: 2,760 grt

Length: 315.0 ft   Beam: 43.0 ft   Draught: 20.5 ft
How Sunk: Torpedoed by *U-13*   Depth: 49 metres

The Swedish-registered steamship *Fram* was built by Sir R. Dixon & Co. of Middles-brough. While at anchor in Aberdour Bay, sheltering from a storm, she was torpedoed by the *U-13* (OL Max Schulte) at 00.43 hrs GMT on 1 February 1940. The position was recorded as 5743N, 0206W.

The vessel broke in two, and the bow section sank immediately, but the stern section drifted for half an hour before going down.

About 12 hours after the sinking, the Aberdeen trawler *Viking Deep* picked up five men from a raft which had drifted to a position about 10 miles north of Troup Head, and took them to Macduff. A further ten survivors were picked up by another trawler after 36 hours adrift in freezing conditions on a second raft. Ten other crewmembers, including the captain and stewardess, were lost.

For many years, only the larger stern section had been located and dived. It lies at 5742.750N, 0213.356W (OSGB 36) (or 5742.748N, 0213.466W in WGS 84) oriented 160/340°, on a white sandy seabed at 49 metres. The stern itself sits almost upright and is fairly intact, rising 9 metres from the seabed. The four-bladed cast iron propeller with a diameter of about 10ft is still in place.

Moving forward, the wreck has collapsed down onto the seabed and is a mass of plates and beams, although much is recognisable – including a spare propeller, hatches, winches and engine. The ship's safe still lies among the wreckage, but the key has not been found! The wreck is strewn with nets and trawl doors, and carpeted with dead men's fingers and anemones.

Despite numerous searches, the bow section was not found until 1995. It lies in 38 metres of water, at 5742.101N, 0213.587W (OSGB 36) (or 5742.099N, 0210.697 in WGS 84) 2 miles west of Rosehearty.

The bow stood vertically, pointing towards the surface in 38 metres, and rising 5-6 metres from the bottom. It therefore presented only a very small echo-sounder target, which perhaps explains why it took so long to find the forward section. The stem has collapsed in on itself since 1999.

Pieces of wreckage lie on the bottom, along the line of the stern section's drift.

The Fram *(Photo: © Collection Tomas Johanneson)*

As currents in this area can run at up to 4 knots, this wreck is best dived at LW slack.

Obvious precautions should be taken due to the depth, currents and offshore location of the wreck – this is a dive only for experienced divers with appropriate training and equipment.

Delayed SMBs are recommended for decompression stops as the current can be strong enough to drag shot-line marker buoys under the surface.

The Rosehearty bombing range may be used from 9 a.m. to 4 p.m. on weekdays. The RAF doesn't take kindly to dive-boats near the range, and in 1995 members of Peterhead BSAC were bombed by four RAF Tornados, which apparently mistook the orange dive-boat for the target float! Fortunately, the bombs missed, but it might be safer to dive this wreck at the weekend!

Underwater visibility along the coast from Kinnaird Head to Buckie is extremely good, with the best visibility of all – rivalling even Scapa Flow – in the stretch between Gardenstown and Rosehearty. Average visibility is around 15 metres, with 25-30 metres visibility quite common after a few settled days in the summer.

This is in complete contrast to the relatively poor underwater visibility from Kinnaird Head down the east coast to Montrose, where average visibility may be only about 5 metres, although at times it can be much better.

It may be worth bearing in mind that a vessel named *Edward Bonaventure* was lost in Pitsligo Bay on 7 November 1556. She encountered severe weather while en route from Russia to Scotland with a cargo of jewels, presents, gold, silver and furs. She anchored in Pitsligo Bay, just west of Rosehearty, but Pitsligo Bay offers no shelter from a northerly gale, and she was blown from her mooring, and driven ashore on the rocks. She must have been smashed to pieces in a very short time, and most of the hundred or so aboard were lost. The wreck was then plundered by locals. There will obviously be nothing left of wooden parts of the ship, but any non-ferrous metal parts that may remain will have been mixed up with metal debris from other wrecks, driven into crevices in the rocks, and covered in kelp.

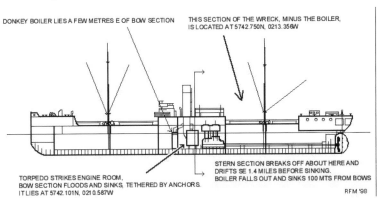

Diagram of Fram (*Drawing by Roger Mathison*)

UNKNOWN – KILDALE ?

Wreck No: 167
Latitude: 57 44 30 N
GPS Lat: 5744.500 N
Location: 8 miles E of Kinnaird Head

Date Sunk:
Longitude: 01 45 40 W
GPS Long: 0145.667 W
Area: Buchan

Type:		Tonnage: grt
Length: ft	Beam: ft	Draught: ft
How Sunk:		Depth: 51 metres

Charted as a wreck with a clearance of at least 51 metres in about 60 metres.
  This is 8¼ miles E of Kinnaird Head, and 12½ miles NE of Rattray Head.
  This might be another position for the *Kildale*, recorded in 574524N, 014500W PD.
Alternatively, this might be the *Trsat*.

KILDALE

Wreck No: 168		Date Sunk: 03 11 1940
Latitude: 57 45 15 N		Longitude: 01 46 00 W
GPS Lat: 5745.250 N		GPS Long: 0146.000 W
Location: 7 miles E of Rattray Head		Area: Buchan
Type: Steamship		Tonnage: 3,877 grt
Length: 363.5 ft	Beam: 51.4 ft	Draught: 22.8 ft
How Sunk: Bombed		Depth: 45 metres

The steamship *Kildale* was built in 1924 by W. Pickersgill of Sunderland.
  At 19.30 hrs on 3 November 1940, while en route from Barahona, in the Dominican
Republic, to London with a cargo of sugar, she was attacked and bombed amidships by
German aircraft off Kinnaird Head. Her crew of thirty-six and one gunner abandoned
the ship in a sinking condition. A search next day by aircraft failed to locate the ship.
  One seaman died in the water, and a steward was missing. The survivors were picked
up by *HMT Pentland Firth*, and *HMT Northern Wave*, the escorting trawlers of convoy
WN45. Twenty-eight survivors were landed at Leith, and five at Methil. Five had been
missing, but four must have been found later, suggesting that there were probably three
vessels involved in the rescue. It is most unlikely that both escorts would have hung
around to pick up survivors whilst the rest of the convoy steamed away.
  British Vessels Lost at Sea gives the position as 574500N, 014500W PA, and the
position has also been described as 7 miles 25° from Rattray Head. This is very close to
the position originally recorded for the *Kildale* at 574524N, 014500W PD.

UNKNOWN

Wreck No: 169		Date Sunk:
Latitude: 57 45 10 N		Longitude: 01 33 40 W
GPS Lat: 5745.167 N		GPS Long: 0133.667 W
Location: 9 miles E of Kinnaird Head		Area: Buchan
Type:		Tonnage: grt
Length: ft	Beam: ft	Draught: ft
How Sunk:		Depth: metres

UNKNOWN – REMUERA ?

Wreck No: 170	Date Sunk: Pre – 1945
Latitude: 57 46 00 N PA	Longitude: 01 54 00 W PA

GPS Lat: 5746.000 N
Location: 5 miles NE of Kinnaird Head
Type:
Length: ft
How Sunk:

GPS Long: 0154.000 W
Area: Buchan
Tonnage: grt
Beam: ft Draught: ft
Depth: 60 metres

Charted as Wk PA with at least 45 metres over it in about 60 metres.

This is considered to be only a very approximate position, but a wreck near here gave off oil in 1945. It is probably the *Remuera* – see wreck no. 175.

WILLIAM ROCKEFELLER

Wreck No: 171
Latitude: 57 46 00 N PA
GPS Lat: 5746.000 N
Location: 21 miles E of Kinnaird Head
Type: Tanker
Length: 430.0 ft
How Sunk: Torpedoed by *UC-58*

Date Sunk: 18 05 1918
Longitude: 01 22 00 W PA
GPS Long: 0122.000 W
Area: Buchan
Tonnage: 7,157 grt
Beam: 58.2 ft Draught: 33.3 ft
Depth: 75 metres

The American tanker *William Rockefeller* was built by William Cramp & Sons in 1916, and owned by the Standard Oil Co. of New Jersey.

DODAS says she was torpedoed by a German submarine in the North Sea on 18 May 1918.

According to the Hydrographic Department two positions were given in 1918 – 5744N, 0121W and 5749N, 0123W. A position midway between these two was chosen to record her at 5746N, 0122W, where she is charted as Wk PA with at least 75 metres of water over her.

Lloyds World War One Losses, which is a hand-written publication, rather than typeset, states that the ship was en route from New York to Glasgow, and records the position of torpedoing as 5744N, 1023W, which is a perfectly feasible position in the North Western Approaches to the Clyde, apparently consistent with the ship's voyage.

It was therefore hard to imagine why the *William Rockefeller* should have been anywhere near the North Sea at all, but the scribe who wrote the longitude as 1023W made a clerical error. He should have written 0123W. Admiralty documents give the position as 5749N, 0123W.

In the Rear Admiral's office in Peterhead a signal was received on the evening of Saturday 18 May 1918: 'SOS. *Rockefeller* torpedoed off Peterhead, 2005.'

All ships in the harbour were ordered to raise steam at once. Longside Airship Station was informed, and Peterhead Signal Station reported that they could see the ship 12 miles NE of the station.

HM Tug *William Poulson* left harbour at 20.25, and at 20.30, HMS *Tyrant* signalled 'Urgent. *Rockefeller* torpedoed 5749N, 0123W.'

The tug *William Poulson* and HMT *Princess Marie Jose* went to the stricken tanker, while no fewer than sixteen other trawlers and drifters equipped with hydrophones carried out a search for the U-boat.

In addition to the auxiliary patrol vessels on the search, Longside Air Station despatched two airships to the position of the wreck, and they carried out a continuous patrol of the vicinity until the hunt was abandoned.

At 22.55 hrs, the trawlers heard depth bombs exploding, and when they went to investigate, found a distinct oily track running NW/SE. Two trawlers proceeded NW, and two SE in that track, but heard nothing. At 11.40am, all ships had to return to Peterhead as they were required for escort duties.

The depth charge they had heard at 22.55 had been a bomb dropped by one of the airships on the oily track. The oily track had not been caused by a submarine, however, but was oil from the torpedoed ship drifting to leeward of the wreck.

UNKNOWN

Wreck No: 172	Date Sunk: Pre – 1965
Latitude: 57 46 20 N	Longitude: 02 14 15 W
GPS Lat: 5746.333 N	GPS Long: 0214.250 W
Location: 5 miles NNE of Troup Head	Area: Buchan
Type:	Tonnage: grt
Length: ft Beam: ft	Draught: ft
How Sunk:	Depth: 100 metres

A wreck at about 574600N, 021312W PA gave off fuel oil in 1965.

The wreck has since been more accurately located in 92 metres of water at 574620N, 021415W.

A fisherman's snag at 574655N, 021411W in 100 metres seems to be a further refinement of the position.

UNKNOWN – FRIENDSHIP ?

Wreck No: 173	Date Sunk: Pre – 1945
Latitude: 57 46 12 N	Longitude: 01 57 42 W
GPS Lat: 5746.200 N	GPS Long: 0157.700 W
Location: 4½ miles NNE of Kinnaird Head	Area: Buchan
Type:	Tonnage: grt
Length: 110.0 ft Beam: ft	Draught: ft
How Sunk:	Depth: 46 metres

This wreck was reported in April 1945 at 574612N, 015748W PA. It is apparently 110 ft long, and stands up 30 ft from the bottom.

Possibly the *Friendship*, sunk 17 July 1924, or the trawler *Norseman*, lost on 26 July 1912.

UNKNOWN

Wreck No: 174	Date Sunk:
Latitude: 57 46 12 N	Longitude: 01 33 42 W
GPS Lat: 5746.200 N	GPS Long: 0133.700 W
Location: 12 miles NE of Rattray Head	Area: Buchan
Type:	Tonnage: grt
Length: ft Beam: ft	Draught: ft
How Sunk:	Depth: 82 metres

Charted as a wreck with at least 30 metres over it in about 82 metres.

REMUERA

Wreck No: 175
Latitude: 57 46 59 N
GPS Lat: 5746.983 N
Location: 6½ miles NE of Kinnaird Head
Type: Steamship
Length: 485.0 ft   Beam: 62.3 ft
How Sunk: Torpedoed by aircraft

Date Sunk: 26 08 1940
Longitude: 01 52 42 W
GPS Long: 0152.700 W
Area: Buchan
Tonnage: 11,445 grt
Draught: 41.0 ft
Depth: 69-45 metres

The steamship *Remuera* was built by W. Denny in 1911 for the New Zealand Shipping Company. Homeward-bound from New Zealand with 4,801 tons of refrigerated cargo and 1,646 tons of general cargo, she was sunk by a direct hit from an aerial torpedo about 12 miles north of Peterhead, when the ship was attacked by four Heinkel 115 torpedo bombers and eight Ju 88 aircraft based at Stavanger, Norway. The tug *William Brady* sailed from Peterhead to her assistance, but by the time she arrived on the scene, *Remeura* had already sunk. All ninety-three crew and one gunner were saved.

The wreck lies on her port side, oriented NNW 080/260°, with her stern towards the SSE and bows NNW. Least depth is 45 metres in a total depth of 69 metres to the seabed.

A non-sub contact in 1944, at 574618N, 015300W, 6 miles off Kinnaird Head in about 30 fathoms, was thought to be either the *Remuera* or the *Trsat*, but the wreck at 574659N, 015242W is about 151 metres long – right for the *Remuera*, but twice the length of the *Trsat*.

Remuera *(Photo: author's collection)*

UNKNOWN

Wreck No: 176
Latitude: 57 46 35 N PA
GPS Lat: 5746.583 N
Location: 11 miles NNE of Rattray Head
Type:

Date Sunk:
Longitude: 01 40 30 W PA
GPS Long: 0140.500 W
Area: Buchan
Tonnage: grt

Length: ft   Beam: ft   Draught: ft
How Sunk: Depth: 64 metres

Charted as Wk PA with at least 30 metres over it in about 64 metres.

LOUISIANA

Wreck No: 177   Date Sunk: 18 04 1917
Latitude: 57 46 45 N PA   Longitude: 01 22 00 W PA
GPS Lat: 5746.750 N   GPS Long: 0122.000 W
Location: 21 miles E of Kinnaird Head Area: Buchan
Type: Steamship   Tonnage: 3015 grt
Length: 319.8 ft   Beam: 46.0 ft Draught: 23.2 ft
How Sunk: Torpedoed by *UC-45*   Depth: metres

Charted as Wk PA with at least 70 metres over it.

The Danish steamship *Louisiana*, built in 1896 by Armstrong & Co. of Newcastle-upon-Tyne, was torpedoed and sunk by the *UC-45* on 18 April 1917, 20 miles NNE of Buchan Ness. The position was also recorded as 5746N, 0138W, and described as 9 miles NE (mag) of Rattray Head.

The *Louisiana* was en route from Copenhagen and North Shields to Boston, Massachusetts with 2,957 tons of general cargo, including wood pulp. Her crew of twenty-seven were rescued by HMT *Balena*, and landed at Peterhead.

HMS *Somali* reported the wreck of a submarine at 574700N, 012200W PA, 21 miles east of Kinnaird Head, in November 1939. The contact is charted as Wk PA with at least 80 metres over it, and recorded by the Admiralty Hydrographic Department as an unknown German submarine.

It was thought this might possibly be the *U-77*, but the wreck of that First World War U-boat was found off Dunbar in 1990.

HMS *Somali* was probably keeping a very sharp lookout for submarines, particularly as this was only a few days after *U-47* had torpedoed the *Royal Oak* in Scapa Flow, and U-boat consciousness was high. It is perhaps understandable that any underwater contact obtained was likely to be assumed to be a U-boat. (A case of 'submarinitis'?)

This position is fairly close to the estimated position for the sinking of the *Louisiana* in 1917, and I suspect this may have been the wreck detected by HMS *Somali*.

TRSAT

Wreck No: 178   Date Sunk: 07 09 1941
Latitude: 57 45 17 N   Longitude: 01 57 04 W
GPS Lat: 5745.286 N   GPS Long: 0157.059 W
Location: 7 miles NE by E of Kinnaird Head   Area: Buchan
Type: Steamship   Tonnage: 1369 grt
Length: 235.6 ft   Beam: 36.2 ft Draught: 15.4 ft
How Sunk: Bombed   Depth: 45 metres

The Faroese vessel *Trsat* (ex-*Allie*) was built in 1919 by Forth S.B. Co. (Jeffreys of Alloa).

At 20.54 hrs on 7 September 1941, while en route from Reykjavik to Hull with 845 tons of fish, she was bombed by a single German aircraft, seven miles NExE of Kinnaird Head. One bomb was a direct hit, and *Trsat* sank. Fraserburgh lifeboat *John and Charles Kennedy* was alerted at 20.57 hrs by a message from Kinnaird Head Coastguards, who also reported flares a few minutes later.

The lifeboat was launched at 22.07 hrs and found first an empty boat, then wreckage, then a waterlogged boat with thirteen men and one body in it. The coxswain passed the body and the boat to HM trawler *Ebor Abbey* then continued to search for two missing men. Of the *Trsat's* seventeen crew, two and one gunner were lost, and fourteen, including some injured, were landed by the lifeboat.

One body was picked up the next day by the *Ebor Abbey*. A total of three lives were lost.

UNKNOWN

Wreck No: 179	Date Sunk:
Latitude: 57 47 05 N PA	Longitude: 01 37 55 W PA
GPS Lat: 5747.083 N	GPS Long: 0137.917 W
Location: 12 miles NE of Rattray Head	Area: Buchan
Type:	Tonnage: grt
Length: ft Beam: ft	Draught: ft
How Sunk:	Depth: 60 metres

Charted as Wk PA with at least 40 metres over it in about 60 metres.

UNKNOWN

Wreck No: 180	Date Sunk:
Latitude: 57 47 10 N PA	Longitude: 01 34 55 W PA
GPS Lat: 5747.167 N	GPS Long: 0134.917 W
Location: 13 miles NE of Cairnbulg Point	Area: Buchan
Type:	Tonnage: grt
Length: ft Beam: ft	Draught: ft
How Sunk:	Depth: 63 metres

Charted as Wk PA with at least 40 metres over it in about 63 metres.
Possibly *Trinity NB*?

SVARTON

Wreck No: 181	Date Sunk: 03 01 1940
Latitude: 57 45 30 N	Longitude: 02 00 02 W
GPS Lat: 5745.506 N	GPS Long: 0200.041 W
Location: 3½ miles N of Kinnaird Head	Area: Buchan
Type: Steamship	Tonnage: 2,475 grt
Length: 296.1 ft Beam: 44.5 ft	Draught: 19.7 ft
How Sunk: Torpedoed by *U-58*	Depth: 64 metres

The Swedish steamship *Svarton* (ex-*Cedargrove*) was en route from Narvik to the Tees with a cargo of iron ore on 3 January 1940, when she was torpedoed by the *U-58* (KL Herbert Kuppisch). Twenty of her crew were lost. Eleven were saved.

The Hydrographic Department originally recorded the *Svarton* at 5750N, 0150W PA, hence the Wk PA charted in that position, but this was subsequently amended in 1957 to 5748N, 0147W PA.

During the course of the action Kuppisch must have been working with his chart, on which he marked the position as AN1856. (He was actually more accurate than that, as he detailed the position as the lower left corner of AN1856.) He also noted that his U-boat was in 38 metres of water at the time of firing the torpedo at 09.11 hrs. After the action, when he was writing up his Ktb, he inadvertently made a transcription error in writing the position as AN1866.

AN1856 equates to about 5745N, 0200W, and there is a wreck in 64 metres at 5745.506N, 0200.041W. Very close by, where Kuppisch was when he fired his torpedo, the depth is 38 metres!

CHALLENGER

Wreck No: 182	Date Sunk: 13 09 1967
Latitude: 57 48 12 N PA	Longitude: 01 41 00 W PA
GPS Lat: 5748.200 N	GPS Long: 0141.000 W
Location: 12½ miles NE of Kinnaird Head	Area: Buchan
Type: Trawler	Tonnage: grt
Length: ft Beam: ft	Draught: ft
How Sunk:	Depth: 60 metres

Charted as Wk PA with at least 35 metres over it in about 60 metres.
This is 12½ miles NNE of Rattray Head.

CALIBAN ?

Wreck No: 183	Date Sunk: 12 04 1917
Latitude: 57 49 15 N	Longitude: 01 48 00 W
GPS Lat: 5749.250 N	GPS Long: 0148.000 W
Location: 8 miles NE ½E of Kinnaird Head	Area: Buchan
Type: Trawler	Tonnage: 215 grt
Length: 112.6 ft Beam: 22.5 ft	Draught: 12.3 ft
How Sunk: By submarine – gunfire	Depth: metres

The steel steam trawler *Caliban* was built by Cook Welton & Gemmell in 1911. She was captured by a German submarine on 12 April 1917, and sunk by gunfire.

Two very different positions have been recorded.

British Vessels Lost at Sea 1914–1918 gives the position as 45 miles NE by N from Rattray Head, and this was obviously the description used by the Hydrographic Department to plot the wreck in 581945N, 013030W PA.

Lloyds War Losses gives the position as 8 miles NE ½E of Kinnaird Head, which plots in 574830N, 014830W PA.

The wreck charted in 97 metres of water at 574915N, 014800W, 10 miles NE ½E of Kinnaird Head, might be the *Caliban*.

TRINITY NB

Wreck No: 184

Latitude: 57 50 00 N PA

GPS Lat: 5750.000 N

Location: 17 miles NE of Rattray Head

Type: Trawler

Length: 116.0 ft   Beam: 22.2 ft

How Sunk: Bombed

Date Sunk: 17 12 1939

Longitude: 01 30 00 W PA

GPS Long: 0130.000 W

Area: Buchan

Tonnage: 203 grt

Draught: 12.2 ft

Depth: 80 metres

The Granton steam trawler *Trinity NB* (GN95) was bombed and sunk at 575000N, 013000W PA, while outward bound from Granton to the fishing grounds on 18 December 1939. Two of the crew were drowned, and a third later died from exposure. The remainder of the crew were picked up by a Danish vessel and landed at a Norwegian port.

    The wreck is charted as Wk PA with at least 80 metres over it.

UNKNOWN

Wreck No: 185 .

Latitude: 57 52 48 N PA

GPS Lat: 5752.800 N

Location: 11 miles N of Kinnaird Head

Type:

Length: ft   Beam: ft

How Sunk:

Date Sunk:

Longitude: 01 57 00 W PA

GPS Long: 0157.000 W

Area: Buchan

Tonnage: grt

Draught: ft

Depth: metres

PRINCESS CAROLINE

Wreck No: 186

Latitude: 57 54 45 N PA

GPS Lat: 5754.750 N

Location: 14mls NE by E ½E Kinnaird Head

Type: Steamship

Length: 238.7 ft   Beam: 33.3 ft

How Sunk: Mined

Date Sunk: 13 10 1915

Longitude: 02 00 30 W PA

GPS Long: 0200.500 W

Area: Buchan

Tonnage: 888 grt

Draught: 16.0 ft

Depth: metres

The British steamship *Princess Caroline* was mined 14 miles NE by E ½E of Kinnaird Head on 13 August 1915.

    It is thought that the mine she struck may have been laid by the German raider *Möewe*.

UNKNOWN

Wreck No: 187

Latitude: 57 55 00 N PA

Date Sunk: Pre – 1945

Longitude: 01 54 00 W PA

GPS Lat: 5755.000 N	GPS Long: 0154.000 W
Location: 13½ miles NNE of Kinnaird Head	Area: Buchan
Type:	Tonnage: grt
Length: 170.0 ft Beam: ft	Draught: ft
How Sunk:	Depth: 73 metres

At 575500N, 015400W PA there is a wreck about 170 ft long.

A wreck about 170 ft long was also reported in 1945 at 575510N, 015715W. Are they the same wreck?

JENNY JENSEN

Wreck No: 188	Date Sunk: 16 02 1975
Latitude: 57 56 00 N PA	Longitude: 01 54 24 W PA
GPS Lat: 5756.000 N	GPS Long: 0154.400 W
Location: 14½ miles NNE of Kinnaird Head	Area: Buchan
Type: MFV	Tonnage: 81 grt
Length: ft Beam: ft	Draught: ft
How Sunk: Foundered	Depth: metres

The Danish MFV *Jenny Jensen* foundered on 16 February 1975.

Her crew were all saved.

GRECIAN PRINCE

Wreck No: 189	Date Sunk: 14 12 1918
Latitude: 57 57 00 N PD	Longitude: 02 08 00 W PD
GPS Lat: 5757.000 N	GPS Long: 0208.000 W
Location: 16½ miles N ½E of Kinnaird Head	Area: Buchan
Type: Trawler	Tonnage: 126 grt
Length: ft Beam: ft	Draught: ft
How Sunk: Trawled up a mine	Depth: metres

The trawler *Grecian Prince* trawled up a mine in her nets 16½ miles N ½E from Kinnaird Head on 14 December 1918. When the mine exploded, the vessel and eight of the crew were lost. Two crewmen were saved.

HORACE E NUTTEN ?

Wreck No: 190	Date Sunk: 14 12 1918
Latitude: 57 49 07 N	Longitude: 02 14 26 W
GPS Lat: 5749.117 N	GPS Long: 0214.443 W
Location: 9 miles NW of Kinnaird Head	Area: Buchan
Type: Trawler	Tonnage: 126 grt
Length: 112.2 ft Beam: 23.1 ft	Draught: 13.2 ft
How Sunk: Bombed	Depth: 90 metres

A Peterhead trawler skipper has reported a wreck in this position 9 miles NW of Kinnaird Head, and 8½ miles NE of Troup Head.

This might possibly be the steam trawler *Horace E Nutten* (ex-*Strathcarron*), which was built in 1913 by Hall Russell of Aberdeen.

On 29 March 1941 she left Aberdeen in ballast for the Faroes, and was last seen off Troup Head at 20.00 hrs that evening. Shortly after that sighting she was bombed and sunk by German aircraft in the Moray Firth, with the loss of all ten crewmembers.

The Joint Arbitration Committee considered she had been lost by war causes, probably on 29 March, and she was finally posted missing on 30 July 1941.

HARRY NOSTT 651

Wreck No: 191		Date Sunk: 25 05 1941	
Latitude: 57 57 36 N PA		Longitude: 02 10 00 W PA	
GPS Lat: 5757.600 N		GPS Long: 0210.000 W	
Location: 15½ miles N by W of Kinnaird Head		Area: Buchan	
Type: Drifter		Tonnage: 125 grt	
Length: 82.2 ft	Beam: 23.5 ft	Draught: 12.0 ft	
How Sunk: Bombed		Depth: metres	

The Faroese drifter *Harry Nostt 651* was bombed by German aircraft at 09.00 hrs on 25 May 1941. She was taken in tow, but this had to be abandoned later that day. She was later found derelict and on fire, and was sunk by gunfire 17 miles N by W ½W of Rattray Head. The position recorded, 575736N, 021000W PA, is 15½ miles N by W of Kinnaird Head. Admiralty files in the PRO state that she sank 37 miles north of Rattray Head.

COMPASS ROSE

Wreck No: 192		Date Sunk: 07 04 1975	
Latitude: 57 59 12 N		Longitude: 01 44 30 W	
GPS Lat: 5759.200 N		GPS Long: 0144.500 W	
Location: 20 miles NE of Fraserburgh		Area: Buchan	
Type: Motorship		Tonnage: 329 grt	
Length: 137.0 ft	Beam: 24.0 ft	Draught: 7.0 ft	
How Sunk: Foundered		Depth: metres	

The Panamanian-registered, wooden-hulled, twin screw motor survey vessel *Compass Rose* was on charter to the French oil company Total.

While en route from the Beryl oilfield to Fraserburgh on 7 April 1975, she was overwhelmed by mountainous seas whipped up by 60-knot winds. An air search was launched on 16 April, by which time the *Compass Rose* had been out of radio contact for over a week. A body from the *Compass Rose* was picked up by a fishing boat about 20 miles north-east of Fraserburgh, but there was no sign of the seventeen others known to have been aboard, and the search was abandoned on the 18th.

On 5 May, fishermen found pieces of wreckage painted the same colour as the *Compass Rose*, and a large wreck contact was obtained on the 6th at 575912N, 014430W.

ASTRONOMER

Wreck No: 193	Date Sunk: 02 06 1940
Latitude: 58 01 50 N	Longitude: 02 02 37 W
GPS Lat: 5801.833 N	GPS Long: 0202.617 W
Location: 20 miles N of Kinnaird Head	Area: Buchan
Type: Steamship	Tonnage: 8401 grt
Length: 482.7 ft Beam: 58.2 ft	Draught: 33.2 ft
How Sunk: Torpedoed by *U-58*	Depth: 56 metres

Astronomer was built in 1917 by D. & W. Henderson, Glasgow. She was requisitioned by the Admiralty for use as a boom carrier in August 1939, and was torpedoed and sunk by the *U-58* (KL H Kuppisch) off Kinnaird Head while carrying boom defence gear from Rosyth to Scapa Flow.

The German grid reference was given as AN1829, which equates to about 575700N, 020000W.

Escorted by HM trawlers *Leicester City* and *Stoke City*, the *Astronomer* had been northbound from Rosyth to Scapa Flow with a large part of the Nevi Skerry boom aboard. At 22.00 hrs on 1 June 1940, acting on information from Rosyth, *Stoke City* had attacked a contact further south. The *Astronomer* was torpedoed (or at the time, it was thought, possibly mined) at 22.53 hrs on 1 June. The explosion took place right aft. A large hole several feet across was blown in the midships portion of the main deck, and the stern of the ship was laid open. The after accommodation was wrecked, and two of the dead, along with the injured, were trapped here.

Wick lifeboat, *City of Edinburgh*, was launched and the A/S trawlers *Paul Rykens* and *Peter Hendricks* were ordered to proceed 'with utmost despatch, to the scene'. *Kelvin* and *Mashona* were also sailed from Scapa but were told to keep to the eastward due to the danger of mines. The tug *St Mellons* sailed from Scapa to tow the damaged vessel to port, but before she arrived, two further explosions occurred at 02.00 hrs and 03.36 hrs on 2 June, which *Stoke City* stated were caused by torpedoes, but at least one was probably a boiler explosion, and the *Astronomer* sank. After the attack, *U-58* was pursued for 43 hours before making her escape.

Surgeon Sub Lieutenant J. Evans RN reported that the explosion took place right aft under the stern and blew a large hole several feet across in the midships portion of the steel main deck. Evans wrote that 'The poop deck was laid open to the sky aft, in the mid line, and the stern was laid open to the sea.' The seamen's quarters were right aft on the main deck port, and the firemen were opposite on the starboard side. Here, partitions were destroyed and cots, tables and sleeping men were thrown against the deckhead above. Casualties had to be extracted from the debris and wreckage of twisted cots in pitch darkness, an exercise that was complicated by the fact that the ship was sinking by the stern.

The initial explosion blew AB W. Spratt from the after well deck right through the smashed hatch covers into no.7 hold. When he landed, this hold was already filling with water. SBA Chief Petty Officer J.W. Andrews RN and an un-named mercantile apprentice were commended by Evans for their coolness and presence of mind during the rescue operation. Fireman C. Ward was trapped against a bulkhead, though a second explosion freed him. By the time he was freed, the water was rising and there was no response to the names of the two missing men, Firemen Tough and Brand. Nor was there any sound of breathing and, as the ship was sinking rapidly, further rescue attempts were abandoned.

The seriously injured were given morphia by mouth in the boats. SBA F. Ford had brought surgical instruments with him on leaving *Astronomer*'s sick bay and these were used by Evans in giving further medical attention once the casualties were aboard rescue ships. Evans had great difficulty in identifying the injured and dying as they were merchant ratings, most of whom had only signed on at Rosyth a few days earlier. None had identity discs and few even knew each other.

According to *Lloyds War Losses* four crew were lost out of fifty-five and one gunner. There were also forty-eight naval ratings aboard. This is slightly at variance with reports held in the PRO which state that two were lost from *Astronomer,* and that *Leicester City* took fifty-five survivors, many badly injured, to Aberdeen. *Stoke City* was ordered to remain in the vicinity but disobeyed orders, and left when *Astronomer* sank, to land fifty-four survivors at Aberdeen. In addition to those lost with the ship, Stoker G.A. Ross died of his injuries on the 2nd and AB J. Smith died of multiple injures on the 5th. None of the RN boom defence party aboard were injured or lost. *BDV Barbican* was sent to the area on 2 June to recover buoys constantly coming to the surface from the wreck.

According to the German records *Astronomer* was torpedoed by *U-58* on 1 June 1940 in AN1829, which equates to about 5757N, 0200W.

Lloyds War Losses gives the position as 5804N, 0212W, which is 23 miles N of Kinnaird Head, but the position of loss has also been described as 15 miles N of Kinnaird Head.

The wreck at 580150N, 020237W, 20 miles N of Kinnaird Head, was first reported in 1986. This is obviously a large wreck, 140 metres long, oriented 016/196°, and standing up 11 metres in a total depth of 67 metres.

It is only 2.75 miles east of the wreck found in 1944 at 580157N, 020717W, which the Hydrographic Department has assumed to be the *Astronomer*, but the length of the wreck at 580150N, 020237W more closely matches the length of the *Astronomer*.

Astronomer (*Photo: JMC*)

DALVEEN

Wreck No: 194	Date Sunk: 28 09 1940
Latitude: 58 01 57 N	Longitude: 02 07 17 W
GPS Lat: 5801.950 N	GPS Long: 0207.283 W
Location: 20 miles N¾W of Kinnaird Head	Area: Buchan

Type: Steamship		Tonnage: 5,193 grt
Length: 406.9 ft	Beam: 52.3 ft	Draught: 28.3 ft
How Sunk: Bombed		Depth: 96 metres

On 28 September 1940, *Dalveen* was one of the ships in convoy HX73A, en route from Montreal to Hull with a cargo of 7,398 tons of wheat. At 20.20 hrs the convoy was attacked by German aircraft.

Kinnaird Head Coastguard Station informed Fraserburgh Lifeboat Station that gun flashes and flares could be seen several miles to the north-west. The *Dalveen* and the steamship *Queen City* (4,814 grt) were damaged, and both vessels were abandoned. *Dalveen* sank within ten minutes, and eleven of her crew were lost. Thirty-one survivors were landed at Lyness. Fraserburgh lifeboat *John and Charles Kennedy* was launched at 22.00 and travelled 18 miles to reach the *Queen City* of Bideford. The Master, Second Engineer and thirteen of the crew of the *Queen City* were picked up by the lifeboat from a ship's boat and landed at Fraserburgh. A further twenty survivors were landed at Thurso by the A/S trawler *Windermere*. The *Queen City* was towed to Aberdeen by the tug *Abeille IV*.

Both *Lloyds War Losses* and *British Vessels Lost at Sea 1939–1945* give the position of attack as 581000N, 021900W PA. This is about 30 miles NNW of Kinnaird Head, and a wreck is charted PA in that position, with at least 40 metres of water over it in about 70 metres total depth.

As gun flashes were seen from Kinnaird Head, however, the position must have been considerably closer than 30 miles away.

Mr F. McQueen, the chief officer of the *Dalveen*, estimated the position of attack as approximately 15 miles north of Kinnaird Head, and Fraserburgh lifeboat records state that the lifeboat travelled 18 miles to reach the *Queen City*. (*Dalveen* had already sunk before the lifeboat was even launched.)

The wreck found in 1944 at 580157N, 020717W is 120 metres long, closely matching the 123-metre length of the *Dalveen*. This wreck is 20 miles N¾W of Kinnaird Head, fairly closely matching the distances given by Mr McQueen and the Fraserburgh lifeboat. It is therefore in about the right position, and apparently the right length, to be the *Dalveen*, which was built in 1927.

The wreck lies 035/215°, and stands up 19 metres in a total depth of 115 metres.

WIGMORE

Wreck No: 195		Date Sunk: 18 11 1939
Latitude: 58 01 12 N PA		Longitude: 01 57 30 W PA
GPS Lat: 5801.200 N		GPS Long: 0157.500 W
Location: 25 miles N by W Rattray Head		Area: Buchan
Type: Trawler		Tonnage: 345 grt
Length: 141.1 ft	Beam: 24.1 ft	Draught: 13.2 ft
How Sunk: Torpedoed by *U-18*		Depth: metres

The steam trawler *Wigmore* (ex-*Embassy*) was built by Cook, Welton & Gemmell of Beverley in 1928. She was in a convoy of trawlers heading from Grimsby to the Icelandic fishing grounds when she was torpedoed 25 miles N by W of Rattray Head by *U-18* (KL Max-Hermann Bauer), at 21.16 hrs on 18 November 1939. Sixteen crewmen were lost.

The destroyers *Imogen*, *Imperial* and *Impulsive* were sent on an A/S sweep, but with no result.

The Hydrographic Department has recorded the *Wigmore* at 580112N, 015730W PA, but the position has also been given as 5759N, 0207W PA and 5759N, 0206W PA.

GLENRAVEL

Wreck No: 196	Date Sunk: 08 08 1915
Latitude: 58 06 30 N PA	Longitude: 02 00 30 W PA
GPS Lat: 5806.000 N	GPS Long: 0200.500 W
Location: 25 miles N of Kinnaird Head	Area: Buchan
Type: Steamship	Tonnage: 1092 grt
Length: 233.5 ft Beam: 33.9 ft	Draught: 14.0 ft
How Sunk: By *U-17* – bomb	Depth: metres

On 8 August 1915 the British steamship *Glenravel* was captured by the *U-17*, 25 miles north of Kinnaird Head, and then sunk with a bomb placed on board.

Another report gives the position as 12 miles NNE of Kinnaird Head, while a third description of the position of loss is 15 miles from Fraserburgh.

The *Glenravel* had been en route from Belfast to Leith with a cargo of 800 tons of iron ore and general goods.

LIANA

Wreck No: 197	Date Sunk: 16 02 1940
Latitude: 58 08 48 N PA	Longitude: 02 12 00 W PA
GPS Lat: 5808.800 N	GPS Long: 0212.000 W
Location: 27 miles N of Kinnaird Head	Area: Buchan
Type: Steamship	Tonnage: 1,664 grt
Length: 265.0 ft Beam: 38.5 ft	Draught: 17.4 ft
How Sunk: Torpedoed by *U-14*	Depth: metres

A sonar contact obtained here in 1945 is thought to be the Swedish steamship *Liana*, which was torpedoed by the *U-14* (OL Herbert Wohlfarth), 24 miles north of Kinnaird Head on 16 February 1940. The vessel had been en route from Blyth to Halmstadt with a cargo of coal. Ten of her crew were lost.

The German grid reference was given as AN1853, which equates to about 575100N, 020000W.

OSMED

Wreck No: 198	Date Sunk: 16 02 1940
Latitude: 58 09 00 N PA	Longitude: 02 08 00 W PA
GPS Lat: 5809.000 N	GPS Long: 0208.000 W
Location: 27 miles N of Kinnaird Head	Area: Buchan
Type: Steamship	Tonnage: ,1526 grt
Length: 243.6 ft Beam: 36.9 ft	Draught: 17.3 ft
How Sunk: Torpedoed by *U-14*	Depth: metres

The Swedish steamship *Osmed* was torpedoed by the *U-14* (Wolfarth), 20 miles north of Kinnaird Head on 16 February 1940, while en route from Blyth to Halmstadt with a cargo of coal. Thirteen of her crew were lost.

DODAS describes the position as 24 miles from Kinnaird Head. The German grid reference was AN1853, which equates to about 5751N, 0200W.

One estimate of the position has been given as 580900N, 020800W PA, where a sonar contact was obtained in 1945.

The trawler *Loch Hope* picked up seventeen survivors from the torpedoed Swedish ships *Liana* and *Osmed* from a raft in 5807N, 0212W and landed them at Scrabster.

At 10.30 hrs on 25 February, HMS *Gallant* picked up twelve survivors from the Swedish steamship *Santos* in 5917N 0042W. *Gallant* had been directed to the raft by a Hudson aircraft, and she landed the survivors at Invergordon at 21.00 hrs. *Santos* had been carrying eight survivors from the *Liana*, of whom two were saved.

The *Santos* (3,840 grt), Kirkwall for Gothenburg, was torpedoed by *U-63* (Lorentz) at 21.54 hrs on the 24th. *Santos* had not been sailing in convoy but was well lit with navigation lights switched on, and two floodlights shining on a Swedish flag painted on a piece of canvas. *U-63* chased her for an hour and a half before firing one torpedo without warning. *Santos* sank quickly. Thirty-one of her crew were lost. There were twelve survivors.

U-63 was sunk by the escort of convoy HN14 before she could report her success.

Some of the Wrecks in the Moray Firth

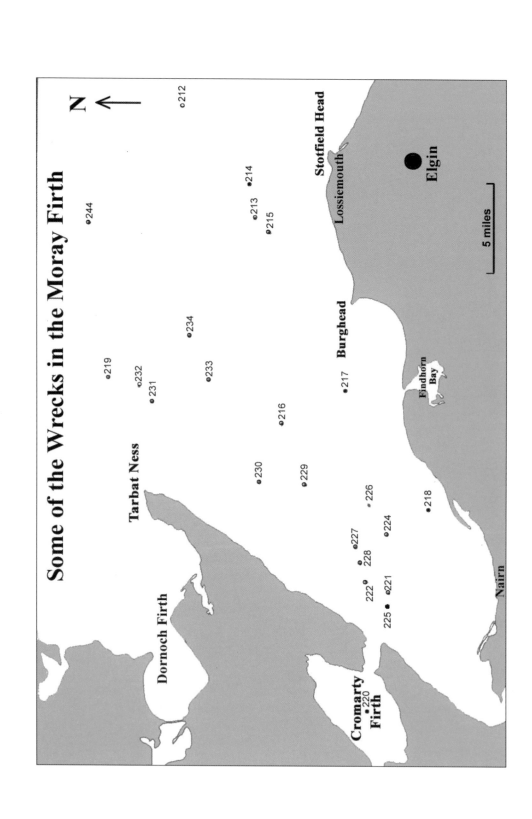

N

Dornoch Firth

Tarbat Ness

Cromarty
Firth
•220

225 •
222 •
•221

•227
228 •

•224

•226

•230

•229

•216

•233

•234

•219

•232
•231

•244

•212

•218

Nairn

•217   Burghead

Findhorn
Bay

Lossiemouth

Stotfield Head

•213
•215

•214

● Elgin

5 miles

3

MORAY

BETTY

Wreck No: 199		Date Sunk: 17 11 1893
Latitude: 57 40 00 N PA		Longitude: 02 20 00 W PA
GPS Lat: 5740.000 N		GPS Long: 0220.000 W
Location: Shark Rock, Gardenstown		Area: Moray
Type: Barque		Tonnage: 373 grt
Length: ft	Beam: ft	Draught: ft
How Sunk: Ran aground		Depth: metres

The 3-masted barque *Betty* of Malmo, Sweden, ran on to Shark Rock 100 yards off Gardenstown, on 17 November 1893, and was smashed to pieces on the shore. She was carrying a cargo of coal. Her anchor was recovered in 1971.

LOCHIE

Wreck No: 200		Date Sunk: 31 03 1966
Latitude: 57 40 00 N PA		Longitude: 02 26 00 W PA
GPS Lat: 5740.000 N		GPS Long: 0226.000 W
Location: 2 miles E of Macduff		Area: Moray
Type: Trawler		Tonnage: grt
Length: ft	Beam: ft	Draught: ft
How Sunk:		Depth: metres

The Macduff trawler *Lochie* was one of a number of boats heading to port from the fishing grounds in rough seas on 31 March 1966. Three miles from Macduff she sprang a leak and began filling rapidly. The crew called for assistance. The *Coastal Boy*, also of Macduff, answered their call and was able to take the crew of four off. A line was fixed between the vessels, but it snapped and could not be secured again. Shortly afterwards, the *Lochie* was driven onto rocks two miles east of Macduff. Before the *Coastal Boy* left the scene, only the tips of her masts could be seen.

EBENEEZER

Wreck No: 201	Date Sunk: 19 02 1900
Latitude: 57 41 05 N	Longitude: 02 34 06 W
GPS Lat: 5741.083 N	GPS Long: 0234.100 W

Location: Salt Rock, Whitehills, Banffshire	Area: Moray
Type: Barque	Tonnage: 533 grt
Length: 130.0 ft	Beam: ft Draught: ft
How Sunk: Ran aground	Depth: 9 metres

The 3-masted wooden barque *Ebeneezer* ran aground on Salt Rock, off Knock Head, Whitehills, on 19 February 1900. The vessel, which was built at Tredestrand, Norway in 1869, had been bound from Porsgrund to Grimsby with a cargo of coal. The very broken remains were scattered amongst kelp-covered rocks and sandy gullies around Salt Rock, which is visible at low water. The bell has been recovered. A brass nail was found in 1982, but it seems nothing else is left now.

UNKNOWN

Wreck No: 202	Date Sunk:
Latitude: 57 42 00 N PA	Longitude: 02 49 00 W PA
GPS Lat: 5742.000 N	GPS Long: 0249.000 W
Location: Cullen Bay, ¼ mile off Cullen	Area: Moray
Type: Steamship?	Tonnage: grt
Length: ft	Beam: ft Draught: ft
How Sunk:	Depth: 8 metres

There is a rumour that a steamship ran aground near Cullen with the loss of twelve crew. As far as I am aware, no date has been associated with the rumour, but a large steel propeller and shaft, reputed to have been found in a depth of 8 metres in Cullen Bay, certainly seem to indicate the loss of a vessel nearby, and give some substance to the rumour.

Caple Rock lies about ¼ mile offshore, and is a potential hazard to vessels entering the bay.

In 1974 the motor trawler *Artemis* stranded near Cullen. (See wreck at 574145N, 024900W PA.)

An aircraft is also said to have been lost in this vicinity on 6 November 1939.

START ?

Wreck No: 203	Date Sunk: 08 08 1940
Latitude: 57 51 42 N	Longitude: 02 29 39 W
GPS Lat: 5751.700 N	GPS Long: 0229.650 W
Location: 12 miles north of Banff	Area: Moray
Type: Steamship	Tonnage: 1168 grt
Length: 227.7 ft	Beam: 36.3 ft Draught: ft
How Sunk: Torpedoed by *U-13*	Depth: metres

The Norwegian steamship *Start* disappeared after leaving Sunderland on 29 January 1940, bound for Oslo with a cargo of 1,478 tons of coal and a crew of sixteen.

She was torpedoed and sunk on 31 January 1940 by *U-13* (Schulte). The position was given as AN1846, which equates to about 5745N, 0236W. The *Start* was built in 1923.

A wreck found 12 miles north of Banff at 575142N, 022939W in about 70 metres depth might be the *Start*.

The Norwegian steamship Start *(Photo: courtesy of World Ship Society)*

LOCH LOYAL

Wreck No: 204	Date Sunk: 08 08 1940
Latitude: 57 47 45 N PA	Longitude: 02 37 45 W PA
GPS Lat: 5747.750 N	GPS Long: 0237.750 W
Location: 9 miles ENE of Portknockie	Area: Moray
Type: Trawler	Tonnage: 196 grt
Length: ft Beam: ft	Draught: ft
How Sunk: Collision	Depth: metres

The steam trawler *Loch Loyal* was built by Halls of Aberdeen.

She sank in the Moray Firth on 8 August 1940 after a collision with a Naval patrol vessel.

Two days later, the Naval patrol vessel *Young Sid* sank in the Moray Firth after a collision. It would seem likely that there is a connection! The position given is the one recorded by the Hydrographic Department.

MORAY FIRTH

Wreck No: 205	Date Sunk: 28 03 1943
Latitude: 57 46 00 N PA	Longitude: 02 49 00 W PA
GPS Lat: 5746.000 N	GPS Long: 0249.000 W
Location: N of Cullen	Area: Moray
Type: Steamship	Tonnage: 541 grt
Length: 160.2 ft Beam: 26.6 ft	Draught: 9.9 ft
How Sunk: Collision	Depth: metres

The British steamship *Moray Firth* was built in 1927 by J. Lewis & Sons, Aberdeen. She was registered in Newcastle, and owned by the Firth Shipping Co. Ltd.

On 28 March 1943, en route from London to Kirkwall with a cargo of cement, she sank after a collision (with what?) at about 574600N, 024700W PA.

In 1945, a sonar contact obtained about 4½ miles north of Cullen at 574600N, 024900W PA was assumed to have been the *Moray Firth*.

The nearest charted wreck is at 575050N, 025000W in about 90 metres depth, 8½ miles N by E of Portknockie. This might be the *Moray Firth*, or possibly even the *Loch Loyal*.

ARTEMIS

Wreck No: 206		Date Sunk: 02 09 1974	
Latitude: 57 41 45 N PA		Longitude: 02 50 00 W PA	
GPS Lat: 5741.705 N		GPS Long: 0250.000 W	
Location: Near Cullen		Area: Moray	
Type: Trawler		Tonnage: grt	
Length: 65.0 ft	Beam: ft	Draught: ft	
How Sunk: Ran aground		Depth: metres	

The Fraserburgh MFV *Artemis* went aground near Cullen in dense fog at about 4.00 a.m. on 2 September 1974 while en route to the Isle of Man.

Her bottom was ripped out on the sharp rocks at Sunnyside Beach, which is in an isolated bay between Logie Head and Findlater Castle. The five crewmen launched an inflatable dinghy and landed safely on the rocky shore, then made their way on foot to Cullen. The *Artemis* was stuck fast on rocks only 100 ft from the high water mark. She was battered by a storm a week later, and broke up.

The position has been recorded by the Hydrographic Department as 574115N, 025000W PA.

BRIAR ROSE

Wreck No: 207		Date Sunk: 10 10 1967	
Latitude: 57 41 00 N PA		Longitude: 02 58 00 W PA	
GPS Lat: 5741.000 N		GPS Long: 0258.000 W	
Location: West Muck Rocks, off Buckie		Area: Moray	
Type: MFV		Tonnage: grt	
Length: ft	Beam: ft	Draught: ft	
How Sunk: Ran aground		Depth: metres	

The wooden MFV *Briar Rose*, with a crew of eight, ran onto West Muck Rocks off her home port of Buckie on 10 October 1967. A strong northerly wind was blowing, with choppy seas. The Buckie lifeboat *Laura Moncur*, under the command of Coxswain George Jappy, put to sea at 1.35 a.m. Coxswain Jappy's first thought was to drop anchor and veer down to the fishing boat, but when the skipper of the *Briar Rose* shouted that his vessel was breaking up, Coxswain Jappy headed straight for the stranded boat. At the first attempt two men were rescued before the lifeboat was swept away by the backwash from the rocks. On the second run in, a nylon rope was made fast to the stem of the casualty, and three men were rescued before the lifeboat was swept away again. Using the rope, Coxswain Jappy was able to get back alongside, and the last three men were rescued. The lifeboat returned to Buckie harbour at 2.10 a.m. The entire rescue had been accomplished in only 45 minutes. For his excellent service, Coxswain Jappy was awarded the Royal National Lifeboat Institution's Thanks on Vellum.

TEAL

Wreck No: 208	Date Sunk: 02 01 1917
Latitude: 57 40 00 N PA	Longitude: 02 56 00 W PA
GPS Lat: 5740.000 N	GPS Long: 0256.000 W
Location: Wrecked off Buckie	Area: Moray
Type: Trawler	Tonnage: 165 grt
Length: 118.2 ft Beam: 20.5 ft	Draught: 10.8 ft
How Sunk: Ran aground?	Depth: metres

The iron screw steam trawler *Teal* was built in 1897 by Edwards Bros of N. Shields, engine by N.E. Marine of Sunderland. She was wrecked off Buckie while in Admiralty service on 2 January 1917.

HIRPA

Wreck No: 209	Date Sunk: 02 01 1918
Latitude: 57 40 00 N PA	Longitude: 02 56 00 W PA
GPS Lat: 5740.000 N	GPS Long:0256.000 W
Location: Wrecked near Buckie	Area: Moray
Type: Whaler	Tonnage: 110 grt
Length: 92.4 ft Beam: 18.5 ft	Draught: 10.7 ft
How Sunk: Ran aground	Depth: metres

The steel steam whaler *Hirpa* was built in 1911 by Akers Mek. Vaerks., Christiania (Oslo), and registered in Leith. She was lost by running aground near Buckie on 2 January 1918.

BPT No. 31

Wreck No: 210	Date Sunk: 1925
Latitude: 57 40 11 N	Longitude: 03 03 03 W
GPS Lat: 5740.183 N	GPS Long: 0303.050 W
Location: Ashore at Speymouth	Area: Moray
Type: Barge	Tonnage: grt
Length: ft Beam: ft	Draught: ft
How Sunk: Ran aground	Depth: metres

BPT 31 (Battle Practice Target 31) was a barge that broke adrift in 1925 and was washed ashore in Spey Bay, 1.2 miles 277° from Port Gordon.

NAR

Wreck No: 211	Date Sunk: 15 12 1904
Latitude: 57 41 30 N PA	Longitude: 03 06 00 W PA

GPS Lat: 5741.500 N	GPS Long: 0306.000 W
Location: Off Speymouth	Area: Moray
Type: Steamship	Tonnage: 281 grt
Length: 145.8 ft Beam: 22.4 ft	Draught: 10.5 ft
How Sunk: Foundered	Depth: 11 metres

The Glasgow steamship *Nar* foundered off Speymouth in a NNE storm on 15 December 1904.

Her crew of nine were all lost. The vessel had been en route from Sunderland to Burghead with a cargo of coal when the storm blew up on the 14th, and she anchored about a mile off Kingston to ride it out. Distress signals were seen after midnight, and the local rocket brigade was called out. Although the brigade fired several star rockets, they received no signals in reply, and because of the distance of the vessel from the shore, were unable to do anything other than wait for daylight. In the morning, wreckage and four bodies were found washed up on the beach, along with two ship's lifeboats, and a lifebuoy bearing the name *Nar*. A week later, the mast of the *Nar* was located floating in the sea, still attached to the hull, about one mile offshore.

UNKNOWN

Wreck No: 212	Date Sunk:
Latitude: 57 49 54 N	Longitude: 03 09 05 W
GPS Lat: 5749.901 N	GPS Long: 0309.080 W
Location: 7½ miles NE of Stotfield Head	Area: Moray
Type: Submarine?	Tonnage: grt
Length: ft Beam: ft	Draught: ft
How Sunk:	Depth: 82 metres

Charted as a wreck at 82 metres, 10½ miles N of Buckie.

It has been said that this is a submarine, found during pipeline work.

CHRISSIE CRIGGIE

Wreck No: 213	Date Sunk: 01 12 1971
Latitude: 57 46 50 N	Longitude: 03 22 30 W PA
GPS Lat: 5746.833 N	GPS Long: 0322.500 W
Location: 4 miles NW of Stotfield Head	Area: Moray
Type: MFV	Tonnage: grt
Length: ft Beam: ft	Draught: ft
How Sunk: Collision with *Spectrum*	Depth: 61 metres

The MFV *Chrissie Criggie* was sunk in collision with the MFV *Spectrum* 4 miles NNE of Lossiemouth on 1 December 1971. The Hydrographic Department gives the position as 574700N, 031400W PA, but the wreck charted at 574650N, 032230W might be the *Chrissie Criggie*.

WELLINGTON AIRCRAFT

Wreck No: 214	Date Sunk: 30 07 1941
Latitude: 57 47 09 N	Longitude: 03 19 40 W

GPS Lat: 5747.150 N   GPS Long: 0319.666 W
Location: 4 miles W by N of Stotfield Head   Area: Moray
Type: Aircraft   Tonnage: grt
Length: ft   Beam: ft   Draught: ft
How Sunk: Depth: 62 metres

Charted as a wreck in about 62 metres, 4 miles north of Stotfield Head.
   This is Wellington aircraft R1170 from 20 OTU (Operational Training Unit).

UNKNOWN

Wreck No: 215   Date Sunk: Pre – 1945
Latitude: 57 46 12 N   Longitude: 03 23 45 W
GPS Lat: 5746.200 N   GPS Long: 0323.750 W
Location: 4½ miles NW of Stotfield Head   Area: Moray
Type: Tonnage: grt
Length: 46.0 ft   Beam: ft   Draught: ft
How Sunk: Depth: 58 metres

The wreck charted 4½ miles NW of Stotfield Head in about 58 metres with a clearance
of at least 50 metres was found in 1945. It is apparently 46 ft long standing up 18 ft, and
oriented 080/260°.
   Possibly an aircraft?

UNKNOWN – YOUNG SID ?

Wreck No: 216   Date Sunk: Pre-1976
Latitude: 57 45 32 N   Longitude: 03 40 25 W
GPS Lat: 5745.533 N   GPS Long: 0340.417 W
Location: 7 miles S by E of Tarbat Ness   Area: Moray
Type: Tonnage: grt
Length: ft   Beam: ft   Draught: ft
How Sunk: Depth: 26 metres

Charted as a wreck at 26 metres in about 26.5 metres, this is apparently the wreck of a
very small vessel which does not protrude much above the sandy seabed.
   In 1963 the position of this wreck was given as 574449N, 033356W.
   The wreck here is thought to be the remains of a wooden vessel.
   Apparently a small boat was washed ashore from a wooden steamship which sank
about 4 miles NW of Burghead. (When?) Two suggestions for the identity of this wreck
are the *Wansbeck*, or the *Commodore*, both lost in February 1900.
   A further suggestion is that this might be the 100-ton steel drifter *Young Sid*, which
was built in 1912 by J. Duthie of Aberdeen, and registered in Lowestoft. She measured
86.1 x 18.7 x 8.8 ft.
   She was requisitioned for use by the Admiralty as an auxiliary patrol vessel in May
1940, and armed with a 3-pdr gun. She sank in the Moray Firth on 10 August 1940, as
a result of a collision.
   The date of sinking is two days after the trawler *Loch Loyal* sank in the Moray Firth

by collision with a naval patrol vessel. It seems likely that the *Young Sid* was the naval patrol vessel which collided with the *Loch Loyal*.

UNKNOWN

Wreck No: 217	Date Sunk: Pre-1964
Latitude: 57 42 39 N	Longitude: 03 38 57 W
GPS Lat: 5742.650 N	GPS Long: 0338.950 W
Location: 8 miles W by N of Burghead	Area: Moray
Type: MFV?	Tonnage: grt
Length: ft Beam: ft	Draught: ft
How Sunk:	Depth: 55 metres

This is the wreck of a small wooden vessel, first reported in 1964.

RONA

Wreck No: 218	Date Sunk:
Latitude: 57 38 39 N	Longitude: 03 48 03 W
GPS Lat: 5738.650 N	GPS Long: 0348.050 W
Location: 3½ miles NE of Nairn	Area: Moray
Type: MFV	Tonnage: grt
Length: ft Beam: ft	Draught: ft
How Sunk: Fire	Depth: 22 metres

The MFV *Rona* was reported lost by fire. Her 4 cwt. propeller has been salvaged.

HARMONY ?

Wreck No: 219	Date Sunk: 15 11 1941
Latitude: 57 53 50 N	Longitude: 03 36 30 W
GPS Lat: 5753.833 N	GPS Long: 0336.500 W
Location: 5 miles NE of Tarbat Ness	Area: Moray
Type: Drifter	Tonnage: 79 grt
Length: ft Beam: ft	Draught: ft
How Sunk: Collision	Depth: 58 metres

The steel-hulled steam drifter *Harmony* (ex-*Unison*) was built in 1910.

She was requisitioned in 1940, and sank in a collision off Invergordon on 15 November 1941.

The intact wreck of a small steel-hulled steam drifter lying upright on a fairly firm seabed in 58m of water, about 5 miles north east of Tarbat Ness Lighthouse, was dived by Jacksac divers in 1995. Because of its exposed position, its distance from a suitable launching point, and its depth, it took several years to build up a reasonable picture of the wreck. These were deep air dives, and the information gathered was very sketchy. It wasn't until she was dived using trimix that a decent picture of the wreck was built up. The wreck could not be identified by name, but a date stamp of 1940 was found on the base of a broken stone jar in her hold. This brought both *Harmony* and *Young*

Sid into the frame. These were both drifters requisitioned for naval use, and would therefore probably have been armed,* but no trace of a gun or shells has been found on the wreck. Both of these vessels were lost in collisions, but a detailed inspection of the hull of this wreck reveals no obvious breaches. The port side does show a pronounced bend inwards, however, and this may be collision damage. Other than that, there is no obvious indication of the reason for sinking.

The wreck is virtually intact, and is about 91 ft long by 17 ft beam and 9 ft draught. The top of the wheelhouse is missing, leaving the remains of the steering wheel still in position. There is a brass centre boss on the wheel, but no name is engraved on it. The wheelhouse telegraph was in poor condition with the face broken, and mostly made of iron. The ship's log was found on the port side decking, along with the compass binnacle. The log was in good condition but the compass had rotted away. The binnacle still had the flinders balls attached and an inclinometer lay next to it. The log showed a distance run of 77 miles.

Two navigation lights were also found on the seabed off the port side.

The funnel is broken in two, one part lying on the port deck, while the other part is stuck into the seabed on the starboard side. The steam engine and boiler can be seen through the hole left by the funnel. The forward decking has rotted away leaving the hold wide open. The base of the foremast is still there, but the mast itself has gone. An Admiralty pattern anchor lies on the starboard forward deck. A fairly substantial 'A' frame, presumably for minesweeping, runs from port to starboard at the stern, with a small winch on the centre of the deck directly below it. An old fishing net is draped over the aft part of the wreck, but the steel propeller and rudder are still visible at the stern. Visibility on the wreck is usually excellent, but it is subject to strong tidal streams.

NATAL

Wreck No: 220		Date Sunk: 31 12 1915
Latitude: 57 41 16 N		Longitude: 04 05 15 W
GPS Lat: 5741.267 N		GPS Long: 0405.250 W
Location: 1½ miles W of Cromarty Light		Area: Moray
Type: Cruiser		Tonnage: 13,550 tons
Length: 505.3 ft	Beam: 73.5 ft	Draught: 27.5 ft
How Sunk: Internal explosion		Depth: 25 metres

The British cruiser HMS *Natal* was built by Vickers in 1907. While at anchor in Cromarty harbour on New Year's Eve 1915, a Christmas/New Year children's party was being held aboard the ship. While the party was in full swing, a fire broke out aboard, and shortly afterwards, the ship's magazine blew up, sinking her immediately. A total of 405 lives were lost. (Some reports say 421.)

There was quite a bit of speculation at the time about the cause of the explosion, and sabotage was feared by some. The official enquiry concluded that the most likely cause was a cordite explosion. Cordite becomes unstable when overheated, and other ships had suffered a similar fate.

The *Natal* lay on her side with part of her keel visible above the surface until 1940, despite the attentions of several salvage operators. The wreck has since been dispersed

---

*Young Sid was hired by the Admiralty for the period 1915–1919 as an armed drifter, returned to her owners and then re-hired from May 1940, when she was again armed with a 3-pdr gun, whereas *Harmony* does not seem to have ever been armed at all!

with explosives, and is now only 2 metres above the seabed at 15-25 metres, about 1½ miles west of Cromarty light.

The wreck is rarely visited. This may be due to a myth which has been spread that because the *Natal* is in the shipping channel, the Cromarty Firth Port Authority should be consulted before diving, and despite the considerable efforts over many years to demolish the wreck completely, it may be classified as a war grave, and that permission to dive the *Natal* should also be sought from the Admiralty at Invergordon.

Some divers have reported being given the run-around when trying to comply with these largely imaginary obstacles to diving the wreck, and have been passed back and forth between the Cromarty Port Authority and the Royal Navy.

In fact the wreck of the cruiser HMS *Natal* has never been officially classified as a war grave,* despite the huge loss of life. The reason may be that the wreck was cut up and salvaged between 1937 and 1939 so that relatively little of the *Natal* remains in the Cromarty Firth.

The work was carried out by the South Stockton Shipbreaking Co., using their salvage vessel *Disperser*. The recovered scrap metal was loaded into small coasters and transported to the shipbreaking company's wharf at Thornaby on Tees.

The work commenced on 1 July 1937, and continued, when the weather allowed, until September 1939, when the *Disperser* was requisitioned by the Admiralty for more urgent salvage work.

Unfortunately, while engaged on salvage work, the ship was lost with all hands during a gale at Kirkwall on the night of 15 April 1940. She was refloated, repaired, and returned to service in 1944, lasting until January 1953, when she arrived at Llanely, in South Wales, to be broken up. I believe even more salvage work has been carried out since then.

Even if the wreck was considered to be a war grave, The Protection of Military Remains Act 1986 does not preclude diving on war graves – merely that nothing should be removed or disturbed.

Nobody seemed to be unduly concerned about the disturbance to the wreck in 1937–1939, at a time when many relatives with memories of those lost would still be alive.

I am indebted to Ian Oxley, Project Officer, Scotland's Maritime Record Enhancement, Scottish Institute of Maritime Studies, University of St Andrews, for drawing my attention to the following quote from the excellent article:

Dromgoole, S., 1996, 'Military remains on and around the coast of the United Kingdom: statutory mechanisms of protection', *International Journal of Marine and Coastal Law*, Vol. 11, No. 1: 23–45:

> Offences under the Act are not subject to strict liability but instead depend on whether the defendant believed, or had reasonable grounds for suspecting, that the place comprised 'any remains of an aircraft or vessel which had crashed, sunk or been stranded while in military service' (PMRA 1986, Section 2(1)(b)).
>
> Where persons have the requisite belief or knowledge, they will commit an offence if, without the authority of a licence, they inter alia tamper with, damage, move, or

---

*The Ministry of Defence announced on 9 November 2001 – eighty-six years after she sank – that the wreck of HMS *Natal* is one of fifteen military maritime graves in waters under UK jurisdiction that are now designated as 'Controlled Sites', and that all diving on 'Controlled Sites' is prohibited without a specific licence. A MoD spokesperson said that 'anyone wishing to dive a controlled site would have to have full MoD permission, and that this would only be granted under stringent conditions and in special circumstances. Divers with no justifiable cause for visiting the site would be excluded, and harsh penalties will be imposed if necessary.'

unearth any remains, or enter any hatch or other opening which encloses part of the interior of the craft. Excavation, diving and salvage operations are prohibited, if carried out for the above purposes.

In view of the extensive salvage work carried out on HMS *Natal* in the past, this must surely be a classic case of locking the stable door after the horse has bolted!

HMS Natal (*Photo: author's collection*)

MARSONA

Wreck No: 221	Date Sunk: 04 08 1940
Latitude: 57 40 28 N	Longitude: 03 55 00 W
GPS Lat: 5740.466 N	GPS Long: 0355.000 W
Location: 4½ miles ESE of Cromarty Firth	Area: Moray
Type: Trawler	Tonnage: 276 grt
Length: 126.0 ft Beam: 23.5 ft	Draught: 12.6 ft
How Sunk: Mined	Depth: 15 metres

The trawler *Marsona* (ex-*James Christopher*) was built in 1918 by J.P. Rennoldson of South Shields for J. Marr of Fleetwood. She was requisitioned for use as a minesweeper in October 1939. In the early morning of 4 August 1940 *Marsona* was pair-sweeping with HMT *George Cousins*, towing an 'M' sweep (magnetic sweep) between them. The vessels' ability to manoeuvre, to execute a turn, was seriously hampered by having to pass between two dan buoys 7 cables apart. These buoys marked a swept channel adjacent to a British minefield. At 07.24 hrs *Marsona* detonated a magnetic mine. The OOW at the observation post on South Sutor asserted that two mines exploded, one on the sweep between *Marsona* and *George Cousins*, the other under the stern of the *Marsona*.

S/Lt E.A.F. Weller, aboard HM Drifter *Industry*, said that at 07.20, while connecting up his minesweeping tackle off the Sutor Buoy, he heard an explosion and observed HMT *Marsona* mined in a position ½ mile SSE of Whistle Buoy and saw a further explosion 250 yards west of the other explosion. The *Industry* proceeded at full speed to the scene of the wreckage to look for survivors, but found none.

Chief Skipper E. Marshall of *George Cousins* said: '*Marsona* and *George Cousins* commenced connecting the "M" sweep at Sutor Buoy at 06.50 and *George Cousins* had veered all magnets and was veering sweep wire and *Marsona* was veering magnets when she was mined.

'Another explosion occurred about 300 yards SSE from our position, which was ½ mile S 66°E from Sutor Whistle Buoy.

'I immediately stopped engines, ordered the sea boat away to pick up survivors, had the sweep wire cut, and steamed to the vicinity of the wreckage. We came close to one man who was unable to grasp lines thrown. C. Wilson, engineman, jumped overboard and fastened a line round the man, and he was pulled aboard.'

Two wrecks are charted very close together at 574028N, 035500W, and 574025N, 035457W but they are probably two pieces of the same wreck. The wreck is well broken up and partly buried in the seabed, but shells dated 1917 can still be found in the wreckage of this armed trawler. There are strong tidal streams here.

The steam trawler Marsona *(Photo: courtesy of World Ship Society)*

DURHAM CASTLE

Wreck No: 222	Date Sunk: 26 01 1940
Latitude: 57 41 30 N	Longitude: 03 54 06 W
GPS Lat: 5741.50 N	GPS Long: 0354.10 W
Location: 3 miles E of Cromarty Firth	Area: Moray
Type: Steamship	Tonnage: 8,240 grt
Length: 475.4 ft Beam: 56.7 ft	Draught: 31.6 ft
How Sunk: Mined	Depth: 14 metres

The 8,240-grt twin screw steamship *Durham Castle* was built in 1904 by Fairfields of Glasgow, for the Union Castle Line.

She was sold for scrap in 1939, and towed to Rosyth for breaking up. Only five days after demolition work began, she was taken over by the Admiralty for use as a blockship at Scapa Flow. She was mined and sunk in a SE gale and severe icy conditions at the entrance to Cromarty Firth on 26 January 1940, while under tow to Orkney by the tug *Watermeyer*. It is thought that the mine she struck had been laid on 22 January by *U-57* (KL Claus Korth).

The wreck was buoyed, and the Northern Lighthouse Board records show that the position of the wreck buoy was 574115N, 035410W. The wreck was deep in soft mud when inspected by Metal Industries divers on 16 February 1940.

It has been suggested to me that the wreck of the *Durham Castle* was later dispersed with explosives. A number of mines strung on a cable laid along the wreck are said to have been used to achieve this. The wreck buoy was presumably removed when this was done, as it is no longer there.

The Hydrographic Department recorded the *Durham Castle* at 574130N, 035406W, but in 1964 the wreck here was reported to be only about 200 ft long, lying on her starboard side, and standing up 4 metres from the hard, flat sandy bottom at 18 metres, with a large hole in her port side.

This description seems to be of a much smaller vessel than the *Durham Castle*, but the Hydrographic Department notes do not mention whether the complete wreck was sitting on the bottom, or if the wreck was deeply embedded in the seabed, leaving only a 200-foot long section of a larger wreck exposed above the seabed.

(If this is a complete wreck, the length and the description of the damage closely match the *Shelbrit I.*)

The description of the nature of the seabed as a hard flat sandy bottom also does not accord with the Metal Industries divers' report of the *Durham Castle* being deeply embedded in soft mud.

The position is very far west for a vessel being towed from Rosyth to Scapa Flow, unless for some reason she was being routed via the Cromarty Firth.

Various sports divers have searched for the wreck of the *Durham Castle*, but as far as I am aware, none have had any success. Perhaps the remains have finally disappeared beneath the mud.

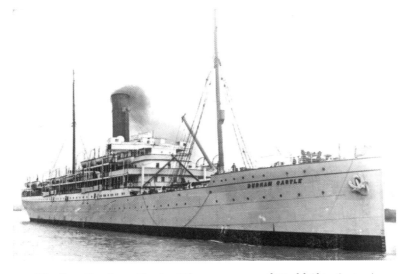

The liner Durham Castle *(Photo: courtesy of World Ship Society)*

UNKNOWN – BARGE ?

Wreck No: 223	Date Sunk:
Latitude: 57 40 11 N	Longitude: 03 49 18 W
GPS Lat: 5740.183 N	GPS Long: 0349.300 W
Location: 5 miles NE of Nairn	Area: Moray
Type:	Tonnage: grt
Length: 452.0 ft Beam: ft	Draught: ft
How Sunk: Mined	Depth: 27 metres

The wreck charted at 574030N, 035000W is recorded by the Hydrographic Department as an Unknown vessel lying N/S, with a least depth of 28 metres in 38 metres, and estimated by side scan sonar to be about 137 metres (452 ft) long. Dimensions obtained from side-scan sonar images are notoriously unreliable, but very close by there is a large wreck at 574011N, 034918W.

Divers have described this wreck as a massive barge, or possibly a floating dock, at 27–35 metres depth, and it has been said to be 'as large as a football pitch'. It has been suggested that it may have been a refuelling barge for Sunderland aircraft which sank in a storm sometime during the Second World War. Despite some considerable effort to investigate this suggestion, I have found no record that any such barge ever existed during the war. The only other plausible candidate to emerge is a floating dock which broke adrift from her tugs off Dunnet Head in 1945. The crew were taken off by a tug. She was later connected up again, and towed towards Invergordon. Did she not make Invergordon?

I am conscious, too, that this wreck is not very far from the reported position of the *Durham Castle*, and the preparation of the *Durham Castle* for use as a blockship might have included removal of the superstructure and engines, making the hull more barge-like?

The apparent length of this wreck also fairly closely matches the length of the *Durham Castle*.

TANTIVY

Wreck No: 224		Date Sunk: 1951	
Latitude: 57 40 31 N		Longitude: 03 49 55 W	
GPS Lat: 5740.519 N		GPS Long: 0349.910 W	
Location: 5 miles NE of Nairn		Area: Moray	
Type: Submarine		Tonnage: 1,090/1,575tons	
Length: 273.3 ft	Beam: 26.6 ft	Draught: 14.8 ft	
How Sunk: Scuttled as a target		Depth: 42 metres	

The T-Class Submarine HMS *Tantivy* was built by Vickers Armstrong at Barrow in 1943.

On 26 September 1949 she was transferred from active service to reserve, prior to breaking up. Instead of going to the breaker's yard, however, she was sunk in the Cromarty area in 1951 as a target for Asdic and A/S weapons trials. The top of the conning tower is at 33 metres, and the seabed is at 42 metres. The wreck is almost completely intact. Before she was scuttled the periscope was removed, and all the hatches were welded shut.

HMS Tantivy *(Photo: author's collection)*

SHELBRIT I

Wreck No: 225   Date Sunk: 19 09 1940
Latitude: 57 40 11 N   Longitude: 03 57 30 W
GPS Lat: 5740.183 N   GPS Long: 0357.500 W
Location: 1.3 miles 109° Cromarty Signal Station Area: Moray
Type: Motor Tanker   Tonnage: 1,025 grt
Length: 230.0 ft.   Beam: 32.7 ft.   Draught: 13.8 ft.
How Sunk: Mined? Torpedoed?   Depth: 15 metres

The tanker *Shelbrit I* (ex-*British Pluck*) either hit a mine or was torpedoed en route from Grangemouth to Inverness at 07.44 hrs on 19 January 1940. She was carrying 300 tons of pool petrol, 200 tons of aviation spirit, and diesel oil in her bunkers. All twenty crew and one gunner were lost when she blew up and went on fire SE of the entrance to the Cromarty Firth, at 574011N, 035730W PA, about 1.3 miles 109° from Cromarty Port War Signal Station. One body was recovered. Fire in the locality on the sea was put out by 16.00 hrs by Invergordon Auxiliary Fire Service and Invergordon Dockyard Fire Party.

As there is apparently no record of any U-boat claiming to have made an attack on her, or any other ship in the area at the time, it seems more likely that she struck a mine, although no mines were found in the area.

The wreck was marked by the Northern Lighthouse Board vessel *Pharos* on 30 September 1940, but no trace of it was found during a sonar search around that position in 1975.

A 'regular dense feature' was found by side scan sonar at 574050N, 035713W in 1974.

That position is fairly close to 574011N, 035730W, which was the approximate position recorded for the *Shelbrit I*. The area was closely examined in 1975, but the 'dense feature' reported the year before was not found. The seabed here is of fine sand.

Could this possibly have been a wreck which is now completely buried in the seabed?

Lloyds also recorded a further position 573900N, 035630W PA, and suggested that her loss was possibly due to an internal cause, and not a magnetic mine.

As the *Shelbrit I* approached the entrance to the Cromarty Firth she was met by the examination trawler *Craik*. At 07.42 hrs, the *Craik* identified the *Shelbrit I* as a friendly vessel proceeding to Inverness.

At 07.45 hrs, from a distance of 3,200 yards, those aboard the *Craik* saw the *Shelbrit I* suddenly burst into flames, apparently after striking a mine, as the flames were preceded by a dull detonation and upheaval of water. Witnesses spoke of a jet of water 50 feet high, approximately midships, and *Shelbrit I* seeming to rise up out of the water. When the ship settled back, the initial explosion was followed by the explosion of her cargo. Marine Knight of the *Craik* stated that the first explosion took place on *Shelbrit I*'s port side, not quite on the bow, but just where the foc'slehead begins. The wind was very changeable, and swept the flames away momentarily, revealing a gaping hole on the port side, just abreast the foc'sle break.

Others, including the master of the *Enid Mary*, which had been in convoy with *Shelbrit I*, gave evidence at the Board of Enquiry that the distinctive noise of a German aircraft had been heard some hours previously, and that the aircraft was seen passing twice over the *Enid Mary*, once heading up the Cromarty Firth, and again coming back down again.

It was postulated that this aircraft may have dropped a mine in the path of the *Shelbrit I.*

SUNDERLAND AIRCRAFT 1

Wreck No: 226	Date Sunk:
Latitude: 57 41 29 N	Longitude: 03 47 25 W
GPS Lat: 5741.483 N	GPS Long: 0347.417 W
Location: 6½ miles NE of Nairn	Area: Moray
Type:	Tonnage: grt
Length: ft Beam: ft	Draught: ft
How Sunk:	Depth: 35 metres

A wreck is charted in 574129N, 034725W at 35 metres.

This is 6½ miles NE of Nairn, and 6½ miles E of the entrance to the Cromarty Firth.

It is also 1½ miles NE of the *Tantivy.*

This is a fairly intact Sunderland aircraft on a muddy seabed at 46 metres.

A Sunderland aircraft *(Photo: author's collection)*

SUNDERLAND AIRCRAFT 2

Wreck No: 227	Date Sunk: Pre-1976
Latitude: 57 41 58 N	Longitude: 03 51 05 W
GPS Lat: 5741.967 N	GPS Long: 0351.083 W
Location: 7½ miles E of Cromarty Firth	Area: Moray
Type:	Tonnage: grt
Length: 132.0 ft Beam: ft	Draught: ft
How Sunk:	Depth: 27 metres

Charted as a wreck with at least 27 metres over it in about 28 metres.

This wreck was found in 1976, and is apparently about 132ft long.

It is the fairly well broken up remains of a Sunderland aircraft.

SUNDERLAND AIRCRAFT 3

Wreck No: 228   Date Sunk: Pre-1976
Latitude: 57 41 48 N   Longitude: 03 52 30 W
GPS Lat: 5741.800 N   GPS Long: 0352.500 W
Location: 6 miles E of Cromarty Firth Area: Moray
Type: Tonnage: grt
Length: 100.0 ft   Beam: ft   Draught: ft
How Sunk: Depth: 31 metres

This wreck was found in 1976. It is approximately 100 feet long, lying NE/SW, and is the remains of a Sunderland aircraft. The fuselage is lying on its side, half buried in the seabed.

Although it is charted as a wreck with 21.5 metres over it in about 25 metres, the wreck is actually lying at a depth of 31 metres.

SUNDERLAND AIRCRAFT 4

Wreck No: 229   Date Sunk: Pre-1976
Latitude: 57 44 21 N   Longitude: 03 45 40 W
GPS Lat: 5744.350 N   GPS Long: 0345.677 W
Location: 6 miles NW of Findhorn Bay   Area: Moray
Type: Tonnage: grt
Length: ft   Beam: ft   Draught: ft
How Sunk: Depth: 38 metres

This is the wreck of yet another Sunderland aircraft, on a muddy seabed. It was located in 1975, and is charted as a wreck with at least 29 metres over it in about 33 metres.

This aircraft has been trawled almost out of existence, but the keel remains, along with the complete wingspan, less its upper skin, exposing the fuel tank bags. The large wing tip floats are still attached, but caught on one of them is what appears to be a large black mine!

SAN TIBURCIO

Wreck No: 230   Date Sunk: 06 05 1940
Latitude: 57 46 34 N   Longitude: 03 45 33 W
GPS Lat: 5746.567 N   GPS Long: 0345.533 W
Location: 003°, 5½ miles to Tarbat Ness Area: Moray
Type: Tanker   Tonnage: 5,995 grt
Length: 413.0 ft   Beam: 53.4 ft Draught: 27.2 ft
How Sunk: Mined   Depth: 24 metres

The London-registered steam tanker *San Tiburcio* was built in 1921 by the Standard S.B. Co., Shooters Island, New York, and was owned by the Eagle Oil & Shipping Co.

On 6 May 1940, *San Tiburcio* was en route from Scapa Flow to Invergordon with a cargo of 2,193 tons of fuel oil and twelve Sunderland flying boat wing floats. Off the Black Isle a mine exploded right under her hull, two thirds of the way aft, in position

165° Tarbat Ness 4.2 miles. The mine had been laid by *U-9* (KL Wolfgang Luth) on 9 February 1940. The ship was carried away for about 1½ miles as damage to the control platform prevented her engines from being stopped. Her steering was also destroyed, and her back was broken. The vessel broke in two 45 minutes after the mine explosion, and sank. She settled on an even keel, thus allowing the boats to be lowered without difficulty, and her crew of forty were all saved.

The escorting trawler *Leicester City* reported no sign of a torpedo track from her position half a cable on the tanker's port beam, and nor did she obtain a U-boat contact.

Note that a magnetic mine was detonated by the M/S trawlers *Marsona* and *George Cousins* off Tarbat Ness in 574000N, 034550W on 28 May 1940. Another was detonated by the M/S trawlers *Bramble* and *Speedy* in 129° Tarbat Ness 4.4 miles on 7 June. Another two, also by *Bramble* and *Speedy*, on 8 June in 136° Tarbat Ness 3.6 miles and 145° Tarbat Ness 3½ miles. Other mines were discovered in the area in July and August 1940.

The wreck is charted at 574634N, 034532W, with a clearance of 19.1 metres in about 30 metres, and is upright and virtually intact, but broken in two, just aft of the bridge superstructure. The forward part of the wreck, about 160 ft long, lies 022/202°, while the 250-foot long stern section lies at right angles to and about 30 metres aft of the forward section. Although the stern gun was reportedly removed by the Royal Navy in 1989, it was merely blown off its mounting and now lies jammed in a hole in the port side of the stern. The wreck is covered in a beautiful profusion of marine growths, and is owned by the Kinloss Branch of the BSAC.

On the Hydrographic printout, there is a note that in 1976 the length of this wreck was given as 175 metres (577 ft), and a naval diver reported that the wreck was lying on its side!

The *San Tiburcio* is definitely not lying on its side. The 175-metre dimension may be an estimate of the sum of the lengths of the two sections of the wreck, plus the distance of the gap between them.

My research has failed to identify any vessel even approaching a length of 577 ft sunk off the north east of Scotland.

The Eagle Oil tanker San Tiburcio (*Photo: National Maritime Museum*)

VERONA

Wreck No: 231
Latitude: 57 51 39 N
GPS Lat: 5751.670 N
Location: 4½ miles SE of Tarbat Ness
Type: HM Yacht
Length: 165.0 ft   Beam: 23.1 ft
How Sunk: Mined

Date Sunk: 24 02 1917
Longitude: 03 38 34 W
GPS Long: 0338.572 W
Area: Moray
Tonnage: 437 grt
Draught: ft
Depth: 38 metres

HM yacht *Verona* (ex-*Tighnamara*, ex-*Katoomba*, ex-*Lord Byron*, ex-*Imogen*) was built in 1890, and hired by the Admiralty in November 1914. At 08.17 hrs on 24 February 1917, she struck a mine and sank very quickly about 4¼ miles 92° from Tarbat Ness. Various witnesses estimated the length of time she took to sink as between half a minute and two minutes. The position given in 1917 was 575140N, 033840W.

The wreck is charted 4½ miles SE of Tarbat Ness at 575000N, 034100W PA with at least 15 metres over it in 25 metres, but no wreck was found here in 1975. The wreck has since been found at 575139N, 033834W. Depth to the top of the bridge is 38 metres, while the seabed of sand and pebbles is at 44 metres. She lies with a list to starboard, and is broken amidships. The fittings are of a very high standard with brass ventilators and ornate decorated toilets. There are at least two small guns on the counter stern. Broken crockery bearing an Admiralty anchor can be found amongst the wreckage. Until 1997 she had a large, impressive bowsprit, but this had disappeared by May 1998 – possibly wrenched off by a trawl net.

The *Verona* carried one depth charge. The Court of Enquiry heard evidence that the safety pin had not been removed. Her depth charge, therefore, did not explode when the vessel sank. Any diver finding this depth charge would be well advised not to try to collect the pin as a souvenir!

HM Yacht Verona (*Photo: E.Jenyns*)

YOUNG FOX

Wreck No: 232
Latitude: 57 52 18 N
GPS Lat: 5752.300 N
Location: 3 miles E of Tarbat Ness

Date Sunk: 06 12 1928
Longitude: 03 37 09 W
GPS Long: 0337.150 W
Area: Moray

Type: Motor-Sailer		Tonnage: 98 grt
Length: ft	Beam: ft	Draught: ft
How Sunk: Foundered		Depth: 43 metres

The motor-sailer *Young Fox* was built in 1893. En route from Sunderland to Portmahomack with a cargo of 139.5 tons of coal she foundered in rough seas about 3 miles east of Tarbat Ness.

Least depth is 43 metres in a total depth of 45 metres. The wreck lies oriented 045/225°.

(The Hydrographic Department gave the position as 575141N, 033831W in 31 metres, but note that this is almost exactly the position of the *Verona*.)

UNKNOWN

Wreck No: 233	Date Sunk: Pre 1974
Latitude: 57 49 02 N	Longitude: 03 36 46 W
GPS Lat: 5749.033 N	GPS Long: 0336.767 W
Location: 6 miles SE of Tarbat Ness	Area: Moray
Type:	Tonnage: grt
Length: 412.0 ft Beam: ft	Draught: ft
How Sunk:	Depth: 27 metres

This wreck, which is charted at 26.5 metres, was located in 1974. It is apparently a large wreck about 125 metres (412 ft) long, lying 070/250°, but only standing up about 3 metres from the seabed of small stones and broken shell. Dimensions obtained by side scan sonar are notoriously unreliable, and the length dimension may be inaccurate.

UNKNOWN – PRE-1976

Wreck No: 234	Date Sunk: Pre 1976
Latitude: 57 49 57 N	Longitude: 03 32 54 W
GPS Lat: 5749.950 N	GPS Long: 0332.900 W
Location: 8 miles N of Burghead	Area: Moray
Type:	Tonnage: grt
Length: ft Beam: ft	Draught: ft
How Sunk:	Depth: 34 metres

Charted as a wreck at 34 metres. This may be either a rock or a small wreck. It only sticks up about one metre from the bottom.

QUESTING

Wreck No: 235	Date Sunk: 20 09 1975
Latitude: 57 51 48 N	Longitude: 03 48 50 W
GPS Lat: 5751.800 N	GPS Long: 0348.833 W
Location: Port Mor, 1½ miles N Portmahomack	Area: Moray
Type: Motor vessel	Tonnage: grt

Length: 54.0 ft   Beam: ft   Draught: ft
How Sunk: Ran aground   Depth: metres

The motor vessel *Questing* broke from her moorings off Portmahomack during a storm on 29 September 1975, and was blown towards the shore. When she grounded in the relatively shallow water close to the shore, her hull was damaged, and the vessel sank. Two feet of her mast showed above the surface at low tide immediately after sinking, but during the following weeks the sunken vessel broke up, large pieces of wreckage being washed ashore. No-one was aboard the *Questing* at the time of her loss.

DUCHESS

Wreck No: 236   Date Sunk: 16 11 1923
Latitude: 57 50 18 N PA   Longitude: 03 50 15 W PA
GPS Lat: 5750.300 N   GPS Long: 0350.250 W
Location: 3 cables 274° Portmahomack Pier   Area: Moray
Type: Trawler   Tonnage: 155 grt
Length: 97.0 ft   Beam: 20.0 ft Draught: 9.0 ft
How Sunk: Depth: metres

The steel ketch *Duchess* ran aground on 14 November 1923, but floated off and sank between Banff and Meikle Ferry on 16 November.

On 26 November her position was described as 3 cables 274° from Portmahomack pier. Salvage had to be abandoned when the wreck broke up in a gale on 20 March 1924. At that time her mast, which was attached to the wreckage by rigging, protruded 2ft above water 1¼ miles NW by N of Portmahomack.

MAYFLOWER

Wreck No: 237   Date Sunk: 01 02 1973
Latitude: 57 50 24 N PA   Longitude: 02 53 24 W PA
GPS Lat: 5750.400 N   GPS Long: 0253.400 W
Location: 8 miles N of Portknockie   Area: Moray
Type: MFV (FR210)   Tonnage: grt
Length: ft   Beam: ft   Draught: ft
How Sunk: Collision with *Devotion*   Depth: 80 metres

The MFV *Mayflower* was sunk in a collision with MFV *Devotion* on 1 February 1973.

MISTY ISLE

Wreck No: 238   Date Sunk: 04 03 1970
Latitude: 57 54 00 N PA   Longitude: 02 58 00 W PA
GPS Lat: 5754.000 N   GPS Long: 0258.000 W
Location: 13 miles N of Buckie   Area: Moray
Type: MFV   Tonnage: grt
Length: 40.0 ft   Beam: ft   Draught: ft
How Sunk: Collision with *Kathleen*   Depth: metres

The MFV *Misty Isle* sank after a collision with MFV *Kathleen* on 13 March 1970.

UNKNOWN

Wreck No: 239	Date Sunk: Pre 1933
Latitude: 57 54 42 N PA	Longitude: 03 43 36 W PA
GPS Lat: 5754.700 N	GPS Long: 0343.600 W
Location: 029°, 3¼ miles Tarbat Ness Light.	Area: Moray
Type:	Tonnage: grt
Length: ft Beam: ft	Draught: ft
How Sunk:	Depth: metres

A wreck was reported in this position on 20 March 1933.

JOHN DUNKIN

Wreck No: 240	Date Sunk: 11 02 1941
Latitude: 57 54 48 N	Longitude: 03 02 50 W
GPS Lat: 5754.800 N	GPS Long: 0302.833 W
Location: 13 miles N by E of Buckie	Area: Moray
Type: Trawler	Tonnage: 202 grt
Length: 115.3 ft Beam: 22.1 ft	Draught: 12.2 ft
How Sunk: Bombed	Depth: 80 metres

The steam trawler *John Dunkin* was bombed 13 miles N by E of Buckie on 11 February 1941, and was taken in tow by the trawler *White Ear*. The tow had to be slipped as the *John Dunkin* was sinking and both trawlers were being strafed. Eight of the nine crew aboard the *John Dunkin* were rescued. One was lost.

The Hydrographic Department recorded the position as 575448N, 030250W, but there is also a wreck charted at 575630N, 030300W, just over a mile away, and this may be the *John Dunkin*.

TOTNES

Wreck No: 241	Date Sunk: 12 01 1937
Latitude: 57 58 20 N PA	Longitude: 03 59 00 W PA
GPS Lat: 5758.333 N	GPS Long: 0359.000 W
Location: Ashore at Golspie, Sutherland	Area: Moray
Type: Steamship	Tonnage: 283 grt
Length: ft Beam: ft	Draught: ft
How Sunk: Ran aground	Depth: metres

The steamship *Totnes* (ex-*Earl of Durham*, ex-*Jolly Christine*, ex-*Tine*) was built in 1918. She went ashore at Littleferry, near Golspie on 12 January 1937, and her back was broken on the 19th. Some material was salvaged from the wreck by Metal Industries in 1940.

HILLFERN

Wreck No: 242	Date Sunk: 31 10 1940
Latitude: 57 57 00 N PA	Longitude: 02 25 30 W PA
GPS Lat: 5757.000 N	GPS Long: 0225.500 W
Location: 35 miles SE of Wick	Area: Moray
Type: Steamship	Tonnage: 1535 grt
Length: 240.9 ft Beam: 36.3 ft	Draught: ft
How Sunk: Mined?	Depth: metres

According to *British Vessels Lost at Sea 1939-45*, the British steamship *Hillfern* (ex-*Tyne Bell*) was lost due to an unknown cause, 35 miles NNW of Kinnaird Head, on 31 October 1940.

This plots in 5814N, 0222W.

Lloyds War Losses describes the position as 35 miles NNW of Buchan Ness, and gives the position as 575700N, 022530W PA. (That position is actually 21 miles NW of Kinnaird Head, and about 39 miles NW of Buchan Ness. It also seems too far south-west of the route from Buchan Ness to Duncansby Head.)

Lloyds also states that the *Hillfern* was sunk by an external explosion, not considered to be a torpedo or a bomb. This leaves a mine as the only alternative possibility. It was known that her degaussing coil was broken, and it is thought that she strayed into a British minefield. At 16.00 hrs her small boat was reported by an aircraft to be in 5834N, 0122W. (Could this be a misprint for 0222W?)

At 04.00 hrs on 3 November, HMS *Douglas* landed eleven survivors from the *Hillfern* at Scapa Flow. The other eight members of *Hillfern*'s nineteen crew were lost.

The *Hillfern* had been en route from Sunderland to Cork with a cargo of 2,150 tons of coal.

Britain's Sea War – a diary of ship losses 1939–1945 states that she was sunk by German aircraft north-*east* of Kinnaird Head. This must surely be a misprint for north-*west*, and the report of her being sunk by an aircraft is not consistent with the Admiralty report in the PRO.

UNKNOWN

Wreck No: 243	Date Sunk:
Latitude: 57 57 55 N	Longitude: 03 29 44 W
GPS Lat: 5757.916 N	GPS Long: 0329.733 W
Location: 10 miles ENE of Tarbat Ness	Area: Moray
Type:	Tonnage: grt
Length: ft Beam: ft	Draught: ft
How Sunk:	Depth: 49 metres

Located in 1963, this charted wreck is thought to be the remains of a ferry.

WYNOR

Wreck No: 244	Date Sunk: 21 02 1923
Latitude: 57 58 16 N	Longitude: 03 20 22 W

GPS Lat: 5758.274 N   GPS Long: 0320.374 W
Location: 16 miles NE of Tarbat Ness   Area: Moray
Type: Steamship   Tonnage: 113 grt
Length: ft   Beam: ft Draught: ft
How Sunk: Foundered   Depth: 54 metres

The small steel steamship *Wynor* was built in 1921 by P. McGregor & Sons of Kirkintilloch.

She foundered in heavy weather 16 miles north-east of Tarbat Ness Lighthouse while en route from Leith to Wick with a cargo of manure on 21 February 1923.

The wreck lies upright and intact in 58m of water. When divers located the wreck in September 1999, underwater visibility was over 30m, and the whole of the wreck was visible from 21m. Her bow has suffered some trawl damage and the hull plating is corroding away. The wooden decking has rotted away completely, giving access to the engine room. The bridge has collapsed over the starboard side, and the bell was found on the seabed there. The maker's plate had become detached from the front of the bridge, and was found lying loose on top of the sacks of manure. The wreck is covered in fish and there are hundreds of conger eels in the holes between the sacks of manure.

The bell recovered from the Wynor *(Photo: Courtesy of Ken Farrow)*

The builder's plate from the Wynor *(Photo: Courtesy of John Leigh)*

UNKNOWN – FERNSIDE ?

Wreck No: 245

Latitude: 57 59 12 N

GPS Lat: 5759.200 N

Location: 9½ miles NE of Buckie

Type:

Length: ft   Beam: ft

How Sunk: By Aircraft ?

Date Sunk:

Longitude: 02 47 30 W

GPS Long: 0247.500 W

Area: Moray

Tonnage: grt

Draught: ft

Depth: metres

This position is also 11 miles NW of Banff.

The 269 grt British steamship *Fernside* was built in 1921 by R.B. Harrison of Newcastle.

She measured 117.1 x 22.2 x 9.1 ft.

On 26 February 1942 she left Hartlepool bound for Wick with a cargo of coal, but neither the ship, nor any of her eight crew and two gunners, were ever seen again. She was presumed to have been sunk by aircraft off Banff on 27 February.

As this is the only wreck charted in the area which appears to meet the criteria 'off Banff' and reasonably on a course to Wick, I have assumed that it might possibly be the *Fernside,* but it seems a very dubious presumption that she would have steamed as far as the Moray Firth by the next day.

If she was sunk on the 27th – and there seems to be no substantial evidence to support that supposition – I would imagine she must have been sunk long before she reached the Moray Firth.

If she was not sunk on the 27th, every day she remained afloat increased the likelihood of her being seen, but there were no reported sightings of her after she departed Hartlepool.

Almost sixty years after the event, a brother of one of the crew, who lives in Peterhead, said he had the notion that the *Fernside* had been blown up off the Bullers of Buchan, 4 or 5 miles south of Peterhead, but he was unable to substantiate this impression.

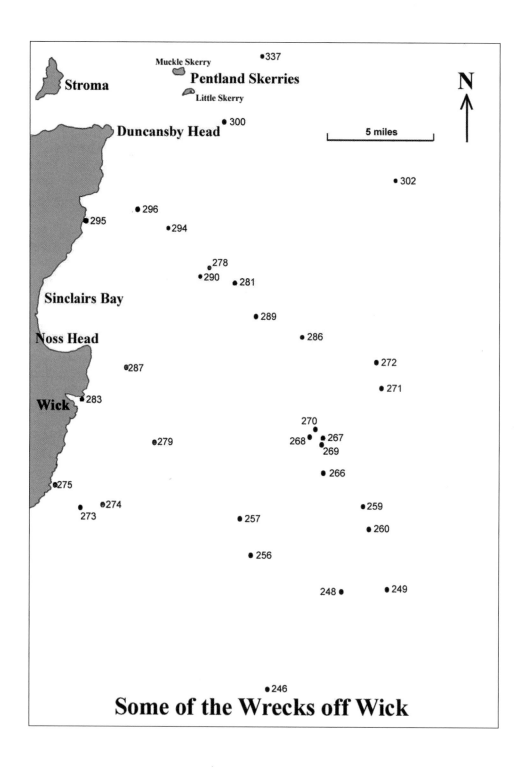

Some of the Wrecks off Wick

4

WICK

MIRANDA

Wreck No: 246	Date Sunk: 21 01 1940
Latitude: 58 00 13 N	Longitude: 02 43 03 W
GPS Lat: 5800.220 N	GPS Long: 0243.050 W
Location: 22 miles NW of Troup Head	Area: Wick
Type: Steamship	Tonnage: 1,328 grt
Length: 237.0 ft Beam: 37.2 ft	Draught: 16.0 ft
How Sunk: Torpedoed by *U-57*	Depth: 68 metres

It had been thought that this wreck might possibly be the Dundee steamship *Jacona*, which was mined on 12 August 1915. The wreck lies 063/243° and stands up 30 ft from the seabed. A sonar contact in 1945 suggested the wreck was about 105 ft long. As this estimate was considerably less than the *Jacona's* 320 ft, however, some doubt existed about the identity of the wreck. (See my comments regarding dimensions obtained by side scan sonar in the introduction.)

The Norwegian steamship *Miranda*, en route from Blyth to Oslo with a cargo of coal, was originally thought to have been torpedoed by *U-22* (KL Karl-Heinrich Jenisch) at 05.40 hrs on 21 January 1940 in German Grid AN1681, which equates to about 582700N, 022400W. The Hydrographic Department, Lloyds and *Axis Submarine Successes*, however, all give the position as 581400N, 020500W PA. This is 32 miles N of Kinnaird Head, and 37 miles ESE of Wick.

We now know that the ship at which *U-22* fired a torpedo at 05.40 hrs on 21 January was the *Cyprian Prince*, but the torpedo either missed, or failed to explode on contact.

The U-boat attacks in this area were subsequently re-assessed, and the *Miranda* is now considered to have been the unidentified ship torpedoed by *U-57* (KL Claus Korth) at 20.26 hrs CET (19.26 hrs British time), on 20 January in German Grid AN1819, which equates to about 575700N, 023600W.

The *Miranda* and the *Tekla* were thought to have been two of the well-lit neutral vessels which had been following the *Cyprian Prince* northwards during the night of 20/21 January, and at least two members of the *Cyprian Prince's* crew stated that two neutral vessels were still in sight a few minutes after 05.40 hrs on the 21st. (See *Exmouth*)

Fourteen of *Miranda's* crew were lost, but three survivors, Ivar Kolbjörn Hansen, Erik Anker Hansen, and Anton Knudsen, were picked up by the British armed boarding vessel *Discovery II* at 11.00 hrs the next day. They were landed in Kirkwall on the 26th, and left there on the 28th aboard the Norwegian steamship *Balta*, bound for Bergen. A 'sjöforklaring' (enquiry) into the loss of the *Miranda* was held in Bergen on 1 February 1940. The three survivors said that the *Miranda* had left Blyth on 19 January, bound for Oslo with a cargo of coal. She was one of five vessels sailing together, without any armed escort. The name and nationality of the ship was painted on the hull, and the Norwegian flag was painted on the bridge roof. The Norwegian flag was hoisted on the after flagstaff, and the vessel was lit up, but the flagstaff was not illuminated. Everything went well until, without warning, their ship was torpedoed in the engine room at about 19.15 hrs on 20 January. This coincides pretty well with the time of Korth's attack, solving the mystery of who sank the *Miranda*.

The *Tekla* and at least one other of the three remaining illuminated neutral ships must have been the vessels seen by those on board *Cyprian Prince* after the *Exmouth* was torpedoed. It is now clear that *Miranda* cannot have been one of them, as she had been sunk about ten hours earlier.

Second mate Ivar Hansen was on the bridge when he heard the giant explosion near the engine room. The force of the explosion threw him from the bridge to the boat deck. Recovering from that, he ran to the poop, where the raft was located. Ivar Hansen was first on the raft, and pulled stoker Knudsen on to it. The two of them pulled donkeyman Pedersen and trimmer Eriksen aboard. Ordinary Seaman Erik Hansen swam to the raft and pulled himself up on to it. The raft capsized when the *Miranda* sank and the five occupants were thrown into the water. They all managed to reboard the raft, but were without any means of propulsion as there was only one oar, the others having been lost when the raft capsized. The raft was equipped with lights, and the men witnessed some of their shipmates sinking and disappearing. After about 15 minutes the area was quiet. It was freezing cold on the raft, and after about three hours trimmer Eriksen perished, and about midnight donkeyman Pedersen died too. They both died of cold and exposure. The three remaining survivors were also frozen, but made use of the fresh water and rusks with which the raft was equipped, and waited for daylight.

The Norwegian steamship Miranda *(Photo: author's collection)*

UNKNOWN

Wreck No: 247	Date Sunk:
Latitude: 58 02 30 N	Longitude: 02 34 30 W
GPS Lat: 5802.500 N	GPS Long: 0234.500 W
Location: 27 miles NW of Kinnaird Head	Area: Wick
Type:	Tonnage: grt

Length: ft   Beam: ft Draught: ft.
How Sunk: Depth: 48 metres

Could this wreck be the *Hillfern*?

LYNX

Wreck No: 248   Date Sunk: 09 08 1915
Latitude: 58 10 32 N   Longitude: 02 30 14 W
GPS Lat: 5810.540 N   GPS Long: 0230.240 W
Location: 24 miles SE of Wick   Area: Wick
Type: Destroyer   Tonnage: 935 tons
Length: 266.0 ft   Beam: 27.0 ft Draught: 9.0 ft
How Sunk: Mined   Depth: 65 metres

HMS *Lynx* was one of the Grand Fleet destroyers on patrol in the Moray Firth on the night of 8 August 1915. An enemy minefield was known to exist, but its exact extent was not accurately known.

Three destroyers normally patrolled together, but HMS *Midge* was the only other destroyer on the patrol line with *Lynx* at the time. The torpedo boat destroyer HMS *Osprey* had been sent to deliver orders to the minesweeping trawlers, and she arrived later.

At 10.40 p.m. on 8 August, *Lynx* received a message that was sent to all of the destroyers on outer patrol in the Moray Firth, ordering them to keep at least five miles to the eastward of the N-R line (Noss Head to Rosehearty), and well clear of the minefield.

She struck a mine and sank at 06.10 hrs on 9 August. Her Captain, Cdr J. Cole, was lost with seventy-three of his crew. There were only twenty-six survivors. At the time *Lynx* was blown up there was no information that the minefield extended north of latitude 58°, but *Lynx* had been warned by *Faulknor* that it was feared the minefield extended across the Firth. A signal made at 12.30 p.m. on 8 August only directed *Lynx* to pass north of latitude 58°. She was sunk in latitude 5808N.

There was no evidence to show the exact position at the time of striking the mine, but survivors were picked up by the SS *Volcano* about 8.30 a.m. in 580700N, 023830W.

The *Midge* had correctly interpreted the order to keep well outside the N-R line, but the court took the view that it would be wrong to censure the late commanding officer of *Lynx* for not having taken the same view, and that recent sweeping had shown mines were laid eight miles outside the N-R line.

The explosion apparently occurred in front of No.1 boiler room, wrecking and severing the fore part of the ship, as far aft as No.1 boiler room.

A second violent explosion also occurred in the vicinity of No.1 boiler room, between 5 and 10 minutes after the first explosion. The Court of Enquiry was of the opinion that this was caused by the after part of the ship drifting against a second mine.

The Hydrographic Dept gives the position of the *Lynx* as 580650N, 023730W PA.

Part of the wreck was found and dived in 2000 at 5810.540N, 0230.240W. The divers descended on a pile of wreckage dominated by four inverted 'V' structures with sides that seemed to be made of tubes – very similar to condenser tubes, but flat slabs – and covered in brass valves of all shapes and sizes, and huge brass pipes. They saw nothing that resembled a ship – no Scotch boilers, engines, bows or stern – and did not realise that the inverted 'V' structures are Yarrow water-tube boilers. These divers did not know what they had dived on, but had the correct impression that it was part of a wreck which had been mined or torpedoed, and broken up.

An echo-sounder search around the position found a further three wrecks, none of which were on the chart. One target at 5810.480N, 0229.980W is only 350 yards away from the one they dived, and is almost certainly another part of HMS *Lynx*.

The dive was carried out from Wick, but the wreck is in range of RIBS from the Moray coast.

The Yarrow water-tube boiler was first used 1896, but not in merchant ships, apart from large turbine-powered liners. Its main use was for warships. British destroyers were first fitted with them in 1896, and from the early 1900s onwards it was customary to have two, three or four water-tube boilers and two steam turbines powering a destroyer. Water-tube boilers were far smaller than traditional scotch boilers of similar output, and their fast steam generating rate and high pressure were ideal for naval use. They could be coal or oil fired.

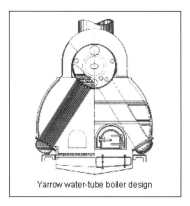

Yarrow water-tube boiler design

U-309

Wreck No: 249		Date Sunk: 16 02 1945	
Latitude: 58 09 39 N		Longitude: 02 22 51 W	
GPS Lat: 5809.650 N		GPS Long: 0222.856 W	
Location: 28 miles SE of Wick		Area: Wick	
Type: Submarine		Tonnage: 769 tons	
Length: 221.4 ft	Beam: 20.5 ft	Draught: 15.8 ft	
How Sunk: Depth-charged		Depth: 55 metres	

U-309 (OL Herbert Loeder) was a Type VIIC Atlantic U-boat, 769 tons surfaced, 871 tons submerged.

On 16 February 1945 the RCN frigate *St John* (Cdr A.F.C. Layard) obtained an asdic contact on a U-boat lying on the bottom, and attacked with depth charges. Some diesel oil and paper came to the surface. A second and third attack with hedgehog anti-submarine mortars produced more oil, and a fourth attack using depth charges resulted in a mass of wreckage, including German charts, signal books and cork insulation. The target was again attacked the following day, producing an aluminium water bottle, French charts of the Caribbean with a stamp showing that they were issued at Kiel, and a tube of sun cream issued from the naval stores at Kiel, but nothing came to the surface to establish how long the submarine had been on the seabed. *U-309* was built with a deck gun, but there is no deck gun on the wreck. (All deck guns were removed in 1943.) A loop antenna on the conning tower dates the U-boat as certainly not before 1943.

It had been rumoured that a body came to the surface, with a jacket from which a Nazi eagle and swastika badge was recovered. This is untrue. No body or jacket came to the surface.

The position has been described as 55 miles NE of Cromarty, and also given as 5809N, 0223W. There were no survivors from the forty-seven crew.

In 1945 the wreck here was estimated to be 177 ft long, and standing up 18 ft from the bottom.

PARKHILL

Wreck No: 250	Date Sunk: 18 11 1939
Latitude: 58 10 14 N	Longitude: 02 29 45 W
GPS Lat: 5810.240 N	GPS Long: 0229.750 W
Location: 30 miles SE of Wick	Area: Wick
Type: Steamship	Tonnage: 500 tons
Length: 161.7 ft Beam: 26.4 ft	Draught: 15.8 ft
How Sunk: Torpedoed by *U-22*	Depth: 52 metres

The British steamship *Parkhill* (ex-*Glenarch*) left Blyth on 17 November 1939, bound for Kirkwall with 449 tons of coal. She failed to arrive, and was finally posted missing on 3 January 1940. After the war it was learned that she had been torpedoed by the *U-22* (KL Karl-Heinrich Jenisch), at 23.10 hrs on 18 November 1939 in German grid square AN1821, which equates to about 5809N, 0224W. All nine of the crew were lost. A wreck found in 1986 at 580934N, 023022W might be the *Parkhill*.

Axis Submarine Successes also gives a position of 5807N, 0218W (apparently from an Allied source), although that position is not mentioned in *Lloyds War Losses*, and nor is any wreck charted there.

CARISBROOK

Wreck No: 251	Date Sunk: 21 06 1915
Latitude: 58 09 57 N	Longitude: 02 30 22 W
GPS Lat: 5809.950 N	GPS Long: 0230.370 W
Location: 24 miles SE of Wick	Area: Wick
Type: Steamship	Tonnage: 2352 grt
Length: 300.3 ft Beam: 42.9 ft	Draught: 20.1 ft
How Sunk: Gunfire from *U-38*	Depth: metres

The British steamship *Carisbrook* was built by J. Blumer of Sunderland in 1907 for the Brook Steamship Co. Ltd of Glasgow. While en route from Montreal to Leith with a cargo of wheat she was captured by *U-38* on 21 June 1915 and sunk by gunfire in the North Sea 70 miles S ¾W from Start Point Lighthouse, Orkney. (This plots in 580730N, 023955W PA.)

Lloyds War Losses gives the position as 40 miles N of Kinnaird Head, which plots in 582045N, 020000W PA. *Carisbrook* had two single-ended boilers and six ribbed furnaces.

A wreck at 582016N, 023958W is about 60 metres long, and stands up 7 metres. Least depth is 48 metres in a general depth of 59 metres. This wreck is in about the right area for the *Carisbrook,* but the apparent length of the wreck is about 120 ft too short. The apparent length, however, may be incorrect – see my comments regarding dimensions obtained by side scan sonar in the introduction.

Two more wrecks lie very close to HMS *Lynx.* One is a small steamship, the other a large one.

The length estimates for the large one vary from about 300 to about 400 ft. This is the wreck at 580957N, 023022W. Four divers saw nothing to suggest a reason for the ship sinking. This may simply be because they swam the length of the wreck at deck level, rather than along the side of the hull, and would therefore probably miss seeing a hole in the hull, such as from a mine, torpedo, collision, or gunfire. The number of holds is not known, nor is it known what cargo, if any, remains in them.

The style of the stern and rudder suggests a fairly old steamship dating from either the turn of the century, or the early twentieth century.

In the absence of any further information to go on, my best guess is that this is the *Carisbrook.*

None of the sparse information about the wreck of the large steamship near the *Lynx* conflicts with that.

The *Jacona* is another possibility. These two ships were of almost identical size. Both were built in Sunderland, and both had two boilers and triple-expansion steam engines made by the same engine builder.

The small steamship is probably the *Parkhill.*

ACTIVE ?

Wreck No: 252	Date Sunk: 18 12 1939
Latitude: 58 17 55 N	Longitude: 02 44 32 W
GPS Lat: 5817.917 N	GPS Long: 0244.533 W
Location: 12 miles SE of Wick	Area: Wick
Type: Trawler	Tonnage: 185 grt
Length: ft Beam: ft	Draught: ft
How Sunk: By aircraft	Depth: 57 metres

Wreckage standing about one metre high, and spread over an area of 80 x 40 metres, oriented NNW/SSE, was located here in 1986 during a survey carried out for the oil industry.

It might be the remains of the steam trawler *Active*, which was attacked and sunk by German aircraft with torpedoes 48 miles NNW of Rattray Head on 18 December 1939.

The position for the sinking of *Active* was recorded in 1972 as 581436N, 024324W PA, and it has also been described as 30 miles N by W of Rattray Head.

COMMANDER BOYLE

Wreck No: 253	Date Sunk: 23 08 1915
Latitude: 58 11 00 N	Longitude: 02 27 30 W
GPS Lat 5811.000 N	GPS Long: 0227.500 W
Location: 25 miles SE of Wick	Area: Wick
Type: Trawler	Tonnage: 242 grt

Length: 115.5 ft   Beam: ft   Draught: ft
How Sunk: Mined   Depth: 58 metres

The trawler *Commander Boyle* was sunk by a mine 40 miles N by W of Rattray Head on 23 August 1915. The position recorded at the time was 581230N, 022530W PA, but a wreck found in October 1944 at 581100N, 022730W is thought to be the *Commander Boyle*.

A more accurate position may be 5810.940N, 0227.480W.

The *Commander Boyle* was built in 1915, and was therefore almost new when she was sunk.

JASPER

Wreck No: 254   Date Sunk: 26 08 1915
Latitude: 58 12 46 N   Longitude: 02 25 40 W
GPS Lat: 5812.767 N   GPS Long: 0225.667 W
Location: 24 miles SE of Wick   Area: Wick
Type: Trawler   Tonnage: 221 grt
Length: 101.0 ft   Beam: 20.5 ft Draught: 11.0 ft
How Sunk: Mined   Depth: 54 metres

The iron-hulled steam trawler *Jasper* (ex-*Rayvernol*) was built in 1912 by Smiths Dock, Middlesbrough. As she was commissioned by the Admiralty as a minesweeper at the time of loss, she will probably have a gun aboard.

The position of sinking was recorded as 581300N, 022130W PA in 1915, but the wreck found in 1982 at 581246N, 022540W is thought to be the *Jasper*.

SERVUS

Wreck No: 255   Date Sunk: 08 12 1959
Latitude: 58 13 42 N   Longitude: 03 26 00 W
GPS Lat: 5813.700 N   GPS Long: 0326.000 W
Location: SE side of Dunbeath Castle   Area: Wick
Type: Motor Vessel   Tonnage: 360 grt
Length: 148.5 ft   Beam: 23.7 ft   Draught: 10.2 ft
How Sunk: Ran aground   Depth: metres

The Leith-registered coaster *Servus* was en route to Wick during a storm when a shaft broke in her engine room. The vessel then began to drift helplessly towards the Caithness shore. Buckie lifeboat went to her assistance, as did the fishery research vessels *Scotia* and *Explorer*, and the trawler *Aberdeen Progress*.

Scotia attempted to tow the *Servus*, but was unable to arrest her westward drift. Buckie lifeboat had to return to harbour for refuelling, and Wick lifeboat could not be launched in the prevailing conditions.

The Cromarty lifeboat *Lilla Marras, Douglas & Will* was able to set out, and finally caught up with the *Servus* when she was only one mile from the shore. All eight of the crew were rescued before the *Servus* went aground and became a total loss at the SE side of Dunbeath Castle.

JACONA

Wreck No: 256	Date Sunk: 12 08 1915
Latitude: 58 13 27 N	Longitude: 02 43 01 W
GPS Lat: 5813.450 N	GPS Long: 0243.017 W
Location: 19 miles SE of Noss Head	Area: Wick
Type: Steamship	Tonnage: 2,969 grt
Length: 320.4 ft Beam: 41.0 ft	Draught: 20.0 ft
How Sunk: Mined	Depth: 48 metres

The Dundee steamship *Jacona* (ex-*Saint Marnock*) was en route from the Tees to Montreal with a general cargo when she struck a mine on 12 August 1915, and sank with the loss of twenty-nine lives.

Lloyds recorded the position as 25 miles NNW of Troup Head, but the wreck here is actually 36 miles NNW of Troup Head, and 19 miles SE of Noss Head.

The *Jacona* was built by J. Laing of Sunderland in 1889. Her triple-expansion steam engine was by J. Dickinson of Sunderland, and she had two double-ended boilers. The wreck is upright and lying 120/300° on a seabed which slopes from 48 to 54 metres. The least depth is 40 metres. Two boilers were seen when the wreck was dived in 1999, but just aft of the boilers there is a sheer break in the hull. The wreck is obviously broken in two pieces. The stern section was not seen, but an echo sounder contact 50 metres to the south east is assumed to be the stern section.

LLANISHEN ?

Wreck No: 257	Date Sunk: 23 08 1940
Latitude: 58 16 16 N	Longitude: 02 44 48 W
GPS Lat: 5816.267 N	GPS Long: 0244.800 W
Location: 14 miles SE of Noss Head	Area: Wick
Type: Steamship	Tonnage: 5,053 grt
Length: 400.5 ft Beam: 54.0 ft	Draught: 25.9 ft
How Sunk: Bombed	Depth: 35–45 metres

The 5053 grt steamship *Llanishen* was built by Bartram of Sunderland in 1929.

At 22.10 hrs BST, on 23 August 1940, while en route from Leith to Baltimore in ballast, she was bombed by German Heinkel aircraft based at Stavanger.

The first bomb hit the starboard side amidships, splitting the deck open. A second bomb exploded near No.4 hold, severely damaging the starboard side forward of the funnel. The vessel took an immediate list to port. Eighteen men got away in the port lifeboat. Nine others attempted to escape in the starboard boat, but one of them was killed in the attempt.

The remaining nine got away in the port jolly boat, but seven of them were lost when the jolly boat capsized, throwing all of the occupants into the water. The Captain reported that when he abandoned ship three or four minutes after the attack, the *Llanishen* was listing about 40° to port, and looked as if she was about to roll over on to the lifeboats at any moment.

Lloyds War Losses and *British Vessels Lost at Sea 1939-45* give the position of attack as 581700N, 022700W, while *DODAS* gives 'about 30 miles N of Banff'.

She is recorded by the Hydrographic Department at 582100N, 023200W PA, 18 miles

SE of Wick, but the wreck charted as 33 metres in about 42 metres, 14 miles SE of Wick at 581616N, 024448W may be the *Llanishen*. This wreck is a 120-metre long steamship oriented 035/215°. It apparently has three large boilers, and contains bottles and other material of Second World War vintage. The *Llanishen* had three single-ended boilers fitted with superheaters, and 9 corrugated furnaces made by Blair & Co. (1926) Ltd.

The attack on the *Llanishen* was seen by Captain Bain of the *Makalla*, one of the vessels in the same convoy, and after abandoning ship, Captain Thomas of the *Llanishen* saw the *Makalla* and the *MV Beacon Grange* (10,119 grt), which had also been attacked, burning in the distance. The *Beacon Grange* was towed in by the tugs *Buccanneer* and *Salvage King*, and beached.

After about two hours, the survivors from the *Llanishen* were picked up by the *Kylebrook* and landed at Lyness.

GRETAFIELD

Wreck No: 258		Date Sunk: 23 02 1940
Latitude: 58 14 45 N PA		Longitude: 03 25 00 W PA
GPS Lat: 5814.750 N		GPS Long: 0325.000 W
Location: Beached near Dunbeath harbour		Area: Wick
Type: Tanker		Tonnage: 10191 grt
Length: 500.2 ft	Beam: 67.9 ft	Draught: 36.9 ft
How Sunk: Torpedoed by *U-57* and beached		Depth: 15 metres

The 10,191-grt British steam tanker *Gretafield* was built in 1928 by Cammell Laird for the Northern Petroleum Tank Steamship Company. Laden with 13,000 tons of aviation spirit and 1,100 tons of fuel oil from Curacao via Halifax to Invergordon in convoy HX18, she was torpedoed by the *U-57* (KL Claus Korth) 12 miles E of Wick at 12.17 a.m. on 14 February 1940.

The ship was hit on the port side, between the bridge and the No. 3 tank. The whole of the bridge, the second officer and one look-out man were smothered in fuel oil. The explosion wrecked the chart room, radio room and wheelhouse. The wheel was blown out of the coxswain's hand, breaking his wrist. One man on the poop was thrown about 5 feet into the air, and five others were blown overboard. The ship immediately took a heavy list to port.

The Admiralty report gives the position of attack as 5820N, 0237W, whereas Lloyds give the position as 5827N, 0233W. Captain Derricks gave the position as about 5840N, 0225W.

Ten minutes later a second very heavy explosion occurred in the vicinity of No. 9 tank and bunker, blowing oil and deck fittings 150 feet in the air and killing the gunner, whose body lay beside his gun.

Despite the tremendous explosions, the tanker did not sink immediately, but burst into flames.

With the ship listing badly, and with oil spreading on the decks and huge flames leaping, the crew had difficulty in getting the lifeboats launched. Three boats which managed to get away had to be rowed through a huge slick of oil which spread over the sea, a foot thick, with flames spreading rapidly over the water towards them.

Two trawlers fishing in the area were first on the scene to pick up survivors, while Wick lifeboat *City of Edinburgh* proceeded to the scene. The decks of the Wick lifeboat were scorched as she attempted to go alongside.

The two trawlers, *Peggy Nutten* and *Strathalpine*, whose skippers were prepared to enter the burning sea to rescue the sailors, landed twenty-seven survivors from the crew of forty-one, including a fifteen-year-old boy, at Wick. The trawlers had cut their nets, thereby losing their catch. Eleven of *Gretafield*'s crew were lost.

The blazing wreck drifted ashore 2.6 cables, 210° from Dunbeath Pier, to the south of Dunbeath Bay, at 14.45 hrs on the 15th, where the fire continued to burn for several days. The tanker *British Tommy* was sent with a view to salvaging oil from *Gretafield*, but she broke in two on the 19th and slewed round, making any salvage impossible. The ship was abandoned as a total loss. Later the bodies of three crew members, so badly burned that a positive identification was impossible, were recovered and buried at Latheron churchyard. One was Danny Sinclair of Wick, who is thought to have escaped, but returned to retrieve presents he had bought for his mother. Another was Gunner Marine Davy of Plymouth.

Both parts of the wreck lie close together. The bow section lies 2.8 cables, 185° from Dunbeath pier. Some salvage work was carried out by Metal Industries in 1940–41.

The tanker Gretafield *on fire off Wick. (Photo: PRO)*

EXMOUTH

Wreck No: 259	Date Sunk: 21 01 1940
Latitude: 58 18 28 N	Longitude: 02 28 56 W
GPS Lat: 5818.467 N	GPS Long: 0228.938 W
Location: 21 miles SE of Noss Head	Area: Wick
Type: Destroyer	Tonnage: 1475 tons
Length: 343.0 ft Beam: 33.7 ft	Draught: 8.7 ft
How Sunk: Torpedoed by *U-22*	Depth: 60 metres

The entire crew of 189 were lost when the 1934-built E-Class destroyer HMS *Exmouth* (Cdr R.S. Benson) was torpedoed north east of Tarbat Ness in the Moray Firth by the

U-22 (KL Karl-Heinrich Jenisch) at 04.44 hrs on 21 January 1940. The German Grid reference was given as AN1684, which equates to about 582100N, 022400W.

Warship Losses of WW2 gives the position of torpedoing as 5818N, 0225W.

The *Exmouth* had met the *Cyprian Prince* (Captain Benjamin T. Wilson) off Aberdeen, to escort her northwards to Scapa Flow. Benson signalled simply 'Follow us. Speed 10 knots. Course 070.' The destroyer was showing 'a very bright stern light'.

Chief Officer Albert Clark was on watch in *Cyprian Prince*, which was following at a safe distance of four cables astern of *Exmouth* on a course of 330° at 10 knots. Both vessels continued to steam northwards as night fell. The sea was calm, and visibility good. The *Exmouth*'s stern light was still in sight of the *Cyprian Prince* at 04.44 hrs when Clark heard one explosion, and thinking *Exmouth* was dropping depth charges, called Captain Wilson, who was in his bunk, to the bridge. Wilson had arrived on the bridge when, at 04.48 hrs there was a second detonation, which Clark described as 'a terrific explosion, much louder than the first'.

At 04.50, the *Cyprian Prince* stopped her engines to look for survivors. Her helm was turned to port to clear the upturned hull of the *Exmouth*. Voices were heard in the water, and flickering or flashing lights were seen, and at 04.51, she went full ahead and put her helm over to starboard to close the men in the water. At 04.53 she stopped engines again and, according to Marine Gunner Ronald Sheen, about ten men could be heard in the water.

Captain Wilson had already ordered men to stand by the boats, ready to go and pick up the survivors, but considered that stopping in good visibility to rescue them carried too great a risk of his own vessel being torpedoed. At 04.56 hrs he rang down for full ahead and turned to port, leaving the men in the water. *Cyprian Prince* continued northwards alone with its urgent cargo of searchlights, anti-aircraft guns, and mobile units, Scammel trucks, cars and ammunition for the defence of Scapa Flow. This was less than three months after HMS *Royal Oak* had been torpedoed in Scapa Flow by *U-47* (KK Gunther Prien).

Cyprian Prince's radio operator William Costello logged at 05.07 hrs 'Called GKR (Wick Radio), giving secret callsign, "SOS. Sinking in 5818N, 0225W"'. Costello then looked out to see the two well-lit neutral ships which had been following *Cyprian Prince* all night. (These were thought to be the Danish *Tekla*, and the Norwegian *Miranda*.) Seaman Cyril Monck in *Cyprian Prince* jumped out of his bunk on hearing the first explosion, and was pulling on his trousers at the time of the second. He went on deck and saw the lights of two neutral steamers on the port beam, apparently heading south. (He would have been confused by the fact that, by then, *Cyprian Prince* had reversed course to close the men in the water.)

George Montgomery, chief engineer of the *Cyprian Prince*, was asleep in his bunk on the starboard side, just above the engine room. He was wakened by a series of small bangs, which he took to be a door banging in the engine room. He got up to investigate, and shouted down to the engine room 'Shut that door', but was told by the second engineer that the door he had thought to be responsible for the banging was securely shut. When questioned at some length by the Court of Enquiry about the noise that had wakened him, he said he heard three or four bangs which sounded like bangs on the ship's side. These were followed two or three minutes afterwards by a very heavy detonation which seemed quite close by.

U-22's Ktb (*Kriegstagebuche* – war diary) reveals that the U-boat was heading south on the surface on a very dark night. The moon was setting behind the clouds when they saw the illuminated neutral ships heading north-west. While Jenisch was looking at them, a blacked-out destroyer, followed by a similarly darkened steamship, unexpectedly moved into his line of sight between the U-boat and the illuminated ships. Had it not been for the lights of the neutral ships, he would not have spotted the darkened ships at all. Caught by surprise, Jenisch accelerated to try to get into a good firing position, but was unable to get ahead of the destroyer. After a pursuit lasting almost an hour he fired one torpedo at the destroyer, and a second at the steamship. The first torpedo exploded after 2 minutes 35 seconds, when it hit *Exmouth* in the starboard side at the forward magazine, sparking off a tremendous secondary explosion and producing thick black smoke.

The second torpedo exploded after a run of 4 minutes 7 seconds. This shot had obviously failed – a dud, or a miss, perhaps due to the steamship changing course after the first detonation was heard.

Jenisch tried to chase the steamer, but had to take avoiding action to prevent his U-boat ramming into the ship as it turned to run west towards the coast at a speed of at least 12.5 knots – *U-22*'s maximum speed. *Cyprian Prince* was actually doing 13 knots, and *U-22* was unable to catch the ship, and had no opportunity to fire any further torpedoes at it.

It would seem that the torpedo fired at the *Cyprian Prince* may not have missed. The banging noise that wakened Chief Engineer Montgomery might possibly have been the torpedo hitting several times against the side of the vessel as it passed at an angle without the contact pistol firing. After the torpedo cleared the ship's side it would continue to the end of its run before sinking. German torpedoes were fitted with two pistols, one contact and one magnetic, one of which the U-boat commander selected before firing. It was found that the magnetic pistol was too sensitive and the contact pistol would only work against a straight surface. Against a curved surface, the torpedo could glance off without exploding.

The Admiralty claimed the first news of the sinking of the *Exmouth* was when *Cyprian Prince* reached Kirkwall at 13.00 hrs. This was despite the fact that Captain Wilson had attempted to send a visual signal by Aldis lamp to Noss Head, Duncansby Head and Muckle Skerry, as he passed each in turn, but had been unable to elicit any response. We also know from *U-22*'s Ktb that they heard either the destroyer or the steamship sending at a very rapid speed 'SOS. Sinking in lat 58°18′N, long 02°25′W', and Wick Radio (GKR) on the 600-metre waveband repeating 'SOS unknown vessel sinking in position 5818N, 0225W'. The war diary of the Admiral Commanding Orkney and Shetland (ACOS) contains an entry for 21 January: '*Cyprian Prince* broadcast SOS at 0400 [*sic*] and made report on arrival at Kirkwall.'

Some hours after her loss two signals were made to *Exmouth*, at 15.46 and 17.25, to report her position, following an earlier order at 12.39 from C-in-C Rosyth to search for a submarine which had sunk a Danish ship – the *Tekla*.

When it was finally realised that *Exmouth* had been lost, the destroyer HMS *Sikh*, the minesweepers HMS *Sphinx*, the tug *St Mellons*, the A/S trawlers *King Sol*, *Loch Monteith*, *St Elstan* and *St Cathan*, and the Wick lifeboat *City of Edinburgh*, immediately rushed to the area and an air search was made. *St Mellons* reported large quantities of oil fuel and surface wreckage, but no survivors. One lifebuoy from the *Exmouth* was found floating amongst a handful of orange crates and other flotsam. HMS *Sphinx* picked up the lifebuoy, and the rescue ships also picked up a raft bearing two dead bodies and marked M/S *Maurija*, in 5817N, 0126W.

On 28 January, nine bodies from the *Exmouth* were washed ashore at Wick. They were found by Donald Sutherland, a ten-year-old schoolboy who was playing truant from school. More bodies came ashore at Lybster. A mass funeral took place in Wick on the 31st. Eighteen ratings were buried in a mass grave. One of them was PO Joe O'Brien, a pre-war athlete of note, who had won 200 medals for swimming.

The Admiralty Board of Enquiry spent some time considering the effectiveness of *Exmouth*'s Asdic, and found that Benson had not given Wilson clear instructions, and that his signal 'Follow me' was wholly inadequate. They also stated that Benson should not have shown a stern light, as this was inviting attack. Normal convoy practice would have been for the escort to take station on the convoy, rather than the other way around. They also debated whether the captain of the *Cyprian Prince* had done the right thing in obeying the Admiralty DMS (Defence of Merchant Shipping) instructions in abandoning the survivors of the destroyer when he might have rescued them, but concluded that his action had been correct.

Captain Wilson was clearly badly affected by the episode and left *Cyprian Prince* after this voyage. He was 'not expected to return'.

Cyprian Prince, 1,988 grt, was bombed at Piraeus on 6 April 1941. Four of her thirty-six crew were killed. The ship was beached near Salamis, and in November 1945 the wreck was found lying at Pesteri (Salamis Island).

This same policy of not stopping to pick up survivors from torpedoed vessels was followed many times during the war, as it was considered that such an action increased to an unacceptable degree the risk of the would-be rescuer's vessel also being torpedoed, leading to additional loss of life, the loss of valuable cargoes, and the loss of further vital cargo-carrying capacity.

In addition to naval escorts, specially-designated rescue vessels sailed with many large wartime convoys. Compared to the bulk of the cargo-carrying ships of the convoy, these were relatively small, shallow-draught vessels.

The Admiralty had recorded the approximate position of the wreck as 5818N, 0225W – the same position that was broadcast by *Cyprian Prince*'s radio operator. On three occasions towards the end of the war, in January, February and March 1945, a bottom contact was located within a few miles of that position. The vessels involved actually reported very slightly different positions for the contact, and they probably all assumed it might have been a U-boat. For fifty-six years no-one seems to have realised that it was the wreck of HMS *Exmouth*.

The fact that this is the *Exmouth* was deduced by Orkney-based wreck researcher Kevin Heath, and the author, after considerable research. The final vital clues came from *U-22*'s Ktb, which Kevin obtained from Washington DC, USA. At 08.45 CET the navigator made a correction adjustment (Versetzung) to the position of the U-boat, putting it about 10 nm south of where he had hitherto supposed the boat to be, but the positions previously recorded in the Ktb were not retrospectively amended to take this correction into account. The AN1684 position was obviously incorrect, and the difficulty of keeping an accurate running plot had been exacerbated by the boats continual course and speed changes during the hours of darkness, resulting in a gradually increasing error.

Kevin divulged the position to Mark Reeves and Alex Deas of the European Technical Diving Centre, Burray, Orkney. The position we gave them was so accurate that it took them only twenty minutes to locate the wreck. They dived and confirmed its identity on 24 June 2001. Alex Deas described the wreck as an underwater garden of stunning beauty, covered with bright hydroids, anemones and starfish. It was teeming with shoals of large fish, with many lobsters, crabs and sea urchins on the wreck. He said, 'It is most fitting that the site has been transformed from one of death and destruction to one of tranquillity and life. I have never seen so much sea life on any other wreck', a point Mark Reeves affirmed. He added 'It is clear why the *Exmouth* sank so quickly after the explosion. The torpedo did not simply make a hole, but it literally blew the ship apart. It was evident from surveying the wreck that the *Exmouth* obviously sank immediately. Now it is a very beautiful site, in clear water.'

The wreck is lying almost upside down, very smashed up, twisted and corroded. The 4.7-inch gun turrets are lying upside down in the wreckage. The 'terrific explosion, much louder than the first', described by those on the *Cyprian Prince*, was very likely *Exmouth*'s forward magazine exploding, and this would be the source of the black cloud of smoke seen by *U-22*. A magazine explosion would also account for a lot of the enormous damage to the wreck.

Exmouth obviously hit the seabed bow first, causing the fore end to bend and distort. The wreck was detected by anti-submarine vessels during the war. They possibly assumed it to be a U-boat, and may have subjected it to depth-charging, causing further damage. We now have about an hour of video footage of the wreck, and several features, including her distinctive anchors, propellers, range finder, etc., have been matched with plans of the ship.

Large quantities of 4.7-inch and anti-aircraft gun shells are strewn around. A 4.7-inch gun shell manufactured in 1937 was recovered. It had reload date stamps of February and April 1938. Her torpedo tubes are loaded with torpedoes – the warhead noses are visible at the front ends of the tubes. Some tubes have the rear end caps in place, but at least one tube has split, and the twin contra-rotating propellers of the torpedo in the tube can be seen. Depth charges are visible at the stern, and the streamlined asdic housing protrudes from the upturned hull. At least one fishing net is snagged on the wreck.

About 160 relatives attended a memorial service for those lost on HMS *Exmouth* at Wick Cemetery, and in Wick Old Parish Church on 1/2 September 2001. The Royal Navy presented a White Ensign.

For further information see the official HMS Exmouth 1940 Association website at:
    http://www.geocities.com/exmouthhms1940assoc/ or
    http://www.hms-exmouth.org.uk/

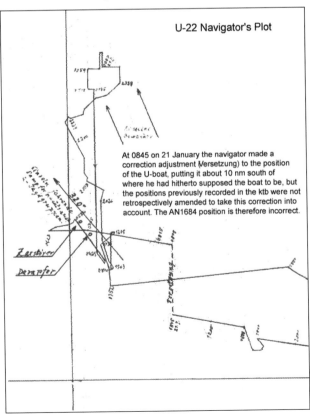

U-22 Navigator's Plot

At 0845 on 21 January the navigator made a correction adjustment (Versetzung) to the position of the U-boat, putting it about 10 nm south of where he had hitherto supposed the boat to be, but the positions previously recorded in the ktb were not retrospectively amended to take this correction into account. The AN1684 position is therefore incorrect.

Photographs of the headstones of the sailors from HMS Exmouth *and HMS* Sphinx *buried in the mass grave in Wick cemetery. (Photos: © R.N. Baird 1999)*

HMS Exmouth (*Photo: IWM*)

TEKLA

Wreck No: 260	Date Sunk: 21 01 1940
Latitude: 58 16 28 N	Longitude: 02 26 33 W
GPS Lat: 5816.473 N	GPS Long: 0226.550 W
Location: 27 miles SE of Noss Head	Area: Wick
Type: Steamship	Tonnage: 1,469 grt
Length: 249.5 ft Beam: 38.1 ft	Draught: 15.0 ft
How Sunk: Torpedoed by *U-22*	Depth: 58 metres

The Danish steamship *Tekla*, belonging to D/S Torm of Copenhagen, was built in Helsingør in 1920. She was torpedoed and sunk while en route from Burntisland to Aarhus with a cargo of coal and coke on 21 January 1940. The ship sank in three minutes with the loss of nine of her eighteen crew.

According to Rohwer's *Axis Submarine Successes 1939–45* she was torpedoed at 05.00 hrs on 21 January 1940. The position was described as 50 minutes (miles?) north-east of Tarbat Ness, and the torpedoing was originally attributed to the *U-55* (KL Werner Heidel).

Admiralty documents in the PRO state that *Tekla* was torpedoed at 05.13 hrs on the 21st in 5818N, 0225W, which is about 40 miles NNW of Kinnaird Head, and this is the position recorded by the Hydrographic Department, Lloyds and *Axis Submarine Successes*. The fact that all three sources give the same position suggests a common original source – probably the radio log of the *Cyprian Prince*, whose radio operator gave that position at 05.07 hrs when he called GKR (Wick Radio): 'SOS. Sinking in 5818N, 0225W.' (Although the vessel he was referring to was HMS *Exmouth*.)

Further consideration has since been given to the U-boat attacks in this area during January 1940, and it is now known that *Tekla* was the ship torpedoed by *U-22* at 06.11 hrs on the 21st (07.11 hrs CET) in AN1681, which equates to about 5827N, 0224W.

About an hour and a half after this grid reference was entered in *U-22*'s Ktb, the U-boat's navigator made a correction to his position plot by 10 miles southwards. This would result in a position for the torpedoing of the *Tekla* as 5817N, 0224W.

A wreck located at 581624N, 022612W in February 1945 was reported to be 130 ft long, and standing up 30 ft from the seabed. The wreck was located and dived by Dave

Dale on 1 June 2001 at 5816.473N, 0226.550W. Although nine of *Tekla*'s crew were lost, there were nine survivors.

An inquest was held in Copenhagen on 25 January and 1 February 1940. Able Seaman Julius Thomsen had taken over the helm at 06.00 hrs on the 21st. The weather was calm with a slight swell. It was dark but still with some visibility. About five minutes before the torpedo struck, Thomsen observed a sharp beam of light coming from low over the water, and flashing towards *Tekla*'s bridge. The light came and went a couple of times before disappearing. He immediately told the mate, Hans Jørgensen, that they probably had a German U-boat to starboard, and shortly afterwards saw at a distance of 300–400 metres the luminous streak of a torpedo coming towards the starboard side of the ship. Thomsen immediately put the helm hard to port, but it was too late. When the torpedo struck there was a violent explosion which killed four members of *Tekla*'s crew. Both hatches flew up in the air before the explosion was even heard. The ship immediately took a list to starboard, which increased rapidly, and she began to sink. The starboard lifeboat was put into the water and ten men jumped into it. Immediately after that the vessel sank. As the *Tekla*'s stern lifted upwards, and the ship capsized, the mainmast hit the lifeboat, crushing it. The ten men who were in the lifeboat fell into the water and five of them drowned. The other five managed to board a raft which had floated free. Four more of *Tekla*'s crew were on another raft. At about 8.30 a.m. these four were taken aboard a Royal Navy vessel and transferred to the Norwegian ship *Iris*, which at the same time took the five men from the second raft. The nine survivors were disembarked in Bergen.

The body of one member of *Tekla*'s crew, Verner Sørensen of Fredericia, was washed ashore and buried in an unmarked grave in Wick cemetery (Plot No. 1026).

The Danish steamship Tekla *(Photo: courtesy of World Ship Society)*

Verner Sørensen's unmarked grave in Wick cemetery (Photo: © R.N. Baird 2001)

SPHINX

Wreck No: 261

Latitude: 58 18 00 N PA

GPS Lat: 5818.000 N

Location: Occumster Cove, 1½ miles N Lybster

Type: Minesweeper

Length: 245.0 ft   Beam: 33.5 ft

How Sunk: Bombed

Date Sunk: 03 02 1940

Longitude: 03 15 24 W PA

GPS Long: 0315.400 W

Area: Wick

Tonnage: 875 tons

Draught: 7.9 ft

Depth: metres

The minesweeper HMS *Sphinx* was built in 1939 by W. Hamilton of Port Glasgow.

On 3 February 1940 the minesweepers *Speedwell*, *Skipjack* and *Sphinx* were sweeping in company at 5737N 0159W, 15 miles north of Kinnaird Head, when they were attacked at 09.15 hrs by two Dornier aircraft. One bomb hit *Sphinx* (Commander J.R.N. Taylor, senior officer of the 5th minesweeping flotilla), passed through her bridge and upper deck, then exploded in her forward mess deck. Her fore ends were wrecked and her upper deck folded back against the bridge. The initial explosion appears to have left four killed, including Cdr Taylor, and three seriously injured. *Speedwell* took her in tow for Invergordon at 10.50 hrs. The tow parted at 12.50 hrs but was passed again. It parted again at 22.00 hrs. At 01.00 on the 4th, *Sphinx* asked for her wounded to be taken off but none of the vessels present could get alongside as she was in immediate danger of sinking in heavy seas. At 03.00 hrs the crew of the *Sphinx* had to abandon ship, and *Speedwell* crashed alongside three times and managed to pick up four men. HMS *Boreas* then made repeated attempts to go alongside and managed to take off another seven. At 04.55 hrs *Sphinx* capsized. Many of the crew were choked to death in her fuel oil which had been pumped into the sea in an attempt to calm the waves. HMS *Boreas* picked up thirty survivors from the sea and sent an urgent signal asking for a medical officer.

HMS Sphinx *after attack by German aircraft. (Photo: PRO) Note the foredeck folded right back against the front of the bridge! Even the bomb entry hole is visible.*

He transferred aboard in the Dornoch Firth at 09.25 hrs. A total of forty-six survivors were landed at Invergordon on the 4th. Commander Taylor, four other officers and forty-nine ratings were killed.

Bodies were washed ashore as far away as Wick, and Walls in Orkney. Of the thirty bodies washed ashore in Caithness, twenty were buried in Wick cemetery.

At 12.00 hrs on the 5th, the wreck of HMS *Sphinx* was washed ashore, bottom up, in Occumster Bay, 1½ miles north of Lybster at 5818N, 0315W PA, and was immediately declared a total loss.

Metal Industries salvaged some material from the wreck in 1940.

The wreck lies broadside to the shore in a gully at the bottom of the cliffs, below the croft owned by the Sutherland family, who make Caithness cheese and sheepskin rugs.

Broken wreckage is scattered along the east side of the bay. Many items have been recovered over the years, but the gun and a safe are among the items remaining.

The bows are missing. The damaged bow section fell off sometime during the afternoon of 4 February 1940, possibly when the *Sphinx* capsized.

One of the Sphinx graves in Wick cemetery. (Photo: © R.N. Baird 2001)

The poignant note reads:
HENRY DUCE aged 25 years
We of today
Of our future we've sighed
We of the past
With no future we've cried
Given the chance
What might have transpired.
1940 ALVIRRA a young bride – came by 1997

EAMONT

Wreck No: 262
Latitude: 58 16 30 N
GPS Lat: 5816.500 N
Location: 0.3 miles N of Latheronwheel
Type: Trawler
Length: 117.4 ft   Beam: 22.5 ft
How Sunk: Bombed

Date Sunk: 11 02 1941
Longitude: 03 22 00 W
GPS Long: 0322.000 W
Area: Wick
Tonnage: 227 grt
Draught: 13.7 f
Depth: 10 metres

The armed steam trawler *Eamont* was bombed three miles off Dunbeath harbour at 5815N, 0326W on 11 February 1941. Two bombs exploded alongside the vessel, but one which fell into the wheelhouse failed to explode. *Eamont* fired at the aircraft with her Lewis gun, but to no effect. She dropped anchor, and her crew of ten abandoned ship, and were taken ashore by the patrol drifter *Harmony*. There were no casualties. The *Eamont* drifted towards the shore about 0.3 miles north of Latheronwheel in an easterly gale the following day, and broke in two. She fetched up next to the Coastguard Station, which was hurriedly evacuated due to the UXB. The forepart lay on its side against a cliff, while the after part sank in deeper water, 300 metres straight out from a triangle of grass. Live ammunition is in the broken wreckage. The boiler is still intact.

ANDALUSIA

Wreck No: 263
Latitude: 58 18 00 N PA ?
GPS Lat: 5818.000 N ?
Location: 39 miles N ¾W of Kinnaird Head
Type: Steamship
Length: 236.1 ft   Beam: 45.2 ft
How Sunk: Torpedoed by *U-55*?

Date Sunk: 21 01 1940
Longitude: 02 25 00 W PA ?
GPS Long: 0225.000 W ?
Area: Wick
Tonnage: 1,284 grt
Draught: 24.2 ft
Depth: metres

The loss of the Swedish steamship *Andalusia* is shrouded in mystery. She left Verdon, near Bordeaux, on 17 January 1940, bound for Gothenburg with a general cargo, including cork, and reported by radio on the 21st (at what time, and where was she then?), but was never heard from again. In the original version of *Axis Submarine Successes 1939–1945*, Professor Dr Jürgen Rohwer suggests she was probably torpedoed by the *U-55* (KL Werner Heidel), on 21 January 1940, in the North Sea. Was she really sunk by the *U-55*, and if so, where?

According to the German records, *U-55* was sent from Kiel on 16 January, to operate off the south of Ireland. She was sunk in that area on 30 January at 4837N, 0746W, by HMS *Fowey* (Cdr H.B. Ellison), HMS *Whitshed*, (Cdr E.R. Condor), the French destroyer *Valmy*, and RAF Sunderland 'Y', N9025 of 228 Squadron (pilot F/O Edward J. Brooks), based at Pembroke Docks. *U-55* was first depth-charged by HMS *Fowey*, and after surfacing was attacked by the Sunderland, which brought in HMS *Whitshed* and the French destroyer *Valmy*. *U-55* had been damaged, and was unable to dive. When these vessels opened fire, Heidel chose to scuttle *U-55*. All of the U-boat's crew survived, except for Heidel, and were picked up by HMS *Fowey*. The U-boat's log must have been lost, as no details of her activities during her one and only patrol have survived.

U-55 had to pass around the north east of Scotland en route to her designated operating area, and it was obviously considered that she may have been in the Moray Firth area on 21 January, as that same day, according to Dr Rohwer, she is said to have torpedoed the 1,387-grt Norwegian motorship *Segovia* off the Moray Firth. (This is questionable, however, as according to *Lloyds War Losses, Volume 2*, the *Segovia* left Oporto on 17 January for Oslo. She was in the Bay of Biscay on 20 January, and in the latitude of Lands End on 23 January.)

It had also been thought that *U-55* torpedoed the Danish steamship *Tekla* on the 21st at 5818N, 0225W, which is off the Moray Firth, about 40 miles NNW of Kinnaird Head.

The German records show that the U-boats operating in the Moray Firth area during that time were the *U-9*, *U-18*, *U-22*, *U-57* and *U-61*, and *Tekla* is now believed to have been sunk by the *U-22*.

Why was the *Andalusia* thought to have been in that area at the time?

If she had sailed via the Straits of Dover and up the North Sea, she should by that time have been in the eastern area of the North Sea, approaching her destination, and several hundred miles from the Moray Firth.

On the other hand, the most direct route was not a practical proposition during the war, and she was forced to take a more circuitous route around the west and north of Britain.

In *Lloyds War Losses, Vol.2*, page 1275, in the Remarks column, against the *Segovia*, it says:

Wreckage passed on Jan 27 in 5830N, 0800W. Jan 28 in 5757N, 0843W.
Feb 10 & 11 in 5920N, 1514W to 5929N, 1310W.

(It was not the *Segovia* which passed this wreckage, but other vessels which reported passing wreckage in these positions, and some of this wreckage was assumed to possibly have been from the *Segovia*.)

This strongly suggests to me that the *Segovia* was known to have been heading from Oporto to Oslo by a route around the west and north of Britain, rather than through the Straits of Dover, and according to *det Norske Veritas*, *Segovia* is believed to have been torpedoed off the west coast of Scotland on 21 January 1940.

As the *Andalusia* left Verdon, near Bordeaux, on the same day as the *Segovia* sailed from Oporto, they were presumably sailing very similar routes, especially after passing Lands End.

One of the vessels was Swedish, the other Norwegian – both neutral countries at that time.

These vessels must have been sailing alone, rather than in convoy, and both disappeared without trace at around the same time. The most likely explanation for their disappearance was that they were torpedoed.

U-55 might well have encountered both the *Andalusia* and the *Segovia* while en route to the south of Ireland, but particularly as the *Segovia* was in the latitude of Lands End on 23 January, it seems to me that any such encounter is likely to have taken place after *U-55* had rounded Cape Wrath. It might therefore be possible that some of the wreckage found could indeed have been from the *Segovia*, and other wreckage perhaps from the *Andalusia*.

All this leads me to think that there is something not quite right about Dr Rohwer's suppositions, and that neither the *Andalusia* nor the *Segovia* was sunk anywhere near the North Sea, let alone the Moray Firth!

According to *Vrakliggare 1982* (Wreck Register 1982), published in Stockholm, *Andalusia* is believed to have been torpedoed NW of Ireland.

U-55 did not return from her patrol, and as no other U-boat claimed to have sunk them, by a process of elimination, *U-55* seems the most likely candidate for having done so.

Why did Dr Rohwer think *U-55* was in the Moray Firth area on the 21st?

I suspect the rationale for thinking that she may have been there on the 21st arose from an attempt to account for the sinking of the *Tekla* in that area on that day.

This sinking was originally attributed to *U-55*, but on further consideration, it is now believed that the *Tekla* was sunk by the *U-22*, which was operating in the Moray Firth area.

Having originally attributed the sinking of the *Tekla* in the Moray Firth on the 21st to the *U-55*, however, and presuming that the *Andalusia* and the *Segovia*, both of which were thought to have been sunk that day, were also sunk by the *U-55*, it logically follows that they must also have been in the Moray Firth area at that time!

It would seem that the only reason *U-55* was thought possibly to have been in the Moray Firth that day was the original attribution to her of sinking the *Tekla* in that area.

With that now being discounted, there is no longer any reason to place *U-55* there on that day.

As she left Kiel on the 16th, she should have been well past the Moray Firth five days later, and possibly even past Cape Wrath by then. As all U-boats were instructed to pass through the Fair Isle Channel rather than the Pentland Firth, it is unlikely *U-55* was ever in the Moray Firth area.

In the revised edition of *Axis Submarine Successes* the entries for *Andalusia* and *Segovia* have been altered to reflect the above.

The Swedish steamship Andalusia *(Photo: Tomas Johanneson collection)*

SLEIPNER

Wreck No: 264	Date Sunk: 15 02 1940
Latitude: 58 18 00 N PA	Longitude: 01 46 00 W PA
GPS Lat: 5818.000 N	GPS Long: 0146.000 W
Location: 50 miles NE of Rattray Head	Area: Wick
Type: Steamship	Tonnage: 1066 grt
Length: 231.2 ft Beam: 35.1 ft	Draught: ft
How Sunk: Torpedoed by *U-14*	Depth: 85 metres

The Danish steamship Sleipner *(ex-*Trondheim*) (Photo: Danmarks Handelsflaade 1939)*

RHONE

Wreck No: 265		Date Sunk: 15 02 1940
Latitude: 58 18 00 N PA		Longitude: 01 46 00 W PA
GPS Lat: 5818.000 N		GPS Long: 0146.000 W
Location:		Area: Wick
Type: Steamship		Tonnage: 1064 grt
Length: 237.1 ft	Beam: 35.6 ft	Draught: 21.6 ft
How Sunk: Torpedoed by *U-14*		Depth: 85 metres

The Danish steamships *Sleipner* and *Rhone* were sailing together from Methil to Esbjerg when they were torpedoed by the *U-14* (OL Herbert Wolfarth) on 15 February 1940, 50 miles north of Rattray Head. The German grid position was given as AN1699, which equates to about 5815N, 0124W, but the position has also been recorded as 5816N, 0143W PA, or 5818N, 0146W PA.

Both vessels were carrying cargoes of coal. *Sleipner* also had eighteen passengers. These were Greek seamen on their way to join a ship in Denmark. *Rhone* was attacked first, just before midnight on the 15th, and sank in two minutes. All twenty on board had to swim for it. *Sleipner* stopped immediately and lowered her three lifeboats to pick up survivors from the *Rhone*. She also sent out a distress message. Five minutes after midnight, she too was torpedoed. There was a violent explosion in her bow. The crew and passengers boarded the lifeboats, and about ten minutes later *Sleipner* sank in an upright position. Three of *Sleipner*'s boats rescued her own crew and thirteen survivors from the *Rhone*. One of these boats disappeared in the dark. The other two boats containing nineteen and twenty survivors, including eleven from the *Rhone* (two of *Rhone*'s crew perished in the lifeboat, and were left on a raft), were found 9 hours later by the Swedish fishing boat *Standard,* which took them the 35 miles to Wick. The missing third boat was found after about 12 hours, and its occupants rescued by HMS *Kipling.* Seven of *Sleipner*'s twenty-three crew and six of her eighteen passengers were lost. Nine of *Rhone*'s crew were lost. HMS *Eclipse* picked up the raft and the two bodies from *Rhone* in 5840N 0105W on 19th. *Sleipner* and *Rhone* were both built in 1915.

MAKALLA ?

Wreck No: 266	Date Sunk: 23 08 1940
Latitude: 58 20 16 N	Longitude: 02 39 58 W
GPS Lat: 5820.267 N	GPS Long: 0239.967 W
Location: 13 miles SE of Noss Head	Area: Wick
Type: Steamship	Tonnage: 6,677 grt
Length: 445.0 ft Beam: 58.2 f	Draught: 31.2 ft
How Sunk: Bombed	Depth: 59 metres

A large dispersed wreck was found here in 1985. The wreck appeared to be about 60 metres long, standing up about 11 metres from the bottom. Least depth is 48 metres in a general depth of 59 metres.

The Brocklebank steamship *Makalla* was built in 1918. While in convoy OA203 from London to Durban, Colombo and Calcutta, via Methil, with 2,500 tons of general cargo, she was attacked and sunk by German Heinkel aircraft based at Stavanger, at about 10.00 p.m. on 23 August 1940.

The position has been recorded as 5817N, 0227W, but her master gave the position as 5816N, 0236W. In addition, the Hydrographic Department has also referred to 5818N, 0246W PA in connection with the *Makalla*.

The first two bombs were near misses, but the second two hit the ship abaft No.4 hold and the funnel, causing a great amount of smoke. The ship shook violently, and the deck cargo caught fire immediately, the flames reaching as high as the cross trees.

The ship was abandoned in six boats and a liferaft.

Twelve of the crew of eighty-four were lost when one of the boats capsized on lowering, and the occupants were thrown into the water. As the boat with the captain, chief officer and two other men drifted along the port side of the *Makalla*, they saw a huge hole in the ship's side, which the captain thought likely to have been caused by an aerial torpedo. The ship was soon lost to sight in the darkness. When last seen, she was listing to port at an angle of 20°.

The survivors were all picked up by HMS *Leith* and landed at Scapa Flow.

Makalla *(Photo: JMC)*

MARSTENEN

Wreck No: 267	Date Sunk: 30 08 1940
Latitude: 58 23 28 N	Longitude: 02 39 31 W
GPS Lat: 5823.467 N	GPS Long: 0239.517 W
Location: 13 miles SE of Noss Head	Area: Wick
Type: Steamship	Tonnage: 1,832 grt
Length: 267.3 ft Beam: 42.9 ft	Draught: 16.5 ft
How Sunk: Bombed	Depth: 58 metres

The Norwegian steamship *Marstenen* was attacked by aircraft while en route from St Johns, Newfoundland to Ridham Dock with a cargo of pulpwood. All of the crew were saved.

The position has been variously reported as 582300N, 023700W PA (Lloyds), 582000N, 023100W PA (Hydrographic Dept.), and 580000N, 023500W PA (*WW2 MSL*).

There is no wreck charted in, or close to, the last two positions given above, but the wreck charted at 582328N, 023931W in 58 metres is close to the position given by Lloyds.

A further possibility is the wreck at 582016N, 023958W, which is a large wreck about 60 metres long, and standing up 7 metres. Least depth is 48 metres in a general depth of 59 metres.

TRIDENT

Wreck No: 268	Date Sunk: 03 10 1974
Latitude: 58 20 26 N	Longitude: 02 39 22 W
GPS Lat: 5820.440 N	GPS Long: 0239.360 W
Location: 13 miles SE of Noss Head	Area: Wick
Type: Trawler (PD III)	Tonnage: 68 grt
Length: 85.0 ft Beam: ft	Draught: ft
How Sunk: Foundered	Depth: 60 metres

The steel MFV *Trident* of Peterhead foundered with the loss of all seven of her crew, 10½ – 12 miles SE of Duncansby Head while en route from Ayr to her home port on 3 October 1974.

She had been built by Tees Marine of Middlesbrough only 18 months previously.

The vessel had been fishing off the Isle of Man, and had landed her catch at Ayr. Leaving there in company with another Peterhead boat, the *Faithful II*, both vessels sailed together until *Faithful II* broke down about 9 miles SSE of Duncansby Head. The Fishery Protection vessel *Switha* passed her a roll of tape to repair a pipe which had burst in her engine room, and while this repair was being carried out, *Faithful II* was in radio contact with the *Trident*. By the time the repair to *Faithful II* had been completed, the *Trident* was seen on her radar about 5 miles ahead.

Faithful II continued to Peterhead, and seeing no sign of the *Trident* there, assumed she must have overtaken her, and that *Trident* would soon follow into the harbour. The *Trident*, however, failed to appear, and no radio contact could be made with the missing vessel.

A full scale sea and air search was launched, and up to 200 herring boxes and four herring baskets – three green and the other red – were found floating in an area 20 miles south of the *Trident's* last known position.

No wreckage was found despite a search by two *Shacklton* aircraft from Lossiemouth, a *Nimrod* aircraft from Kinloss, Wick and Macduff lifeboats, HMS *Switha* and fishing boats from several north east towns. Fishermen at Peterhead became increasingly convinced that the *Trident* must have been overwhelmed by a huge sea, and turned over.

The wreck was found in June 2001, lying on its starboard side on a sandy seabed at 60 metres. The hold contained blue plastic fish boxes, and even after 27 years blue paint was still visible on the hull, and white paint on the superstructure. The number on the bow was too encrusted to be legible, but the name TRIDENT was clearly visible on the stern.

MINSK

Wreck No: 269	Date Sunk: 19 03 1940
Latitude: 58 22 35 N	Longitude: 02 41 02 W
GPS Lat: 5822.583 N	GPS Long: 0241.033 W
Location: 13 miles SE of Wick	Area: Wick
Type: Steamship	Tonnage: 1,229 grt
Length: 252.0 ft Beam: 37.0 ft	Draught: 15.0 ft
How Sunk: Torpedoed by *U-19*	Depth: 60 metres

The Danish steamship *Minsk* was torpedoed by the *U-19* (Schepke), at 22.21 hrs on 19 March 1940 while en route from Manchester via Kirkwall to Esbjerg. She was hit in the engine room, and quickly lost way. She sank in 5½ minutes, and eleven of her twenty crew were lost.

Axis Submarine Successes gives the German grid position as AN1680.

Lloyds War Losses and the Hydrographic Department both give the position as 5807N, 0239W PA.

The Danish steamship Minsk *(Photo: Danmarks Handelsflaade 1939)*

CHARKOW

Wreck No: 270	Date Sunk: 19 03 1940
Latitude: 58 24 12 N	Longitude: 02 42 11 W
GPS Lat: 5824.200 N	GPS Long: 0242.183 W
Location: 12 miles ESE of Wick	Area: Wick
Type: Steamship	Tonnage: 1,026 grt
Length: 236.0 ft Beam: 36.0 ft	Draught: 21.0 ft
How Sunk: Torpedoed by *U-19*	Depth: 68 metres

The Danish DFDS steamship *Charkow* was built in 1913 by Helsingors Jernskibs.

She left Kirkwall, in ballast, on 19 March 1940, bound for Methil and Esbjerg, and disappeared. A raft with the body of one member of her crew was found some days later, and wreckage was recovered near Fraserburgh. The vessel was finally posted missing on 29 May.

It was only after the war that it was learned that she had been torpedoed by the *U-19* (KL Joachim Schepke), at 22.37 hrs on 19 March 1940, with the loss of the entire crew. *Charkow* was hit in the engine room, and sank quickly by the stern. She hung vertically for a short time with her bow in the air, before sinking within four minutes.

Axis Submarine Successes gives the German grid position as AN1680, and the Allied estimate of her position as 5807N, 0239W. This was the position Lloyds gave for the *Minsk*, and I suspect this position was used also for the *Charkow* because these two ships were torpedoed only 16 minutes apart. The wrecks certainly cannot be very far apart, and two wrecks found fairly close together in this area are probably *Charkow* and *Minsk*.

The wreck lies 105/285°, with a least depth of 65 metres in a general depth of 68 metres.

The Danish steamship Charkow (*Photo: Danmarks Handelsflaade 1939*)

BOTHAL

Wreck No: 271	Date Sunk: 20 03 1940
Latitude: 58 25 12 N	Longitude: 02 27 40 W
GPS Lat: 5825.200 N	GPS Long: 0227.667 W
Location: 20 miles E of Wick	Area: Wick

Type: Steamship   Tonnage: 1,026 grt
Length: 275.0 ft   Beam: 41.0 ft   Draught: 18.0 ft
How Sunk: Torpedoed by *U-19*   Depth: 60 metres

The Danish steamship *Bothal* was built in 1920 by Ferguson Bros. En route from Frederikshaven to Blyth in ballast she was torpedoed by the *U-19* (Schepke), at 05.18 hrs on 20 March 1940, only 21 minutes after he had torpedoed the *Viking*. Both ships must therefore lie close to each other. The German grid reference was given as AN1680. Lloyds gave the position as 5808N, 0238W. All the lights on the ship went out when the torpedo exploded, and at the same time flames were seen extending from both sides of the quarterdeck. Almost instantaneously, a second explosion followed, and the *Bothal* broke in two. The two halves folded into each other and hung vertically for a few moments. The stern section sank almost immediately, and within 4 minutes, the bow section also sank. Some crewmembers who tried to save themselves on a raft on the foredeck were sucked down, along with the raft, when *Bothal* sank. The men taking to the raft heard the screams of the men trapped below. When the raft came up again five men saved themselves on it. Fifteen of the twenty crew were lost. Seven survivors (two from *Viking* and five from *Bothal*) were spotted by an aircraft which directed Wick lifeboat to the scene 20 hours after the sinkings. Four of the seven were injured.

The wreck in this position was found in 1986. It stands up about 5 metres from the seabed.

The Danish steamship Bothal (*Photo: Danmarks Handelsflaade 1939*)

VIKING

Wreck No: 272   Date Sunk: 20 03 1940
Latitude: 58 27 24 N   Longitude: 02 28 00 W
GPS Lat: 5827.400 N   GPS Long: 0228.000 W
Location: 20 miles E of Wick   Area: Wick
Type: Steamship   Tonnage: 1,153 grt
Length: 231.0 ft   Beam: 34.0 ft   Draught: 14.0 ft
How Sunk: Torpedoed by *U-19*   Depth: 60 metres

The Danish steamship *Viking* (built Flensburg in 1893) was en route from Frederikshaven to Blyth in ballast when she was torpedoed by *U-19* (KL Joachim Schepke), at 04.57 hrs on 20 March 1940. A violent explosion occurred in the forepart of the vessel. One minute later another explosion occurred amidships, after which the ship hung vertically in the water with the stern upwards. According to a Danish report the ship hung there for half an hour before sinking. Two crewmembers succeeded in saving themselves on a raft. Wick lifeboat picked them up at 13.30 hrs on the 21st. The other fourteen members of the sixteen-man crew were lost. The same U-boat sank the Danish vessel *Bothal* 21 minutes later. *Axis Submarine Successes* gives the position for both *Bothal* and *Viking* as 5821N, 0222W, while *Lloyds War Losses* gives 5808N, 0238W for both ships.

The German grid reference for the sinking of both vessels was given as AN1680, but this is only a very rough approximation, as no German grid square ends in zero. AN1681 equates to about 5827N, 0224W. Two wrecks fairly close together in that area are the *Viking* and the *Bothal*.

In fact the weather conditions in the area at the time were poor. Darkness, a heavy swell and rain severely curtailed visibility, and Schepke was uncertain about his position. At 02.40 hrs on 20 March he surfaced, loaded the torpedo tubes and ran to the west, towards the coast, in order to be in a position to intercept any steamers that might come through the Duncansby Head/Pentland Skerries gap, and to obtain a fix to check his position. Patrolling towards the east of that area, at 04.15 hrs he sighted the lights of two steamers sailing together. The steamships were gradually approaching *U-19*'s position on a zig-zag course. Watching the first steamer, he established its mean course as 240° towards the Moray Firth. On its zig-zag course, the second steamer was the first to come near *U-19*.

Schepke fired a torpedo which detonated after 46 seconds. The *Viking* was hit in the engine room, and stopped dead in the water. A second explosion occurred moments later – apparently a boiler explosion, producing a cloud of black smoke. According to Schepke's report the *Viking* hung vertically in the water before sinking in two minutes.

He then ran after the first steamer, and soon caught up, especially as it turned to run on a reciprocal course, apparently heading back towards the *Viking*, presumably to rescue any survivors.

The wreck here was found when the trawler *Antares* caught her gear in it in October 1979.

Local fishermen refer to this wreck as 'Valhalla', and use 5827.123N, 00227.755W.

The Danish steamship Viking *(ex-*Taygeta*) (Photo: Danish Maritime Museum, Kronborg)*

FREYA

Wreck No: 273	Date Sunk: 09 01 1959
Latitude: 58 21 12 N PA	Longitude: 03 04 24 W PA
GPS Lat: 5821.200 N	GPS Long: 0304.400 W
Location: 1½ miles E of Sarclet Head	Area: Wick
Type: Fishery Protection	Tonnage: 274 grt
Length: 157.1 ft Beam: 24.2 ft	Draught: ft
How Sunk: Foundered	Depth: 76 metres

The fishery protection vessel *Freya* had been anchored off Wick when a storm blew in from the east, and her anchor started to drag. Setting off in a southerly direction for Invergordon in increasingly heavy seas, she was struck on the port beam by three successive big waves which threw her over on her side and capsized her in rough seas before any radio distress call could be sent out. Some of the crew managed to board a liferaft which floated free as the vessel sank. They fired flares, which were seen by the Belgian trawler *St Jan Berchmans*. She picked up sixteen survivors, but three others were lost. The 17-year-old cabin boy, Ian Taylor of Leith, sang pop songs on the raft while waiting to be picked up.

According to Richard Larn, after she capsized the *Freya* drifted ashore in the Haven, north of Sarclet Head.

The Hydrographic Department gives the position as 582112N, 030424W, but it was assumed that the wreck charted at 582136N, 030124W at 67 metres must be the *Freya*.

This theory was shattered when the bell was recovered. It is engraved MORAY.

Perhaps *Freya* is the wreck at 582100N, 030630W, 1½ miles S of Sarclet Head in 42 metres.

MORAY

Wreck No: 274	Date Sunk: 17 11 1893
Latitude: 58 21 36 N	Longitude: 03 01 24 W
GPS Lat: 5821.600 N	GPS Long: 0301.400 W
Location: 5 miles S of Wick	Area: Wick
Type: Steamship	Tonnage: 438 grt
Length: 162.5 ft Beam: 24.1 ft	Draught: 10.5 ft
How Sunk: Foundered	Depth: 67 metres

The steel steamship *Moray* of Burghead was built by Grangemouth Dockyard Co. in 1889. She foundered with all hands during a storm of hurricane force on 17 November 1893, while en route from Sunderland to Burghead with a cargo of coal.

During the storm of 17–19 November 1893 almost fifty vessels were lost around Scotland, at least nine of them off the north-east of Scotland, including one small vessel (*Lillie*) in Sandend Bay.

Lots of wreckage was washed ashore at Sandend, including two steering wheels, port and starboard light boxes, deck fittings and cabin furniture. Much wreckage was later cast ashore on the Moray coast – that found at Portsoy was assumed to be from the *Moray*; she was the most significant vessel reported lost, and thought to be in the area as she was bound for Burghead from Sunderland.

On the 17th the wind was NW 11, veered NNE 12 by the 18th and dropped to Force 7 on the 19th.

Given the weather conditions on the 17th, after rounding Rattray Head the *Moray* would probably have kept her head towards the huge seas, to seek shelter from the violent NW storm in the lee of the Caithness coast. Turning to port to head for Burghead would not have been a viable option, as she would then have the violent seas bearing down on her starboard beam, rendering her liable to be capsized. As the wind veered NNE and increased to hurricane force 12 she would have been at the mercy of mountainous seas running down from the Arctic.

The wreckage that was washed ashore at Sandend, and assumed to be from the *Moray*, must actually have come from one or more of the other vessels that were lost. In August 2000 divers who thought they were diving the *Freya* off Wick found themselves on the wreck of a much older steamship, and recovered a bell engraved MORAY, and this is the only vessel named *Moray* recorded as lost in the Moray area.

The divers all commented on how badly corroded the metalwork of the wreck was for a ship that sank in the 1950s. Back on the surface the bell didn't initially reveal a name due to the covering of encrusted dirt, but after cleaning, the name MORAY was uncovered. The records show no ships of that name lost off Wick, but this wreck is the right size, and must be the same *Moray* as that believed lost between Buckie and Portsoy on the Moray Coast in a NW force 11 storm in 1983, almost 50 miles from the wreck's position.

The bell of the Moray *(Photo: Courtesy of John Leigh)*

SCORPIO

Wreck No: 275		Date Sunk: 27 09 1907	
Latitude: 58 22 26 N		Longitude: 03 05 36 W	
GPS Lat: 5822.433 N		GPS Long: 0305.600 W	
Location: Sarclet Head		Area: Wick	
Type: Trawler		Tonnage: 145 grt	
Length: 102.3 ft	Beam: 19.8 ft	Draught: 9.9 ft	
How Sunk: Ran aground		Depth: metres	

The iron-hulled steam trawler *Scorpio* ran aground on Sarclet Head, about three miles south of Wick, on 27 September 1907.

REIN

Wreck No: 276	Date Sunk: 13 04 1937
Latitude: 58 24 15 N PA	Longitude: 03 05 00 W PA
GPS Lat: 5824.250 N	GPS Long: 0305.000 W
Location: Helman Head, 2 miles S of Wick	Area: Wick
Type: Steamship	Tonnage: 1,157 grt
Length: 241.2 ft Beam: 35.3 ft	Draught: 14.7 ft
How Sunk: Ran aground	Depth: 15 metres

On 13 April 1937 the Norwegian steamship *Rein* was heading north towards the Pentland Firth when she ran ashore in fog and darkness on Helman Head, south of Wick. She grounded at the foot of the cliff, and her distress flares were not seen on shore, but they were spotted by the local fishing boat *Smiling Morn*, which approached as close as the rocks would allow, and stood by to pick up the crew, who left the stranded vessel in their two small boats. In the dawn light the crew reboarded the stricken vessel to salvage their belongings before again being taken off by the *Smiling Morn* and landed at Wick. By the next high tide, the *Rein* was submerged, and the broken remains now lie in 15 metres of water. Her builder's plate was recovered in 1995, and is on display at the Wick Society Heritage Centre (Framnaes Mek Vaerks., Sandefjord).

The Rein *aground at Helman Head. (Photo: author's collection)*

BERRIEDALE

Wreck No: 277	Date Sunk: 19 05 1943
Latitude: 58 19 00 N PA	Longitude: 02 59 00 W PA
GPS Lat: 5819.000 N	GPS Long: 0259.000 W
Location: 7 miles SSE of Wick	Area: Wick
Type: Steamship	Tonnage: 614 grt
Length: 168.3 ft Beam: 26.4 ft	Draught: 14.0 ft
How Sunk: Foundered	Depth: metres

The 614-grt steamship *Berriedale* (ex-*Almascos*, ex-*Royal Regis*) was built in 1922. She foundered 7 miles SSE of Wick on 19 May 1943, while carrying a cargo of coal from Blyth to Stornoway.

GARDAR ?

Wreck No: 278	Date Sunk: 21 05 1943
Latitude: 58 32 28 N	Longitude: 02 52 14 W
GPS Lat: 5832.467 N	GPS Long: 0252.233 W
Location: 6½ mile NE of Noss Head	Area: Wick
Type: Trawler	Tonnage: 462 grt
Length: ft Beam: ft	Draught: ft
How Sunk: Collision with *Miguel de Larrinaga*	Depth: 56 metres

The Icelandic trawler *Gardar* (GK25) was built by Smiths Dock, Middlesbrough in 1930.

While en route from Iceland to Hull with fish she was sunk in collision with the Liverpool steamship *Miguel de Larrinaga*, in dense fog at 13.00 hrs on 21 May 1943.

The *Miguel de Larrinaga* was proceeding north in convoy EN31. She was the fourth ship in the port column, and the convoy speed had been reduced to 7½ knots because of the fog.

The trawler's speed was estimated at about 10 knots, and she sank within minutes. Three of her crew were lost, but ten were picked up by the *Miguel de Larrinaga*. They were transferred to the Grimsby trawler *Belldock*, which was nearby, and she landed them at Aberdeen.

The collision position given in the convoy records was 5832N, 0246W, but this was probably a dead-reckoning position, as it was thick fog at the time, and none of the vessels in the area had radar to get a fix on Duncansby Head or the Pentland Skerries.

There is no wreck charted in that position. The nearest unidentified charted wreck is at 583228N, 025214W. The wreck here lies 000/180° and is 50 metres long x 11 metres beam, and stands up 7.2 metres from the seabed at 64 metres. It may be the *Gardar*.

Miguel de Larringa apparently also rammed another ship near Scotland only a few days before.

SOUND FISHER

Wreck No: 279	Date Sunk: 13 01 1957
Latitude: 58 24 30 N	Longitude: 02 56 50 W
GPS Lat: 5824.500 N	GPS Long: 0256.833 W
Location: 4 miles ESE of Wick	Area: Wick
Type: Steamship	Tonnage: 1,130 grt
Length: 226.0 ft Beam: 34.0 ft	Draught: 14.0 ft
How Sunk: Foundered	Depth: 70 metres

The steamship *Sound Fisher* had left Lyness with a cargo of scrap recovered from the German fleet, and was bound for Ghent. Not long after sailing the cargo shifted and she developed a list which increased until the port rail was awash. Distress flares were fired and an SOS transmitted. This was heard by the Aberdeen trawlers *Woodbine* and *Dulcibelle* fishing nearby. Before dawn the port lifeboat was launched in a choppy sea, but it was crushed between the ship's side and the *Woodbine*. When the Captain climbed in to try to free the boat it was swept away with seven men in it. They were picked up by the *Dulcibelle* and landed at Aberdeen. Meanwhile, the *Woodbine* had rigged a breeches buoy to the stern of the *Sound Fisher* and had taken off six men, a seventh jumping on to the trawler's bow. The *Sound Fisher* sank five hours after being abandoned four miles ESE of Wick. The position of sinking has been variously described as 8 miles E of Noss Head, 5.4 miles 120° from Noss Head, and 4 miles ESE of Wick, while the Hydrographic Department gives the position as 582557N, 025400W PA. The *Sound Fisher* is the wreck charted 4 miles ESE of Wick at 582430N, 025650W (49 metres in a total depth of about 65 metres), although the real depth is 70 metres.

Sound Fisher *(ex-*Benveg, *ex-*Polperro*) (Photo: author's collection)*

ST NICHOLAS and EMS

Wreck No: 280	Date Sunk: 17 06 1914
Latitude: 58 26 15 N	Longitude: 03 03 30 W
GPS Lat: 5826.250 N	GPS Long: 0303.500 W
Location: Proudfoot Rocks, North Head, Wick	Area: Wick
Type: Steamship	Tonnage: 787 grt
Length: 228.0 ft Beam: 27.0 ft	Draught: 15.4 ft
How Sunk: Ran aground	Depth: 22 metres

The iron steamship *St Nicholas*, built in 1877, ran aground in fog on Proudfoot Rocks while en route from Scrabster to Wick. She slipped off the rocks six hours after stranding, and sank in 22 metres.

The wreckage of several other vessels also lies at the Proudfoot Rocks, including the 158-grt iron steamship *Ems*, which had just left Wick en route to Stettin with a cargo of fish when she ran on to the Proudfoot Rocks on 18 July 1882.

THE EMPEROR

Wreck No: 281	Date Sunk: 12 09 1940
Latitude: 58 31 06 N	Longitude: 02 49 20 W
GPS Lat: 5831.100 N	GPS Long: 0249.333 W

Location: 10 miles SE of Duncansby Head | Area: Wick
Type: Steamship | Tonnage: 824 grt
Length: 195.1 ft | Beam: 30.3 ft | Draught: 12.1 ft
How Sunk: Collision with HMS *Saon* | Depth: 69 metres

At 02.20 hrs on 12 September 1940 the 824-grt steamship *The Emperor*, in convoy EN5, collided with the escorting HMS *Saon* 10 miles S by E ¾E from Duncansby Head, in 5836N, 0255W. *The Emperor* sank and her master was lost. HMS *Saon* picked up the rest of her crew.

The Emperor was carrying a cargo of cement clinker from London to Glasgow. She was built by the Ailsa Shipbuilding Co. of Troon in 1930, and owned by J. Hay & Sons of Glasgow.

The wreck here is a 60-metre long x 12-metre beam 3-island vessel lying upright, 160/340°.

OLIVE LEAF

Wreck No: 282 | Date Sunk: 16 01 1974
Latitude: 58 26 24 N | Longitude: 03 02 48 W
GPS Lat: 5826.400 N | GPS Long: 0302.800 W
Location: North Head, Wick | Area: Wick
Type: MFV | Tonnage: 52 grt
Length: ft | Beam: ft | Draught: ft
How Sunk: Ran aground | Depth: metres

The Lossiemouth fishing boat *Olive Leaf* stranded on the rocks at North Head, at the entrance to Wick Bay, about a mile from Wick on 16 January 1974.

She had been on her way into the harbour when she grounded on a spur of Proudfoot Rocks. The crew of four were taken off by the Wick fishing boat *Boy Andrew* which also tried, unsuccessfully, to tow the *Olive Leaf* off the rocks.

The following day, *Boy Andrew* and two other Wick boats, the *Good Hope* and the *Avalon*, tried again, but the *Olive Leaf* was hard aground and listing heavily to port. A third attempt was made at high water the next day, and this time she was towed off, but sank at 582624N, 030248W.

ISLEFORD

Wreck No: 283 | Date Sunk: 25 01 1942
Latitude: 58 26 29 N | Longitude: 03 03 47 W
GPS Lat: 5826.483 N | GPS Long: 0303.783 W
Location: 74°, 4¾ cables S Pier Light | Area: Wick
Type: Steamship | Tonnage: 423 grt
Length: 150.0 ft | Beam: 26.4 ft | Draught: ft
How Sunk: Ran aground | Depth: 12-17 metres

The munitions carrier *Isleford* was lost near Wick on 25 January 1942. She was blown ashore in a gale on the north side of Wick Bay, while en route from Scapa Flow to Invergordon with a cargo of ammunition. Wick lifeboat could not be launched due to the heavy seas, and Cromarty lifeboat was called. Wick LSA fired four rockets with lines, but the crew were unable to hold and fix them, and all fifteen of them were lost. The vessel broke in two and foundered.

The wreck is scattered over a fairly wide area in 12-17 metres.

As far as is known, the ammunition has yet to be found, but perhaps most of it has been removed. The Royal Navy inspects the wreck from time to time to make sure there is no danger of explosion.

DROMARA

Wreck No: 284	Date Sunk: 14 02 1941
Latitude: 58 25 00 N PA	Longitude: 03 05 15 W PA
GPS Lat: 5826.500 N	GPS Long: 0305.250 W
Location: Brig o'Trams, Wick	Area: Wick
Type: Steamship	Tonnage: 723 grt
Length: 181.0 ft Beam: 30.7 ft	Draught: 13.5 ft
How Sunk: Ran aground	Depth: 15 metres

The Belfast steamship *Dromara* was en route from Londonderry to London on 14 February 1941 when her cargo of bog-ore shifted, causing a severe list. The vessel was abandoned eight miles E by N of Wick, and Wick lifeboat rescued the crew of thirteen. According to Lloyds, the *Dromara* drifted ashore at the Old Man of Wick.

The Hydrographic Department recorded her at 582630N, 030330W, but the remains of the *Dromara* have been found at Gote o' Tram, about one mile south of South Head, Wick.

This location is known as 'Brig o' Trams' ('Gote o' Tram' on the Ordnance Survey map).

The 'Brig' is a sea stack which is joined to the mainland at the top.

The wreckage is fairly well spread out in about 15 metres of water. The two boilers are still intact, along with much of the triple expansion engine.

There is no slip at Wick, but boats can be launched at Staxigoe Harbour.

CARENCY

Wreck No: 285	Date Sunk: 28 06 1957
Latitude: 58 27 10 N	Longitude: 03 03 05 W PA
GPS Lat: 5827.167 N	GPS Long: 0303.083 W
Location: Greenigoe, 1 mile N of Wick	Area: Wick
Type: Trawler	Tonnage: 233 grt
Length: ft Beam: ft	Draught: ft
How Sunk: Ran aground	Depth: 6 metres

The Aberdeen-registered steam trawler *Carency* was built in 1919 by Cook Welton & Gemmell of Beverley. She ran aground in fog a mile north of Wick at Greenigoe, Broadhaven, on 28 June 1957.

Wick LSA arrived and succeeded in putting a line aboard the stranded vessel while the Wick lifeboat stood by. The crew did not take the opportunity to leave immediately, as they were of the opinion that their vessel might be saved, and preferred to await the arrival of another trawler, the *Gilmar*.

When she arrived, a towline was attached, and Wick lifeboat took off the thirteen crew and transferred the *Carency*'s skipper to the *Gilmar*, which was only able to move the *Carency* about twenty feet before she stuck on the rocks again, finally rolling over and sinking.

The wreck lies in 6 metres of water, and is in a very broken state. The boiler, steam engine, and various other items such as her cast iron propeller, rudder, winch and sections of hull plating, are still there. Again, due to the shallow depth, the remains tend to be covered in a thick layer of kelp during the summer months, but are relatively weed-free in the winter months.

SWORD DANCE

Wreck No: 286
Latitude: 58 28 21 N
GPS Lat: 5828.350 N
Location: 10 miles E by S ¼S of Noss Head
Type: Trawler
Length: 160.5 ft   Beam: 27.5 ft
How Sunk: Collision

Date Sunk: 05 07 1942
Longitude: 02 42 50 W
GPS Long: 0242.833 W
Area: Wick
Tonnage: 530 grt
Draught: 10.5 ft
Depth: 70 metres

HMS *Sword Dance* was built by Henry Robb of Leith in 1940 as a minesweeper for the Royal Navy, but was almost exclusively employed on escort work with coastal convoys. In the early morning of 5 July 1942, while escorting an eastbound convoy, she was rammed in dense fog by one of the merchant ships. She was holed in the starboard coal bunker. Her boiler and engine rooms immediately flooded, and she sank in less than an hour. Another escort vessel rescued all of the crew. One report describes the position of her loss as 'off the north east of Scotland'. Another says 'in the Moray Firth'. The Hydrographic Department recorded the position as 582812N, 024300W PA, but the wreck is now charted at 582821N, 024250W in a depth of 70 metres. The wreck is oriented 110/290°.

PITSTRUAN

Wreck No: 287
Latitude: 58 27 55 N
GPS Lat: 5827.917 N
Location: 2 miles SE of Noss Head
Type: Trawler
Length: 115.4 ft   Beam: 22.1 ft
How Sunk: Mined

Date Sunk: 13 04 1917
Longitude: 02 59 29 W
GPS Long: 0259.483 W
Area: Wick
Tonnage: 206 grt
Draught: 12.0 ft
Depth: 51metres

The steel steam trawler *Pitstruan* was built in 1913 by A. Hall, Aberdeen.

While she was in Admiralty service as a minesweeper, escorting a fishing boat about two miles south-east of Noss Head, two mines were spotted floating on the surface. The crew were all on deck looking out for any more floating mines when she struck a moored mine and sank immediately. The drifter *Lapwing* picked up two injured survivors and landed them at Wick.

The wreck is an armed steam trawler, well smashed up and broken in two, lying on a sandy seabed. The bow section has been flattened. A small gun lies adjacent to the boiler. Aft of the boiler is a tangle of engine remains and condenser tubes, then the stern section. The wreck rises 4 metres from the bottom.

JEAN STEPHEN

Wreck No: 288	Date Sunk: 18 01 1958
Latitude: 58 30 00 N PA	Longitude: 03 07 30 W PA
GPS Lat: 5830.000 N	GPS Long: 0307.500 W
Location: Sinclairs Bay	Area: Wick
Type: Trawler	Tonnage: 212 grt
Length: 115.0 ft Beam: 22.0 ft	Draught: 12.9 ft
How Sunk: Ran aground	Depth: metres

Jean Stephen (ex-*Savitrie*) was built in 1917 by A. Hall & Co., Aberdeen, and was immediately requisitioned by the Admiralty for use as a minelayer and minesweeper. It was only after the war that she was able to be used for her original intended purpose as a fishing trawler.

On 18 January 1958 she was sheltering in Sinclairs Bay in company with several other trawlers, and was just preparing to leave when a blizzard struck, blowing her ashore on the beach.

Wick lifeboat and LSA crew were called, and while the lifeboat stood by a little way off, the crew were taken ashore by breeches buoy.

UNKNOWN

Wreck No: 289	Date Sunk:
Latitude: 58 29 18 N	Longitude: 02 48 20 W
GPS Lat: 5829.300 N	GPS Long: 0248.333 W
Location: 11½ miles SE of Duncansby Head	Area: Wick
Type:	Tonnage: grt
Length: ft Beam: ft	Draught: ft
How Sunk:	Depth: 65 metres

The wreck in this position was found in 1986.

CLAN MACKINLAY

Wreck No: 290	Date Sunk: 06 11 1940
Latitude: 58 32 05 N	Longitude: 02 53 00 W
GPS Lat: 5832.083 N	GPS Long: 0253.000 W
Location: 6 miles NE of Noss Head	Area: Wick
Type: Steamship	Tonnage: 6,365 grt
Length: 420.0 ft Beam: 54.5 ft	Draught: 34.0 ft
How Sunk: Bombed	Depth: 53 metres

The 6,365-grt British steamship *Clan Macinlay* was built in 1918 by W. Hamilton & Co. She was the Commodore ship in convoy WN31. Lt Cdr H. Nicholas was the convoy commodore. The vessel was bombed and set on fire by a German aircraft on

6 November 1940 while en route from Bombay to London with 5,960 tons of general cargo.

The position of attack was given as 583500N, 025300W, south east of the Pentland Firth, but despite being hit by three bombs at 18.15 hrs, she did not sink immediately. Efforts were made to take her towards land, but she eventually had to be abandoned 4¾ miles 52° from Noss Head. She capsized an hour later, and sank at 20.00 hrs in 583205N, 025300W, 6 miles NE of Noss Head. Five of the crew of eighty-two were lost. The wreck is covered in lost fishing nets.

STAR OF VICTORY

Wreck No: 291	Date Sunk: 24 10 1939
Latitude: 58 32 00 N PA	Longitude: 03 06 30 W PA
GPS Lat: 5832.000 N	GPS Long: 0306.500 W
Location: Keiss, near Wick	Area: Wick
Type: Trawler	Tonnage: 235 grt
Length: 120.0 ft Beam: 23.0 ft	Draught: 14.0 ft
How Sunk: Ran aground	Depth: metres

The Admiralty Strath-Class trawler *Star of Victory* was built by Duthies of Aberdeen as the *William Ashton*.

She was temporarily renamed *City of Perth* while on loan to the US Navy from 1919, but reverted to her original name when returned to civilian ownership. She operated out of Grimsby until 1929, when she was bought by the Walker Steam Trawl Fishing Co. Ltd, who renamed her *Star of Victory*. She was wrecked at Keiss, near Wick, on 24 October 1939. The position of the wreck was recorded in 1942 as 583100N, 030700W PA.

HASSETT

Wreck No: 292	Date Sunk: 18 09 1953
Latitude: 58 33 30 N PA	Longitude: 03 04 30 W PA
GPS Lat: 5833.500 N	GPS Long: 0304.500 W
Location: Ruff of Auckengill, Sinclairs Bay	Area: Wick
Type: Trawler	Tonnage: 349 grt
Length: 141.0 ft Beam: 24.6 ft	Draught: 133.2 ft
How Sunk: Ran aground	Depth: metres

While outward bound for the fishing grounds in heavy seas, the Grimsby trawler *Hassett* struck rocks at the Rough of Auckengill, Sinclairs Bay, in the early hours of 18 September 1953. She sent out a distress call, and Wick lifeboat and LSA team spent several hours searching for the stranded trawler. By the time they found her, five of the crew had been swept away and drowned while trying to get away in the ship's boat. The destroyer HMS *Scorpion* also picked up the SOS and sped to the scene, but the heavily-breaking seas forced her to stand by with the lifeboat some distance offshore.

The LSA team on the shore succeeded in firing two lines aboard the stranded trawler, but they were out of reach of the crew, who had taken refuge in the wheelhouse to avoid being swept overboard. A third line fired aboard was near enough to be grabbed, and fifteen survivors were hauled ashore by daybreak. The lifeboat picked up one body from the sea, and three more bodies were washed ashore. The fifth body was never found.

According to the Hydrographic Department, who attribute the information to *Lloyds List*, the vessel was reported to be breaking up in 1953 at 582845N, 030245W. As this position is near the lighthouse at Noss Head, some seven miles south of Auckengill, it suggests that the true location may have been the Rough of Ackergill.

Hassett (ex-*Runswick Bay*, ex-*Gambri*) was built by Cook Welton & Gemmell in 1929.

V-81

Wreck No: 293	Date Sunk: 21 06 1919
Latitude: 58 33 40 N PA	Longitude: 03 05 00 W PA
GPS Lat: 5833.666 N	GPS Long: 0305.000 W
Location: Sinclairs Bay	Area: Wick
Type: Destroyer (German)	Tonnage: 1,188 tons
Length: 269.0 ft Beam: 24.0 ft	Draught: ft
How Sunk: Foundered	Depth: 8 metres

The German destroyer *V-81* was scuttled in Scapa Flow on 21 June 1919. She was subsequently raised, and was being towed to the Forth for breaking up when she broke free and foundered in Sinclairs Bay on 20 September 1937. The Hydrographic Department recorded the position of foundering as 583000N, 030500W PA, but the wreck lies about three miles further north, in 8 metres of water to the south of Buchollie Castle. She was later sold for scrap, and all that remains are two steam turbines and what may be a generator, or possibly a gearbox. Underwater visibility here is usually in excess of 15 metres. Boats may be launched at Keiss or Staxigoe.

IMOGEN

Wreck No: 294	Date Sunk: 16 07 1940
Latitude: 58 34 13 N	Longitude: 02 56 09 W
GPS Lat: 5834.217 N	GPS Long: 0256.150 W
Location: 4 miles ESE of Freswick Bay	Area: Wick
Type: Destroyer	Tonnage: 1,370 tons
Length: 323.0 ft Beam: 32.0 ft	Draught: 8.5 ft
How Sunk: Collision with HMS *Glasgow*	Depth: 73 metres

This position is also 6½ miles NE of Noss Head.

The destroyer HMS *Imogen* was built by Hawthorne Leslie in 1936.

At 22.10 hrs on 16 July 1940, Force 'C', consisting of four cruisers – *Southampton, Sussex, Shropshire* and *Glasgow* – accompanied by eight destroyers – *Cossack, Sikh, Fortune, Fury, Inglefield, Imogen, Zulu* and *Maori* – were again approaching the Pentland Skerries, after having previously turned back because of fog. The cruisers were in single line ahead in close order, in the above sequence. The destroyers were also in line ahead, in two groups of four, and the groups were steaming parallel to each other, to starboard, and maintaining a position approximately one mile astern of the rear cruiser (*Glasgow*).

The destroyers had been ordered to take station astern, and conform generally to the movements of the cruisers, but their orders were insufficiently precise.

At 22.50 hrs, fog was again encountered, and the cruisers were ordered to turn 180° to port in succession. The destroyers executed their turns by flag signals. During the next hour, the cruisers ran in and out of fog banks, performed three more large alterations of course, and disappeared into a fog bank before the destroyers could conform to the last course change. At 23.55 hrs HMS *Glasgow* loomed out of the fog and struck HMS *Imogen* at an angle of about 45° on the port side of her foc'sle, just abaft 'A' gun. The ships met at about 30 knots, and HMS *Glasgow*'s stem cut into the side of the ship, and was deeply embedded in HMS *Imogen* by the .5-inch gun deck between her funnels. The ships remained locked in this position. Immediately on impact, an explosion and fire broke out on HMS *Imogen*. This was probably caused by the combustion of two 5-gallon drums of petrol which were stowed in the ready-use petrol rack situated at the break of the foc'sle, against the superstructure. The stem of HMS *Glasgow* came in contact with the 4.7-inch ready-use ammunition locker, clips from which were subsequently found on the foc'sle of HMS *Glasgow*. Just aft of this ready-use locker was a firework tank, and the ready-use petrol storage rack. Sparks were seen, caused by the collision, and the DG coil, which was live at the time, was also cut. There were, therefore, ample sources of ignition for the intense fire which started instantly, and spread into the fuel in the foremost tanks, then the oil fuel in Nos. 1 and 2 boiler rooms. Steam was lost immediately, and HMS *Imogen* was left with no fire-fighting capability. Prompt action was taken aboard HMS *Glasgow* by means of hoses to put out the fire aboard HMS *Imogen*, but to no avail.

Orders were given to abandon HMS *Imogen*, and this was carried out within 30 minutes by Carley float, the starboard whaler, and lines directly to HMS *Glasgow*. At least three members of HMS *Glasgow*'s crew boarded *Imogen* to ensure that no survivors remained, and one of them was lost.

Because of the danger of HMS *Imogen*'s fore magazine exploding, HMS *Glasgow* broke away as soon as possible after ten officers and 135 ratings had been transferred to HMS *Glasgow*.

Eighteen of *Imogen*'s crew were lost and nine injured. When last seen, HMS *Imogen* was burning fiercely. She later blew up and sank at about 5834N, 0254W PA.

According to a lifeboat report *Imogen* broke in two, and the after part drifted west with the ebb, north of Stroma, and sank about four miles WNW of Stroma Lighthouse with eighteen hands. (It is interesting to note that the Admiralty report in the PRO and the lifeboat report both agree that eighteen were lost.) Distress signals were repeatedly fired by gun and rocket, and aid was summoned by the Stroma Coastguards, but owing to fog and strong tides she was not located in time to save the crew.

STELLATUS

Wreck No: 295		Date Sunk: 03 03 1959
Latitude: 58 34 35 N PA		Longitude: 03 03 45 W PA
GPS Lat: 5834.583 N		GPS Long: 0303.750 W
Location: Just South of Buchollie Castle		Area: Wick
Type: Steamship		Tonnage: 1,827 grt
Length: 313.5 ft	Beam: 42.9 ft	Draught: 19.8 ft
How Sunk: Ran aground		Depth: metres

The Swedish steamer *Stellatus*, bound from Turku, Finland, to Ellesmere Port with a cargo of wood pulp, ran aground in fog just south of Buchollie Castle, Caithness on 3 March 1959. Wick lifeboat took the twenty-six crew off the ship, which was lying parallel to the shore with a slight list to starboard. A week later, she broke in two during a south-east gale, and the stern section sank.

The Stellatus *ashore near Buchollie Castle (Photo: D.Robertson, Wick)*

HESSEN

Wreck No: 296	Date Sunk: 25 06 1987
Latitude: 58 35 00 N	Longitude: 02 59 00 W
GPS Lat: 5835.000 N	GPS Long: 0259.000 W
Location: 2 miles SE of Skirza Head	Area: Wick
Type: Fish factory ship	Tonnage: 998 grt
Length: 240.4 ft Beam: 36.6 ft	Draught: 24.1 ft
How Sunk: Ran aground	Depth: 34 metres

At 8.00 p.m. on 25 June 1987 Wick Radio received a message from the West German stern-trawling fish factory ship *Hessen*, stating that she had water in her engine room, and was drifting with nineteen people on board. She was lowering her lifeboats, and asked for immediate assistance. The MFV *Shepherd Lad* was alongside. The aircraft carrier HMS *Ark Royal* reported at 8.20 that she was in the vicinity and had launched a helicopter with a water pump at 9.00 p.m. At the same time the passenger ferry *Pentland Venture* reported that she was proceeding to the casualty to stand by. In the meantime the *Shepherd Lad* took the sinking vessel in tow at 8.37 pm, but as the *Hessen* settled deeper into the sea, the trawler *Nordic Pride* began to take off her crew. Two helicopters from the *Ark Royal* assisted in the evacuation. One man was picked out of the sea by helicopter, while the Orkney lifeboat took the rest off the deck. The *Hessen* foundered at 9.40 p.m. None of the survivors were injured, and all were landed at John o' Groats. When the *Hessen* sank she still had 300 tons of diesel in her bunkers, but the valves were closed.

NAVARRE

Wreck No: 297	Date Sunk: 02 09 1939
Latitude: 58 35 50 N PA	Longitude: 03 02 30 W PA

GPS Lat: 5835.833 N

GPS Long: 0302.500 W

Location: Skirza Head, S of Duncansby Head

Area: Wick

Type: Trawler

Tonnage: 276 grt

Length: 126.3 ft

Beam: 23.5 ft   Draught: 12.7 ft

How Sunk: Ran aground

Depth: metres

The Grimsby trawler *Navarre* ran aground in dense fog at the foot of high cliffs on Skirza Head. Two other trawlers failed in an attempt to tow her off the rocks, and the vessel's small boat was washed away by the waves and smashed on the rocks. In the darkness, fog and heavy seas, Wick lifeboat succeeded in manoeuvring alongside and took off nine of the crew, shortly after the trawler's crew had fired a line ashore. The local lifesaving brigade brought the remaining two crew members ashore by means of this line.

Navarre (ex-*Cesar de Paepe*, ex-*John Davis*) was built in 1918 by Bow McLachlan of Paisley.

THYRA

Wreck No: 298

Date Sunk: 11 06 1914

Latitude: 58 37 45 N PA

Longitude: 03 02 00 PA

GPS Lat: 5837.750 N

GPS Long: 0302.000 W

Location: E side of Duncansby Head

Area: Wick

Type: Steamship

Tonnage: 3,742 grt

Length: 339.0 ft

Beam: 48.0 ft   Draught: 29.0 ft

How Sunk: Ran aground

Depth: 10 metres

On 11 June 1914 the steamship *Thyra* of Tonsberg ran aground on the Stacks of Duncansby while en route from Dundee to New York. The weather at the time was calm, and some of her cargo, which included pianos, spirits, lime juice, tea, star antimony and copper matte, was recovered, but the vessel itself was beyond recovery.

The Hydrographic Department gives the position as 583630N, 030118W PD.

The *Thyra* was built in 1899 by Osbourne, Graham & Co. of Sunderland.

GEORGE ROBB

Wreck No: 299

Date Sunk: 07 12 1959

Latitude: 58 37 30 N PA

Longitude: 03 02 00 W PA

GPS Lat: 5837.500 N

GPS Long: 0302.000 W

Location: Duncansby Head

Area: Wick

Type: Trawler

Tonnage: 217 grt

Length: 118.0 ft

Beam: 22.2 ft   Draught: 14.3 ft

How Sunk: Ran aground

Depth: metres

All twelve of the crew were lost when the Aberdeen trawler *George Robb* ran aground on the Stacks of Duncansby during a storm on 7 December 1959. Wick lifeboat could not be launched in the prevailing sea state, and the lifesaving crew had to search the shore on foot. The wind was so severe that huge sheets of spray from the breaking waves were being blown up and over the cliffs. By the time the *George Robb* was located in the beam of a searchlight, she was lying on her port side, totally submerged by the heavy seas. As there was no sign of survivors, nor any possibility of rendering assistance even if there had been, the lifesaving crew retired to the shelter of Duncansby Head lighthouse to wait until dawn to resume their search. One of the Wick coastguards collapsed and died on the cliffs while directing the search operation.

Only two bodies from the *George Robb*'s crew of twelve were washed ashore.

George Robb (ex-*Elise I. Carnie*) was built in 1930 by Hall Russell of Aberdeen. She was originally a steam trawler, but had been converted to diesel in 1959.

U-1020

Wreck No: 300	Date Sunk: 01 01 1945
Latitude: 58 38 08 N	Longitude: 02 46 11 W
GPS Lat: 5838.013 N	GPS Long: 0246.191 W
Location: SE of Sandy Riddle	Area: Wick
Type: Submarine	Tonnage: 173 grt
Length: ft Beam: ft	Draught: ft
How Sunk:	Depth: 65 metres

U-1020 was a type VIIC/41 U-boat of 769 tons surfaced, 871 tons submerged. Under the command of OL Otto Eberlein, she patrolled off the Pentland Firth from 7 December 1944 until the end of the month, but sighted no targets. On New Year's Eve, she headed south, and is thought to have been mined in the deep minefield outside the Moray Firth on, or shortly after, 1 January 1945. There were no survivors.

At 10.30 hrs on 11 January 1945, Liberator 'A' of 224 Sqdn spotted a 500-yard long smoke trail on the water north of Banff at 5748N, 0226W. A hydrophone transmitting buoy was dropped and churning noises were heard. The aircraft reported that it was investigating a suspicious object, possibly a schnorkel. The smoke vanished very rapidly, and the aircraft resumed its course, without making any attack on the suspected U-boat.

This might have been *U-1020*, but there has also been speculation that *U-1020* was sunk in an attack on 1 January 1945 by the R.N. destroyer HMS *Onslaught* and a Polish destroyer, off the Orkneys, and that several survivors were rescued by the Polish ship but that none were put ashore when the ship docked. The implication, of course, is that they ended up as fish food.

This rumour was published in 1998 in Peter Sharpe's *U-boat Fact File*, and it has also been the subject of discussion in U-boat forums on the Internet in 2000.

As far as I am aware, no corroborating evidence has ever been produced.

The rumour seems to have originated from a book entitled *Arctic Destroyers* by Gordon Connell, a wartime Royal Navy officer who wrote several books on the subject of destroyers. This book contains a reference to HMS *Onslaught* and an un-named Polish destroyer being involved in the sinking of a U-boat, and suggests that the Polish destroyer took aboard sixteen of the U-boat's crew, but never landed them.

Onslaught on patrol with a Polish destroyer found a U-boat by 'asdic' contact, and both destroyers delivered a series of coordinated attacks that drove the U-boat to the surface where her crew abandoned ship, at the same time scuttling their boat. The Pole picked up sixteen survivors and in company with *Onslaught* returned to Scapa Flow. As soon as his ship was at her berth in the destroyer trots, Gutta Sound, Pleydell-Bouverie sent his cutter with an escort over to the Allied destroyer to collect the U-boat prisoners of war. His men received a chilling but understandable response from the men whose country had been raped by the Nazi invasion, 'Oh yes we had sixteen U-boat crew men, we have tried them, they were found guilty before we entered harbour'. There were no prisoners to be collected.

The Naval Historical Branch endeavoured to investigate this claim in 1983, but could find nothing in naval records that might have a bearing on it, and concluded that the claim was entirely fictional.

This view was reinforced by Connell's failure to name either the Polish destroyer, or the U-boat, and nor did he give a position or a date for the alleged incident. Lt George Gordon Connell, DSC has since died. Was he writing from personal knowledge, or was this something he had heard about?

It was relatively easy to confirm that Cdr The Hon Anthony Pleydell-Bouverie was indeed in command of HMS *Onslaught* in late 1944 until at least 19 June 1945, when he was awarded the DSC. Some evidence relating to the alleged incident with the Polish destroyer should surely be found in *Onslaught*'s deck log. That logbook should be held in the Public Records Office at Kew, in the ADM53 series. It is not there. It has been destroyed! I wonder why?

Andrezej Bartelski's Polish Navy website confirms the identity of the Polish destroyer as ORP *Piorun*, but Bartelski merely says *U-1020* was sunk by *Piorun* and *Onslaught*, and that all the U-boat's crew were lost. He does not give details of the action and nor does he mention prisoners.

According to BdU's records, *U-1020* left Christiansand on 24 November to go to AF77 (NW of Shetland).

On 3 December, she was ordered to proceed via AN12 and AN14 to AN16, SE of S Ronaldsay.

On 30 December she was told she had a free hand to proceed to the Moray Firth, and was expected to arrive in AN1756 (i.e. 5745N, 0348W) on 1 January.

(Compare this with the report that a U-boat was sighted by Liberator 'A' of 224 Sqdn north of Banff at 5748N, 0226W at 10.30 hrs on 11 January 1945.)

BdU further instructed that if conditions in the Moray Firth proved unfavourable, she was to patrol off Aberdeen, but nothing was heard from *U-1020* after she left Christiansand.

These grid references show that *U-1020* was never intended to be west of Orkney at any time, and therefore she could not possibly have been responsible for the torpedoing of HMS *Zephyr* in 5857N, 0400W on 31 December, as given in *Axis Submarine Successes*. When the damage to HMS *Zephyr* was examined, it was not clear how it had been inflicted, and there was some doubt about whether it had been caused by a torpedo. A mine was considered the likely cause.

The wreck at 583808N, 024611W is known to local fishermen as 'The Submarine', and is possibly *U-1020*. This position is within grid square AN1645.

DARING

Wreck No: 301	Date Sunk: 18 02 1940
Latitude: 58 27 00 N PA	Longitude: 01 36 00 W PA
GPS Lat: 5827.000 N	GPS Long: 0136.000 W
Location: 50 miles E of Duncansby Head	Area: Wick
Type: Destroyer	Tonnage: 1,375 tons
Length: 326.0 ft Beam: 33.0 ft	Draught: 8.5 ft
How Sunk: Torpedoed by *U-23*	Depth: metres

The destroyer HMS *Daring* was built by Thorneycroft in 1932.

She was once commanded by Lord Louis Mountbatten, but at the time of her loss she was under the command of Cdr S.A. Cooper, escorting ships of convoy HN12 carrying iron ore from Bergen to Methil. Other escorting ships were HMS *Ilex* and HMS/M *Thistle* and HMS *Inglefield*.

The *Daring* broke in two and sank with the loss of 157 of the 162 aboard when she was torpedoed by *U-23* (KL Otto Kretschmer), about 50 miles east of Duncansby Head at 02.56 hrs on 18 February 1940. The ship turned bottom up in less than 30 seconds. When last seen about half an hour later, the ship was still afloat with the stern blown off, and floating vertically.

Daring was the first Royal Navy ship acknowledged to have been sunk by a U-boat torpedo in the Second World War. In an attempt to play down the menace of the U-boats, previous losses due to that cause had been attributed to the vessel possibly having struck a mine.

The German grid reference was given as AN1692, which equates to about 5827N, 0136W.

HMS/M *Thistle* estimated the position by Dead Reckoning as 5840N, 0140W.

A wreck charted at 582432N, 013612W at a depth of 106 metres might be HMS *Daring*.

NESSUS

Wreck No: 302	Date Sunk: 08 09 1918
Latitude: 58 33 00 N	Longitude: 02 12 45 W
GPS Lat: 5833.000 N	GPS Long: 0212.750 W
Location: 26 miles E of Noss Head	Area: Wick
Type: Destroyer	Tonnage: 1,025 tons
Length: 271.5 ft Beam: 26.7 ft	Draught: 10.2 ft
How Sunk: Collision with HMS *Amphitrite*	Depth: 75 metres

On the afternoon of 7 September 1918 the cruiser HMS *Amphitrite* (11,000 tons), which was acting as a minelayer, was being escorted back to her base at Rosyth by the destroyers HMS *Nessus* and *Maenad*. The destroyers were stationed about five cables on *Amphitrite*'s starboard and port bows respectively, and the convoy was zig-zagging at 16 knots on a mean course of S6°E. The sea was smooth, and the wind was S by E force 3–4. At 14.27 hrs the ships ran into fog, and *Amphitrite* signalled to the escorts 'I shall not zig-zag while it is as thick as this'.

At 14.45 the fog closed in and *Nessus* lost sight of *Amphitrite*. Five minutes later *Nessus* caught a brief glimpse of *Amphitrite* in the correct relative position, but almost immediately lost sight of her again. At 14.58 *Nessus* reduced speed to 11 knots and steadied ship on S15°E – an alteration of 9° towards *Amphitrite* – intending to drop astern of the cruiser. At about 15.01 *Nessus* again sighted *Amphitrite*, and found herself close to the cruiser's bow.

Amphitrite attempted to manoeuvre clear of *Nessus*, but at 15.03, the cruiser struck the destroyer on her port side amidships at a very slight angle. The position of the collision was 5832N, 0029W.

The main damage sustained by *Nessus* was a large hole in her after boiler room, which flooded. The bulkhead between engine room and boiler room was badly buckled and fractured, and water was leaking into the engine room. There was also a hole in the engine room, below the water line, her port side was dented in, and all rivets started in the ship's side in the engine room. Her warhead oil fuel tank was punctured, and an auxiliary steam pipe in the engine room was fractured. There was superficial damage all along the port side to the stern.

As soon as possible after the collision *Maenad* took *Nessus* in tow, and proceeded WNW at 6½–7 knots for Scapa. A message was sent asking for salvage tugs, and every effort was made to stop water coming into the ship. About three quarters of an hour after the collision, sufficient repairs had been made to work the pumps, and the water level in the engine room (about 6 feet) was kept level.

At 16.15 *Amphitrite* parted company and proceeded alone towards Rosyth, having ascertained that *Nessus* was sufficiently seaworthy to reach port under the conditions then prevailing.

At about 19.00 a signal from Orkney warned of approaching bad weather, and ordered that *Nessus'* crew should be removed, if necessary. By 21.00 the weather had increased and *Nessus* and *Maenad* were hove-to. At midnight the weather was worse, and the water in the ship was slowly gaining.

At 04.00 on the 8th HMS *Paladin* and the tug *Labour* arrived. The tug also took *Nessus* in tow, but was unable to make much headway in the wind and sea which had increased considerably during the night. The wind was now SSE force 6–7, Sea State 5.

At 08.50 the pumps stopped due to lack of steam, and the ship began to settle down rapidly. It was then decided to abandon ship. The *Paladin* came alongside and all eighty officers and men transferred to her. At 10.25 *Nessus* sank in 593300N, 021245W.

The 3-funnelled destroyer HMS *Nessus* was built by Swan Hunter & Wigham Richardson in 1915.

An obstruction charted in 582945N, 021250W at 71 metres in a general depth of about 77 metres might be HMS *Nessus*.

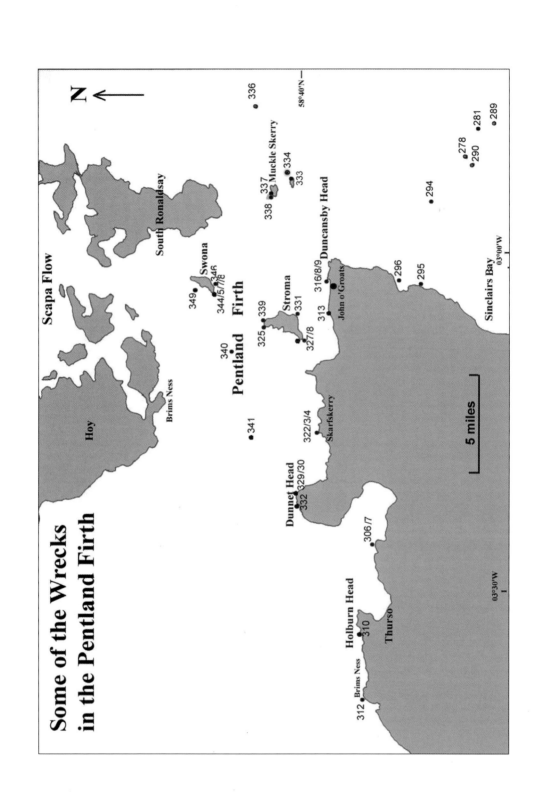

Some of the Wrecks
in the Pentland Firth

N

Scapa Flow

South Ronaldsay

Hoy

Brims Ness

Swona

Pentland   Firth

349

344/5/7/8   346

340

339

Stroma

325   331

341

327/8

313

316/8/9

John o' Groats

322/3/4

Skarfskerry

Dunnet Head   329/30

332

306/7

Holburn Head   310

Thurso

Brims Ness   312

336

Muckle Skerry

337

338   334

333

Duncansby Head

294

296

295

Sinclairs Bay

278

290   281

289

58°40'N

03°00'W

03°30'W

5 miles

5
PENTLAND

HARTY

Wreck No: 303
Latitude: 58 35 50 N PA
GPS Lat: 5835.833 N
Location: Near Strathy Point
Type: Drifter
Length: ft
How Sunk: Ran aground in fog

Date Sunk: 12 08 1932
Longitude: 04 01 30 W PA
GPS Long: 0401.500 W
Area: Pentland
Tonnage: grt
Beam: ft Draught: ft
Depth: metres

The steel steam drifter *Harty* ran aground in fog at the west side of Strathy Point on 12 August 1932. Strathy Point is at 583600N, 040100W.

BALMORAL

Wreck No: 304
Latitude: 58 35 00 N PA
GPS Lat: 5835.000 N
Location: Near Strathy Point
Type: Trawler
Length: ft
How Sunk: Ran aground

Date Sunk: 01 06 1951
Longitude: 04 00 00 W PA
GPS Long: 0400.000 W
Area: Pentland
Tonnage: grt
Beam: ft Draught: ft
Depth: metres

The Lossiemouth seine net wooden fishing boat *Balmoral* struck in a gap between two steep faces of rock near Strathy Point in dense fog, and was badly holed.

The crew of six scrambled ashore before their vessel sank, and spent hours on a ledge in darkness, not knowing where they were. Had the *Balmoral* struck the steep cliffs on either side of the gap, the crew would probably have been unable to get ashore, and might not have been heard of again.

AVENEL

Wreck No: 305
Latitude: 58 36 10 N PA
GPS Lat: 5836.167 N
Location: W side of Thurso breakwater
Type: Steamship
Length: ft
How Sunk: Ran aground

Date Sunk: 25 01 1906
Longitude: 03 30 54 W PA
GPS Long: 0330.900 W
Area: Pentland
Tonnage: 271 grt
Beam: ft Draught: ft
Depth: metres

The steel steamship *Avenel* ran aground on the west side of Thurso breakwater on 25 January 1906.

JURA

Wreck No: 306	Date Sunk: 09 10 1926
Latitude: 58 36 30 N PA	Longitude: 03 25 00 W PA
GPS Lat: 5836.500 N	GPS Long: 0325.000 W
Location: Off Murkle, Caithness	Area: Pentland
Type: Steamship	Tonnage: 2,280 grt
Length: 285.0 ft Beam: 42.0 ft	Draught: 19.0 ft
How Sunk: Ran aground	Depth: metres

The steel steamship *Jura* was built by Harland & Wolff, Belfast. She ran aground off Murkle on 9 October 1926.

SUNLIGHT

Wreck No: 307	Date Sunk: 17 02 1953
Latitude: 58 36 32 N	Longitude: 03 25 27 W
GPS Lat: 5836.533 N	GPS Long: 0325.450 W
Location: Murkle reef	Area: Pentland
Type: Trawler	Tonnage: 203 grt
Length: 115.0 ft Beam: 22.0 ft	Draught: 12.0 ft
How Sunk: Ran aground	Depth: 3 metres

The wooden trawler *Sunlight* struck Murkle reef during a storm on 17 February 1953. Only the boiler remains, heavily covered in weed, and visible at low water.

UNKNOWN AIRCRAFT

Wreck No: 308	Date Sunk: 08 06 1943 ?
Latitude: 58 36 35 N PA	Longitude: 03 31 50 W PA
GPS Lat: 5836.583 N	GPS Long: 0331.833 W
Location: 700 yards E of Scrabster harbour	Area: Pentland
Type: Aircraft	Tonnage: grt
Length: ft Beam: ft	Draught: ft
How Sunk:	Depth: 13 metres

This might be a Walrus aircraft which crashed into the sea near Thurso on 8 June 1943. The position has also been recorded as 583745N, 033100W PA.

BEECH

Wreck No: 309	Date Sunk: 22 06 1941
Latitude: 58 36 39 N	Longitude: 03 31 54 W
GPS Lat: 5836.650 N	GPS Long: 0331.900 W

Location: 1 mile off Thurso/Scrabster   Area: Pentland
Type: Trawler   Tonnage: 540 grt
Length: ft   Beam: ft   Draught: ft
How Sunk: Bombed by Aircraft   Depth: 9 metres

Built in 1929 as the *Lord Dawson*, this trawler was hired by the Admiralty for use as a minesweeper in 1939, and was bombed at Scrabster on 22 June 1941. The position was recorded as Littlehead light 0.3 miles, 147°. Little of the wreck remains above the seabed.

BEN RINNES

Wreck No: 310   Date Sunk: 27 03 1928
Latitude: 58 37 26 N PA   Longitude: 03 32 28 W PA
GPS Lat: 5837.440 N   GPS Long: 0332.480 W
Location: ¼ m W of Spear Point, Holburn Hd.   Area: Pentland
Type: Trawler   Tonnage: 183 grt
Length: 108.0 ft   Beam: 21.0 ft   Draught: 12.4 ft
How Sunk: Ran aground   Depth: metres

The steam trawler *Ben Rinnes* was built by Hall Russell in 1901.
   She ran aground in fog ¼ mile west of Spear Point near Holburn Head at Scrabster on 27 March 1928. Her crew were all saved.

CLARKWOOD

Wreck No: 311   Date Sunk: 22 08 1975
Latitude: 58 35 00 N PA   Longitude: 03 55 00 W PA
GPS Lat: 5835.000 N   GPS Long: 0355.000 W
Location: 5 miles W of Holburn Head   Area: Wick
Type: Trawler   Tonnage: grt
Length: ft   Beam: ft   Draught: ft
How Sunk: Ran aground   Depth: metres

The trawler *Clarkwood* ran aground 5 miles west of Holburn Head, near Dounreay Atomic Establishment. The crew were taken off as the vessel was being pounded against the rocks.

ASSE

Wreck No: 312   Date Sunk: 16 03 1928
Latitude: 58 37 00 N PA   Longitude: 03 40 00 W PA
GPS Lat: 5837.000 N   GPS Long: 0340.000 W
Location: Brims Ness, Sutherland   Area: Pentland
Type: Steamship   Tonnage: 952 grt
Length: 222.4 ft   Beam: 32.5 ft   Draught: 11.3 ft
How Sunk: Ran aground   Depth: metres

The German steamship *Asse* was wrecked at Ushat Head, just west of Brims Ness, Sutherland on 16 March 1928. She was en route from Dublin to Danzig with a cargo of scrap iron. Scrabster lifeboat and LSA team went to her assistance, but the crew landed in their own boat. The *Asse* became a total wreck.

MALIN HEAD

Wreck No: 313	Date Sunk: 22 10 1910
Latitude: 58 38 37 N	Longitude: 03 07 36 W
GPS Lat: 5838.617 N	GPS Long: 0307.600 W
Location: Ness of Huna, Gills Bay	Area: Pentland
Type: Steamship	Tonnage: 3,467 grt
Length: 346.5 ft Beam: 42.9 ft	Draught: 26.4 ft
How Sunk: Ran aground	Depth: metres

The Belfast steamship *Malin Head* ran aground on an outlying reef off Huna Ness while en route from Middlesbrough to Montreal with a cargo of 2,500 tons of pig iron.

In spite of her broken back, twisted hull and flooded compartments, she was refloated early in November, but had to be beached in Gills Bay as she was taking in so much water.

WILSTON

Wreck No: 314	Date Sunk: 15 02 1916
Latitude: 58 38 59 N	Longitude: 02 31 02 W
GPS Lat: 5838.667 N	GPS Long: 0231.040 W
Location: 23 miles ENE of Wick	Area: Pentland
Type: Steamship	Tonnage: 2,611 grt
Length: 310.0 ft Beam: 46.0 ft	Draught: 20.0
How Sunk: Mined	Depth: 62 metres

The British steamship *Wilston* struck a mine about 23 miles ENE of Wick at 2.30 a.m. on 15 February 1916 and sank in six minutes. The captain and seven of the crew were killed. The vessel was built in 1909, and was carrying 4,000 tons of coal from the Tyne to Scapa Flow. The survivors were picked up by the steamship *Express*, and were landed at Fraserburgh.

BENACHIE

Wreck No: 315	Date Sunk: 24 11 1971
Latitude: 58 38 48 N PA	Longitude: 03 02 00 W PA
GPS Lat: 5838.800 N	GPS Long: 0302.000 W
Location: 1 mile E of John o' Groats	Area: Pentland
Type: MFV	Tonnage: grt
Length: ft Beam: ft	Draught: ft
How Sunk: Ran aground	Depth: metres

The wreck of the MFV *Benachie* lies about one mile east of John o' Groats.

SALVAGE KING

Wreck No: 316
Latitude: 58 38 50 N PA
GPS Lat: 5838.833 N
Location: W of Duncansby Head
Type: Tug
Length: 186.3 ft   Beam: 36.2 ft
How Sunk: Ran aground

Date Sunk: 12 09 1940
Longitude: 03 03 20 W PA
GPS Long: 0303.333 W
Area: Pentland
Tonnage: 1,164 grt
Draught: 16.2 ft
Depth: metres

The tug *Salvage King* was built in 1925 by Bow, McLachlan & Co., Paisley.
    She ran aground and was wrecked 1½ miles west of Duncansby Head on 12
September 1940.

ST OLAVES

Wreck No: 317
Latitude: 58 38 55 N PA
GPS Lat: 5838.917 N
Location: Off Duncansby Head
Type: Tug
Length: 135.6 ft   Beam: 29.1 ft
How Sunk: Ran aground

Date Sunk: 21 09 1942
Longitude: 03 02 00 W PA
GPS Long: 0302.000 W
Area: Pentland
Tonnage: 468 grt
Draught: 13.6 ft
Depth: metres

HM tug *St Olaves* was built by Harland & Woolf in 1919. She ran aground on 21
September 1942 while towing the barge *Golden Crown*. The barge was later salvaged,
along with part of the tug's gear.

ARDMORE

Wreck No: 318
Latitude: 58 38 55 N PA
GPS Lat: 5838.917 N
Location: Duncansby Ness
Type: Steamship
Length: 216.9 ft   Beam: 30.2 ft
How Sunk: Ran aground

Date Sunk: 20 08 1899
Longitude: 03 03 00 W PA
GPS Long: 0303.000 W
Area: Pentland
Tonnage: 903 grt
Draught: 15.2 ft
Depth: metres

The iron steamship *Ardmore* was en route from Gothenburg to Ayr with a cargo of pit
props when she ran onto the rocks at Duncansby Ness in calm conditions, and became
a total loss.

ARALIA

Wreck No: 319
Latitude: 58 38 55 N PA
GPS Lat: 5838.917 N

Date Sunk: 29 03 1923
Longitude: 03 03 20 W PA
GPS Long: 0303.333 W

Location: Duncansby Ness   Area: Pentland
Type: Trawler   Tonnage: 229 grt
Length: 122.1 ft   Beam: 21.6 ft Draught: 11.45 ft
How Sunk: Ran aground   Depth: metres

The iron trawler *Aralia* ran aground on Duncansby Ness on 29 March 1923, while en route from Iceland to Grimsby.

BRACONBUSH

Wreck No: 320   Date Sunk: 29 01 1942
Latitude: 58 39 00 N PA   Longitude: 03 00 00 W PA
GPS Lat: 5839.000 N   GPS Long: 0300.000 W
Location: 2 miles SE of Duncansby Head   Area: Pentland
Type: Trawler   Tonnage: 204 grt
Length: 115.4 ft   Beam: 22.2 ft Draught: 12.1 ft
How Sunk: Mined   Depth: metres

The Fleetwood steam trawler *Braconbush* (ex-*John Conne*), built in 1919 by Hawthorns of Leith, was mined off Duncansby Head on 29 January 1942, while en route from Aberdeen to the fishing grounds in the Minch. She was taken in tow by another trawler towards Scrabster, but sank before reaching there. Her eleven crew were all saved.

ISABELLA

Wreck No: 321   Date Sunk: 01 11 1918
Latitude: 58 39 00 N PA   Longitude: 03 01 00 W PA
GPS Lat: 5839.000 N   GPS Long: 0301.000 W
Location: Off Duncansby Head   Area: Pentland
Type: Schooner   Tonnage: 109 grt
Length: 84.0 ft   Beam: 21.5 ft Draught: 10.0 ft
How Sunk: Foundered   Depth: metres

The 109-ton Wick schooner *Isabella*, en route from Sunderland to Stromness with a cargo of coal, was last seen leaving Sinclairs Bay on 1 November 1918.

She was never seen again, but a body washed ashore at John o' Groats later that month was presumed to have been one of her crew of four. This led to speculation that the *Isabella* had foundered in heavy seas off Duncansby Head.

VICTORIA

Wreck No: 322   Date Sunk: 04 03 1891
Latitude: 58 39 08 N   Longitude: 03 16 45 W
GPS Lat: 5839.133 N   GPS Long: 0316.750 W
Location: Scarfskerry, Caithness   Area: Pentland
Type: Steamship   Tonnage: 2,128 grt
Length: 290.6 ft   Beam: 40.1 ft Draught: 20.2 ft
How Sunk: Ran aground   Depth: 12 metres

The Sunderland-registered steamship *Victoria* was built in 1882 by Short Bros, Belfast.

En route from Hamburg to New York with a general cargo which included sugar and dynamite detonators, her engine failed in heavy seas off the Butt of Lewis. She was then blown by the westerly gale towards the Pentland Firth. Her crew were all taken off by Longhope lifeboat and landed in Orkney before the derelict steamship finally drifted ashore and was wrecked at Scarfskerry. The detonators in her cargo exploded, and the ship broke up.

The remains of the *Victoria* now lie scattered in rocky gullies just west of the small harbour at Scarfskerry.

JORGEN BUGGE

Wreck No: 323	Date Sunk: 07 06 1895
Latitude: 58 39 20 N	Longitude: 03 16 30 W
GPS Lat: 5839.333 N	GPS Long: 0316.500 W
Location: Scarfskerry Point	Area: Pentland
Type: Steamship	Tonnage: 894 grt
Length: 219.4 ft Beam: 29.3 ft	Draught: 16.6 ft
How Sunk: Ran aground	Depth: 12 metres

The iron steamship *Jorgen Bugge (ex-West Riding)* was built in 1871 by Doxford of Sunderland. She ran onto the rocks at Scarfskerry Point while en route from Sundswall to Fleetwood with a cargo of wood pulp on 7 June 1895. Her engine shows above water at all states of the tide, and there is plenty of wreckage scattered on the bottom. Some of that wreckage may be from the *Victoria*.

LINKMOOR

Wreck No: 324	Date Sunk: 10 11 1930
Latitude: 58 39 10 N	Longitude: 03 16 42 W
GPS Lat: 5839.166 N	GPS Long: 0316.700 W
Location: 50 yards off Scarfskerry	Area: Pentland
Type: Steamship	Tonnage: 3175 grt
Length: 331.0 ft Beam: 47.7 ft	Draught: 22.5 ft
How Sunk: Ran aground	Depth: 10 metres

The British steamship *Linkmoor* was built in 1913 by J. Blumer & Co. En route from Liverpool to Blyth in ballast, she was driven ashore in a northerly gale at Scarfskerry Head, Brough Bay on 30 November 1930. Both anchors had been dropped, but they did not hold, and the *Linkmoor* ended up on the rocks at the entrance to Scarfskerry harbour. There was only a 10-foot gap between the wreck and the end of the harbour, and several vessels were blocked inside the harbour until the wreck was eventually broken up for scrap in 1934/5. Her boilers remained on site, standing vertically, and from a distance could be mistaken for an eroded sandstone stack, until they fell over during a storm in 1993/4. The remains of the *Linkmoor* lie in 6 to 10 metres of water. Her rudder lies propped up against the base of a cliff. Underwater visibility is usually about 10 metres.

COPELAND

Wreck No: 325	Date Sunk: 25 07 1888
Latitude: 58 41 40 N	Longitude: 03 07 30 W
GPS Lat: 5841.667 N	GPS Long: 0307.500 W
Location: Langaton Point, Stroma	Area: Pentland
Type: Steamship	Tonnage: 798 grt
Length: 226.5 ft Beam: 29.4 ft	Draught: 15.5 ft
How Sunk: Ran aground	Depth: 24-38 metres

The iron steamship *Copeland* was built in Glasgow in 1874.

On 25 July 1888, while en route from Reykjavik to Granton with a cargo of fish, wool, 482 ponies, eleven passengers, and a crew of thirty-two, she encountered thick fog in the Pentland Firth.

Everything went well until they passed Dunnet Head, about half a mile from land. The ship was steering due east, with the tide running strongly in the same direction. The *Copeland* was going at half-speed, and had stopped previously to take soundings. When within sight of land they hailed the fishing boat *Isabella Sinclair,* and took the skipper, Andrew Sinclair, on board to land telegrams. As a local fisherman, Mr Sinclair had an intimate knowledge of the tides and currents of the Pentland Firth. He offered to pilot the steamship through the Pentland Firth, but his offer was declined. The *Copeland* then continued on her way at full speed, with the tide. At 11.35 Captain Charles Thompson slowed to half-speed, and altered course to ESE. At 11.45 he changed course to SE, and breakers were seen only fifty yards ahead. Captain Thompson immediately ordered the helm to be turned to port, and went full astern, but his vessel had run aground before her way could be taken off. He kept the engines running astern for a couple of minutes after the vessel struck, but to no avail, and water gradually filled the hold.

The *Copeland* had run aground on rocks about 500 yards from Langaton Point, the extreme north point of the island of Stroma. The *Copeland* carried five boats, and all the passengers (among them Sir Rider Haggard, a well-known writer of that period) and crew reached shore safely in the ship's boats. Most of the ponies were put overboard to swim ashore after being lowered over the ship's side in slings, but 128 of them were drowned in hold 2. The remainder landed on Stroma. The wrecked ship broke in two a week later. The stern section sank in 25 metres, but the bow remained on the rocks.

Captain Thompson, who had been a master for thirty years, was aware that the currents in the Pentland Firth were strong and uncertain, and varied with the wind. He attributed the stranding of the vessel to the fact that he had made insufficient allowance for the current. Although the log was out, it was of very little use.

He had been on deck from Tuesday morning till Wednesday, and had not taken his clothes off for five and a half days.

KOORAH

Wreck No: 326	Date Sunk: 11 02 1954
Latitude: 58 40 04 N	Longitude: 03 23 22 W
GPS Lat: 5840.067 N	GPS Long: 0323.367 W
Location: ½ mile W of Dunnet Head	Area: Pentland
Type: Trawler	Tonnage: 227 grt
Length: 117.0 ft Beam: 22.5 ft	Draught: 13.0 ft
How Sunk: Ran aground	Depth: metres

The steam trawler *Koorah* was built in 1912 by Hall Russell, Aberdeen.

During the hours of darkness in the early morning of 11 February 1954, she ran onto rocks half a mile west of Dunnet Head (this suggests on the Neback Reef).

The crew of twelve left in their small boat and were picked up by the Thurso fishing boat *Oor Lassie*, and taken to Scrabster. The wreck lies below Sherrie Geo, and has been partly buried under fallen rocks.

NORTH SEA

Wreck No: 327	Date Sunk: 08 05 1896
Latitude: 58 40 07 N PA	Longitude: 03 03 30 W PA
GPS Lat: 5840.167 N	GPS Long: 0303.500 W
Location: SW corner of Island of Stroma	Area: Pentland
Type: Steamship	Tonnage: 1,076 grt
Length: 230.0 ft Beam: 30.9 ft	Draught: 15.9 ft
How Sunk: Ran aground	Depth: metres

The British steamship *North Sea*, built in 1881, was wrecked on the south-west corner of the island of Stroma in the Pentland Firth on 8 May 1896. The vessel had been en route from the Clyde to Copenhagen with a cargo of coal.

BETTINA DANICA

Wreck No: 328	Date Sunk: 13 02 1993
Latitude: 58 40 07 N PA	Longitude: 03 03 00 W PA
GPS Lat: 5840.167 N	GPS Long: 0303.000 W
Location: SW tip of Stroma Island	Area: Pentland
Type: Motor Vessel	Tonnage: 1,354 grt
Length: ft Beam: ft	Draught: ft
How Sunk: Ran aground	Depth: metres

The Danish motor vessel *Bettina Danica* ran aground on the south-west tip of Stroma Island in the Pentland Firth at 4.00 a.m. on Saturday 13 February 1993.

The ship had been en route from Greenock to Oslo. Thurso lifeboat and Wick Coastguard stood by as two tugs from Orkney, the *Harald* and the *Einar*, tried in vain to tow her off the rocks. Five of the six crewmembers and a salvageman were airlifted to the *Einar* and taken to Orkney. The captain and two other salvagemen remained aboard the stranded vessel to pump 40 tons of diesel from a forward tank to a higher tank aft in the vessel, to minimise the risk of pollution if the tank ruptured during further salvage attempts, and to make it easier to transfer the fuel to another vessel if this should prove necessary. Attempts to refloat the ship over the next few days were unsuccessful, and on 18 February she started to break up.

PETER BERG

Wreck No: 329	Date Sunk: 26 05 1906
Latitude: 58 40 15 N PA	Longitude: 03 23 00 W PA
GPS Lat: 5840.250 N	GPS Long: 0323.000 W

Location: On Dunnet Head	Area: Pentland
Type: Steamship	Tonnage: 1,832 grt
Length: 260.7 ft Beam: 36.3 ft	Draught: 19.8 ft
How Sunk: Ran aground	Depth: metres

The Danish iron steamship *Peter Berg* (ex-*Almandine*) stranded off Dunnet Head on 26 May 1906, while en route from Glasgow to Norway with a cargo of coal.

COTHERSTONE

Wreck No: 330	Date Sunk: 29 08 1877
Latitude: 58 40 15 N PA	Longitude: 03 23 00 W PA
GPS Lat: 5840.250 N	GPS Long: 0323.000 W
Location: Dunnet Head	Area: Pentland
Type: Steamship	Tonnage: 1,467 grt
Length: 290.4 ft Beam: 36.3 ft	Draught: 26.4 ft
How Sunk: Ran aground	Depth: metres

The British steamship *Cotherstone* ran aground on Dunnet Head in thick fog during the night of 29 August 1887 while en route, in ballast, from Dublin to Sunderland.
Her crew all managed to reach the shore, but the vessel became a total loss.

EMPIRE PARSONS

Wreck No: 331	Date Sunk: 12 01 1942
Latitude: 58 40 15 N PA	Longitude: 03 06 00 W PA
GPS Lat: 5840.250 N	GPS Long: 0306.000 W
Location: Scarton Point, Stroma Island	Area: Pentland
Type: Steamship	Tonnage: 6742 grt
Length: 434.5 ft Beam: 57.3 ft	Draught: ft
How Sunk: Ran aground	Depth: metres

The British steamship *Empire Parsons* ran aground on her maiden voyage at Scarton Point on the Island of Stroma on 12 January 1942. She had been the leading ship in a convoy heading west in a SE gale with snow and sleet which reduced visibility. Her crew were taken off by breeches buoy. Salvage work was carried out by Metal Industries, and only the keel and propeller shaft with steel propeller remain.

DALEWOOD

Wreck No: 332	Date Sunk: 03 03 1974
Latitude: 58 40 18 N	Longitude: 03 22 29 W
GPS Lat: 5840.300 N	GPS Long: 0322.483 W
Location: On Dunnet Head	Area: Pentland
Type: Trawler	Tonnage: 234 grt
Length: 115.0 ft Beam: 25.0 ft	Draught: 11.0 ft
How Sunk: Ran aground	Depth: metres

The wooden MFV *Dalewood* left Aberdeen at about 10.15 hrs on 3 March 1974, bound for the Faroese fishing grounds, and at about 21.20 hrs was driven at full speed onto rocks in a small cove almost under the west side of Dunnet Head lighthouse, at the foot of 400-foot cliffs.

The skipper sent out a Mayday, giving his position as Duncansby Head, which misled rescuers for a time. The eleven crew took to two liferafts, and were picked up by the Admiralty tug *Cyclone* and the trawler *Sealgair*. All were eventually landed at Scrabster.

BEN BARVAS

Wreck No: 333	Date Sunk: 03 01 1964
Latitude: 58 40 30 N	Longitude: 02 54 27 W
GPS Lat: 5840.500 N	GPS Long: 0254.450 W
Location: Little Pentland Skerry	Area: Pentland
Type: Trawler	Tonnage: 235 grt
Length: ft Beam: ft	Draught: ft
How Sunk: Ran aground	Depth: metres

The Aberdeen trawler *Ben Barvas* ran onto Little Skerry in heavy weather at night on 3 January 1964. An SOS radio message was sent out, and five of the crew took to a life raft. They were picked up by their sister trawler *Ben Screel*.

Despite floating debris and diesel oil, the nine remaining members of her crew were saved by means of breeches buoy after the Longhope lifeboat anchored about 100 yards away and fired a line across in the heaving seas, which were breaking over the stricken trawler. Longhope lifeboat Coxswain Daniel Kirkpatrick was awarded his second silver medal for this rescue, which was almost a carbon copy of another rescue he had performed five years previously, and for which he had been awarded his first silver medal. That was the rescue of the fourteen crew from the Aberdeen trawler *Strathcoe*, which had gone on to the rocks in a narrow crevice at the bottom of 400-foot cliffs. Coxswain Kirkpatrick took the lifeboat into the gully while huge seas were breaking over the grounded trawler wedged at the head of the narrow gap. In mountainous seas, and with rocks only about 70 yards away on either side, he dropped an anchor and fired a line to the trawler. A breeches buoy was rigged up, and the trawler's crew were successfully taken off their vessel.

The wreck of the *Ben Barvas* lies on its port side, with the bows pointing north east, on the eastern extremity of Little Skerry. As might be expected, she has been rather broken by wave action, although she is still high and dry.

FIONA

Wreck No: 334	Date Sunk: 06 09 1917
Latitude: 58 41 01 N	Longitude: 02 53 30 W
GPS Lat: 5841.167 N	GPS Long: 0253.500 W
Location: Wrecked on Pentland Skerries	Area: Pentland
Type: Steamship	Tonnage: 1,161 grt
Length: 280.0 ft. Beam: 36.1 ft	Draught: 18.0 ft
How Sunk: Ran aground	Depth: 10-12 metres

The armed boarding steamship *Fiona* was built in 1905 by Caledon, Dundee. On 6 September 1917 she ran aground on a ridge of rocks running northeasterly from Louther Skerry towards Clettack Skerry, the most easterly of the Pentland Skerries.

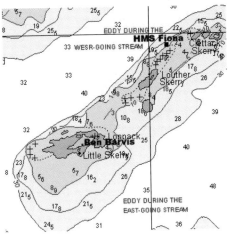

The locations of the wrecks of Ben Barvas *and* Fiona *in the Pentland Skerries*

UB-83

Wreck No: 335		Date Sunk: 10 09 1917
Latitude: 58 42 00 N PA		Longitude: 02 56 00 W PA
GPS Lat: 5842.000 N		GPS Long: 0256.000 W
Location: 'Near the Pentland Skerries'		Area: Pentland
Type: Submarine		Tonnage: 516 tons surfaced, 647 tons submerged
Length: 183.2 ft	Beam: 19.0 ft	Draught: ft
How Sunk: Depth-charged		Depth: metres

UB-83 (OL H Buntebardt) was depthcharged 'in the Pentland Firth' by the destroyer HMS *Ophelia* on 10 September 1917. All thirty-five of the U-boat's crew died.

One report gives the position as 5828N, 0150W, 'near the Pentland Skerries', but that position is actually about 35 miles SE of the Pentland Skerries! It is, however, near Pentland Skerries Ground, and a wreck which might be *UB-83* is charted in 90 metres at 582920N, 015745W.

The position recorded by the Hydrographic Department is 584200N, 025600W PA, and one diver claims to have dived a U-boat in 26 metres, between Muckle Skerry and Little Skerry, at about 584040N, 025500W.

A conning tower trawled up by a fishing boat in the early 1980s was thought to possibly have been from *U-18*, but the conning tower of *U-18* is still in position on the wreck. The conning tower that was trawled up might, therefore, have come from *UB-83*.

U-18

Wreck No: 336	Date Sunk: 23 11 1914
Latitude: 58 42 09 N	Longitude: 02 48 00 W

GPS Lat: 5842.150 N   GPS Long: 0248.000 W
Location: 4 miles E of Pentland Skerries   Area: Pentland
Type: Submarine   Tonnage: 564 tons surfaced,
                                             691 tons submerged
Length: 204.6 ft   Beam: 19.7 ft Draught: ft
How Sunk: Rammed, Ran aground, Scuttled   Depth: 76 metres

On 23 November 1914 *U-18* (KL Heinrich von Hennig) had entered Scapa Flow by following a steamer through the Hoxa Sound entrance, only to discover that there were no British Naval ships in the anchorage at that time. On the way back out of Hoxa Sound, *U-18's* periscope was seen, and she was rammed one mile off the entrance, first by the armed trawler *Dorothy Gray*, and then by the destroyer *Garry*. With her hydroplanes damaged by the ramming, *U-18* was difficult to control, and she rose and sank erratically while attempting to escape eastwards, away from the British vessels intent on finishing off their victim. Caught in the powerful currents for which the Pentland Firth is notorious, she was carried onto the rocks of the Pentland Skerries, and then a further four miles eastwards, where she was scuttled by her crew at 15.10 hrs on 23 November 1914. Twenty-two survivors were picked up by the *Garry*. The Hydrographic Department has recorded the *U-18* at 584209N, 024800W, four miles east of Muckle Skerry, where a wreck is charted at 65 metres.

The wreck is lying upright, partially embedded in sand, and surrounded by massive sand hills. The wreck is obviously scoured by shifting sand, as it is clean, and practically devoid of marine growths.

There is an open hatch near the stern, through which the whole of the aft compartment can be seen, with plates and bottles scattered inside. Further towards the stern there is a huge gash across the outer casing where the *Garry* rammed the U-boat. The conning tower is intact with the top hatch closed and the tiny portholes on each side also still intact. The periscope is either retracted or missing. (It is most likely missing, as the trawler *Dorothy Gray* rammed the periscope, blinding the U-boat.) The bows have the most damage, with the plating rotted through to reveal the bow torpedo tubes. This damage was probably caused when the submarine hit the Pentland Skerries whilst trying to escape the pursuing British ships. The hydroplane ribs are still visible but their covering skin has corroded away. The starboard hydroplane is also bent and damaged – caused by one of the ramming vessels.

Diving conditions in the Pentland Firth are always unpredictable. There does not seem to be any real slack water at all, but underwater visibility is wonderful – on the descent the whole of the U-boat can be seen from 50 metres, 25 metres below.

U-18 *(Photo: National Maritime Museum)*

KIRUNA

Wreck No: 337	Date Sunk: 12 08 1915
Latitude: 58 41 28 N	Longitude: 02 55 51 W
GPS Lat: 5841.466 N	GPS Long: 0255.850 W
Location: Muckle Skerry, Pentland Skerries	Area: Pentland
Type: Steamship	Tonnage: 4638 grt
Length: 389.4 ft Beam: 52.8 ft	Draught: ft
How Sunk: Ran aground	Depth: 22-26 metres

The Swedish steamship *Kiruna* ran aground on Muckle Skerry, the largest of the Pentland Skerries, on 12 August 1945 while en route from Philadelphia to Stockholm with a cargo of coal.

The wreck is very broken up, and lies between the *Kathe Niederkirchner* and Muckle Skerry light.

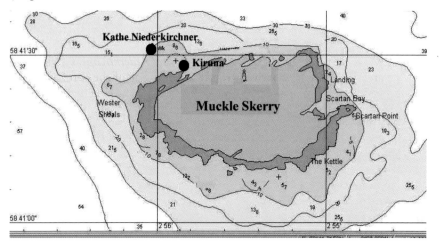

The locations of the wrecks of Kathe Niederkirchner *and* Kiruna *off Muckle Skerry*

KATHE NIEDERKIRCHNER

Wreck No: 338	Date Sunk: 23 08 1965
Latitude: 58 41 31 N	Longitude: 02 56 02 W
GPS Lat: 5841.517 N	GPS Long: 0256.034 W
Location: Wrecked on Pentland Skerries	Area: Pentland
Type: Motor vessel	Tonnage: 8,003 grt
Length: 467.0 ft Beam: 61.0 ft	Draught: 24.0 ft
How Sunk: Ran aground	Depth: 16 metres

The East German motor vessel *Kathe Niederkirchner* was en route from Havana to Rostock, East Germany with a cargo of sugar when she ran aground off the NW corner of Muckle Skerry in thick fog at 5.30 a.m. on 23 August 1965. Visibility was down to about 200 yards when the ship struck the skerry. Most on board were asleep, apart from those on duty, but within seven minutes the forty-eight crew and two passengers abandoned ship in a lifeboat, and made for the island, which was inhabited only by the three lighthouse keepers. On hearing the ship running onto the rocks, the principal lighthouse keeper, David Leslie, called Wick Radio. All three keepers then ran through the fog to the edge of the cliff and saw the lifeboat immediately below, looking for a place to land. At great personal risk, Mr Leslie jumped aboard the lifeboat, and piloted it to the lighthouse landing stage. In their haste to abandon ship, the East Germans had had to leave all their personal belongings behind. Some were wearing only their pyjamas. The cold and hungry survivors were looked after by the lighthouse keepers, and they ate practically everything in the lighthouse. Meanwhile, alerted by Wick Radio, Longhope lifeboat had been launched. She made for Muckle Skerry, and picked up forty-eight of the survivors. The Captain, Horst Wentzel, and the bosun, Erwin Westphalen, remained on the skerry to await instructions from the owners.

Shortly before midday, some 6½ hours after the stranding, a boat skippered by fisherman Willie Mowat of South Ronaldsay arrived at the wreck site. On board were the receiver of wrecks, a coastguard officer, Mr William Jolly, representing the ship's owners, and a police constable.

Mr Jolly was the Kirkwall agent of the Shipwrecked Fishermen's and Mariner's Royal Benevolent Society, and had already, that morning, arranged for the survivors to be fed and clothed and taken care of in Kirkwall, and organised a charter aircraft to fly them to London.

While Mr Mowat's boat was taking one of the *Kathe Niederkirchner's* lifeboats, which was full of water, in tow, a boat arrived from the other side of the Pentland Firth, and attempted to take the ship's lifeboat in tow itself, defying instructions to the contrary from the official party.

Apparently the hijackers succeeded in getting away with the boat, but were forced to abandon it when it sank near the south-east corner of Muckle Skerry.

The *Kathe Niederkirchner* rolled over and sank at 2.30 p.m., nine hours after stranding.

The *Orcadian* newspaper of Thursday 26 August 1965 contains a fascinating report of 'piracy on the high seas like the days of Morgan and Captain Kidd':

> Some hours later, between 9.00 and 10.00 p.m., as darkness was falling, Mr Mowat's boat was again at the Skerries, and had taken another ship's lifeboat in tow. He had also found the ship's lifeboat of the morning, which was still partially submerged, and also taken it in tow. There were some South Ronaldsay men in the second ship's lifeboat, and the police constable was again in Mr Mowat's boat. As the 'train' of three boats set off for South Ronaldsay, a new intruder arrived from Caithness. This was a fishing boat with about a dozen men on board. These men apparently had 'knives, grapples and spears', which they brandished in a very threatening manner, and attempted to take over the tow of the two ship's lifeboats.
>
> It appears they got a grapple on to the tow rope between Mr Mowat's boat and the next ship's lifeboat. The South Ronaldsay men cut the tow with an axe and the two boats drifted clear.
>
> There was a bit of a 'stramash' in the Firth and the seiner, it is said, tried to ram the ship's boat and did, indeed, strike her. There was a melée and the South Ronaldsay boat succeeded in picking up the tow once more. They made for the Skerry again and went in so close that the 'pirate' seiner, with its much greater draught, dared not follow, in case of running aground. Frustrated, the seiner eventually made off towards Caithness.
>
> The Captain and bosun of the *Kathe Niederkirchner*, who were still on Muckle Skerry, witnessed the attempted hijacking. Orkney police are making a full investigation of the incidents, and the District Coastguard Officer is also making a full report to his headquarters.

Kathie Niederkircher *(Photo: courtesy of* The Orcadian*)*

After the furore surrounding her sinking died down, the *Kathe Niederkirchner* was almost forgotten for thirty-three years until South Ronaldsay fisherman Willie Mowat dropped a bombshell in August 1998, when the BBC's Northern Isles Reporter John Johnston followed up the story:

> It is claimed by eyewitnesses at the time, like fisherman Willie Mowat, that once the cargo of sugar spilled out, a strange metal cylinder with radioactive markings was visible, fixed to the bottom of the hold.

Willie Mowat is convinced there was a secret cargo on board, related to the Cuban missile crisis of 1962. He said, 'It is a known thing that the nuclear weapons the Russians had sent to Cuba had to be returned, and the only way it could be concealed was in the sugar.'

Willie's son Lawrence is a diver, and while exploring the wreck in 1972, he spotted this container amongst the wreckage. He recognised it as strongly resembling missiles which had been shipped to Cuba ten years earlier. When news of his dive came to the attention of the police in Orkney, he was ordered to stay away from the wreck.

(Remember that the police constable and the others aboard Willie Mowat's boat must surely also have seen the container before the *Kathe Niederkirchner* sank.)

Willie believes there is something suspicious about it, and thinks it should be investigated. This point was put to Orkney Islands Council's Harbour Director, Captain Bob Sclater, who doubted if a salvage operation would be practical. At that time the wreck had been there for thirty-three years, and with the weather and tidal conditions at the Pentland Skerries, he considered the wreck would be smashed up and a lot of it washed away, but no detailed survey of the wreck had been carried out.

In any case, it would not be the responsibility of Orkney Islands Council's Harbours Department to investigate the matter as the wreck lies outside the harbour area. It would probably be up to the government to consider whether the wreckage should be examined to see if there was anything there that might eventually cause a problem. The Admiralty Hydrographic Department's records contain no suggestion that the ship was carrying anything other than sugar. The wreck now lies 070/250° about 200 metres offshore in 16 metres of water with a least depth of 7 metres. With the wreck lying

Kathie Niederkircher *(Photo: courtesy of* The Orcadian*)*

in such shallow water, it was thought that after the passage of more than thirty years, anything suspicious would probably have been found.

Muckle Skerry is not an easy place for many divers to reach, and the weather and tidal conditions are such that the occasions when it is possible to dive here are very limited.

It is doubtful whether many divers have visited this wreck.

Without any firm evidence to the contrary, there are people in Orkney who remain to be convinced that there is no secret radioactive cargo lying at the bottom of the Pentland Firth.

As the *Kathe Niederkirchner* was built in 1964, two years after the missile crisis of 1962, she was obviously not involved in the original transporting of missiles to Cuba. The container, therefore, cannot simply be a left-over fitment to the vessel, dating from these shipments.

CORINTHIA

Wreck No: 339	Date Sunk: 07 06 1903
Latitude: 58 41 38 N	Longitude: 03 06 22 W
GPS Lat: 5841.640 N	GPS Long: 0306.367 W
Location: Wardie Geo, Swilkie Point, N Stroma	Area: Pentland
Type: Steamship	Tonnage: 1,378 grt
Length: 252.1 ft Beam: 32.2 ft	Draught: 21.3 ft
How Sunk: Ran aground	Depth: 23 metres

The 1,378-grt steamship *Corinthia* (ex-*Author*) ran aground in fog and was wrecked at Swilkie Point, the north point of the island of Stroma, in 1903. She was carrying a cargo of railway sleepers from Danzig to Liverpool. The vessel capsized and sank after the twenty-one crew abandoned ship.

The wreck was dived by Kevin Heath in 2001.

The stern section of the wreck is upside down in 22 metres. Half of one of the four blades of her large cast iron propeller is missing. The bow, engine and boiler were not seen but a good magnetometer reading was obtained to the west (inshore) of the stern.

DRANGAJOKULL

Wreck No: 340	Date Sunk: 28 06 1960
Latitude: 58 43 10 N PA	Longitude: 03 08 00 W PA
GPS Lat: 5843.167 N	GPS Long: 0308.000 W
Location: 1½ miles NW of Stroma	Area: Pentland
Type: Motor vessel	Tonnage: 621 grt
Length: 170.0 ft Beam: 29.0 ft	Draught: 14.0 ft
How Sunk: Foundered	Depth: 55 metres

The Icelandic motor vessel *Drangajokull* was en route from Antwerp to Reykjavik with a 500-ton general cargo including potatoes and a tractor when she capsized and sank 1½ miles NW of Stroma on 28 June 1960. The crew were all saved.

X-22

Wreck No: 341	Date Sunk: 07 02 1944
Latitude: 58 43 42 N	Longitude: 03 18 00 W
GPS Lat: 5843.700 N	GPS Long: 0318.000 W
Location: 4 miles NE of Dunnet Head	Area: Pentland
Type: Submarine X-Craft	Tonnage: 30 tons
Length: 51.6 ft Beam: 5.8 ft	Draught: 7.4 ft
How Sunk: Collision with *Syrtis*	Depth: metres

On 7 February 1944, *X-22* was being towed by the submarine *Syrtis* (Lt M.H. Jupp), from Loch Cairnbawn to Scapa Flow. While passing through the Pentland Firth on the surface, the sea conditions were very rough. Those on board the towing submarine had to hang on to avoid falling over as the waves threw the boat about, and visibility was seriously impaired by the blown spray. At about 03.55 hrs Lt C. Blythe, one of the officers on the bridge, was washed overboard by a huge wave which came crashing down from astern. When the water drained away, it was noticed that the tow line had gone slack, and others left on the bridge thought they could see Lt Blythe in the water off the starboard quarter. It was very quickly realised that what they had thought to be the shape of a man, was in fact *X-22*, which was swept directly under the bows of the *Syrtis*. The larger submarine hit the X-craft three times as she rode over her. There was a smell of fuel oil in the air, but neither Lt Blythe nor *X-22* with her crew of four was seen again. Those lost in *X-22* were two Australians, Lt B.M. McFarlane and Lt W.S. Marsden, along with ERA C. Ludbrooke and AB J. Pretty.

Lt Jupp had taken the precaution of having a lifebuoy on the bridge, but it was the Board of Enquiry's opinion that in the particular circumstances, Lt Blythe could not have been saved even if he had been wearing a life jacket. It was known that the use of rope lashings is not liked. They restrict movement about the bridge, and there is a danger that a man may not be able to free himself in time if the submarine has to dive quickly. As a result of this incident, special safety belts were approved to be fitted to all submarines 'as occasion serves'.

GERTRUD

Wreck No: 342	Date Sunk: 01 06 1934
Latitude: 58 41 44 N	Longitude: 03 07 24 W
GPS Lat: 5841.733 N	GPS Long: 0307.400 W
Location: NW corner of Stroma	Area: Pentland
Type: Steamship	Tonnage: 1,691 grt
Length: 260.7 ft Beam: 36.3 ft	Draught: 20.9 ft
How Sunk: Ran aground	Depth: metres

The Finnish steamship *Gertrud* (ex-*Maun Hartmann*) struck Langaton Point while en route from Manchester to Finland in ballast. Her crew of twenty-two were taken off by Stroma fishermen.

TERN

Wreck No: 343	Date Sunk: 12 05 1976
Latitude: 58 41 45 N PA	Longitude: 03 07 30 W PA
GPS Lat: 5841.750 N	GPS Long: 0307.500 W
Location: NW corner of Stroma	Area: Pentland
Type: MFV	Tonnage: grt
Length: ft Beam: ft	Draught: ft
How Sunk: Ran aground	Depth: metres

The MFV *Tern* ran onto a rock at the north-west corner of Stroma on 12 May 1976. Her pump was unable to cope with the inflowing water, and the vessel sank. Her three crewmen were rescued.

ROSS TERN

Wreck No: 344	Date Sunk: 09 02 1973
Latitude: 58 44 08 N	Longitude: 03 03 52 W
GPS Lat: 5844.133 N	GPS Long: 0303.867 W
Location: Tarf Tail, Swona Island	Area: Pentland
Type: Trawler	Tonnage: 288 grt
Length: ft Beam: ft	Draught: ft
How Sunk: Ran aground	Depth: metres

The MFV *Ross Tern* was en route from Aberdeen to the west-coast fishing grounds, and had entered the Pentland Firth in darkness. The GPS navigator was not working efficiently, and the radar showed land about five miles off the port beam, but no sighting ahead or to starboard, because of a snow shower. The helmsman was uncertain of the vessel's position, but considered her to be too far north. Before the situation could be properly ascertained, the vessel struck the rocks at Little Windy Skerry, very near Tarf Tail, Swona Island. Longhope lifeboat picked up six men from a liferaft, and in a difficult and dangerous manoeuvre, plucked the remaining five of the crew directly from the stricken vessel.

ST CLAIR

Wreck No: 345	Date Sunk: 25 08 1949
Latitude: 58 44 08 N	Longitude: 03 03 52 W
GPS Lat: 5844.133 N	GPS Long: 0303.867 W
Location: Tarf Tail, Swona Island	Area: Pentland
Type: Trawler	Tonnage: 255 grt
Length: ft Beam: ft	Draught: ft
How Sunk: Ran aground	Depth: metres

The Grimsby steam trawler *St Clair* ran aground at Tarf Tail, Swona Island on 25 August 1949.

The Hydrographic Department gives the position as 584455N, 030335W PA.

CROMA

Wreck No: 346	Date Sunk: 14 08 1899
Latitude: 58 44 13 N	Longitude: 03 03 27 W
GPS Lat: 5844.217 N	GPS Long: 0303.450 W
Location: SE side, Swona Island	Area: Pentland
Type: Steamship	Tonnage: 3,187 grt
Length: 330.3 ft Beam: 43.7 ft	Draught: 27.3 ft
How Sunk: Ran aground	Depth: metres

The British steamship *Croma* ran aground in thick fog at the south-east side of Swona Island in the Pentland Firth on 14 August 1899, while en route from Dundee to New York with 550 tons of general cargo. The master and chief officer imprudently attempted to pass through the Pentland Firth in darkness, thick fog, and against the flood tide, which was estimated to be running at 8 or 9 knots.

As the *Croma* had gone aground at high tide, it was impossible to refloat her, but during the month she lay there before breaking up and slipping into deeper water, over 300 tons of cargo were recovered, including beer and spirits, bales of jute and flax goods. Other recovered items included cases of marmalade, books, carpets and rolls of canvas.

The vessel was built by J.L. Thompson & Sons of Sunderland in 1883.

The photograph below was successfully used by Stromness diver Kevin Heath to find the wreck in 2000. The wreck is now completely broken up.

Croma (*Photo: courtesy of Kirkwall Library Archives*)

JOHANNA THORDEN

Wreck No: 347	Date Sunk: 12 01 1937
Latitude: 58 44 20 N	Longitude: 03 04 10 W
GPS Lat: 5844.333 N	GPS Long: 0304.167 W
Location: SW tip of Tarf of Swona	Area: Pentland
Type: Motorship	Tonnage: 3,223 grt
Length: 362.0 ft Beam: 51.0 ft	Draught: 18.0 ft
How Sunk: Ran aground	Depth: 50 metres

The Finnish motor ship *Johanna Thorden* was on her maiden voyage, returning from Baltimore and New York to Gothenburg, and had had a rough crossing of the Atlantic. She had reached the Butt of Lewis in the afternoon of 11 January 1937, and was approaching the Pentland Firth in the hours of darkness that night. A new lighthouse had been commissioned on Tor Ness, at the south of Hoy, only a few days earlier. That light had not been there when the *Johanna Thorden* made her outbound voyage a few weeks earlier, and there is evidence to suggest that its unexpected appearance may have caused confusion on the bridge as to exactly where the ship was. Just after midnight, the engines were suddenly ordered to be put full astern. Crewmembers who rushed on deck to investigate the reason for this unexpected manoeuvre were shocked to see a high black cliff into which they had nearly crashed. It is supposed that this must have been Dunnet Head. Having so narrowly avoided disaster, the ship was hove-to for several hours between Dunnet Head and Tor Ness, while the captain tried to work out where he was. At 5.20 a.m. the ship went full speed ahead again, but only half an hour later, at 5.50 a.m. on the 12th, the ship ran aground at her full speed of 12 knots. She rode right up on to a rock and stopped dead. (Her speed at the moment of impact was probably in excess of 12 knots, due to assistance by the east-going tidal stream.) A southerly gale was blowing with high seas and driving rain. Captain Lahja Simola told the radio operator, George Moliis, to send an SOS, and to say that the ship was aground on the Pentland Skerries – either Louther Skerry or Clettack Skerry. Moliis tried for about twenty minutes to broadcast an SOS, but without success. He then found that the impact of the ship's grounding had been so severe that her radio aerial had snapped, making it impossible to transmit any message. Forty distress rockets were fired, and clothes soaked in petrol were set alight, but no-one saw the flares or fires. Captain Simola ordered everyone to the lifeboats, and the first boat, with twenty-five people, including two women and two children, left at 6.15 a.m. It failed to make the shore, and all aboard were lost. Bodies were washed ashore on five different Orkney islands, while the boat itself washed ashore on Deerness.

Olof Pehkonen, the steward on the *Johanna Thorden*, said that when the first lifeboat left, he could see a low strip of land not far away on the left hand side, where a light was shining. Another light could be seen miles away. The visibility suddenly became poorer, and the wind and waves began to roll the ship violently.

Shortly after the first boat left, *Johanna Thorden* broke in two. All those still on board were on the stern section, and their impression was that the bow section broke loose and was washed away by the swift stream. I suspect they had not immediately realised that with the bow section breaking off, the stern section was no longer anchored to the rock, and it was they who were being washed away!

When the first boat had got away, the ship had been listing dangerously, but when she broke in two, just forward of the bridge, the aft part floated and came on to an even keel. Visibility at that time was only about 200 metres, and no land could be seen.

The second boat with the captain and his remaining twelve crew left an hour later. After a horrendous three hours the boat was capsized in the surf off Kirkhouse Point on the east side of South Ronaldsay. All the occupants were thrown out of the boat, and only eight survivors managed to reach the shore. They told of the stranded ship breaking in two, and had only gone 300 metres away from the stern section when they saw it rise up and sink vertically. The last glimpse they had of her as she disappeared beneath the surface was the Finnish flag on the stern.

Captain Simola was not one of the survivors. His body was one of three washed ashore.

The arrival of these survivors was the first the islanders knew about the shipwreck.

Longhope lifeboat was alerted at midday, and was launched twenty minutes later. Not long after the lifeboat set out, word was received that their services were not required, and the lifeboat was recalled. The seas were too heavy for the lifeboat to return to its station at Brims, so she beat her way round to the more sheltered Longhope pier instead. By the time she arrived there, however, another message had been received that a ship's lifeboat was still missing, and that the lifeboat services were needed after all. Coxswain Dass and his crew immediately set off again towards Swona to search for the missing lifeboat. Just off the Clett of Swona they saw the bow and foremast of a vessel, and concluded that this was the scene of the wreck that had called them out.

Because of what their captain had told them, however, the survivors said that they had run aground on Louther Rock in the Pentland Skerries. If that had been the case, it would have meant that the bow section had been swept six miles by the gale before being driven ashore at Tarf Tail, at the south end of Swona. Coxswain Dass and other local seamen doubted very much that the bow part of the ship would drift, after the vessel broke up, from the Skerries to Swona. Their opinion was that the flood tide would carry the ship eastward, and this is borne out by the positions at which the two lifeboats came ashore.

Speculation and controversy as to exactly where the *Johanna Thorden* ran aground lasted for years.

Another unlikely suggestion was that the *Johanna Thorden* had actually struck Lother Rock off the south-western tip of South Ronaldsay, before breaking in two, and that the bow section had been swept four miles westwards to Tarf Tail on Swona.

There are extremely strong currents around this location. The wreck of the bow section is lying in a steep gully in 15–40 metres of water off the tip of Tarf Tail. Her cargo included 100 cars, tractors, radio receivers, hides, apples, tobacco, paraffin wax, tyres and 250 tons of copper, a considerable quantity of which was salvaged from the wreck by Keith Jessop in 1969.

The location of the bow section was pointed out to him by James Rosie of Swona, who showed the divers exactly where the vessel went down. They found it immediately.

The motor ship Johanna Thorden *(Photo: author's collection)*

The copper recovered by Keith Jessop was in coils. In searching for the stern section, which contained over 100 tons of copper ingots, he followed the debris along its line of drift from Tarf Tail, until he saw a huge pile of copper bars lying on the bottom. They had obviously spilled from the wreck as it broke in two and drifted down the tide. Unfortunately he did not have a sufficiently long line with him to mark the spot, and was never able to find it again.

It will still be there, but it would be prudent to remember that Tarf Tail is where the turbulence known as the Westerbirth takes place, and along with Swilkie Point off the north tip of Stroma, this is reputed to be among the most difficult tide races in the Pentland Firth – you have been warned!

Some of the wrecks around Swona (© Bob Baird)

GUNNAREN

Wreck No: 348	Date Sunk: 19 08 1935
Latitude: 58 44 48 N	Longitude: 03 03 36 W
GPS Lat: 5844.800 N	GPS Long: 0303.600 W
Location: On W side of Swona Island	Area: Pentland
Type: Motorship	Tonnage: 3,229 grt
Length: 354.1 ft Beam: 50.1 ft	Draught: 21.7 ft
How Sunk: Ran aground	Depth: metres

The Swedish motorship *Gunnaren* was en route from New York to Stockholm with mail and general cargo, when she went ashore in dense fog at 5.00 a.m. on 19 August 1935. Her bottom was ripped out when she struck a pinnacle of rock on the west side of Swona Island in the Pentland Firth, and the vessel broke in two. Longhope lifeboat rescued her crew and the mail. Some of her general cargo was salvaged, and Swedish and German ships made attempts to refloat the *Gunnaren*, without success, even after the wreck had been cut into sections. She was finally abandoned as a total loss. The stern lies 100 yards offshore, north of Dyke End at 5844.7888N, 0303.7480W (WGS84), and parts of the wreck are visible at all states of the tide. The bow section lies in 9 metres of water north of Selki Skerry at 5844.4290N, 0304.1495W (WGS84).

The vessel was built in 1930 by Lindholmen-Motala.

Gunnaren *(Photo: A. Duncan)*

PENNSYLVANIA

Wreck No: 349	Date Sunk: 27 07 1931
Latitude: 58 44 52 N	Longitude: 03 03 35 W
GPS Lat: 5844.867 N	GPS Long: 0303.583 W
Location: W side of Swona Island	Area: Pentland
Type: Steamship	Tonnage: 3,759 grt
Length: ft Beam: ft	Draught: ft
How Sunk: Ran aground	Depth: 12 metres

En route from New York to Copenhagen the 3,759-grt steamship *Pennsylvania* encountered thick fog on 27 July 1931, and struck a rock pinnacle, which is awash at low water, north of Dyke End, close to the west side of Swona.

The *Pennsylvania* was carrying a general cargo, including copper. Longhope lifeboat went to rescue the crew, but they abandoned ship in their own boats and landed on Swona. The stranded vessel broke her back within a week, and parts of her cargo were washed ashore in Caithness and Orkney.

The wreck remained perched on the rocks above water for some time, and was pillaged by men from Stroma and the mainland. Their first raid enabled the men from the mainland to pay off the outstanding debt for the engine of their boat. Eventually, they took off so much from the wreck that they felt obliged to buy the *Pennsylvania* for

£100. The mainland men clubbed together with the men from Stroma, and created a syndicate with fifty £2 shares. They took everything off the wreck and held a big sale. The shareholders all received about £100 from the proceeds.

The shallowest part of the wreck lies 12 metres down the west side of the rock pinnacle, with more wreckage scattered down the slope. The stern of the wreck, with prop shaft, engines and keel, lies at the base of the pinnacle in 27 metres.

STRATHMIGLO

Wreck No: 350	Date Sunk: 02 09 1932
Latitude: 58 41 20 N	Longitude: 04 00 39 W
GPS Lat: 5841.333 N	GPS Long: 0400.650 W
Location: 6 miles off Strathy Point	Area: Pentland
Type: Trawler	Tonnage: 203 grt
Length: 115.5 ft Beam: 23.1 ft	Draught: ft
How Sunk: Collision	Depth: 105 metres

The wreck found here is apparently 132 ft long, and is probably the steel trawler *Strathmiglo* (ex-*Ocean Clipper*), which was sunk in a collision 6 miles off Strathy Point on 2 September 1932.

ORLOCK HEAD

Wreck No: 351	Date Sunk: 28 07 1940
Latitude: 58 41 46 N	Longitude: 04 02 35 W
GPS Lat: 5841.767 N	GPS Long: 0402.583 W
Location: 6.7 miles 320° Strathy Point	Area: Pentland
Type: Steamship	Tonnage: 1,563 grt
Length: 240.0 ft Beam: 36.3 ft	Draught: 19.3 ft
How Sunk: Bombed by aircraft	Depth: 102 metres

The *Orlock Head* was built by the Dublin Dockyard Co. in 1921.

While en route from London to Liverpool with a cargo of 2,065 tons of cement, she was set on fire when bombed and gunned by German aircraft at 584100N, 042100W on 28 July 1940.

She finally sank 320°, 6.7 miles from Strathy Point, and was recorded at 584230N, 040530W PA in 1940. Six of the twenty-five crew were lost.

DUCKBRIDGE

Wreck No: 352	Date Sunk: 22 02 1916
Latitude: 58 42 00 N PA	Longitude: 04 00 00 W PA
GPS Lat: 5842.000 N	GPS Long: 0400.000 W
Location: 6 miles N of Strathy Point	Area: Pentland
Type: Steamship	Tonnage: 1,491 grt
Length: 240.0 ft Beam: 36.2 ft	Draught: 20.1 ft
How Sunk: Mined	Depth: metres

The collier *Duckbridge* was built in 1914, by Craig Taylor & Co.

She was mined and sunk 6 miles north of Strathy Point with the loss of nineteen of her crew.

Her approximate position is recorded as 584200N, 040000W PA.

FREIDIG ?

Wreck No: 353	Date Sunk: 08 02 1944
Latitude: 58 49 36 N	Longitude: 04 00 35 W
GPS Lat: 5849.600 N	GPS Long: 0400.583 W
Location: 14 miles N of Strathy Point	Area: Pentland
Type: Steamship	Tonnage: 1,333 grt
Length: 237.0 ft Beam: 35.2 ft	Draught: 16.0 ft
How Sunk: Foundered	Depth: 70 metres

The Norwegian steamship *Freidig* was en route from Aberdeen to Liverpool with a cargo of rye when she foundered in the vicinity of Strathy Point after her cargo shifted.

In the afternoon of 8 February 1944 it is recorded that she was reported '14 miles off Cape Wrath'.

(I suspect this may be an error, and that the report should read '14 miles off Strathy Point'!)

Thurso lifeboat *H.C.J.* was launched at 15.00 hrs into a gale and heavy snow in response to reports of two dinghies drifting towards the shore.

At 16.30 hrs the rafts were sighted being driven towards the shore off Melvich, to the east of Strathy Point. The lifeboat coxwain, John McLeod, made for the raft nearest the shore and rescued Second Mate Anders Lovaas and Seaman Oddbar K. Clausen. They then found five dead on the other raft. Crewmen Willie Sinclair and David Thompson went aboard the raft and had great difficulty recovering the bodies as their arms and legs were entwined. Another sixteen had left *Freidig* in a boat but were not found. A total of twenty-one lives were lost.

The wreck here lies N/S. It is apparently about 60 metres long, and stands up 7 metres. Note that it is very close to the position recorded for the sinking of the Norwegian steamship *Navarra* on 6 April 1940, and the length dimension more closely matches the *Navarra* than the *Freidig*.

KING EDWARD VII

Wreck No: 354	Date Sunk: 16 01 1916
Latitude: 58 42 22 N	Longitude: 03 53 34 W
GPS Lat: 5842.367 N	GPS Long: 0353.567 W
Location: 7 miles NE of Strathy Point	Area: Pentland
Type: Battleship	Tonnage: 16350 tons
Length: 453.7 ft Beam: 78.0 ft	Draught: 26.7 ft
How Sunk: Mined	Depth: 115 metres

The battleship *King Edward VII* was built in 1905 at Devonport Dockyard. She was armed with four 12-inch guns, four 9.2-inch, ten 6-inch, fourteen 12-pounders, two machine guns and four torpedo tubes.

On 16 January 1916, en route from Scapa Flow to Belfast for refitting, she struck a mine some 25 miles west of Swona. Both engine rooms were flooded, and the ship took a list to starboard. Guns and rocket signals attracted the attention of the steamship *Princess Melita* about five miles away, and when she arrived a towing wire was passed to her. While she was preparing to tow, HMS *Kempenfelt* arrived and a towing wire was also passed to her. Both vessels started to tow *King Edward VII* at 2.15 p.m., but due to a strong wind and sea the ship was unmanageable. At 2.40 p.m., *Kempenfelt's* tow wire parted. It was obvious that any further attempt to take the battleship in tow would be useless. The ship was settling in the water, and *Princess Melita's* tow was slipped. With the ship having taken so much water, the increasing heavy weather, the towing having failed, and darkness approaching, Captain C. Maclachlan decided to abandon ship for the night. The destroyer *Musketeer* came alongside at 2.45 p.m., followed by *Marne*, *Fortune* and *Nessus*, and took off all the officers and men. Tugs and *Nessus* were ordered to stand by the ship, while the other destroyers were sent back to Scapa with all the men from the battleship. *King Edward VII* turned over and sank at 8.10 p.m.

In April 1997, a team of divers led by Leigh Bishop became the first divers to visit the battleship. Although the minimum depth of the wreck is charted as 94 metres, *King Edward VII* lies at a depth of 115 metres at the western entrance to the Pentland Firth, off the north coast of Scotland. The main object of the expedition was to confirm the identity of the wreck.

Leigh Bishop said, 'This was pretty immediate on the first dive with visibility of about 25m revealing the wreck lying upside down, listing to her starboard side, but at an angle that still showed her superstructure, and a row of 6-inch guns. The first few metres of the ship's bow, blown off by the mine blast, were nowhere to be seen. Sundry items in the wreck's debris field included boxes of very large shells and some enormous portholes.'

The team made twenty-four dives on the wreck over four days to depths ranging from 105–115m.

One of their biggest problems was coping with the cold during the 2½ hours of decompression required after only sixteen minutes on the wreck in 6°C water.

The expedition achieved one of the first known European amateur dives to a wreck lying totally below 100 metres, and proved that the systems and procedures used by the group are among the best in the world.

HMS King Edward VII *(Photo: author's collection)*

THUNFISCH

Wreck No: 355

Latitude: 58 42 04 N

GPS Lat: 5842.066 N

Location: ¾ mile NE of Muckle Skerry Light

Type: Trawler

Length: 219.0 ft   Beam: 31.0 ft

How Sunk: Ran aground

Date Sunk: 31 01 1975

Longitude: 02 54 08 W

GPS Long: 0254.132 W

Area: Pentland

Tonnage: 824 grt

Draught: 14.0 ft

Depth: 26 metres

The German trawler *Thunfisch* struck Clettack Skerry in heavy weather and sank ¾ mile NE of the lighthouse on Muckle Skerry. A red flare had been sighted about 8 miles NE of Duncansby Head, and Longhope lifeboat was launched. Wick lifeboat also went out to search in the area of the Pentland Skerries. Longhope lifeboat took off three men from a liferaft. Several vessels in the area joined the search for the missing men. A total of eight survivors were picked up from rafts. The remaining twelve members of *Thunfisch*'s crew landed on Swona, and were picked up from there by helicopter. All twenty crew were saved.

The Hydrographic Department gives the position as 5840N, 0300W. This is one mile NE of Duncansby Head, and must be only a very approximate position in the general area of Pentland/Duncansby.

The Pentland Skerries lighthouse keeper stated that the *Thunfisch* struck Clettack Skerry and then sank ¾ mile NE of the lighthouse on Muckle Skerry.

Others believe the wreck may actually be west of the Pentland Skerries.

Some of the Wrecks off Cape Wrath

6

CAPE WRATH

JOHN RANDOLPH

Wreck No: 356		Date Sunk: 05 09 1952
Latitude: 58 32 00 N PA		Longitude: 04 15 00 W PA
GPS Lat: 5832.000 N		GPS Long: 0415.000 W
Location: Torrisdale Bay, Sutherland		Area: Wrath
Type: Steamship		Tonnage: 7191 grt
Length: 441.5 ft	Beam: 57.0 ft	Draught: 27.0 ft
How Sunk: Ran aground – tow broke		Depth: metres

The Liberty ship *John Randolph* was built by Bethlehem-Fairfield in February 1942. She sailed to Russia in convoy PQ-16, and was one of thirty-five ships returning from North Russia in convoy QP-13. Approaching Iceland in poor visibility, on 5 July 1942, six of these ships inadvertently went into a British minefield off the north-west of Iceland. These were the minesweeper HMS *Niger*, 815 tons, and the US ships *Heffron*, 7,611 grt, *Hybert*, 6,120 grt, *John Randolph*, 7,191 grt, *Massmar*, 5,828 grt, and the Russian *Rodina*, 4,441 grt.

All six ships hit mines and four of them sank, but the bow section of the *John Randolph* was beached at Flateyri, Iceland. It was later refloated and towed to Falcon Point, Reyjkavik, where it was used as a storage hulk, a boat landing stage, and a cargo-handling platform.

On 1 September 1952, while being towed to Bo'ness in the Forth for scrapping, the bow section broke adrift from the Dutch tug *Oceanis* in rough seas at 5920N, 0733W, and had to be abandoned. The derelict forepart was washed ashore and wrecked four days later on 5 September, on the sandy beach in Torrisdale Bay, Sutherland.

The rough weather on the north coast of Scotland continued for several days, and local opinion was that unless early efforts were made to refloat the hulk, it would become firmly embedded in the sand.

Several writers in the past have incorrectly reported this wreck to be the Liberty ship *Richard Bland*, which was returning from North Russia in convoy RA53 when she was torpedoed by the *U-255* (Reche), at 09.26 hrs on 5 March 1943 in position 7244N, 1127E, SW of Bear Island. Another American ship, the *Executive*, 4,978 grt, was hit by one of the three torpedoes fired at both vessels, and was sunk.

U-boats and air reconnaissance reported both ships to be sinking, but the *Richard Bland* was only damaged, and remained afloat until found five days later on 10 March at 6653N, 1410W, again by the *U-255*. At 16.36 hrs, Reche fired another three torpedoes, and the *Richard Bland* broke in two. The stern portion sank, but the forward section was taken in tow by the tug *Horsa*, which grounded at 6538N, 1354W on 16 March.

The bow section of the *Richard Bland* was driven ashore near Akureyri, Iceland at 6536N, 1405W.

The Liberty Ship John Randolph *under construction (Photo: Project Liberty Ship)*

The wreck in Torrisdale Bay has also been incorrectly identified in the past as the *Paulus Potter* (ex-*Empire Johnson*), a 7,168-grt Liberty ship built in 1942, and owned by the Dutch government in exile in London.

She was carrying a cargo of aircraft in the ill-fated PQ-17 convoy from Reykjavik to Archangel when she was attacked by German *Ju-88* aircraft of KG30 in the Barents Sea on 5 July 1942. Her engine and steering gear were put out of action, and with the vessel taking in water, the crew abandoned ship in four lifeboats. Three other ships nearby had also been hit by bombs, and the German aircraft then fired incendiary shells into all four vessels. Three of them sank, but the *Paulus Potter* remained afloat, and was found derelict, 600 miles north of Murmansk, eight days later by the *U-255*. A boarding party from the U-boat found the engine room flooded, and recovered secret papers which had not been thrown overboard in the haste to abandon the ship, which was in any case presumed to be about to founder.

Reche then torpedoed the ship with his last remaining torpedo, and the *Paulus Potter* caught fire and sank within two minutes at about 70N, 52E. A photograph of the vessel sinking by the stern was taken by *U-255*, and it clearly shows the ship to be intact, complete with its bows.

ASHBURY

Wreck No: 357	Date Sunk: 08 01 1945
Latitude: 58 32 48 N	Longitude: 04 24 32 W
GPS Lat: 5832.800 N	GPS Long: 0424.533 W
Location: Dubh-Sgeir Mohr, Kyle of Tongue	Area: Wrath
Type: Steamship	Tonnage: 3901 grt

Length: 356.5 ft   Beam: 50.0 ft   Draught: 24.7 ft
How Sunk: Ran aground   Depth: 22 metres

The British steamship *Ashbury* (ex-*Cairnhill*, ex-*Nitedal*) was built by William Gray & Co. of West Hartlepool in 1924. She was one of the fleet belonging to the Alexander Shipping Co. Ltd of London, whose normal peacetime route was from the River Plate to London, with regular sailings from the Argentine.

At the time of loss she was en route from Workington to the Tyne in ballast, and had already been in difficulties in Loch Ewe. In the early hours of 4 January 1945 a signal was received from HM Drifter *Fairweather*, of the Loch Ewe Harbour Patrol, stating that *Ashbury* was dragging and was unwilling to move without a pilot aboard.

The tug *Empire Ivy* was ordered to proceed to the assistance of *Ashbury*, and the tug contacted the *Ashbury* at approximately 01.30 to find that she had lost her starboard anchor and two shackles of cable, and was dragging badly. Assisted by the *Empire Ivy*, *Ashbury* was anchored in various areas of Loch Ewe, and was undoubtedly prevented from fouling other vessels, and from dragging ashore, by the efforts of the tug.

After leaving Loch Ewe to resume their northward journey, convoy WN67 encountered very heavy weather, and the ships became scattered. On the evening of 7 January, efforts were being made by the escorts to round up the stragglers and re-form the convoy, but without much success, owing to the gale and heavy seas.

A signal transmitted in plain language by W/T from the *Ashbury* at 10.00 p.m. on 7 January said: 'Unmanageable. Require tug to stand by urgently. Drifting towards the shore. Position 20 miles west of Dunnet Head. Am drifting quickly, practically on shore. Is any help being sent?'

This was the first intimation that *Ashbury* was in distress, but the message was not received by the Admiral Commanding Orkney and Shetland until 23.25 hrs on 7 January. HMCS *SteTherese*, one of the convoy escorts which had been searching for stragglers, was informed of *Ashbury*'s position. This ship made contact with both *Ashbury* and the Norwegian steamship *Bestik* at 02.05 on 8 January, and found them both close to a lee shore with anchors down. Weather conditions were very bad, wind northerly force 8–9, with very high seas, and intermittent rain and hail squalls. Between 02.30 and 03.30, three attempts were made to close *Ashbury* sufficiently to pass a line, but conditions were much too hazardous. Shoals were visible close to leeward, and due to darkness and the lack of landmarks or lights, the ship's position was not accurately known, so attempts were abandoned. *Ashbury* dragged rapidly and struck Dubh Sgeir Mhor reef at the mouth of Talmine Bay at 03.30 hrs. She sank with the loss of all forty-two aboard. *Bestik* escaped, and finally anchored in Scapa Flow at 13.00 hrs on 8 January. Wreckage from the *Ashbury* and twenty-six bodies were washed ashore at Talmine and Tongue the following day. Nineteen of them were buried at Thurso, and 300 people attended the funeral.

The Court of Inquiry found that the primary cause of her stranding was that, being under Admiralty orders during a critical period of the war, she was obliged to sail 'in a ballast condition which in the abnormally heavy sea and weather conditions at the time, prevented her from maintaining speed and place in the convoy and from keeping off the rocks on which she was ultimately stranded'.

Although her loss was war-related, there is no suggestion that she was sunk or damaged by enemy action.

Lloyds regarded this and all such cases as marine losses. Her loss was considered due to an ordinary marine risk, namely a low-powered ship in ballast becoming unmanageable and running ashore in heavy weather.

The *Ashbury*'s boiler lies on a sandy bottom at the foot of a 20-metre vertical drop at the north side of Dubh Sgeir Mhor reef, part of the Talmine Skerries. The south side of the reef drops more gently with many gullies and a kelp forest. The ship's spare iron propeller lies in one of the gullies. Her 7-ton bronze propeller and 4-inch gun lay at the south side of the reef but they, along with the bell, have been raised. The gun was displayed outside a house near Talmine for several years until the owner moved to Bettyhill.

Ashbury (*Photo: courtesy of World Ship Society*)

VULTURE II

Wreck No: 358		Date Sunk: 16 03 1918	
Latitude: 58 29 15 N		Longitude: 04 40 12 W	
GPS Lat: 5829.250 N		GPS Long: 0440.200 W	
Location: In Loch Erribol		Area: Wrath	
Type: Trawler		Tonnage: 190 grt	
Length: 115.5 ft	Beam: 21.0 ft	Draught: 11.2 ft	
How Sunk: Collision		Depth: 50 metres	

The iron-hulled steam trawler *Vulture II* was built in 1899 by Cook Welton & Gemmell, Hull, engine by C.D. Holmes of Hull, and owned by the St Andrews Steam Fishing Co. Ltd.

The wreck lies about 600 metres NW of White Head light, near the edge of the 50-metre depth contour.

TERN

Wreck No: 359		Date Sunk: 23 02 1915	
Latitude: 58 31 15 N PA		Longitude: 04 39 15 W PA	
GPS Lat: 5831.250 N		GPS Long: 0439.250 W	
Location: Wrecked in Loch Erribol		Area: Wrath	
Type: Trawler		Tonnage: 199 grt	
Length: 110.6 ft	Beam: 21.6 ft	Draught: 11.5 ft	
How Sunk: Ran aground?		Depth: 18 metres	

The steel fishing trawler *Tern* was built in 1907 by Goole SB & Rprng. Co. She was hired by the Admiralty in 1914 as a minesweeper, and was wrecked in Loch Erribol on 23 February 1915.

Six members of her crew were lost.

BULLEN

Wreck No: 360	Date Sunk: 06 12 1944
Latitude: 58 43 46 N	Longitude: 04 51 16 W
GPS Lat: 5843.767 N	GPS Long: 0451.267 W
Location: 7½ miles NE of Cape Wrath	Area: Wrath
Type: Destroyer	Tonnage: 1,300 grt
Length: 306.0 ft Beam: 37.0 ft.	Draught: 13.5 ft
How Sunk: Torpedoed by *U-775*	Depth: 77 metres

The British destroyer HMS *Bullen* was an ex-US Buckley Class destroyer, built in 1943.

On 6 December 1944 she was one of the ships of 19 Escort Group on an anti-submarine sweep off the north of Scotland. Other ships in the group were HMS *Hesperus*, HMS *Goodall*, HMS *Loch Insh* and HMS *Antigua*. At 09.48 hrs, 7 miles 037° from Cape Wrath, *Bullen* was torpedoed by the *U-775* (OL Erich Taschenmacher).

She was struck amidships and broke in two. The bow section sank first, and the stern section sank about two hours later. Ninety-seven men were rescued by HMS *Hesperus*.

A Board of Enquiry was held on 18 December 1944 in HMS Defender, a Western Approaches shore establishment at Liverpool.

First Lieutenant William Daniel told the enquiry that he believed the torpedo had struck on the starboard side, at the bulkhead between the engine room and No.2 boiler room. The upper deck immediately began to buckle at an angle of 100°, right across the ship from the point of impact. Both the engine room and No.2 boiler room flooded and the ship broke in two.

Stoker Petty Officer Frank Hughes told the Board of Enquiry that he had been in the forward (No.1) Boiler Room with Stokers Dale, Moss and Biggs. All the lights had gone out, but he put the emergency lights on and got out his torch to have a look at the bilges to see if there was any water in them. There was no water there, so they all felt pretty safe. The communication system was out of action, and no one had been down to tell the men what was going on. Stoker Dale was detailed to go up top and find out what was happening. He came back a couple of minutes later and said that he thought the after boilers had blown off. P/O Hughes thought that unlikely, but the after boilers were out of action so he started to raise steam again.

A long time seemed to pass, and still no-one had come to tell them anything.

Stoker Dale was sent back up top again to see what he could find out, and he came back to say that everybody was in the water swimming and all covered in oil. There were rafts over the side and nets.

P/O Hughes didn't think it could possibly be that bad. There was a slight list on the ship, but they were dry and there was no water. He thought Dale must be joking until the engineer officer passed by and said, 'You had better come up, they are abandoning ship.'

Everyone got out of the boiler room and shut the hatches down. The ship was in a very bad condition. She was sinking. The foc'sle was awash. There were only a few left on the foc'sle by that time, and everybody was abandoning ship.

Stoker Dale went over the starboard side, and P/O Hughes went over the port side.

He swam for about two hours before he saw a whaler. There were too many round it so he then swam to a raft, which he hung on to. Shortly before reaching the raft he turned round and saw *Bullen* broken in two.

All lifesaving apparatus except for the whaler and the motor boat was got away safely. The whaler had been stove in two days previously, while escorting a convoy during a storm off the north coast of Ireland, and it had not been repaired. There was no time to launch her motor boat, but life rafts were thrown overboard before the crew abandoned ship.

Navigating Officer Lieutenant John Winstanley RNR recalled that the captain was seen going over the side wearing a lifejacket. Two ratings from *Hesperus*, which had stopped to pick up survivors, climbed down the scrambling net, but they could not get hold of him. *Hesperus* manoeuvred and they tried to catch him again. They succeeded in giving him a line, which he managed to get one arm through, and his head. The ratings got him three feet above the water before he slipped and was never seen again.

Several injured men were found below after the *Bullen* was torpedoed, among them a petty officer lying amid a pool of oil on the floor of the senior rates' bathroom. One man was trapped in the crack across the upper deck. Desperate efforts were made to free him but he went down with the ship. Bow and stern stood upright as she sank and, according to the enquiry findings, this class of vessel was known for its lack of longitudinal strength.

Goodall dropped her whaler to help pick up survivors, then she and *Antigua* carried out an anti-submarine sweep. *Hesperus* stopped and *Goodall's* whaler came alongside her with about ten survivors from *Bullen*.

Just at that moment, Commander George Levassick in *Hesperus* moved ahead and turned her into the wind. *Goodall's* whaler was swamped and two of her ratings were lost along with at least two of *Bullen's* survivors. Four officers and ninety-three ratings survived and were picked up by HMS *Hesperus*.

The enquiry found that there was evidence of disorganisation in *Bullen* – poor damage control and the fact that the whaler had not been repaired after two days were blamed on Lieutenant Daniel, though he was commended for his efforts to save life when the ship was abandoned. It also turned out that, when the torpedo struck, all the officers with the exception of Sub Lieutenant Clark as OOW were in the wardroom for a conference about a forthcoming inspection.

Commander George Levassick of HMS *Hesperus*, who was senior officer of the escort group, was criticised for stopping to pick up survivors instead of leading the counter-attack on the U-boat.

The frigates HMS *Loch Insh* and *Goodall* hunted *U-775* for 14 hours before losing Asdic contact. The U-boat escaped and returned to her base at Bergen on 21 December.

More RN ships swept the area the following day, and depth-charges dropped on one contact produced hammocks, greatcoats and naval caps, identifying the target as part of HMS *Bullen*.

The Hydrographic Department gave an estimate for the position of the sinking of the *Bullen* as 5842N, 0412W PA, but this is some 20 miles to the east of the position of attack, and no wreck is charted near that position. The wreck at 584346N, 045116W is in about the right position for the attack on the *Bullen*. This wreck lies SSE/NNW, and has been estimated to be about 180 ft long by about 50 ft beam, and standing up 19 ft from the seabed.

The length of the wreck could very well correspond to the length of the forward section of the *Bullen*, but the beam dimension is somewhat greater than that of the *Bullen*.

(The dimensions may be wrong, however, as they were probably estimated using side scan sonar, and dimensions obtained with this equipment are notoriously inaccurate.)

The Hydrographic Department suggests this wreck might possibly be the *Fornebo*, but the dimensions do not fit that vessel either.

CARIBBEAN

Wreck No: 361	Date Sunk: 27 09 1915
Latitude: 58 12 52 N	Longitude: 05 43 53 W
GPS Lat: 5812.870 N	GPS Long: 543.880 W
Location: 12 miles W of Point of Stoer	Area: Wrath
Type: Steamship	Tonnage: 5,824 grt
Length: 420.0 ft Beam: 49.8 ft	Draught: 25.0 ft
How Sunk: Foundered	Depth: 88 metres

This wreck was found during a sonar sweep in 1970. From side scan sonar images, it appears to be the wreck of a two-funnelled passenger ship about 390ft long. The wreck lies 34 miles SW of Cape Wrath, oriented NW/SE and standing up about 14 metres from the bottom which is at 103 metres.

The Royal Mail Steam Packet Co. steamship *Caribbean* (ex-*Dunottar Castle* of the Union Castle Line) was built by Fairfields at Govan in 1890. She was requisitioned by the Admiralty during the First World War for service first as a transport and later as an auxiliary cruiser. It was then decided to use her as a fleet base ship at Scapa Flow, and during the summer of 1915 HMS *Caribbean* was in Cammell Laird's yard at Birkenhead being fitted out as an accommodation ship for dockyard workers. Extensive structural alterations were made throughout the ship to provide accommodation for messing and sleeping 600 men. Several extra cabins were fitted, along with many additions to the upper deck in the way of sheds for machinery, corrugated tops to the superstructure, etc. In addition, six large angle irons were placed on each side of the ship to take a very large landing stage. These alterations were compensated for by an extra 1,500 tons of iron ballast. The ship came out of dock on 24 September 1915, and immediately headed north towards Cape Wrath.

When Commander Henry Leonard Bethune was called to take command of the *Caribbean*, he had last been at sea twelve years previously, and his crew was comprised of men not accustomed to the ship. Some had not boarded the ship until the day before she sailed, so that the ship sailed with practically a new set of officers and men. The carpenter had only been on the ship for ten or eleven days. He knew very little about ships, and seemed quite strange to most of his duties.

As she entered the lower Minch, the *Caribbean* ran into heavy weather. At about noon on the 26th it was first reported to her captain, Cdr Bethune, that the ship was making water.

At about 08.00 a.m. the chief engineer had reported water coming down into the stokehold from the port foremost cross bunker, but the pumps were dealing with it satisfactorily. The shutter door was shored up and caulked, but owing to the flimsy nature of the door it was distorted and water continued to leak through.

The pumps became choked with ashes and eventually the water could not be contained. Some portholes in the room directly above this bunker were found to be open. The carpenter and chief officer went round together closing all the scuttles and securing the deadlights. These scuttles had been reported closed when the ship left the dock, before going down the Mersey. The foreman and chief officer between them went round and saw every scuttle closed as they were leaving the basin. Four or five miles from Cape Wrath the chief engineer reported that the ship must turn its head to sea, as water was coming down the stokehold and lifting the floor plates. The wind was from the north east, and the ship's head was duly turned to point in that direction. The chief engineer reported that water was gaining on the pumps, and the ship's head was pointed to the west, so as to get clear of the land.

Cdr Bethune was concerned that if the engines stopped and they were caught to the east, they should have very little chance of saving the ship. At about 12.30–1.00 p.m. the navigating officer was told to get as far west as he could into the open sea. The ship would thus have a chance to drift clear of the land. The engines stopped at 2.15 p.m.

Before that, the ship could make about 6 knots. The navigating officer said that the nearest port, Stornoway, was 23 miles away, and as the water was gaining, Bethune did not think it expedient to try and make a port where he might get a lee shore. He thought they should have more chance of being picked up by drifting in mid-channel.

The very large angle irons threw up a lot of water as the ship proceeded, and Bethune thought this might have caused plates to strain and make a leak. Average speed on the journey was 11.7 knots. The ship took a heavy list to port. A lifeboat was tipped by the stern while being lowered.

An SOS was sent about 1.00 p.m., and at 1.30 p.m., Rear Admiral Tupper in Stornoway received a telegram advising him of the distressed state of the *Caribbean*. He immediately ordered the yachts *Hersilia* and *Calanthe* to sea from Stornoway, along with the Cape Wrath trawlers.

Calanthe reported the sea too bad to proceed as she was taking water below, and after four hours attempting to make progress northward, *Hersilia* reported similarly. Both yachts were ordered to return to shelter.

The trawlers *Princess Alice*, *Lily Melling* and *Ijuin* were sheltering in the lee of Bulgie Island when they received a radio message at 1.30 p.m. on the 26th, and immediately proceeded to sea to search for the *Caribbean*. The sea was so bad that they did not find the stricken vessel until 3.00 p.m. A tug was also sent for, but it never found the ship.

The trawlers stood by the ship, and watched for the tug *Flying Kestrel* and the cruiser HMS *Birkenhead*. The *Kestrel* did not arrive at all, but *Birkenhead* arrived at 9.00 p.m. Because of the very bad weather conditions *Birkenhead* was unable to take *Caribbean* in tow, and stood by also.

There was no moonlight, and searchlights were not used, in case they attracted the unwelcome attention of a U-boat.

At midnight *Princess Alice* picked three men out of the water. They were from a smashed boat. The sea was very bad, but the cruiser lowered two well-manned lifeboats, which *Lily Melling* and *Princess Alice* towed to the wreck. By that time *Caribbean* had a heavy list to port

They first tried to get alongside to leeward, and then they succeeded in getting the boat close-to by going to windward, and the men jumped into the boat from the ship. *Princess Alice* also picked up one boat from *Caribbean* containing twenty-three men. *Lily Melling* made two trips with the lifeboat. The first lot of nineteen men she took on board herself, while the second lot went to the cruiser. *Birkenhead*'s boat managed to take twenty-four of the crew off the weather side, and the remaining forty to fifty were also taken off by that boat on its second trip. The men slid down the side of *Caribbean* into the boat. It appears, therefore, that five boatloads were saved, namely two boats from *Caribbean* and two boats from *Birkenhead*, one of which made two trips.

Caribbean was still afloat with *Birkenhead* and *Ijuin* standing by when the trawlers left at 4.00 a.m. They steered for Stornoway, and near the entrance to the harbour at 5.30 a.m., they saw the tug *Flying Kestrel* at anchor, and gave her the position of the wreck, 8 miles east of Tiumpan Head. The tug put to sea again.

The trawlers got alongside the wharf at 6.00 a.m. Arrangements were made to billet the men, who had already been given hot refreshments. Three men were taken to hospital with bruised and sprained ankles, presumably sustained in jumping from the *Caribbean* into the boats.

At 9.45 a.m. *Flying Kestrel* returned to Stornoway and reported they had seen nothing of the wreck, and concluded that it had sunk.

At 10.25 a.m. the trawler *Ijuin* arrived and reported that the *Caribbean* had sunk in 5814N, 0542W at 7.15 a.m. On making the final plunge her stern came right out of the water, and she went down bows first at an angle of 90°, with fifteen members of her crew who could not be taken off in time.

Birkenhead went south down the Minch, and the survivors from *Caribbean*'s crew were sent to Scapa in the tug. It left at 6.00 p.m. to arrive at Scapa in daylight.

The Court of Enquiry was of the opinion that blame was directly attributable to the carpenter for not having made himself acquainted with the ship, and having reported all scuttles closed when three were left open. *Birkenhead* did everything possible after her arrival, and her captain was justified in not showing lights, which might have attracted an enemy submarine. With no lights being shown, it was easy for the tug *Flying Kestrel* to miss the *Caribbean* in the dark.

Dunottar Castle *became HMS* Caribbean *(Photo: courtesy of World Ship Society)*

HYLAS

Wreck No: 362	Date Sunk: 15 08 1917
Latitude: 58 38 53 N	Longitude: 05 46 42 W
GPS Lat: 5838.883 N	GPS Long: 0546.700 W
Location: 24 miles W of Cape Wrath	Area: Wrath
Type: Steamship	Tonnage: 4,240 grt
Length: 379.5 ft Beam: 49.5 ft	Draught: ft
How Sunk: Torpedoed by *U-80*	Depth: 110 metres

The British steamship *Hylas* was en route from Archangel to Belfast with a cargo of flax when she was torpedoed and sunk by the *U-80* on 15 August 1917, 10 miles east of the Butt of Lewis. This would suggest a position of about 583000N, 055500W, but the wreck located in 1983 at 583853N, 054642W is probably the *Hylas*. This wreck is 140 metres long by 30 metres wide, and stands up 9.5 metres from the bottom.

This wreck is 18 miles NE of the Butt of Lewis and 24 miles W of Cape Wrath.

NOREEN MARY

Wreck No: 363	Date Sunk: 05 07 1944
Latitude: 58 30 59 N	Longitude: 05 33 24 W
GPS Lat: 5830.983 N	GPS Long: 0533.400 W
Location: 18 miles SW of Cape Wrath	Area: Wrath
Type: Trawler	Tonnage: 207 grt
Length: 118.8 ft Beam: 23.1 ft	Draught: ft
How Sunk: By submarine – gunfire (*U-247*)	Depth: 114 metres

This intact wreck lies oriented 090/270° in about 124 metres total depth. It is estimated to be about 45m long, and a sonar trace shows a mast still sticking up 10.3 metres.

At 20.45 hrs on 5 July 1944 the steam trawler *Noreen Mary* (GN17) (ex-*Kate Lewis*) signalled *Starbank* that she had seen a U-boat and had been missed by two torpedoes. At about 21.00 hrs the U-boat's conning tower broke the surface and it opened fire with its deck gun.

Noreen Mary had sunk by 22.00 hrs in 240° Cape Wrath 14 miles. *HMT Lady Madeleine* picked up two survivors at 04.25 hrs on the 6th.

The U-boat was *U-247* (OL Gerhard Matschulat), who gave the position as AM3682, which equates to about 5827N, 0536W.

Lloyds recorded the position as 5830N, 0523W, which is 15 miles SW of Cape Wrath.

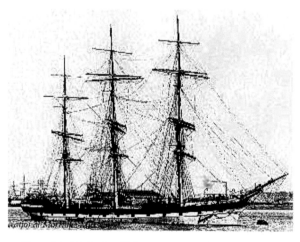

The sailing ship Majorka *(Photo: National Maritime Museum)*

MAJORKA

Wreck No: 364	Date Sunk: 14 08 1917
Latitude: 58 34 05 N	Longitude: 05 13 45 W
GPS Lat: 5834.083 N	GPS Long: 0513.750 W

Location: 3 miles NW of Am Balg   Area: Wrath
Type: Sailing Vessel   Tonnage: 1,684 grt
Length: 259.5 ft   Beam: 38.2 ft Draught: 23.1 ft
How Sunk: By submarine   Depth: 57 metres

The iron sailing ship *Majorka* (ex-*Clan Mackenzie*) was built in 1882 by R. Duncan of Port Glasgow, and registered in Drammen, Norway. She was sunk by a submarine on 14 August 1917.

Lloyds War Losses gives the position of attack as 5830N, 0520W.

The wreck lies WNW/ESE in 57 metres, and stands up 3.75 metres from the bottom.

According to one report, a mast showed 6 feet above the surface at low water for a time after she sank.

The bell from the Majorka, *showing the vessel's original name* Clan Mackenzie *(Photo: Courtesy of Ken Farrow)*

U-905

Wreck No: 365   Date Sunk: 23 03 1945
Latitude: 58 35 31 N   Longitude: 05 46 06 W
GPS Lat: 5835.517 N   GPS Long: 0546.100 W
Location: 23 miles W of Cape Wrath   Area: Wrath
Type: Submarine   Tonnage: 769/871 dwt
Length: 221.4 ft   Beam: 20.5 ft Draught: 15.8 ft
How Sunk: Depth-charged   Depth: 130 metres

Type VIIC Atlantic U-boat *U-905* (OL Bernhard Schwarting) might have been the U-boat attacked by a Liberator aircraft of 86 Sqdn (F/Lt N. E. M. Smith), north of Cape Wrath on 20 March 1945, but there was no direct evidence of a kill.

Three days later, on 23 March, the frigate HMS *Conn* of the 21st Escort Group depth-charged a U-boat 23 miles west of Cape Wrath.

The identity disc of one of *U-905*'s crewmen was recovered. There were no survivors.

BEACON LIGHT

Wreck No: 366	Date Sunk: 11 11 1940
Latitude: 58 27 24 N	Longitude: 05 44 59 W
GPS Lat: 5827.400 N	GPS Long: 0544.983 W
Location: 24 miles SW of Cape Wrath	Area: Wrath
Type: Steamship	Tonnage: 2,768 grt
Length: 312.8 ft Beam: 40.4 ft	Draught: 28.3 ft
How Sunk: Torpedoed by *U-91*	Depth: 102 metres

The oiler (tanker) *Beacon Light* was en route from Liverpool to Scapa Flow with a cargo of fuel oil when she was torpedoed 15 miles SE of the Butt of Lewis by the *U-91* on 19 February 1918. There were no survivors from her crew of thirty-three. The *Beacon Light* was armed with a defensive gun, but it was not used as the crew did not see their attacker before their ship was hit.

The wreck was located and examined in 1984. It is apparently intact and upright, lying 049/229° in 112 metres. Least depth is 102 metres.

SUNNYVALE

Wreck No: 367	Date Sunk: 16 12 1971
Latitude: 58 36 30 N PA	Longitude: 05 00 30 W PA
GPS Lat: 5836.500 N	GPS Long: 0500.500 W
Location: ½ mile S of Am Bodach	Area: Wrath
Type: Trawler	Tonnage: grt
Length: ft Beam: ft	Draught: ft
How Sunk: Ran aground	Depth: 30 metres

The MFV *Sunnyvale* ran aground one mile south of Cape Wrath on 16 December 1971.

HAMNAVOE

Wreck No: 368	Date Sunk: 01 04 1981
Latitude: 58 38 21 N	Longitude: 04 55 37 W
GPS Lat: 5838.350 N	GPS Long: 0455.617 W
Location: 2 miles E of Cape Wrath	Area: Wrath
Type: Trawler	Tonnage: grt
Length: ft Beam: ft	Draught: ft
How Sunk:	Depth: 33 metres

The British MFV *Hamnavoe* was abandoned on fire on 1 April 1981. She later sank 074° 2.3 miles from Cape Wrath light. The wreck lies oriented N/S in an area of sand waves, whose crests are over 2 metres high, and spaced about 6 metres apart. As the height of the wreck is only 2 metres, it may cover and uncover as the sand shifts.

PARNU

Wreck No: 369		Date Sunk: 18 04 1941	
Latitude: 58 27 21 N		Longitude: 05 48 57 W	
GPS Lat: 5827.350 N		GPS Long: 0548.950 W	
Location: 285° 8 miles from Cape Wrath		Area: Wrath	
Type: Steamship		Tonnage: 1,578 grt	
Length: 247.5 ft	Beam: 36.3 ft	Draught: ft	
How Sunk: Collision		Depth: 103 metres	

The steamship *Parnu* (ex-*Corness*, ex-*Westgarth*) was carrying a cargo of coal from Barry to London when she was involved in a collision 285° 8 miles from Cape Wrath on 18 April 1941. This must have been at about 584000N, 051300W. She was taken in tow, evidently for Stornoway, but sank 15 miles ESE of the Butt of Lewis at 572721N, 054857W. The wreck is apparently intact, lying 060/240° standing up 7.5 metres in 111 metres total depth.

The vessel was built in 1909 by Sir R. Dixon & Co. of Middlesbrough.

The Manipur (*Photo: JMC*)

MANIPUR

Wreck No: 370		Date Sunk: 17 07 1940	
Latitude: 58 41 15 N		Longitude: 05 11 50 W	
GPS Lat: 5841.250 N		GPS Long: 0511.833 W	
Location: 7 miles NW of Cape Wrath		Area: Wrath	
Type: Steamship		Tonnage: 8,652 grt	
Length: 473.0 ft	Beam: 64.0 ft	Draught: 37.0 ft	
How Sunk: Torpedoed by *U-57*		Depth: 68 metres	

The Brocklebank steamship *Manipur* was built in 1920 by Lithgows of Port Glasgow. On 17 July 1940, while en route from Baltimore and Halifax, Nova Scotia to London with a general cargo including iron, steel, lumber, zinc slabs, copper and explosives, she was torpedoed by *U-57* (KL Erich Topp). The German grid square was given as AM3662, which equates to about 5845N, 0500W. The *Manipur* was hit in No.2 hold at 23.17 hrs, and about 30 seconds later another torpedo hit the stokehold and she sank in four to five minutes.

At 01.45 hrs, HMS *Skeena* reported the torpedoing of the *Manipur*, and that she had picked up sixty-four survivors before rejoining the convoy. Seven Europeans and seven 'Asiatics' were lost.

Lloyds notes that she sank about 6 miles NW of Cape Wrath, and the Hydrographic Department recorded the position as 584117N, 051143W, but the wreck is now charted at 584115N, 051150W. The position has also been recorded as 584122N, 051152W.

In 1971 Risdon Beazley/Ulrich Harms found the wreck in a very badly broken condition. Their salvage vessel *Foremost 18* recovered a total of 489 tons of copper and 149 tons of zinc.

FORNEBO

Wreck No: 371	Date Sunk: 17 06 1917
Latitude: 58 41 38 N	Longitude: 04 54 27 W
GPS Lat: 5841.633 N	GPS Long: 0454.450 W
Location: 5 miles NE of Cape Wrath	Area: Wrath
Type: Steamship	Tonnage: 4,401 grt
Length: 363.0 f Beam: 52.8 ft	Draught: ft
How Sunk: Torpedoed by *U-78*	Depth: 80 metres

The Admiralty tanker *Fornebo* was bringing a cargo of fuel oil from Port Arthur, Texas, to the UK when she was torpedoed by *U-78* four miles north of Cape Wrath on 17 June 1917.

This would give a position of about 584200N, 050200W PA, but no wreck is charted near that position. The Hydrographic Department suggested the wreck at 584346N, 045116W, 7 miles NE of Cape Wrath, might be the *Fornebo*, but that wreck is apparently only about 180 ft long, whereas the *Fornebo* was 363 ft long.

The uncharted wreck at 584138N, 045427W, five miles 35° from Cape Wrath, is the nearest recorded wreck to the description 'four miles north of Cape Wrath'. This wreck was thought by the Hydrographic Department to be the *Prince Rupert City*, but the dimensions and construction of the wreck found in 1984 at 584603N, 044701W, 11 miles NE of Cape Wrath, appear to match those of the *Prince Rupert City*. The wreck at 584138N, 045427W might, therefore, be the *Fornebo*.

OILFIELD

Wreck No: 372	Date Sunk: 16 03 1918
Latitude: 58 42 39 N PA	Longitude: 05 27 29 W PA
GPS Lat: 5842.650 N	GPS Long: 0527.483 W
Location: 15 miles NW of Cape Wrath	Area: Wrath
Type: Tanker	Tonnage: 4,000 grt
Length: 346.5 ft Beam: 46.2 ft	Draught: ft
How Sunk: Torpedoed by *U-90*	Depth: metres

The tanker *Oilfield* was en route from Grangemouth and Methil to New York in ballast on 16 March 1918 when she was torpedoed and damaged by *U-90* 15 miles NW of Cape Wrath. Three of the crew were lost. She was beached and refloated, but became a total loss. Where was she beached? There are not many places to beach a ship around Cape Wrath!

UNKNOWN

Wreck No: 373	Date Sunk:
Latitude: 58 42 48 N	Longitude: 04 29 24 W
GPS Lat: 5842.800 N	GPS Long: 0429.400 W
Location: 17 miles ENE of Cape Wrath	Area: Wrath
Type:	Tonnage: grt
Length: ft Beam: ft	Draught: ft
How Sunk:	Depth: 56 metres

It had been assumed this was the wreck of *U-297*, but a U-boat found 16 miles west of Yesnaby, Orkney is now known to be *U-297*.

The wreck here might be the *Albula*, and perhaps it was detected and depth-charged by HMS *Loch Insh* and *Goodall* during the hunt for the U-boat that sank HMS *Bullen*?

ALBULA

Wreck No: 374	Date Sunk: 10 08 1940
Latitude: 58 38 00 N PA	Longitude: 04 35 30 W PA
GPS Lat: 5838.000 N	GPS Long: 0435.500 W
Location: 3 miles N of Whiten Head	Area: Wrath
Type: Motorship	Tonnage: 329 grt
Length: 135.9 ft Beam: 24.0 ft	Draught: 9.1 ft
How Sunk: Collision with *Countess*	Depth: 45 metres

On 10 August 1940 the destroyer HMS *Jaguar* rescued the crew of the Dutch motorship *Albula*, rammed by SS *Countess* in convoy, in position 583800N, 043530W.

A subsequent search both by air and the tug *Thames* from Stornoway failed to locate the *Albula*. It was therefore considered that she had probably sunk.

The position given is three miles north of Whiten Head in a depth of about 45 metres to a sand and shingle seabed. No wreck is charted there, but *Albula* may have drifted some distance before finally foundering. The *Albula* was built by Gute Hoffnungshutte at Walsum in 1935, and was powered by a 4-cylinder Sulzer oil engine.

ALWAKI

Wreck No: 375	Date Sunk: 10 07 1940
Latitude: 58 43 15 N	Longitude: 04 29 04 W
GPS Lat: 5843.250 N	GPS Long: 0429.067 W
Location: 17 miles NE of Cape Wrath	Area: Wrath
Type: Steamship	Tonnage: 4,533 grt
Length: 372.9 ft Beam: 52.8 ft	Draught: 26.4 ft
How Sunk: Torpedoed by *U-61*	Depth: 56 metres

The Dutch steamship *Alwaki* was built in 1922 by Werf. Maasdijk.

At 12.45 hrs on 10 July 1940 HMCS *St Laurent* reported the *Awalki* sinking 12 miles north east of Cape Wrath after what was thought to be internal, engine room explosions. As a result, the sinking of the *Alwaki* is not included in *Lloyds War Losses*.

HMS *Coventry* took off her crew, and although it was not realised at the time that the ship had been torpedoed, an A/S sweep was mounted. The position of sinking was estimated as 584600N, 044600W PA, and also described as 10 miles NE of Cape Wrath.

In fact the *Alwaki* had been torpedoed by *U-61* (KL Jürgen Oesten), in German grid AN1542, which equates to about 5845N, 0436W.

The wreck at 584138N, 045427W, which was originally thought possibly to have been the *Prince Rupert City*, might be the *Alwaki*. The dimensions of these vessels were fairly similar.

The wreck at 584315N, 042904W is in almost the exact position recorded for *U-297* at 5844N, 0429W. The wrecks of both *Alwaki* and *Prince Rupert City* were already lying in the vicinity of the attacks on the U-boat responsible for sinking HMS *Bullen*, and perhaps one (or more) of the asdic contacts attacked could have been an existing wreck.

The position of this wreck has also been recorded as 5843.008N, 0429.400W (OSGB36).

It lies oriented 020/200°, and is apparently 200 ft long, stands up 53 ft, and has a beam of 53 ft.

UNKNOWN – ALWAKI?

Wreck No: 376	Date Sunk:
Latitude: 58 46 25 N	Longitude: 04 55 10 W
GPS Lat: 5846.417 N	GPS Long: 0455.167 W
Location: 9 miles N of Cape Wrath	Area: Wrath
Type:	Tonnage: grt
Length: ft Beam: ft	Draught: ft
How Sunk:	Depth: 72 metres

This may be the Dutch steamship *Alwaki*, torpedoed by *U-61* (Oesten), on 10 July 1940 in German grid AN1542, which equates to about 5845N, 0436W.

The position of sinking was estimated as 584600N, 044600W PA, and also described as 10 miles NE of Cape Wrath.

The position of this wreck seems to meet that description rather better than the wreck at 584315N, 042904W.

The sinking of the *Alwaki* is not included in *Lloyds War Losses*. She sank after an explosion in the engine room, but it was not realised at the time that the explosion was due to a torpedo. It was assumed that the explosion was an internal one, and that her loss was not war-related.

PRINCE RUPERT CITY

Wreck No: 377	Date Sunk: 02 06 1941
Latitude: 58 46 03 N	Longitude: 04 47 01 W
GPS Lat: 5846.050 N	GPS Long: 0447.017 W

Location: 11 miles NE of Cape Wrath   Area: Wrath

Type: Steamship   Tonnage: 4,749 grt

Length: 400.5 ft   Beam: 54.3 ft   Draught: 25.6 ft

How Sunk: Bombed   Depth: 71 metres

Built in 1924 by W. Gray of Sunderland, the steamship *Prince Rupert City* was en route in ballast from Britain to the St Lawrence when she was attacked by German aircraft at 11.30 pm on 1 June 1941. Admiralty records state that she was bombed and sunk in 5846N, 0441W, off Cape Wrath, whereas Lloyds give the position of attack as 584630N, 044130W PA.

The vessel was abandoned after midnight, when at 01.35 hrs forty survivors, including her master, were rescued by the trawler *Arran* and taken to Oban. *Prince Rupert City* finally sank at 6.15 a.m. on 2 June. Four lives were lost, but there were forty-five survivors.

The Hydrographic Department recorded the wreck at 584138N, 045427W, 35° 5 miles from Cape Wrath, as the *Prince Rupert City*.

The dimensions and apparent construction of the wreck found in 1984 at 584603N, 044701W, however, 11 miles NE of Cape Wrath, match those of the *Prince Rupert City*.

CHELSEA

Wreck No: 378   Date Sunk: 30 08 1940

Latitude: 58 45 00 N PA   Longitude: 07 00 00 W PA

GPS Lat: 5845.000 N   GPS Long: 0700.000 W

Location: N of Lewis   Area: Wrath

Type: Steamship   Tonnage: 4,084 grt

Length: 396.1 ft   Beam: 52.8 ft   Draught: 27.2 ft

How Sunk: Torpedoed by *U-32*   Depth: metres

In the early hours of 30 August 1940 three ships from convoy HX66A were torpedoed and sunk north of Lewis by *U-32* (KL Hans Jenisch). These were the SS *Chelsea* (Br 4,804 grt), SS *Mill Hill* (Br 4,318 grt) and the MV *Norne* (Nw 3,971 grt).

Lloyds gives the position as 5848N, 0649W PA, which appears to correspond very closely to the German grid position recorded as AM3538 (5851N, 0700W), but no wrecks are charted in, or near, that position.

The chief officer of the *Chelsea* estimated the position as 5945N, 0400W PA, and three wrecks are charted around that position at 5945N, 0402W, 5944N, 0359W and 5947N, 0355W.

The *Chelsea* had been en route from Montreal to Methil and London with 7,600 tons of maize. Twenty-four, including one gunner, were missing out of the *Chelsea's* thirty-five crew.

The eleven survivors were landed at Thurso by the trawler *Lord Cecil* on the 31st.

UNKNOWN – LILY ?

Wreck No: 379   Date Sunk: 29 05 1940

Latitude: 58 48 25 N   Longitude: 04 35 18 W

GPS Lat: 5848.417 N   GPS Long: 0435.300 W

Location: 17 miles NE of Cape Wrath   Area: Wrath

Type: Steamship		Tonnage: 1281 grt
Length: 224.4 ft	Beam: 33.0 ft	Draught: ft
How Sunk: Torpedoed by *U-13*		Depth: 63 metres

The 1,281-grt Danish steamship *Lily* sailed from Fowey, Cornwall, on 2 April 1940, bound for Aarhus with a cargo of china clay. Her route took her around the north of Scotland, and she called in to Kirkwall for examination. On 9 April the Germans invaded Denmark. There was no question of her being allowed to leave for her now-occupied homeland. Instead, she left Kirkwall on 25 April 1940, bound for Preston, but disappeared en route. The Joint Arbitration Committee considered that she was lost due to war causes, and she was finally posted missing on 26 June.

She was in fact torpedoed by *U-13* (Schulte) at 01.17 hrs on 26 April. *U-13* fired two torpedoes, one of which hit the bow of the *Lily*, and broke off her foc'sle. The *Lily* sank in 45 seconds, with the loss of all her crew.

The German grid position was recorded as AN1524, which equates to about 5857N, 0412W.

Twelve minutes later, however, *U-13* torpedoed the British steamship *Scottish American* (6,999 grt) in German grid AN1545, which equates to about 5839N, 0436W.

These two positions are 23 miles apart. To cover that distance in 12 minutes, *U-13* would have to be doing 115 knots! That is obviously completely out of the question!

Scottish American was not sunk – only damaged. Her crew gave the position of attack as 5841N, 0440W.

This wreck lies oriented 045/225° and is apparently 60 metres long, standing up 6 metres from the bottom. It might be the *Lily*. Alternatively, the wreck at 584315N, 042904W, recorded as the *Alwaki*, could be the *Lily*.

The Swedish steamship Murjek *(Photo: Tomas Johanneson collection)*

MURJEK ?

Wreck No: 380		Date Sunk: 11 03 1916
Latitude: 58 49 50 N		Longitude: 04 39 15 W
GPS Lat: 5849.833 N		GPS Long: 0439.250 W
Location: 16 miles NE of Cape Wrath		Area: Wrath
Type: Steamship		Tonnage: 4,146 grt
Length: 353.1 ft	Beam: 49.5 ft	Draught: ft
How Sunk: Mined		Depth: 72 metres

The Swedish steamship *Murjek* was mined 12 miles NE of Cape Wrath on 11 March 1916 while en route from Philadelphia to Narvik with a cargo of coal and machinery.

UNKNOWN

Wreck No: 381   Date Sunk:
Latitude: 58 52 00 N   Longitude: 04 59 20 W
GPS Lat: 5852.000 N   GPS Long: 0459.333 W
Location: 14 miles N of Cape Wrath   Area: Wrath
Type: Tonnage: grt
Length: ft   Beam: ft   Draught: ft
How Sunk: Depth: 53 metres

A wreck is charted very close SW of Nun Rock, which rises to 5.4 metres from the surface. This suggests the possibility that a vessel may have sunk after striking the rock.

There is, however, apparently some doubt that this is a wreck. It may be a rock.

JUNONA

Wreck No: 382   Date Sunk: 25 08 1917
Latitude: 58 44 00 N   Longitude: 05 36 00 W
GPS Lat: 5844.000 N   GPS Long: 0536.000 W
Location: 20 miles NW of Cape Wrath   Area: Wrath
Type: Steamship   Tonnage: 3,462 grt
Length: 345.3 ft   Beam: 46.1 ft   Draught: 15.4 ft
How Sunk: Torpedoed by *U-80*   Depth: metres

The Russian steamship *Junona* was built in 1898 by Wigham Richardson.

On 25 August 1917, while en route from Archangel to Barry with 400 tons of pit props, she was torpedoed and sunk at 5844N, 0436W by *U-80*. HM Whaler *Cowwhale* rescued thirty-seven of *Junona*'s crew.

BLAKE

Wreck No: 383   Date Sunk: 24 07 1917
Latitude: 58 59 10 N   Longitude: 05 21 30 W
GPS Lat: 5859.177 N   GPS Long: 0521.500 W
Location: 24 miles NW of Cape Wrath   Area: Wrath
Type: Steamship   Tonnage: 3,740 grt
Length: 342.1 ft   Beam: 46.6 ft   Draught: 24.8 ft
How Sunk: Torpedoed by *UC-49*   Depth: 81 metres

The British steamship *Blake* was a Doxford turret ship built in 1906.

On 24 July 1917 she was torpedoed and sunk by *UC-49* while en route from Penarth to Archangel with a cargo of coal. Five of the crew were lost. The *Blake* had a gun.

British Vessels Lost at Sea 1949–1918 describes the position as 30 miles N by W ½W from Cape Wrath, while Lloyds describe the position as 14 miles S 40° E of North Rona, which would plot very close to 585910N, 052130W.

MANINA

Wreck No: 384	Date Sunk: 08 04 1968
Latitude: 59 01 25 N	Longitude: 04 30 18 W
GPS Lat: 5901.417 N	GPS Long: 430.300 W
Location: East side of Stack Skerry	Area: Wrath
Type: Motor ship	Tonnage: 1,333 grt
Length: 263.8 ft Beam: 40.2 ft	Draught: 16.2 ft
How Sunk: Ran aground	Depth: 26 metres

On 8 April 1968 the Greek motor vessel *Manina* (ex-*Corvus*, built in Gothenburg in 1947) was en route in ballast from Bergen to Glasgow. Just before 5.00 a.m. she radioed an SOS message saying she had run onto the 120-foot Stack five miles south-west of Sule Skerry Lighthouse. She said that one of her holds was full of water and that the fourteen crew were abandoning ship. Red flares fired by the *Manina* were seen by the Sule Skerry lightkeepers.

A sea and air rescue operation was immediately launched, with two Orkney lifeboats, various ships in the area, and a Shackleton aircraft from RAF Kinloss all converging on the scene.

A force 7 westerly wind was blowing, and there was a short steep swell. The *Manina* was taking a very heavy pounding, and by midday she had broken up and disappeared.

The Shackleton developed engine trouble and had to return to her base but she was replaced by another aircraft. On his return to Kinloss Squadron Leader D.C. Matheson reported:

'When we were flying at 500 feet we saw three of the survivors on a raft. They were near a Swedish vessel which had nets slung over the side to help to get the men on board. There were several empty lifejackets in the water and a lot of wreckage.' He had seen a body about a quarter of a mile away from the rocks where the *Manina* had grounded.

The Swedish vessel was the tanker *Vassijaure*, which, with a British cargo ship, the *Afghanistan*, had quickly arrived at the Stack.

Stromness lifeboat and the long-range lifeboat *Grace Paterson Ritchie*, which had been based in Kirkwall while undergoing winter trials, were also on their way to the scene. Sule Skerry is about 37 miles west of Orkney, and it would take the two lifeboats four or five hours to get there.

The *Kalgalos*, another ship assisting in the search, picked up a body 5½ miles from the rock.

The *Ross Kipling*, which was 25 miles NNW from the Stack, radioed that she was making for the Skerry. The fishery protection vessel *Norna*, 55 miles away, was also making for the scene. The *Vassijaure* radioed at 7.30 a.m. that she had picked up five survivors on rafts. Twenty-five minutes later she reported that she had come upon five dead seamen on an upturned lifeboat and rafts. At 8.10 a.m. the *Afghanistan* located a raft and an empty upturned lifeboat with twelve life jackets, but with no survivors, either on or near it. She continued her search, as far as 10 miles down wind from Stack Skerry. The drama continued all morning. By that time, the two lifeboats had also joined the ships. Stromness lifeboat picked up two bodies about a quarter of a mile from the Stack. At 11.45 a.m. the aircraft signalled that she considered the search area had been adequately covered. The surface ships were thanked for their help and they proceeded on their voyages, leaving behind the two lifeboats and the aircraft to continue the search.

The *Grace Paterson Ritchie* circled round the Stack and radioed that there was nobody on the rock, and no sign of the *Manina*, which had by then completely disappeared, leaving two large oil slicks, a mass of wreckage and an upturned lifeboat to mark the spot where the ship had sunk.

At midday the *Vassijaure* left for Lewis with the five survivors, and the five dead men, who included the master, Captain Victor Kaprokefalos. Stornoway lifeboat met the Swedish tanker 12 miles off the mainland of Lewis and took the survivors and bodies back to Stornoway.

The survivors included Vassilias Kyriacou, the second mate, who said 'Nearly everyone was asleep this morning when this happened. The ship struck a rock and the forward hold started to fill up. We abandoned ship, and seconds later she keeled over and broke up. I was on a raft with some others. We could see some of the men in the water, but we could do nothing because we had no ropes or lifebelts to throw them. It was really terrible. Within minutes all our clothes were wet and we had to rub ourselves to keep warm. Every time a wave came we thought we would capsize. Georgios Domitriades, apprentice engineer, was in the sea for a long time. We found him hanging on to a lifeboat, which had overturned. We must have been adrift for about three hours before we were picked up. We were given tea and I don't remember much more. It was really terrible, so very cold.'

Stromness lifeboat had been unable to transfer the two bodies she had picked up to the *Vassijaure* because of the heavy swell, and left for home with them.

Coxswain Alfred Sinclair said 'There was absolutely no sign of the *Manina*, only lots of wreckage of lifeboats, doors and tables. The seas were heavy and the spray was breaking almost up to the top of the rock. We picked up the two bodies floating in the water with lifejackets a quarter of a mile off the Stack. They were about 100 yards apart.'

The search by the aircraft and the *Grace Paterson Ritchie* continued until late in the afternoon, but no further survivors were found. Nine of the *Manina's* fourteen crew were lost.

Her well-broken remains lie at depths of 12 to 44 metres in a rocky gully immediately adjacent to Stack Skerry. Underwater visibility here is around 35 metres. The bridge and midships section lies at 26 metres. The top of her mast is at 12 metres, and it leads down to the bows. The stern, with a large stainless steel propeller and three spare blades, is at a depth of 44 metres.

U-36 ?

Wreck No: 385	Date Sunk: 24 07 1915
Latitude: 59 04 30 N	Longitude: 05 16 00 W
GPS Lat: 5904.500 N	GPS Long: 0516.000 W
Location: 28 miles NW of Cape Wrath	Area: Wrath
Type: Submarine	Tonnage: grt
Length: ft Beam: ft	Draught: ft
How Sunk: Gunfire	Depth: 97 metres

U-36 (KL Ernst Graeff) was sunk by gunfire from HMS *Prince Charles* on 24 July 1915.

Prince Charles was a decoy ship – merchant vessels with concealed armament, and with their holds filled with empty barrels to give additional buoyancy in the event of the vessel being damaged. *U-36* approached the ostensibly innocuous merchant ship *Prince Charles*, fired a warning shot, and ordered her to stop. *Prince Charles'* 'panic party' – members of the crew acting as merchant seamen – abandoned the Q-ship in a small boat. As soon as they were clear, *U-36* started to shell the apparently deserted vessel. When the U-boat approached to within 600 yards, *Prince Charles* ran up her white ensign, dropped the hatch covers and sides of deckhouses, exposing her concealed guns, and opened fire on the unsuspecting submarine, which sank stern first. There were fifteen survivors, but eighteen other members of the U-boat's crew were lost. *U-36* was the first U-boat to be sunk by a Q-ship.

The position has been given as 5907N, 0530W, and 5905N, 0601W, but no wreck is charted in either of these positions. The unknown wreck charted at 590430N, 051600W might be *U-36* (or possibly the *Graciosa*).

PAJALA

Wreck No: 386	Date Sunk: 18 01 1940
Latitude: 59 05 20 N	Longitude: 05 56 00 W
GPS Lat: 5905.333 N	GPS Long: 0556.000 W
Location: 4 miles WSW of North Rona	Area: Wrath
Type: Motor vessel	Tonnage: 6,873 grt
Length: ft	Beam: ft Draught: ft
How Sunk: Torpedoed by *U-25*	Depth: 71 metres

The Swedish motor vessel *Pajala* was torpedoed and sunk by *U-25* (KK Victor Schutze) on 18 January 1940. *Pajala* had been en route from Buenos Aires to Gothenburg with a cargo of 9,150 tons of grain and cattle food. Her crew were all saved. The trawler *Northern Duke* had been escorting the *Pajala* (presumably into Kirkwall to be examined for contraband) and noted the torpedo explosion at 17.15 hrs. At 17.30 hrs, *Northern Duke* shelled and depth-charged a U-boat 072°, North Rona 10 miles. The armed trawlers *Kimberley* and *Ashanti* were sent on a sweep. *Kimberley* reported wreckage, probably from the *Pajala*, but found nothing else. (*U-25* recorded the position as AM3488, which equates to about 5909N, 0536W.)

The Swedish steamship Pajala *(Photo: Tomas Johanneson collection)*

GRACIOSA

Wreck No: 387	Date Sunk: 24 08 1918
Latitude: 59 06 00 N PA	Longitude: 05 00 00 W PA

GPS Lat: 5906.000 N	GPS Long: 0500.000 W
Location:	Area: Wrath
Type: Sailing ship	Tonnage: 2,276 grt
Length: 280.5 ft Beam: 39.6 ft	Draught: ft
How Sunk: By submarine	Depth: metres

The steel four-masted Portuguese sailing vessel *Graciosa* was sunk by a submarine on 24 August 1918, while en route from North Shields to Lobito Bay with a cargo of coal.

Lloyds War Losses gives the position as 5906N, 0500W.

UNKNOWN – U-36 ?

Wreck No: 388	Date Sunk:
Latitude: 59 10 20 N	Longitude: 05 52 20 W
GPS Lat: 5910.333 N	GPS Long: 552.333 W
Location: 3 miles NW of North Rona	Area: Wrath
Type:	Tonnage: grt
Length: ft Beam: ft	Draught: ft
How Sunk:	Depth: 80 metres

This might be *U-36*. Or possibly the *Emmaplein*?

BOTUSK

Wreck No: 389	Date Sunk: 31 01 1941
Latitude: 59 11 00 N PA	Longitude: 05 45 00 W PA
GPS Lat: 5911.000 N	GPS Long: 0545.000 W
Location: 6 miles NE of North Rona	Area: Wrath
Type: Steamship	Tonnage: 3,091 grt
Length: 333.3 ft Beam: 46.8 ft	Draught: 23.3 ft
How Sunk: Mined	Depth: metres

The British steamship *Botusk* was en route from St John, New Brunswick to Cardiff with a cargo of 4,221 tons of grain when she struck a mine about 6 miles NE of North Rona on 31 January 1941. Four of her crew were lost. The remaining thirty-four were saved.

The *Botusk* and the Dutch steamship *Emmaplein* were in convoy HX103, and strayed into the North Rona minefield. *Botusk* detonated a mine and sank. The survivors were landed at Thurso by the cable ship *Ariel* on 1 February.

Botusk (ex-*Transit*, ex-*Molton*) was built in 1919 by Ropner S.B. & Rpg. Co. of Stockton.

EMMAPLEIN

Wreck No: 390	Date Sunk: 31 01 1941
Latitude: 59 11 00 N PA	Longitude: 05 45 00 W PA
GPS Lat: 5911.000 N	GPS Long: 5045.000 W
Location: 6 miles NE of North Rona	Area: Wrath

Type: Steamship	Tonnage: 5.436 grt
Length: ft	Beam: ft Draught: ft
How Sunk: Mined	Depth: metres

The Dutch steamship *Emmaplein* was en route from St John, New Brunswick to the Tyne with 4,000 tons of timber and 3,000 tons of scrap metal when she struck a mine on 31 January 1941, about 6 miles NE of North Rona. Her crew of thirty-four were all saved.

Emmaplein was last seen by an aircraft at 18.00 hrs. The survivors were landed at Thurso by the cable ship *Ariel* on 1 February.

POWHATAN

Wreck No: 391	Date Sunk: 06 04 1917
Latitude: 59 32 00 N PA	Longitude: 06 30 00 W PA
GPS Lat: 5932.000 N	GPS Long: 0630.000 W
Location: 25 miles N by W North Rona	Area: Wrath
Type: Steamship	Tonnage: 6,117 grt
Length: 420.4 ft Beam: 53.2 ft	Draught: 29.1 ft
How Sunk: Torpedoed by *U-66*	Depth: metres

The British steam tanker *Powhatan* (ex-*Tuscarora*) was built in 1898 by Sir J. Laing, Sunderland for the Tank Storage & Carriage Co. Ltd. She was torpedoed by the *U-66* 25 miles N by W from North Rona on 6 April 1917, while en route from Sabine to Kirkwall with a cargo of fuel oil. Thirty-six of the crew were lost, and her master was taken prisoner.

LAGAHOLM

Wreck No: 392	Date Sunk: 01 03 1940
Latitude: 59 34 00 N PA	Longitude: 05 10 00 W PA
GPS Lat: 5934.000 N	GPS Long: 0510.000 W
Location: 65 miles N of Cape Wrath	Area: Wrath
Type: Motor Vessel	Tonnage: 2.818 grt
Length: 336.1 ft Beam: 50.0 ft	Draught: 20.3 ft
How Sunk: By *U-32* – gunfire	Depth: 120 metres

On 1 March 1940 the Swedish motor vessel *Lagaholm* was en route from Baltimore and New York for Gothenburg and Malmo when she was sunk by gunfire from the *U-32* (OL Hans Jenisch), about 80 miles west of Kirkwall. One member of her crew was lost. On 2 March, an aircraft of 269 Sqdn reported that the *Lagaholm* was burning furiously in 5934N, 0510W.

At 11.36 hrs a lifeboat was seen in the same position. *Lagaholm* sank in the afternoon, and the Norwegian *Bel Pamela* landed fourteen survivors at Kirkwall and another thirteen at North Ronaldsay.

U-32 had fired three torpedoes at the *Bel Pamela* earlier that morning, but all three had exploded prematurely. Jenisch had obviously lost faith in his torpedoes, and this is why he resorted to gunfire to sink the *Lagaholm*.

The *Lagaholm* was carrying mail and 4,000 tons of general cargo, including 100 tons of aluminium ingots, 62 tons of copper and 53 tons of brass.

The Swedish steamship Lagaholm (*Photo: Tomas Johanneson collection*)

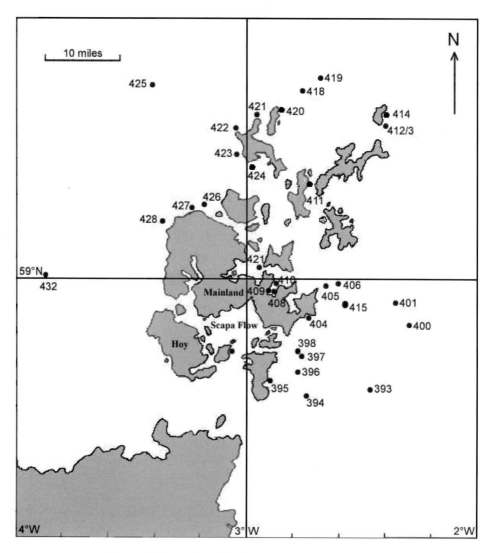

Some of the wrecks off Orkney. Map (© R.N. Baird)

7

ORKNEY

A number of authors have written extensively about Scapa Flow and the scuttling of the German fleet, the subsequent salvaging of most of the ships, and descriptions of those that remain today.

There seemed little point in me regurgitating what others have already done so well, so I made a deliberate decision not to include these wrecks, preferring instead to concentrate on wrecks which others have not already written about.

For information on wrecks in Scapa Flow, the blockships, HMS *Royal Oak* and HMS *Vanguard*, I would refer the reader to the following books: *Jutland to Junkyard*, by S.C. George; *The Man who Bought a Navy* by G. Bowman; *Dive Scapa Flow*, by Rod MacDonald; *Dive Scotland*, Vol. 3, by Gordon Ridley; *Shipwrecks of Orkney, Shetland and Pentland Firth*, by David M. Ferguson; *The Grand Scuttle*, by Dan van der Vat; *Scapa*, by James Miller; *Black Saturday*, by Alexander McKee; *Nightmare at Scapa Flow*, by H.J. Weaver; and *The Royal Oak Disaster*, by Gerald S. Snyder. There are also others.

DUKE OF ALBANY

Wreck No: 393	Date Sunk: 24 08 1916
Latitude: 58 45 25 N	Longitude: 02 27 37 W
GPS Lat: 5845.417 N	GPS Long: 0227.617 W
Location: 8 miles NE of Pentland Skerries	Area: Orkney
Type: Steamship	Tonnage: 1,997 grt
Length: 331.0 ft Beam: 41.0 ft	Draught: 17.0 ft
How Sunk: Torpedoed by *UB-27*	Depth: 60 metres

The British steamship *Duke of Albany* was built in 1907 for the Lancashire & Yorkshire Railway. During the First World War she was requisitioned by the Admiralty for use as an Armed Boarding Steamer. On 24 August 1916, in company with the *Duke of Clarence*, she was steaming eastwards at 14½ knots towards her patrol area east of the Pentland Skerries. The vessels were proceeding in line abreast, about 1½ miles apart. *Duke of Albany* was to the northward. At 09.00 hrs in position 5844N, 0228W a torpedo track was spotted about 300 yards away, running near the surface, approaching the *Duke of Albany* from her port beam. The officer of the watch, Lt Norman Leslie RNR, immediately rang down for full ahead, and put the helm hard over to starboard in an attempt to avoid the torpedo, which, however, struck the ship under the port engine room, a few feet below the water line, at 9.03 a.m. The emergency bells were rung, and all hands were at their action stations by the time the explosion took place. A few seconds later, a second torpedo passed close astern, running deep. The ship immediately began to settle by the stern, and six minutes later the bows reared up and the ship sank quickly, stern first. At the time the position was noted as 5842N, 0223W.

One of the lifeboats was blown to pieces – fragments reached the height of the top of the funnel. Another was capsized as the ship sank, but the two remaining lifeboats got clear away. Survivors included eleven officers and seventy-six ratings. One of the officers and four men were seriously injured.

The *Duke of Clarence* at once proceeded at full speed towards the *Duke of Albany*, slipping two boats close to the men swimming in the water, and endeavoured to ram the U-boat, whose position was indicated by a swirl on the surface of the sea. She may have been partially successful, as a slight metallic shock was felt in the engine room, but the U-boat was not sunk.

Duke of Albany *(Photo: courtesy of Lancashire & Yorkshire Railway Society)*

TAMARA XII ?

Wreck No: 394	Date Sunk: 18 02 1923
Latitude: 58 44 16 N	Longitude: 02 40 36 W
GPS Lat: 5844.267 N	GPS Long: 0240.600 W
Location: 8 miles E of Old Head, S Ronaldsay	Area: Orkney
Type: Sailing ship	Tonnage: 1,767 grt
Length: ft Beam: ft	Draught: ft
How Sunk: Foundered	Depth: 67 metres

Strong easterly winds lashed the north of Scotland on Saturday 18 February 1923. Shortly after 7 o'clock in the evening the lighthouse keeper on Copinsay observed distress signals from a ship between Copinsay and the Pentland Skerries.

The vessel was apparently brightly illuminated with electric light. Later reports stated that the bright lights had given place to a dim one, and eventually this too disappeared.

Stromness and Longhope lifeboats were summoned and launched with all possible speed. The Stromness boat headed across Scapa Flow for Holm, intending to enlist the services of a pilot to take the boat through the obstructions in Holm Sound. By the time the lifeboat reached Holm, however, the lights of the vessel had disappeared. The Stromness lifeboat therefore returned home.

Despite the terrible sea conditions, Longhope lifeboat made its way through the Pentland Firth, and searched for some time between the Pentland Skerries and Copinsay, but found nothing, before they were forced to return to port. With the coming of daylight the next morning, the lighthouse keepers scanned the troubled waters but could find no trace of any vessel. This led to the surmise that the vessel must either have foundered or had been able to proceed on her voyage.

On Monday 20th it was reported that wreckage had been washed ashore on a number of the Orkney islands. Part of a ship's boat marked *Tamara XII* was reported.

Large quantities of wreckage had been passing Copinsay for some days, including seamen's bunks. Planks and part of a mahogany table had also come ashore.

At Deerness, a lifebuoy marked *Jupiter*, Bergen – the name of the regular mail steamer which sailed between Newcastle & Bergen – was picked up.

Lifebuoys marked 'Hamburg' were also found washed ashore at various places on the east Mainland, and it was reported from Copinsay that papers belonging to a German vessel had been found.

A deck house was washed ashore on Shapinsay, but there was no indication as to the name of the ship to which it belonged, but it was of a larger type than found on trawlers.

On the island of Eday, a door with the words 'Officers Mess Room' had been found, as well as other wreckage including the 'billboard' for an anchor, apparently belonging to a vessel of some size.

On Tuesday 21 February, a ship's figurehead of some considerable size came ashore at Howquoy Head, Holm. On that same day, a badly damaged ship's boat marked 'Tamara XII, Hamburg' with the body of a young man aboard, wearing a lifebelt, was picked up near Start Sound, Sanday. Another boat similar to the one found at Start Sound also came ashore at Sanday, but there was nothing to identify the vessel to which it belonged. The body of a young seaman also came ashore near the same spot. From a post-mortem examination it appeared that the man died of exposure. There was nothing to identify the body, but it seemed to be that of a foreign seaman clothed in oilskins, a seaman's jacket, and sea-boots.

Tamara XII, a steel full-rigged sailing ship of 1,767 grt, was built by W. Pickersgill of Sunderland, in 1892. She was originally named *Naworth Castle*. The vessel was later bought by a German firm and renamed *Tarpenbek*. Later still she was renamed *Tamara XII*. *Tamara XII* had left Leith on 6 February for Hamburg, thus encountering the full force of the ESE gales.

The wreck here is 110 metres long. (See also *Loch Maddy*.)

OPAL & NARBOROUGH

Wreck No: 395	Date Sunk: 12 01 1918
Latitude: 58 46 15 N	Longitude: 02 55 48 W
GPS Lat: 5846.250 N	GPS Long: 0255.800 W
Location: Clett of Crura, S Ronaldsay	Area: Orkney
Type: Destroyers	Tonnage: 1,025 dwt
Length: 273.0 ft Beam: 26.7 ft	Draught: 10.2 ft
How Sunk: Ran aground	Depth: 8-11 metres

The M-Class destroyers *Opal* and *Narborough* were returning to Scapa Flow on the pitch dark night of 12 January 1918, in a blizzard and gale, when both ships ran ashore on the east coast of South Ronaldsay, below Ward Hill.

HMS *Opal* had been the leading ship, and the Court of Enquiry found that she had either steered an incorrect course, or failed to make sufficient allowance for the wind and tide, causing both vessels to run ashore under high cliffs in terrible weather conditions.

When it was realised that the two destroyers were missing, a search over a wide area around the Pentland Skerries was carried out. At 9.20 a.m. on 14 January, wreckage of HMS *Opal* and *Narborough* was sighted on the Clett of Crura in Windwick Bay. HM trawler *Michael Maloney* lowered her boat to examine the wreckage. The sea was calm but there was a heavy swell from the south-east, making examination of wrecks difficult and dangerous. A man was sighted ashore who signalled by semaphore that he was a survivor from the *Opal*. Michael Maloney's boat managed to rescue the man, Able Seaman William Sissons of HMS *Opal*, who was the only survivor from the combined ships' companies of 189 men.

He was suffering from exposure and shock, and was taken to the hospital ship *China*.

At the time of his ship striking he was one of the crew at the midship gun. Despite his condition he was able to provide lucid information about the loss of the ships. About 9.30 p.m. on Saturday 12 January, HMS *Opal* and *Narborough* were in company. *Opal* was leading. There was a thick blizzard at the time and a heavy following sea. *Opal* struck heavily about three times, and shortly after appeared to slide into deep water. Almost immediately after striking, *Opal* was pooped by the following sea which filled up her after part and carried away her funnels and mast. After apparently sliding into deeper water her fore part broke off at the break of the fo'c'sle, and the remainder foundered about a quarter of an hour later. According to Sissons, *Opal* had been sounding with her sounding machine, and immediately upon striking the rocks she blew three blasts on her siren, which were answered by *Narborough*, which appeared to pass *Opal* on the port quarter, strike heavily and heel well over. Nothing more of *Narborough* was seen by the survivor. He stated that the captain and sub-lieutenant of *Opal* were on the bridge at the time of striking, and gave orders to abandon ship. He did not observe any boat manage to get away safely and stated that the Carley Floats were launched, but owing to the sea state, no one could remain on them. He managed to swim ashore and reached a ledge, with crevices well sheltered from the wind, with about 50 yards to walk about on. Huddled on the narrow cliff ledge for thirty-six hours, suffering from exposure, he kept himself alive with shellfish and snow, and at one time managed to scale the cliff to within a few feet of the top but fell back again. He considered that men on deck before the midship gun-platform should have had some chance of saving themselves but could give no information about anyone from *Narborough*.

Both ships lie broken up to the south of the rock named Clett of Crura. The remains of a deck housing lies on the shore below the memorial at 5846.000N, 0256.311W.

A substantial quantity of non-ferrous metal, including the propellers, was recovered during salvage operations carried out in 1932.

Plaque on the memorial at Wind Wick (Photo: R.N. Baird)

GIRALDA

Wreck No: 396	Date Sunk: 30 01 1940
Latitude: 58 47 48 N	Longitude: 02 45 54 W
GPS Lat: 5847.800 N	GPS Long: 0254.900 W
Location: 3 miles SE Grimness, S Ronaldsay	Area: Orkney
Type: Steamship	Tonnage: 2,178 grt
Length: 280.0 ft Beam: 41.0 ft	Draught: 19.0 ft
How Sunk: Bombed	Depth: 66 metres

The Leith steamship *Giralda* was bound from Ayr to Kirkwall with a cargo of coal when she was bombed and strafed by German aircraft about 8 miles SE of Copinsay, or about 3 miles SE of Grimness, South Ronaldsay on 30 January 1940. *Giralda* sank, and her crew left in a boat. The weather conditions were stormy, with a strong easterly wind, and the boat with her crew of twenty-three aboard capsized in Water Sound, throwing them all into the sea. There were no survivors.

DAGHESTAN

Wreck No: 397	Date Sunk: 26 03 1940
Latitude: 58 49 51 N	Longitude: 02 45 51 W
GPS Lat: 5849.856 N	GPS Long: 0245.852 W
Location: 212° 9 miles from Copinsay Light	Area: Orkney
Type: Steam tanker	Tonnage: 5,742 grt
Length: 409.2 ft Beam: 52.8 ft	Draught: ft
How Sunk: Torpedoed by *U-57*	Depth: 57 metres

The British RFA steam tanker *Daghestan* was en route from Scapa Flow to Sullom Voe with 7,600 tons of crude oil when she was torpedoed and sunk by the *U-57* (Korth), at 20.13 hrs on 25 March 1940, 212° 9 miles from Copinsay Lighthouse. The *Daghestan* had previously been damaged by a bomb from a German aircraft on the 20th, and had also been attacked previously in the Fair Isle Channel by *U-19* (Schepke), on 20 February, while bound from Sullom Voe for Scapa. On that occasion the torpedo exploded off her starboard bow and she was undamaged.

Nineteen of the crew were rescued by the *Northern Dawn*, and six others by *HMT Brontes*, which had been escorting the *Daghestan*.

Three of the thirty-three crew and one gunner aboard were lost. One body was recovered from the sea.

The wreck is said to lie oriented 140/320° in 57 metres.

REMUS

Wreck No: 398	Date Sunk: 23 02 1918
Latitude: 58 50 25 N	Longitude: 02 46 02 W
GPS Lat: 5850.417 N	GPS Long: 0246.333 W
Location: 4.75 miles SW of Copinsay Light	Area: Orkney
Type: Steamship	Tonnage: 1,079 grt
Length: 222.3 ft Beam: 34.4 ft	Draught: 13.1 ft
How Sunk: Torpedoed by *UC-59*	Depth: 60 metres

The British steamship *Remus* was built in 1908. On 23 February 1918 she was torpedoed and sunk by *UC-59*, at about 5850N, 0242W, while en route from Longhope to ? with a cargo of coal. Five of her crew were lost. The *Remus* had a gun. The position was also described as 4.75 miles SW of Copinsay Light. This plots in 585025N, 024602W, very close NW of the *Daghestan*.

GLEN FARG

Wreck No: 399	Date Sunk: 04 10 1939
Latitude: 58 52 00 N PA	Longitude: 01 54 00 W PA
GPS Lat: 5852.000 N	GPS Long: 0154.000 W
Location: 30 miles East of S.Ronaldsay	Area: Orkney
Type: Steamship	Tonnage: 876 grt
Length: 198.0 ft Beam: 29.7 ft	Draught: ft
How Sunk: Torpedo & gunfire by *U-23*	Depth: metres

The British steamship *Glen Farg* was torpedoed by the *U-23* (Kretschmer) at 06.00 hrs on 4 October 1939 in German grid square AN2679, which equates to about 5909N, 0048W. She had been en route from Trondheim to Methil and Grangemouth with a general cargo including pulp, carbide, paper and ferro-chrome. One member of her crew was lost.

Lloyds War Losses gives the position as 585200N, 013100W.

The Hydrographic Department gives the position as 585200N, 015400W.

BANCREST

Wreck No: 400	Date Sunk: 30 01 1940
Latitude: 58 53 08 N	Longitude: 01 52 25 W
GPS Lat: 5853.134 N	GPS Long: 0152.407 W
Location: 24 miles E of Copinsay	Area: Orkney
Type: Steamship	Tonnage: 4,450 grt
Length: ft Beam: ft	Draught: ft
How Sunk: Bombed	Depth: 86 metres

The British steamship *Bancrest* was en route from Philadelphia to Leith with 7,449 tons of wheat in bulk, when she was attacked by German aircraft on 20 January 1940.

Bancrest was bombed and strafed 24 miles east of Copinsay, or in 5853N 0152W according to Lloyds. One member of the crew of thirty-six was missing. The rest of her crew were rescued by HMS *Javelin* from Scapa Flow.

VESTFOSS

Wreck No: 401	Date Sunk: 01 03 1940
Latitude: 58 54 00 N PA	Longitude: 02 23 00 W PA
GPS Lat: 5854.000 N	GPS Long: 0223.000 W
Location: 9 miles E of Copinsay	Area: Orkney
Type: Steamship	Tonnage: 1,388grt

Length: 254.0 ft   Beam: ft   Draught: ft
How Sunk: Bombed   Depth: metres

The Norwegian steamship *Vestfoss* was built by Nylands of Kristiania in 1909.

En route from Partington to Oslo with a cargo of coal on 1 March 1940 she was bombed by German aircraft 6 miles SE of Auskerry. She was taken in tow by the Aberdeen trawler *Star of Liberty*, but sank about 9 miles E of Copinsay, according to her Master. *DODAS* gives the position as 12 miles SE of Copinsay. Her crew of twenty-one were landed at Kirkwall.

URANIA

Wreck No: 402   Date Sunk: 28 03 1917
Latitude: 58 57 30 N PA   Longitude: 02 21 00 W PA
GPS Lat: 5857.500   GPS Long: 0221.000 W
Location: 10-12 miles E Copinsay Light Area: Orkney
Type: Sailing barque   Tonnage: 1,688 grt
Length: 255.0 ft   Beam: 39.0 ft   Draught: 22.0 ft
How Sunk: Torpedoed by *UC-42*   Depth: 68 metres

The Norwegian steel-hulled sailing barque *Urania* was built by Alexander Stephen of Linthouse, Glasgow in 1891. On a voyage from New York to Aalborg, Denmark she had called in to Kirkwall for inspection, but on leaving she was torpedoed by the German U-boat *UC-42*, 10 to 12 miles east of Copinsay lighthouse. *Urania* was struck on the port side by the mizzen mast, and sank in less than a minute with seven of her crew of twenty. The thirteen survivors were rescued by the Norwegian barque *Fremad I*, and taken into Kirkwall. Four of these survivors died later, when the vessel taking them back home was sunk too.

UNKNOWN

Wreck No: 403   Date Sunk:
Latitude: 59 14 30 N   Longitude: 02 12 40 W
GPS Lat: 5914.506 N   GPS Long: 0212.668 W
Location: 6 miles SE of Start Point   Area: Orkney
Type: Tonnage: grt
Length: ft   Beam: ft   Draught: ft
How Sunk: Mined?   Depth: 61 metres

In the mid-1990s fishermen found a wreck in the above position. They apparently believe it is the wreck of a fairly sizeable ship, but offer no suggestion as to its identity.

One fishing vessel trawled up a mine, complete with its concrete sinker, very close to the wreck.

This suggests the vessel probably sank after striking a British defensive mine.

I have been unable to find any obvious candidate for the identity of this wreck. Although it is by no means unknown for vessels to disappear without trace, especially if there are no survivors, it is a relatively unusual circumstance. This wreck may more likely be from the First rather than the Second World War. I make this suggestion at least partially because I would more readily have expected to find some reference elsewhere to a vessel sunk in this area in the Second World War – either some reference in British records, or a German claim of success, for example.

There were, of course, a number of ships lost off Orkney, even in the Second World War, whose positions are only approximately known, but none of these approximate positions are sufficiently close to the position of this wreck for any likely candidate to stand out.

FARO

Wreck No: 404	Date Sunk: 27 01 1940
Latitude: 58 54 46 N	Longitude: 02 45 52 W
GPS Lat: 5854.767 N	GPS Long: 0245.867 W
Location: Taracliff Bay, Deerness	Area: Orkney
Type: Steamship	Tonnage: 844 grt
Length: 212.9 ft Beam: 31.4 ft	Draught: 13.2 ft
How Sunk: Torpedoed by *U-20*	Depth: metres

The Norwegian steamship *Faro* (ex-*Randi*) was en route, in ballast, from Sarpsborg to Methil when she was torpedoed by *U-20* (von Klot-Heydenfeldt), 15 miles SE of Copinsay lighthouse, at 20.03 hrs on 27 January 1940.

The crew abandoned ship in two lifeboats, and stayed close to the ship, which remained afloat. One of the boats, containing eight men, drifted away in the darkness. At dawn next day the master decided to board the ship, which was still afloat, but down by the head. An attempt was made to steer the *Faro* out to sea, as by this time she had drifted into Taracliff Bay, Deerness. This was not successful, however, as the propeller was out of the water, and racing ineffectually. The ship drove ashore when the starboard anchor chain parted, and the seven crew were taken off by breeches buoy. The missing lifeboat was washed ashore on Copinsay later that day, with only one man alive, and three bodies.

The Norwegian steamship Faro *ashore in Taracliff Bay, Deerness (Photo: author's collection)*

COTOVIA

Wreck No: 405	Date Sunk: 22 07 1917
Latitude: 58 58 15 N	Longitude: 02 38 28 W
GPS Lat: 5858.125 N	GPS Long: 0238.379 W
Location: 3 miles E of Mull Head	Area: Orkney
Type: Steamship	Tonnage: 4,020 grt
Length: 372.2 ft Beam: 52.5 ft	Draught: 24.7 ft
How Sunk: Mined	Depth: 40 metres

The British steamship *Cotovia* was built by Irvine's SB & DD Co. Ltd. of West Hartlepool in 1911.

En route from Archangel to Dundee with a cargo of flax on 22 July 1917, she struck a mine laid by *UC-49*, and sank in 40 metres of water, two miles SW of Auskerry, or 2 miles E of Mull Head, Orkney.

She lay forgotten until 1997 when she was found accidentally by Mark Halsted, skipper of the dive boat *Sunrise,* while en route to the Northern Isles – even the local fisherman seemed to be unaware of the existence of this wreck.

The wreck sits with its bow pointing east and stern to the west, on a hard seabed with sand patches. Underwater visibility is normally very good in Orkney, but it is outstanding here. From 15m down, the top of her engine block, covered in dead men's fingers, can be seen. The wreck is flattened, with her three boilers and engine block standing up three metres from the bottom. The ship was armed with one 3-pounder gun, and shell cases are strewn about the stern, where the prop shaft ends. This is a big wreck and it will take several dives to see it all.

The Svinta *on fire after the German bomb attack (Photo: author's collection)*

SVINTA

Wreck No: 406	Date Sunk: 22 03 1940
Latitude: 58 59 00 N PA	Longitude: 02 35 30 W PA
GPS Lat: 5859.000 N	GPS Long: 0235.500 W
Location: Copinsay Light 40° 4.7 miles	Area: Orkney
Type: Steamship	Tonnage: 1,267 grt
Length: 237.6 ft. Beam: 36.3 ft.	Draught: 16.2 ft.
How Sunk: Bombed then torpedoed or mined?	Depth: 38 metres

From 18.30 to 19.52 hrs on 20 March 1940 three air attacks were mounted on Kirkwall, and portions of the outbound and inward Norwegian convoys ON21 and HN20. The Bergen steamship *Svinta*, which was en route from Preston to Oslo with coal and coke, was damaged and had to be abandoned. The tug *St Mellons* took the *Svinta* in tow towards Orkney, but at 22.10 hrs *Svinta* sank in 040° Copinsay 4.7 miles, after what was thought to be a torpedo explosion. However, there is no record of any U-boat claiming to have fired a torpedo at her. Perhaps she struck a mine? Or perhaps the fire raging aboard the ship sparked off a coal dust explosion? The wreck is charted PA with a clearance of 38 metres in a total depth of about 46 metres. The *Svinta* was built in 1916 in Ablasserdam, Holland.

DANMARK

Wreck No: 407		Date Sunk: 12 01 1940
Latitude: 58 58 47 N		Longitude: 02 53 04 W
GPS Lat: 5858.783 N		GPS Long: 0253.067 W
Location: Inganess Bay		Area: Orkney
Type: Tanker		Tonnage: 1,0517 grt
Length: 491.7 ft	Beam: 66.0 ft	Draught: ft
How Sunk: Torpedoed by *U-23*		Depth: 12 metres

The Danish motor tanker *Danmark* was lying at anchor in Inganess Bay, Orkney, when she was torpedoed by *U-23* (Kretschmer) at 06.50 hrs CET on 12 January 1940. The explosion lifted the deck and left a 20-foot hole in her side, but none of the crew was injured. The *Danmark* had been carrying 8,200 tons of petrol and 5,760 tons of kerosene. The tanker remained afloat until 21.01 when her stern section sank. A German torpedo was discovered in this position on the 21st. The forward section of the ship also sank, but was later refloated and towed to Inverkeithing, where it was used as a storage hulk for fuel oil.

A Northern Lighthouse Board note dated 21 January 1949 – nine years later – lists the wreck of the stern section in Inganess Bay as one to be dispersed after its oil had been removed.

The bow section of the tanker Danmark *(Photo: World Ship Society)*

HALF SUNK BENEATH THE WAVES
The 5,000-ton Glasgow steamer ' Loch Maddy ' was torpedoed by a U-boat on February 22, 1940.
The photographs above show: left, the bow half of the ' Loch Maddy ' sinking beneath the waves;
right, the stern half of the vessel taken in tow by another ship.

Loch Maddy *bow and stern (Photo: Kirkwall Archives)*

LOCH MADDY

Wreck No: 408	Date Sunk: 22 02 1940
Latitude: 58 58 03 N	Longitude: 02 53 39 W
GPS Lat: 5858.058 N	GPS Long: 0253.656 W
Location: Inganess Bay	Area: Orkney
Type: Steamship	Tonnage: 4,996 grt
Length: 415.8 ft Beam: 56.1 ft	Draught: ft
How Sunk: Torpedoed by *U-57* & *U-23*	Depth: 12 metres

The Glasgow steamship *Loch Maddy* was one of the ships in convoy HX19, and was carrying 2,000 tons of wheat, 6,000 tons of lumber and aircraft from Vancouver to Leith. At 18.09 hrs on 21 February 1940 she was hit amidships by a torpedo from *U-57* (Korth), and abandoned in AN1654, which equates to about 5839N, 0224W. HMS *Diana* picked up thirty-three of her crew of thirty-nine and was herself attacked. HMS *Gallant* and HMS *Griffin* carried out a search for the U-boat responsible. Survivors reported that destroyers appeared in answer to their flares about 90 minutes after they left the ship, then left. Shortly afterwards they heard two heavy explosions.

Seven hours later, *U-23* (Kretschmer) found the *Loch Maddy* still afloat, and torpedoed the ship again at 01.07 hrs on the 22nd. This time the *Loch Maddy* broke in two. Both parts must have remained afloat for some time, as photographs of the bow section sinking, and the stern section under tow to Orkney, were obviously taken in daylight. The position given by Kretschmer was AN1651, which equates to about 5845N, 0224W.

The wreck charted in 62 metres at 5844.404N, 0229.481W, 10 miles SE of Copinsay, might be the bow section of the *Loch Maddy*, which was reported a danger to shipping until it sank. On the other hand, from the photograph of *Loch Maddy's* stern section under tow, it looks as if the ship broke in two just forward of the aft hold forward bulkhead. This suggests the aft portion was about 100ft long, leaving the forward section, which sank, about 320ft (or about 100m) long. This ties in quite nicely in length and position with the wreck at 5844.276N, 0240.600W – see *Tamara XII*.

The tug *St Mellons* took the stern section in tow to Inganess Bay, Orkney, where it was beached in 12 metres west of Weethick Head. Up to 24 February 234 tons of cargo was recovered from the after part, but it was considered unlikely that any more could be salvaged. Divers have reported that Oregon pine logs are still in the wreck.

VARDEFJELL

Wreck No: 409		Date Sunk: 13 12 1942	
Latitude: 58 57 59 N		Longitude: 02 54 31 N	
GPS Lat: 5857.981		GPS Long: 0254.522 W	
Location: Inganess Bay		Area: Orkney	
Type: Tanker		Tonnage: 8,316 grt	
Length: 486.3 ft	Beam: 61.1 ft	Draught: 26.8 ft	
How Sunk: Broke in two in heavy seas		Depth: metres	

The Norwegian tanker *Vardefjell* was built in September 1939 by Eriksbergs mek. Verkstad A/B of Gothenburg, and was owned by Olsen & Ugelstad of Oslo. She was delivered from the builders on 4 April 1940, and then just escaped the German occupation of Norway five days later.

According to information from Norway, at the time of her loss, her voyage was recorded as UK – USA with a cargo of oil. This did not make any sense, especially in 1942. Had the voyage record been transposed? Should it have read USA – UK? This would be more credible. What was the truth?

Under the command of Captain Nils A. Ambjørnsen, she left the Clyde on 11 December 1942 with a cargo of oil, in a convoy for North Africa, as part of 'Operation Torch' – the North Africa landings.

While en route, she broke in two in heavy seas, 250 miles west of Lewis, on the 13th, and the forepart with twelve men on it, including all the officers and the others who were on duty there, drifted off and disappeared! Thirty-two were left on the after part. Two of them died when efforts were made to lower boats to rescue the twelve on the bow section, but due to the weather their attempts at reaching their shipmates had to be abandoned. At first it was presumed that the ship had been torpedoed. It was only much later that it became known that she had broken in two due to stress of heavy weather. The twelve men on the bow section included the radio officers and all the navigators. The remaining thirty of the crew on the after part managed to trim that section, and tried to reach the UK. They drifted northwards, with no navigation equipment or navigators, and after eleven days some fishermen at Våg in the Faroe Islands encountered half a tanker on Christmas Eve, and went out to assist. Quite a Christmas present for the crew!

Boatswain Einar Halvorsen had been elected 'leader' after the forepart of *Vardefjell* had been lost. In spite of the continuous hurricane blowing, and notwithstanding his lack of navigational skills, he was able to get them all through an eleven-day ordeal. He had painted 'VARDEFJELL – SEND HELP S.O.S.' in big, bold letters on each side of the ship. On 18 December a British aircraft flew over the wreckage and circled for two hours. Before it departed it dropped two red smoke flares, but no-one knew what this meant. On the 22nd a Sunderland aircraft came over, sending signals in morse code to them, but again nobody understood what they meant. When land was spotted on the night leading up to Christmas Eve, Halvorsen guessed it to be either Ireland or

Scotland, but when the fishermen came close enough later that day, and called to them in Danish, they learned they had reached the Faroe Islands.

(Note: According to an account published in *Krigsseileren* (*The Warsailor*) in 1972, the captain, three mates, the steward and five others were on the foreship, twenty-nine on the afterpart. The last time they saw the foreship was around 07.00 hrs on the morning of 14 December.)

The fishermen took the sailors to port, while the stern section of *Vardefjell* was taken in tow to Kirkwall. It was even possible to save 3,000 tons of her oil.

It had been thought that the forward section must have sunk with twelve of the crew, but on 28 December the forward section was located, derelict and abandoned, 6 miles NE of the Faroes. This section was also towed into Inganess Bay, and beached.

The stern section was subsequently towed to the Tyne, where a new bow section was built and fitted in Sunderland, and the ship was returned to service in July 1944.

The last entry in the 1941 *Lloyds Loss Book* for the *Vardefjell* states simply, '19/7/44 Left Tyne for New York'.

In 1951 she was sold to Rio Guaba Cia. Nav., Panama and renamed *Vigilant*. She was renamed *Andros Vigor* in 1956 and *Andros Cloud* in 1957, and was finally broken up in 1959.

The original bow section still lies ashore in the south-west corner of Inganess Bay.

The stern section of the Norwegian tanker Vardefjell *(Photo: Olsen & Ugelstad, Oslo)*

Vardefjell *bow section in Inganess Bay, Dec. 2001 (Photo: Ian Potten)*

The Norwegian tanker Vardefjell *before she broke in two (Photo: author's collection)*

DISPERSER & ENDEAVOUR

Wreck No: 410		Date Sunk: 15 04 1940
Latitude: 59 01 43 N		Longitude: 02 56 52 W
GPS Lat: 5901.710 N		GPS Long: 0256.870 W
Location: The String, Orkney		Area: Orkney
Type: BDV & Trawler		Tonnage: 313 grt
Length: 112.6 ft	Beam: 31.7 ft	Draught: 11.7 ft
How Sunk: Foundered		Depth: 23 metres

The wreck of a boom defence vessel, complete with bow horns, boiler, engine and steel prop, was reported by divers to lie in the above position. It was assumed to be the salvage vessel *Disperser* (ex-*T.I.C.Limpet*, ex-*Mauch Chauk*), which was built by Harlan & Hollingsworth of Wilmington, Delaware in 1912. (Note: T.I.C. = Tyne Improvement Commission.)

She was used between 1937 and 1939 to undertake salvage on HMS *Natal*, which blew up in the Cromarty Firth on 31 December 1915. While engaged in salvage operations she foundered in Kirkwall Bay with a cargo of scrap iron, in a gale on the night of 15 April 1940.

Admiralty records, however, state that the *Disperser* was refloated on 23 June 1943 and towed to Lyness. She left there on 11 August 1943 to be refitted and returned to service.

There is a record that the *Disperser* was finally broken up at Llanelly, South Wales in 1953.

This leaves the question, what is lying off Kirkwall Bay?

The *Endeavour* (A 493), a trawler built in 1894, was used by the Royal Navy as a boom boat. She was lost after a collision on 10 March 1918 and was found about 1990 by clam diver Keith Bichan. The wreck sits upright and intact in 24m. There is access to the holds and engine room, and a small bridge is still in place.

The local diving club from Kirkwall were looking for this wreck one evening, saw the mark on the sounder, dropped the shot, and on diving were convinced that what they had found was the wreck of the 313-ton salvage vessel *Disperser*. They described the wreck as sitting upright in 23m, with the bow fairly intact and complete with two large lifting horns. Just aft of this the wreck was broken up and the boiler and engine could clearly be seen. The steel propeller was also seen under the stern.

With the *Endeavour* apparently having been used by the Royal Navy as a boom boat, I wonder if there is any possibility that she might have been fitted with a lifting device like bow horns to enable her to act as a boom vessel?

Two positions, extremely close together, have been given for the wreck: 5901.71N, 0256.87W and 5901.47N, 0256.64W. Are there really two separate wrecks?

This seems unlikely, particularly as there is evidence that one of them was refloated.

Furthermore, *Disperser* was not in that position in the first place, as she sank 7.9 cables 342° from the pier head light at Kirkwall at 5859.967N, 0257.600W, nearly two miles further south, off Crow Ness, in much shallower water.

OCEANA

Wreck No: 411		Date Sunk: 18 10 1918	
Latitude: 59 12 24 N		Longitude: 02 44 45 W	
GPS Lat: 5912.400 N		GPS Long: 0244.750 W	
Location: Mill Bay, Eday		Area: Orkney	
Type: Tug		Tonnage: 311 grt	
Length: 140.0 ft	Beam: 22.7 ft	Draught: 13.1 ft	
How Sunk: Collision		Depth: 12 metres	

An unidentified wreck about 30 metres long and standing up 6 metres in a general depth of 12 metres, lies in Mill Bay on the east side of Eday.

The wreck is oriented 115/295°, and is lying on its starboard side with bow and stern intact. The midships section is broken, but the boiler is intact. The wreck has two engines and twin screws.

It is known locally as the '*Char*', and is said to have sunk in 1915.

It is rumoured to be a First World War armed tug, but there is no sign of any gun or ammunition in the wreck, but a box of ammunition has been found about 100 metres away from the wreck.

Oceana (ex-*Cerberus* ex-*Oceana*) was run down on 18 October 1918 while at anchor 'at Scapa Flow' by another Admiralty tug, *Stobo Castle*.

I suspect the use of the description 'at Scapa Flow' might easily mean 'somewhere/anywhere in the Orkney area'.

However, she was not declared a total loss until 31 Jan 1919, which seems to imply there was some salvage attempt. This probably accounts for the broken centre section and the lack of a gun and ammunition – they would almost certainly have been salvaged.

Oceana was a two-engined twin-screw tug, built in 1889 by Gourlay Bros, Dundee for William Watkins, London.

MIM

Wreck No: 412		Date Sunk: 01 11 1939	
Latitude: 59 21 00 N		Longitude: 02 22 16 W	
GPS Lat: 5921.000 N		GPS Long: 0222.267 W	
Location: Reef Dyke, N Ronaldsay		Area: Orkney	
Type: Steamship		Tonnage: 4,996 grt	
Length: 416.5 ft	Beam: 56.4 ft	Draught: 25.0 ft	
How Sunk: Ran aground		Depth: metres	

The Norwegian steamship *Mim* was built in 1938. She was driven ashore in heavy weather and broke up on Reef Dyke, North Ronaldsay, 125° from the Free Kirk manse. At the time of loss she was owned by Skibs, A.S. Skytteren, and was carrying a cargo of wheat from Fremantle to Bergen. Eleven members of her crew reached shore in one of the ship's boats. The twenty left on board were taken off by Stromness lifeboat.

The *Mim* broke up completely in three days. The wreck can still be seen at low water, but it is completely covered most of the time.

MISTLEY

Wreck No: 413		Date Sunk: 19 06 1957
Latitude: 59 21 00 N		Longitude: 02 22 00 W
GPS Lat: 5921.000 N		GPS Long: 0222.000 W
Location: Reef Dyke, N Ronaldsay		Area: Orkney
Type: Steamship		Tonnage: 485 grt
Length: 159.0 ft	Beam: 25.2 ft	Draught: 11.7 ft
How Sunk: Ran aground		Depth: metres

The British steamship *Mistley* (ex-*Coe-Pam*, ex-*Western*) was built by Cochranes of Selby in 1920. While carrying a cargo of coal she ran aground on Reef Dyke, about 1½ miles off the south-west corner of North Ronaldsay on 19 June 1957 and became a total loss.

HANSI

Wreck No: 414		Date Sunk: 08 11 1939
Latitude: 59 23 00 N PA		Longitude: 02 23 04 W PA
GPS Lat: 5923.000 N		GPS Long: 0223.067 W
Location: Linklet Bay, N Ronaldsay		Area: Orkney
Type: Steamship		Tonnage: 1,028 grt
Length: 221.1 ft	Beam: 33.0 ft	Draught: ft
How Sunk: Ran aground		Depth: metres

The engine of the Norwegian steamship *Hansi* broke down while she was en route from Homelvik to Ellesmere Port with a cargo of wood and pulp. In her disabled condition she drifted onto Reef Dyke, off the south-west of North Ronaldsay. The ship was holed, and her engine room flooded. The ship took on a heavy list, but at high tide she floated off the rocks, only to be driven ashore again in Linklet Bay, where the crew abandoned ship in their lifeboats.

RUBY

Wreck No: 415		Date Sunk: 28 03 1917
Latitude: 58 56 50 N		Longitude: 02 33 11W
GPS Lat: 5856.829 N		GPS Long: 0233.019 W
Location: 2½ miles S of Auskerry Light		Area: Orkney
Type: Steamship		Tonnage: 234 grt
Length: 124.7 ft	Beam: 22.2 ft	Draught: 9.2 ft
How Sunk: Mined		Depth: 65 metres

The steamship *Ruby*, belonging to W. Cooper & Sons of Kirkwall, was built by J. Fullerton & Co. of Paisley in 1882.

On 28 March 1917 she was en route from Leith to Kirkwall with a general cargo, when at 10.10 a.m. she struck a mine. The explosion was very violent, and the *Ruby* sank before either of her two lifeboats could be swung out. One crewman who had been working in the ship's galley jumped into the sea and swam to an empty barrel. He then swam to one of the ship's lifeboats which had floated free as the *Ruby* sank. He succeeded in getting into the boat, from which he was picked up thirty minutes later by a patrol vessel, and landed at Kirkwall.

The wreck 2½ miles SE of Mull Head, Deerness, and 2½ miles south of Auskerry Light is in exactly the right position for a ship going from Leith to Kirkwall. This wreck is also the right size for the *Ruby*, and has only one boiler.

The Ruby (*Photo: author's collection*)

FOXEN

Wreck No: 416	Date Sunk: 17 01 1940
Latitude: 58 52 00 N PA	Longitude: 00 22 00 W PA
GPS Lat: 5822.000 N	GPS Long: 0022.000 W
Location: E of the Orkneys	Area: Orkney
Type: Steamship	Tonnage: 1,304 grt
Length: 240.0 ft Beam: 37.0 ft	Draught: 16.0 ft
How Sunk: Torpedoed by *U-55*?	Depth: metres

According to Swedish reports, the steamship *Foxen* was sunk by a mine on 17 January 1940, while en route from Garston to Gothenburg with a cargo of coal or coke. Eight of the crew were lost.

British reports say she was sunk by a U-boat, but there is no record of any U-boat claiming to have sunk the *Foxen*. It may be possible that she was sunk by *U-55* (KL Werner Heidel), but that U-boat was sunk, and no records of her patrol survived.

U-92

Wreck No: 417	Date Sunk: 08 09 1918
Latitude: 59 00 00 N PD	Longitude: 01 30 00 W PD
GPS Lat: 5900.000 N	GPS Long: 0130.000 W
Location: Fair Isle Channel	Area: Orkney
Type: Submarine	Tonnage: 998 dwt
Length: 216.0 ft Beam: 20.0 ft	Draught: ft
How Sunk: Mined	Depth: metres

U-92 sailed for the Irish Sea on 4 September 1918. Her last radio message was on 9 September, when she reported that she was just south of the Fair Isle passage. She was possibly mined there later that day, and may be one of the wrecks charted in the Fair Isle Channel.

ISLAND LASS

Wreck No: 418	Date Sunk: 03 03 1962
Latitude: 59 26 00 N PA	Longitude: 02 43 12 W PA
GPS Lat: 5926.000 N	GPS Long: 0243.200 W
Location: 6 miles NE Mull Head, Papa Westray	Area: Orkney
Type:	Tonnage: grt
Length: ft Beam: ft	Draught: ft
How Sunk: Foundered	Depth: 60 metres

A despatch box from the Foula mail boat *Island Lass*, which sank off Orkney on 3 March 1962, was picked up on the Holm of Papa in Papa Westray. The wooden box contained four loaves, newspapers and 6s 3½d in change for Betty Humphrey of Foula.

The damaged *Island Lass* was abandoned by her four-man crew and one passenger during gales as she made the trip from Scalloway to Foula. She drifted for two days before being taken in tow by the Northern Lighthouse ship *Pole Star*. As the *Pole Star* tried to tow her to safety, however, the *Island Lass* foundered about 6 miles north-east of Mull Head, Papa Westray.

The *Island Lass* was a wooden vessel built in 1949, and an appeal was launched in Shetland to replace her. She was the only vessel providing a 'regular' service for the people of the isolated community on the island of Foula.

VARING

Wreck No: 419	Date Sunk: 07 02 1917
Latitude: 59 29 33 N	Longitude: 02 33 37 W
GPS Lat: 5929.545 N	GPS Long: 0233.610 W
Location: 12 mls NE Mull Head, Papa Westray	Area: Orkney
Type: Steamship	Tonnage: 2,107 grt
Length: 290.6 ft Beam: 43.3 ft	Draught: 20.3 ft
How Sunk: Torpedoed	Depth: metres

The Swedish steamship *Varing* was reportedly torpedoed and sunk 10 miles ENE of Noup Head, Orkney on 7 February 1917, while en route from Savannah, Georgia to Helsingborg with a cargo of oil cake. Her captain claimed that his ship was sunk by a British submarine. (How would he know?)

The wreck charted 12 miles NE of Mull Head, Papa Westray at 5929.533N, 0233.542W is the *Varing*.

The Swedish steamship Varing *(Photo: Tomas Johanneson collection)*

BELLAVISTA

Wreck No: 420		Date Sunk: 29 07 1948	
Latitude: 59 22 34 N		Longitude: 02 51 54 W	
GPS Lat: 5922.567 N		GPS Long: 0251.900 W	
Location: Fowl Craig, Papa Westray		Area: Orkney	
Type: Steamship		Tonnage: 3,527 grt	
Length: 350.4 ft	Beam: 50.0 ft	Draught: 23.6 ft	
How Sunk: Ran aground		Depth: 15 metres	

The Panamanian steamship *Bellavista* ran aground in dense fog at Fowl Craig, Papa Westray on 29 July 1948, while carrying a cargo of iron ore from Narvik to Ardrossan.

The vessel was built in 1917 by Campbeltown S.B. Co. as the *Lady Charlotte*, but changed hands several times, becoming *South Lea, Ioannis Carras, Spyridon, Spyridon II,* and then finally *Bellavista*. Efforts to refloat the ship were unsuccessful.

The wreck lies very broken up, pointing in a westerly direction over a ledge, with the bow in 5 metres and the stern in 15 metres.

BIRKA

Wreck No: 421	Date Sunk: 10 01 1916
Latitude: 59 21 45 N	Longitude: 02 57 09 W
GPS Lat: 5921.750	GPS Long: 0257.150 W
Location: Bow Rock, N Westray	Area: Orkney

Type: Steamship		Tonnage: 1,790 grt
Length: 282.0 ft	Beam: 33.9 ft	Draught: 24.9 ft
How Sunk: Ran aground		Depth: metres

The Swedish iron steamship *Birka* (ex-*Orchis*) of Stockholm was built in Glasgow in 1870.

En route from Swansea to Gothenburg with a cargo of coal, she ran aground on the Bow Rock off the extreme north point of Westray, late in the evening of 10 January 1916, and broke up almost immediately. A tremendous sea was running, and there was a north-westerly gale. There were no survivors. All eighteen crew and one passenger were lost. Next day five bodies washed ashore on the Holm of Aikerness, and four in Papa Westray. One of the bodies was that of Captain Bennett; another was that of his wife. Wreckage and some of the cargo of coal was also washed ashore.

Two more bodies, both wearing lifejackets, also came ashore at Rapness at the extreme south of Westray, but these were thought to have come from a different vessel.

The Swedish steamship Birka (*Photo: Tomas Johanneson collection*)

TOMMELINE

Wreck No: 422		Date Sunk: 20 05 1988
Latitude: 59 20 02 N		Longitude: 03 04 12 W
GPS Lat: 5920.033 N		GPS Long: 0304.200 W
Location: Noup Head, Westray		Area: Orkney
Type: MFV		Tonnage: grt
Length: 100 ft	Beam: ft	Draught: ft
How Sunk: Ran aground		Depth: 26 metres

The Norwegian ex-fishing vessel *Tommeline* (ex-*Antonsen Jnr*), carrying young salmon worth about £150,000 from Oban to a fish farm in Shetland, ran aground below Noup Head lighthouse on 20 May 1988. The cause of her grounding remains a bit of a mystery as the skipper claimed he lost steering two miles from the Noup, but it was suspected that the watch-keeper had fallen asleep. The other three crew members first became aware of the problem only when they were thrown out of their bunks as the boat struck the rocks. Although their vessel did not seem to be in imminent danger of sinking, the crew launched their inflatable life raft. About three quarters of an hour later, however, the *Tommeline* suddenly started to sink. The four men boarded the life raft and made for the shore, only about 50 feet away. By the time they reached the shore and looked round, all they could see was the top of the mast sticking out of the water. The four men were saved by the rescue helicopter from Sumburgh. Several unsuccessful attempts were made to raise the *Tommeline*, but she now sits intact and upright, in a narrow steep-sided gully no more then a metre wider than the ship itself, just off Noup Head. This is a very scenic wreck to dive. The depth is about 26m to the seabed and 20m to the deck. It is possible to enter the cabins and engine room of this wreck. There is even a stove sitting in the galley. In the bow section are two large plastic containers used as an oxygenation plant to keep the cargo of fish healthy.

TOSTO

Wreck No: 423			Date Sunk: 17 06 1917
Latitude: 59 16 40 N			Longitude: 03 04 54 W
GPS Lat: 5916.610 N			GPS Long: 0304.900 W
Location: 1½ miles W of Inga Ness, Westray			Area: Orkney
Type: Steamship			Tonnage: 1,234 grt
Length: 240.0 ft	Beam: 35.5 ft	Draught: 17.9 ft	
How Sunk: Mined			Depth: 60 metres

The Norwegian steamship *Tosto* (ex-*Heimdal*) was built by J. Priestman of Sunderland in 1904.

On the Kirkwall to Lerwick leg of a voyage from Methil to Haugesund with a cargo of coal, she struck a mine on 17 June 1917, and sank within three minutes.

The mine was part of German minefield 113, laid by the U-boat *UC-49* (Oberleutnant zur see H. Kukenthal) on 9 June 1917.

Some of *Tosto*'s crew managed to launch a lifeboat, which then picked up other members of the crew who had to jump into the sea. They were all rescued by an auxiliary trawler of the convoy escort, and taken into Lerwick.

Slack water is a must for diving this one as the wreck lies in an area of very strong tides, but with excellent underwater visibility. She is very broken up, the bows and boiler being the most prominent pieces of wreckage. The bell, inscribed 'Heimdal 1904 Christiania', was recovered in May 1998.

The Norwegian steamship Tosto *(Photo: Erling Skjold)*

SCANDINAVIC

Wreck No: 424

Latitude: 59 14 34 N

GPS Lat: 5914.567 N

Location: 0.6 miles W of Skea Skerries

Type: Steamship

Length: 326.5 ft   Beam: 47.2 ft

How Sunk: Ran aground

Date Sunk: 01 02 1917

Longitude: 02 59 34 W

GPS Long: 0259.567 W

Area: Orkney

Tonnage: 3,072 grt

Draught: 22.4 ft

Depth: 13 metres

The Swedish steamship *Scandinavic* (ex-*Dagmar*) was built by Furness & Co. of West Hartlepool in 1904.

In thick fog she ran aground on Skea Skerry, Westray on 1 February 1917, while carrying a cargo of cotton from Galveston to Gothenburg, via Kirkwall for inspection by Contraband Control.

Within a week the ship had broken up. The wreck lies in the centre of a reef about 200 yards wide, about 0.6 miles west of the south end of Skea Skerries. It is heavily overgrown with kelp in summer; this obscures the wreck and makes it hard to find, but in winter, the keel, stern and propshaft can be seen. The bow is badly damaged, and the hull is flattened and overgrown. The engine and boilers lie half buried in gullies some distance from the wreck.

The Swedish steamship Scandinavic *(Photo: Tomas Johanneson collection)*

O.A. BRODIN

Wreck No: 425

Latitude: 59 27 30 N

GPS Lat: 5927.500 N

Location: 15 miles NW of Noup Head

Type: Steamship

Length: 266.1 ft   Beam: 42.8 ft

How Sunk: Torpedoed by *U-57*

Date Sunk: 17 07 1940

Longitude: 03 29 15 W

GPS Long: 0329.250 W

Area: Orkney

Tonnage: 1,960 grt

Draught: 18.4 ft

Depth: 80 metres

The Swedish steamship *O.A. Brodin* was carrying a cargo of about 2,765 tons of pulpwood from Burlington, Newfoundland, and St John's, Newfoundland to Ridham Dock via Kirkwall, when she was torpedoed and sunk by *U-57* (OL Erich Topp), on

17 July 1940. Three of her twenty-four crew were lost. The German grid position was recorded as AN1368, which equates to about 5927N, 0324W. The position recorded by the survivors of the *O.A. Brodin* was 5922N, 0340W PA.

The wreck charted at 592730N, 032915W may be the *O.A. Brodin*.

O.A.Brodin *(Photo: courtesy of World Ship Society)*

FREESIA

Wreck No: 426	Date Sunk: 01 01 1922
Latitude: 59 09 47 N	Longitude: 03 10 45 W
GPS Lat: 5909.780 N	GPS Long: 0310.750 W
Location: Eynhallow Sound	Area: Orkney
Type: Trawler	Tonnage: 285 grt
Length: 132.0 ft Beam: 22.5 ft	Draught: 11.7 ft
How Sunk: Ran aground/foundered	Depth: 40 metres

At about 9.15 a.m. on Sunday morning, 1 January 1922, Mr George L. Thomson, Hon. Secretary of Stromness Lifeboat, received a telegram advising him that a steamer had struck the rocks and was damaged near Birsay, and that she was burning flares. Mr Thomson immediately called out the lifeboat crew and notified the Rocket Brigade, all of whom responded to the call very quickly, and the lifeboat left the harbour at 9.40 to render assistance. The weather at the time was very rough, and a heavy sea was breaking on the shore all along the west side.

Mr Thomson and a party of signallers left by car for Costa, Evie and other vantage points from where they could signal and direct the lifeboat on her arrival from Stromness. Meanwhile Mr Thomson had arranged for two boats from Evie and one boat from Rousay to be launched to render any assistance possible.

The Grimsby steam trawler *Freesia* was returning from fishing off the Faroes when she struck rocks west of Costa Head at about 07.30 a.m., and was very severely damaged. She had struck the face of the cliff bow-on, but had bounced off, breaking her propshaft, then drifted east with the tide, out of control, until she rounded Costa Head. Immediately off the farm at Midhouse, Costa, Evie and about half a mile from the head, her anchor was dropped to arrest her drift into Eynhallow Sound, away from the land. Because of the damage she had sustained against the rocks, however, *Freesia* was making water fairly quickly, and settling down.

The *Freesia* had lost her small boat in very rough weather off Faroe, and the crew had constructed a raft. When the trawler sank, nine members of *Freesia's* crew boarded the raft, which was dragged under as the vessel sank, and the nine men on it were sucked down and drowned. Two other members of the crew who could not get on to the raft clung to a lifebuoy until the raft floated free again, and they held on to it until saved by Stromness lifeboat.

It was only when the two survivors had been landed that it became known which vessel had been lost. The lifeboat returned to Stromness at 6.40 p.m. She had been at sea, in terrible conditions off a lee shore, for nine hours. Coxswain Johnstone was awarded the RNLI Bronze medal and vellum.

Today the wreck lies fairly broken up in 40 metres, with the boiler and the engine block, still with brass oil boxes inside. Her steel propeller lies just off to the side of the engine. The bow is a bit of a swim away to the south across a sand and rock bottom, but underwater visibility is usually excellent. The tip of the bows, with two anchor hawse pipes, and the trawl winch nearby, are the main points of interest.

HESSONITE

Wreck No: 427		Date Sunk: 04 10 1924	
Latitude: 59 09 20 N PA		Longitude: 03 13 20 W PA	
GPS Lat: 5909.300 N		GPS Long: 0313.300 W	
Location: Hellyalonga, W of Costa Head		Area: Orkney	
Type: Trawler		Tonnage: 290 grt	
Length: 125.4 ft	Beam: 23.1 ft	Draught: ft	
How Sunk: Ran aground		Depth: metres	

The steam trawler *Hessonite* (H222) (ex-*Cape Hatteras*, ex-*William Darnold*), was built in 1918. En route from the Faroes to Hull, with a cargo of fish valued at £1,500, she stranded on rocks at Hellyalonga between Skippi Geo and Costa Head, in dense fog about 2.20 a.m. on 4 October 1924. Fortunately there was little or no wind, and the sea was smooth at the time.

The trawler's whistle attracted the attention of people residing in the neighbourhood, and they sent a telegram for the Stromness Lifeboat and rocket brigade. The message was received at Stromness shortly after 4.00 a.m. and no time was lost in getting the lifeboat crew and rocket brigade together. The lifeboat was the first to leave for the stranded vessel, but the rocket brigade, who travelled by bus, were first to reach the top of the cliffs above the vessel. They quickly established communications with *Hessonite's* crew of ten, but the trawler men preferred to wait for the lifeboat, which took them off and landed them at Stromness shortly after 10.00 a.m.

The wrecked trawler was visited the following day by a number of people from Stromness, who reported that the vessel had been washed higher up on the rocks, which are large and flat as a table. It appeared to be undamaged and it was hoped to save the vessel should the weather keep favourable. The *Hessonite* was so close to the cliff edge at Hellyalonga on the north side of Birsay, about a mile east of the Brough of Birsay, that she could not be seen from above.

It was expected that an attempt would soon be made to refloat the vessel.

Three weeks later, the underwriters engaged the East Coast Salvage Company of Dundee to attempt to salvage the trawler. Representatives of that company visited the wreck and boarded her, making a close and careful examination, and found the vessel still undamaged. They expected their salvage steamer and recovery gear to arrive in a day or two, when they hoped to get suitable weather to float the vessel. Part of the cargo of fish was thrown overboard, wires were run out and every preparation made for towing the vessel off the rocks at the first suitable tide, if the weather continued favourable. Everything depends on the weather, especially on a rock-bound coast like Birsay.

The photo of the wreck shows the *Hessonite* sitting under the high cliffs to the south of Costa Head, where she sat for six weeks before slipping into deeper water.

It is not known whether the salvers assisted her slipping off the rocks, but it does seem amazing that the *Hessonite* remained in her precarious position for such a long time.

As far as is known the wreck has not been found, and is therefore un-dived.

The trawler Hessonite *ashore near Costa Head (Photo: Kirkwall Archives)*

HAMPSHIRE

Wreck No: 428		Date Sunk: 05 06 1916
Latitude: 59 07 05 N		Longitude: 03 23 51 W
GPS Lat: 5907.078 N		GPS Long: 0323.851 W
Location: 1½ miles NW Marwick Head		Area: Orkney
Type: Cruiser		Tonnage: 18,850 dwt
Length: 473.5 ft	Beam: 68.5 ft	Draught: 24.0 ft
How Sunk: Mined		Depth: 70 metres

At the outbreak of the First World War Lord Kitchener was appointed Secretary of State for War. In that capacity he was responsible for recruiting the volunteer British

army, and his famous rallying slogan raised an army of volunteer soldiers so vast that insufficient resources existed to train and equip it. But he was unable to confine his attentions to recruitment, and by 1916 he had made bitter enemies amongst the War Cabinet and the General Staff by his interference and outspoken criticisms – not the least of which was his expressed doubts as to whether Britain could win the war without appalling loss of life. Events subsequently proved him to be correct, but to publicly make such statements was politically unacceptable.

Field Marshal Lord Kitchener was difficult to control, and regarded as something of a liability. A plan was devised to send him to Russia to reform the army there. He was to carry secret papers intended for the Czar's eyes only, and his ship was laden with gold bullion – or so it is claimed.

Kitchener and his party were to travel to Archangel in northern Russia on the cruiser HMS *Hampshire,* which was to pass up the east side of Orkney on a route that was regularly swept for mines, and to maintain a speed of not less than 18 knots. Two destroyers would escort her as far as midway between Norway and the Faroes. From there on she would proceed alone at 16 knots, keeping not less than 200 miles from the Norwegian coast, and zigzagging to avoid torpedo attack.

On the afternoon of 5 June, however, a gale was blowing from the north-east and a heavy sea was battering the east coast, hampering minesweeping operations. It was realised that the sea conditions would make it difficult for the two destroyers to keep up with the bigger and more powerful cruiser, and Jellicoe tried to persuade Kitchener to delay his journey, but Kitchener refused.

Only about 15 minutes before departure Admiral Jellicoe ordered Captain Saville of the *Hampshire* to change his route, and proceed instead around the west of Hoy, to provide some shelter from the weather for the start of the voyage and enable the destroyers to keep up with the *Hampshire.*

HMS Hampshire *(Photo: Imperial War Museum)*

Fleet auxiliaries often used that route, but it was not regularly swept for mines as it was thought that no German submarine mine-layer had sufficient range to reach there.

The *Hampshire* left Scapa Flow by the southern route through Hoxa Sound at about 4.40 p.m. then turned west past Cantick Head and into the Pentland Firth. Off Tor Ness at the south-west of Hoy, the destroyers *Victor* and *Unity* were waiting to escort her. The weather forecast had been badly misjudged. By the time *Hampshire* arrived at the rendezvous, the wind had shifted to the northwest. Rounding the south-west corner of Hoy the trio of ships entered the open seas, and faced a head-on gale. This was exactly the opposite of what had been expected, and the ships now experienced the very conditions they had sought to avoid by altering their route from the east to the west side of Orkney. The destroyers were soon having trouble keeping up and at 6.20 p.m. they were ordered to turn back. The *Hampshire* continued alone into a force-nine gale, and terrible seas, against which even the *Hampshire* struggled to make progress. She was only able to make 13.5 knots and was about 1½ miles from shore between Marwick Head and the Brough of Birsay, when at 7.40 p.m. a violent explosion shook the whole ship. Fire flashed through the ship, followed by other explosions and smoke. The steering gear jammed and the lights faded and went out as the generators failed. Without power it was impossible to radio for assistance. According to some survivors the explosion seemed to be on the port side under the foremost stokehold. Other survivors said there was also an explosion forward and the ship immediately began to settle into the water. Flames and a cloud of hot, suffocating smoke came up from below, where most of the crew were, with the hatches closed for the night. The men began to open them and proceed to their stations. As the crew hurried aft away from the explosions, PO Wilfred

Wesson, one of the survivors, saw Lord Kitchener in the gun room flat with a naval officer who was heard to call out, 'Make way for Lord Kitchener'. They both passed by and went up the after hatch to the quarterdeck just before him. He saw no other military officers nor any more of Lord Kitchener after getting on deck.

The cruiser was settling quickly by the bows. There was no power to work the lifeboat derricks, although there would have been alternative manual gear to launch the ship's boats, but none of the larger boats could be hoisted out in the 15 minutes before the ship sank. One smaller boat was lowered into the water with fifty men in it, but it could not get away from the ship. It rose to the crest of a wave and was swept against the *Hampshire*'s side with terrific force, leaving nothing but a tangled mass of bodies struggling for survival amongst swirling flotsam.

None of the survivors saw any boat get clear of the ship. Although the large boats could not be lowered, some men sat in them, in the hope that as the ship went down these boats would float free. But at about 7.50pm the *Hampshire* rolled over to starboard as she sank bows first, carrying the boats and men down with her.

Smoke and flames poured from just behind the bridge, and as her stern lifted out of the water Stoker Frederick Sims saw her propellers still turning as she sank. Only 10 to 15 minutes had elapsed since she struck the mine.

Three Carley floats got away from the sinking ship. One of them had only six men in it, and in the severe conditions it was flung over twice, throwing the men into the sea. When it reached the shore at Skaill Bay only two men were alive. Many of the forty-seven men crowded on the second Carley raft were almost immediately swept from it by the fury of the water, and when it washed ashore just north of Skaill Bay at 1.15 a.m., only four of them were still alive.

About forty men were in the third Carley raft when it left the *Hampshire*. All of them were soaked, and in the cold and wind, they were soon suffering from exposure, losing consciousness and dying with appalling swiftness. When it finally washed up on the rocks half a mile north of Skaill Bay five hours later at 1.00 a.m. only six of them were still alive.

These twelve men were the only survivors from the ship's company of 655 men.

They miraculously clambered up the precipitous rocks to the safety of a crofter's dwelling.

Scores of others were dashed to pieces on the rocks, and wreckage of boats was washed ashore as far south as Aberdeen.

A subsequent search located thirteen mines in the vicinity of the wreck site, laid at a depth of seven to nine metres. They were deep enough to let smaller vessels such as fishing boats or minesweepers pass over the top of them, but would catch the bigger vessels. A spread of thirty-four mines had been laid by *U-75* (KL Kurt Beitzen) on 29 May.

In 1959 the *Orcadian* newspaper published a fairly lengthy article about the sinking of the *Hampshire*. At that time some of the people who remembered the event were still alive. There were very few people who had witnessed the tragedy, one or two in Marwick, and Joe Angus of Stromness, who was then a gunner in the Orkney Territorial Forces. He saw 'a cloud of smoke and flame burst up behind the bridge of the *Hampshire*', and instantly gave the alarm to the man in charge of the watching post, Corporal Drever, who in his turn raced to the post office. The cruiser was about a mile and a half from the shore. In fifteen minutes she had disappeared.

At 7.45 p.m. on 5 June 1916, a telegraph message was sent from Birsay Post Office to Kirkwall and Stromness. It read: 'Battle cruiser seems in distress between Marwick Head and the Brough of Birsay.' A second telegram saying 'vessel down' followed twenty minutes later.

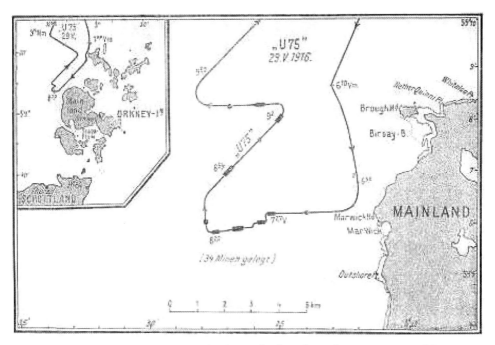

This map shows the route U-75 *took when it laid its thirty-four mines on 29 May 1916*

The service authorities in Kirkwall and Stromness were caught unprepared for this disaster and were slow to react, and seemed to be in the grip of panic. They failed to make an urgent search of the coast, which might have saved the lives of a few who survived the waves, only to be killed by the rocks, and they violently discouraged civilians who wanted to help. There are claims that the Admiralty had forbidden the local coastguard to search for survivors for four hours after the ship had sunk. In Birsay, the few who knew of the disaster and who wanted to help were in some cases 'forcibly prevented under dire threats'. A soldier told one man 'all civilians were to remain in their houses and not to venture near the shore or we should be fired on'. It was local opinion that if people in the neighbourhood had been allowed to take a hand in the rescue operations more lives could have been saved.

News of the cruiser's loss quickly reached Mr G.L. Thomson, honorary secretary of the Stromness Lifeboat. He rushed to Stromness Naval HQ with an offer to launch the lifeboat, but his offer was declined by a senior officer who told him: 'you have no right to interfere in Naval matters. It is none of your bloody business. And, what's more, if you attempt to launch a lifeboat it's mutiny. Mutiny do you hear? Any more nonsense or argument and I'll have the whole lot of you locked up.'

It was not until 9.45 p.m. that a tug and two trawlers left Stromness for Birsay. A little after 10 p.m. four destroyers followed, then other boats. Observers in Birsay were adamant that none reached the scene of the sinking before midnight. Cars from Kirkwall lost their way and had to be re-directed. A party from Stromness made a more effective search, but were hampered by lack of information.

One or two men reached a farmhouse after their ordeal at sea. Others were found on the rocks more dead than alive. Bodies were washed ashore, or were picked up by ships. Not a single man was rescued from the sea itself. Someone remembered two lorry-loads of bodies coming to Stromness Pier, little attempt being made to cover them from public view. Some were almost naked. They were sent down a chute into the hold of a Naval tug to be taken for burial at Lyness.

In his day, Lord Kitchener was almost as famous and revered as, for example, John F. Kennedy, or Princess Diana, and exactly as happened after their deaths, the nation went into a period of shocked disbelief and mourning. He was a legend in his own lifetime, and the sudden loss of this symbol of national unity sparked off many rumours as people struggled to accept it, and to come to terms with it. Everyone who remembered the death of Kitchener recollected exactly what they were doing at the time, just as those who remember the deaths of President Kennedy, or Princess Diana, can remember where they were, and what they were doing at the time. I know I can.

In 1916, the most renowned figure of his time disappeared, and many refused to believe the Empire's greatest soldier had simply drowned.

Controversy raged for years following the sinking of the *Hampshire*. Was it really a mine, or was it a bomb planted by German, Irish or even British saboteurs? Great significance was attached to the fact that Stromness lifeboat had not put to sea to pick up survivors and that locals trying to help in a shore search were turned back at bayonet point by armed soldiers posted on the cliffs around Birsay.

Ten years after the sinking the Admiralty published a white paper on the loss of HMS *Hampshire*.

This may have been, at least in part, an attempt to quash the rumours, but the report has never been universally accepted as satisfactory. It has been claimed that it contains factual errors, that it whitewashes naval and other personnel, and implies that errors of judgement were made and lack of co-operation shown by Orcadians, who were greatly offended by any suggestion that they were at fault for not launching Stromness lifeboat. It did not tell the whole story, and fuelled strong suspicion that something was still being kept secret by the Admiralty. Because of the continuing secrecy many stories spread around, some plausible, others utterly fantastic.

Even after the passage of more than eighty years since Kitchener went down with the *Hampshire*, rumours still persist that there was a cover-up, and that his death was no accident.

As recently as 1992 it was reported in the *Orcadian* newspaper that local people were not allowed to help and that some who tried to do so were turned away – at the point of a soldier's gun.

Of the 655 men aboard the ship, only twelve survived – and they were ordered to say nothing of what had happened that night.

Years after the event, one man even claimed to have been told by 'a reasonably credible authority' that some of the survivors who reached the shore were shot by our own soldiers.

The controversy was alive and kicking in 1988 when *The Sunday Times* published an article describing some of the plethora of bizarre theories surrounding Kitchener's death seventy-two years before:

It is a tribute to Kitchener's enormous public prestige that many people would rather believe anything, however absurd, than accept the truth.

Bizarre conspiracy theories are not confined to Elvis Presley, Marilyn Monroe, John F. Kennedy or Princess Diana. It seems the coincidence of sudden, untimely death and cult status combine to create an overwhelming blend that increases credulity and leaves even normally sensible people open to outlandish suggestions.

It is amazing how gullible people can be! If Kitchener's body had been recovered, none of the bizarre stories would ever have been told.

One theory (by no means the most far-fetched) was that he had gone to Russia, and became Joseph Stalin!

Or he had been taken prisoner by a U-boat, or was living on a remote island. There were reports that he had been seen in Washington, Cairo, Rome and Cyprus.

Horatio Herbert Kitchener. Born near Ballylongford, County Kerry in 1850. Died 5 June 1916 on HMS *Hampshire*.

Joseph Stalin. Born Iosif Vissarion-ovich Dzhugashvili, in 1879 in Gori, Georgia. He died in 1953.

A more plausible story was that German spies in Britain had finally destroyed their worst enemy. Ernst Carl, Germany's master spy in England, and Fritz Joubert Duquesne, 'The Man who Killed Kitchener', both wrote allegedly factual accounts of their exploits.

Even Kitchener's sister, Millie Parker, claimed that her failure to contact him in the spirit world was proof that he was still alive!

Arthur Vectis Freeman, a journalist who wrote under the pseudonym of Frank Power, perpetrated the most elaborate hoax inflicted on the gullible public. He reported that Kitchener had not sailed on the *Hampshire* at all, but had been impersonated by a double. The longer Kitchener failed to appear, however, the less credible that story became, so Power came up with another: Kitchener had suffered a last agonising fight for life clinging to a rock in Orkney, and had finally succumbed. He claimed the Admiralty had deliberately sent Kitchener to his death as an act of vengeance and had made little attempt to rescue any survivors.

All that could be done to honour the national hero was to bring his body back from where it lay in an unmarked grave in Norway. Power invented another story that a 'sea-soaked epaulette of an officer of the British Army, upon which were the insignia of the rank of Field Marshal' had been found in the hut of a Norwegian fisherman, who had taken it from a dead body.

Accompanied by a film cameraman, Power went off to recover the hero's body, which he intended to bring back for interment in Westminster Abbey. A funeral procession was arranged for the benefit of the camera, and a coffin allegedly containing Kitchener's remains was ceremoniously carried aboard a boat. Power arrived in London by train and the coffin was transported to a nearby chapel. It remained there all night, draped in a flag, and with candles burning. But Power had overlooked the fact that a body cannot be buried in England without a death certificate, and for that a coroner must examine the remains. In full view of the press, the police moved the coffin to Lambeth mortuary, where it was opened in the presence of the famous pathologist Sir Bernard Spilsbury – to reveal nothing but tar, which had been poured in to give it weight.

There was disgust at this abuse of the public's feelings for Kitchener, and outrage that anyone could have committed such a cruel hoax, which had people doffing their caps and standing to attention when a box full of tar was conveyed through the streets.

It was 'well known local knowledge' that the sinking was no accident and that the Admiralty had sent Kitchener to his death.

The truth about the sinking of the *Hampshire* was much simpler. The ship should not have been allowed to sail in seas so high that mine-sweeping operations were impossible and the escorting destroyers could not keep pace with her. The Royal Navy's commander-in-chief, Admiral Sir John Jellicoe, who had lunch with Kitchener the day he died, must have realised this, as he considered himself responsible for the loss of the *Hampshire* and for Kitchener's death.

Shortly after 9 p.m. the commander-in-chief of the Grand Fleet 'directed Officer Commanding Western Patrol to take any action to warn all inhabitants along the coast to assist in any possible manner. A motor cyclist was despatched within a short period.'

Within 12 hours, the commander-in-chief could inform the Admiralty: 'I greatly fear there is little hope of there being any survivors as the whole shore has been searched.'

With all hope gone that further lives could be saved, other priorities took over. Shortly after 1 p.m. on 6 June, the Admiralty flashed an urgent message: 'Lord Kitchener had a number of most secret and important official documents. Any wreckage floating about should be examined and precautions taken to watch the coast for wreckage drifting in.'

All communication between Orkney and the mainland was suspended and strict censorship of letters and papers in Scotland was ordered. It was emphasised that no indication could be given of the *Hampshire*'s position when it sank. It was then that the Orcadians were turned back. It would be hard to devise a better scheme to arouse suspicion that the Admiralty had something to hide!

It is almost certain that there is a secret report on the disaster. Kitchener's friend and biographer, Sir George Auther, wrote to *The Times* on 10 February 1926: 'Early in 1920 the first Lord of Admiralty (the late Lord Long) asked me to read the secret and unpublished report on the sinking of the *Hampshire* on the understanding that I would not divulge a word to anybody.'

Further evidence that something remains secret came in 1959 when Donald McCormick, the author of *The Mystery of Lord Kitchener's Death,* disclosed that for the purposes of researching his book he would be granted free access to the Admiralty files if he would permit the Admiralty to amend any part of his book for 'reasons of public interest, regardless of the source from which your information is obtained'. Mr McCormick declined to agree to these conditions, but he was nevertheless given access to many sources previously unexplored. He also took care to rely on valuable testimony from people still alive in Orkney who could vouch for certain happenings.

From time to time rumours emerge that one part of HMS *Hampshire*'s mission was to take not just Lord Kitchener, but gold to Russia. Enquiries as to whether there was any gold on board the *Hampshire* have always been met with official denial, but in 1933 a group of divers working under a Captain Brandt claimed to have removed over £60,000 worth of gold from her strong room. The salvage had been aborted when one of the divers was killed and others seriously injured. They claimed that more than £2 million was still on board. (That was at 1933 prices. At today's prices it would be worth considerably more!)

The Admiralty claimed to know nothing about this, and stated that the *Hampshire* remained the property of HM Government and could not be touched.

One woman claimed that her grandfather worked as a diver in the Royal Navy and that he was involved in an official dive on the *Hampshire* in 1916 in a search to recover bodies. It seems most unlikely to this author that any dive would be carried out for that

At the top of the 300-foot high cliffs at Marwick Head, overlooking the site of the tragedy stands the very prominent Kitchener Memorial, erected in 1926 with money raised by the people of Orkney.
The plaque on the monument reads:

This tower was raised by the people of Orkney in memory of Field Marshal Earl Kitchener of Khartoum on that corner of his country, which he had served so faithfully, nearest to the place where he died on duty.

He and his staff perished, along with the officers and nearly all of the men of HMS Hampshire, on 5th June 1916.

purpose – especially some time after the event, and in the middle of a war that resulted in thousands of bodies. If there was gold on board the *Hampshire*, though, this would have provided sufficient reason to carry out a diving operation to recover it.

The wreck of the *Hampshire* is a war grave and nothing should be removed from it. It was surveyed in 1977 and again in 1983, when a German salvage company illegally raised one of its large bronze propellers. Their recovery vessel called in to Peterhead, where the propeller they had recovered aroused great curiosity when it was spotted lying on the deck. Recovered material was impounded by the receiver of wrecks. The propeller lay ashore at Peterhead harbour for a time, but was later taken to Lyness museum, Orkney. In fact a whole container-load of artefacts recovered from the *Hampshire* was shipped back to Lyness! As the activities of the German divers continued over a period of several weeks, in full view of people in Orkney, there should have been plenty of opportunity to investigate what they were doing while they were there, rather than wait until they came into Peterhead. Was it only by chance that they went to Peterhead? Why did they not proceed directly to Germany?

Perhaps it was no accident that the activity of these divers was not disturbed. What better way could there be to conceal a secret salvage operation of *Hampshire*'s gold than to carry it out in full view, under the pretext of a 'survey', and to reinforce the

The author's wife with the Hampshire *propeller at Lyness (Photo: R.N. Baird)*

'innocence' of the activity by publicly seizing artefacts 'illegally-recovered' from the war grave? – Or am I merely fuelling the rumours?

The evidence from these surveys confirms the Admiralty version that the *Hampshire* struck a mine. It was claimed that the bow plating at the site of the explosion was blown inwards and not outwards as one would expect with an internal explosion, but in fact a lot of the hull plating is missing, and a very large part is bent outwards. This may not all have happened on 5 June 1916. Some of this may be due to subsequent salvage operations.

Certainly, the wreck seems to show evidence of salvage work having been carried out at some time prior to the 'survey' of 1977. The *Hampshire* is lying almost completely upside down, and the whole of the keel plating appears to have been neatly removed from the fore end of the ship, right back to the forward boiler room, and peeled to the port side, out of the way of grabs. It is unlikely that a mine explosion on its own could have made such a tidy job, although one theory is that the plating may have torn off at a row of rivets around one of the ship's ribs. Someone appears to have been looking for something, and knew where to look. It would seem that their search may have been successful, as the exposed area of the forepart of the ship appears to have been cleared right down to the underside of the main deck, and contains nothing of any great value – only ship wreckage.

Some survivors apparently indicated that the initial explosion was just aft of the bridge and that the bottom was ripped out of a boiler room.

As the ship turned over on or near the surface, parts of the superstructure and the guns fell off. What did not fall off immediately was swept off on the way down. The debris field is huge and the guns are about 200 yards away from the ship, sticking out of the sand. The seabed is littered with various artefacts. The decks have collapsed into about seven feet of tangled wreckage.

This wreck is a very sensitive war grave of particular interest to the Ministry of Defence and to the people of Orkney. The Protection of Military Remains Act (1986) made it an offence to disturb or remove anything from the wreck of any Royal Navy ship, or merchant vessel in government service which has human remains aboard, but no great effort has been made to enforce it.

As recently as 9 November 2001, Dr Lewis Mooney, the Under Secretary of State for Defence, announced that greater protection would be given to military wrecks and maritime graves, following rising concern over disturbance and trophy hunting by an irresponsible minority of divers. HMS *Hampshire* was one of sixteen wrecks designated as 'Controlled Sites', with all diving prohibited without a specific licence.

ETHEL DUNCAN

Wreck No: 429		Date Sunk: 18 10 1916
Latitude: 59 25 00 N PA		Longitude: 04 36 00 W PA
GPS Lat: 5925.000 N		GPS Long: 0436.000 W
Location: 40 miles WNW of Noup Head		Area: Orkney
Type: Steamship		Tonnage: 2,510 grt
Length: 286.5 ft	Beam: 43.4 ft.	Draught: 18.8 ft
How Sunk: Torpedoed by *U-20*		Depth: metres

The collier *Ethel Duncan* was built in 1912 by Mackay Bros of Alloa, triple expansion engine by N.E. Marine of Sunderland.

She was owned by the Ethel Duncan Steamship Co., later J.T. Duncan of Cardiff.

Under the command of Captain A.R. Murphy, she was captured and torpedoed by *U-20* on 18 October 1916, 40 miles WNW from Noup Head, Orkney in position 5925N, 0436W, while en route from Cardiff to ? with a cargo of coal. No lives were lost. The *Ethel Duncan* did not have a gun.

EXCELLENT

Wreck No: 430		Date Sunk: 09 01 1917
Latitude: 59 37 00 N PA		Longitude: 04 18 00 W PA
GPS Lat: 5937.000 N		GPS Long: 0418.000 W
Location: 40 miles NW of Noup Head, Orkney		Area: Orkney
Type: Steamship		Tonnage: 1,944 grt
Length: 280.0 ft.	Beam: 40.5 ft.	Draught: 18.2 ft.
How Sunk: By *U-70* – gunfire		Depth: metres

On 9 January 1917 the unarmed British steamship *Excellent* was en route from Penarth to Lerwick with a cargo of coal when she was captured by *U-70* 40 miles NE from Noup Head, Orkney. Her crew were given time to man the boats before *Excellent* was sunk by gunfire. Her skipper was taken back to Germany as a prisoner of war.

The *Excellent* was built in 1907 by S.P. Austin of Sunderland, engine by J. Dickinson of Sunderland.

Excellent *(Photo: courtesy of World Ship Society)*

LEELANAW

Wreck No: 431	Date Sunk: 25 07 1915
Latitude: 59 32 00 N PA	Longitude: 04 22 00 W PA
GPS Lat: 5932.000 N	GPS Long: 0422.000 W
Location: 40 miles NW of Noup Head	Area: Orkney
Type: Steamship	Tonnage: 1,924 grt
Length: ft Beam: ft	Draught: ft
How Sunk: Torpedoed	Depth: metres

On 25 July 1915 the 1,924-grt American steamship *Leelanaw* was torpedoed while en route from Archangel to Belfast with a cargo of flax and hemp.

The position recorded was 595800N, 045000W, but in February 1954 Risdon Beazley gave the position of the wreck as 593200N, 042200W.

U-297

Wreck No: 432	Date Sunk: 06 12 1944
Latitude: 59 00 51.5 N	Longitude: 03 53 45.3 W
GPS Lat: 5900.858 N	GPS Long: 0353.755 W
Location: 16 miles W of Yesnaby, Orkney	Area: Orkney
Type: Submarine	Tonnage: 769 grt
Length: 220.5 ft Beam: 20.3 ft	Draught: 15.7 ft
How Sunk: Depth-charged	Depth: 77 metres

On 6 December 1944 the frigates HMS *Loch Insh* and *Goodall* were hunting for the U-boat which had torpedoed HMS *Bullen*. Aircraft had been called in to assist in the search, and Sunderland 'Y' of 201 Squadron (F/Lt D.R. Hatton), already on patrol off the Butt of Lewis, arrived in the vicinity at 10.55 hrs, in time to see HMS *Bullen* sinking. The aircraft circled the survivors on rafts, then continued to search the area. During the

course of the search for the attacker a series of depth charges were dropped by *Loch Insh* and *Goodall* on an Asdic contact at about 5844N, 0429W. Splintered wooden wreckage and oil came to the surface, and it was assumed the U-boat had been destroyed. Sunderland 'Y' observed the frigates throwing out frequent patterns of depth charges.

Later that afternoon, at 16.43 hrs, in position 5844N, 0420W, three minutes after sunset in fading light, Sunderland 'Y' sighted white smoke and a periscope wake at a distance of 5 miles. The Sunderland dropped from 400 ft to 50 ft as she flew up the wake. Her first attack failed, as the depth-charges hung up. In a second attack, however, 6 depth charges straddled the U-boat's wake at 16.52 hrs. Three of the depth charges entered the wake, the other three dropped slightly ahead – spaced 60 ft apart. The wake and smoke disappeared immediately as the U-boat sank. The aircraft circled, and five minutes lated a pear-shaped oil patch and ochre-coloured scum appeared on the surface. Twenty minutes later, this had grown to a large oil slick measuring one mile by half a mile.

The first depth charge attack by the frigates was on *U-775*, which had sunk the *Bullen*, but that U-boat escaped and returned to base at Bergen on 21 December.

The U-boat attacked and sunk by the Sunderland was Type VIIC/41 U-boat *U-297* (OL Wolfgang Aldegarmann), which had been patrolling in the adjacent area off the north coast of Scotland, south of Hoy and in the Pentland Firth. There were no survivors.

For almost sixty years it seems not to have been realised that the attack by the Sunderland was on a different U-boat from that attacked by *Loch Insh* and *Goodall*, and most sources have recorded the position of loss of *U-297* as 5844N, 0429W. A wreck is charted exactly one mile south of this position at 5843N, 0429W (56 metres in about 60 metres total depth). This is 17 miles ENE of Cape Wrath, or 9 miles NNE of Whiten Head, or 16 miles NW of Strathy Point.

It was tempting to assume that this must be the *U-297*, but the wreck charted at 590051N, 035345W (77 metres in about 84 metres) was found to be a Type VIIC/41 U-boat when dived in May 2000 by Ian Trumpess and Kevin Heath of Stromness. It lies in 285 feet of water (86 metres), 16 miles west of Yesnaby in the Orkney Islands. (Yesnaby is near Neban Point, about 2 miles N of Stromness.) The wreck is oriented 100/280°.

It was assumed that this must be the *U-297*, but according to *Axis Submarine Successes* the destroyer HMS *Zephyr* was damaged at 5857N, 0400W in a torpedo attack made by *U-1020* at 03.30 hrs on 31 December 1944. That position must have been recorded by the *Zephyr*, as *U-1020* was never heard from again. Was a counter-attack carried out by vessels accompanying *Zephyr*? The position of the attack on *Zephyr* is only 5 miles from the position of this wreck.

We have the wreck of a Type VIIC U-boat at 590051.5N, 035345.3W, 16 miles W of Yesnaby, Orkney. (This is a long way from 5844N, 0429W – bearing 50°, 27 miles away!)

The wreck is lying upright, but with a list to starboard. There is no glaringly obvious damage to the wreck, other than a slight bend in the forward part of the hull (which might very well have been caused by the submarine hitting the seabed bow first). The snorkel is retracted into its recess, and the three AA guns lie on the seabed beside the wreck. (Dragged off by a trawler perhaps?)

The top hatch of the conning tower is open, but the bottom hatch is closed. (Was the top hatch dislodged by depth charges, or did someone escape from the conning tower?)

The U-boat has four liferaft hatches in the forward casing. (They are closed.) This was a feature peculiar to U-boats based in Norway.

U-297 and *U-1020* were both based in Norway. These U-boats were of the same type, and looked identical. U-boat numbers were not painted on the conning tower during the war, and nor were the boats fitted with external nameplates. How could the U-boat off Orkney be identified?

Without entering the U-boat to look for some evidence of its identity, there is only one way. The vent holes in the outer casing are grouped in the forecasing, below the conning tower, and in the aft casing. The groupings and patterns of the vent holes in *U-297* and *U-1020* were identical, except in one very minor respect below the conning tower on the starboard side only.

Instead of 20 vent holes in two rows of 10, as shown in the photograph of *U-995*, *U-297* had a pattern of holes grouped 4, 8, 4 on the top row, and a row of 8 holes on the bottom row. *U-1020* had a pattern of holes 2, 8, 4 on the top row, and a row of 8 holes on the bottom row.

Examination of the vent hole patterns on the wreck enabled the U-boat to be identified as *U-297*.

The photograph below is of Type VIIC/41 U-boat *U-995*, which is on display at Laboe, Germany. The double rows of 10 vent holes in the centre casing below the conning tower are very obvious. Also visible in this photograph are the vent holes in the forward casing (at bottom right of photo).

F/Lt Hatton was killed at 02.03 hrs on 14 March 1945 when Sunderland 'A' of 201 Sqdn crashed into a hill north of Killybegs, in County Donegal, Ireland. There were no survivors.

Various authors have referred to *U-297*:

Sharpe: (*U-boat Fact File*)
6.12.44 Depth charged by RN Frigates *Goodall* and *Loch Insch* (5844Nx0429W) 18 miles ENE of Cape Wrath and lost with all fifty hands.

Starboard side of U-995 *on display at Laboe, Kiel, Germany (Photo: Susanne Giehler)*

Kemp: (*U-boats Destroyed*)

On 6 December *U-775* torpedoed the frigate *Bullen*. The hunt for the culprit turned up *U-297* instead. HMS *Loch Insch* and *Goodall* carried out a series of attacks which brought wooden wreckage and oil to the surface. Aircraft were ordered to search the area. Later that afternoon Sunderland 'Y' of No 201 Squadron sighted white smoke and a periscope wake. In its first attack the depth charges hung up but in a second run the wake was straddled and afterwards a large slick of oil was sighted. *U-775* survived the war and was sunk in Operation 'Deadlight'.

Wynn: (*U-boat Operations of the Second World War*)

25.11.44 Left Kiel for British coastal waters.

U-297 patrolled S of Hoy and off Scapa Flow. On 6.12.44 she was located by the destroyers HMS *Goodall* (Lt. Cdr. J.V. Fulton) and the frigate HMS *Loch Insch* (Lt. Cdr. E.W.C. Dempster), which were searching for *U-775*. Their depth-charge attacks sank *U-297* NW of Strathy Point. There were no survivors, fifty dead.

Sunderland III ML882 NS-Y

Crew: F/Lt. D.R. Hatton; F/Sgt. R.D.A Becker; F/Sgt. S.B. Frith; Flg. Off. V. Howkins; Sgt. J.R. Mansfield; F/Sgt. J.G. Robinson; F/Sgt. G.R. Kennedy; Sgt. F.N.G. Ford; F/Sgt. D.J.T. Twist; F/Sgt. C.J. Ryder; Flg. Off. R. Dalby; Sgt. R.F. Woodward. (*Howkins* is as shown on the Form 541)

Took-off 07.10 hrs on 6.12.44; landed back 21.23 hrs.

F/Lt. Hatton's report stated:

Patrol commenced at 10.08 in position 58.30N 06.15W. At 10.40, message received from Group to proceed to position 58.40N 04.05W and co-operate with escort vessels to search for suspected U-boat. Aircraft arrived in vicinity at 10.55 and at once sighted a sinking escort vessel that had been torpedoed and, after it sank, aircraft circled the survivors on rafts and continued searching the area. Nothing was seen all morning or afternoon except that other escort vessels were throwing out frequent patterns of DCs in the vicinity. At 16.43, in position 58.44N, 04.20W, three minutes after sunset in fading light, with the aircraft at 400 feet, white smoke was sighted at approx five miles, bearing 045° Green. Aircraft at once altered course to investigate and lost height to 200 feet. At one mile range a considerable wake was seen, 1,100 feet long as later measured by the navigator as aircraft flew up its track. The source of the smoke, though not visible, was travelling at a speed of 10-12 knots (undoubtedly the schnorkel of a U-boat). Aircraft crossed wake track ahead of the smoke, turned to port and made an attacking run at a height of 50 feet along track of wake from astern. The DCs failed to release; as no faults were found, aircraft again made a similar attack at the still-moving wake and smoke from 50 feet. This time the DCs functioned and a straddle of six fell in a straight line up the wake at 16.52 hrs. Three DCs entered the actual wake, the other three being ahead – spacing 60 feet. The wake and smoke at once disappeared. Aircraft circled and five minutes later a pear-shaped oil patch and ochre-coloured scum was noted. Twenty minutes later, this had reached a size of one mile by half a mile. At 16.57, aircraft flew over to the nearest escort vessel and contacted them on R/T and by visual signals. Aircraft then returned to vicinity of attack. Signals had been sent to base and at 17.33 PLE (prudent limit of endurance) had been reached. Aircraft set course for base, noting that the first escort vessel was now nearing scene of attack. The escort vessels could find no Asdic contacts that night in rough seas. It is probable that the U-boat was damaged; the photographs were failures due to fading light. No radar contacts were made.

The escort vessel reported as torpedoed would appear to be the frigate *Bullen*.

The Coastal Command Staff History contains some further information:

U-296 was in the North Minch area from 14/11/44 and *U-775* from 25/11/44, but on 3 December BdU decided to take action against the carriers conducting sweeps off Norway and *U-775* was ordered in towards the Hoy Sound area. *U-296* remained off the Butt of Lewis (her presence was known – that was why the Sunderland was patrolling that area) and sighted nothing, but reported hearing distant explosions all day on 6/12. *U-775* sighted EG19 (Escort Group 19) at daybreak about 10 miles north-east of Cape Wrath and sank HMS *Bullen*. The A/S hunt for the U-boat lasted 14 hours.

Sunderland 'Y' of 201 Sqdn, already on patrol off the Butt of Lewis, joined the hunt at 10.53 hrs on the 6th in time to see the two halves of *Bullen* sinking in 5846N, 0449W, and was ordered to search between the sinking destroyer and the shore. One series of attacks by *Loch Insh* and *Goodall* at 11.30 hrs brought up oil and splintered woodwork. In the afternoon, the Sunderland circled EG19 who were attacking asdic contacts. Weather 6/10ths cloud, moderate sea and moderate wind 250°.

At 16.52 hrs Sunderland 'Y' sighted a jet of whitish smoke or steam issuing from the sea five miles away in 5844N, 0429W, but could get no contact on her ASV Mk.3 radar. A snorkel was sighted travelling at 10–12 knots on course 050°. Six depth charges were dropped, straddling the head of the wake, then the Sunderland flew off to EG19, which was about eight miles away. Returning to the scene of the attack, the Sunderland saw a large area of smooth discoloured water.

In 1955, the compilers of the *Coastal Command Staff History* concluded that the Sunderland had attacked a 'williwaw' and that credit for sinking *U-297* should go to EG19. They noted that, in November, the same aircrew had reported a snorkel in the Minch, which apparently turned out to be a williwaw.

Those who carried out the 1955 assessment were of the opinion that *U-297* ran into the hunt for *U-775*.

This seems unlikely to me. From her position 50 miles away off the Butt of Lewis, *U-296* was able to hear the explosions of the depth charges dropped on *U-775*. *U-297*, less

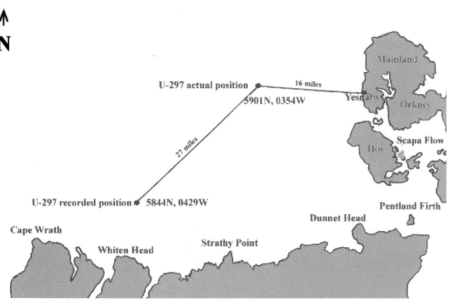

The location of U-297 *(Map © Bob Baird)*

than 30 miles away, would also be able to hear these explosions. Far from running into the hunt for *U-775*, *U-297*'s course of 50° as described by the Sunderland, was running in exactly the opposite direction! (Note that the wreck off Yesnaby is also 50° from the position of the attacks on *U-775*!)

U-1020 was sent to AN16 – an area south-east of Orkney. She arrived on 7 December and stayed until the end of the month, but saw nothing. She was then ordered to go south into the Moray Firth.

The first Arctic boat, *U-312*, arrived on 23 December but left on 26 December after damaging her rudder while attempting to get into Scapa Flow via Hoxa Sound.

U-278 and *U-313* took up this patrol at the end of December, but saw nothing and complained of fierce currents.

According to *Axis Submarine Successes*, *U-278* (KL Joachim Franze) reported that he had torpedoed one ship, but gave no date, nor any details about the target. Note that he did not claim to have sunk the ship – merely that he had torpedoed a ship.

The German *xB-Dienst* reported that the Norwegian steamship *Bestik* (2,684 grt) had anchored in a damaged condition at 13.00 hrs on 8 January 1945 in the Scapa Flow area and that the British *Ashbury* (3,901 grt) had become a total loss. We know that neither *Bestik* nor *Ashbury* were attacked by a U-boat, therefore the ship *U-278* claimed to have torpedoed cannot have been either of these.

After 6 December, when the *Bullen* was sunk, only one ship was torpedoed in this area off the north of Scotland during the rest of the war. That ship was the destroyer HMS *Zephyr*.

Axis Submarine Successes shows the *Zephyr* as damaged by a torpedo at 03.30 hrs on 31 December 1944 in 5857N, 0400W, off the west of Orkney. Prof. Dr Jürgen Rohwer attributes this attack to *U-1020*, but as *U-1020* was east of Orkney she could not have made an attack in the position given. At first glance it seemed possible, therefore, that *U-278* torpedoed the *Zephyr* – not *U-1020*. Closer examination of the records, however, indicates that *U-278* did not carry out that attack either.

In *U-boat Operations of the Second World War*, Kenneth Wynn notes that *U-278* left Bergen on 23 December 1944 and went to an area off northeast Scotland between the Pentland and Moray Firths. The boat was to operate against British carrier groups but saw only merchant ships and patrol boats.

She radioed a request on 15 January to be permitted to leave that area to operate further east, owing to currents in her assigned operating area, low battery capacity and heavy noise level generated by the boat during submerged passage. No mention was made of torpedoes fired or hits achieved. This was only made in a further message on 1 February when she reported that a torpedo fired at a steamship detonated after 8 minutes 2 seconds, and that two further torpedoes fired at a steamer and its escort inexplicably missed, but no date or time was given for these attacks. This must be the same report Dr Rohwer referred to. *U-278* put in to Narvik on 13 February 1945.

U-1020 (OL Otto Eberlein) patrolled off the Pentland Firth from 7 December 1944 until the end of the month, but sighted no targets. On New Year's Eve, she was ordered to head south, to patrol close in around AN1756 (5745N, 0348W). If Eberlein found conditions unfavourable there, he was to go to patrol around AN1894 (5727N, 0148W), off Buchan/Aberdeen. The southern boundary of this patrol area was AN0126 (5709N, 0200W), but it is not known if she ever got to that area.

U-1020 was never heard from again, and is thought to have been mined in the deep minefield outside the Moray Firth on, or shortly after, 1 January 1945. There were no survivors.

She might have been the U-boat sighted by Liberator 'A' of 224 Sqdn north of Banff at 5748N, 0226W at 10.30 hrs on 11 January 1945.

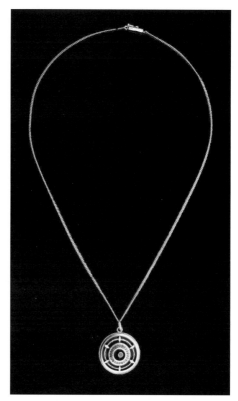

The Aldegarmann necklace (Photo: © R.N. Baird)

It is worth noting that during the first nine months of the war, U-boats heading from Germany to the Atlantic were ordered to pass through the Fair Isle Gap between Orkney and Shetland. This instruction was issued by Dönitz's deputy, Victor Oehrn, who had been a U-boat commander before the war. In May 1940, Dönitz ordered him to take command of *U-37* and go out to prove that problems with the German torpedoes had been cured. (Malfunctions of the magnetic detonating pistols of their torpedoes had demoralised the U-boat men, and severely damaged their faith in the weapons.)

Despite his misgivings concerning the advisability of doing so, but not wishing to be seen to depart from his own instructions to the other U-boat commanders, he took *U-37* through the Fair Isle Gap. Just west of the Gap *U-37* was sighted and attacked by a British aircraft so accurately that its crew reported her sunk. Oehrn did not enjoy the experience! Henceforth all U-boats were ordered to take the longer but safer route around the north of Shetland!

At no time during the war did U-boats attempt to break out into the Atlantic through the Pentland Firth, and nor was it used as a route to return to Germany. In full flow, the tidal stream through the Pentland Firth runs faster than the maximum surfaced speed of Type VII U-boats, and at twice their submerged speed. It would certainly not have been a practical proposition for a U-boat to attempt to pass through the constricted waters of the Pentland Firth.

The east-coast portion of inward-bound convoys came round the north of Scotland and down to Methil where ships were dispersed to their ports or joined the south-bound east coast of England convoys. Outgoing convoys sailed from Methil northabout out to the Atlantic through the Pentland Firth. The timing of convoys was intended to ensure that they passed through the Pentland Firth in daylight with the tide, but as can be imagined, it was not always possible to stick to this.

A booklet about the finding of *U-297*, written by Richard W. Skinner, was published in 2002. A copy was sent to Wolfgang Aldegarmann's widow, Hilde, who was pleased to finally learn, after almost sixty years, what had happened to her husband's boat, and where his body lies.

Hilde, who is now in her eighties, sent a gold and sapphire pendant, which her husband had given her, and which she wore for many years, to be dropped into *U-297*'s conning tower as a declaration of her love, and as a last farewell gesture to her husband. This moving tribute will be carried out by Kevin Heath and Ian Trumpess, owner of the Orkney dive boat *Radiant Queen*, while Hilde's nephew Thomas Bergmeier of Detmold, Germany, places a wreath on the sea above.

NAVARRA

Wreck No: 433		Date Sunk: 06 04 1940
Latitude: 59 00 00 N PA		Longitude: 04 07 00 W PA
GPS Lat: 5900.000 N		GPS Long: 0407.000 W
Location: 25 miles W of Orkney		Area: Orkney
Type: Steamship		Tonnage: 2,118 grt
Length: 285.0 ft	Beam: 43.5 ft	Draught: 19.1 ft
How Sunk: Torpedoed by *U-59*		Depth: 70 metres

The Norwegian steamship *Navarra* was completed in January 1921 by Osbourne Graham & Co. of Sunderland for D/S Garonne, owned by Fearnley & Eger of Oslo. Engine by G. Clark of Sunderland. She was a three-island steamship classed by Norsk Veritas (the Norwegian equivalent of Lloyds).

The *Navarra* was bound from Swansea to Oslo with a cargo of 3,000 tons of coal on 6 April 1940, and was proceeding with the usual lights showing to indicate that she was a neutral vessel. In addition, she was flying the Norwegian flag. Despite that, she was torpedoed and sunk by the *U-59* (KL Harald Jürst), NW of Scotland, in German grid AN1537, which equates to about 5851N, 0336W. The wreck charted at 585045N, 034250W, nine miles west of Rora Head, is very close to that position, but this wreck is thought to be the MFV *Daystar*, sunk 10 March 1982.

The *Navarra* sank in about three minutes, and ten of her crew and two passengers were lost.

A coastal command aircraft sighted a lifeboat on 6 April at LK002014 (a wartime coastal command grid position off the north coast of Scotland), and guided the Finnish steamer *Atlas* to the scene. The lifeboat contained survivors from the Norwegian steamship *Navarra*, which had been torpedoed in a gale at 02.30 hrs on the 6th, about 25 miles N of Strathie Point.

Lloyds recorded the position as 5900N, 0400W, which is about 25 miles west of the Orkneys.

The wreck at 584936N, 040035W is apparently about 60 metres long, and stands up 7 metres. It is very near the position recorded by Lloyds, but the length dimension is a little less than the *Navarra*.

All the officers and nine of the crew were killed, but fourteen survivors were picked up from the lifeboat by the Finnish steamship *Atlas* and landed at Kirkwall on the 7th. Six of the twelve who were missing were believed to have been killed by the explosion of the torpedo. The captain, three officers and two passengers were lost when one of the ship's two lifeboats was dragged under by the sinking ship. Two survivors from this boat were able to jump into the sea and were saved by the other lifeboat, which contained the remaining twelve survivors.

When landed by the *Atlas*, a vessel of one thousand tons, the fourteen survivors were exhausted and able to speak only incoherently. Two of the men had leg injuries. One of the survivors' watches had stopped at 2.22 a.m., and this was presumed to have been the time he abandoned ship.

Although no submarine had been seen at the time of the attack, a German U-boat surfaced when the *Navarra* sank, came to within ten or fifteen yards of the lifeboat and flashed a light on the boat and its occupants. Although within easy hailing distance of the survivors, the occupants of the submarine conning tower did not question or address the men, but left them to sink or swim in heavy seas, torrential rain and poor visibility.

Several of the survivors stated that they had been able to see the submarine in the vicinity for about half an hour after the sinking of the *Navarra*, but the Germans offered no help.

Without their captain and officers, the survivors were in low spirits, but determined to keep their boat from disaster until daylight, when they thought they had a chance of being picked up.

So big were the seas after daylight that the men's range of visibility was very limited, and only when on the crest of a wave were they able to see any distance.

The U-boat was not in sight when the dawn broke. The exhausted men, most of them suffering from shock and exposure, had not long to wait for a good sign, once the daylight came.

An aircraft was seen, and the pilot appeared to spot the lifeboat, for he left his course and made towards the small craft. The aircraft circled over the lifeboat once or twice, and was seen to be a British warplane. Having indicated to the lifeboat that he had noted their plight, the pilot sped away out of sight. The master of the Finnish steamer *Atlas* which effected the rescue said:

> A British coastal patrol airplane came over my ship and made a signal to me as he flew around. I realised that he wanted to tell me the way to some place where assistance was needed. I altered course and followed the way shown by the airplane. About 11 o'clock in the forenoon the airplane showed me a ship's lifeboat which was occupied by fourteen men. We had a difficult job to get them on board because of the terrible seas, but we did so without injuring any of them. I then put about to the nearest port and landed them ten hours later. On the way to port, my officers and I tried to learn from the rescued men what exactly had happened to them, but they were in a bad state and very incoherent. We just had to nurse them as best we could for fear some of them would die before we got them ashore.

The *Navarra* was sunk three days before the German invasion of Norway. She had no gun or deck cargo, and had been heading to Kirkwall for examination, before proceeding to Oslo.

The fourteen men who were landed at Kirkwall on 7 April 1940 subsequently sailed for home – a neutral country when their ship was sunk – but now at war with Germany. If their vessel had not been sunk on 6 April, they would have been steaming up Oslo Fiord on the morning of 9 April, in the midst of the German Navy invading Norway!

On 9 April 1940, one of the *Navarra*'s lifeboats was found in North Ronaldsay Sound, and on 2 May a liferaft from the *Navarra* was found at Ness Point, Burray, Orkney, and on 3 May another was found at Old Head, South Ronaldsay.

On 4 May a lifebuoy from the *Navarra* was found at Stew Haven, on the east side of South Ronaldsay.

A very dark photograph of the Navarra *with a high deck cargo (probably pit props supported by vertical stakes), which obscures some detail of the ship itself. The photograph appears to show the bell attached to the foremast of the* Navarra. *(Photo: courtesy of World Ship Society)*

Marstonmoor *(Photo: courtesy of World Ship Society)*

MARSTONMOOR

Wreck No: 434

Latitude: 59 28 00 N PA

GPS Lat: 5928.000 N

Location: 55 miles NNE from Cape Wrath

Type: Steamship

Length: 314 .0ft   Beam: 46.5 ft

How Sunk: Torpedoed by *U-107*

Date Sunk: 14 04 1918

Longitude: 04 24 00 W PA

GPS Long: 0424.000 W

Area: Orkney

Tonnage: 2,744 grt

Draught: 20.6 ft

Depth: metres

The British steamship *Marstonmoor* was built in September 1906 by J. Blumer & Co., Sunderland. Triple expansion engine by Denny of Dumbarton. The ship was owned by Moorline, and managed by W. Runciman. Under the command of Captain W. Evans, she was torpedoed and sunk by *U-107* on 14 April 1918, 55 miles NNE from Cape Wrath, or 50 miles W by N of Noup Head, while en route from Barry to Archangel with mails, coal and general cargo (Lloyds gives her route as Milford Haven to Murmansk). The *Marstonmoor* was armed with a defensive gun (see photo). Her position was recorded as 5934N, 0454W, but an obstruction charted at 593130N, 043112W in 71 metres might be the *Marstonmoor*.

UB-116

Wreck No: 435	Date Sunk: 28 10 1918
Latitude: 58 50 07 N	Longitude: 03 04 06 W
GPS Lat: 5850.117 N	GPS Long: 304.100 W
Location: Panhope Bay, Flotta	Area: Orkney
Type: Submarine	Tonnage: 516/641tons
Length: 181.0 ft Beam: 19.0 ft	Draught: 12.0 ft
How Sunk: Mined	Depth: 26 metres

On 28 October 1918 *UB-116* (OL Hans-Joachim Emsmann) was entering Scapa Flow through the Hoxa Sound entrance. Her presence beneath the surface was detected by hydrophones, and on shore her progress was monitored. After waiting for the U-boat to penetrate deep into the controlled minefield at 5850N, 0304W, mines were electrically detonated from the shore. Emsmann and his entire crew were lost.

UB-116 was the last U-boat to be sunk in British waters during the First World War. According to one report she was raised in 1919 and resunk in 26 metres.

During the First World War a Royal Navy diving team, commanded by Captain G.C.C. Damant, was involved in recovering intelligence material from sunken U-boats. Damant had been involved in experiments related to research into decompression tables conducted for the Admiralty by Dr J.S. Haldane and Dr W.E.Boycott in 1906. During these experiments Commander Damant and another diver, A. Catto, attained the world record depth of 210 ft.

A member of Damant's team, Warrant Shipwright E.C. Miller, was told to dive on a submarine sunk in a minefield off Orkney.

After blasting open the conning-tower hatch Miller went inside. It was pitch black and he kept bumping into bodies. By the light of his torch he could see that all the bodies were wearing officers' uniforms, and he thought the whole crew were officers. He found a stack of leather suitcases and prised several of them open to find that they all contained suits of smart civilian clothes, shirts, collars, cravats and shoes, along with sums of money and various other things. By October 1918 it must have been obvious that the war was about to end in defeat for Germany. Were the crew intending to land somewhere in Britain? A bit unlikely, perhaps, immediately after carrying out an attack on a British target in Scapa Flow. Or did they intend to try to make for Spain after their mission, and wear the civilian clothes there, rather than end up in a prison camp? In his log Captain Damant says the cases were recovered and taken away by Naval authorities. He did not mention that all the bodies were dressed in officers' uniforms, but he did identify the U-boat with the suitcases as *UB-116*.

UB-116 was a new U-boat commanded by Oberleutnant Hans-Joachim Emsmann, the son of an admiral. She had a crew of thirty-five and was armed with ten torpedoes. Emsmann had been ordered to enter Scapa Flow by Hoxa Sound, which, he was wrongly informed, was not mined or netted. Before he sailed on 24 October, Emsmann told a colleague ashore that he knew he would not return.

Did he say that out of a sense of foreboding, or was that related to the suitcases with civilian clothes?

The U-boat was spotted on the surface off Hoy, to the west of the Hoxa entrance, which was both mined and netted. The defences were alert and waiting for him when he attempted to enter Scapa Flow, and the U-boat was detected by hydrophones. Its progress was monitored, and just before midnight, when it was right over a line of mines, the button to detonate them was pressed.

At dawn, a trail of oil emanated from *UB-116*. It is said that the hydrophones detected tapping noises from the submarine that morning, but nevertheless a destroyer dropped more depth charges.

The wreck of *UB-116* lies at the entrance to Pan Hope Bay. It was sold for salvage in 1969, and during salvage operations in 1975 a number of charges had been placed to crack open the hull. When they were detonated, the live torpedoes in the forward tubes exploded, blasting the wreck apart. All that remains now are pieces of bent and twisted steel plating, pipes, wires and broken electrical items, spread over the seabed, and partially buried in soft sand.

After the war, Miller returned to recovering gold from the *Laurentic,* which had struck a mine and sunk off the north west of Ireland on 23 January 1917. He had started that task during the war, but diving on sunken U-boats was even more important at that time. For the dangerous and secret work he had done, recovering intelligence material from within the wrecks of U-boats, Warrant Shipwright Miller RN was awarded the MBE on 1 January 1919. Later that same year he was awarded the Distinguished Service Cross for his accomplishments in connection with the hazardous and important salvage work he had carried out.

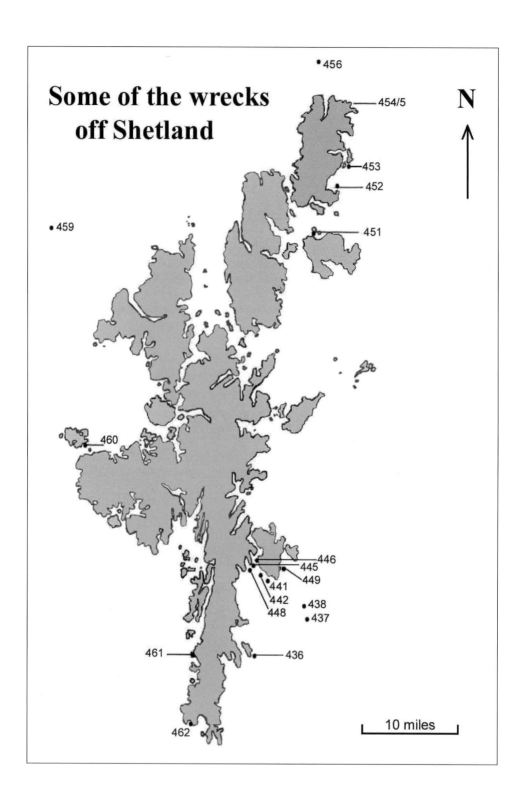

Some of the wrecks off Shetland

8
SHETLAND

ST SUNNIVA

Wreck No: 436	Date Sunk: 10 04 1930
Latitude: 59 59 51 N	Longitude: 01 09 24 W
GPS Lat: 5959.850 N	GPS Long: 0109.400 W
Location: SE corner of Mousa	Area: Shetland
Type: Steamship	Tonnage: 864 grt
Length: 237.8 ft Beam: 29.7 ft	Draught: ft
How Sunk: Ran aground	Depth: 25-30 metres

The *St Sunniva* was built by Hall Russell of Aberdeen in 1887 for the North of Scotland Orkney and Shetland Steam Navigation Company. She spent her first twenty-one years cruising the Norwegian Fiords in the summer months. In the autumn, she voyaged round the British Isles. In 1908 she was chartered for voyages around the Mediterranean, but that part of her career was short-lived due to severe competition. In 1909 she was altered to make her suitable for the Aberdeen–Orkney–Shetland run. By April 1930 she had done that run about 3,000 times, and had become one of the most popular ships in Shetland.

At 3.45 a.m. on 10 April 1930 she struck the island of Mousa in dense fog, hitting submerged rocks between the Muckle Bard and the Swarf.

Immediately she went aground, an SOS was sent to the radio station at Wick, stating that the vessel was sinking fast, and water was coming into the cabins. Sea conditions deteriorated, and the increasing swell continually pounded the ship on the rocks. The engine room staff had a narrow escape when machinery was driven violently inboard by the force of the stranding, and the stokehold flooded rapidly.

Lerwick coastguard received a telegram at about 6.00 a.m., and with all due speed, the Life Saving Company in Lerwick left for Mousa on the trawler *Fort James*, along with the *Earl of Zetland* and the small wooden fishery cruiser *Vaila*. Stromness lifeboat, over 70 miles away, was also sent for.

Two of her own boats were launched on the starboard side, but they were smashed to pieces against *St Sunniva*'s hull. Three other boats were then launched on the port side, and the survivors set off to attempt a landing on Mousa. There were rocks only 50 yards away, but due to the strength of the swell it was obviously impossible to get ashore there. The lifeboats had no choice but to row round to the more sheltered west side of the island. It took about two hours to achieve this, and once there, about forty passengers and crew, including men, women and children, were able to scramble over the rocks to safety. No-one was lost. The captain set off for Sandlodge on the Mainland to raise the alarm, while the passengers sheltered in a shepherd's bothy. Later that morning the survivors on Mousa were taken off and landed at Lerwick, most still in their night attire, having had no chance to dress or save any belongings. The wreck broke up and sank completely in a south-easterly gale later that month.

Very little had been saved. Most of the mail on board was lost. This included payment in the form of postal orders and bank drafts to the value of several thousand pounds, intended as payment for knitwear workers on the islands, and no compensation could be obtained for their loss.

The wreck of the *St Sunniva* lies in 25 to 30 metres close to the shore at the north-east entrance to a sandy bay known as the Swarf. Wreckage is strewn in rock gullies which run in a north-south direction. Bollards, bits of condenser, a winch, a large anchor with a broken stock, and a pile of chain can be seen. An iron propeller lies at the end of a shallow gully running in towards the shore.

The mail boat St Sunniva *aground on Mousa (Photo: Shetland Museum)*

UC-55

Wreck No: 437		Date Sunk: 29 09 1917	
Latitude: 60 01 56 N		Longitude: 00 57 15 W	
GPS Lat: 6001.930 N		GPS Long: 0057.254 W	
Location: 6½ miles E of Helliness		Area: Shetland	
Type: Submarine		Tonnage: 493 t	
Length: 163.0 ft	Beam: 17.3 ft	Draught: 12.2 ft	
How Sunk: Gunfire and depth-charging		Depth: 101 metres	

UC-55 left Germany with orders to mine the entrance to both Kirkwall and Lerwick harbours, the weapons to be laid in equal numbers and at irregular distances, but not more than five miles from the shore. While laying mines off Lerwick on 29 September 1917 she lost trim and began to sink rapidly bow first, going down to 50 metres (165 feet) at which point her hull plating split since this was beyond her diving depth. The resultant inrush of salt water reached her batteries, causing chlorine gas to be produced, and one battery caught fire. She was forced to surface immediately to ventilate the boat and recharge her air banks. While on the surface *UC-55* was sighted by the trawlers

HMS *Sylvia* and HMS *Moravia*, both armed with 6-pdr guns. A shell from *Sylvia's* gun hit the conning tower, killed her commanding officer, Ruhle von Lilienstern, and disabled the steering gear. A second shell struck the hull and she began to sink, after which two depth-charges were dropped right alongside and the U-boat blew up. The *Moravia* then arrived, put two more shots into the wreck and dropped another depth-charge. Seventeen officers and men were taken prisoner. The remaining ten members of her crew were killed.

The position has been described as 4 miles ENE of Mousa Lighthouse.

The wreck charted at 600156N, 005715W, in 101 metres, is a reasonably close fit to that position description, and might be the *UC-55*.

FLYNDERBORG

Wreck No: 438
Latitude: 60 03 13 N
GPS Lat: 6003.212 N
Location: 4½ miles SE of Bard Head
Type: Steamship
Length: 254.1 ft   Beam: 36.3 ft
How Sunk: Torpedoed by *UC-40*

Date Sunk: 21 10 1917
Longitude: 00 58 03 W
GPS Long: 0058.055 W
Area: Shetland
Tonnage: 1,400 grt
Draught: ft
Depth: 97 metres

The Danish steamship *Flynderborg* was in a convoy on 21 October 1917. At 5.40 p.m., off the Bard of Bressay, about 5 nm from Ness Head (presumably Feadda Ness), a torpedo was seen close to the ship. Immediately afterwards, a violent explosion occurred, and *Flynderborg* began to sink. The crew managed to get into the lifeboats, and shortly afterwards, *Flynderborg* sank. At 6.30 p.m. the crew was taken aboard a Royal Navy vessel and put ashore that same evening at Lerwick.

The wreck at 6003.2121N, 0058.0547W, in 97 metres, is the right distance from Feadda Ness, and at least one Shetland fisherman knows this wreck as the *Flynderborg*.

SLAVONIC

Wreck No: 439
Latitude: 60 05 03 N
GPS Lat: 6005.052N
Location: Off Bard of Bressay
Type: Steamship
Length: 346.2 ft   Beam: 50.3 ft
How Sunk: Torpedoed by *UC-40*

Date Sunk: 19 10 1917
Longitude: 01 04 32 W
GPS Long: 104.538W
Area: Shetland
Tonnage: 3,604 grt
Draught: 22.9 ft
Depth: 85 metres

The Russian steamship *Slavonic* was en route from Archangel to Lerwick with a cargo of timber when she was torpedoed by *UC-40*, 6 cables SSW of Bard Head on 19 October 1917.

She was taken in tow for 30 minutes before she sank.

The wreck is charted with a depth of 71 metres, at 6005.0573N, 0104.5456W (WGS84), but the actual depth is 85 metres.

This is a fairly large wreck, at least 300 ft long, with two large boilers. There is no sign of any cargo. *Slavonic* (ex-*Teutonic*) was built by W. Gray & Co. of West Hartlepool in 1905.

ASIA

Wreck No: 440	Date Sunk: 24 10 1917
Latitude: 60 06 04 N	Longitude: 01 07 23 W
GPS Lat: 6006.065 N	GPS Long: 0107.389 W
Location: 1¼ mile S of Kirkabister Light	Area: Shetland
Type: Trawler	Tonnage: 309 grt
Length: 147.4 ft Beam: 23.4 ft	Draught: 11.5 ft
How Sunk: Mined	Depth: 69 metres

The wreck here is the steel steam trawler *Asia*, built by Earles of Hull in 1905. Her stern was severely damaged when she struck a mine and sank off Kirkabister light on 12 September 1917. Small calibre gun shells have been found in the wreck.

LEONATUS

Wreck No: 441	Date Sunk: 12 12 1917
Latitude: 60 06 22 N	Longitude: 01 06 05 W
GPS Lat: 6006.364 N	GPS Long: 0106.084 W
Location: 2 miles E by S Kirkabister Light	Area: Shetland
Type: Steamship	Tonnage: 2099 grt
Length: 292.1 ft Beam: 42.3 ft	Draught: 19.7 ft
How Sunk: Torpedoed by *UC-40*	Depth: 60 metres

The Glasgow steamship *Leonatus* (ex-*Scarsdale*) was built in 1903 by Richardson, Duck & Co. of Stockton-on-Tees.

En route from Swansea via Loch Ewe to Lerwick with a cargo of coal she was torpedoed by the *UC-40* at 9.00 a.m. on 12 December 1917, two miles east by south of Kirkabister Lighthouse. She was taken in tow for Lerwick, but foundered between Bard Head and The Ord at 12.45 p.m. The survivors were picked up by a patrol vessel and landed in Lerwick.

The *Leonatus* lies in 60m of water in two parts lying at an angle to each other, suggesting she either broke on the surface or on the way down, rather than on impact with the seabed. There is a gap of about 6m between the two halves at the nearest point. The wreck is in an area where the tide eddies, the tide running from stern to bow, but it is diveable at all states of the tide.

Landing on the bow, the top of the wreck is at 52m, lying upright, her anchors still dogged in place. The shot-line is normally tied to the winch here. Immediately aft of the winch, the wooden upper decking has all gone, but the lower decking is still in place leading to a hatch and the foc'sle stores. A ladder leads down to the stores, which contained an assortment of items, including spare navigation lights (now in the Lerwick museum), porthole glass, crockery, and various cargo-handling equipment spares, as well as a few tins of paint. The bulkhead from the stores aft is corroded, but not enough to swim through, so you have to exit the same way you came in, past the ever-present shoals of fish. You will pass over more winches and cargo-handling items as you swim aft over the hold full of coal. The wreck is covered in prolific marine growth due to the tide running over her. The bow section is about 150ft long and ends cleanly just forward of the engines. On the seabed here lie the remains of her bridge and accommodation, seemingly having slid off the ship as she sank. The compass binnacle was raised in 2000, and will be displayed in the Lerwick museum. The stand design is of three entwined heraldic dolphins. The compass itself has corroded away, but the round glass face remains. A tangle of flattened remains on the seabed in 60-62m leads across to the stern section.

One boiler stands clear, seemingly huge, as the decking has collapsed all around the engines, making it easy to see the structure of the fairly basic triple expansion steam engine. There are two boilers in place. The gratings are still around the engine, so when swimming aft it feels almost as if you are wandering along a companionway. As you move aft over the stern holds the huge spare prop is still higher than the rest of the ship, the decking reinforced below it. It is now very unstable and liable to fall any time! Next to the propeller is the gun, completely intact. It was mounted on a steel 'box', through the decking. The whole structure has collapsed forward and lies in one piece, surrounded by shells, all dated 1911. A brass (or bronze) fretwork beneath the shells is perhaps some sort of storage system for them – maybe wood with a brass frontage?

Aft of here the deck rises up to about 52m from the more general 55-56m. The stern lockers are inaccessible, beams having fallen across the entrance. The aft railing is still in place and looks stunning with the sun shining down, like a basket work covered in growth. Swimming over the stern and down, the propeller stands in the scour at 62m.

I am indebted to Fiona Watson of Voe, Shetland for the above description of the wreck.

ANGLO DANE

Wreck No: 442	Date Sunk: 21 10 1917
Latitude: 60 06 31 N	Longitude: 01 07 35 W
GPS Lat: 6006.525N	GPS Long: 0107.574 W
Location: ¾ miles S of Kirkabister Light	Area: Shetland
Type: Steamship	Tonnage: 808 grt
Length: 217.0 ft	Beam: 28.2 ft	Draught: 15.8 ft
How Sunk: Mined or torpedoed by *UC-40*	Depth: 69 metres

The Danish steamship *Anglo Dane* was an iron steamship of 708grt, 203.4 x 26.7 x 14.4 ft, built by Andrew Leslie & Co. of Hebburn on Tyne in 1866 for the Anglo Danish and Baltic Steam Navigation Co. Ltd (C.P.A. Koch).

Due to financial problems in that steamship company, however, she remained in the ownership of the builder, Andrew Leslie, until she was bought by DFDS, Copenhagen in 1867 for £16,000.

For some years she plied the routes Hull/Antwerp–Copenhagen–Baltic and Copenhagen–Iceland.

In 1874 she was rebuilt by Burmeister & Wain, Copenhagen, and became 217 x 28.2 x 15.8 ft and 808 grt. Her original boiler was replaced by a single Scotch boiler, and her 2-cylinder Thompson and Boyd engine was rebuilt as a 4-cylinder by Burmeister and Wain.

In 1895 another new boiler was installed by Burmeister and Wain.

On 21 October 1917, while in convoy on a voyage from South Shields to Elsinore, she either struck a mine, or was torpedoed by *UC-40*, about half a mile from Kirkabister light. The ship broke in two, and the forward section sank immediately. The stern section remained afloat for about four minutes before sinking. One crew member, stoker Niels Jonsberg of Copenhagen, was lost. The rest of the crew took to a lifeboat and were shortly taken aboard the British torpedo-boat *Arab*, and put ashore at Lerwick.

The wreck lies upright with the bows pointing towards Lerwick. From the stern, the propeller is still in place at 68-69m. Her beautiful counter stern is almost completely intact. The seabed is white sand, which reflects the ambient light, and even at this depth a torch is often not needed.

Moving forward over the holds the decking and upper works are all gone, but the cross beams are close together, making her still seem very solid. The smashed remains of a toilet are on the port side about halfway down the hold. The holds themselves are filled with thick coal dust and sludge.

Coming to the forward edge of the hold, a pile of green glass beer bottles is in a corner, and above is a big winch where the shot line is often tied. From the vantage point of the winch you can look forward over the engines. Immediately aft of the engines is a big open metal cylinder with sides about an inch thick. It is big enough for a diver to enter from the top, and looks as though it may have had a lid on it at some time.

The engine seems to be relatively complex, and apparently more advanced than those on similar wrecks nearby such as the *Leonatus* and *Glenisla*. On the port side the iron helm has fallen through the deck and remains wedged underneath. Just in front of this a large wolf fish is in residence. It has been seen on every dive to date!

A large copper soup tureen was found below decks on the starboard side. This must have been the galley. The boiler seems to have been dislodged slightly, possibly as a result of the torpedo explosion. Her bows are completely gone forward of the boiler, and lie close by in 68 metres. There is a debris field around where they split off, as the guts of the ship spilled out on to the seabed – it might be worth spending a little time rummaging around this area.

Again, I am grateful to Fiona Watson for her description of this wreck, which was long assumed to be the *Parkmill*. However, crockery bearing the DFDS crest, recovered from the wreck, coupled with no sign of torpedo damage on the starboard side, cast serious doubt upon its identity as the *Parkmill*. This wreck is almost certainly the *Anglo Dane*.

The Danish steamship Anglo Dane *(Photo: author's collection)*

PARKMILL? or WORON?

Wreck No: 443	Date Sunk: 10 09 1917
Latitude: 60 06 22 N	Longitude: 01 05 06 W
GPS Lat: 6006.364 N	GPS Long: 0105.105 W
Location: ½ mile W of Bard Head	Area: Shetland
Type: Steamship	Tonnage: 1,316 grt
Length: 236.4 ft Beam: 36.3 ft	Draught: 15.2 ft
How Sunk: Torpedoed by *UC-40*	Depth: 45 metres

This charted wreck might be the steamship *Parkmill,* which was built by the Clyde S.B. & E. Co., Port Glasgow in 1909.

On 10 September 1917 she was en route from Blyth to Lerwick with a cargo of 1,780 tons of coal. Just as she was about to enter Bressay Sound she was torpedoed by the German U-boat *UC-40.*

The torpedo struck the starboard side just forward her engine room at 10.40 a.m., and the crew abandoned ship. *Parkmill* sank 15 minutes later. She was *UC-40*'s second victim that morning.

There are those who think the *Leonatus* and *Parkmill* struck mines laid by *UC-40,* but according to German Rear Admiral Arno Spindler, who was in a position to know, they were sunk by torpedo.

The wreck at 6006.525N, 0107.574W was long assumed to be the *Parkmill,* but crockery bearing the DFDS crest has been recovered from that wreck, casting doubt on its identity as the *Parkmill.*

The *Parkmill* must lie elsewhere.

Another even larger wreck which has not been found yet, but which must be somewhere in the area, is the 3,342-grt Russian steamship *Woron* (ex-*Snowdon Range*), torpedoed by *UC-40* off the south entrance to Bressay Sound on 24 October 1917. She was built by Irvine of West Hartlepool in 1906, and measured 326.9 x 47.3 x 13.7 ft.

GWLADMENA

Wreck No: 444	Date Sunk: 02 01 1918
Latitude: 60 08 12 N	Longitude: 01 08 38 W
GPS Lat: 6008.201N	GPS Long: 0108.637 W
Location: South side of Breiwick	Area: Shetland
Type: Steamship	Tonnage: 928 grt
Length: 221.3 ft Beam: 30.2 ft	Draught: 16.2 ft
How Sunk: Collision with *Flora*	Depth: 34-39 metres

The iron steamship *Gwladmena* (ex-*Mary Hough*, ex-*Maggie Warrington*) was built by R. Irvine of West Hartlepool in 1878.

Coming in to Lerwick with a cargo of coal from Methil on 2 January 1918, she was involved in a collision with the Danish steamship *Flora. Gwladmena* sank, but her crew of twenty-two were all saved.

The wreck is almost intact and upright in 39m, with her bows pointing toward the coastguard station on the Knab. The bridge lies off to the starboard side, and its cargo of coal is strewn everywhere. The wreck is normally buoyed, with a line attached to the bow. Descending to the wreck, the whole bow section comes into view at around

2om, with the top of the wreck at around 34m. It is possible to see the whole wreck all at once, and visibility rarely drops below 10m. Many divers have raved about the amazingly good underwater visibility on this wreck, but this is true of all the wrecks around Shetland! The foc'sle store is open and still contains hoses, coiled hawsers and paint tins. The bulkhead between the store and the forward hold has corroded away allowing in plenty of natural light. The stump of a wooden mast stands between the foc'sle store and the hold. The hole in the decking above, through which the mast used to penetrate, can be clearly seen. Lying on the bottom, on the starboard side are a winch and hawser. The port anchor is also on the sand.

The engine, built by Blair and Co. of Stockton-on-Tees, lies on its side. It has been dragged over the two boilers and is now in front of them. The propeller has been salvaged, and the shaft is exposed, still with its stern gland of lignum vitae. In February 1998, a klondiker's anchor ripped off the decking at the stern, opening up that area for the first time. The gun lies on the seabed off the starboard side. A few shells also lie on the seabed, periodically covered and uncovered by the sand. There is almost no tide on the wreck, but a surface current sometimes runs here.

SAMBA

Wreck No: 445	Date Sunk: 28 12 1956
Latitude: 60 07 41 N	Longitude: 01 09 22 W
GPS Lat: 6007.678 N	GPS Long: 0109.369 W
Location: Ruggen, Ness of Sound	Area: Shetland
Type: Motor vessel	Tonnage: 663 grt
Length: 151.8 ft Beam: 26.4 ft	Draught: ft
How Sunk: Ran aground	Depth: 35 metres

The minesweeping trawler HMS *Olive* was built in 1940 by Hall Russell of Aberdeen. In 1948 she was sold to a Swedish company, who converted her to a tanker for carrying fuel oil and renamed her *Samba*. On Christmas Day, 1956, she was en route, in ballast, from Rotterdam to Odda in Sweden, when she broke down in the North Sea, about 30 miles west of southern Norway. The engineer tried to repair the fault, but to no avail. Radio power was weak, and it was not until the following day that her distress call was heard. By then she was about 130 miles east of Peterhead, adrift in a gale force wind.

Eleven ships and an RAF Shackleton aircraft searched for the *Samba*. She was finally located by the Shackleton, which dropped flares to guide the searching ships to the vessel's position. First to arrive was the Hull trawler *Cape Mariata*, which was soon joined by another trawler, the *Robert Croan*. Both boats stood by the *Samba* until 10.30 a.m. on 26 December, when *Cape Mariata* was relieved by her sister trawler, *Cape Adair*. At 4.00 p.m. on the 27th, the Dutch tug *Noord Holland* arrived.

By that time the *Samba* had been driven so far by the gale that she was 38 miles ESE of Bard Head, Bressay! The Dutch skipper's plan was to get a line aboard the *Samba* as soon as daylight broke, but in the high seas all attempts failed. The situation was becoming more critical as the *Samba* had by then drifted to a position 19 miles ESE of Bard Head.

At 11.25 a.m. Lerwick lifeboat *Lady Jane & Martha Ryland* was launched. Great seas swept over her as she left the harbour. Local people gathered at the pier in Lerwick, deeply concerned for the lives of those aboard the crippled ship. Others tuned their radios to follow the drama.

The motor vessel Samba *(Photo: author's collection via Shetland Sub Aqua Club)*

At 12.15 p.m., 13 miles south-by-east from Bard Head, the *Samba* was drifting north-west at four knots. It was looking like she could end up in the Sandwick area. Another hour passed before the lifeboat reported its own position as four miles south-by-east of Bard Head, making painfully slow progress in very difficult conditions. She had had to slow down, as her cockpit was filling with water. By 1.30 p.m. the lifeboat had radio contact with the *Noord Holland*, but was unable to see any of the nearby vessels.

The tug's radio operator had a tone of urgency in his voice when he said: 'We don't know if you will reach us or not. If you don't it will be dangerous for the *Samba*.'

In the 1950s the lifeboat had neither radar nor direction-finder. Because of this, the tug fired rockets to indicate her position, but conditions were so bad that the lifeboat crew could not see them.

During this time, the ferry *St Clair* was anchored in Lerwick harbour, unable to dock at Victoria Pier. She still had all her passengers on board from Aberdeen. At 2.30 p.m. the *St Clair* came on the air to relay to the tug a bearing given by Wick Radio. At this time the *Samba* was only about two miles south of the Bard, and it seemed she would clear the cliffs and drift into Bressay Sound.

After a long silence, at 3.17 p.m. the tug reported she had six survivors on board. It was not possible to repeat this feat, since the tug itself was now dangerously close to the shore.

It was dark when the *St Clair* weighed anchor and offered assistance by pumping oil on to the waves. By now the *Samba* was less than half a mile from the rocks, and the lifeboat skipper asked *St Clair* to provide a lee for a rescue attempt. The survivors managed to jump on to the lifeboat as she came up under the *Samba*'s stern. Six times this feat was accomplished, first saving one man, then two, then another one. Two attempts failed, and then finally Captain Bloomberg was saved on the sixth run.

At 4.48 p.m. the lifeboat broke radio silence to announce: 'We have got them all off the ship now'. A crowd stood on the storm-lashed pier to welcome the lifeboat shortly after 5.00 p.m.

Coxswain Sales and his lifeboat crew had done an amazing job. In the most appalling conditions, they had repeatedly risked the *Samba* crashing down on top of them.

Coxswain John Sales was awarded a Bronze Medal by the RNLI for this rescue.

The six survivors on board the tug *Noord Holland* were taken to Denmark, while the remaining crew were landed at Lerwick. The *St Clair* could not get back into the harbour and had to stand off all night. She finally berthed at 9.30 a.m., and the fifty-five passengers disembarked from one of the more extraordinary voyages from Aberdeen to Lerwick.

At about the same time as the lifeboat returned to Lerwick, the *Samba* crashed ashore on the rocks at Ruggen, on the Ness of Sound.

Her anchor chain is still visible on the rocks, and divers can follow it down through the kelp and over large boulders to a rocky slope where large sections of the wreck lie at 20 metres.

Continuing down the steep slope to 35 metres, the largely intact forepeak lies on its port side, while beyond that is a large tank. The *Samba* had apparently been engaged in shipping acid.

GLENISLA

Wreck No: 446		Date Sunk: 24 11 1917
Latitude: 60 07 53 N		Longitude: 01 08 04 W
GPS Lat: 6007.882 N		GPS Long: 0108.067 W
Location: Bressay Sound		Area: Shetland
Type: Steamship		Tonnage: 1.263 grt
Length: 251.5 ft	Beam: 32.8 ft	Draught: 20.4 ft
How Sunk: Collision with *Glenelg*		Depth: 39-46 metres

The iron steamship *Glenisla* was built by W.B. Thompson of Dundee in 1878.

On 24 November 1917, the *Glenisla* was waiting at Kirkwall to join a convoy to cross the North Sea with a cargo of coal for Slemmestad, Norway, when she was sunk in a collision with the Glasgow steamship *Glenelg*. The collision occurred in the middle of Bressay Sound, where the *Glenisla* was at anchor, ¾ mile north of Kirkabister Light, in the main fairway between Bressay and Ness of Sound. All twenty-three members of her crew were rescued.

The *Glenelg* was under tow at the time, having been torpedoed, but at the subsequent enquiry the *Glenisla* was held responsible for the collision, as she was not showing any lights. A local diver was sent down to check if the *Glenisla's* light shutters were open, and he reported that they were.

This was not the first collision the *Glenisla* had been involved in. She had had an eventful and chequered career. When she was only a few months old, she was involved in a collision with the *Albanian* in the Thames, whilst racing another vessel. She was scuttled twice, once at Brest in 1902 and again at Lisbon in 1908 after her cargo of esparto grass caught fire. After the second scuttling she lay for almost a month before being raised. Her damage was comparatively minor, and she headed back to the Tyne for repairs under her own steam. In 1914, just before the outbreak of the war, she sliced a French trawler in two, drowning four of the crew. She then became a decoy vessel (a Q Ship) for the Admiralty until 1916. Then in 1917 she was involved in yet another collision, this time with the *Glenelg*.

The wreck lies in 45 metres of water, upright and intact on a sandy seabed, with her bow pointing north towards Lerwick. As she lies within the harbour limits, permission to dive her must be obtained from Lerwick Port Control. Her wooden decking has largely rotted away, together with all the superstructure, leaving the wreck open and easy to explore. The highest point of the wreck is the engine and boilers. There are three boilers lying together, two low down in the ship, with the third much larger one up-ended in the middle. The engine room is open with a large square engine, and tools were still hanging in the engine room.

Moving forward the wreck is more broken, perhaps due to vessels dropping their anchors into it. Just below a tangle of anchors (not all of which belonged to the *Glenisla*) part of her starboard side near the bow has collapsed due to the collision damage, and a winch is precariously balanced on what remains of the decking. Her large steel mast lies on the seabed off the port side, and on a clear day the mast is visible from the deck 5m above.

Aft of the engines is the tiled galley. The stern is reasonably intact, and contains a few shell heads, but the gun lies on the sand 5m off the port side of the wreck. Pieces of white phosphorus lie around the stern of the wreck, looking like underwater wedges of cheese. They stand out brightly against the steel hull and the sand. Phosphorous is hazardous. If brought to the surface and exposed to air, it will start to smoke, and ignite spontaneously. Her propeller has been salvaged, but the spare iron propeller is still in the wreck amongst a tangle of girders.

Tidal streams over the *Glenisla* are negligible. The position has also been recorded as 6007.882N, 00108.067W.

The ship's bell, mounted between two cast iron dolphins, has been recovered, along with a number of portholes. A toilet bowl (well flushed!) was recovered and presented to Shetland Museum.

The bell of the Glenisla *(Photo: Shetland Museum)*

LUNOKHODS-1

Wreck No: 447	Date Sunk: 09 11 1993
Latitude: 60 07 11 N	Longitude: 01 07 15 W
GPS Lat: 6007.189 N	GPS Long: 0107.243 W
Location: Below Kirkabister Lighthouse	Area: Shetland
Type: Motor vessel	Tonnage: 2,774 grt
Length: 276.8 ft Beam: 46.3 ft	Draught: 18.8 ft
How Sunk: Ran aground	Depth: 2-45 metres

Russian fish factory ships, or Klondikers, as they are generally known, anchor in Bressay Sound to the south of Lerwick. They have a reputation for dragging their anchors in heavy storms and failing to get their engines started in time to prevent themselves from being driven ashore.

The Latvian-registered Klondiker *Lunokhods-1* dragged her anchors and was driven ashore against Kirkabister Ness, below Kirkabister Lighthouse on Bressay, during a severe southerly storm on 9 November 1993.

The Shetland Coastguard helicopter 'Oscar Charlie' lifted off all of her 156 crew. The full capacity of the S-61 helicopter is normally eighteen passengers. She crammed in thirty-two on one trip! That still holds the record as the biggest single rescue lift by one helicopter in Britain. The ship's cat was rescued from the vessel a few days later. Keiran Murray, the helicopter winchman, kindly provided the photo!

The ship was driven stern first into a geo, and remains tightly wedged there today. The stern section is still fairly intact, and runs from 2–18m of water, with easy access inside past the machinery and refrigeration coils. These areas are largely open to daylight, and silt free. The engine room, a workshop and switch rooms are all accessible through large holes. The propeller is still attached, but is under the wreckage at the very back of the geo, where it is likely to remain for the foreseeable future. The bow section, about 30m long, broke off and slid down the slope to 45m where it now lies on its port side. It is, at least theoretically, possible to shot the bow and gradually work back up the slope and work off the deco on the stern. The wreck is well sheltered from the north and east, but it quickly becomes undiveable if there is any wind from the south.

There are no scrap merchants in Shetland, and a large amount of stainless steel and brass is still on the wreck. There are also many portholes, but unfortunately, they are all made of iron!

The stern lies at 6007.189N, 00107.243W, and the bow at 6007.237N, 00107.258W.

Lunokhods-1 *(Photo: courtesy of Keiran Murray)*

PIONERSK

Wreck No: 448
Latitude: 60 07 13 N
GPS Lat: 6007.219 N
Location: SW tip of Trebister Ness
Type: Motor ship (Fish Factory Ship)
Length: 546.2 ft   Beam: 70.4 ft
How Sunk: Ran aground

Date Sunk: 31 10 1994
Longitude: 01 10 42 W
GPS Long: 0110.707 W
Area: Shetland
Tonnage: 10035 grt
Draught: 26.7 ft
Depth: 0-22 metres

A week after the *Lunohods-1* disaster, the *Borodynskye Polye*, a 103-metre long klondiker, raised her anchor to steam north, but was caught by the wind and grounded on Unicorn rock. Today she is well broken up and covered in kelp, in a general depth of 20m at 6013.399N, 0108.706W.

On 31 October 1994, a third Latvian klondiker ran aground. A much larger vessel, the *Pionersk*, was built in 1963. She was driven ashore and wrecked on the south-east shore of Gulberwick, near the south-west tip of Trebister Ness, in yet another severe southerly gale, and broke in two the same night. Her crew of 137 men all escaped. For several months the ship lay on the rocks, before the winter gales broke her up further, leaving just the tip of the bow showing above the water. The *Pionersk* is an excellent dive, full of colour and life, with depths varying from the surface down to 22m at the stern. Because of the size of this ship, and the area covered by the wreckage, several dives are required to see the whole wreck. The bow section is very shallow, mainly less than 10m, although there can be more surge here. The wreckage lies east-west with the bow to the east. Amidships, large sections are still recognisable, with engines, pumps and winches all jumbled up with sections of an accommodation area. The derricks and masts lie across the wreck in depths of 10–15m. Towards the stern, the ship is more intact, with railings and two or three deck levels lying at an angle of about 45° with floor tiles spilling out. The canning room has opened up and is littered with hundreds of gold-coloured tin lids. Many refrigeration coils can be seen, and the wreck contains an amazing amount of brass, including many brass portholes with brass deadlights. The strange thing was that they could be removed without tools! I believe there are now not many portholes left on the wreck. The stern chute is relatively undamaged and open, at around 20m. More winches and gear lie around the wreck at this point.

When the *Pionersk* ran aground, there were questions about safety, pollution and insurance.

Although it was clear where responsibility lay, it was not clear whether anyone would receive any compensation, because there was no insurance. These vessels carry immense amounts of packaging, both cardboard and plastic. The cardboard does not cause any major problems, as it quickly becomes waterlogged and breaks up. The plastics however pose a major headache. They are washed up, blown about and evenly distributed over large areas of coast near the wreck.

Also released are all the medical supplies and instruments, including syringes and drugs. These items, along with food supplies, wood and other debris from the wreck, wash up intermingled with the plastics. This means the operatives cleaning up the debris, or members of the public beach combing, cannot see the hidden dangers.

Quite often, the plastics and other debris are also covered with oil from the wreck, which makes disposal and handling of the refuse even more difficult.

It is reasonable to assume, given the track record of both the Klondikers and the oil tankers, that more groundings will occur. Whilst there are adequate systems and procedures for cost recovery in the case of the oil tankers through the Oil Pollution Compensation Fund, no such system operates for other vessels. Lerwick Harbour Trust responded to the grounding of the *Pionersk* by arresting a vessel owned by the same company. Recovery of the costs in this case took two years. The impacts of shipping disasters affect coastal communities. Marine litter and illegal discharges spoil coastlines, harm wildlife and have implications for public health.

The wrecks do, however, provide lasting tourist attractions for visiting divers.

Pionersk *ashore (Photo: courtesy of Keiran Murray)*

GREEN LILY

Wreck No: 449		Date Sunk: 19 11 1997	
Latitude: 60 06 00 N		Longitude: 01 04 00 W	
GPS Lat: 6006.000 N		GPS Long: 0104.000 W	
Location: N of Bard Head, Bressay		Area: Shetland	
Type: Motor ship		Tonnage: 3,624 grt	
Length: 355.4 ft	Beam: 48.6 ft	Draught: 18.0 ft	
How Sunk: Ran aground		Depth: 24 metres	

Despite bad weather, forecast to become worse, and contrary to earnest advice not to do so, the Bahamian-registered refrigerated cargo ship *Green Lily* left Lerwick in the early morning of 19 November 1997, bound for the Ivory Coast with a cargo of frozen fish. At the time of setting out the weather was southeast force 7, and this was forecast to increase to severe gale force 9, followed by storm force 10 winds. The vessel had not got very far when a sea water supply line fractured in the engine room, and she broke down in appalling conditions 15 miles SE of Bressay. Unsuccessful attempts were made to restart the engine while the vessel drifted northwest at about 1½ – 2 knots. Shetland Coastguard was advised of the situation, and three tugs, the harbour tug *Tystie* and the anchor-handling tug *Gargano,* proceeded to the scene of the casualty. A second anchor-handling tug, *Maersk Champion*, got underway after her deck cargo had been discharged. A coastguard helicopter was called and the Lerwick lifeboat *Michael and Jane Vernon* was launched.

Green Lily *ashore (Photo: Jonathan Wills)*

Gargano succeeded in securing a towline, and started to pull the *Green Lily* towards Lerwick, but the line parted after 51 minutes. An attempt by the Coastguard helicopter 'Lima Charlie' to lift off non-essential crew proved impossible due to the vessel's violent movements in the severe sea conditions, and had to be aborted. The weather by that time was SE gale force 10–11, gusting to force 12, with a heavy swell. *Tystie* then succeeded in making a second tow connection but this broke after only five minutes. By mid-afternoon the *Green Lily* had drifted toward the east coast of Bressay, and her starboard anchor was dropped in an attempt to slow the vessel's drift towards the shore. With the rocks growing ever closer coxswain Clark made numerous attempts to put the lifeboat alongside, often having to back away because of the violent motion of the two boats in the vicious seas. Every time the lifeboat went alongside she was slammed into the side of the ship, and the crew were convinced that she must eventually suffer serious damage.

Green Lily was now so close in that the waves were being reflected from the cliffs, sometimes reaching 50-feet high and breaking heavily. In these violent conditions, and with only yards to spare, Clark took the lifeboat between the casualty and the shore five times, each time snatching one person to safety.

Maersk Champion passed close across *Green Lily*'s bow and managed to grapple her anchor cable. As the tug pulled her head into the wind the slight lee on *Green Lily*'s port side disappeared and the lifeboat could no longer get alongside. Just 200 yards from the shore she broke clear with five survivors aboard and stood by.

Although this manoeuvre had stopped the lifeboat working, it was now possible for the helicopter to move in, for with the ship now head to wind the motion was considerably reduced. As 'Lima Charlie' lifted off the ten remaining crewmembers *Green Lily*'s anchor chain parted and she was driven ashore by the stern, swung round beam-on and pounded by the huge breakers.

Tragically, the helicopter winchman Bill Deacon, who had remained on deck as the last two members of *Green Lily*'s crew were winched up to the helicopter, was swept into the sea by a huge breaking wave, and lost. He had helped ten men to safety before he lost his own life – a dreadful waste of the life of a very brave man. The helicopter's winch wire became snagged on the *Green Lily* shortly afterwards and had to be cut to free the aircraft. With conditions so extreme close to the shore, the lifeboat dared not venture in close enough to search for Bill Deacon and returned to Lerwick to land the survivors. Bill Deacon's body was found some distance away the next day.

The *Green Lily* grounded on the rocks north of Bard Head and started to break up almost immediately. Within hours nothing of the ship remained above water. Within a month of stranding, the only recognisable part of the ship was the very tip of the bow in about 24m. The rest of the wreck, lying in 10-15m, was completely smashed to pieces.

Coxswain Hewitt Clark of the Lerwick lifeboat was awarded a gold medal by the RNLI for his part in the rescue of the *Green Lily*'s crew, and the other five members of the lifeboat crew were all awarded bronze medals. The RNLI also recognised Bill Deacon's courage with a posthumous Thanks on Vellum, with another Vellum also going to the remainder of the aircraft's crew.

LEO DAWSON

Wreck No: 450	Date Sunk: 04 02 1940
Latitude: 60 12 10 N	Longitude: 00 31 20 W
GPS Lat: 6012.167 N	GPS Long: 0031.333 W
Location: 15 miles E of Bressay	Area: Shetland
Type: Steamship	Tonnage: 4,330 grt
Length: 363.2 ft Beam: 51.0 ft	Draught: 26.3 ft
How Sunk: Torpedoed by *U-37*	Depth: 104 metres

The British steamship *Leo Dawson* left Narvik on 29 January 1940 with a crew of thirty-five and a cargo of iron ore for Immingham. She was torpedoed east of Shetland by *U-37* (KK Werner Hartmann) at 21.25 hrs on 4 February in German grid square AN2184, which equates to about 6009N, 0036W.

The wreck charted at 601210N, 003120W, with a least depth of 104 metres, might be the *Leo Dawson*.

JANE

Wreck No: 451	Date Sunk: 20 07 1923
Latitude: 60 38 21 N	Longitude: 00 56 31 W
GPS Lat: 6038.355 N	GPS Long: 0056.519 W
Location: ¼ mile S of Sound Gruney Island	Area: Shetland
Type: Steamship	Tonnage: 840 grt
Length: 198.4 ft Beam: 28.4 ft	Draught: 15.1 ft
How Sunk: Ran aground	Depth: 20 metres

The Swedish steamship *Jane* (ex-*Jane Cory*) was built by Alexander Withy of Hartlepool in 1870.

On 19 July 1923 she had loaded 475 barrels of herring at Baltasound, and was en route from there to Lerwick to pick up some more cargo. After rounding the south of Unst, and entering the sound between Unst and Fetlar, instead of then turning south into Colgrave Sound, between Fetlar and Yell, for some inexplicable reason the pilot turned north into Bluemull Sound, between Unst and Yell, and then tried to go round the north end of the island of Linga. It was a fine summer night, and the vessel's course was being watched with increasing concern by men in Gutcher, Yell.

On board the *Jane*, Captain Osterman was also alarmed, and expressed his anxiety to the pilot. Moments later the ship struck rocks. It was obvious to those on shore that the ship had been holed, as she started to blow off steam.

One of the ship's boats was lowered, and a member of the crew landed two women on Linga.

Meanwhile the ship swung round and floated off the rocks. Having lost her steam the vessel was not under power, and drifted with the tidal stream. Four men from Gutcher set out in a boat and reached the *Jane* at 00.45 a.m., just as the vessel sank. They were surprised to see the canvas round the *Jane*'s hatches tear, and the hatches fly up in the air as the rising water level increased the air pressure inside the holds, blowing the hatch covers off.

The *Jane* sank about ¼ mile south of the island of Sound Gruney. The crew of fourteen, including the two women, were accommodated in Gutcher that night, and next day the *Earl of Zetland* took them to Lerwick.

The wreck lies on its port side in 20 metres, with the highest part rising up 4 metres from the sandy seabed. It is gradually collapsing, but the anchors, propeller and rudder are still there. The bell has been recovered, and is on display in the Shetland Museum in Lerwick.

There are strong currents over the wreck, and the sea life is prolific.

The Swedish steamship Jane *(Photo: Sjöfartsmuseet, Göteborg)*

The propeller of the Jane *(Photo: Shetland Museum)*

TONIS CHANDRIS

Wreck No: 452

Latitude: 60 42 29 N

GPS Lat: 6042.478 N

Location: Vere Rock, Unst

Type: Steamship

Length: 304.2 ft   Beam: 45.5 ft

How Sunk: Ran aground

Date Sunk: 09 01 1940

Longitude: 00 48 59 W

GPS Long: 0048.986 W

Area: Shetland

Tonnage: 3,161grt

Draught: 18.8 ft

Depth: metres

The Greek steamship *Tonis Chandris* (ex-*Efxinos*, ex-*Karl Leonhardt*, ex-*Hornburg*) was built in Rostock in 1904.

On 8 January 1940 she was en route from Kirkenes to Barrow-in-Furness with a cargo of iron ore, when she sighted a U-boat. The ship immediately increased speed and began to zig-zag. The sea was calm, but visibility was reduced by fog. Two or three hours later, in the early hours of the 9th, the *Tonis Chandris* ran aground on the half-submerged Vere Reef about one mile north-west of Ham Ness, Unst.

Water started coming in the forward hold, but the pumps were able to cope, and the ship was in no immediate danger. The weather continued fine the next day and Captain Andreas Cockinos told the crew that if the cargo in the forward hold was discharged, it might be possible to float the vessel off at high tide. But the crew of seventeen Greeks, three Yugoslavs, a Belgian and a Russian were not prepared to carry out the work of unloading the ore. It was clear that they only wanted to go home.

Some of the islanders of Unst volunteered to do the job, and were taken out to the stranded *Tonis Chandris* to jettison the cargo in the forward hold. A lot of time had already been lost, and the weather could not be relied on to continue favourable indefinitely, especially in January. It was planned to pull the ship off the rocks when sufficient cargo had been discharged, and anchor her in Baltasound, where repairs could be carried out. If this was not possible, she could be beached there on a soft bottom where she would be safe while her future could be considered. About 100 tons of her iron ore cargo had been thrown overboard to lighten her by the time a tug arrived from Lerwick around noon on 10 January. The weather had deteriorated by then, and the tug's services were urgently required elsewhere. Despite the fact that it was low tide, and the amount of ore that had been jettisoned was not enough to make a significant impression on the trim of the vessel, it was decided to pull the ship off immediately. As the tug attempted to pull her off the rocks, the ship sustained further damage and

E-14, *a near sister of* E-49. *From 1915 these boats were fitted with a deck gun*

the pumps were no longer able to cope with the greater volume of water pouring in. It was obvious that if the tug continued to pull, the *Tonis Chandris* would merely sink in deeper water. The crew abandoned ship and boarded the tug, which returned to Lerwick. The *Tonis Chandris* remained on the rocks for several more days until she broke up in severe weather from the north-east on 16 January 1940.

The wreck now lies about 50 metres off the north-east corner of the Vere in depths of 15-20 metres. Two boilers, the engine and a propeller shaft casing lie there, and broken pieces of hull plate are scattered in rock gullies at the edge of the reef. Very little remains of the rest of the ship.

A wreck is charted about 300 metres south of Vere rock at 6042.111N, 0048.934W, in about 35 metres of water. Is this a different wreck, or might it be part of the *Tonis Chandris*?

E-49

Wreck No: 453	Date Sunk: 12 03 1917
Latitude: 60 44 13 N	Longitude: 00 48 02 W
GPS Lat: 6044.224 N	GPS Long: 0048.038 W
Location: 500m SSW Balta Light	Area: Shetland
Type: Submarine	Tonnage: 662/807 dwt
Length: 181.0 ft Beam: 22.5 ft	Draught: 12.5 ft
How Sunk: Mined	Depth: 29-33 metres

On 9 March 1917 the German mine-laying U-boat *UC-76* laid mines off Cromarty before going on to Shetland, where she laid a minefield off Baltasound, Unst the following day.

HM Submarines *G-13* and *E-49* were patrolling off the north-east of Shetland on 10 March, *G-13* about 12 miles north of Muckle Flugga, and *E-49* about 30 miles east of Fetlar. An easterly gale was blowing, and *E-49* was being battered by high seas. Her radio mast was damaged, and her commander, Lt Basil Beal, took the boat into Baltasound for shelter to repair the mast, and to wait for the storm to subside. *E-49* reached Baltasound at 10.05 a.m. on 11 March. *G-13* continued her patrol, and at about 4.00 p.m. she sighted the German *UC-43* on the surface 7 miles WNW of Muckle Flugga. In an attack between snow showers, *G-13* torpedoed and sank *UC-43*. At 12.55 hrs on 12 March, *E-49* left Baltasound to resume her patrol, passing through the south channel between the islands of Balta and Huney. She had disappeared from view behind the island of Huney, to the south of the entrance, when those ashore heard a loud explosion, and saw a column of smoke, debris and water rise high above the island. When the submarine failed to appear from behind the island, Naval drifters went to investigate and found naval caps and a grating floating on the surface. The position was buoyed so that divers could investigate the wreck. Later, a close examination showed that *E-49*'s bow had been completely blown off. There were no survivors.

The wreck is now almost completely sunk into the seabed of white sand. The conning tower is folded over at right angles to the buried hull, and lies on its starboard side. The periscope extends horizontally about 6 feet above the sand. Forward of the conning tower the hull ends abruptly. More wreckage is almost completely buried in the seabed off the starboard side – probably the missing bow section. Aft of the conning tower, the submarine's deck gun lies in the sand and the hull of the submarine slopes gradually until it too disappears under the sand. This wreck is a war grave, but in 1990 a group of English divers came ashore with the telescopic radio mast of the *E-49*. In its folded down (i.e. telescoped) condition, it is about 20ft long. They were fined £75 each for making this unauthorised recovery. The periscope is still in Shetland, where it is intended to be displayed in a new, larger, Shetland Museum.

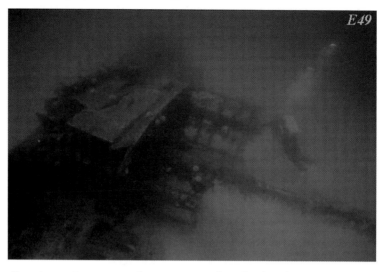

E-49's conning tower is lying on its starboard side (Photo: Ian Potten)

SRT 4442

Wreck No: 454	Date Sunk: 16 10 1958
Latitude: 60 50 00 N	Longitude: 00 46 00 W
GPS Lat: 6050.000 N	GPS Long: 0046.000 W
Location: Holm of Skaw, Unst	Area: Shetland
Type: MFV	Tonnage: grt
Length: ft Beam: ft	Draught: ft
How Sunk: Ran aground	Depth: metres

One of the features of shipping in Shetland over the past 40–50 years has been the large number of Eastern Bloc fishing vessels which have operated around the islands. They have not been immune to disasters.

Four Russian trawlers have been lost around the islands: the *CPT 611* went ashore in thick fog at Spoo Ness, Unst on 27 March 1956; the *SRT 4442 (Urbe)* (SRT stands for 'Sredniy Rybolovnyy Trauler', which translates as 'medium fishing trawler') was wrecked on Holm of Skaw, Unst on 16 October 1958; the *Maia* ran aground on Broch of Houbie, Fetlar on 2 February 1961; and the *SRT 4240* stranded on Skaw Point on 4 March 1967.

Three Russian fish factory ships have also come to grief, all through dragging their anchors and going onto rocks in severe weather: the *Lunohods I* near Bard Head on 9 November 1993; the *Borodinskoye-Polye* on Unicorn Rock off Hawks Ness; and the *Pionersk* on Trebister Ness on 31 October 1994.

The Russian trawler *SRT 4442 (Urbe)* broke down during the night of 16 October 1958, and drove ashore in a northerly gale close to the lighthouse on the Holm of Skaw. Balta Sound rocket apparatus crew were called out, but it was impossible for them to cross over to the Holm because of heavy seas. The Lerwick lifeboat was therefore launched, and proceeded to assist, calling in at Balta Sound to pick up a local pilot, enabling the lifeboat to get close to the casualty and take off three survivors by breeches buoy. A trawl net from the casualty became wrapped round one of the lifeboat's propellers, and that engine had to be closed down throughout the rescue. Twenty-two Russian seamen were lost in the wreck, and many problems were caused by the total lack of Russian co-operation. The Lerwick lifeboat covered a distance of over 100 miles in this rescue, which resulted in Coxswain John Sales receiving a silver medal from the RNLI, and the local pilot Andrew Mouat was awarded a bronze medal for assisting in the rescue.

The Russian trawler SRT 4240 *aground (Photo: author's collection via Shetland Sub Aqua Club)*

SRT 4240

Wreck No: 455		Date Sunk: 04 03 1967	
Latitude: 60 50 00 N		Longitude: 00 46 10 W	
GPS Lat: 6050.000 N		GPS Long: 0046.167 W	
Location: Skaw Point, Unst		Area: Shetland	
Type: Trawler		Tonnage: 264 grt	
Length: 129.2 ft	Beam: ft	Draught: ft	
How Sunk: Ran aground		Depth: metres	

The Russian trawler *SRT 4240* ran aground at the Point of Skaw on 4 March 1967. At 9.00 p.m. she drew attention to her plight by sending up flares, which were spotted by Coastguard Albert Gray, who phoned the Unst Rescue Unit.

Duncan Mouat had also noticed the flares from his home in Haroldswick, and set out towards them to see what assistance he could offer. The trawler was hard aground, wedged between the shore and a rock. Some Russians were already ferrying themselves ashore in a rubber dinghy. Four men got ashore, but the rope broke, and one of them was swept back out to sea. Duncan ran half a mile to phone Lerwick coastguard, who called out the lifeboat.

A force 4–5 south-westerly was blowing when the Unst Coast Rescue Volunteers arrived and found about a dozen Russian sailors ashore. Lights were blazing from another Russian trawler which was standing by. It came so close to the shore that the watchers expected a second wreck at any moment.

The rescue unit set up their own searchlight and breeches buoy between ship and shore. With some Russians assisting, they started conveying personal belongings ashore. The second Russian trawler floated a raft across and ferried some of the crew aboard. They evidently did not want to stay on Unst. The Russians made several trips to and from the wreck to collect whatever they could, until at 1.00 a.m. the last man to leave the wreck cast off the life-saving equipment the rescue team had used. He waved to the Unst Volunteers and shouted 'OK. Thank you.'

Lerwick lifeboat and the oil rig tender *Viking Blazer* were north of Fetlar when they received the message from the Soviet parent ship informing them that all the crew of *SRT 4240* were now safe.

The sea bottom off the Point of Skaw ranges in depth from 5 to 10 metres with massive rock pinnacles and huge boulders rising towards the surface. Part of the trawler lies close inshore, densely overgrown with seaweed. Pieces of copper and brass, and the vessel's steel propeller, have been found, but little else remains.

The Norwegian steamship Enid *(Photo: Dag Bakka Jnr)*

ENID

Wreck No: 456		Date Sunk: 17 01 1940
Latitude: 60 57 20 N		Longitude: 00 52 05 W
GPS Lat: 6057.333 N		GPS Long: 0052.083 W
Location: 6 miles N of Muckle Flugga		Area: Shetland
Type: Steamship		Tonnage: 1,140 grt
Length: 227.7 ft	Beam: 36.3 ft	Draught: ft
How Sunk: Torpedoed & gunned by *U-25*		Depth: 95 metres

The Norwegian steamship *Enid* was torpedoed and gunned by the *U-25* (Schutze) at 13.10 hrs on 17 January 1940, 6–7 miles N of Muckle Flugga, Shetland. She was en route from Trondheim to Dublin with wood pulp. The German grid position was given as AF7889. One report says *Enid* sank at 14.03 hrs, but ACOS war diary says she continued to burn throughout the night.

At 1400 hrs on the 17th, the radio station on Hermaness hill, at the north tip of Unst, just behind Muckle Flugga, reported that a Norwegian vessel was being attacked by a U-boat with gunfire. At 17.00 hrs on the 17th one of *Enid*'s boats with the chief officer in charge reached Burra Firth. He reported that shortly before being attacked he saw a British ship, apparently carrying iron ore, being torpedoed, and that she sank in a few minutes. That must have been the *Polzella*.

POLZELLA

Wreck No: 457
Latitude: 61 00 00 N PA
GPS Lat: 6100.000 N
Location: Off Muckle Flugga
Type: Steamship
Length: 402.6 ft   Beam: 52.8 ft
How Sunk: Torpedoed by *U-25*

Date Sunk: 17 01 1940
Longitude: 00 01 00 W PA
GPS Long: 0001.000 W
Area: Shetland
Tonnage: 4,751 grt
Draught: ft
Depth: metres

The British steamship *Polzella* left Narvik and Lodingen on 13 January 1940, bound for Methil and the Tees with a cargo of iron ore. She was torpedoed and sunk off Muckle Flugga by *U-25* (KK Victor Schutze) at 12.55 on 17 January 1940. The position was given as AF7887. *Polzella* was built in 1929, and had a crew of thirty-seven – none of whom was ever seen again.

Despite the fact that the chief officer of the Norwegian steamship *Enid* had reported seeing a British ship with a cargo of ore being torpedoed and sunk, amazingly no-one seemed to connect that with the *Polzella*.

The *Polzella* was finally posted missing on 20 March 1940. For the purposes of insurance the Joint Arbitration Committee considered that her loss was ¾ war risk and ¼ marine risk.

SWAINBY

Wreck No: 458
Latitude: 61 00 40 N
GPS Lat: 6100.663 N
Location: 25 miles 65° Muckle Flugga
Type: Steamship
Length: 393.0 ft   Beam: ft
How Sunk: Torpedoed by *U-13*

Date Sunk: 17 04 1940
Longitude: 00 08 35 W
GPS Long: 0008.583 W
Area: Shetland
Tonnage: 4,935 grt
Draught: ft
Depth: 117 metres

The British steamship *Swainby* was torpedoed and sunk by the *U-13* (OL Max Schulte) at 17.33 hrs on 17 April 1940 at 6100N, 0005W, 25 miles, 65° from Muckle Flugga, while en route, in ballast, from Maaloysund, Norway to Kirkwall. She would not normally have been sailing empty from Norway, but must have left in a hurry to escape before being captured by the Germans who had invaded Norway on 9 April.

At 04.35 hrs on the 18th reports were received of a ship torpedoed in 060° Muckle Flugga 23 miles. This was the *Swainby*. Her crew of thirty-eight landed on Unst later in the day and were taken to Lerwick.

The wreck charted in 117 metres at 6100.663N, 0008.538W is probably the *Swainby*.

DON EMILIO

Wreck No: 459
Latitude: 60 40 00 N PA
GPS Lat: 6040.000 N
Location: 10 miles NW by W Esha Ness Light

Date Sunk: 01 07 1917
Longitude: 01 50 00 W PA
GPS Long: 0150.000 W
Area: Shetland

Type: Steamship

Length: 352.0 ft

How Sunk: Torpedoed by *U-80*

Tonnage: 3,651 grt

Beam: 50.5 ft   Draught: 23.3 ft

Depth: 120 metres

The British steamship *Don Emilio* was torpedoed by the German submarine *U-80* on 1 July 1917 while en route from Barry to Yukanski (Archangel) with a cargo of coal. One member of the crew was lost. *Don Emilio* was built by J.L. Thompson of Sunderland in 1906.

HIGHCLIFFE

Wreck No: 460

Latitude: 60 19 09 N

GPS Lat: 6019.148 N

Location: Forewick Holm, Papa Stour

Type: Steamship

Length: 366.4 ft

How Sunk: Ran aground

Date Sunk: 06 02 1940

Longitude: 01 39 42 W

GPS Long: 0139.703 W

Area: Shetland

Tonnage: 3,847 grt

Beam: ft   Draught: ft

Depth: 6-26 metres

The British steamship *Highcliffe* left Narvik on 4 February 1940, with a cargo of iron ore for Immingham. To minimise the risk of encountering U-boats, Captain Henderson intended to steam down the west coast of Shetland, rather than the east. As she approached Shetland in poor weather and pitch darkness after midnight on 6 February, the ship was slowed down, and soundings were taken. Land dimly seen ahead was thought to be Fitful Head, at the south-west of Shetland, and the ship's head was altered slightly to starboard, to head a little more westerly, away from the land. Suddenly the bottom shelved up from 18 to 4 to 3 fathoms, and the *Highcliffe* grounded on Forewick Holm, Papa Stour. What had been mistaken for Fitful Head was, in fact, the Neep of Norby, in Sandness. The crew were ordered to stand by the lifeboats, and an SOS was

Highcliffe *(Photo: author's collection)*

transmitted to Wick Radio. Water was coming into No.1 hold, but the pumps were still working. The ship's siren aroused many of the island's inhabitants, who gathered on the shore. Smoke from the *Highcliffe*'s funnel was blowing in the direction of one old woman's house. She ran to her neighbour, believing the Germans had arrived and were trying to gas her!

At 8.00 a.m. *Highcliffe* sent up rockets. Aith lifeboat responded, arriving on the scene two hours later, and took off twenty-eight members of the crew, who were landed on Papa Stour. Captain Henderson remained aboard with six other crewmen until the next day, when it was obvious that the vessel was a total loss and they, too, were taken off by the lifeboat.

It was not long before the wrecked ship broke in two, but it remained visible at all states of the tide for several years before finally disappearing beneath the surface. Most of her cargo of iron ore was salvaged. Wreckage now extends from just below the surface at the north-east corner of Forewick Holm in an easterly direction to a sandy bottom at 26 metres. The forward part of the ship – the shallowest part – is completely broken up. The boiler and engine lie 12 metres down, and below that, large sections of the wreck are still recognisable. The stern section is the most intact part of the wreck, and it is complete with a stern gun, from which a plate dated 1918 has been recovered.

Goodwill Merchant *sinking (Photo: author's collection)*

GOODWILL MERCHANT

Wreck No: 461		Date Sunk: 18 01 1976	
Latitude: 59 59 38 N		Longitude: 01 20 43 W	
GPS Lat: 5959.630 N		GPS Long: 0120.717	
Location: Ness of Ireland		Area: Shetland	
Type: Motor vessel		Tonnage: 468 grt	
Length: 197.8 ft	Beam: 33.8 ft	Draught: 12.7 ft	
How Sunk: Ran aground		Depth: 9-27 metres	

The Dutch motor vessel *Goodwill Merchant* was en route from Grangemouth to Lerwick when she ran aground early in the morning of 18 January 1976. Wick Radio received a message from the vessel: '3.26am GMT, aground on rocks on Fair Isle, on the west side. Require immediate assistance.' The Lerwick lifeboat was launched, and set out to assist. The coastguard also called out the Fair Isle Coast Rescue Equipment Company. A seismic survey ship *Vickers Viscount*, an oil rig supply boat *Wimpey Seadog*, and the frigate HMS *Bacchante*, all diverted from their respective courses to search for the casualty around Fair Isle, while the Fair Isle Coastguard Volunteers scoured the coastline for signs of the vessel. Later, the Fair Isle mail boat, *Good Shepherd*, also joined the search. After six hours, when no trace of the ship had been found, it began to be suspected that the ship must have given a wrong position. A British Airways helicopter was requested to look for the ship on the south Mainland coast, and at 10.08 a.m. sent a radio message for the Lerwick lifeboat to advise that a ship was ashore at the Ness of Ireland, two miles north of St Ninian's Isle, off Bigton, Shetland. At 10.35 a.m. the same helicopter lifted the crew from the vessel, and all the distress radio traffic ceased. Shortly after the men had been lifted from the ship, the vessel sank by the stern. When the captain, first mate Cornelius Veestra and the five other members of the crew were winched into the helicopter, they asked where they were. On being told 'Ireland', they admitted they did not know where they were, but could not believe they were so far off course as to run aground in Ireland! The survivors were landed at Sumburgh.

By that afternoon, only the mast of their ship stuck out of the water. The vessel had been carrying an assorted cargo ranging from cars to kit houses and heavy machinery for the construction of the Sullom Voe oil terminal. After the *Goodwill Merchant* sank, she broke up, and apparently all the Land Rovers in Shetland sported new tyres for some time thereafter!

The wreck is now completely smashed to pieces close under the cliffs, the wreckage running from 9 to 27 metres deep. The propeller was recovered around 1988, and the bell was recovered the following year.

The position of the *Goodwill Merchant* has also been recorded as 5959.758N, 00120.866W.

BRAER

Wreck No: 462		Date Sunk: 05 01 1993	
Latitude: 59 53 24 N		Longitude: 01 21 24 W	
GPS Lat: 5953.400N		GPS Long: 0121.400W	
Location: Garth's Ness		Area: Shetland	
Type: Tanker		Tonnage: 44,989 grt	
Length: 797.0 ft	Beam: 132.2 ft	Draught: 46.8 ft	
How Sunk: Ran aground		Depth: 18 metres	

The Liberian-registered tanker *Braer* (ex-*Hellespont Pride*, ex-*Brae Trader*) left Mongstad oil terminal, north of Bergen, on 3 January 1993 with a cargo of 84,413 tonnes of Norwegian oil for Canada. She also carried 1,700 tonnes of heavy fuel oil and 125 tonnes of diesel. A gale was blowing when she left, and as the tanker made for the Fair Isle Channel, she ran into even worse weather, with waves 100-feet high. On her port quarter she carried a number of 16-foot long steel pipes, welded to a rack outside the 'inert gas room'. This was a compartment where the engine exhaust gases were cooled before being pumped into the air spaces above the oil in her tanks. The heavy breaking seas caused these pipes to break loose, and roll about the deck. In the severe motion conditions it was too dangerous for anyone to venture on deck to secure the pipes again, and eventually they smashed open vent pipes which let air into the ship's fuel tanks as fuel was consumed by her main and auxiliary engines, including the generator. The breaches in these vent pipes allowed sea water to enter, contaminating the ship's fuel supplies. The contaminated fuel caused her auxiliary boiler to fail. This boiler heated the heavy fuel oil for her main engine, to make it fluid enough to flow through the engine's fuel injectors. With the loss of this heating source, the ship's main engine was switched over to running on diesel fuel, but at 4.40 a.m. on 5 January, the water contamination, which affected all the ship's fuel supplies, including the diesel tank, shut down all her machinery and stopped the main engine. The ship was now dead in the water, drifting towards Shetland at 2 knots, without power. With heavy seas breaking over the ship it was impossible for the crew to reach the bows to drop the anchors and slow her drift.

Captain Alexandros Gelis was initially not too worried about the proximity of Sumburgh Head, as he considered that the south-westerly wind would blow his ship to the north-east, past Shetland and into the open sea. But he had reckoned without the effect of the Sumburgh Roost, and delayed telling the coastguards about the extent of the problem until 5.19 a.m. It was not until 6.05 a.m. that he finally asked for a tug to be sent. By 6.32 a.m. the *Braer* was less than 7 miles from Sumburgh Head, and Captain Gelis asked for his thirty-four crew to be taken off. The Coastguard S61 Helicopter 'Oscar Charlie' was already airborne, and seven minutes later it was hovering over the ship, whose mast and funnel were wildly gyrating. It took over an hour to take sixteen men off the *Braer*. By that time another RAF helicopter had arrived from Lossiemouth, and took off the remaining eighteen crewmen. The tug *Star Sirius* arrived from Lerwick at 9.38 a.m., but no one was left on the *Braer* to assist in connecting a towline, and there were no anchor chains to get a hold of. Two of *Braer*'s crewmembers, along with Jim Dickson, the Shetland Islands Council's Pollution Control Officer, and helicopter winchman Freide Manson, were lowered back onto the ship to try to attach a line fired from the *Star Sirius,* but at 11.13 a.m., before a line could be secured, the tanker went aground on the rocks in Garth's Wick, at the west side of Garth's Ness, near Quendale Bay. The four men who had been put aboard the ship were then taken off again.

The wind had risen to 80 mph, and the waves in Garth's Wick were 20–30 feet high.

The single-hulled *Braer* immediately started to break up, and her oil gushed out, creating a potentially major environmental disaster in an internationally known wildlife area.

She was carrying almost 25 million gallons of oil – nearly twice the amount of crude that was aboard the *Exxon Valdez* when it ran aground in Alaska in 1989. It was feared that the spill would have a significant effect on nearby bird and fish populations.

In contrast to the *Exxon Valdez,* which went aground on a reef in Alaska's Prince William Sound on 24 March 1989, the *Braer* was carrying 'light crude', a type of oil which evaporates more quickly and this process was helped by the bad weather.

This was the second major oil spill in a month, and environmentalists called for tougher regulation of oil tankers. Only the month before, a Greek tanker, the *Aegean Sea,* ran aground near La Coruna in northwest Spain during a storm and caught fire, spilling 21.5 million gallons of crude along the coastal fishing area.

The *Braer* had only a single hull, rather than a more damage-resistant double hull, and questions were asked as to why a single-hulled tanker, banned around sensitive coastlines in other countries, was allowed to be in one of Britain's most vulnerable sites for marine wildlife.

The Oil Pollution Act, signed by President Bush in 1990, requires all new US tankers carrying oil to be double-hulled. Single-hulled vessels must be retrofitted or phased out over time.

The bows of the *Braer* showed above the surface for several years before they finally disappeared. In 1999 an attempt was made to recover the propeller, and tow it, slung beneath lifting bags, towards Levenwick, on the east coast of Shetland. This was the nearest place where a crane could lift it ashore, but the attempt failed when the propeller sank just off Garth's Ness.

The tanker Braer *aground at Garth's Ness (Photo: Kieran Murray)*

OCEANIC

Wreck No: 463	Date Sunk: 08 09 1914
Latitude: 60 07 03 N	Longitude: 01 58 23 W
GPS Lat: 6007.044N	GPS Long: 0158.384 W
Location: Hoevdi Reef, 2.4 miles E of Foula	Area: Shetland
Type: Steamship	Tonnage: 1,7274 grt
Length: 704.0 ft Beam: 68.6 ft	Draught: 44.6 ft
How Sunk: Ran aground	Depth: 2-10 metres

When the Great War began on 4 August 1914, RMS *Oceanic* was at sea, en route from New York to Southampton. When she reached the Irish coast, she was met by two Royal Navy cruisers and escorted for the remainder of her voyage. She was quickly requisitioned as HMS *Oceanic* upon her arrival at Southampton and converted into an armed merchant cruiser. The conversion took two weeks. The Royal Navy appointed their own captain, William Slayter, to command the ship, but *Oceanic's* master of two years, Captain Henry Smith, was to remain aboard in an advisory capacity.

When *Oceanic* left Southampton on 25 August 1914, her destination was Scapa Flow, to join the 10th Cruiser Squadron. Arriving at Orkney, *Oceanic* was sent to patrol the Western Approaches, west of Fair Isle. She then made a courtesy call at Reykjavik, Iceland and returned to Scapa Flow where gunnery practice for her inexperienced crew began. The ship's civilian crew now included several Shetland Island fishermen.

Oceanic was to patrol the 150-mile gap between Scotland and the Faroe Islands, to ensure that passing ships did not contain contraband or German sympathisers.

So that gun crews' watch endings would not always coincide with the morning's general alert, Slayter ordered the ship's clock set back forty minutes. Now the ship had two times, Greenwich Mean Time and ship's time, two captains and three crews. Needless to say, more confusion resulted.

Informally, Smith and Slayter agreed that the former would be in command during the day and the latter at night, even though the two were still at odds over how to manage the ship. Slayter, being of the Royal Navy, was in overall command, and he ordered *Oceanic* to search for German submarines and patrol craft around the island of Foula. She would spend much of her time on zigzag courses to evade German submarines. The duty of recording the course changes would be handled by the navigator David Blair. He was originally to be second officer of *Titanic*, but was displaced by Charles Lightoller, who was now *Oceanic*'s first officer.

Foula was sighted on 7 September 1914, and she continued to zigzag despite thick fog. The fog cleared up the next morning. By this time, Blair calculated that *Oceanic* was well south of Foula. Slayter then ordered *Oceanic* on a course to take her back to Foula before retiring. Blair made the calculations, and after that was done, he too retired for a nap.

Smith arrived to look over the chart while Blair slept and concluded that *Oceanic* was fourteen miles to the south and west of Foula. Fearing that their course would result in the ship's running aground on the reefs around the island, Smith ordered a course change to the west to the open sea without consulting Slayter. When Blair awoke and reported for duty, he suggested that soundings be taken to determine the exact position of the ship, but Smith vetoed the idea. Half-an-hour later, Foula was sighted dead ahead. Smith turned the ship several points to starboard to avoid the southern end of the reef known as Da Shaalds (The Shallows) and bring the ship into a narrow channel between reef and island, the latter of which Smith estimated to be four miles off.

Hearing the lookout's cry, Slayter rushed to the bridge. Seeing that the ship was closer to Foula than Smith had thought, Slayter ordered a sharp turn to starboard to leave the area as soon as possible. At that moment, with a large amount of grinding, *Oceanic* was pushed into Da Shaalds, stern first into the reef. The next tide, instead of freeing her, drove her further into the reef.

The Aberdeen trawler *Glenogil* and the HMS *Forward* put lines around *Oceanic*, but *Oceanic* was pushed in much too far. The tow lines snapped and *Oceanic* stayed where she was. Soundings then showed that the double bottom was so badly breached that, even if she were to be freed, she would sink. Orders to abandon ship were given late that afternoon. By evening, all of the ship's 600 crewmembers were evacuated without incident, ferried to other vessels standing by via lifeboats. Lightoller, who had been off watch and in his cabin at the time of *Oceanic*'s grounding, once again found himself supervising the lowering and loading of lifeboats. This was a very sad moment for Lightoller. To see *Oceanic* broken up on the Shaalds reef was almost too much for him to bear. He had some of his men row him back to the ship and he walked about her empty decks one last time, taking the clock from the navigation room wall as a souvenir. The ship was declared a total loss on 11 September.

For the next three weeks, the Admiralty salvage vessel *Lyons* recovered all the guns, all but one of the gun shields, and most of the ammunition and other naval fittings. There was a long period of quiet weather around Foula afterwards, until an incredibly fierce storm struck on 29 September. On the morning of 30 September, *Oceanic* had disappeared.

At first, it was thought that the storm had lifted *Oceanic* off the rocks and carried her to deeper water to sink, but it was later discovered that the storm had pounded the ship to pieces against the rocks. Her remains lay scattered in relatively shallow water. Smith, Slayter, and Blair were all court-martialled. Comparing *Oceanic*'s log and the ship's last movements as witnessed by the inhabitants of Foula, and noting their inconsistencies, Smith and Slayter were exonerated and Blair was mildly reprimanded. The hearings resulted in changes in the armed merchant cruisers' administration, and the mercantile officers were given more responsibility.

The wreck was purchased by J.W.Robertson for £200. He attempted to carry out salvage using hard hat diving techniques, but was defeated by the currents flowing over the wreck site, and declared the wreck to be undiveable.

The wreck was later salvaged by Alex Crawford and Simon Martin.

For further details I would recommend Simon Martin's book *The Other Titanic*.

The White Star liner Oceanic *(Photo: author's collection)*

ST NIDAN

Wreck No: 464	Date Sunk: 28 10 1939
Latitude: 60 29 17 N	Longitude: 04 18 53.02 W
GPS Lat: 6029.283 N	GPS Long: 0418.884 W
Location: 100 miles W of Esha Ness	Area: Shetland
Type: Trawler	Tonnage: 565 grt
Length: 172.2 ft. Beam: 29.1 ft	Draught: 14.7 ft
How Sunk: By *U-59*	Depth: metres

This is the wreck of a trawler 32 x 7 x 2.3 metres high. Two cables, one 180 metres long, the other 40 metres long, extend from the wreck. This is probably the Grimsby trawler *St Nidan*, sunk by the *U-59* (KL Harald Jürst), with gunfire and scuttling charges on 28 October 1939.

LYNX II

Wreck No: 465
Latitude: 60 18 47.59 N
GPS Lat: 6018.793 N
Location: 100 miles W of Esha Ness
Type: Trawler
Length: 127.0 ft
How Sunk: By *U-59*

Date Sunk: 28 10 1939
Longitude: 04 16 54.84 W
GPS Long: 0416.914 W
Area: Shetland
Tonnage: 250 grt
Beam: 22.1 ft Draught: 11.5 ft
Depth: metres

The Hull trawler *Lynx II* was built in 1906 by Cochranes of Selby. She was sunk by the *U-59* (Jürst) with gunfire and scuttling charges on 28 October 1939.

ALGIER

Wreck No: 466
Latitude: 60 17 00 N PA
GPS Lat: 6017.000 N
Location: W of Shetland
Type: Steamship
Length: 217.7 ft
How Sunk: Torpedoed by *U-38*

Date Sunk: 21 03 1940
Longitude: 03 10 00 W PA
GPS Long: 0310.000 W
Area: Shetland
Tonnage: 1,654 grt
Beam: 40.4 ft Draught: 16.6 ft
Depth: 180 metres

The Danish steamship *Algier* was built in 1938.

En route from New York to Copenhagen she was torpedoed by *U-38* (KL Heinrich Leibe) at 01.11 hrs on 21 March 1940 in 6017N, 0310W. She took a list to port and sank by the stern in ten minutes. Lloyds gave the position as 6017N, 0249W.

A lifeboat containing twenty of the crew was picked up 15 miles NNW of Foula on 21 March by the trawler *Manx King*. Four others of the crew and one passenger were lost.

Algier's general cargo included 302 tons of copper, 228 tons of tin, and 130 bottles of quicksilver (mercury), weighing over 4 tons.

Other items listed in *Algier*'s manifest include 11 Studebaker motor cars, 4 tons of Ford auto parts, silk underwear, blank recording discs, and musical instruments.

CHRISTIANSBORG

Wreck No: 467
Latitude: 60 13 00 N PA
GPS Lat: 6013.000 N
Location: 25 miles WNW of Foula
Type: Steamship
Length: ft
How Sunk: Torpedoed by *U-38*

Date Sunk: 21 03 1940
Longitude: 02 49 00 W PA
GPS Long: 0249.000 W
Area: Shetland
Tonnage: 3,270 grt
Beam: ft Draught: ft
Depth: 150 metres

En route from Philadelphia to Copenhagen with 4,107 tons of maize, the Danish steamship *Christiansborg* had called into Kirkwall to be examined for contraband. Shortly after leaving there, by a route advised by the Naval authorities in Kirkwall, to pass around the west and then north of the Shetlands, she was torpedoed by *U-38* (Leibe) at 03.26 hrs on 21 March 1940.

At 02.00 hrs Leibe sighted three steamers, and started a submerged approach to attack them.

At 02.56 he fired a torpedo which missed due to Leibe overestimating the *Christiansborg's* speed.

Despite the bright moonlight, Leibe surfaced to make a second attack from 400 metres away. He saw the torpedo explosion, and *Christiansborg* break in two. The bow section sank, but the stern remained afloat. The sinking took place near the *Algier's* lifeboat, and Leibe did not want to fire another torpedo at the stern section, so as not to weaken the possible belief that *Christiansborg* might have struck a mine – assuming that *U-38* had not been spotted.

The U-boat had been spotted on the surface, however, both before and after the attack, by the *Christiansborg's* third mate, who was on the bridge.

Captain Jonni Rasnussen of the *Christiansborg* gave the position as 6009N, 0255W, which is about 30 miles west of the Ve Skerries.

The torpedo struck the *Christiansborg* on her starboard side, below the bridge, and the ship immediately broke in two. The whole of her forepart, including the bridge, was blown away and sank. The stern section remained afloat, but her engine and boiler room was flooded, and the crew abandoned ship in two lifeboats. All but one were picked up at 08.30 hrs by the British armed boarding vessel *Discovery II*. Officers from the *Discovery II* boarded the after part of the *Christiansborg* and found the foremost bulkhead leaking badly. The engine room and boiler room were flooded, and there was no hope of towing the slowly sinking stern section in. *Discovery II* sank it with gunfire at 6016N, 0250W. This was the position given by the commander of *Discovery II*, and it is close to the course the *Christiansborg* was ordered to sail.

The Danish steamship Christiansborg *(Photo: author's collection)*

BRITTA

Wreck No: 468
Latitude: 60 00 00 N PA
GPS Lat: 6000.000 N
Location: 100 miles W of Shetland
Type: Steamship

Date Sunk: 25 03 1940
Longitude: 04 19 00 W PA
GPS Long: 0419.000 W
Area: Shetland
Tonnage: 1,146 grt

Length: 231.5 ft   Beam: 34.6 ft   Draught: 14.1 f
How Sunk: Torpedoed by *U-47*   Depth: metres

The Danish steamship *Britta* was built in 1921.

En route from Kalundborg, Denmark to Liverpool in ballast, she was torpedoed and sunk by the *U-47* (KL Gunther Prien) at 06.00 hrs on 25 March 1940, in German grid position AN1184, which equates to about 6009N, 0412W.

Thirteen of her eighteen crew were missing. The Danish steamship *Nancy* took five survivors to Swansea.

The Admiralty Hydrographic Department has recorded the *Britta* at 6002N, 0355W PA, and *Lloyds War Losses* gives two more positions – 6000N, 0419W and 5945N, 0430W.

DODAS describes the position as 45 miles N of Sule Skerry, and Admiralty documents describe the position as 40 miles north-west of Sule Skerry.

Britta *(Photo: courtesy of World Ship Society)*

COMETA

Wreck No: 469   Date Sunk: 26 03 1940
Latitude: 60 06 00 N PA   Longitude: 04 36 00 W PA
GPS Lat: 6006.000 N   GPS Long: 0436.000 W
Location: 65 miles NW of Noup Head, Orkney   Area: Shetland
Type: Motor vessel   Tonnage: 3,794 grt
Length: 367.0 ft   Beam: 51.5 ft   Draught: 22.3 ft
How Sunk: Torpedoed by *U-38*   Depth: metres

The Norwegian motor vessel *Cometa* was built in 1921.

En route from Oslo to Buenos Aires with 3,250 tons of general cargo, she was torpedoed and sunk by *U-38* (Leibe) on 26 March 1940, in German grid AN2624. This equates to about 5951N, 0036W, which is some 30 miles east of Sumburgh Head. *DODAS* describes the position as 'outside Kirkwall'.

Lloyds gives the position as 6006N, 0436W, which is consistent with the Norwegian description of the position as 65 miles NW of Noup Head, Orkney.

The *Cometa* had been intercepted by the Northern Patrol vessel *Kingston Peridot*, which had put an armed guard of one officer and four ratings on board to take her in to Kirkwall for examination. Shortly before midnight the *Cometa* was stopped by *U-38*, which first opened fire on her, and then sank her by a torpedo after the crew and passengers had abandoned ship. Among the latter were three women, a child, and a baby in arms. Leibe had given the passengers and crew one hour to abandon the vessel, so there were no casualties. The patrol vessel *Northern Sky* found three lifeboats full of survivors on 26 March.

The Norwegian steamship Cometa *(Photo: Dag Bakka Jnr.)*

ARGENTINA

Wreck No: 470	Date Sunk: 17 03 1940
Latitude: 60 53 53 N	Longitude: 00 33 09 W
GPS Lat: 6053.881 N	GPS Long: 0033.149 W
Location: 6 miles NE of Holm of Skaw, Unst	Area: Shetland
Type: Motor Vessel	Tonnage: 5,371 grt
Length: 378.0 ft Beam: 52.5 ft	Draught: 32.6 ft
How Sunk: Torpedoed by *U-38*	Depth: 112 metres

The Danish motor vessel *Argentina* left Copenhagen on 13 March 1940, bound for South America, via Las Palmas in ballast. She reported by radio on 17 March, then disappeared.

According to *Rohwer's Axis Submarine Successes 1939–45*, she was torpedoed by *U-38* (Leibe) at 23.25 hrs on 17 March in German grid AN1129, which equates to about 6039N, 0348W.

The position has also been recorded as 6030N, 0330W.

It is curious that Dr Rohwer gives the position as AN1129 in the German grid system, as at this early stage of the war, Leibe did not use the coded system, and no AN numbers are given in his Ktb. Some of the positions he gives are in the old pre-war code, but most are in Lat/Long.

In his Ktb, the position Leibe gives for the sinking of the *Argentina* is 6047N, 0030W. This position is on the east side of Shetland, 8 miles east of The Nev, Unst, in about 106 metres depth.

He also says that *Argentina* sank in 10 minutes. *U-38* then passed around the north of Shetland. After that he did not get a navigation fix for four days, and then finally discovered that he was 45 miles north-east of his dead reckoning position, and that he was not even in his patrol area!

The wreck charted at 6053.881N, 0033.149W in 112 metres is probably the *Argentina*.

Argentina (*Photo: author's collection*)

HURSTSIDE

Wreck No: 471	Date Sunk: 04 07 1917
Latitude: 60 17 43.25 N	Longitude: 04 14 57.70 W
GPS Lat: 6017.721 N	GPS Long: 0414.962 W
Location: 100 miles W of Shetland	Area: Shetland
Type: Steamship	Tonnage: 3,149 grt
Length: 330.5 ft Beam: 47.8 ft	Draught: 21.8 ft
How Sunk: Torpedoed by *UC-54*	Depth: 400 metres

In 1996 the wreck of a three-island steamship was found in BP's Foinaven oilfield, about 100 miles west of Shetland. The wreck has a stern gun. There is coal in her holds, and a lot of coal on the seabed, particularly near the huge hole in her aft starboard side, where the hull plates have been blown outwards. She obviously sank stern first, and some of the damage must have been caused by the ship's impact with the seabed. The wreck is oriented 099/249°.

She also has a deck cargo of four tracked vehicles, three of which are American Holt tractors, built under licence by Ruston Proctor of Lincoln, and the fourth is a tractor designed by the Ministry of Munitions and built by Clayton and Shuttleworth of Lincolnshire.

The bridge telegraph (made by McLeods of Cheapside, Liverpool), the binnacle (made by Hutchinson & Jackson of Sunderland), and part of a Marconi radio were recovered in December 1996.

The three-island steamship *Portreath* was completed in 1907 by J. Blumer of Sunderland for the Portfield SS Co., and registered in Cardiff. Her engine was by J. Dickinson of Sunderland.

Her name was changed to *Hurstside* in 1916 when she was bought by the Charlton SS Co. of Newcastle. A 12-cwt 12-pdr gun was fitted on her stern.

On 4 July 1917, while en route from Barry to Archangel with a cargo of 5250 tons of coal and four tractors, she was torpedoed and sunk by the *UC-54* (KL Heinrich XXXVII Prinz Reuss), 108 miles NNE ¼E of Cape Wrath at about 6025N, 0438W.

No lives were lost when the *Hurstside* was sunk. If she had been torpedoed without warning, and all of the damage had occurred on the surface, she would have sunk too quickly to allow anyone a chance to get off. A considerable amount of the damage to the wreck must, therefore, have been caused by her impact with the seabed, and the passage of time.

From the German records, the report by KL Heinrich XXXVII Prinz Reuss, the commander of *UC-54*, tells how he came across the *Hurstside* on 4 July, while the U-boat was heading from Kiel, via the Shetlands, towards the Mediterranean to lay mines.

In accordance with routing and sailing instructions issued by the Transport Office in Cardiff, the *Hurstside* had been zig-zagging since leaving Barry at midnight on 30 June.

At about 8.00 p.m. on 4 July the chief officer reported to the master that a sail had been sighted about 5 miles off the starboard beam. This appeared to be a schooner, which suspiciously worked its way round to the port quarter and then to a position right astern of the *Hurstside*, at a distance of 4 to 5 miles. The dubious vessel had one mast and a fore and aft sail up, and looked as if disguised. She then steered after the ship, heading into the north-easterly wind, and did not approach nearer than 3 miles, keeping out of range of the ship's 12-pdr gun.

At 8.20 p.m. the master increased speed to the maximum of 8½ knots, and altered his zig-zag pattern to an irregular one, every 5 or 10 minutes altering course 4 points, first to W then to E of mean course. The suspicious sail continued to follow in an unwarranted way, through the north-easterly swell and rough sea. (The wind was variously described as NE Force 5, or NE Force 1-2.)

This was considered suspicious by the captain and chief officer, but there is no further reference to this vessel in the captain's report held in the PRO, and nor is there any mention in the brief German report by KL Reuss that he attempted to disguise his U-boat as a sailing vessel.

At about 9.15 p.m. the ship was struck by a torpedo on the starboard side, between No. 3 and No. 4 hold, blowing up No. 4 hatch cover, and splintering the main topmast. The starboard bulwarks fell inboard, and the vessel settled down quickly by the stern. Captain Howe gave orders for a wireless SOS message to be sent out, but afterwards found the aerial been broken and carried away by the splitting main topmast. Eric Ford, the radio operator, stayed in his Marconi office and tried to get a message through, until the master himself finally had to get him to leave after all the remainder of the crew had been placed in boats. Two bags of secret mail and all the confidential papers were sunk by the master.

After the crew had abandoned ship in two boats, the submarine surfaced and fired four shells into the ship to precipitate her foundering. One missed, and the other three hit the deck as the ship was sinking by the stern.

The two lifeboats pulled about half a mile away from the sinking *Hurstside*, the chief officer and eleven men in one boat, the master and twelve men in the other.

The surfaced submarine approached the chief officer's boat, and told him to tell the master's boat to come alongside. In very good English, KL Reuss questioned Captain Howe about the *Hurstside*'s cargo, where she had come from and where she was bound.

On being told by the chief officer, Ernest Beckford, that they had no food, KL Reuss provided six loaves and a tin of jam to be distributed between the two boats. He then saluted and said goodnight. The U-boat was last seen heading east on the surface.

The *Hurstside* finally sank at 10.20 p.m. The position recorded by Lloyds at 60°25′N, 04°38′W is 13¾ miles from the position of the wreck at 60°17′43″N, 04°14′58″W.

The MOD Historical Branch has a microfilmed copy of the log of *UC-54*.

Part of it tells us that the *Hurstside* was torpedoed in the lower left corner of the German coded grid square 1057 Gamma, which appears to equate to about 60°13′N, 04°11′W. (This is somewhat more accurate than Captain Howe's estimate of the position).

The torpedo was fired at a range of 600 metres from the *Hurstside* at 11.25 p.m. German time (this was two hours ahead of British time) and the U-boat surfaced at 11.41 p.m. German time.

Hurstside's master, Captain John Howe and his crew of twenty-six steered SW for about four hours before being picked up from their lifeboats by the Aberdeen trawler *Owl*, which landed them at Pierowall, Westray, Orkney at 1.00 p.m. on the 5th.

The survivors included twenty-one British, one Norwegian, two Swedes, two Dutch and one Russian Finn.

An incredible story of the unhelpful and hostile attitude experienced by the unfortunate shipwrecked seamen is revealed in a statement by Captain Howe:

> I am Master of the British SS *Hurstside*, Admiralty Transport.
>
> My ship was torpedoed and sunk by a German submarine on the fourth of July, between the Orkneys and Faroes. My crew were saved. We were some hours in open boats. We were picked up by the trawler *Owl* of Aberdeen and landed at Peirowall in Westray, Orkneys, on the fifth of July. We were all shaken and exhausted and hungry and were in want of food and clothing.
>
> I went to the hotel at Peirowall, kept by Mrs Irvine. I saw Mrs Irvine and told her we were shipwrecked, that our ship had been sunk by the enemy and we wanted food and lodging. I had money with me and told Mrs Irvine I would pay for food and accommodation.
>
> Mrs Irvine said 'I can't do anything for you'. She refused to let my men enter the hotel and refused to supply us with food or lodging. I was informed by local residents there was ample accommodation in the hotel and no guests were staying there. The men sat about in the open street for two hours till I found people to take them in. Various private houses took them in and were very kind to us, especially Mrs Hewison of the Post Office.
>
> I make this statement because I think my crew were treated very badly by Mrs Irvine, they being shipwrecked at Peirowall after being torpedoed in an Admiralty ship in the performance of their duty to the country.

The statement was signed by John Howe, Master; E. Beckford, 1st Mate; Christian Borries, 1st Engineer, and was witnessed by Alfred le Dewan, Commander RN.

I would imagine Mrs Hewison, and the other Orkney residents who took the distressed seamen into their homes and looked after them, are more typical of today's Orcadians than was the owner of the Pierowall Hotel in 1917. But I would equally have expected that to be the case in 1917.

Although the documentary records do not specifically suggest that the sail seen by the *Hurstside's* crew was the U-boat in disguise, the fact that this vessel is not mentioned again in any of the records makes me wonder if this could have been the case.

It strikes me as strange that the records do not include any mention of the vessel disappearing from view as the *Hurstside* tried to outrun it, and further, if it was an innocent vessel, it seems odd that it did not attempt to offer assistance to the *Hurstside's* crew in the lifeboats.

It may seem a very far-fetched notion for a U-boat to attempt such a disguise, but more than a year before *UC-54* sank the *Hurstside,* the mine-laying U-boat *U-74* (Weisbach) was caught on the surface by four armed trawlers (*Sea Ranger, Oku, Rodino* and *Kimberley*) before she could lay her mines. She was sunk by ramming and gunfire from the *Kimberley*, with the loss of all thirty-four of her crew, 25 miles SE of Peterhead at 12.55 hrs on 27 May 1916.

In *U-boats Destroyed*, Cdr Paul Kemp mentions that the four armed trawlers caught *U-74* on the surface, disguised as a sailing vessel.

Before taking command of *UC-54*, Heinrich Reuss had been at the German U-boat training college. He would, therefore, be aware of this ruse. Indeed, it may have been standard practice to use this form of disguise.

Hurstside *(Photo: Welsh Industrial & Maritime Museum)*

A Ruston Tractor similar to those on the Hurstside *(Photo: author's collection)*

The propeller of the Hurstside, *partially sunk into the seabed – note the rudder is missing*

NORTHERN ROVER

Wreck No: 472	Date Sunk: 28 10 1939
Latitude: 59 57 00 N PA	Longitude: 04 24 00 W PA
GPS Lat: 5957.000 N	GPS Long: 0424.000 W
Location: 100 miles W of Sumburgh Head	Area: Shetland
Type: Trawler	Tonnage: 655 grt
Length: 189.2 ft Beam: 28.2 ft	Draught: 15.5 ft
How Sunk: Torpedoed by *U-59*	Depth: 140 metres

The trawler *Northern Rover* was requisitioned for naval service as a patrol vessel, and was armed with a 4-inch gun mounted on her fo'c'sle. She was last seen on patrol in the Fair Isle Channel on 30 October 1939. When she failed to arrive at Kirkwall as expected on 5 November, she was presumed to have been lost some time between 31 October and 5 November.

Letters sent to all of the crewmembers' next of kin stated that presumption of death should be made for 5 November, but in fact *Northern Rover* was torpedoed and sunk by *U-59* (KL Harald Jürst) at 23.35 hrs on 30 October 1939.

The German grid position was given as AN1313, which equates to about 5957N, 0424W.

HMT Northern Rover *(Photo: author's collection)*

WLADIMIR REITZ

Wreck No: 473	Date Sunk: 04 04 1917
Latitude: 60 40 11 N	Longitude: 02 30 52 W
GPS Lat: 6040.153 N	GPS Long: 0230.872 W
Location: 40 miles NW by N of Foula	Area: Shetland
Type: Steamship	Tonnage: 2,128 grt
Length: 296.7.0 ft Beam: 42.2 ft	Draught: 19.5 ft
How Sunk: Torpedoed by *U-78*	Depth: 120 metres

The Danish steamship *Wladimir Reitz* was torpedoed and sunk by *U-78* (Volbrecht), 40 miles NW by N of Foula Island on 4 April 1917, while en route from Galveston to

Aarhus with a cargo of oilcake. The vessel was built in Glasgow in 1905. The wreck lies two miles from an oil wellhead.

GUSTAV E REUTER

Wreck No: 474	Date Sunk: 25 11 1944
Latitude: 59 44 46 N	Longitude: 01 51 02 W
GPS Lat: 5944.775 N	GPS Long: 0151.031 W
Location: 14 miles WNW of Fair Isle	Area: Shetland
Type: Motor Tanker	Tonnage: 6,336 grt
Length: 421.2 ft　　Beam: 55.4 ft	Draught: 32.2 ft
How Sunk: Torpedoed by *U-48*	Depth: 96 metres

The Swedish tanker *Gustav E Reuter* was built by Eriksbergs of Gothenburg in 1928.

Outward bound in ballast from Sweden to Curacao, she reported that she had been mined or torpedoed at 23.55 hrs on 26 November 1939 in the Fair Isle Channel, and was adrift 130° Sumburgh Head 12 miles. She had, in fact, been torpedoed by Kapitänleutnant Herbert Schultze in *U-48*, which had sailed from Kiel on 20 November as one of several U-boats ordered to operate against British naval forces around Orkney. Lerwick lifeboat *Lady Jane and Martha Ryland* was launched. The lifeboat must have been sheltered from the worst of the weather until she rounded Sumburgh Head, when she would have encountered the seas whipped up by the strong westerly gale. The lifeboat returned to station at 12.00 hrs the next day after failing to find the casualty in very bad weather. Aith lifeboat *The Rankin* was launched but the *Gustav E Reuter* was found by *HMT Kingston Beryl,* which succeeded in taking off eight of the tanker's crew. The weather moderated overnight and the tug *St Mellons* from Kirkwall was able to take the *Gustav E Reuter* in tow by the stern on the 27th. Aith lifeboat returned to station. The gale returned with renewed force from the north-west on the 28th and the *Gustav E Reuter* became unmanageable. She tried to assist the tug by going astern, but the tow parted. Lerwick lifeboat was then launched again and made contact at 15.45 hrs on the 28th. The lifeboat reported that the fore end had been blown off the *Gustav E Reuter*. Nineteen crew were already aboard the tug and the lifeboat took off another fourteen. *St Mellons* brought the master and eighteen crew into Lerwick at 23.00 hrs on the 28th. One member of the crew was lost.

The position of the torpedoing was recorded by *U-48* as AN1452, which equates to about 5939N, 0212W. The combined effects of the gales and seas, assisted by the towing attempt, probably moved the floating stern section of the *Gustav E Reuter* some

The Swedish steam tanker Gustav E Reuter *(Photo: Tomas Johanneson collection)*

distance north-eastward before the salvage effort had to be abandoned, and the vessel was sunk by HM ships – probably by the *Kingston Beryl*.

There are several wrecks charted in the Fair Isle Channel. The wreck charted in 96 metres depth at 594446N, 015102W, 14 miles WNW of Fair Isle might be the *Gustav E Reuter*.

Appendix I
THE GERMAN NAVY GRID SQUARE CODE SYSTEM

During the Second World War the Germans used charts with a secret grid square superimposed to encode positions. Positions given in German records almost exclusively refer to these grid square notations.

The grid charts consisted of large squares, each designated by two capital letters, subdivided to form nine sub-squares, numbered from 1 to 9 corresponding to the modern pushbutton telephone layout. These sub-squares had sides measuring 54 nm, and they were in turn further subdivided into nine small squares with sides of 6 nm each. One small square, for example, was designated AN4173.

The 'normal' large square (e.g. BD) had a side length of 54 x 9 (or 81 x 6) nm = 486 nm, corresponding to 8.1 degrees of latitude.

In the Mercator projection the longitudinal geographic extension of the chart required an adaptation to latitude zone. If ten small squares of 6 nm are equal to one degree of longitude at the equator, it would take only two small squares in the polar regions.

The dimension of a normal large square was always 81/10 degrees of latitude and 81/M degrees of longitude. (Where M is the longitude factor applied to a particular latitude zone.)

For instance, if M = 4 for the large square AE, then the longitudinal dimension of the large square will be 81/4 = 20.25 degrees of longitude.

The large squares AH to AM in the North Atlantic extend over two latitude zones, the north and south sections, requiring their own longitude adjustment factors.

During the war, the Germans referred to their special grid square charts to interpret positions, but it is possible to calculate the latitude/longitude position of a German coded grid square.

I have done this for the grid squares around Scotland, to produce the unique reference tables given in the following pages. Even the Germans themselves never produced these tables.

The calculated lat/long positions are the centres of the small squares, each of which covers an area of 6 x 6 nm = 36 sq. miles. In theory, therefore, the calculated positions should be accurate to within about 3 nm of the true position, always supposing that the Germans' navigation was 100 per cent accurate in the first place! I have no reason to believe, however, that the Germans' navigation was necessarily any better, or worse, than that of the Allies.

Sometimes the German grid notation is the only position information available for the sinking of a ship.

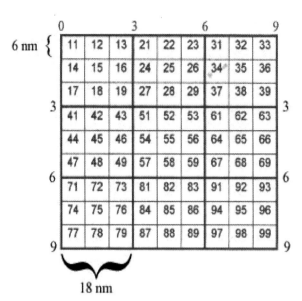

Die Gewässer um England

	Square	Lat	N	Long	W		Square	Lat	N	Long	W
AM	0111	57	15	13	48	AM	0172	56	39	13	36
AM	0112	57	15	13	36	AM	0173	56	39	13	24
AM	0113	57	15	13	24	AM	0174	56	33	13	48
AM	0114	57	09	13	48	AM	0175	56	33	13	36
AM	0115	57	09	13	36	AM	0176	56	33	13	24
AM	0116	57	09	13	24	AM	0177	56	27	13	48
AM	0117	57	03	13	48	AM	0178	56	27	13	36
AM	0118	57	03	13	36	AM	0179	56	27	13	24
AM	0119	57	03	13	24	AM	0181	56	39	13	12
AM	0121	57	15	13	12	AM	0182	56	39	13	00
AM	0122	57	15	13	00	AM	0183	56	39	12	48
AM	0123	57	15	12	48	AM	0184	56	33	13	12
AM	0124	57	09	13	12	AM	0185	56	33	13	00
AM	0125	57	09	13	00	AM	0186	56	33	12	48
AM	0126	57	09	12	48	AM	0187	56	27	13	12
AM	0127	57	03	13	12	AM	0188	56	27	13	00
AM	0128	57	03	13	00	AM	0189	56	27	12	48
AM	0129	57	03	12	48	AM	0191	56	39	12	36
AM	0131	57	15	12	36	AM	0192	56	39	12	24
AM	0132	57	15	12	24	AM	0193	56	39	12	12
AM	0133	57	15	12	12	AM	0194	56	33	12	36
AM	0134	57	09	12	36	AM	0195	56	33	12	24
AM	0135	57	09	12	24	AM	0196	56	33	12	12
AM	0136	57	09	12	12	AM	0197	56	27	12	36
AM	0137	57	03	12	36	AM	0198	56	27	12	24
AM	0138	57	03	12	24	AM	0199	56	27	12	12
AM	0139	57	03	12	12	AM	0211	57	15	10	12
AM	0141	56	57	13	48	AM	0212	57	15	10	00
AM	0142	56	57	13	36	AM	0213	57	15	09	48
AM	0143	56	57	13	24	AM	0214	57	09	10	12
AM	0144	56	51	13	48	AM	0215	57	09	10	00
AM	0145	56	51	13	36	AM	0216	57	09	09	48
AM	0146	56	51	13	24	AM	0217	57	03	10	12
AM	0147	56	45	13	48	AM	0218	57	03	10	00
AM	0148	56	45	13	36	AM	0219	57	03	09	48
AM	0149	56	45	13	24	AM	0221	57	15	09	36
AM	0151	56	57	13	12	AM	0222	57	15	09	24
AM	0152	56	57	13	00	AM	0223	57	15	09	12
AM	0153	56	57	12	48	AM	0224	57	09	09	36
AM	0154	56	51	13	12	AM	0225	57	09	09	24
AM	0155	56	51	13	00	AM	0226	57	09	09	12
AM	0156	56	51	12	48	AM	0227	57	03	09	36
AM	0157	56	45	13	12	AM	0228	57	03	09	24
AM	0158	56	45	13	00	AM	0229	57	03	09	12
AM	0159	56	45	12	48	AM	0231	57	15	09	00
AM	0161	56	57	12	36	AM	0232	57	15	08	48
AM	0162	56	57	12	24	AM	0233	57	15	08	36
AM	0163	56	57	12	12	AM	0234	57	09	09	00
AM	0164	56	51	12	36	AM	0235	57	09	08	48
AM	0165	56	51	12	24	AM	0236	57	09	08	36
AM	0166	56	51	12	12	AM	0237	57	03	09	00
AM	0167	56	45	12	36	AM	0238	57	03	08	48
AM	0168	56	45	12	24	AM	0239	57	03	08	36
AM	0169	56	45	12	12	AM	0241	56	57	10	12
AM	0171	56	39	13	48	AM	0242	56	57	10	00

	Square	Lat	N	Long	W		Square	Lat	N	Long	W
AM	0243	56	57	09	48	AM	0314	57	9	06	36
AM	0244	56	51	10	12	AM	0315	57	9	06	24
AM	0245	56	51	10	00	AM	0316	57	9	06	12
AM	0246	56	51	09	48	AM	0317	57	3	06	36
AM	0247	56	45	10	12	AM	0318	57	3	06	24
AM	0248	56	45	10	00	AM	0319	57	3	06	12
AM	0249	56	45	09	48	AM	0321	57	15	06	00
AM	0251	56	57	09	36	AM	0322	57	15	05	48
AM	0252	56	57	09	24	AM	0323	57	15	05	36
AM	0253	56	57	09	12	AM	0324	57	9	06	00
AM	0254	56	51	09	36	AM	0325	57	9	05	48
AM	0255	56	51	09	24	AM	0326	57	9	05	36
AM	0256	56	51	09	12	AM	0327	57	3	06	00
AM	0257	56	45	09	36	AM	0328	57	3	05	48
AM	0258	56	45	09	24	AM	0329	57	3	05	36
AM	0259	56	45	09	12	AM	0331	57	15	05	24
AM	0261	56	57	09	00	AM	0332	57	15	05	12
AM	0262	56	57	08	48	AM	0333	57	15	05	00
AM	0263	56	57	08	36	AM	0334	57	9	05	24
AM	0264	56	51	09	00	AM	0335	57	9	05	12
AM	0265	56	51	08	48	AM	0336	57	9	05	00
AM	0266	56	51	08	36	AM	0337	57	3	05	24
AM	0267	56	45	09	00	AM	0338	57	3	05	12
AM	0268	56	45	08	48	AM	0339	57	3	05	00
AM	0269	56	45	08	36	AM	0341	56	57	06	36
AM	0271	56	39	10	12	AM	0342	56	57	06	24
AM	0272	56	39	10	00	AM	0343	56	57	06	12
AM	0273	56	39	09	48	AM	0344	56	51	06	36
AM	0274	56	33	10	12	AM	0345	56	51	06	24
AM	0275	56	33	10	00	AM	0346	56	51	06	12
AM	0276	56	33	09	48	AM	0347	56	45	06	36
AM	0277	56	27	10	12	AM	0348	56	45	06	24
AM	0278	56	27	10	00	AM	0349	56	45	06	12
AM	0279	56	27	09	48	AM	0351	56	57	06	00
AM	0281	56	39	09	36	AM	0352	56	57	05	48
AM	0282	56	39	09	24	AM	0353	56	57	05	36
AM	0283	56	39	09	12	AM	0354	56	51	06	00
AM	0284	56	33	09	36	AM	0355	56	51	05	48
AM	0285	56	33	09	24	AM	0356	56	51	05	36
AM	0286	56	33	09	12	AM	0357	56	45	06	00
AM	0287	56	27	09	36	AM	0358	56	45	05	48
AM	0288	56	27	09	24	AM	0359	56	45	05	36
AM	0289	56	27	09	12	AM	0361	56	57	05	24
AM	0291	56	39	09	00	AM	0362	56	57	05	12
AM	0292	56	39	08	48	AM	0363	56	57	05	00
AM	0293	56	39	08	36	AM	0364	56	51	05	24
AM	0294	56	33	09	00	AM	0365	56	51	05	12
AM	0295	56	33	08	48	AM	0366	56	51	05	00
AM	0296	56	33	08	36	AM	0367	56	45	05	24
AM	0297	56	27	09	00	AM	0368	56	45	05	12
AM	0298	56	27	08	48	AM	0369	56	45	05	00
AM	0299	56	27	08	36	AM	0371	56	39	06	36
AM	0311	57	15	06	36	AM	0372	56	39	06	24
AM	0312	57	15	06	24	AM	0373	56	39	06	12
AM	0313	57	15	06	12	AM	0374	56	33	06	36

	Square	Lat	N	Long	W		Square	Lat	N	Long	W
AM	0375	56	33	06	24	AM	1146	60	27	15	12
AM	0376	56	33	06	12	AM	1147	60	21	15	36
AM	0377	56	27	06	36	AM	1148	60	21	15	24
AM	0378	56	27	06	24	AM	1149	60	21	15	12
AM	0379	56	27	06	12	AM	1151	60	33	15	00
AM	0381	56	39	06	00	AM	1152	60	33	14	48
AM	0382	56	39	05	48	AM	1153	60	33	14	36
AM	0383	56	39	05	36	AM	1154	60	27	15	00
AM	0384	56	33	06	00	AM	1155	60	27	14	48
AM	0385	56	33	05	48	AM	1156	60	27	14	36
AM	0386	56	33	05	36	AM	1157	60	21	15	00
AM	0387	56	27	06	00	AM	1158	60	21	14	48
AM	0388	56	27	05	48	AM	1159	60	21	14	36
AM	0389	56	27	05	36	AM	1161	60	33	14	24
AM	0391	56	39	05	24	AM	1162	60	33	14	12
AM	0392	56	39	05	12	AM	1163	60	33	14	00
AM	0393	56	39	05	00	AM	1164	60	27	14	24
AM	0394	56	33	05	24	AM	1165	60	27	14	12
AM	0395	56	33	05	12	AM	1166	60	27	00	00
AM	0396	56	33	05	00	AM	1167	60	21	14	24
AM	0397	56	27	05	24	AM	1168	60	21	14	12
AM	0398	56	27	05	12	AM	1169	60	21	14	00
AM	0399	56	27	05	00	AM	1171	60	15	15	36
AM	1111	60	51	15	36	AM	1172	60	15	15	24
AM	1112	60	51	15	24	AM	1173	60	15	15	12
AM	1113	60	51	15	12	AM	1174	60	09	15	36
AM	1114	60	45	15	36	AM	1175	60	09	15	24
AM	1115	60	45	15	24	AM	1176	60	09	15	12
AM	1116	60	45	15	12	AM	1177	60	03	15	36
AM	1117	60	39	15	36	AM	1178	60	03	15	24
AM	1118	60	39	15	24	AM	1179	60	03	15	12
AM	1119	60	39	15	12	AM	1181	60	15	15	00
AM	1121	60	51	15	00	AM	1182	60	15	14	48
AM	1122	60	51	14	48	AM	1183	60	15	14	36
AM	1123	60	51	14	36	AM	1184	60	09	15	00
AM	1124	60	45	15	00	AM	1185	60	09	14	48
AM	1125	60	45	14	48	AM	1186	60	09	14	36
AM	1126	60	45	14	36	AM	1187	60	03	15	00
AM	1127	60	39	15	00	AM	1188	60	03	14	48
AM	1128	60	39	14	48	AM	1189	60	03	14	36
AM	1129	60	39	14	36	AM	1191	60	15	14	24
AM	1131	60	51	14	24	AM	1192	60	15	14	12
AM	1132	60	51	14	12	AM	1193	60	15	14	00
AM	1133	60	51	14	00	AM	1194	60	09	14	24
AM	1134	60	45	14	24	AM	1195	60	09	14	12
AM	1135	60	45	14	12	AM	1196	60	09	14	00
AM	1136	60	45	14	00	AM	1197	60	03	14	24
AM	1137	60	39	14	24	AM	1198	60	03	14	12
AM	1138	60	39	14	12	AM	1199	60	03	14	00
AM	1139	60	39	14	00	AM	1211	60	51	13	48
AM	1141	60	33	15	36	AM	1212	60	51	13	36
AM	1142	60	33	15	24	AM	1213	60	51	13	24
AM	1143	60	33	15	12	AM	1214	60	45	13	48
AM	1144	60	27	15	36	AM	1215	60	45	13	36
AM	1145	60	27	15	24	AM	1216	60	45	13	24

	Square	Lat	N	Long	W		Square	Lat	N	Long	W
AM	1217	60	39	13	48	AM	1278	60	03	13	36
AM	1218	60	39	13	36	AM	1279	60	03	13	24
AM	1219	60	39	13	24	AM	1281	60	15	13	12
AM	1221	60	51	13	12	AM	1282	60	15	13	00
AM	1222	60	51	13	00	AM	1283	60	15	12	48
AM	1223	60	51	12	48	AM	1284	60	09	13	12
AM	1224	60	45	13	12	AM	1285	60	09	13	00
AM	1225	60	45	13	00	AM	1286	60	09	12	48
AM	1226	60	45	12	48	AM	1287	60	03	13	12
AM	1227	60	39	13	12	AM	1288	60	03	13	00
AM	1228	60	39	13	00	AM	1289	60	03	12	48
AM	1229	60	39	12	48	AM	1291	60	15	12	36
AM	1231	60	51	12	36	AM	1292	60	15	12	24
AM	1232	60	51	12	24	AM	1293	60	15	12	12
AM	1233	60	51	12	12	AM	1294	60	09	12	36
AM	1234	60	45	12	36	AM	1295	60	09	12	24
AM	1235	60	45	12	24	AM	1296	60	09	12	12
AM	1236	60	45	12	12	AM	1297	60	03	12	36
AM	1237	60	39	12	36	AM	1298	60	03	12	24
AM	1238	60	39	12	24	AM	1299	60	03	12	12
AM	1239	60	39	12	12	AM	1311	59	57	15	36
AM	1241	60	33	13	48	AM	1312	59	57	15	24
AM	1242	60	33	13	36	AM	1313	59	57	15	12
AM	1243	60	33	13	24	AM	1314	59	51	15	36
AM	1244	60	27	13	48	AM	1315	59	51	15	24
AM	1245	60	27	13	36	AM	1316	59	51	15	12
AM	1246	60	27	13	24	AM	1317	59	45	15	36
AM	1247	60	21	13	48	AM	1318	59	45	15	24
AM	1248	60	21	13	36	AM	1319	59	45	15	12
AM	1249	60	21	13	24	AM	1321	59	57	15	00
AM	1251	60	33	13	12	AM	1322	59	57	14	48
AM	1252	60	33	13	00	AM	1323	59	57	14	36
AM	1253	60	33	12	48	AM	1324	59	51	15	00
AM	1254	60	27	13	12	AM	1325	59	51	14	48
AM	1255	60	27	13	00	AM	1326	59	51	14	36
AM	1256	60	27	12	48	AM	1327	59	45	15	00
AM	1257	60	21	13	12	AM	1328	59	45	14	48
AM	1258	60	21	13	00	AM	1329	59	45	14	36
AM	1259	60	21	12	48	AM	1331	59	57	14	24
AM	1261	60	33	12	36	AM	1332	59	57	14	12
AM	1262	60	33	12	24	AM	1333	59	57	14	00
AM	1263	60	33	12	12	AM	1334	59	51	14	24
AM	1264	60	27	12	36	AM	1335	59	51	14	12
AM	1265	60	27	12	24	AM	1336	59	51	14	00
AM	1266	60	27	12	12	AM	1337	59	45	14	24
AM	1267	60	21	12	36	AM	1338	59	45	14	12
AM	1268	60	21	12	24	AM	1339	59	45	14	00
AM	1269	60	21	12	12	AM	1341	59	39	15	36
AM	1271	60	15	13	48	AM	1342	59	39	15	24
AM	1272	60	15	13	36	AM	1343	59	39	15	12
AM	1273	60	15	13	24	AM	1344	59	33	15	36
AM	1274	60	09	13	48	AM	1345	59	33	15	24
AM	1275	60	09	13	36	AM	1346	59	33	15	12
AM	1276	60	09	13	24	AM	1347	59	27	15	36
AM	1277	60	03	13	48	AM	1348	59	27	15	24

	Square	Lat	N	Long	W		Square	Lat	N	Long	W
AM	1349	59	27	15	12	AM	1421	59	57	13	12
AM	1351	59	39	15	00	AM	1422	59	57	13	00
AM	1352	59	39	14	48	AM	1423	59	57	12	48
AM	1353	59	39	14	36	AM	1424	59	51	13	12
AM	1354	59	33	15	00	AM	1425	59	51	13	00
AM	1355	59	33	14	48	AM	1426	59	51	12	48
AM	1356	59	33	14	36	AM	1427	59	45	13	12
AM	1357	59	27	15	00	AM	1428	59	45	13	00
AM	1358	59	27	14	48	AM	1429	59	45	12	48
AM	1359	59	27	14	36	AM	1431	59	57	12	36
AM	1361	59	39	14	24	AM	1432	59	57	12	24
AM	1362	59	39	14	12	AM	1433	59	57	12	12
AM	1363	59	39	14	00	AM	1434	59	51	12	36
AM	1364	59	33	14	24	AM	1435	59	51	12	24
AM	1365	59	33	14	12	AM	1436	59	51	12	12
AM	1366	59	33	00	00	AM	1437	59	45	12	36
AM	1367	59	27	14	24	AM	1438	59	45	12	24
AM	1368	59	27	14	12	AM	1439	59	45	12	12
AM	1369	59	27	14	00	AM	1441	59	39	13	48
AM	1371	59	21	15	36	AM	1442	59	39	13	36
AM	1372	59	21	15	24	AM	1443	59	39	13	24
AM	1373	59	21	15	12	AM	1444	59	33	13	48
AM	1374	59	15	15	36	AM	1445	59	33	13	36
AM	1375	59	15	15	24	AM	1446	59	33	13	24
AM	1376	59	15	15	12	AM	1447	59	27	13	48
AM	1377	59	09	15	36	AM	1448	59	27	13	36
AM	1378	59	09	15	24	AM	1449	59	27	13	24
AM	1379	59	09	15	12	AM	1451	59	39	13	12
AM	1381	59	21	15	00	AM	1452	59	39	13	00
AM	1382	59	21	14	48	AM	1453	59	39	12	48
AM	1383	59	21	14	36	AM	1454	59	33	13	12
AM	1384	59	15	15	00	AM	1455	59	33	13	00
AM	1385	59	15	14	48	AM	1456	59	33	12	48
AM	1386	59	15	14	36	AM	1457	59	27	13	12
AM	1387	59	09	15	00	AM	1458	59	27	13	00
AM	1388	59	09	14	48	AM	1459	59	27	12	48
AM	1389	59	09	14	36	AM	1461	59	39	12	36
AM	1391	59	21	14	24	AM	1462	59	39	12	24
AM	1392	59	21	14	12	AM	1463	59	39	12	12
AM	1393	59	21	14	00	AM	1464	59	33	12	36
AM	1394	59	15	14	24	AM	1465	59	33	12	24
AM	1395	59	15	14	12	AM	1466	59	33	12	12
AM	1396	59	15	14	00	AM	1467	59	27	12	36
AM	1397	59	09	14	24	AM	1468	59	27	12	24
AM	1398	59	09	14	12	AM	1469	59	27	12	12
AM	1399	59	09	14	00	AM	1471	59	21	13	48
AM	1411	59	57	13	48	AM	1472	59	21	13	36
AM	1412	59	57	13	36	AM	1473	59	21	13	24
AM	1413	59	57	13	24	AM	1474	59	15	13	48
AM	1414	59	51	13	48	AM	1475	59	15	13	36
AM	1415	59	51	13	36	AM	1476	59	15	13	24
AM	1416	59	51	13	24	AM	1477	59	09	13	48
AM	1417	59	45	13	48	AM	1478	59	09	13	36
AM	1418	59	45	13	36	AM	1479	59	09	13	24
AM	1419	59	45	13	24	AM	1481	59	21	13	12

	Square	Lat	N	Long	W		Square	Lat	N	Long	W
AM	1482	59	21	13	00	AM	1553	58	45	14	36
AM	1483	59	21	12	48	AM	1554	58	39	15	00
AM	1484	59	15	13	12	AM	1555	58	39	14	48
AM	1485	59	15	13	00	AM	1556	58	39	14	36
AM	1486	59	15	12	48	AM	1557	58	33	15	00
AM	1487	59	09	13	12	AM	1558	58	33	14	48
AM	1488	59	09	13	00	AM	1559	58	33	14	36
AM	1489	59	09	12	48	AM	1561	58	45	14	24
AM	1491	59	21	12	36	AM	1562	58	45	14	12
AM	1492	59	21	12	24	AM	1563	58	45	14	00
AM	1493	59	21	12	12	AM	1564	58	39	14	24
AM	1494	59	15	12	36	AM	1565	58	39	14	12
AM	1495	59	15	12	24	AM	1566	58	39	0	00
AM	1496	59	15	12	12	AM	1567	58	33	14	24
AM	1497	59	09	12	36	AM	1568	58	33	14	12
AM	1498	59	09	12	24	AM	1569	58	33	14	00
AM	1499	59	09	12	12	AM	1571	58	27	15	36
AM	1511	59	03	15	36	AM	1572	58	27	15	24
AM	1512	59	03	15	24	AM	1573	58	27	15	12
AM	1513	59	03	15	12	AM	1574	58	21	15	36
AM	1514	58	57	15	36	AM	1575	58	21	15	24
AM	1515	58	57	15	24	AM	1576	58	21	15	12
AM	1516	58	57	15	12	AM	1577	58	15	15	36
AM	1517	58	51	15	36	AM	1578	58	15	15	24
AM	1518	58	51	15	24	AM	1579	58	15	15	12
AM	1519	58	51	15	12	AM	1581	58	27	15	00
AM	1521	59	03	15	00	AM	1582	58	27	14	48
AM	1522	59	03	14	48	AM	1583	58	27	14	36
AM	1523	59	03	14	36	AM	1584	58	21	15	00
AM	1524	58	57	15	00	AM	1585	58	21	14	48
AM	1525	58	57	14	48	AM	1586	58	21	14	36
AM	1526	58	57	14	36	AM	1587	58	15	15	00
AM	1527	58	51	15	00	AM	1588	58	15	14	48
AM	1528	58	51	14	48	AM	1589	58	15	14	36
AM	1529	58	51	14	36	AM	1591	58	27	14	24
AM	1531	59	03	14	24	AM	1592	58	27	14	12
AM	1532	59	03	14	12	AM	1593	58	27	14	00
AM	1533	59	03	14	00	AM	1594	58	21	14	24
AM	1534	58	57	14	24	AM	1595	58	21	14	12
AM	1535	58	57	14	12	AM	1596	58	21	14	00
AM	1536	58	57	14	00	AM	1597	58	15	14	24
AM	1537	58	51	14	24	AM	1598	58	15	14	12
AM	1538	58	51	14	12	AM	1599	58	15	14	00
AM	1539	58	51	14	00	AM	1611	59	03	13	48
AM	1541	58	45	15	36	AM	1612	59	03	13	36
AM	1542	58	45	15	24	AM	1613	59	03	13	24
AM	1543	58	45	15	12	AM	1614	58	57	13	48
AM	1544	58	39	15	36	AM	1615	58	57	13	36
AM	1545	58	39	15	24	AM	1616	58	57	13	24
AM	1546	58	39	15	12	AM	1617	58	51	13	48
AM	1547	58	33	15	36	AM	1618	58	51	13	36
AM	1548	58	33	15	24	AM	1619	58	51	13	24
AM	1549	58	33	15	12	AM	1621	59	03	13	12
AM	1551	58	45	15	00	AM	1622	59	03	13	00
AM	1552	58	45	14	48	AM	1623	59	03	12	48

Square	Lat	N	Long	W	Square	Lat	N	Long	W
AM 1624	58	57	13	12	AM 1685	58	21	13	00
AM 1625	58	57	13	00	AM 1686	58	21	12	48
AM 1626	58	57	12	48	AM 1687	58	15	13	12
AM 1627	58	51	13	12	AM 1688	58	15	13	00
AM 1628	58	51	13	00	AM 1689	58	15	12	48
AM 1629	58	51	12	48	AM 1691	58	27	12	36
AM 1631	59	03	12	36	AM 1692	58	27	12	24
AM 1632	59	03	12	24	AM 1693	58	27	12	12
AM 1633	59	03	12	12	AM 1694	58	21	12	36
AM 1634	58	57	12	36	AM 1695	58	21	12	24
AM 1635	58	57	12	24	AM 1696	58	21	12	12
AM 1636	58	57	12	12	AM 1697	58	15	12	36
AM 1637	58	51	12	36	AM 1698	58	15	12	24
AM 1638	58	51	12	24	AM 1699	58	15	12	12
AM 1639	58	51	12	12	AM 1711	58	09	15	36
AM 1641	58	45	13	48	AM 1712	58	09	15	24
AM 1642	58	45	13	36	AM 1713	58	09	15	12
AM 1643	58	45	13	24	AM 1714	58	03	15	36
AM 1644	58	39	13	48	AM 1715	58	03	15	24
AM 1645	58	39	13	36	AM 1716	58	03	15	12
AM 1646	58	39	13	24	AM 1717	57	57	15	36
AM 1647	58	33	13	48	AM 1718	57	57	15	24
AM 1648	58	33	13	36	AM 1719	57	57	15	12
AM 1649	58	33	13	24	AM 1721	58	09	15	00
AM 1651	58	45	13	12	AM 1722	58	09	14	48
AM 1652	58	45	13	00	AM 1723	58	09	14	36
AM 1653	58	45	12	48	AM 1724	58	03	15	00
AM 1654	58	39	13	12	AM 1725	58	03	14	48
AM 1655	58	39	13	00	AM 1726	58	03	14	36
AM 1656	58	39	12	48	AM 1727	57	57	15	00
AM 1657	58	33	13	12	AM 1728	57	57	14	48
AM 1658	58	33	13	00	AM 1729	57	57	14	36
AM 1659	58	33	12	48	AM 1731	58	09	14	24
AM 1661	58	45	12	36	AM 1732	58	09	14	12
AM 1662	58	45	12	24	AM 1733	58	09	14	00
AM 1663	58	45	12	12	AM 1734	58	03	14	24
AM 1664	58	39	12	36	AM 1735	58	03	14	12
AM 1665	58	39	12	24	AM 1736	58	03	14	00
AM 1666	58	39	12	12	AM 1737	57	57	14	24
AM 1667	58	33	12	36	AM 1738	57	57	14	12
AM 1668	58	33	12	24	AM 1739	57	57	14	00
AM 1669	58	33	12	12	AM 1741	57	51	15	36
AM 1671	58	27	13	48	AM 1742	57	51	15	24
AM 1672	58	27	13	36	AM 1743	57	51	15	12
AM 1673	58	27	13	24	AM 1744	57	45	15	36
AM 1674	58	21	13	48	AM 1745	57	45	15	24
AM 1675	58	21	13	36	AM 1746	57	45	15	12
AM 1676	58	21	13	24	AM 1747	57	39	15	36
AM 1677	58	15	13	48	AM 1748	57	39	15	24
AM 1678	58	15	13	36	AM 1749	57	39	15	12
AM 1679	58	15	13	24	AM 1751	57	51	15	00
AM 1681	58	27	13	12	AM 1752	57	51	14	48
AM 1682	58	27	13	00	AM 1753	57	51	14	36
AM 1683	58	27	12	48	AM 1754	57	45	15	00
AM 1684	58	21	13	12	AM 1755	57	45	14	48

	Square	Lat	N	Long	W		Square	Lat	N	Long	W
AM	1756	57	45	14	36	AM	1827	57	57	13	12
AM	1757	57	39	15	00	AM	1828	57	57	13	00
AM	1758	57	39	14	48	AM	1829	57	57	12	48
AM	1759	57	39	14	36	AM	1831	58	09	12	36
AM	1761	57	51	14	24	AM	1832	58	09	12	24
AM	1762	57	51	14	12	AM	1833	58	09	12	12
AM	1763	57	51	14	00	AM	1834	58	03	12	36
AM	1764	57	45	14	24	AM	1835	58	03	12	24
AM	1765	57	45	14	12	AM	1836	58	03	12	12
AM	1766	57	45	0	00	AM	1837	57	57	12	36
AM	1767	57	39	14	24	AM	1838	57	57	12	24
AM	1768	57	39	14	12	AM	1839	57	57	12	12
AM	1769	57	39	14	00	AM	1841	57	51	13	48
AM	1771	57	33	15	36	AM	1842	57	51	13	36
AM	1772	57	33	15	24	AM	1843	57	51	13	24
AM	1773	57	33	15	12	AM	1844	57	45	13	48
AM	1774	57	27	15	36	AM	1845	57	45	13	36
AM	1775	57	27	15	24	AM	1846	57	45	13	24
AM	1776	57	27	15	12	AM	1847	57	39	13	48
AM	1777	57	21	15	36	AM	1848	57	39	13	36
AM	1778	57	21	15	24	AM	1849	57	39	13	24
AM	1779	57	21	15	12	AM	1851	57	51	13	12
AM	1781	57	33	15	00	AM	1852	57	51	13	00
AM	1782	57	33	14	48	AM	1853	57	51	12	48
AM	1783	57	33	14	36	AM	1854	57	45	13	12
AM	1784	57	27	15	00	AM	1855	57	45	13	00
AM	1785	57	27	14	48	AM	1856	57	45	12	48
AM	1786	57	27	14	36	AM	1857	57	39	13	12
AM	1787	57	21	15	00	AM	1858	57	39	13	00
AM	1788	57	21	14	48	AM	1859	57	39	12	48
AM	1789	57	21	14	36	AM	1861	57	51	12	36
AM	1791	57	33	14	24	AM	1862	57	51	12	24
AM	1792	57	33	14	12	AM	1863	57	51	12	12
AM	1793	57	33	14	00	AM	1864	57	45	12	36
AM	1794	57	27	14	24	AM	1865	57	45	12	24
AM	1795	57	27	14	12	AM	1866	57	45	12	12
AM	1796	57	27	14	00	AM	1867	57	39	12	36
AM	1797	57	21	14	24	AM	1868	57	39	12	24
AM	1798	57	21	14	12	AM	1869	57	39	12	12
AM	1799	57	21	14	00	AM	1871	57	33	13	48
AM	1811	58	09	13	48	AM	1872	57	33	13	36
AM	1812	58	09	13	36	AM	1873	57	33	13	24
AM	1813	58	09	13	24	AM	1874	57	27	13	48
AM	1814	58	03	13	48	AM	1875	57	27	13	36
AM	1815	58	03	13	36	AM	1876	57	27	13	24
AM	1816	58	03	13	24	AM	1877	57	21	13	48
AM	1817	57	57	13	48	AM	1878	57	21	13	36
AM	1818	57	57	13	36	AM	1879	57	21	13	24
AM	1819	57	57	13	24	AM	1881	57	33	13	12
AM	1821	58	09	13	12	AM	1882	57	33	13	00
AM	1822	58	09	13	00	AM	1883	57	33	12	48
AM	1823	58	09	12	48	AM	1884	57	27	13	12
AM	1824	58	03	13	12	AM	1885	57	27	13	00
AM	1825	58	03	13	00	AM	1886	57	27	12	48
AM	1826	58	03	12	48	AM	1887	57	21	13	12

	Square	Lat	N	Long	W		Square	Lat	N	Long	W
AM	1888	57	21	13	00	AM	1959	56	45	14	36
AM	1889	57	21	12	48	AM	1961	56	57	14	24
AM	1891	57	33	12	36	AM	1962	56	57	14	12
AM	1892	57	33	12	24	AM	1963	56	57	14	00
AM	1893	57	33	12	12	AM	1964	56	51	14	24
AM	1894	57	27	12	36	AM	1965	56	51	14	12
AM	1895	57	27	12	24	AM	1966	56	51	00	00
AM	1896	57	27	12	12	AM	1967	56	45	14	24
AM	1897	57	21	12	36	AM	1968	56	45	14	12
AM	1898	57	21	12	24	AM	1969	56	45	14	00
AM	1899	57	21	12	12	AM	1971	56	39	15	36
AM	1911	57	15	15	36	AM	1972	56	39	15	24
AM	1912	57	15	15	24	AM	1973	56	39	15	12
AM	1913	57	15	15	12	AM	1974	56	33	15	36
AM	1914	57	09	15	36	AM	1975	56	33	15	24
AM	1915	57	09	15	24	AM	1976	56	33	15	12
AM	1916	57	09	15	12	AM	1977	56	27	15	36
AM	1917	57	03	15	36	AM	1978	56	27	15	24
AM	1918	57	03	15	24	AM	1979	56	27	15	12
AM	1919	57	03	15	12	AM	1981	56	39	15	00
AM	1921	57	15	15	00	AM	1982	56	39	14	48
AM	1922	57	15	14	48	AM	1983	56	39	14	36
AM	1923	57	15	14	36	AM	1984	56	33	15	00
AM	1924	57	09	15	00	AM	1985	56	33	14	48
AM	1925	57	09	14	48	AM	1986	56	33	14	36
AM	1926	57	09	14	36	AM	1987	56	27	15	00
AM	1927	57	03	15	00	AM	1988	56	27	14	48
AM	1928	57	03	14	48	AM	1989	56	27	14	36
AM	1929	57	03	14	36	AM	1991	56	39	14	24
AM	1931	57	15	14	24	AM	1992	56	39	14	12
AM	1932	57	15	14	12	AM	1993	56	39	14	00
AM	1933	57	15	14	00	AM	1994	56	33	14	24
AM	1934	57	09	14	24	AM	1995	56	33	14	12
AM	1935	57	09	14	12	AM	1996	56	33	14	0
AM	1936	57	09	14	00	AM	1997	56	27	14	24
AM	1937	57	03	14	24	AM	1998	56	27	14	12
AM	1938	57	03	14	12	AM	1999	56	27	14	00
AM	1939	57	03	14	00	AM	2111	60	51	12	00
AM	1941	56	57	15	36	AM	2112	60	51	11	48
AM	1942	56	57	15	24	AM	2113	60	51	11	36
AM	1943	56	57	15	12	AM	2114	60	45	12	00
AM	1944	56	51	15	36	AM	2115	60	45	11	48
AM	1945	56	51	15	24	AM	2116	60	39	11	36
AM	1946	56	51	15	12	AM	2117	60	39	12	00
AM	1947	56	45	15	36	AM	2118	60	39	11	48
AM	1948	56	45	15	24	AM	2119	60	39	11	36
AM	1949	56	45	15	12	AM	2121	60	51	11	24
AM	1951	56	57	15	00	AM	2122	60	51	11	12
AM	1952	56	57	14	48	AM	2123	60	51	11	00
AM	1953	56	57	14	36	AM	2124	60	45	11	24
AM	1954	56	51	15	00	AM	2125	60	45	11	12
AM	1955	56	51	14	48	AM	2126	60	45	11	00
AM	1956	56	51	14	36	AM	2127	60	39	11	24
AM	1957	56	45	15	00	AM	2128	60	39	11	12
AM	1958	56	45	14	48	AM	2129	60	39	11	00

	Square	Lat	N	Long	W		Square	Lat	N	Long	W
AM	2131	60	51	10	48	AM	2192	60	15	10	36
AM	2132	60	51	10	36	AM	2193	60	15	10	24
AM	2133	60	51	10	24	AM	2194	60	09	10	48
AM	2134	60	45	10	48	AM	2195	60	09	10	36
AM	2135	60	45	10	36	AM	2196	60	09	10	24
AM	2136	60	45	10	24	AM	2197	60	03	10	48
AM	2137	60	39	10	48	AM	2198	60	03	10	36
AM	2138	60	39	10	36	AM	2199	60	03	10	24
AM	2139	60	39	10	24	AM	2211	60	51	10	12
AM	2141	60	33	12	00	AM	2212	60	51	10	00
AM	2142	60	33	11	48	AM	2213	60	51	09	48
AM	2143	60	33	11	36	AM	2214	60	45	10	12
AM	2144	60	27	12	00	AM	2215	60	45	10	00
AM	2145	60	27	11	48	AM	2216	60	45	09	48
AM	2146	60	27	11	36	AM	2217	60	39	10	12
AM	2147	60	21	12	00	AM	2218	60	39	10	00
AM	2148	60	21	11	48	AM	2219	60	39	09	48
AM	2149	60	21	11	36	AM	2221	60	51	09	36
AM	2151	60	33	11	24	AM	2222	60	51	09	24
AM	2152	60	33	11	12	AM	2223	60	51	09	12
AM	2153	60	33	11	00	AM	2224	60	45	09	36
AM	2154	60	27	11	24	AM	2225	60	45	09	24
AM	2155	60	27	11	12	AM	2226	60	45	09	12
AM	2156	60	27	11	00	AM	2227	60	39	09	36
AM	2157	60	21	11	24	AM	2228	60	39	09	24
AM	2158	60	21	11	12	AM	2229	60	39	09	12
AM	2159	60	21	11	00	AM	2231	60	51	09	00
AM	2161	60	33	10	48	AM	2232	60	51	08	48
AM	2162	60	33	10	36	AM	2233	60	51	08	36
AM	2163	60	33	10	24	AM	2234	60	45	09	00
AM	2164	60	27	10	48	AM	2235	60	45	08	48
AM	2165	60	27	10	36	AM	2236	60	45	08	36
AM	2166	60	27	10	24	AM	2237	60	39	09	00
AM	2167	60	21	10	48	AM	2238	60	39	08	48
AM	2168	60	21	10	36	AM	2239	60	39	08	36
AM	2169	60	21	10	24	AM	2241	60	33	10	12
AM	2171	60	15	12	00	AM	2242	60	33	10	00
AM	2172	60	15	11	48	AM	2243	60	33	09	48
AM	2173	60	15	11	36	AM	2244	60	27	10	12
AM	2174	60	09	12	00	AM	2245	60	27	10	00
AM	2175	60	09	11	48	AM	2246	60	27	09	48
AM	2176	60	09	11	36	AM	2247	60	21	10	12
AM	2177	60	03	12	00	AM	2248	60	21	10	00
AM	2178	60	03	11	48	AM	2249	60	21	09	48
AM	2179	60	03	11	36	AM	2251	60	33	09	36
AM	2181	60	15	11	24	AM	2252	60	33	09	24
AM	2182	60	15	11	12	AM	2253	60	33	09	12
AM	2183	60	15	11	00	AM	2254	60	27	09	36
AM	2184	60	09	11	24	AM	2255	60	27	09	24
AM	2185	60	09	11	12	AM	2256	60	27	09	12
AM	2186	60	09	11	00	AM	2257	60	21	09	36
AM	2187	60	03	11	24	AM	2258	60	21	09	24
AM	2188	60	03	11	12	AM	2259	60	21	09	12
AM	2189	60	03	11	00	AM	2261	60	33	09	00
AM	2191	60	15	10	48	AM	2262	60	33	08	48

	Square	Lat	N	Long	W		Square	Lat	N	Long	W
AM	2263	60	33	08	36	AM	3234	60	45	05	24
AM	2264	60	27	09	00	AM	3235	60	45	05	12
AM	2265	60	27	08	48	AM	3236	60	45	05	00
AM	2266	60	27	08	36	AM	3237	60	39	05	24
AM	2267	60	21	09	00	AM	3238	60	39	05	12
AM	2268	60	21	08	48	AM	3239	60	39	05	00
AM	2269	60	21	08	36	AM	3241	60	33	06	36
AM	2271	60	15	10	12	AM	3242	60	33	06	24
AM	2272	60	15	10	00	AM	3243	60	33	06	12
AM	2273	60	15	09	48	AM	3244	60	27	06	36
AM	2274	60	09	10	12	AM	3245	60	27	06	24
AM	2275	60	09	10	00	AM	3246	60	27	06	12
AM	2276	60	09	09	48	AM	3247	60	21	06	36
AM	2277	60	03	10	12	AM	3248	60	21	06	24
AM	2278	60	03	10	00	AM	3249	60	21	06	12
AM	2279	60	03	09	48	AM	3251	60	33	06	00
AM	2281	60	15	09	36	AM	3252	60	33	05	48
AM	2282	60	15	09	24	AM	3253	60	33	05	36
AM	2283	60	15	09	12	AM	3254	60	27	06	00
AM	2284	60	09	09	36	AM	3255	60	27	05	48
AM	2285	60	09	09	24	AM	3256	60	27	05	36
AM	2286	60	09	09	12	AM	3257	60	21	06	00
AM	2287	60	03	09	36	AM	3258	60	21	05	48
AM	2288	60	03	09	24	AM	3259	60	21	05	36
AM	2289	60	03	09	12	AM	3261	60	33	05	24
AM	2291	60	15	09	00	AM	3262	60	33	05	12
AM	2292	60	15	08	48	AM	3263	60	33	05	00
AM	2293	60	15	08	36	AM	3264	60	27	05	24
AM	2294	60	09	09	00	AM	3265	60	27	05	12
AM	2295	60	09	08	48	AM	3266	60	27	05	00
AM	2296	60	09	08	36	AM	3267	60	21	05	24
AM	2297	60	03	09	00	AM	3268	60	21	05	12
AM	2298	60	03	08	48	AM	3269	60	21	05	00
AM	2299	60	03	08	36	AM	3271	60	15	06	36
AM	3211	60	51	06	36	AM	3272	60	15	06	24
AM	3212	60	51	06	24	AM	3273	60	15	06	12
AM	3213	60	51	06	12	AM	3274	60	09	06	36
AM	3214	60	45	06	36	AM	3275	60	09	06	24
AM	3215	60	45	06	24	AM	3276	60	09	06	12
AM	3216	60	45	06	12	AM	3277	60	03	06	36
AM	3217	60	39	06	36	AM	3278	60	03	06	24
AM	3218	60	39	06	24	AM	3279	60	03	06	12
AM	3219	60	39	06	12	AM	3281	60	15	06	00
AM	3221	60	51	06	00	AM	3282	60	15	05	48
AM	3222	60	51	05	48	AM	3283	60	15	05	36
AM	3223	60	51	05	36	AM	3284	60	09	06	00
AM	3224	60	45	06	00	AM	3285	60	09	05	48
AM	3225	60	45	05	48	AM	3286	60	09	05	36
AM	3226	60	45	05	36	AM	3287	60	03	06	00
AM	3227	60	39	06	00	AM	3288	60	03	05	48
AM	3228	60	39	05	48	AM	3289	60	03	05	36
AM	3229	60	39	05	36	AM	3291	60	15	05	24
AM	3231	60	51	05	24	AM	3292	60	15	05	12
AM	3232	60	51	05	12	AM	3293	60	15	05	00
AM	3233	60	51	05	00	AM	3294	60	09	05	24

	Square	Lat	N	Long	W		Square	Lat	N	Long	W
AM	3295	60	09	05	12	AM	3466	59	33	05	00
AM	3296	60	09	05	00	AM	3467	59	27	05	24
AM	3297	60	03	05	24	AM	3468	59	27	05	12
AM	3298	60	03	05	12	AM	3469	59	27	05	00
AM	3299	60	03	05	00	AM	3471	59	21	06	36
AM	3411	59	57	06	36	AM	3472	59	21	06	24
AM	3412	59	57	06	24	AM	3473	59	21	06	12
AM	3413	59	57	06	12	AM	3474	59	15	06	36
AM	3414	59	51	06	36	AM	3475	59	15	06	24
AM	3415	59	51	06	24	AM	3476	59	15	06	12
AM	3416	59	51	06	12	AM	3477	59	09	06	36
AM	3417	59	45	06	36	AM	3478	59	09	06	24
AM	3418	59	45	06	24	AM	3479	59	09	06	12
AM	3419	59	45	06	12	AM	3481	59	21	06	00
AM	3421	59	57	06	00	AM	3482	59	21	05	48
AM	3422	59	57	05	48	AM	3483	59	21	05	36
AM	3423	59	57	05	36	AM	3484	59	15	06	00
AM	3424	59	51	06	00	AM	3485	59	15	05	48
AM	3425	59	51	05	48	AM	3486	59	15	05	36
AM	3426	59	51	05	36	AM	3487	59	09	06	00
AM	3427	59	45	06	00	AM	3488	59	09	05	48
AM	3428	59	45	05	48	AM	3489	59	09	05	36
AM	3429	59	45	05	36	AM	3491	59	21	05	24
AM	3431	59	57	05	24	AM	3492	59	21	05	12
AM	3432	59	57	05	12	AM	3493	59	21	05	00
AM	3433	59	57	05	00	AM	3494	59	15	05	24
AM	3434	59	51	05	24	AM	3495	59	15	05	12
AM	3435	59	51	05	12	AM	3496	59	15	05	00
AM	3436	59	51	05	00	AM	3497	59	09	05	24
AM	3437	59	45	05	24	AM	3498	59	09	05	12
AM	3438	59	45	05	12	AM	3499	59	09	05	00
AM	3439	59	45	05	00	AM	3611	59	03	06	36
AM	3441	59	39	06	36	AM	3612	59	03	06	24
AM	3442	59	39	06	24	AM	3613	59	03	06	12
AM	3443	59	39	06	12	AM	3614	58	57	06	36
AM	3444	59	33	06	36	AM	3615	58	57	06	24
AM	3445	59	33	06	24	AM	3616	58	57	06	12
AM	3446	59	33	06	12	AM	3617	58	51	06	36
AM	3447	59	27	06	36	AM	3618	58	51	06	24
AM	3448	59	27	06	24	AM	3619	58	51	06	12
AM	3449	59	27	06	12	AM	3621	59	03	06	00
AM	3451	59	39	06	00	AM	3622	59	03	05	48
AM	3452	59	39	05	48	AM	3623	59	03	05	36
AM	3453	59	39	05	36	AM	3624	58	57	06	00
AM	3454	59	33	06	00	AM	3625	58	57	05	48
AM	3455	59	33	05	48	AM	3626	58	57	05	36
AM	3456	59	33	05	36	AM	3627	58	51	06	00
AM	3457	59	27	06	00	AM	3628	58	51	05	48
AM	3458	59	27	05	48	AM	3629	58	51	05	36
AM	3459	59	27	05	36	AM	3631	59	03	05	24
AM	3461	59	39	05	24	AM	3632	59	03	05	12
AM	3462	59	39	05	12	AM	3633	59	03	05	00
AM	3463	59	39	05	00	AM	3634	58	57	05	24
AM	3464	59	33	05	24	AM	3635	58	57	05	12
AM	3465	59	33	05	12	AM	3636	58	57	05	00

	Square	Lat	N	Long	W		Square	Lat	N	Long	W
AM	3637	58	51	05	24	AM	3698	58	15	05	12
AM	3638	58	51	05	12	AM	3699	58	15	05	00
AM	3639	58	51	05	00	AN	0111	57	15	03	00
AM	3641	58	45	06	36	AN	0112	57	15	02	48
AM	3642	58	45	06	24	AN	0113	57	15	02	36
AM	3643	58	45	06	12	AN	0114	57	9	03	00
AM	3644	58	39	06	36	AN	0115	57	9	02	48
AM	3645	58	39	06	24	AN	0116	57	9	02	36
AM	3646	58	39	06	12	AN	0117	57	03	03	00
AM	3647	58	33	06	36	AN	0118	57	03	02	48
AM	3648	58	33	06	24	AN	0119	57	03	02	36
AM	3649	58	33	06	12	AN	0121	57	15	02	24
AM	3651	58	45	06	00	AN	0122	57	15	02	12
AM	3652	58	45	05	48	AN	0123	57	15	02	00
AM	3653	58	45	05	36	AN	0124	57	09	02	24
AM	3654	58	39	06	00	AN	0125	57	09	02	12
AM	3655	58	39	05	48	AN	0126	57	09	02	00
AM	3656	58	39	05	36	AN	0127	57	03	02	24
AM	3657	58	33	06	00	AN	0128	57	03	02	12
AM	3658	58	33	05	48	AN	0129	57	03	02	00
AM	3659	58	33	05	36	AN	0131	57	15	01	48
AM	3661	58	45	05	24	AN	0132	57	15	01	36
AM	3662	58	45	05	12	AN	0133	57	15	01	24
AM	3663	58	45	05	00	AN	0134	57	09	01	48
AM	3664	58	39	05	24	AN	0135	57	09	01	36
AM	3665	58	39	05	12	AN	0136	57	09	01	24
AM	3666	58	39	05	00	AN	0137	57	03	01	48
AM	3667	58	33	05	24	AN	0138	57	03	01	36
AM	3668	58	33	05	12	AN	0139	57	03	01	24
AM	3669	58	33	05	00	AN	0141	56	57	03	00
AM	3671	58	27	06	36	AN	0142	56	57	02	48
AM	3672	58	27	06	24	AN	0143	56	57	02	36
AM	3673	58	27	06	12	AN	0144	56	51	03	00
AM	3674	58	21	06	36	AN	0145	56	51	02	48
AM	3675	58	21	06	24	AN	0146	56	51	02	36
AM	3676	58	21	06	12	AN	0147	56	45	03	00
AM	3677	58	15	06	36	AN	0148	56	45	02	48
AM	3678	58	15	06	24	AN	0149	56	45	02	36
AM	3679	58	15	06	12	AN	0151	56	57	02	24
AM	3681	58	27	06	00	AN	0152	56	57	02	12
AM	3682	58	27	05	48	AN	0153	56	57	02	00
AM	3683	58	27	05	36	AN	0154	56	51	02	24
AM	3684	58	21	06	00	AN	0155	56	51	02	12
AM	3685	58	21	05	48	AN	0156	56	51	02	00
AM	3686	58	21	05	36	AN	0157	56	45	04	42
AM	3687	58	15	06	00	AN	0158	56	45	02	12
AM	3688	58	15	05	48	AN	0159	56	45	02	00
AM	3689	58	15	05	36	AN	0161	56	57	01	48
AM	3691	58	27	05	24	AN	0162	56	57	01	36
AM	3692	58	27	05	12	AN	0163	56	57	01	24
AM	3693	58	27	05	00	AN	0164	56	51	01	48
AM	3694	58	21	05	24	AN	0165	56	51	01	36
AM	3695	58	21	05	12	AN	0166	56	51	01	24
AM	3696	58	21	05	00	AN	0167	56	45	01	48
AM	3697	58	15	05	24	AN	0168	56	45	01	36

Square	Lat	N	Long	W		Square	Lat	N	Long	W
AN	0169	56	45	01	24	AN	0541	56	03	03	55
AN	0171	56	39	03	00	AN	0542	56	03	03	45
AN	0172	56	39	02	48	AN	0543	56	03	03	35
AN	0173	56	39	02	36	AN	0544	55	57	03	55
AN	0174	56	33	03	00	AN	0545	55	57	03	45
AN	0175	56	33	02	48	AN	0546	55	57	03	35
AN	0176	56	33	02	36	AN	0547	55	51	03	55
AN	0177	56	27	03	00	AN	0548	55	51	03	45
AN	0178	56	27	02	48	AN	0549	55	51	03	35
AN	0179	56	27	02	36	AN	0551	56	03	03	25
AN	0181	56	39	02	24	AN	0552	56	03	03	15
AN	0182	56	39	02	12	AN	0553	56	03	03	05
AN	0183	56	39	02	00	AN	0554	55	57	03	25
AN	0184	56	33	02	24	AN	0555	55	57	03	15
AN	0185	56	33	02	12	AN	0556	55	57	03	05
AN	0186	56	33	02	00	AN	0557	55	51	03	25
AN	0187	56	27	02	24	AN	0558	55	51	03	15
AN	0188	56	27	02	12	AN	0559	55	51	03	05
AN	0189	56	27	02	00	AN	0561	56	03	02	55
AN	0191	56	39	01	48	AN	0562	56	03	02	45
AN	0192	56	39	01	36	AN	0563	56	03	02	35
AN	0193	56	39	01	24	AN	0564	55	57	02	55
AN	0194	56	33	01	48	AN	0565	55	57	02	45
AN	0195	56	33	01	36	AN	0566	55	57	02	35
AN	0196	56	33	01	24	AN	0567	55	51	02	55
AN	0197	56	27	01	48	AN	0568	55	51	02	45
AN	0198	56	27	01	36	AN	0569	55	51	02	35
AN	0199	56	27	01	24	AN	0571	55	45	03	55
AN	0511	56	21	03	55	AN	0572	55	45	03	45
AN	0512	56	21	03	45	AN	0573	55	45	03	35
AN	0513	56	21	03	35	AN	0574	55	39	03	55
AN	0514	56	15	03	55	AN	0575	55	39	03	45
AN	0515	56	15	03	45	AN	0576	55	39	03	35
AN	0516	56	15	03	35	AN	0577	55	33	03	55
AN	0517	56	09	03	55	AN	0578	55	33	03	45
AN	0518	56	09	03	45	AN	0579	55	33	03	35
AN	0519	56	09	03	35	AN	0581	55	45	03	25
AN	0521	56	21	03	25	AN	0582	55	45	03	15
AN	0522	56	21	03	15	AN	0583	55	45	03	05
AN	0523	56	21	03	05	AN	0584	55	39	03	25
AN	0524	56	15	03	25	AN	0585	55	39	03	15
AN	0525	56	15	03	15	AN	0586	55	39	03	05
AN	0526	56	15	03	05	AN	0587	55	33	03	25
AN	0527	56	09	03	25	AN	0588	55	33	03	15
AN	0528	56	09	03	15	AN	0589	55	33	03	05
AN	0529	56	09	03	05	AN	0591	55	45	02	55
AN	0531	56	21	02	55	AN	0592	55	45	02	45
AN	0532	56	21	02	45	AN	0593	55	45	02	35
AN	0533	56	21	02	35	AN	0594	55	39	02	55
AN	0534	56	15	02	55	AN	0595	55	39	02	45
AN	0535	56	15	02	45	AN	0596	55	39	02	35
AN	0536	56	15	02	35	AN	0597	55	33	02	55
AN	0537	56	09	02	55	AN	0598	55	33	02	45
AN	0538	56	09	02	45	AN	0599	55	33	02	35
AN	0539	56	09	02	35	AN	1111	60	51	04	48

	Square	Lat	N	Long	W		Square	Lat	N	Long	W
AN	1112	60	51	04	36	AN	1173	60	15	04	24
AN	1113	60	51	04	24	AN	1174	60	09	04	48
AN	1114	60	45	04	48	AN	1175	60	09	04	36
AN	1115	60	45	04	36	AN	1176	60	09	04	24
AN	1116	60	45	04	24	AN	1177	60	03	04	48
AN	1117	60	39	04	48	AN	1178	60	03	04	36
AN	1118	60	39	04	36	AN	1179	60	03	04	24
AN	1119	60	39	04	24	AN	1181	60	15	04	12
AN	1121	60	51	04	12	AN	1182	60	15	04	00
AN	1122	60	51	04	00	AN	1183	60	15	03	48
AN	1123	60	51	03	48	AN	1184	60	09	04	12
AN	1124	60	45	04	12	AN	1185	60	09	04	00
AN	1125	60	45	04	00	AN	1186	60	09	03	48
AN	1126	60	45	03	48	AN	1187	60	03	04	12
AN	1127	60	39	04	12	AN	1188	60	03	04	00
AN	1128	60	39	04	00	AN	1189	60	03	03	48
AN	1129	60	39	03	48	AN	1191	60	15	03	36
AN	1131	60	51	03	36	AN	1192	60	15	03	24
AN	1132	60	51	03	24	AN	1193	60	15	03	12
AN	1133	60	51	03	12	AN	1194	60	09	03	36
AN	1134	60	45	03	36	AN	1195	60	09	03	24
AN	1135	60	45	03	24	AN	1196	60	09	03	12
AN	1136	60	45	03	12	AN	1197	60	03	03	36
AN	1137	60	39	03	36	AN	1198	60	03	03	24
AN	1138	60	39	03	24	AN	1199	60	03	03	12
AN	1139	60	39	03	12	AN	1211	60	51	03	00
AN	1141	60	33	04	48	AN	1212	60	51	02	48
AN	1142	60	33	04	36	AN	1213	60	51	02	36
AN	1143	60	33	04	24	AN	1214	60	45	03	00
AN	1144	60	27	04	48	AN	1215	60	45	02	48
AN	1145	60	27	04	36	AN	1216	60	45	02	36
AN	1146	60	27	04	24	AN	1217	60	39	03	00
AN	1147	60	21	04	48	AN	1218	60	39	02	48
AN	1148	60	21	04	36	AN	1219	60	39	02	36
AN	1149	60	21	04	24	AN	1221	60	51	02	24
AN	1151	60	33	04	12	AN	1222	60	51	02	12
AN	1152	60	33	03	48	AN	1223	60	51	02	00
AN	1153	60	33	03	48	AN	1224	60	45	02	24
AN	1154	60	27	04	12	AN	1225	60	45	02	12
AN	1155	60	27	04	00	AN	1226	60	45	02	00
AN	1156	60	27	03	48	AN	1227	60	39	02	24
AN	1157	60	21	04	12	AN	1228	60	39	02	12
AN	1158	60	21	04	00	AN	1229	60	39	02	00
AN	1159	60	21	03	48	AN	1231	60	51	01	48
AN	1161	60	33	03	36	AN	1232	60	51	01	36
AN	1162	60	33	03	24	AN	1233	60	51	01	24
AN	1163	60	33	03	12	AN	1234	60	45	01	48
AN	1164	60	27	03	36	AN	1235	60	45	01	36
AN	1165	60	27	03	24	AN	1236	60	45	01	24
AN	1166	60	27	03	12	AN	1237	60	39	01	48
AN	1167	60	21	03	36	AN	1238	60	39	01	36
AN	1168	60	21	03	24	AN	1239	60	39	01	24
AN	1169	60	21	03	12	AN	1241	60	33	03	00
AN	1171	60	15	04	48	AN	1242	60	33	02	48
AN	1172	60	15	04	36	AN	1243	60	33	02	36

	Square	Lat	N	Long	W		Square	Lat	N	Long	W
AN	1244	60	27	03	00	AN	1315	59	51	04	36
AN	1245	60	27	02	48	AN	1316	59	51	04	24
AN	1246	60	27	02	36	AN	1317	59	45	04	48
AN	1247	60	21	03	00	AN	1318	59	45	04	36
AN	1248	60	21	02	48	AN	1319	59	45	04	24
AN	1249	60	21	02	36	AN	1321	59	57	04	12
AN	1251	60	33	02	24	AN	1322	59	57	04	00
AN	1252	60	33	02	12	AN	1323	59	57	03	48
AN	1253	60	33	02	00	AN	1324	59	51	04	12
AN	1254	60	27	02	24	AN	1325	59	51	04	00
AN	1255	60	27	02	12	AN	1326	59	51	03	48
AN	1256	60	27	02	00	AN	1327	59	45	04	12
AN	1257	60	21	04	42	AN	1328	59	45	04	00
AN	1258	60	21	02	12	AN	1329	59	45	03	48
AN	1259	60	21	02	00	AN	1331	59	57	03	36
AN	1261	60	33	01	48	AN	1332	59	57	03	24
AN	1262	60	33	01	36	AN	1333	59	57	03	12
AN	1263	60	33	01	24	AN	1334	59	51	03	36
AN	1264	60	27	01	48	AN	1335	59	51	03	24
AN	1265	60	27	01	36	AN	1336	59	51	03	12
AN	1266	60	27	01	24	AN	1337	59	45	03	36
AN	1267	60	21	01	48	AN	1338	59	45	03	24
AN	1268	60	21	01	36	AN	1339	59	45	03	12
AN	1269	60	21	01	24	AN	1341	59	39	04	48
AN	1271	60	15	03	00	AN	1342	59	39	04	36
AN	1272	60	15	02	48	AN	1343	59	39	04	24
AN	1273	60	15	02	36	AN	1344	59	33	04	48
AN	1274	60	09	03	00	AN	1345	59	33	04	36
AN	1275	60	09	02	48	AN	1346	59	33	04	24
AN	1276	60	09	02	36	AN	1347	59	27	04	48
AN	1277	60	03	03	00	AN	1348	59	27	04	36
AN	1278	60	03	02	48	AN	1349	59	27	04	24
AN	1279	60	03	02	36	AN	1351	59	39	04	12
AN	1281	60	15	02	24	AN	1352	59	39	03	48
AN	1282	60	15	02	12	AN	1353	59	39	03	48
AN	1283	60	15	02	00	AN	1354	59	33	04	12
AN	1284	60	09	02	24	AN	1355	59	33	04	00
AN	1285	60	09	02	12	AN	1356	59	33	03	48
AN	1286	60	09	02	0	AN	1357	59	27	04	12
AN	1287	60	03	02	24	AN	1358	59	27	04	00
AN	1288	60	03	02	12	AN	1359	59	27	03	48
AN	1289	60	03	02	00	AN	1361	59	39	03	36
AN	1291	60	15	01	48	AN	1362	59	39	03	24
AN	1292	60	15	01	36	AN	1363	59	39	03	12
AN	1293	60	15	01	24	AN	1364	59	33	03	36
AN	1294	60	09	01	48	AN	1365	59	33	03	24
AN	1295	60	09	01	36	AN	1366	59	33	03	12
AN	1296	60	09	01	24	AN	1367	59	27	03	36
AN	1297	60	03	01	48	AN	1368	59	27	03	24
AN	1298	60	03	01	36	AN	1369	59	27	03	12
AN	1299	60	03	01	24	AN	1371	59	21	04	48
AN	1311	59	57	04	48	AN	1372	59	21	04	36
AN	1312	59	57	04	36	AN	1373	59	21	04	24
AN	1313	59	57	04	24	AN	1374	59	15	04	48
AN	1314	59	51	04	48	AN	1375	59	15	04	36

	Square	Lat	N	Long	W		Square	Lat	N	Long	W
AN	1376	59	15	04	24	AN	1447	59	27	03	00
AN	1377	59	09	04	48	AN	1448	59	27	02	48
AN	1378	59	09	04	36	AN	1449	59	27	02	36
AN	1379	59	09	04	24	AN	1451	59	39	02	24
AN	1381	59	21	04	12	AN	1452	59	39	02	12
AN	1382	59	21	04	00	AN	1453	59	39	02	00
AN	1383	59	21	03	48	AN	1454	59	33	02	24
AN	1384	59	15	04	12	AN	1455	59	33	02	12
AN	1385	59	15	04	00	AN	1456	59	33	02	00
AN	1386	59	15	03	48	AN	1457	59	27	04	42
AN	1387	59	09	04	12	AN	1458	59	27	02	12
AN	1388	59	09	04	00	AN	1459	59	27	02	00
AN	1389	59	09	03	48	AN	1461	59	39	01	48
AN	1391	59	21	03	36	AN	1462	59	39	01	36
AN	1392	59	21	03	24	AN	1463	59	39	01	24
AN	1393	59	21	03	12	AN	1464	59	33	01	48
AN	1394	59	15	03	36	AN	1465	59	33	01	36
AN	1395	59	15	03	24	AN	1466	59	33	01	24
AN	1396	59	15	03	12	AN	1467	59	27	01	48
AN	1397	59	09	03	36	AN	1468	59	27	01	36
AN	1398	59	09	03	24	AN	1469	59	27	01	24
AN	1399	59	09	03	12	AN	1471	59	21	03	00
AN	1411	59	57	03	00	AN	1472	59	21	02	48
AN	1412	59	57	02	48	AN	1473	59	21	02	36
AN	1413	59	57	02	36	AN	1474	59	15	03	00
AN	1414	59	51	03	00	AN	1475	59	15	02	48
AN	1415	59	51	02	48	AN	1476	59	15	02	36
AN	1416	59	51	02	36	AN	1477	59	09	03	00
AN	1417	59	45	03	00	AN	1478	59	09	02	48
AN	1418	59	45	02	48	AN	1479	59	09	02	36
AN	1419	59	45	02	36	AN	1481	59	21	02	24
AN	1421	59	57	02	24	AN	1482	59	21	02	12
AN	1422	59	57	02	12	AN	1483	59	21	02	00
AN	1423	59	57	02	00	AN	1484	59	15	02	24
AN	1424	59	51	02	24	AN	1485	59	15	02	12
AN	1425	59	51	02	12	AN	1486	59	15	02	00
AN	1426	59	51	02	00	AN	1487	59	09	02	24
AN	1427	59	45	02	24	AN	1488	59	09	02	12
AN	1428	59	45	02	12	AN	1489	59	09	02	00
AN	1429	59	45	02	00	AN	1491	59	21	01	48
AN	1431	59	57	01	48	AN	1492	59	21	01	36
AN	1432	59	57	01	36	AN	1493	59	21	01	24
AN	1433	59	57	01	24	AN	1494	59	15	01	48
AN	1434	59	51	01	48	AN	1495	59	15	01	36
AN	1435	59	51	01	36	AN	1496	59	15	01	24
AN	1436	59	51	01	24	AN	1497	59	09	01	48
AN	1437	59	45	01	48	AN	1498	59	09	01	36
AN	1438	59	45	01	36	AN	1499	59	09	01	24
AN	1439	59	45	01	24	AN	1511	59	03	04	48
AN	1441	59	39	03	00	AN	1512	59	03	04	36
AN	1442	59	39	02	48	AN	1513	59	03	04	24
AN	1443	59	39	02	36	AN	1514	58	57	04	48
AN	1444	59	33	03	00	AN	1515	58	57	04	36
AN	1445	59	33	02	48	AN	1516	58	57	04	24
AN	1446	59	33	02	36	AN	1517	58	51	04	48

	Square	Lat	N	Long	W		Square	Lat	N	Long	W
AN	1518	58	51	04	36	AN	1579	58	15	04	24
AN	1519	58	51	04	24	AN	1581	58	27	04	12
AN	1521	59	03	04	12	AN	1582	58	27	04	00
AN	1522	59	03	04	00	AN	1583	58	27	03	48
AN	1523	59	03	03	48	AN	1584	58	21	04	12
AN	1524	58	57	04	12	AN	1585	58	21	04	00
AN	1525	58	57	04	00	AN	1586	58	21	03	48
AN	1526	58	57	03	48	AN	1587	58	15	04	12
AN	1527	58	51	04	12	AN	1588	58	15	04	00
AN	1528	58	51	04	00	AN	1589	58	15	03	48
AN	1529	58	51	03	48	AN	1591	58	27	03	36
AN	1531	59	03	03	36	AN	1592	58	27	03	24
AN	1532	59	03	03	24	AN	1593	58	27	03	12
AN	1533	59	03	03	12	AN	1594	58	21	03	36
AN	1534	58	57	03	36	AN	1595	58	21	03	24
AN	1535	58	57	03	24	AN	1596	58	21	03	12
AN	1536	58	57	03	12	AN	1597	58	15	03	36
AN	1537	58	51	03	36	AN	1598	58	15	03	24
AN	1538	58	51	03	24	AN	1599	58	15	03	12
AN	1539	58	51	03	12	AN	1611	59	03	03	00
AN	1541	58	45	04	48	AN	1612	59	03	02	54
AN	1542	58	45	04	36	AN	1613	59	03	02	36
AN	1543	58	45	04	24	AN	1614	58	57	03	00
AN	1544	58	39	04	48	AN	1615	58	57	02	48
AN	1545	58	39	04	36	AN	1616	58	57	02	36
AN	1546	58	39	04	24	AN	1617	58	51	03	00
AN	1547	58	33	04	48	AN	1618	58	51	02	48
AN	1548	58	33	04	36	AN	1619	58	51	02	36
AN	1549	58	33	04	24	AN	1621	59	03	02	24
AN	1551	58	45	04	12	AN	1622	59	03	02	12
AN	1552	58	45	03	48	AN	1623	59	03	02	00
AN	1553	58	45	03	48	AN	1624	58	57	02	24
AN	1554	58	39	04	12	AN	1625	58	57	02	12
AN	1555	58	39	04	00	AN	1626	58	57	02	00
AN	1556	58	39	03	48	AN	1627	58	51	02	24
AN	1557	58	33	04	12	AN	1628	58	51	02	12
AN	1558	58	33	04	00	AN	1629	58	51	02	00
AN	1559	58	33	03	48	AN	1631	59	03	01	48
AN	1561	58	45	03	36	AN	1632	59	03	01	36
AN	1562	58	45	03	24	AN	1633	59	03	01	24
AN	1563	58	45	03	12	AN	1634	58	57	01	48
AN	1564	58	39	03	36	AN	1635	58	57	01	36
AN	1565	58	39	03	24	AN	1636	58	57	01	24
AN	1566	58	39	03	12	AN	1637	58	51	01	48
AN	1567	58	33	03	36	AN	1638	58	51	01	36
AN	1568	58	33	03	24	AN	1639	58	51	01	24
AN	1569	58	33	03	12	AN	1641	58	45	03	00
AN	1571	58	27	04	48	AN	1642	58	45	02	48
AN	1572	58	27	04	36	AN	1643	58	45	02	36
AN	1573	58	27	04	24	AN	1644	58	39	03	00
AN	1574	58	21	04	48	AN	1645	58	39	02	48
AN	1575	58	21	04	36	AN	1646	58	39	02	36
AN	1576	58	21	04	24	AN	1647	58	33	03	00
AN	1577	58	15	04	48	AN	1648	58	33	02	48
AN	1578	58	15	04	36	AN	1649	58	33	02	36

	Square	Lat	N	Long	W		Square	Lat	N	Long	W
AN	1651	58	45	02	24	AN	1722	58	09	04	00
AN	1652	58	45	02	12	AN	1723	58	09	03	48
AN	1653	58	45	02	00	AN	1724	58	03	04	12
AN	1654	58	39	02	24	AN	1725	58	03	04	00
AN	1655	58	39	02	12	AN	1726	58	03	03	48
AN	1656	58	39	02	00	AN	1727	57	57	04	12
AN	1657	58	33	04	42	AN	1728	57	57	04	00
AN	1658	58	33	02	12	AN	1729	57	57	03	48
AN	1659	58	33	02	00	AN	1731	58	09	03	36
AN	1661	58	45	01	48	AN	1732	58	09	03	24
AN	1662	58	45	01	36	AN	1733	58	09	03	12
AN	1663	58	45	01	24	AN	1734	58	03	03	36
AN	1664	58	39	01	48	AN	1735	58	03	03	24
AN	1665	58	39	01	36	AN	1736	58	3	03	12
AN	1666	58	39	01	24	AN	1737	57	57	03	36
AN	1667	58	33	01	48	AN	1738	57	57	03	24
AN	1668	58	33	01	36	AN	1739	57	57	03	12
AN	1669	58	33	01	24	AN	1741	57	51	04	48
AN	1671	58	27	03	00	AN	1742	57	51	04	36
AN	1672	58	27	02	48	AN	1743	57	51	04	24
AN	1673	58	27	02	36	AN	1744	57	45	04	48
AN	1674	58	21	03	00	AN	1745	57	45	04	36
AN	1675	58	21	02	48	AN	1746	57	45	04	24
AN	1676	58	21	02	36	AN	1747	57	39	04	48
AN	1677	58	15	03	00	AN	1748	57	39	04	36
AN	1678	58	15	02	48	AN	1749	57	39	04	24
AN	1679	58	15	02	36	AN	1751	57	51	04	12
AN	1681	58	27	02	24	AN	1752	57	51	03	48
AN	1682	58	27	02	12	AN	1753	57	51	03	48
AN	1683	58	27	02	00	AN	1754	57	45	04	12
AN	1684	58	21	02	24	AN	1755	57	45	04	00
AN	1685	58	21	02	12	AN	1756	57	45	03	48
AN	1686	58	21	02	00	AN	1757	57	39	04	12
AN	1687	58	15	02	24	AN	1758	57	39	04	00
AN	1688	58	15	02	12	AN	1759	57	39	03	48
AN	1689	58	15	02	00	AN	1761	57	51	03	36
AN	1691	58	27	01	48	AN	1762	57	51	03	24
AN	1692	58	27	01	36	AN	1763	57	51	03	12
AN	1693	58	27	01	24	AN	1764	57	45	03	36
AN	1694	58	21	01	48	AN	1765	57	45	03	24
AN	1695	58	21	01	36	AN	1766	57	45	03	12
AN	1696	58	21	01	24	AN	1767	57	39	03	36
AN	1697	58	15	01	48	AN	1768	57	39	03	24
AN	1698	58	15	01	36	AN	1769	57	39	03	12
AN	1699	58	15	01	24	AN	1771	57	33	04	48
AN	1711	58	09	04	48	AN	1772	57	33	04	36
AN	1712	58	09	04	36	AN	1773	57	33	04	24
AN	1713	58	09	04	24	AN	1774	57	27	04	48
AN	1714	58	03	04	48	AN	1775	57	27	04	36
AN	1715	58	03	04	36	AN	1776	57	27	04	24
AN	1716	58	03	04	24	AN	1777	57	21	04	48
AN	1717	57	57	04	48	AN	1778	57	21	04	36
AN	1718	57	57	04	36	AN	1779	57	21	04	24
AN	1719	57	57	04	24	AN	1781	57	33	04	12
AN	1721	58	09	04	12	AN	1782	57	33	04	00

	Square	Lat	N	Long	W		Square	Lat	N	Long	W
AN	1783	57	33	03	48	AN	1854	57	45	02	24
AN	1784	57	27	04	12	AN	1855	57	45	02	12
AN	1785	57	27	04	00	AN	1856	57	45	02	00
AN	1786	57	27	03	48	AN	1857	57	39	04	42
AN	1787	57	21	04	12	AN	1858	57	39	02	12
AN	1788	57	21	04	00	AN	1859	57	39	02	00
AN	1789	57	21	03	48	AN	1861	57	51	01	48
AN	1791	57	33	03	36	AN	1862	57	51	01	36
AN	1792	57	33	03	24	AN	1863	57	51	01	24
AN	1793	57	33	03	12	AN	1864	57	45	01	48
AN	1794	57	27	03	36	AN	1865	57	45	01	36
AN	1795	57	27	03	24	AN	1866	57	45	01	24
AN	1796	57	27	03	12	AN	1867	57	39	01	48
AN	1797	57	21	03	36	AN	1868	57	39	01	36
AN	1798	57	21	03	24	AN	1869	57	39	01	24
AN	1799	57	21	03	12	AN	1871	57	33	03	00
AN	1811	58	09	03	00	AN	1872	57	33	02	48
AN	1812	58	09	02	48	AN	1873	57	33	02	36
AN	1813	58	09	02	36	AN	1874	57	27	03	00
AN	1814	58	03	03	00	AN	1875	57	27	02	48
AN	1815	58	03	02	48	AN	1876	57	27	02	36
AN	1816	58	03	02	36	AN	1877	57	21	03	00
AN	1817	57	57	03	00	AN	1878	57	21	02	48
AN	1818	57	57	02	48	AN	1879	57	21	02	36
AN	1819	57	57	02	36	AN	1881	57	33	02	24
AN	1821	58	09	02	24	AN	1882	57	33	02	12
AN	1822	58	09	02	12	AN	1883	57	33	02	00
AN	1823	58	09	02	00	AN	1884	57	27	02	24
AN	1824	58	03	02	24	AN	1885	57	27	02	12
AN	1825	58	03	02	12	AN	1886	57	27	02	00
AN	1826	58	03	02	00	AN	1887	57	21	02	24
AN	1827	57	57	02	24	AN	1888	57	21	02	12
AN	1828	57	57	02	12	AN	1889	57	21	02	00
AN	1829	57	57	02	00	AN	1891	57	33	01	48
AN	1831	58	09	01	48	AN	1892	57	33	01	36
AN	1832	58	09	01	36	AN	1893	57	33	01	24
AN	1833	58	09	01	24	AN	1894	57	27	01	48
AN	1834	58	03	01	48	AN	1895	57	27	01	36
AN	1835	58	03	01	36	AN	1896	57	27	01	24
AN	1836	58	03	01	24	AN	1897	57	21	01	48
AN	1837	57	57	01	48	AN	1898	57	21	01	36
AN	1838	57	57	01	36	AN	1899	57	21	01	24
AN	1839	57	57	01	24	AN	2111	60	51	01	12
AN	1841	57	51	03	00	AN	2112	60	51	01	00
AN	1842	57	51	02	48	AN	2113	60	51	00	48
AN	1843	57	51	02	36	AN	2114	60	45	01	12
AN	1844	57	45	03	00	AN	2115	60	45	01	00
AN	1845	57	45	02	48	AN	2116	60	45	00	48
AN	1846	57	45	02	36	AN	2117	60	39	01	12
AN	1847	57	39	03	00	AN	2118	60	39	01	00
AN	1848	57	39	02	48	AN	2119	60	39	00	48
AN	1849	57	39	02	36	AN	2121	60	51	00	36
AN	1851	57	51	02	24	AN	2122	60	51	00	24
AN	1852	57	51	02	12	AN	2123	60	51	00	12
AN	1853	57	51	02	00	AN	2124	60	45	00	36

	Square	Lat	N	Long	W		Square	Lat	N	Long	W
AN	2125	60	45	00	24	AN	2186	60	09	00	12
AN	2126	60	45	00	12	AN	2187	60	03	00	36
AN	2127	60	39	00	36	AN	2188	60	03	00	24
AN	2128	60	39	00	24	AN	2189	60	03	00	12
AN	2129	60	39	00	12	AN	2191	60	15	00	00
AN	2131	60	51	00	00	AN	2192	60	15	00	-12
AN	2132	60	51	00	-12	AN	2193	60	15	00	-24
AN	2133	60	51	00	-24	AN	2194	60	09	00	00
AN	2134	60	45	00	00	AN	2195	60	09	00	-12
AN	2135	60	45	00	-12	AN	2196	60	09	00	-24
AN	2136	60	45	00	-24	AN	2197	60	03	00	00
AN	2137	60	39	00	00	AN	2198	60	03	00	-12
AN	2138	60	39	00	-12	AN	2199	60	03	00	-24
AN	2139	60	39	00	-24	AN	2611	59	57	01	12
AN	2141	60	33	01	12	AN	2612	59	57	01	00
AN	2142	60	33	01	00	AN	2613	59	57	00	48
AN	2143	60	33	00	48	AN	2614	59	51	01	12
AN	2144	60	27	01	12	AN	2615	59	51	01	00
AN	2145	60	27	01	00	AN	2616	59	51	00	48
AN	2146	60	27	00	48	AN	2617	59	45	01	12
AN	2147	60	21	01	12	AN	2618	59	45	01	00
AN	2148	60	21	01	00	AN	2619	59	45	00	48
AN	2149	60	21	00	48	AN	2621	59	57	00	36
AN	2151	60	33	00	36	AN	2622	59	57	00	24
AN	2152	60	33	00	24	AN	2623	59	57	00	12
AN	2153	60	33	00	12	AN	2624	59	51	00	36
AN	2154	60	27	00	36	AN	2625	59	51	00	24
AN	2155	60	27	00	24	AN	2626	59	51	00	12
AN	2156	60	27	00	12	AN	2627	59	45	00	36
AN	2157	60	21	00	36	AN	2628	59	45	00	24
AN	2158	60	21	00	24	AN	2629	59	45	00	12
AN	2159	60	21	00	12	AN	2631	59	57	00	00
AN	2161	60	33	00	00	AN	2632	59	57	00	-12
AN	2162	60	33	00	-12	AN	2633	59	57	00	-24
AN	2163	60	33	00	-24	AN	2634	59	51	00	00
AN	2164	60	27	00	00	AN	2635	59	51	00	-12
AN	2165	60	27	00	-12	AN	2636	59	51	00	-24
AN	2166	60	27	00	-24	AN	2637	59	45	00	00
AN	2167	60	21	00	00	AN	2638	59	45	00	-12
AN	2168	60	21	00	-12	AN	2639	59	45	00	-24
AN	2169	60	21	00	-24	AN	2641	59	39	01	12
AN	2171	60	15	01	12	AN	2642	59	39	01	00
AN	2172	60	15	01	00	AN	2643	59	39	00	48
AN	2173	60	15	00	48	AN	2644	59	33	01	12
AN	2174	60	09	01	12	AN	2645	59	33	01	00
AN	2175	60	09	01	00	AN	2646	59	33	00	48
AN	2176	60	09	00	48	AN	2647	59	27	01	12
AN	2177	60	03	01	12	AN	2648	59	27	01	00
AN	2178	60	03	01	00	AN	2649	59	27	00	48
AN	2179	60	03	00	48	AN	2651	59	39	00	36
AN	2181	60	15	00	36	AN	2652	59	39	00	24
AN	2182	60	15	00	24	AN	2653	59	39	00	12
AN	2183	60	15	00	12	AN	2654	59	33	00	36
AN	2184	60	09	00	36	AN	2655	59	33	00	24
AN	2185	60	09	00	24	AN	2656	59	33	00	12

	Square	Lat	N	Long	W		Square	Lat	N	Long	W
AN	2657	59	27	00	36	AN	4128	58	51	00	24
AN	2658	59	27	00	24	AN	4129	58	51	00	12
AN	2659	59	27	00	12	AN	4131	59	03	00	00
AN	2661	59	39	00	00	AN	4132	59	03	00	-12
AN	2662	59	39	00	-12	AN	4133	59	03	00	-24
AN	2663	59	39	00	-24	AN	4134	58	57	00	00
AN	2664	59	33	00	00	AN	4135	58	57	00	-12
AN	2665	59	33	00	-12	AN	4136	58	57	00	-24
AN	2666	59	33	00	-24	AN	4137	58	51	00	00
AN	2667	59	27	00	00	AN	4138	58	51	00	-12
AN	2668	59	27	00	-12	AN	4139	58	51	00	-24
AN	2669	59	27	00	-24	AN	4141	58	45	01	12
AN	2671	59	21	01	12	AN	4142	58	45	01	00
AN	2672	59	21	01	00	AN	4143	58	45	00	48
AN	2673	59	21	00	48	AN	4144	58	39	01	12
AN	2674	59	15	01	12	AN	4145	58	39	01	00
AN	2675	59	15	01	00	AN	4146	58	39	00	48
AN	2676	59	15	00	48	AN	4147	58	33	01	12
AN	2677	59	09	01	12	AN	4148	58	33	01	00
AN	2678	59	09	01	00	AN	4149	58	33	00	48
AN	2679	59	09	00	48	AN	4151	58	45	00	36
AN	2681	59	21	00	36	AN	4152	58	45	00	24
AN	2682	59	21	00	24	AN	4153	58	45	00	12
AN	2683	59	21	00	12	AN	4154	58	39	00	36
AN	2684	59	15	00	36	AN	4155	58	39	00	24
AN	2685	59	15	00	24	AN	4156	58	39	00	12
AN	2686	59	15	00	12	AN	4157	58	33	00	36
AN	2687	59	09	00	36	AN	4158	58	33	00	24
AN	2688	59	09	00	24	AN	4159	58	33	00	12
AN	2689	59	09	00	12	AN	4161	58	45	00	00
AN	2691	59	21	00	00	AN	4162	58	45	00	-12
AN	2692	59	21	00	-12	AN	4163	58	45	00	-24
AN	2693	59	21	00	-24	AN	4164	58	39	00	00
AN	2694	59	15	00	00	AN	4165	58	39	00	-12
AN	2695	59	15	00	-12	AN	4166	58	39	00	-24
AN	2696	59	15	00	-24	AN	4167	58	33	00	00
AN	2697	59	09	00	00	AN	4168	58	33	00	-12
AN	2698	59	09	00	-12	AN	4169	58	33	00	-24
AN	2699	59	09	00	-24	AN	4171	58	27	01	12
AN	4111	59	03	01	12	AN	4172	58	27	01	00
AN	4112	59	03	01	00	AN	4173	58	27	00	48
AN	4113	59	03	00	48	AN	4174	58	21	01	12
AN	4114	58	57	01	12	AN	4175	58	21	01	00
AN	4115	58	57	01	00	AN	4176	58	21	00	48
AN	4116	58	57	00	48	AN	4177	58	15	01	12
AN	4117	58	51	01	12	AN	4178	58	15	01	00
AN	4118	58	51	01	00	AN	4179	58	15	00	48
AN	4119	58	51	00	48	AN	4181	58	27	00	36
AN	4121	59	03	00	36	AN	4182	58	27	00	24
AN	4122	59	03	00	24	AN	4183	58	27	00	12
AN	4123	59	03	00	12	AN	4184	58	21	00	36
AN	4124	58	57	00	36	AN	4185	58	21	00	24
AN	4125	58	57	00	24	AN	4186	58	21	00	12
AN	4126	58	57	00	12	AN	4187	58	15	00	36
AN	4127	58	51	00	36	AN	4188	58	15	00	24

	Square	Lat	N	Long	W		Square	Lat	N	Long	W
AN	4189	58	15	00	12	AN	4461	57	51	00	00
AN	4191	58	27	00	00	AN	4462	57	51	00	-12
AN	4192	58	27	00	-12	AN	4463	57	51	00	-24
AN	4193	58	27	00	-24	AN	4464	57	45	00	00
AN	4194	58	21	00	00	AN	4465	57	45	00	-12
AN	4195	58	21	00	-12	AN	4466	57	45	00	-24
AN	4196	58	21	00	-24	AN	4467	57	39	00	00
AN	4197	58	15	00	00	AN	4468	57	39	00	-12
AN	4198	58	15	00	-12	AN	4469	57	39	00	-24
AN	4199	58	15	00	-24	AN	4471	57	33	01	12
AN	4411	58	09	01	12	AN	4472	57	33	01	00
AN	4412	58	09	01	00	AN	4473	57	33	00	48
AN	4413	58	09	00	48	AN	4474	57	27	01	12
AN	4414	58	03	01	12	AN	4475	57	27	01	00
AN	4415	58	03	01	00	AN	4476	57	27	00	48
AN	4416	58	03	00	48	AN	4477	57	21	01	12
AN	4417	57	57	01	12	AN	4478	57	21	01	00
AN	4418	57	57	01	00	AN	4479	57	21	00	48
AN	4419	57	57	00	48	AN	4481	57	33	00	36
AN	4421	58	09	00	36	AN	4482	57	33	00	24
AN	4422	58	09	00	24	AN	4483	57	33	00	12
AN	4423	58	09	00	12	AN	4484	57	27	00	36
AN	4424	58	03	00	36	AN	4485	57	27	00	24
AN	4425	58	03	00	24	AN	4486	57	27	00	12
AN	4426	58	03	00	12	AN	4487	57	21	00	36
AN	4427	57	57	00	36	AN	4488	57	21	00	24
AN	4428	57	57	00	24	AN	4489	57	21	00	12
AN	4429	57	57	00	12	AN	4491	57	33	00	00
AN	4431	58	09	00	00	AN	4492	57	33	00	-12
AN	4432	58	09	00	-12	AN	4493	57	33	00	-24
AN	4433	58	09	00	-24	AN	4494	57	27	00	00
AN	4434	58	03	00	00	AN	4495	57	27	00	-12
AN	4435	58	03	00	-12	AN	4496	57	27	00	-24
AN	4436	58	03	00	-24	AN	4497	57	21	00	00
AN	4437	57	57	00	00	AN	4498	57	21	00	-12
AN	4438	57	57	00	-12	AN	4499	57	21	00	-24
AN	4439	57	57	00	-24	AN	4711	57	15	01	12
AN	4441	57	51	01	12	AN	4712	57	15	01	00
AN	4442	57	51	01	00	AN	4713	57	15	00	48
AN	4443	57	51	00	48	AN	4714	57	9	01	12
AN	4444	57	45	01	12	AN	4715	57	9	01	00
AN	4445	57	45	01	00	AN	4716	57	9	00	48
AN	4446	57	45	00	48	AN	4717	57	3	01	12
AN	4447	57	39	01	12	AN	4718	57	3	01	00
AN	4448	57	39	01	00	AN	4719	57	3	00	48
AN	4449	57	39	00	48	AN	4721	57	15	00	36
AN	4451	57	51	00	36	AN	4722	57	15	00	24
AN	4452	57	51	00	24	AN	4723	57	15	00	12
AN	4453	57	51	00	12	AN	4724	57	9	00	36
AN	4454	57	45	00	36	AN	4725	57	9	00	24
AN	4455	57	45	00	24	AN	4726	57	9	00	12
AN	4456	57	45	00	12	AN	4727	57	3	00	36
AN	4457	57	39	00	36	AN	4728	57	3	00	24
AN	4458	57	39	00	24	AN	4729	57	3	00	12
AN	4459	57	39	00	12	AN	4731	57	15	00	00

	Square	Lat	N	Long	W		Square	Lat	N	Long	W
AN	4732	57	15	00	-12	AN	4793	56	39	00	-24
AN	4733	57	15	00	-24	AN	4794	56	33	00	00
AN	4734	57	9	00	00	AN	4795	56	33	00	-12
AN	4735	57	9	00	-12	AN	4796	56	33	00	-24
AN	4736	57	9	00	-24	AN	4797	56	27	00	00
AN	4737	57	3	00	00	AN	4798	56	27	00	-12
AN	4738	57	3	00	-12	AN	4799	56	27	00	-24
AN	4739	57	3	00	-24	AN	5111	56	21	02	25
AN	4741	56	57	01	12	AN	5112	56	21	02	15
AN	4742	56	57	01	00	AN	5113	56	21	02	05
AN	4743	56	57	00	48	AN	5114	56	15	02	25
AN	4744	56	51	01	12	AN	5115	56	15	02	15
AN	4745	56	51	01	00	AN	5116	56	15	02	05
AN	4746	56	51	00	48	AN	5117	56	09	02	25
AN	4747	56	45	01	12	AN	5118	56	09	02	15
AN	4748	56	45	01	00	AN	5119	56	09	02	05
AN	4749	56	45	00	48	AN	5121	56	21	01	55
AN	4751	56	57	00	36	AN	5122	56	21	01	45
AN	4752	56	57	00	24	AN	5123	56	21	01	35
AN	4753	56	57	00	12	AN	5124	56	15	01	55
AN	4754	56	51	00	36	AN	5125	56	15	01	45
AN	4755	56	51	00	24	AN	5126	56	15	01	35
AN	4756	56	51	00	12	AN	5127	56	09	01	55
AN	4757	56	45	00	36	AN	5128	56	09	01	45
AN	4758	56	45	00	24	AN	5129	56	09	01	35
AN	4759	56	45	00	12	AN	5131	56	21	01	25
AN	4761	56	57	00	00	AN	5132	56	21	01	15
AN	4762	56	57	00	-12	AN	5133	56	21	01	05
AN	4763	56	57	00	-24	AN	5134	56	15	01	25
AN	4764	56	51	00	00	AN	5135	56	15	01	15
AN	4765	56	51	00	-12	AN	5136	56	15	01	05
AN	4766	56	51	00	-24	AN	5137	56	09	01	25
AN	4767	56	45	00	00	AN	5138	56	09	01	15
AN	4768	56	45	00	-12	AN	5139	56	09	01	05
AN	4769	56	45	00	-24	AN	5141	56	03	02	25
AN	4771	56	39	01	12	AN	5142	56	03	02	15
AN	4772	56	39	01	00	AN	5143	56	03	02	05
AN	4773	56	39	00	48	AN	5144	55	57	02	25
AN	4774	56	33	01	12	AN	5145	55	57	02	15
AN	4775	56	33	01	00	AN	5146	55	57	02	05
AN	4776	56	33	00	48	AN	5147	55	51	02	25
AN	4777	56	27	01	12	AN	5148	55	51	02	15
AN	4778	56	27	01	00	AN	5149	55	51	02	05
AN	4779	56	27	00	48	AN	5151	56	03	01	55
AN	4781	56	39	00	36	AN	5152	56	03	01	45
AN	4782	56	39	00	24	AN	5153	56	03	01	35
AN	4783	56	39	00	12	AN	5154	55	57	01	55
AN	4784	56	33	00	36	AN	5155	55	57	01	45
AN	4785	56	33	00	24	AN	5156	55	57	01	35
AN	4786	56	33	00	12	AN	5157	55	51	01	55
AN	4787	56	27	00	36	AN	5158	55	51	01	45
AN	4788	56	27	00	24	AN	5159	55	51	01	35
AN	4789	56	27	00	12	AN	5161	56	03	01	25
AN	4791	56	39	00	00	AN	5162	56	03	01	15
AN	4792	56	39	00	-12	AN	5163	56	03	01	05

	Square	Lat	N	Long	W		Square	Lat	N	Long	W
AN	5164	55	57	01	25	AN	5235	56	15	00	-15
AN	5165	55	57	01	15	AN	5236	56	15	00	-25
AN	5166	55	57	01	05	AN	5237	56	9	00	-05
AN	5167	55	51	01	25	AN	5238	56	9	00	-15
AN	5168	55	51	01	15	AN	5239	56	9	00	-25
AN	5169	55	51	01	05	AN	5241	56	3	00	55
AN	5171	55	45	02	25	AN	5242	56	3	00	45
AN	5172	55	45	02	15	AN	5243	56	3	00	35
AN	5173	55	45	02	05	AN	5244	55	57	00	55
AN	5174	55	39	02	25	AN	5245	55	57	00	45
AN	5175	55	39	02	15	AN	5246	55	57	00	35
AN	5176	55	39	02	05	AN	5247	55	51	00	55
AN	5177	55	33	02	25	AN	5248	55	51	00	45
AN	5178	55	33	02	15	AN	5249	55	51	00	35
AN	5179	55	33	02	05	AN	5251	56	3	00	25
AN	5181	55	45	01	55	AN	5252	56	3	00	15
AN	5182	55	45	01	45	AN	5253	56	3	00	05
AN	5183	55	45	01	35	AN	5254	55	57	00	25
AN	5184	55	39	01	55	AN	5255	55	57	00	15
AN	5185	55	39	01	45	AN	5256	55	57	00	05
AN	5186	55	39	01	35	AN	5257	55	51	00	25
AN	5187	55	33	01	55	AN	5258	55	51	00	15
AN	5188	55	33	01	45	AN	5259	55	51	00	05
AN	5189	55	33	01	35	AN	5261	56	3	00	-05
AN	5191	55	45	01	25	AN	5262	56	3	00	-15
AN	5192	55	45	01	15	AN	5263	56	3	00	-25
AN	5193	55	45	01	05	AN	5264	55	57	00	-05
AN	5194	55	39	01	25	AN	5265	55	57	00	-15
AN	5195	55	39	01	15	AN	5266	55	57	00	-25
AN	5196	55	39	01	05	AN	5267	55	51	00	-05
AN	5197	55	33	01	25	AN	5268	55	51	00	-15
AN	5198	55	33	01	15	AN	5269	55	51	00	-25
AN	5199	55	33	01	05	AN	5271	55	45	00	55
AN	5211	56	21	00	55	AN	5272	55	45	00	45
AN	5212	56	21	00	45	AN	5273	55	45	00	35
AN	5213	56	21	00	35	AN	5274	55	39	00	55
AN	5214	56	15	00	55	AN	5275	55	39	00	45
AN	5215	56	15	00	45	AN	5276	55	39	00	35
AN	5216	56	15	00	35	AN	5277	55	33	00	55
AN	5217	56	9	00	55	AN	5278	55	33	00	45
AN	5218	56	9	00	45	AN	5279	55	33	00	35
AN	5219	56	9	00	35	AN	5281	55	45	00	25
AN	5221	56	21	00	25	AN	5282	55	45	00	15
AN	5222	56	21	00	15	AN	5283	55	45	00	05
AN	5223	56	21	00	05	AN	5284	55	39	00	25
AN	5224	56	15	00	25	AN	5285	55	39	00	15
AN	5225	56	15	00	15	AN	5286	55	39	00	05
AN	5226	56	15	00	05	AN	5287	55	33	00	25
AN	5227	56	9	00	25	AN	5288	55	33	00	15
AN	5228	56	9	00	15	AN	5289	55	33	00	05
AN	5229	56	9	00	05	AN	5291	55	45	00	-05
AN	5231	56	21	00	-05	AN	5292	55	45	00	-15
AN	5232	56	21	00	-15	AN	5293	55	45	00	-25
AN	5233	56	21	00	-25	AN	5294	55	39	00	-05
AN	5234	56	15	00	-05	AN	5295	55	39	00	-15

	Square	Lat	N	Long	W			Square	Lat	N	Long	W
AN	5296	55	39	00	-25		AN	5298	55	33	00	-15
AN	5297	55	33	00	-05		AN	5299	55	33	00	-25

Appendix II
BIBLIOGRAPHY

The following is a list of sources and publications that were used for reference:

The Admiralty Hydrographic Department, Taunton

Axis Submarine Successes 1939–1945 by Jürgen Rohwer. Patrick Stephens, 1983

Axis Submarine Successes of World War Two by Jürgen Rohwer. Greenhill Books, 1999

Lloyds War Losses, WW1

Lloyds War Losses, WW2, Vols. 1 & 2

Lloyds Register of Shipping

British Merchant Ships sunk by U-boats in the 1914–18 War by A.J. Tennent, 1990

Caithness and the War 1939–1945 by Norman Glass. Peter Reid & Co., 1948

Dive Scotland, Vol.3, by Gordon Ridley. Underwater World Publications, 1992

Goldfinder by Keith Jessop. Simon & Schuster, 1998

Off Scotland by Ian G. Whittaker. C-Anne Publishing, 1998

The Liberty Ships by L.A. Sawyer & W.H. Mitchell. Lloyds, 1985

The Real Price of Fish by George F. Ritchie. Hutton Press, 1991

The Scots Magazine. D.C.Thompson

The Tip of the Spear by Pamela Mitchell. Richard Netherwood, 1993

Shipwreck Index of the British Isles, Vol 4, by Richard & Briget Larn. Lloyds, 1998

Shipwrecks of North East Scotland 1444–1990 by David M. Ferguson. Aberdeen Univ. Press, 1991

U-boats Destroyed by Paul Kemp. Arms & Armour Press, 1997

U-boat Operations of the Second World War by Kenneth Wynn. Chatham, 1997

Warship Losses of WW2, by David Brown. Arms & Armour Press, 1990

Wealth from the Sea by Alan C. Crothall. Starr Line, 1993

Various Admiralty documents held in the PRO Kew

PHOTOGRAPHIC ACKNOWLEDGEMENTS

Illustration	**Copyright**	**Page No.**
Kenilworth	Aberdeen City Art Gallery & Museums	9
G. Koch	Aberdeen City Art Gallery & Museums	12
Ben Screel	Aberdeen City Art Gallery & Museums	13
Highlander	H.H. Rodmel	21
Coastal Emperor	G. Prentise	25
Archangel	World Ship Society	28
St Clement	Aberdeen Art Gallery & Museums	32
Brightside	World Ship Society	37
City of Osaka	Aberdeen City Art Gallery & Museums	41
Nymphaea	Aberdeen City Art Gallery & Museums	42
Easdale	Author's collection	44
Star of the Isles	Arbuthnot Museum, Peterhead	44
Frederick Snowden	Aberdeen Art Gallery & Museums	46
Ben Tarbert	Maritime Photo Library	57
Sea Reefer	Author's collection	58
Atland	World Ship Society	60
Muriel builders' plate	Roger Mathison	64
St Magnus	Aberdeen City Art Gallery & Museums	66
Ebro	Author's collection	69
Kiev	World Ship Society	72
Port Denison	National Maritime Museum	76
Anna	Aberdeen Journals	78
Sovereign	Roger Mathison	81
Antonio	David C. Buchan/*Fraserburgh Herald*	82
Prestonian	Author's collection	84
Noordpool	Arbuthnot Museum, Peterhead	86
Fram	Tomas Johanneson collection	88
Remuera	Author's collection	93
Astronomer	J. & M. Clarkson	101
Start	World Ship Society	109
HMS *Natal*	Author's collection	117
Marsona	World Ship Society	118
Durham Castle	World Ship Society	119
HMS *Tantivy*	Author's collection	120
Sunderland aircraft	Author's collection	122
San Tiburcio	National Maritime Museum	124
Verona	E. Jenyns	125
Wynor bell	Ken Farrow	130
Wynor builders' plate	John Leigh	130

Illustration	Copyright	Page No.
Hessonite	Kirkwall Archives	261
HMS *Hampshire*	Imperial War Museum	263
Kitchener	Author's collection	267
Stalin	Author's collection	267
Marwick Head	Author's collection	269
Hampshire propeller	R.N. Baird	270
Excellent	World Ship Society	272
U-995	Susanne Giehler	274
Aldegarmann necklace	R.N. Baird	278
Navarra	World Ship Society	281
Marstonmoor	World Ship Society	281
St Sunniva	Shetland Museum	286
Samba	Author's collection	293
Glenisla bell	Shetland Museum	295
Lunokhods-1	Kieran Murray	296
Pionersk ashore	Kieran Murray	298
Green Lily	Jonathan Wills	299
Jane	Sjöfartsmuseet, Göteborg	301
Jane propeller	Shetland Islands Council	301
E-14	Submarine Museum, Gosport	302
E-49 conning tower	Ian Potten	304
SRT-4240	Author's collection via Shetland SAC	305
Enid	Dag Bakka Jnr	306
Highcliffe	Author's collection via Shetland SAC	308
Goodwill Merchant	Author's collection via Shetland SAC	309
Braer	Kieran Murray	312
Oceanic	Author's collection	314
Christiansborg	Author's collection	316
Britta	World Ship Society	317
Cometa	Dag Bakka Jnr	318
Argentina	Author's collection	319
Hurstside	Welsh Industrial & Maritime Museum	322
Ruston tractor	Author's collection	322
Hurstside propeller	Author's collection	322
HMT *Northern Rover*	Author's collection	323
Gustav E Reuter	Tomas Johanneson collection	324

Over the years I have been gathering information, I have also collected a large number of photographs. Some photographs were taken by myself, or obtained directly from copyright holders, while others were either found in a variety of publications and websites, or sent to me by various individuals. Some of these sources did not include any information about the copyright owners.

A considerable effort has been made to trace and acknowledge copyright holders, and to obtain permission to use photographs, but it has not been possible to trace them all.

I apologise for any apparent negligence.

INDEX OF WRECKS BY NAME

Name	Latitude	Longitude	Area	Wreck	Page
Aberdeenshire	57 27 43 N	01 46 43 W	Buchan	99	53
Active ?	58 17 55 N	02 44 32 W	Wick	252	138
Albula	58 38 00 N PA	04 35 30 W PA	Wrath	374	225
Alcora	57 34 40 N PA	01 48 54 W PA	Buchan	127	68
Alder	57 41 00 N PA	01 56 00 W PA	Buchan	153	80
Algier	60 17 00 N PA	02 49 00 W PA	Shetland	466	315
Alirmay	57 02 48 N	02 07 00 W	Aberdeen	5	3
Alwaki	58 43 15 N	04 29 04 W	Wrath	375	225
Alwyn	57 05 30 N PA	01 55 30 W PA	Aberdeen	14	7
Andalusia	58 18 00 N PD	02 25 00 W PD	Wick	263	152
Anglo Dane	60 06 31 N	01 07 35 W	Shetland	442	289
Anna	57 39 37 N	01 54 30 W	Buchan	147	78
Antonio	57 41 50 N	02 01 31 W	Buchan	157	82
Anvers	57 41 15 N	01 47 45 W	Buchan	154	80
Aralia	58 38 55 N PA	03 03 20 W PA	Pentland	319	185
Archangel	57 16 00 N PA	02 00 12 W PA	Aberdeen	58	27
Ardmore	58 38 55 N PA	03 03 00 W PA	Pentland	318	185
Argentina	60 53 53 N	00 33 09 W	Shetland	470	318
Artemis	57 41 45 N PA	02 50 00 W PA	Moray	206	110
Ashbury	58 32 48 N	04 24 32 W	Durness	357	212
Asia	60 06 04 N	01 07 23 W	Shetland	440	288
Asse	58 37 36 N PA	03 38 30 W PA	Pentland	312	183
Astrea	57 23 24 N PA	01 51 00 W PA	Buchan	80	42
Astronomer ?	58 01 50 N	02 02 37 W	Buchan	193	100
Atland	57 29 47 N	01 40 40 W	Buchan	111	60
Auric	57 40 30 N	01 54 45 W	Buchan	149	79
Avenel	58 36 10 N PA	03 30 54 W PA	Pentland	305	181
Balmoral	58 35 00 N PA	04 00 00 W PA	Pentland	304	181
Bancrest	58 53 08 N	01 52 25 W	Orkney	400	242
Baron Minto	57 37 30 N PA	01 49 30 W PA	Buchan	135	71
Beacon Light	58 27 24 N	05 44 59 W	Wrath	366	222
Beech	58 36 39 N	03 31 54 W	Pentland	309	182
Belcher	57 21 00 N PA	01 55 27 W PA	Buchan	72	37
Bellavista	59 22 34 N	02 51 54 W	Orkney	420	255
Bel Lily	57 32 45 N	01 42 20 W	Buchan	116	62
Belvoir Castle	57 17 00 N PA	01 30 00 W PA	Aberdeen	62	30
Ben Barvas	58 40 30 N	02 54 27 W	Pentland	333	191
Ben More	57 40 00 N PA	01 54 52 W PA	Buchan	148	78
Ben Rhydding	57 15 00 N PA	02 02 15 W PA	Aberdeen	57	27
Ben Rinnes	58 37 26 N PA	03 32 28 W PA	Pentland	310	183
Ben Screel	57 08 20 N PA	02 02 40 W PA	Aberdeen	26	13
Ben Tarbert	57 29 39 N	01 46 14 W	Buchan	105	56
Ben Torc	57 07 42 N	02 02 48 W	Aberdeen	23	11

Name	Latitude	Longitude	Area	Wreck	Page
G Koch	57 08 18 N	02 02 40 W	Aberdeen	25	12
Gardar ?	58 32 28 N	02 52 14 W	Wick	278	165
Garrawalt	57 03 11 N	02 06 30 W	Aberdeen	6	3
Gelsina	57 06 45 N PA	01 57 00 W PA	Aberdeen	17	8
George Robb	58 37 45 N PA	03 02 00 W PA	Wick	299	175
Gertrud	58 41 44 N	03 07 24 W	Pentland	342	199
Giralda	58 47 48 N	02 45 54 W	Orkney	396	241
Glen Farg	58 52 00 N PA	01 54 00 W PA	Orkney	399	242
Glenisla	60 07 53 N	01 08 04 W	Shetland	446	294
Glenravel	58 06 30 N PA	02 00 30 W PA	Buchan	196	103
Glentanar	57 09 45 N	02 01 40 W	Aberdeen	40	19
Goodwill Merchant	59 59 38 N	01 20 43 W	Shetland	461	309
Graciosa	59 06 00 N PA	05 00 00 W PA	Wrath	387	232
Grecian Prince	57 57 00 N PD	02 08 00 W PD	Buchan	189	98
Green Lily	60 06 00 N	01 04 00 W	Shetland	449	298
Gretafield	58 14 45 N PA	03 25 00 W PA	Wick	258	141
Gunnaren	58 44 48 N	03 03 36 W	Pentland	348	203
Gustav E Reuter	59 44 46 N	01 51 02 W	Shetland	474	324
Gwladmena	60 08 12 N	01 08 38 W	Shetland	444	291
Hampshire	59 07 05 N	03 23 51 W	Orkney	428	261
Hamnavoe	58 38 21 N	04 55 37 W	Wrath	368	222
Hansi	59 23 00 N PA	02 23 04 W PA	Orkney	414	252
Harmony ?	57 53 50 N	03 36 30 W	Moray	219	114
Harry Nostt	57 57 36 N PA	02 10 00 W PA	Buchan	191	99
Hartfell	57 23 24 N PA	01 51 00 W PA	Buchan	81	43
Harty	58 35 00 N PA	04 00 00 W PA	Pentland	303	181
Hassett	58 33 30 N PA	03 04 30 W PA	Wick	292	171
Hessen	58 35 00 N	02 59 00 W	Wick	296	174
Hessonite	59 09 20 N PA	03 13 20 W PA	Orkney	427	260
Highcliffe	60 19 09 N	01 39 42 W	Shetland	460	308
Hillfern	57 57 00 N PA	02 25 30 W PA	Moray	242	129
Hirpa	57 40 00 N PA	02 56 00 W PA	Moray	209	111
Horace E Nutten ?	57 49 07 N	02 14 26 W	Buchan	190	98
Hurstside	60 17 43.25 N	04 14 57.70 W	Shetland	471	319
Hylas	58 30 45 N	05 46 20 W	Wrath	362	219
Imogen	58 34 13 N	02 56 09 W	Wick	294	172
Imperial Prince	57 13 00 N PA	02 03 00 W PA	Aberdeen	51	24
Integrity	57 24 00 N PA	01 43 00 W PA	Buchan	88	47
Isabella	58 39 00 N PA	03 01 00 W PA	Pentland	321	186
Island Lass	59 26 00 N PA	02 43 12 W PA	Orkney	418	254
Isleford	58 26 29 N	03 03 47 W	Wick	283	167
Jacona	58 13 27 N	02 43 01 W	Wick	256	140
James Hall	57 09 26 N	02 04 22 W	Aberdeen	36	17
Jane	60 38 21 N	00 56 31 W	Shetland	451	300
Jasper	58 12 46 N	02 25 40 W	Wick	254	139
Jean Stephen	58 30 00 N PA	03 07 30 W PA	Wick	288	170
Jenny Jensen	57 56 00 N PA	01 54 24 W PA	Buchan	188	98
Johanna Thorden	58 44 20 N	03 04 10 W	Pentland	347	201
John Dunkin	57 54 48 N	03 02 50 W	Moray	240	128
John Randolph	58 31 20 N	04 15 30 W	Durness	356	211
Jorgen Bugge	58 39 20 N	03 16 30 W	Pentland	323	187
Junona	58 44 00 N PA	05 36 00 W PA	Wrath	382	229
Jura	58 36 30 N PA	03 25 00 W PA	Pentland	306	182
Karemma	57 18 30 N PA	01 59 00 W PA	Aberdeen	65	31
Kathe Neiderkirchner	58 41 31 N	02 56 02 W	Pentland	338	194

Name	Latitude	Longitude	Area	Wreck	Page
Tekla	58 16 28 N	02 26 33 W	Wick	260	148
Tern	58 41 45 N PA	03 07 30 W PA	Pentland	343	199
Tern	58 31 15 N PA	04 39 15 W PA	Wrath	359	214
Teutonia	57 04 00 N PA	02 05 30 W PA	Aberdeen	10	5
Thunfisch	58 42 04 N	02 54 08 W	Pentland	355	208
Thyra	58 37 45 N PA	03 02 00 PA	Wick	298	175
Tommeline	59 20 02 N	03 04 12 W	Orkney	422	256
Tonis Chandris	60 42 29 N	00 48 59 W	Shetland	452	302
Torgrim	57 37 20 N	01 50 45 W	Buchan	139	73
Tosto	59 16 40 N	03 04 54 W	Orkney	423	257
Totnes	57 58 20 N PA	03 59 00 W PA	Moray	241	128
Trebartha	57 06 08 N	02 04 12 W	Aberdeen	16	7
Trevorian	57 10 00 N PA	01 54 00 W PA	Aberdeen	42	19
Trident	58 20 26 N	02 39 22 W	Wick	268	157
Trieste	57 31 30 N PA	01 46 45 W PA	Buchan	114	62
Trinity NB	57 50 00 N PA	01 30 00 W PA	Buchan	184	97
Trsat	57 47 00 N PA	01 51 00 W PA	Buchan	178	94
U-18	58 42 09 N	02 48 00 W	Pentland	336	192
U-36 ?	59 10 20 N	05 52 20 W	Wrath	388	233
U-36 ?	59 04 30 N	05 16 00 W	Wrath	385	231
U-40	57 00 00 N PA	01 50 00 W PA	Aberdeen	1	1
U-63	58 40 00 N PA	00 10 00 W PA	Shetland	198	104
U-74	57 15 00 N PA	01 09 00 W PA	Aberdeen	56	26
U-92	59 00 00 N PD	01 30 00 W PD	Orkney	417	254
U-297	59 00 52 N	03 53 45 W	Orkney	432	272
U-309	58 09 39 N	02 22 51 W	Moray	249	136
U-905	58 35 31 N	05 46 06 W	Wrath	365	221
U-1020	57 38 08 N	02 46 11 W	Wick	300	176
U-1206	57 21 18 N	01 39 12 W	Buchan	73	38
UB-83	58 42 00 N PA	02 56 00 W PA	Pentland	335	192
UB-116	58 50 07 N	03 04 06 W	Pentland	435	282
UC-55	60 01 56 N	00 57 15 W	Shetland	437	286
Ulster	57 04 30 N PA	02 05 30 W PA	Aberdeen	12	6
Union	57 37 00 N PA	01 47 00 W PA	Buchan	133	70
Unknown	57 46 20 N	02 14 15 W	Buchan	172	92
Unknown	58 52 00 N	04 59 20 W	Wrath	381	229
Unknown	57 46 12 N	03 23 45 W	Moray	215	113
Unknown	57 42 39 N	03 38 57 W	Moray	217	114
Unknown	57 57 55 N	03 29 44 W	Moray	243	129
Unknown	57 45 10 N	01 33 40 W	Buchan	169	90
Unknown	58 42 48 N	04 29 24 W	Wrath	373	225
Unknown	57 49 54 N	03 09 05 W	Moray	212	112
Unknown	57 47 05 N PA	01 37 55 W PA	Buchan	179	95
Unknown	57 46 35 N PA	01 40 30 W PA	Buchan	176	93
Unknown	57 40 30 N	01 45 38 W	Buchan	151	79
Unknown	57 38 30 N PA	01 33 25 W PA	Buchan	145	77
Unknown	57 42 00 N PA	02 49 00 W PA	Moray	202	108
Unknown	57 52 48 N PA	01 57 00 W PA	Buchan	185	97
Unknown	57 34 35 N	01 33 35 W	Buchan	122	66
Unknown	57 46 12 N	01 33 42 W	Buchan	174	92
Unknown	57 49 02 N	03 36 46 W	Moray	233	126
Unknown	57 55 00 N PA	01 54 00 W PA	Buchan	187	97
Unknown	57 54 42 N PA	03 43 36 W PA	Moray	239	128
Unknown	57 41 20 N PA	01 43 50 W PA	Buchan	155	81
Unknown	57 14 30 N PA	01 40 00 W PA	Aberdeen	55	26

INDEX OF WRECKS BY LATITUDE

Latitude	Longitude	Name	Area	Wreck	Page
57 10 00 N PA	01 32 00 W PA	Prince of Wales	Aberdeen	44	20
57 10 00 N PA	01 54 00 W PA	Trevorian	Aberdeen	42	19
57 10 10 N PA	01 51 55 W PA	St.Catherine	Aberdeen	46	21
57 11 00 N PA	02 04 00 W PA	Nurzec	Aberdeen	47	22
57 11 49 N	01 49 36 W	Rattray Head	Aberdeen	48	22
57 12 06 N	02 03 45 W	Sheriffmuir	Aberdeen	49	23
57 12 30 N PA	01 47 30 W PA	Emperor	Aberdeen	50	23
57 13 00 N PA	02 03 00 W PA	Imperial Prince	Aberdeen	51	24
57 13 12 N	02 03 06 W	Coastal Emperor	Aberdeen	52	24
57 13 48 N PA	01 50 00 W PA	Unknown – pre-1945	Aberdeen	53	25
57 14 00 N PA	02 02 30 W PA	Fairy	Aberdeen	54	26
57 14 30 N PA	01 40 00 W PA	Unknown	Aberdeen	55	26
57 15 00 N PA	02 02 15 W PA	Ben Rhydding	Aberdeen	57	27
57 15 00 N PA	01 09 00 W PA	U-74	Aberdeen	56	26
57 16 00 N PA	02 00 12 W PA	Archangel	Aberdeen	58	27
57 16 21 N	02 01 00 W	Ross Khartoum	Aberdeen	59	29
57 16 24 N	02 01 00 W	Star of the Wave	Aberdeen	60	29
57 16 42 N	01 41 18 W	Unknown	Aberdeen	61	29
57 17 00 N PA	01 30 00 W PA	Belvoir Castle	Aberdeen	62	30
57 17 00 N PA	01 25 00 W PA	Ennismore	Aberdeen	63	30
57 18 30 N PA	01 59 00 W PA	Karemma	Aberdeen	65	31
57 18 30 N	01 58 30 W	Roslin	Aberdeen	64	30
57 19 00 N PA	01 50 00 W PA	St Clement	Aberdeen	66	31
57 20 16 N	01 56 42 W	Nairn	Buchan	67	35
57 20 20 N	01 56 42 W	Brightside	Buchan	70	36
57 20 45 N PA	01 57 15 W PA	Lesrix	Buchan	69	36
57 20 50 N	01 55 48 W	Ladybird	Buchan	71	37
57 20 57 N	01 55 13 W	Santa Catarina	Buchan	68	35
57 21 00 N PA	01 55 27 W PA	Belcher	Buchan	72	37
57 21 18 N	01 39 12 W	U-1206	Buchan	73	38
57 21 45 N PA	01 55 00 W PA	Solvang	Buchan	75	39
57 22 09 N	01 53 51 W	Ben Wyvis	Buchan	74	39
57 22 35 N	01 52 52 W	City of Osaka	Buchan	77	40
57 22 34 N	01 52 52 W	Nymphaea	Buchan	78	41
57 22 40 N PA	01 52 45 W PA	Contender	Buchan	76	40
57 23 00 N	01 47 48 W	Frederick Snowden	Buchan	86	46
57 23 18 N PA	01 38 30 W PA	Ormonde	Buchan	79	42
57 23 24 N PA	01 51 00 W PA	Astrea	Buchan	80	42
57 23 24 N PA	01 51 00 W PA	Easdale	Buchan	82	43
57 23 24 N PA	01 51 00 W PA	Hartfell	Buchan	81	43
57 23 24 N PA	01 50 00 W PA	Milwaukee	Buchan	84	45
57 23 24 N PA	01 51 00 W PA	Star of the Isles	Buchan	83	44
57 23 30 N	01 51 18 W	Maria W	Buchan	85	45
57 23 43 N	01 41 31 W	Unknown – Pretoria ?	Buchan	87	46
57 24 00 N PA	01 43 00 W PA	Integrity	Buchan	88	47
57 24 03 N	01 37 12 W	Freidrich Bolte	Buchan	89	47
57 24 28 N	01 34 45 W	Mercator	Buchan	90	48
57 24 50 N	01 49 45 W	Philorth	Buchan	91	48
57 24 54 N	01 49 46 W	Chicago	Buchan	92	49
57 25 37 N	01 45 17 W	Windward Ho	Buchan	95	51
57 25 51 N	01 35 52 W	St Glen	Buchan	93	50
57 26 05 N	01 36 14 W	Sofie Bakke	Buchan	94	50
57 26 10 N	01 49 00 W	Wistow Hall	Buchan	96	51
57 27 12 N	01 47 42 W	Zitella	Buchan	100	53
57 27 24 N	01 22 12 W	Unknown – Annemeike ?	Buchan	97	52

Latitude	Longitude	Name	Area	Wreck	Page
57 40 11 N	03 57 30 W	Shelbrit I	Moray	225	121
57 40 11 N	03 49 18 W	Unknown – Barge	Moray	223	119
57 40 28 N	03 55 03 W	Marsona	Moray	221	117
57 40 30 N	01 54 45 W	Auric	Buchan	149	79
57 40 30 N PA	01 46 30 W PA	Charles Goodanew	Buchan	150	79
57 40 30 N	01 45 38 W	Unknown	Buchan	151	79
57 40 30 N PA	02 10 30 W PA	William Hope	Buchan	160	84
57 40 31 N	03 49 55 W	Tantivy	Moray	224	120
57 40 40 N PA	01 34 00 W PA	Chancellor ?	Buchan	152	79
57 40 52 N	02 09 54 W	Prestonian	Buchan	159	83
57 40 56 N	01 56 30 W	Sovereign	Buchan	156	81
57 41 00 N PA	01 56 00 W PA	Alder	Buchan	153	80
57 41 00 N PA	02 58 00 W PA	Briar Rose	Moray	207	110
57 41 00 N PA	02 58 00 W PA	Teal	Moray	208	111
57 41 05 N	02 34 06 W	Ebeneezer	Moray	201	107
57 41 15 N	01 47 45 W	Anvers	Buchan	154	80
57 41 16 N	04 05 15 W	Natal	Moray	220	115
57 41 20 N PA	01 43 50 W PA	Unknown	Buchan	155	81
57 41 24 N	01 33 06 W	Cape York	Buchan	158	82
57 41 25 N	01 45 36 W	Port Denison	Buchan	142	75
57 41 29 N	03 47 25 W	Sunderland Aircraft 1	Moray	226	122
57 41 30 N PA	03 06 00 W PA	Nar	Moray	211	111
57 41 30 N	03 54 06 W	Durham Castle	Moray	222	118
57 41 45 N PA	02 50 00 W PA	Artemis	Moray	206	110
57 41 48 N	03 52 30 W	Sunderland Aircraft 3	Moray	228	123
57 41 50 N	02 07 35 W	G 103	Buchan	162	85
57 41 50 N	02 01 31 W	Antonio	Buchan	157	82
57 41 58 N	03 51 05 W	Sunderland Aircraft 2	Moray	227	122
57 42 00 N PA	02 49 00 W PA	Unknown	Moray	202	108
57 42 02 N	02 03 49 W	Craigforth	Buchan	164	87
57 42 06 N	02 10 35 W	Fram (Bows)	Buchan	166	87
57 42 07 N	02 07 07 W	Noordpool	Buchan	163	86
57 42 39 N	03 38 57 W	Unknown	Moray	217	114
57 42 45 N	02 13 22 W	Fram (Stern)	Buchan	166	87
57 42 50 N PA	01 42 00 W PA	Bretagne	Buchan	165	87
57 44 30 N	01 45 40 W	Unknown – Kildale ?	Buchan	167	89
57 44 21 N	03 45 40 W	Sunderland Aircraft 4	Moray	229	123
57 45 00 N PA	02 36 00 W PA	Start	Moray	203	108
57 45 10 N	01 33 40 W	Unknown	Buchan	169	90
57 45 15 N	01 46 00 W	Kildale ?	Buchan	168	90
57 45 32 N	03 40 25 W	Unknown – Young Sid ?	Moray	216	113
57 45 30 N	02 00 02 W	Svarton	Buchan	181	95
57 46 00 N PA	02 49 00 W PA	Moray Firth	Moray	205	109
57 46 00 N PA	01 54 00 W PA	Unknown – Remuera ?	Buchan	170	90
57 46 00 N PA	01 22 00 W PA	William Rockefeller	Buchan	171	91
57 46 12 N	03 23 45 W	Unknown	Moray	215	113
57 46 12 N	01 33 42 W	Unknown	Buchan	174	92
57 46 12 N PA	01 57 42 W PA	Unknown – Friendship ?	Buchan	173	92
57 46 20 N	02 14 15 W	Unknown	Buchan	172	92
57 46 34 N	03 45 32 W	San Tiburcio	Moray	230	123
57 46 35 N PA	01 40 30 W PA	Unknown	Buchan	176	93
57 46 45 N PA	01 22 00 W PA	Louisiana	Buchan	177	94
57 46 50 N	03 22 30 W	Chrissie Criggie	Moray	213	112
57 46 59 N	01 52 42 W	Remuera	Buchan	175	93
57 47 00 N PA	01 51 00 W PA	Trsat	Buchan	178	94

Latitude	Longitude	Name	Area	Wreck	Page
58 16 30 N	03 22 00 W	Eamont	Wick	262	152
58 17 55 N	02 44 32 W	Active ?	Wick	252	138
58 18 00 N PA	02 25 00 W PA	Andalusia	Wick	263	152
58 18 00 N PA	03 14 45 W PA	Sphinx	Wick	261	150
58 18 00 N PA	01 46 00 W PA	Sleipner	Wick	264	154
58 18 00 N PA	01 46 00 W PA	Rhone	Wick	265	155
58 18 28 N	02 28 56 W	Exmouth	Wick	259	142
58 20 16 N	02 39 58 W	Makalla	Wick	266	156
58 21 12 N	03 04 24 W	Freya	Wick	273	162
58 21 36 N	03 01 24 W	Moray	Wick	274	162
58 22 26 N	03 05 36 W	Scorpio	Wick	275	163
58 22 35 N	02 41 02 W	Minsk	Wick	269	158
58 23 28 N	02 39 31 W	Marstenen	Wick	267	157
58 29 26 N	02 39 22 W	Trident	Wick	268	157
58 24 12 N	02 42 11 W	Charkow	Wick	270	159
58 24 15 N PA	03 05 00 W PA	Rein	Wick	276	164
58 24 30 N	02 49 24 W	Berriedale ?	Wick	277	164
58 24 30 N	02 56 50 W	Sound Fisher	Wick	279	165
58 25 00 N PA	03 05 15 W PA	Dromara	Wick	284	168
58 25 12 N	02 27 40 W	Bothal	Wick	271	159
58 26 15 N	03 03 30 W	St.Nicholas and Ems	Wick	280	166
58 26 24 N	03 02 48 W	Olive Leaf	Wick	282	167
58 26 29 N	03 03 47 W	Isleford	Wick	283	167
58 27 00 N PA	01 36 00 W PA	Daring	Wick	301	177
58 27 10 N	03 03 05 W	Carency	Wick	285	168
58 27 24 N	02 28 00 W	Viking	Wick	272	160
58 27 24 N	05 44 59 W	Beacon Light	Wrath	366	222
58 27 55 N	02 59 29 W	Pitstruan	Wick	287	169
58 28 21 N	02 42 50 W	Sword Dance	Wick	286	169
58 29 15 N	04 40 12 W	Vulture II	Wrath	358	214
58 29 18 N	02 48 20 W	Unknown	Wick	289	170
58 30 00 N PA	03 07 30 W PA	Jean Stephen	Wick	288	170
58 30 00 N	05 23 00 W	Noreen Mary	Wrath	363	220
58 30 45 N	05 46 20 W	Hylas	Wrath	362	219
58 31 15 N PA	04 39 15 W PA	Tern	Wrath	359	214
58 31 06 N	02 49 20 W	The Emperor	Wick	281	166
58 31 20 N	04 15 30 W	John Randolph	Durness	356	211
58 32 00 N PA	03 06 30 W PA	Star of Victory	Wick	291	171
58 32 05 N	02 53 00 W	Clan Mackinlay	Wick	290	170
58 32 28 N	02 52 14 W	Gardar ?	Wick	278	165
58 32 48 N	04 24 32 W	Ashbury	Durness	357	212
58 33 00 N	02 12 45 W	Nessus	Wick	302	178
58 33 30 N PA	03 04 30 W PA	Hassett	Wick	292	171
58 33 40 N PA	03 05 00 W PA	V-81	Wick	293	172
58 34 05 N	05 13 45 W	Majorka	Wrath	364	220
58 34 13 N	02 56 09 W	Imogen	Wick	294	172
58 34 35 N PA	03 03 45 W PA	Stellatus	Wick	295	173
58 35 00 N PA	04 00 00 W PA	Balmoral	Pentland	304	181
58 35 00 N PA	03 55 00 W PA	Clarkwood	Pentland	311	183
58 35 00 N PA	04 00 00 W PA	Harty	Pentland	303	181
58 35 00 N	02 59 00 W	Hessen	Wick	296	174
58 35 31 N	05 46 06 W	U-905	Wrath	365	221
58 35 50 N PA	03 02 30 W PA	Navarre	Wick	297	174
58 36 10 N PA	03 30 54 W PA	Avenel	Pentland	305	181
58 36 30 N PA	03 25 00 W PA	Jura	Pentland	306	182

Latitude	Longitude	Name	Area	Wreck	Page
58 43 46 N	04 51 16 W	Bullen	Wrath	360	215
58 44 00 N PA	05 36 00 W PA	Junona	Wrath	382	229
58 44 08 N	03 03 52 W	Ross Tern	Pentland	344	199
58 44 08 N	03 03 52 W	St Clair	Pentland	345	200
58 44 13 N	03 03 27 W	Croma	Pentland	346	200
58 45 25 N	02 27 37 W	Duke of Albany	Orkney	393	237
58 44 16 N	02 40 36 W	Tamara XII	Orkney	394	238
58 44 20 N	03 04 10 W	Johanna Thorden	Pentland	347	201
58 44 48 N	03 03 36 W	Gunnaren	Pentland	348	203
58 44 52 N	03 03 35 W	Pennsylvania	Pentland	349	204
58 45 00 N PA	07 00 00 W PA	Chelsea	Wrath	378	227
58 46 03 N	04 47 01 W	Prince Rupert City	Wrath	377	226
58 46 15 N	02 55 48 W	Opal & Narborough	Orkney	395	239
58 46 25 N	04 55 10 W	Unknown – Alwaki ?	Wrath	376	226
58 47 48 N	02 45 54 W	Giralda	Orkney	396	241
58 48 25 N	04 35 18 W	Unknown – Lily ?	Wrath	379	227
58 49 50 N	04 39 15 W	Murjek ?	Wrath	380	228
58 49 51 N	02 45 51 W	Daghestan	Orkney	397	241
58 50 07 N	03 04 06 W	UB-116	Orkney	435	282
58 50 25 N	02 46 02 W	Remus	Orkney	398	241
58 52 00 N PA	01 54 00 W PA	Glen Farg	Orkney	399	242
58 52 00 N PA	00 22 00 W PA	Foxen	Orkney	416	253
58 52 00 N	04 59 20 W	Unknown	Wrath	381	229
58 53 08 N	01 52 25 W	Bancrest	Orkney	400	242
58 54 00 N PA	02 23 00 W PA	Vestfoss	Orkney	401	242
58 54 46 N	02 45 52 W	Faro	Orkney	404	244
58 56 50 N	02 33 11 W	Ruby	Orkney	415	252
58 57 30 N PA	02 21 00 W PA	Urania	Orkney	402	243
58 57 59 N	02 54 31 N	Vardefjell	Orkney	409	248
58 58 03 N	02 53 39 W	Loch Maddy	Orkney	408	247
58 58 15 N	02 38 28 W	Cotovia	Orkney	405	245
58 58 47 N	02 53 04 W	Danmark	Orkney	407	246
59 00 00 N PD	01 30 00 W PD	U-92	Orkney	417	254
58 59 00 N PA	02 35 30 W PA	Svinta	Orkney	406	245
59 01 43 N	02 56 52 W	Disperser & Endeavour	Orkney	410	250
58 59 10 N	05 21 30 W	Blake	Wrath	383	229
59 00 00 N PA	04 07 00 W PA	Navarra	Orkney	433	279
59 00 51.5 N	03 53 45.3 W	U-297	Orkney	432	272
59 01 25 N	04 30 18 W	Manina	Wrath	384	230
59 04 30 N	05 16 00 W	U-36 ?	Wrath	385	231
59 05 20 N	05 56 00 W	Pajala	Wrath	386	232
59 06 00 N PA	05 00 00 W PA	Graciosa	Wrath	387	232
59 07 05 N	03 23 51 W	Hampshire	Orkney	428	261
59 09 20 N PA	03 13 20 W PA	Hessonite	Orkney	427	260
59 09 47 N	03 10 45 W	Freesia	Orkney	426	259
59 10 20 N	05 52 20 W	U-36 ?	Wrath	388	233
59 11 00 N PA	05 45 00 W PA	Botusk	Wrath	389	233
59 11 00 N PA	05 45 00 W PA	Emmaplein	Wrath	390	233
59 12 24 N	02 44 45 W	Oceana ?	Orkney	411	251
59 14 30 N	02 12 40 W	Unknown	Orkney	403	243
59 14 34 N	02 59 34 W	Scandinavic	Orkney	424	258
59 16 40 N	03 04 54 W	Tosto	Orkney	423	257
59 20 02 N	03 04 12 W	Tommeline	Orkney	422	256
59 21 00 N	02 22 16 W	Mim	Orkney	412	251
59 21 00 N	02 22 00 W	Mistley	Orkney	413	252